FROM PARENTS
TO CHILDREN

DATE DUE

FROM PARENTS TO CHILDREN

THE INTERGENERATIONAL TRANSMISSION OF ADVANTAGE

JOHN ERMISCH, MARKUS JÄNTTI,
AND TIMOTHY SMEEDING,
EDITORS

Russell Sage Foundation · New York

The Russell Sage Foundation

Library of Congress Cataloging-in-Publication Data

From parents to children : the intergenerational transmission of advantage / John Ermisch, Markus Jäntti, and Timothy Smeeding, editors.
    p. cm.
    Includes bibliographical references and index.
    ISBN 978-0-87154-045-4 (pbk. : alk. paper) — ISBN 978-1-61044-780-5 (ebook)
1. Inheritance and succession. 2. Social mobility. 3. Parent and child. 4. Intergenerational relations. I. Ermisch, John. II. Jäntti, Markus, 1966– III. Smeeding, Timothy M.
    HB715.F76 2012
    306.874—dc23

2011053537

Text design by Suzanne Nichols.

RUSSELL SAGE FOUNDATION
112 East 64th Street, New York, New York 10065
10 9 8 7 6 5 4 3 2 1

We dedicate this volume to the memory of the "captain" and leader of the German team, Joachim R. Frick, an expert in international comparative research in the field of economic inequality and mobility. Joachim played an important role at our meetings and in arranging all of the German contributions. He passed away much too early, at age forty-nine, on December 16, 2011. He leaves us the following epitaph, which brilliantly reflects his way with people and life, in his own words:

When you think of me, don't be sad.
Talk about me, and let yourselves laugh.
Leave me a space among you
like the place I had with you when I was alive.

This is the way Joachim lived his life and made great contributions to research, analysis, and friendship. There will always be a place for Joachim in our hearts and in our memories. May he rest in peace.

Contents

About the Authors

John Ermisch is professor of family demography at the University of Oxford and senior research fellow at Nuffield College, Oxford.

Markus Jäntti is professor of economics at the Swedish Institute for Social Research, Stockholm University.

Timothy Smeeding is Distinguished Professor of Public Affairs and Economics at the La Follette School of Public Affairs and director of the Institute for Research on Poverty, University of Wisconsin–Madison.

Silke Anger is senior researcher at the German Institute for Economic Research (DIW Berlin).

Lars Bergman is professor of economics and president, Stockholm School of Economics.

Erik Bihagen is associate professor of sociology at the Swedish Institute for Social Research (SOFI), Stockholm University.

Paul Bingley is research professor at the Danish National Centre for Social Research.

Anders Björklund is professor of economics at the Swedish Institute for Social Research, Stockholm University.

Jo Blanden is lecturer and economics program director at the University of Surrey and research associate at the Centre for Economic Performance, London School of Economics.

Bruce Bradbury is senior research fellow at the Social Policy Research Centre, University of New South Wales.

Massimiliano Bratti is associate professor of economics at the Department of Economics, Business, and Statistics (DEAS), Università degli Studi di Milano.

Lorenzo Cappellari is professor of economics at the Università Cattolica di Milano.

Miles Corak is professor at the Graduate School of Public and International Affairs, University of Ottawa.

Emilia Del Bono is senior research fellow at the Institute for Social and Economic Research, University of Essex.

Kathryn Duckworth is faculty of policy and society at the Institute of Education, University of London.

Christelle Dumas is assistant professor at the Université de Cergy-Pontoise.

Greg J. Duncan is Distinguished Professor of Education at the University of California–Irvine.

Olaf Groh-Samberg is junior professor of sociology at the Bremen International Graduate School of Social Sciences, University of Bremen.

Robert Haveman is professor emeritus of public affairs and economics and faculty affiliate, Institute for Research on Poverty, at the University of Wisconsin–Madison.

John Jerrim is research fellow in the Department of Quantitative Social Science at the Institute of Education, University of London.

Jan O. Jonsson is professor of sociology at the Swedish Institute for Social Research (SOFI), Stockholm University.

Ilan Katz is professor and centre director at the Social Policy Research Centre, University of New South Wales.

Katja Kokko is academy research fellow at the University of Jyväskylä.

Arnaud Lefranc is professor of economics at the Université de Cergy-Pontoise.

Henning Lohmann is professor of social sciences at the University of Osnabrück and research professor at the German Institute for Economic Research (DIW Berlin).

Anna-Liisa Lyyra is researcher, data analyst, and data manager in the Department of Psychology, University of Jyväskylä.

Katherine Magnuson is associate professor in the School of Social Work, University of Wisconsin–Madison.

Molly Metzger is a graduate student at Northwestern University.

John Micklewright is professor of quantitative social science at the Institute of Education, University of London.

Carina Mood is associate professor of sociology at the Swedish Institute for Social Research (SOFI), Stockholm University.

Martin Nybom is a graduate student at the Swedish Institute for Social Research (SOFI), Stockholm University.

Frauke H. Peter is research fellow at the German Institute for Economic Research (DIW Berlin).

Patrizio Piraino is senior lecturer at the University of Cape Town, South Africa.

Lea Pulkkinen is professor emerita in psychology at the University of Jyväskylä.

Gerry Redmond is associate professor at the School of Social and Policy Studies, Flinders University of South Australia.

John Roemer is Elizabeth S. and A. Varick Professor of Political Science and Economics at Yale University.

Sharon Simonton is research investigator at the Institute for Social Research, University of Michigan.

C. Katharina Spiess is university professor at the Free University of Berlin.

Jane Waldfogel is professor of social work and public affairs at the Columbia University School of Social Work and visiting professor at the Centre for Analysis of Social Exclusion at the London School of Economics.

Elizabeth Washbrook is research associate in the Centre for Multilevel Modelling at the University of Bristol.

Niels Westergård-Nielsen is professor at the Aarhus School of Business, Aarhus University.

James A. Wilson is senior program officer at the Russell Sage Foundation.

Kathryn Wilson is professor of economics at Kent State University.

Acknowledgements

The volume was generously supported and financed by the Russell Sage Foundation (RSF), the Pew Economic Mobility project, and the Sutton Trust, who hosted many meetings, conferences, and discussions to harmonize data and present drafts of the results herein. These formative meetings were held in London, New York, and at the Institute for Research on Poverty (IRP) in Madison, Wisconsin. We thank all our hosts at these institutions. The editors want to thank Russell Sage and Eric Wanner for their chance to formulate and plan this volume right after their 2007–2008 terms as RSF visiting scholars, and for its generous summer support in 2010 providing the time and setting that helped us finish the volume. We are indebted to many of the RSF staff, but especially to our colleague, coauthor, and program manager, James Wilson, who worked with us at every stage of the project and whose continued diligence and attention made the book and the project much better than it would otherwise have been. All are indebted to the IRP staff for helping with editorial work and preparation of the manuscript, especially David Chancellor, Dawn Duren, and Deborah Johnson; and also April Rondeau and Suzanne Nichols at RSF, who shepherded the volume along and chased down its long list of global authors to produce a wonderful volume. We are indebted to Paul Gregg, Oddbjorn Raum, Bob Michael, Stephen Jenkins, and two anonymous referees for their excellent comments, which greatly improved the project and the book. The editors especially want to thank all the author teams for their contributions and are happy to see that many of the teams are still working together to further this research.

PART I

INTRODUCTION

Chapter 1

Advantage in
Comparative Perspective

JOHN ERMISCH, MARKUS JÄNTTI,
TIMOTHY SMEEDING, AND JAMES A. WILSON

O F ALL THE potential consequences of rising economic inequality, none is more worrisome, or more difficult to study, than the possibility that rising inequality will have the long-term effect of reducing equality of opportunity and intergenerational mobility. The reasoning underlying this worry is straightforward. Families clearly have a strong interest in investing in the future social and economic well-being of their children. Although some of these investments may not require financial resources, many others obviously do—among them, paying for quality child care and early childhood education, buying books and computers, living in higher-priced neighborhoods with access to good public schools, assisting with college costs, and providing support for young adults to help them get started in their independent economic lives once their education is completed. As financial resources have become more unequal in a number of countries over the last three decades, the differences in the capacities of rich and poor families to invest in their children also have become more unequal. This change is occurring in a period when relatively more educational investment is needed to meet ongoing labor market changes (Goldin and Katz 2008). It follows that unless these inequities are offset by public policies designed to moderate their effects, the children of the rich will have a relatively better chance of staying rich in the future, and the children of the poor will have less chance of escaping poverty or low socioeconomic status (SES).

Investments in children are even broader than this discussion suggests. An *investment* is a diversion of current resources, such as time or money, from use for immediate consumption of goods and services we value, to activities that pay off in the future in terms of additional resources, including those that benefit our children. A prime example is of course education, but many activities that parents carry out on behalf of their children are investments in a similar sense. Some of them may involve a low monetary cost, but require an investment of time, such as undertaking many different types of activities with children (for example, teaching them to swim or reading to them). In engaging in such activities, parents increase their own enjoyment and current well-being as well as benefitting their children in later life. Other child-related activities can be quite costly, such as paying university tuition. And some activities may benefit children in a different dimension than the initial investment. For example, in addition to aiding their cognitive development, parents and schools help socialize children, teach them to behave courteously, provide motivations, and work in a variety of ways to aid their socioemotional development. These traits may not only pay off in the social and behavioral dimension, but ready them for school so that their cognitive development is enhanced as well. Social and behavioral traits may also be more important for future earnings and jobs as employers may highly value such traits. In economic parlance, there is complementarity between investments in the social (socioemotional) and cognitive dimensions.

Further, all such investments take place in institutional contexts that provide leeway for parents and governments to influence how effective such investments may be. For instance, universal early childhood education for all children might be especially beneficial for the lowest-SES children if all such programs had comparable resources. However, to the extent that the quality of preschools and teachers is subject to neighborhood effects as in elementary and secondary schooling in many nations, low-SES children are likely to be excluded from the best preschools and thereby lessen the equalizing effect of early childhood education. Other childhood investments may also be subject to institutional constraints, nepotism, ability to pay and co-funding, including tuition for colleges and universities (for example, on U.S.-Canadian differences in financial aid and tertiary school completion, see Belley, Frenette, and Lochner 2010).

Although there is evidence that parental investments in children have become more unequal over the past thirty years in some countries (Kaushal, Magnuson, and Waldfogel 2011), analysis of the best multigenerational data available in the United States (from the Panel Study of Income Dynamics) does not show a clear decline in intergenerational mobility between children born in the 1950s and those born in the late 1970s, just before inequality began to rise (Lee and Solon 2009). Part of the problem may be measurement error. The individuals in the cohort born during the period of rising inequality are only in their early thirties, still a bit too young to provide reliable estimates of lifetime income. Another possibility is that the gradual, thirty-year rise in inequality in the United States and smaller increases elsewhere are still too small

Figure 1.1   Estimates of Intergenerational Income Elasticities for Fathers and Sons, Early 1980s

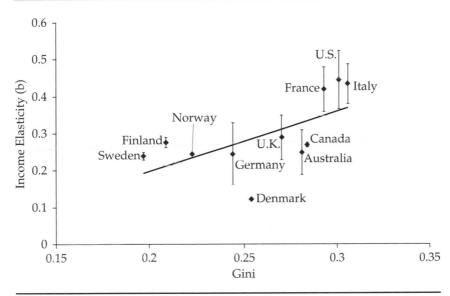

Source: Authors' calculations based on data from Bjorklund and Jäntti (2009, figure 20.1).

to have the types of negative effects suggested by increased economic inequality.

Of course, it is also possible that the prediction that high inequality leads to low mobility is simply wrong. But one compelling reason to doubt this is the recent discovery that the predicted relationship does show up in cross-national comparisons. Figure 1.1 presents the relationship between income inequality (measured by the Gini coefficient for the parents' generation) and the intergenerational income elasticity—a measure of the strength of the relationship between the incomes of parents and the incomes of their grown children. Mobility is measured as the inverse of the elasticity in figure 1.1, hence the lower the elasticity the greater the mobility. Indeed, most measures of mobility are actually measures of persistence of the younger generation's place in the order of outcomes compared to their parents. So when elasticities are high, the parent–adult child relationship is strongest. This plot includes eleven industrialized countries where both measures are now available and demonstrates wide variance in intergenerational mobility across those countries (Björklund and Jäntti 2009).

As figure 1.1 shows, the relationship between inequality and intergenerational elasticity is moderately positive. Higher levels of inequality are associated with lower rates of mobility—the rank order correlation is 0.62. Although we cannot lean too heavily on a regression based on only eleven data points, there are multiple estimates of both inequality and mobility rates in most of these nations, adding credence to the estimates shown in figure 1.1 (Blanden 2011). What is most interesting here is that these countries seem to vary a great deal in the degree to which they manage to attenuate the estimated relationship between inequality and intergenerational mobility. Some countries lie alongside the least squares regression line indicating levels of mobility close to what their levels of inequality might predict (for example, Norway, Germany, and the United Kingdom). Sweden and Finland are low inequality countries that lie slightly above the regression line, with slightly less mobility than their levels of inequality predict. Denmark shows intermediate levels of inequality but stands out with much higher rates of mobility than expected. Canada and Australia tend to fall between intermediate and high levels of inequality, but like Denmark, also show higher levels of mobility than expected. A final group of countries (Italy, the United States, and France) generally have high levels of inequality and lower levels of intergenerational mobility than one would predict.

If this pattern is real, and not just a matter of random variation around the plotted regression line, it suggests that there may be significant differences in the types and effectiveness of public and private investments and institutions that different countries deploy in their efforts to equalize opportunities across the income distribution. These differences may be due to institutional design. For example, some countries may intervene earlier in the lives of disadvantaged individuals, and early intervention may be particularly effective, as many believe (Knudsen et al. 2006). Or, countries may differ in the sheer size of their social welfare expenditures or in the distribution of expenditures across various areas of social welfare, such as health or education. This could make a difference if expenditures in some areas are more effective than others in promoting mobility, one of the questions this book attempts to address. Finally, the effectiveness of institutions designed to promote mobility may depend in part on the amount of inequality they have to cope with. For example, a universal preschool program may be effective in countries where differences in the private resources available to families are modest. But where family differences are great, they may swamp even a well-designed, well-funded preschool program.

Inequality has increased over time relative to the levels of income inequality shown in figure 1.1. This is the case in all the countries shown here, except for France where it has fallen over the past twenty-five years (Smeeding, Erikson, and Jäntti 2011; Brandolini and Smeeding 2009, as shown in chapter 14, this volume). Most countries investigated here have higher inequality now than at any time in the past, but the rank order of countries by levels of income inequality is about the same now as it was for prior generations. The amount of income available to low income families with children is also important in determining life chances as high child poverty means less parental economic resources. Child poverty rates for these countries in the most recent Luxemburg Income Study (LIS) year generally follow the same patterns as do current measures of inequality, where low-inequality nations in Scandinavia have low child poverty rates (5 percent or below at half the median income poverty level), middle-inequality central European countries have poverty rates of 10 to 11 percent, Australia and the United Kingdom are at about 14 percent and the highest rates in Canada, Italy, and the United States are 17 percent or above.[1] This makes it all the more interesting to know how countries like Canada with both above average inequality and above average child poverty rates do so well on mobility outcomes. If the ability to invest more in children increases among the rich and declines among the poor as inequalities increase, greater inequality may lead to even less mobility. If intergenerational mobility is driven by cumulative forces of advantage and disadvantage over the life course, mobility outcomes may become worse for the current generation of children because of increasingly higher inequality (DiPrete and Eirich 2006). These effects might come about in two ways.

First, if the children of higher-SES parents do well in school, they are more likely to attend and graduate from college, are better able to rely on parental help as they establish careers, and ultimately, will earn more income as the wage distribution rewards higher-skilled workers with better earnings. This pattern of development is a form of "cumulative advantage" where success begets more success within generations. But there is also the possibility that greater inequality increases the SES gradient from one generation to the next, and if so, this process of cumulative advantage might make an even larger difference across generations. Patterns of cumulative advantage within generations can be established only if SES-related differences are followed across children's lives. To establish between-generation cumulative advantage requires observations from a minimum of three generations. These requirements are generally beyond currently available data, but offer an appealing framework for how one might expect growing economic inequality to affect intergenerational mobility.

In this volume, we report the results of a coordinated set of mobility studies across ten countries with different levels of inequality. It is a first step toward understanding how and why mobility is sustained at higher rates in some countries than in others. The conceptual framework for making cross-national comparisons is based on a life-course approach, and is detailed in the description that follows. We expect that the life-course approach in a comparative perspective will allow us to see where divergences in outcomes between high-and low-SES children occur in the life cycle and how those differences are related to policies, processes, and institutions operating at various life-course stages.

In most countries where measures are available, there is a moderate to large positive correlation between parental and adult offspring socioeconomic status, and the strength of this association varies across countries (Björklund and Jäntti 2009). But we know relatively little about how advantage is transmitted from parent to child, how that transmission varies across the life course, whether it accumulates within generations, and what structural arrangements mediate that transmission. A major focus of discussion in the United States in recent years has been the discovery of differences in cognitive and socioemotional (noncognitive) outcomes during early childhood that are positively correlated with parents' socioeconomic status.[2] However, there is evidence from a number of other countries that intermediate outcomes after early childhood also have a steep socioeconomic gradient.

A Model of Intergenerational Mobility

The conceptual model shown in figure 1.2 describes the different life points in childhood and young adulthood that are crucial to understanding how advantage is transmitted from parents to their children. In figure 1.2 we begin with parents' socioeconomic status (*Parental$_{SES}$*). Each subsequent box refers to child outcomes at different stages over the child's life course: the birth year (up to one year, or *C_0*), early childhood (ages two through six, or *C_1*), middle childhood (ages seven through eleven, or *C_2*), adolescence (ages twelve through seventeen, or *C_3*), early adulthood (ages eighteen through twenty-nine, or *C_4*), and adulthood (ages thirty-plus, or *O_A*). This same terminology, sometimes using the C stages, is common to all chapters in this volume.

In this model, it may turn out that some ages are particularly important in understanding how advantage is transmitted. One of these, for example, may be around age eleven in middle childhood, when children move from primary to secondary school in many countries. Another may be at age seventeen or eighteen, as adolescents make the transition to early adulthood. Throughout this model, a host of different mobility-relevant skills, attributes, achievements and outcomes are measured. These might include differences in outcomes as varied as birth weights or initial health status, cognitive abilities, educational achievement or attainments, or socioemotional and behavioral outcomes.

Next, and displayed under *Parental$_{SES}$* in the model, *Investments$_{-t}$* and *Institutions$_{-t}$* are the various public and private investments and institutional contexts that may influence or contribute to differences at each life-course stage. Investments might include public programs such as

Figure 1.2   Intergenerational Transmission of Advantage by Life Stage

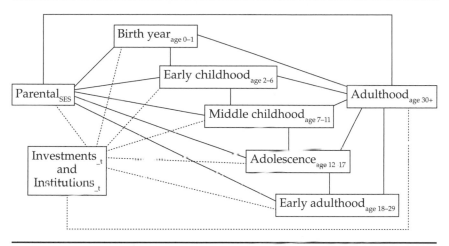

Source: Authors' figure.
Notes: Parental socioeconomic variables and measures: education, income, earnings, SES, occupation, wealth, employment; childhood and early adulthood measures: educational attainment, cognitive measures, socioemotional behavior, employment and labor market, health-physical; investments and institutions assumed to be different public and private investments and institutions contributing to children's development that vary by country; adulthood measures: child SES, income, education, employment, labor market attachment.

day care, universal early education, afterschool or summer programs, or access to health care or health programs, among others. The institutional contexts might refer to processes such as how schools are organized, the presence of educational tracking, or differences in private costs of attending college.

The final stage in the model, adulthood (ages thirty-plus, or *O_A*), refers to offspring outcomes as an adult that are likely to reflect the combination of investments, opportunities, and choices (for example, marriage) that occur through the life course. These might include such characteristics as adult SES, education, occupation, household income, labor market attachment, earnings, or other advantages and disadvantages in the labor market. For instance, labor market institutions and macro-economic factors (or *Institutions_t*) might provide differential returns to the same credentials across countries and thereby independently affect *O_A*. Looking at one important component of SES, individual earnings, Jo Blanden and her colleagues (2011) show that differences in intergenerational earnings outcomes between the United States and the United Kingdom depend most heavily on labor market returns to education. Because the earnings distributions are more unequal in the United States, particularly with much higher rewards among the more highly educated, young adults with the same level of university attainments will do better in terms of earnings in the United States compared to the United Kingdom. It follows that heterogeneity in outcomes across generations within countries will depend on processes that we cannot fully capture in our implementation of the model due to data limitations and poor information about institutional contexts across nations.

It is implicit in figure 1.2 that parental SES may be associated with any stage or outcome of the development process, and any outcome at an earlier life stage may be related to later outcomes all the way up to adulthood. For example, parental education or income (*Parental$_{SES}$*) may be related to birth weights in the birth year, or to test scores and socioemotional behavior in early childhood, which, in turn, may be associated with various outcomes at any of the subsequent developmental stages up to adulthood. Ultimately, offspring adult socioeconomic status, *O_A*, is the outcome of a whole series of parental and other inputs from the birth year on, including the formation of partnerships. This schema is consistent with Flavio Cunha and James Heckman's (2007, 2009) dynamic multistage model of skill development, in which intermediate outcomes at each stage not only affect subsequent outcomes but may also affect the productivity of inputs at subsequent stages. For example, children who were not read to as preschoolers may find it more difficult to learn to read at school. This initial disadvantage can then be reinforced if a poor secondary education limits one's choices and opportunities in terms of preparation for or success in higher education. On the other hand, if this same child were fortunate enough to attend a resource-rich secondary school that specializes in college preparedness, this may offset some of the initial disadvantage, and do a better job of connecting schooling and improving performance between these two levels. The entire process may therefore allow for cumulative advantages within cohorts.

Making Use of a Cross-National Comparative Approach

To generate cross-national evidence on how socioeconomic advantage is likely to be transmitted over the life course, this project consists of sixteen studies that examine for a number of different countries the ways in which different child outcomes vary with parental socioeconomic status at multiple stages of the life course. In some studies, the investigators consider how outcomes at one stage are associated with outcomes at previous stages. And where possible, we look at how these intermediate associations contribute to the correlation between parent and adult-child outcomes (for example, earnings or education). It was clear from the outset of the project that there are a number of national and international datasets, both cross-sectional and longitudinal, which include comparable tests of cognitive ability, health and academic achievement that tap what are thought to be mobility-relevant skills and attributes at various points during an individual's development. Some of these data sources also include information on socioemotional skills and behavioral traits that may be associated with subsequent mobility. Using data like these, plus administrative data in countries where it is available, we undertake a small number of strategically selected cross-national and national studies to estimate correlations of childhood outcomes (at various points along the life course) with parental income, education, or other measures of parental socioeconomic status.

With these results it should then be possible to compare countries in terms of the effectiveness of their efforts to promote mobility at various levels of individual development. So, for example, if a country shows relatively low correlations between parental SES and cognitive skills at the preschool level (a relatively flat SES gradient), it would be important to find out what kinds of investments in families and young children that country is making to narrow the gap between the children of the poor and the children of the rich. Other countries might exhibit higher correlations between parental SES and children's early test scores, but show lower correlations between SES and cognitive skills at later stages of development—perhaps because their primary or secondary educational institutions permit the children of the poor to have second-chance opportunities, allowing some degree of catch-up. Alternatively, there may be countries with institutional arrangements that effectively freeze, or perhaps even exacerbate, inequalities in early cognitive skills by placing students with disparate test scores on different academic tracks, or by placing poor students into remedial education or low-quality schools that are ineffective in enhancing the skills necessary for mobility. In sum, a set of comparably designed national studies of this type can reveal how family resources are correlated with individual outcomes at various points during the early life course, and may be able to shed light on the structural differences that moderate intergenerational mobility in different ways in different countries. Another advantage of the cross-national perspective is that genetic transmission in the outcome (for example, cognitive ability) should be the same across countries, and so cross-country differences should reflect different environments, policy and otherwise.

We are especially interested in cross-national comparisons that might prove to be particularly informative. Figure 1.1 suggests that it might be especially revealing to consider comparisons between Germany and Denmark, where both show Gini coefficients of about 0.25 in the father's generation, but in which the intergenerational income elasticity estimate in Germany (0.25) is double that in Denmark (0.12). Other strategic comparisons might include one or more of the high inequality–low mobility countries (the United States, Italy, and France) with similar inequality but higher mobility countries like Canada or Australia, or comparisons of estimates from Canada or Australia with those generated for Denmark. It is also important to keep in mind the longitudinal nature of the life-cycle model. For example, comparisons between Germany and Denmark may yield similar estimates at one life stage, but fundamentally different estimates at a subsequent point later in the life course. Understanding where and when across different life stages such differences emerge might provide evidence about the public investments that are especially critical for later stages in life.

Research Questions

The model of intergenerational transmission described in figure 1.2 engenders a number of important research questions, and the investigators in this project employed twenty-nine datasets across ten countries to shed light on some of these questions about intergenerational mobility. We draw on the empirical evidence generated by those studies to specifically address four main questions motivated by that model. Even with such a broad spectrum of data, certain constraints existed and we could not make all the comparisons we hoped to achieve.[3] Nevertheless, the breadth and diversity of the data employed has provided us with solid insights into our core questions.

Do differences by parental SES emerge, and if so, when?

Do the differences change over the life course?

How do the childhood differences contribute to intergenerational mobility?

How do answers to these questions vary among countries?

The first three questions can be more formally addressed by a model in which changes in the gaps between SES groups in skills or achievements (for example, cognitive test scores) might occur over childhood and into adulthood. The online appendix to this chapter provides an example based on a simple value-added model of the evolution of skills as the child ages (as in Todd and Wolpin 2003, 2007).[4] It relates skills at a given age or life stage to investments or actions undertaken by families and schools to improve skills at that age or life stage and to the level of skills achieved previously. There may be depreciation in skills over time, making it necessary to continue to invest sufficiently at each age in order to maintain skills. Whether skill differentials by parents' SES widen, narrow, or remain stable as the child ages depends on the pattern of investment at each age in each SES group and the degree to which skills depreciate without investments.

Figure 1.3   SES Skill Differentials, Fanning Out

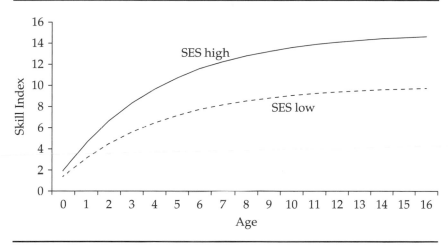

Source: Authors' model.

As children pass into and through school, the SES investment differential may alter. Figures 1.3 through 1.5 illustrate how absolute SES skill differentials might change as children age. For instance, it is possible that differentials diverge systematically as a child moves to adulthood because of cumulative advantage or disadvantage within a generation, causing the investment differential to widen. It is also possible that children from more affluent families experience less depreciation because

Figure 1.4   SES Skill Differentials, Convergence

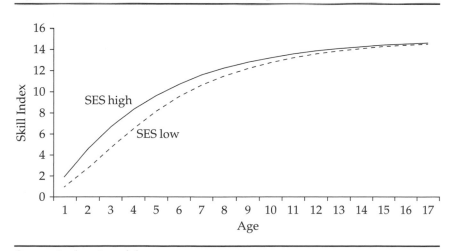

Source: Authors' model.

Figure 1.5   SES Skill Differentials, Constant Gap

Source: Authors' model.

of environmental differences or dinner conversation or school quality (see figure 1.3). Alternatively, equalizing schools (or other institutions or investments) may cause the SES investment differential to narrow as schools substitute more for families in skill acquisition (see figure 1.4). Finally, it may be that absolute SES differentials remain constant over time. As an example, if processes of cumulative advantage are in place, schools may act to simply offset continued gains in advantage, effectively keeping the absolute differences stable over time (see figure 1.5). Because of difficulties in the comparability of outcome measures over time, it is often necessary to make comparisons in standardised or relative SES differentials—that is, adjusting for changing means and variances of the measures over ages. Chapter 10 in this volume compares these two approaches to the evolution of SES differentials over childhood. Neither approach is inherently superior to the other.

The final two questions addressing how childhood differences contribute to intergenerational mobility and how differences in the SES gradients vary among countries are answered in two different ways throughout the rest of the volume. First, a meta-study, in which all participating authors have provided comparative SES gradients for all countries and measures for which data is available, is carried out in chapter 2 (and described in more detail shortly). Second, the individual chapters in this volume provide richer but more limited evidence across a set of countries for specific stages of the child's life course. Both of these allow us to directly draw some conclusions in the penultimate chapter.

In most chapters and in the overall conclusions, we do not distinguish between the sexes in studying the evolution of the SES gradients over the life course. Absence of analysis of such differences does not imply that they are not important, but they are not the focus of this study.

Measuring Parents' SES

To harmonize parental SES, we mainly employ a four-category education ranking for parents' education using the more highly educated of the two parents (or the education of single parents—some authors will also use income, earnings, or occupation). We prefer education as our measure of SES because it is a measure of permanent income and because people with different educational qualifications face different labor markets with different rewards and opportunities and make different career-path choices (artist or banker). Education is positively correlated with parental age at the child's birth and in many countries with stability of marriage as well. More educated parents also have fewer children and do so later in life (Moynihan, Smeeding, and Rainwater 2004). Education is also the indicator of parental SES that is most commonly available for all of the countries examined here, is the most malleable in terms of being made comparable across countries, and is usually constant over the child's life.[5]

For purposes of comparability, education is coded using the International Standard Classification of Education (ISCED) (UNESCO 2006). We distinguish four groups: low (ISCED 0–2, for example, high school dropouts in the United States), medium (ISCED 3–4, for example, a high school diploma in the United States), medium-high (ISCED 5b, higher education below degree level), and high (ISCED 5a-6, degree level or higher). Some of the papers use other more aggregated or disaggregated educational attainment measures, but in the chapter that follows we use this categorization of parents' education to study the gradients that emerge.

This rough classification is for one point in time, and will miss the trends in attainment across nations. Moreover, as percentages are observed at different years, the underlying measures of cross-national educational inequality may differ. Figure 1.6 presents one such trend—in postsecondary education across nations. In all but two countries, Germany and the United States, the pattern is for increasing educational attainment by cohort at the postsecondary school level. Some of the earlier generations who are now forty-five and older will be the parents in our studies, but in studies that focus more on early childhood measures, they will look more like the two younger cohorts—ages up to twenty-four or twenty-five through thirty-four. But the U.S. difference is especially striking in that they were the world leader in educational attainment in the oldest generation and are now experiencing

Figure 1.6   Adults with Associate Degree or Higher

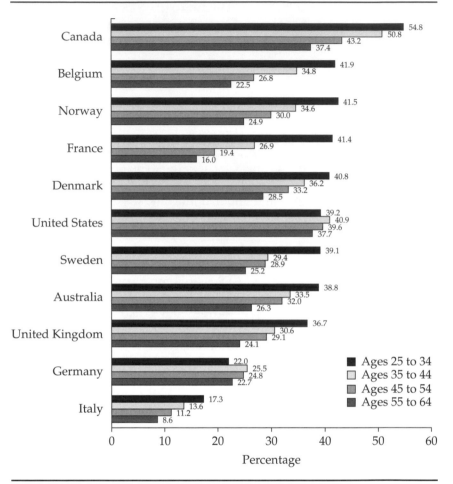

Source: Authors' calculations based on data from OECD (2008).

flat attainment of postsecondary degrees while all other nations, save Germany, are rapidly advancing.

There are clearly other ways to characterize family background. Some of the chapters use differences in parents' income to complement the analysis based on parents' highest education (for example, chapter 4, this volume). Another possibility is to describe family background by parents' social class or occupational group, which is very common in the sociology literature on intergenerational mobility. Yet another approach is to combine a number of indicators to assess the family's SES. For instance, Alissa Goodman and her colleagues (2011) construct a measure of socioeconomic position based on parents' income, social class, housing tenure, and a self-reported measure of financial difficulties. The measure is used in the analysis of children's cognitive attainments in four British data sets. In our view, no measure is ideal, and the strength of family background in distinguishing outcomes of children is often qualitatively the same with the different measures.

Contributions of the Book

In what ways does this volume contribute to our understanding of the emergence of cross-country differences in the association of adult outcomes, such as earnings, with parents' socioeconomic position? This book is part of an integrated effort to better understand the mechanisms that produce the intergenerational transmission of economic and social persistence. Markus Jäntti and his colleagues (2006), in a carefully done study using harmonized panel datasets, suggest large differences across nations in the persistence of intergenerational mobility. In particular, the study notes a probability that someone born in the lowest parental income quintile group in the United States would end up there as an adult is twice as high compared with any other country examined. This finding led the leaders of this project and editors of this volume to ask if we could assess the mechanisms that produced this outcome. As a precursor to this work, we recently published a volume showing the state of the literature on the intergenerational transmission of advantage in 2009 and 2010 and pointing to fruitful avenues for further research, which were followed up in this volume (Smeeding, Erikson, and Jäntti 2011). Most important, the book, *Persistence, Privilege, and Parenting,* suggested that certain data would allow one to more systematically and carefully trace the life course of the transmission of advantage across nations, if we could assemble the right teams of researchers and the right comparable cross-national datasets.

The editors and project leaders began to unravel this mystery by undertaking a multiyear, multiteam cross-national effort to identify the channels through which parental advantage affected mobility. In so doing, we were able to bring together teams of scholars to examine the SES gradient for children of the same age, in the same outcome domain, in different nations using harmonized cross-national longitudinal household, administrative, and other data that are as comparable as possible. The premise of our project was the belief that comparison of socioeconomic gradients for two or more countries at specific points of a child's development would help us to identify the pathways connecting parental success to child success and the pathways through which that generation took place.

Our findings point to promising avenues for future causal modeling. The picture that emerges is both complex and robust. For instance, we address the very important ongoing debate about the importance of early childhood education as the prime policy intervention point for leveling opportunities for success across children whose parents differ in terms of SES (Knudsen et al. 2006). We find that while cross-country differences in the SES gradient in cognitive skills do appear early on, it is not clear that these either increase as children age or that they are the sole determinants of the SES gradient in adult outcomes. We also are the first to discover that comparative gradients in socioemotional behaviors are much shallower than those in cognitive outcomes, suggesting that they contribute less to gradients in adult outcomes than do cognitive achievements. Moreover, the comparative evidence suggests that part of the gradient in SES outcomes in adulthood is due to factors that emerge in labor markets, such as social networks and institutions that set salaries and pay. One of our important contributions then is to show that SES gradients develop early on, but later outcomes in schooling, earnings, and so on are affected by many factors as children age. This, in turn, suggests that there are many stages at which interventions may diminish disadvantages, not just at one early point in a child's life course. Indeed, the reason we do not find strong evidence of widening disparities as children age may be that in most countries education policy does to some extent reduce (or at least not increase) SES disadvantages throughout school.

We were also able to create a secondary dataset (chapter 2, this volume) that includes more than three hundred parental SES gradients for different outcomes and countries, allowing us to assess both the strength of the parental SES association for each outcome across countries, and the ability to compare these countries across multiple outcomes. One of the most robust findings is that parental SES gradients in the United States are the most steep among all ten countries for almost every outcome. These findings suggest that the country with the least intergenerational mobility and the least equal opportunity for children to advance is the United States, a finding entirely consistent with those of Markus Jäntti and his colleagues (2006). Such findings suggest that if one wants to improve opportunity in the United States, policy must be used to flatten these gradients without undermining the ability of parents to do all they can for their children.

The research reported in this volume therefore breaks entirely new ground in terms of both depth and breadth of findings. It attests to the usefulness of having access to comparable cross-national data in exploring the importance of family background for child outcomes. While it is often very difficult to find research designs that allow for convincing causal models in most nations, we have advanced the field in important ways. We have shown that comparing the strength of the association between outcomes and origins at different stages of child development across countries does provide a means to map out where it may—and where it may not—be fruitful to search for answers.

Chapter Organization

In the end, the available data that could be reasonably harmonized limited the range of comparisons we could achieve across age groups and countries. Table 1.1 summarizes the sixteen studies that are the foundation of this volume. It shows the countries, domains of inquiry, measures of parental SES, and different life stages explored in each chapter. Children are observed at different times in different countries and at different stages of development. For instance, the later life-course outcomes are visible only when parents are observed before 1980. The older outcomes after this period cannot yet be fully observed. In contrast, the younger child outcome data (for example, primary school and younger) are largely observed in 1990 and beyond. Only a few nations allow us repeated observation of different cohorts, for example, children under age six. Some of the observations are therefore after the onset of widespread inequality in some countries (for example, in Anglo-Saxon nations where income inequality has grown since 1980). Further, using parent education to measure SES suggests that the patterns of postsecondary achievement in figure 1.6 may well come into play as different cohorts are viewed in different countries at different times.

Introductory Chapters: Meta-Analysis and Prototype

Chapter 2 investigates common elements and differences in the relationship between parental education and outcomes across all the life-cycle stages, domains, and countries in our study. It provides an unvarnished view of the relationships for all results in all chapters. To gain more general insights, rather than list in detail the specific coefficient estimates from each chapter, we chose to ask the participating research groups to provide data in a standardized format to enable us to examine the patterns in the data more broadly. The goal of chapter 2 is to use these data as a separate meta-analytic database and examine how the association of child outcomes with parental SES varies across domains, countries, and child's age in an admittedly broad but informative way. Our regressions, based on 292 data points linking parental SES (as standardized by education) to various child and adult outcomes, suggest important ways in which the intergenerational gradients differ, and some in which they do not, across these dimensions. The meta-analysis offered here, though broadly consistent with the findings of the individual chapters, is intended to complement rather than replace a more detailed reading of

Table 1.1   Summary of Domains, Countries, and Life Stages Distributed by Projects

Projects, by chapter	3	4	5	6	7	8
Domains						
Cognitive	X	X		X	X	
Socioemotional-noncognitive	X	X	X	X		
Health-physical	X					
Education	X				X	X
Labor market	X				X	X
Countries						
Australia		X		X		
Canada		X				
Denmark						X
Finland						
France					X	
Germany			X			
Italy						
Sweden	X					
United Kingdom		X	X	X		
United States		X				
Life stage						
Birth year (0 to 1)						
Early childhood (2 to 6)		X	X	X	X	X
Middle childhood (7 to 11)				X	X	X
Adolescence (12 to 17)	X				X	X
Early adulthood (18 to 29)	X				X	
Adulthood (30+)	X				X	X
Parental SES						
Education	X	X	X	X	X	X
Income	X	X	X			X
Other					X	
Year P_{SES} measured	1962–1965	2000–2004	2000–2003	1999–2001	1978, 1980, 1989, 1993	1984–1991

Source: Authors' compilation.
Note: United Kingdom includes Scotland and England.

9	10	11	12	13	14	15	16	17	18
X	X	X	X	X	X	X	X	X	
X	X						X		
					X			X	
X				X	X	X			X
						X		X	X
			X						
		X	X		X				X
		X							X
X									
		X	X						
		X	X	X			X		
		X		X		X			
X		X					X	X	
X	X	X	X					X	
X	X	X	X		X				
					X			X	
	X								
X	X	X		X	X				
X	X	X	X	X	X		X	X	
		X	X	X	X	X	X		X
								X	X
X	X	X	X	X		X	X		X
	X				X	X		X	X
		X				X	X		X
1958, 1965, 1968, 1970, 1982	1991–1992, 1994–1996 1998	2001–2003, 2006	2000, 2004	1998–2007,	1994, 1997	2004	2005–2006	1970, 1973	1965–1976, 1982–1986

the studies we have based it on and to provide a broader framework for summing up the individual effects.

We identify large differences in the level of intergenerational association across domains, the educational and cognitive being highest, the physical and socioemotional behavior being clearly the lowest, and the economic in between. The evidence across countries strongly suggests that the gradient in the United States is the steepest across the countries we study and that therefore the United States is likely to have the least mobility and the most persistence in the comparative chapters that follow. Finally, we find mixed evidence for whether the intergenerational associations grow stronger as children age, with the cognitive outcome domain most clearly suggesting this pattern.

The remaining chapters in this volume, on which data we have based the meta-analysis, offer studies of the same data that exploit in greater detail the possibilities offered by simultaneously including multiple control variables and different decomposition techniques. Almost all of the chapters are multinational and comparative by design, though we begin by highlighting one—chapter 3—that has unique data allowing the authors to fill in many of the links in figure 1.2 for the same children in one nation.

Chapter 3, written by Carina Mood and her colleagues, illustrates how one might ideally explore the way that skills and traits acquired earlier in life feed into the intergenerational correlations in completed education and income. Because it also illustrates the power and accuracy afforded by the use of administrative data, albeit in one country (Sweden), it offers something of a prototype for future research in this field of inquiry. It takes apart the correlation between fathers' and their sons' incomes (and their respective adult educational attainments), which is the point of departure for this book. In particular, it performs decompositions of these correlations into the contributions attributable to well-measured mobility-relevant skills when the son was aged eighteen. It contains a large number of potentially mediating variables, which include four measures of cognitive ability, four of personality traits, and three of physical traits, as well as the grade point average in the last grade of compulsory secondary school at sixteen. The chapter finds that father's education is strongly related to son's education in large part through the fact that father's education and son's cognitive ability are correlated, and that son's cognitive ability is strongly related to his educational attainment. His personality characteristics at eighteen play only a small role. Although the son's cognitive ability also contributes strongly to the intergenerational correlation in income, partly through the higher education of the son, an important part of the father-son income correlation comes from the association of the son's personality traits with father's income and a strong relationship between his personality traits and his adult income. Physiological characteristics contribute little to either correlation.

The remaining chapters of this volume focus on particular parts of childhood. Five deal with early childhood, particularly before children begin primary school. Another four are concerned with middle childhood to adolescence, and the next five are mainly concerned with late adolescence and early adulthood, and participation in tertiary education. Chapter 18 studies the role of parents' networks in their son's transition to the labor market and their contribution to the father-son correlation in earnings.

Early Childhood

It may be that early differences in achievement are more susceptible to policy changes than older ones are, because the link between family and outcome is less affected by other national institutions and policies that come later in a child's life. Interventions at this stage may also be more cost effective in terms of improving long-term outcomes (Knudsen et al. 2006). We are therefore especially interested in the early stage differences in gradients that come about because of parenting, child care quality and uniformity, and early childhood education.

In chapter 4, Bruce Bradbury and his colleagues document that significant differences in mobility-relevant skills by parental education and income are discernible as early as the age of five in all four countries examined: Australia, Canada, the United Kingdom, and the United States. These differences are generally larger in the United States and the United Kingdom than in Canada and Australia, the United States showing the greatest cognitive differences by parental SES of all four countries.

In chapter 5, John Ermisch, Frank Peter, and Katharina Spiess concentrate on how family change during children's preschool years, such as parental separation or the mother living with a new partner, is associated with their socioemotional behavior. They find similar associations for the United Kingdom and Germany, and conclude that stable family environments are associated with better child behavior in both countries. Family instability is more common among parents with lower education, and this association contributes a moderate fraction to the gradient in socioemotional behavior by parental education.

Chapter 6, by Jo Blanden, Ilan Katz, and Gerry Redmond, takes a more dynamic perspective on cognitive development during preschool and into primary school in the United Kingdom and Australia. The authors find that the gradient in cognitive outcomes by parental education over ages three to seven in the United Kingdom and four to eight in Australia remains relatively constant, neither narrowing nor widening as they start school. Their evidence also indicates that persistence in low cognitive scores over these ages is much higher in the low parental education group, particularly so in the United Kingdom.

The evidence of preschool differences in cognitive and socioemotional development that are related to parental SES could in part reflect differences by SES in child-care arrangements and preschool education, but no evidence is presented on this issue in the previous three chapters. Chapter 7, by Christelle Dumas and Arnaud Lefranc, investigates the impact of universal preschool education in France on children's achievements during school and beyond. Dumas and Lefranc exploit preschool extension that varies over time and municipalities to identify both short- and long-term effects of preschool education on schooling and labor market outcomes, with children from lower SES groups benefiting more. Their evidence suggests that universal preschool education compresses SES differentials in outcomes during school and in adult earnings, thereby enhancing intergenerational mobility. Chapter 8, a complementary study by Paul Bingley and Niels Westergård-Nielsen, uses Danish administrative data to examine the contribution of daycare availability to the intergenerational association of educational attainments and income. The authors find that the educational mobility of children of low-educated parents improves with the availability of daycare in the municipality, but that children from more affluent homes are not affected.

Middle Childhood to Adolescence

Four chapters study the evolution of the achievement gradient with respect to parental SES as the child ages from six to sixteen. Greg Duncan and his colleagues assess in chapter 9 how much differences in cognitive and socioemotional outcomes in relation to parents' educational attainments at ages seven to ten and in adolescence contribute to the parent-child gradient in educational attainment. Their comparative analysis of four countries—Finland, Sweden, the United States, and the United Kingdom—indicates that childhood and adolescent skills account for one-third to one-half of the intergenerational correlation in completed schooling in these countries.

Chapter 10, by Katherine Magnuson, Jane Waldfogel, and Elizabeth Washbrook, compares England and the United States as a child ages from six to fourteen. Evidence is strong that gaps in cognitive achievement by parental education or income widen in England between the ages of eleven and fourteen. In the United States, whether these gaps widen after age seven depends on whether you think of achievement in terms of absolute skill levels (number of questions answered correctly) or relative skill levels (standardized scores).

In chapter 11, John Jerrim and John Micklewright study changes in the relation between family background and scores in two internationally standardized achievement tests taken at ages ten and fifteen, respectively, for a number of the countries studied in other chapters of the book. They find a striking similarity in the relationship between test scores and a measure of family background—the number of books in the home—at both ages in all countries. There is some evidence that this relationship is stronger at age fifteen than age ten in England and Scotland, echoing the finding of Katherine Magnuson and her colleagues in chapter 10, but in most countries the relationship is stable between the two ages.

In chapter 12, John Ermisch and Emilia Del Bono focus on England and find a widening of the gradient in school results with respect to parental education between ages eleven and fourteen and maintenance of the gradient at sixteen, in line with the results from the previous two chapters. They exploit the clustering of their sample by school to show that the widening is strongly related to the association between the quality of secondary school that children attend and their parents' SES, which is stronger than the association between primary school quality and parents' SES. The chapter also presents evidence that the gradient between parents' education and cognitive or school achievement around the age of fourteen is steepest in England and the United States and smallest in Canada and Australia.

Late Adolescence and Beyond

The next six chapters follow children beyond school into university education and the labor market. Chapter 13, by Massimiliano Bratti and his colleagues, investigates the role of educational tracking systems in producing associations between parental background and educational achievements in Italy and Germany. They find a strong association between parents' education and children's achievements in Germany and Italy before tracking takes place—similar to that in other countries studied in this volume. The study demonstrates inequality by parental education in entry to tracks, and this does not weaken during school (for example, it exists for repeating grades and changing tracks). There is a larger attenuation of parental effects as the child progresses through school in Germany than in Italy. Even after controlling for prior academic performance and school track, however, an association between university enrollment and parental education exists for both countries. The chapter concludes that the nature of tracking systems is more important for the strength of SES gradients than age at tracking.

In chapter 14, Robert Haveman and his colleagues compare the United States and Canada during middle childhood, adolescence, and early adulthood. They find remarkably similar gradients in outcomes with respect to parental income in both countries, although the associations generally tend to be lower in Canada. With respect to college attendance, there is a larger penalty from having low-income parents in the United States and a bigger boost from upper-income parents in Canada.

In chapter 15, Massimiliano Bratti and Lorenzo Cappellari study a particular university reform in Italy, which shortened the time that students had to study to obtain a university degree, but also offered the option to study for a further degree. Although the reform widened participation in university, the financial return to the shorter degree in the new system is found to be smaller than that from the old system's long degree. Because the offspring of parents with higher education are more likely to continue their studies beyond the short degree, the reform increased inequality in labor market outcomes among university graduates. These results point to the importance of examining all outcomes of a reform in evaluating its consequences.

In chapter 16, Silke Anger estimates the correlations between German parents and their adolescent children in cognitive abilities and personality traits. She finds similar correlations for cognitive ability (of the order of 0.5) as have been found in Norway, Sweden, and the United States (and slightly higher correlations than in the United Kingdom). Correlations in personality traits are smaller, and none of the correlations are affected by controls for parents' education.

In chapter 17, Anders Björklund, Markus Jäntti, and Martin Nybom study the contribution of early child health, achievements at the end of compulsory schooling, and educational attainments in Sweden and the United Kingdom to the correlation between parents' education and the child's weekly earnings in adulthood. It strongly suggests that the weaker relationship between a child's earnings as an adult and parental education in Sweden than in the United Kingdom mainly arises because there are lower labor market returns to education in Sweden than in the United Kingdom.

Finally, in chapter 18, Paul Bingley, Miles Corak, and Niels Westergård-Nielsen compare Canada and Denmark in the degree to which a son's main employer in adulthood is the same as the father's, showing remarkable similarities in this respect in the two countries. They show that the transmission of employers is strongly and positively related to fathers' earnings, particularly at the top end. They find less intergenerational earnings mobility in Canada than in Denmark, but that the difference narrows higher up within the sons' earnings distribution. Preservation of high income status is strongly related to the tendency of their sons to have the same main employer among higher income fathers in both countries.

Limits and Cautions

The aim of the book is to present new descriptive material on intergenerational transmission. For the most part there are no estimates of causal effects in the strict sense (although Dumas and Lefranc's chapter 7 may be an exception), but that does not mean that the evidence presented is not strongly suggestive about causal mechanisms and the policy strategies that may be implied by them, particularly when it is interpreted in the context of findings from other studies. In the penultimate chapter of the book we present the policy lessons that have emerged from the study.

In the end, it has been impossible to put together all life-cycle stages for any one country, or to cover all countries at any given stage. As a consequence, we cannot present a full picture of the extent to which outcomes at one stage feed into another, nor can we partition out the importance of particular stages in producing the overall intergenerational correlation of status, such as adult income or education in the child generation. For instance, the data we do have, and that was recently published by others, suggest that different labor markets reward the same skills at different rates. Hence, although the earnings rewards to higher skills are greater in the United Kingdom than in Sweden (see chapter 17), research on the United States and the United Kingdom finds much larger rewards for a given set of education credentials in the United States than in the United Kingdom (Blanden 2011).

Immigrants and racial gaps are given only minimal treatment in a few of the chapters because we take these countries as they are in terms of their make-up. Hence countries must adjust policies to meet the realities of the populations that they contain. And sometimes factoring out minorities makes little difference in the results. For instance, Markus Jäntti and his colleagues (2006) find that 42 percent of all U.S. children observed around age thirty-five whose parents were in the lowest quintile group of earnings when they were fifteen years of age remain there as adults. If we exclude blacks from this population, the proportion who remain in the lowest quintile group is 38 percent, still much higher than all of the other countries observed.

In any case, developing common measures of immigrant status is in its infancy within many nations, and these measures are difficult to harmonize across countries (Parsons and Smeeding 2006). The results in chapter 4 of this volume suggest that immigrants do not play a large role, even in Canada and Australia, where immigration is largest, where the data are most recent, and where gradients are less than in other Anglo-Saxon nations. Hence, we do not believe that these factors will affect the results of the findings in this book. Finally, although socioemotional traits appear to be important for economic outcomes (see chapter 3), these traits tend to be measured in variable ways across countries.

Conclusions

Chapter 19, the penultimate chapter, discusses the book's main messages, which we summarize here. Gaps in outcomes by parental SES emerge early in childhood in all countries for which we have evidence. They exist for both cognitive and socioemotional outcomes and are usually larger for the former. Gaps in either school achievement or cognitive test scores during adolescence exist for all of the large number of countries for which we have measures. Cross-national comparisons indicate that differences in the environment matter, with the United States generally having the largest gaps and Canada the smallest. We find only limited evidence of fanning out (that is, gaps become larger as a child ages) during childhood, hence little cross-national evidence for within-generation cumulative disadvantage. Robust evidence from three data sources, however, indicates that SES gaps in achievement for one country—the United Kingdom—become substantially bigger between the ages of eleven (the end of primary school) and fourteen. The widening gap is mainly related to the association between the quality of secondary school that children attend and their parents' SES, driven by residential choices, which is stronger than the association between primary school quality and parents' SES. In other countries, the SES gaps in outcomes are substantial but stay more or less the same through middle childhood and secondary school. But in no case do we find convergence in SES gaps at older ages and life stages, and hence early childhood education and socialization of lower-SES children may hold some promise for reducing the early gradients.

Overall, the evidence suggests that childhood gaps contribute significantly to intergenerational correlations in education and income in all nations. High-quality evidence from Sweden indicates that whereas cognitive ability influences both the son's educational attainment and his earnings, attributes such as social maturity, emotional stability, and leadership capacity measured in later adolescence and early adulthood pay off directly in the labor market rather than through education. About two-fifths of the father-son income correlation can be accounted for by cognitive and personality attributes, leaving a considerable remainder unaccounted for.

Differences between countries in intergenerational income mobility are not, however, necessarily driven entirely, or even mainly, by cross-country variation in the relationship between parental SES and childhood achievements, such as grades during adolescence or final education attainment. For instance, evidence indicates that the weaker relationship between a child's earnings as an adult and parental education in Sweden than in the United Kingdom mainly arises because labor market returns to education in Sweden are lower than in the United Kingdom. Parental influence continues into adulthood in terms of getting good jobs because of parental status or social networks.

Although the United States stands out in having the largest SES gaps and Canada as having some of the smallest, similarities across countries are numerous. Parents are important early in life, in school and related neighborhood choices, including secondary school systems with tracking. High-quality preschool experience—in terms of exposure to books, quality of preschool, formation of socioemotional (noncognitive) skills—has an influence everywhere. Also, the net effect of education systems is not to reduce the relationship between parental SES and child achievement, and, at best, education systems may be offsetting existing processes of cumulative advantage in keeping the overall gradients stable as children age. Parental influence through networks continues into the labor market in early adulthood, but smaller earnings returns to ability and education may reduce the midlife parent-child income correlation in some countries.

An important policy lesson from the research is that it is possible to provide more equal life chances than is the case in the United States without violation of the autonomy of the family or the principle of merit in assigning income positions (for example, jobs) in society. The experience of Canada is a particularly prime example. We also find that certain policies, such as universal preschool education, reduce the influence of family background on children's life chances, even in a country with relatively low intergenerational mobility and high income inequality—France.

This volume ends with a short postscript chapter by John Roemer that summarizes and reflects on the importance of parental rights. As we have seen in most chapters, parental inputs or lack thereof have long-term effects on children's mobility, especially in the very early years of life. Parental rights and responsibilities are especially important and sometimes differentially limited by culture, belief, institutions, and law. But, parents with more money, time, and other resources can have large effects on children's development and well-being. Parents will do all they can to help their children, and so parental rights may place important limits on the ability of policy to enhance mobility, including policies that are targeted to help the poor.

Notes

1. Based on LIS key figures, at http://www.lisdatacenter.org/lis-ikf-webapp/app/search-ikf-figures (accessed November 28, 2011), and Gornick and Jäntti (2010).

2. In referring to certain measures and abilities, we often use the terminology *socioemotional* or *sociobehavioral* rather than the more common *noncognitive* to refer to the diverse sets of behavior (for example, attention, anti- or prosocial behaviors, mental health, locus of control, and so on) generally lumped together as noncognitive traits (see chapter 9, this volume).

3. Of the eleven countries shown in figure 1.1, data from Norway are not included in the current studies.

4. The online appendix can be found at: http://www.russellsage.org/Ermisch_et_al_OnlineAppendix.pdf.

5. Some might argue that we should consider the association with mother's and father's education separately, but we are only using parents' education as a descriptive categorization, not trying to measure their causal impacts. To do the latter requires particular identification strategies (for example, see Ermisch and Pronzato 2011).

References

Belley, Philippe, Marc Frenette, and Lance Lochner. 2010. "Post-Secondary Attendance by Parental Income: Comparing the U.S. and Canada." CIBC Centre for Human Capital and Productivity Working Paper 2010–3. London, Canada: University of Western Ontario.

Björklund, Anders, and Markus Jäntti. 2009. "Intergenerational Income Mobility and the Role of Family Background." In *The Oxford Handbook of Economic Inequality*, edited by Wiemer Salverda, Brian Nolan, and Timothy M. Smeeding. New York: Oxford University Press.

Blanden, Jo. 2011. "Cross-Country Rankings in Intergenerational Mobility: A Comparison of Approaches for Economics and Sociology." *Journal of Economic Surveys*. DOI: 10.1111/j.1467–6419.2011.00690.x.

Blanden, Jo, Robert Haveman, Kathryn Wilson, and Timothy M. Smeeding. 2011. "Understanding the Mechanisms Behind Intergenerational Persistence: A Comparison Between the United States and U.K." In *The Comparative Study of Intergenerational Mobility*, edited by Timothy M. Smeeding, Robert Erickson, and Markus Jäntti. New York: Russell Sage Foundation.

Brandolini, Andrea, and Timothy M. Smeeding. 2009. "Income Inequality in Richer and OECD Countries." In *The Oxford Handbook of Economic Inequality*, edited by Wiemer Salverda, Brian Nolan, and Timothy Smeeding. New York: Oxford University Press.

Cunha, Flavio, and James J. Heckman. 2007. "The Technology of Skill Formation." *American Economic Review* 97(1): 31–47.

———. 2009. "The Economics and Psychology of Inequality and Human Development." *Journal of the European Economic Association* 7(2–3): 320–64.

DiPrete, Thomas A., and Gregory M. Eirich. 2006. "Cumulative Advantage as a Mechanism for Inequality: A Review of Theoretical and Empirical Developments." *Annual Review of Sociology* 32: 271–97.

Ermisch, John, and Chiara Pronzato. 2011. "Causal Effects of Parents' Education on Children's Education." In *Persistence, Privilege, and Parenting*, edited by Timothy M. Smeeding, Robert Erikson, and Markus Jäntti. New York: Russell Sage Foundation.

Goldin, Claudia, and Lawrence F. Katz. 2008. *The Race Between Education and Technology*. Cambridge, Mass.: Harvard University Press.

Gornick, Janet C., and Markus Jäntti. 2010. "Child Poverty in Upper-Income Countries: Lessons from the Luxembourg Income Study." In *From Child Welfare to Child Wellbeing: An International Perspective on Knowledge in the Service of Making Policy*, edited by Sheila B. Kamerman, Shelley Phipps, and Asher Ben-Arieh. New York: Springer.

Goodman, Alissa, Paul Gregg, and Elizabeth Washbrook. 2011. "Children's Educational Attainment and the Aspirations and Behaviours of Parents and Children Through Childhood in the U.K." *Longitudinal and Life Course Studies* 2(1):1–18.

Jäntti, Markus, Bernt Bratsberg, Knut Røed, Oddbjørn Raaum, Robin Naylor, Eva Österbacka, Anders Björklund, and Tor Eriksson. 2006. "American Exceptionalism in a New Light: A Comparison of Intergenerational Earnings Mobility in the Nordic Countries, the United Kingdom, and the United States." IZA Discussion Paper 1938. Bonn, Switzerland, January 2006.

Kaushal, Neeraj, Katherine Magnuson, and Jane Waldfogel. 2011. "How Is Family Income Related to Investments in Children's Learning?" In *Whither Opportunity: Rising Inequality and the Uncertain Life Chances of Low-Income Children*, edited by Greg J. Duncan and Richard Murnane. New York: Russell Sage Foundation.

Knudsen, Eric I., James J. Heckman, Judy L. Cameron, and Jack P. Shonkoff. 2006. "Economic, Neurobiological, and Behavioral Perspectives on Building America's Future Workforce." *Proceedings of the National Academy of the Sciences* 103(27): 10155–62. Available at: http://jenni.uchicago.edu/papers/Knudsen-etal_PNAS_v103n27_2006.pdf (accessed November 29, 2011).

Lee, Chulin, and Gary Solon. 2009. "Trends in Intergenerational Income Mobility." *The Review of Economics and Statistics* 91(4): 766–72.

Moynihan, Daniel P., Timothy M. Smeeding, and Lee Rainwater, eds. 2004. *The Future of the Family*. New York: Russell Sage Foundation.

Organisation for Economic Co-Operation and Development (OECD). 2008. *Education at a Glance 2008: OECD Indicators*. Paris: Organisation for Economic Co-Operation and Development. Available at: http://www.oecd.org/data-oecd/23/46/41284038.pdf (accessed December 15, 2011).

Parsons, C., and Timothy M. Smeeding, eds. 2006. *Immigration and the Transformation of Europe*. Cambridge: Cambridge University Press.

Smeeding, Timothy M., Robert Erikson, and Markus Jäntti. 2011. *Persistence, Privilege, and Parenting: The Comparative Study of Intergenerational Mobility*. New York: Russell Sage Foundation.

Todd, Petra E., and Kenneth I. Wolpin. 2003. "On the Specification and Estimation of the Production Function for Cognitive Ability." *The Economic Journal* 113(485): F3–F33.

———. 2007. "The Production of Cognitive Achievement in Children: Home, School, and Racial Test Score Gaps." *Journal of Human Capital* 1(1): 91–135.

UNESCO. 2006. *ISCED 1997: International Standard Classification of Education*, 2d ed. Montreal: UNESCO Institute for Statistics. Available at: http://www.uis.unesco.org/TEMPLATE/pdf/isced/ISCED_A.pdf (accessed December 15, 2011).

Chapter 2

Socioeconomic Gradients in Children's Outcomes

JOHN ERMISCH, MARKUS JÄNTTI,

AND TIMOTHY SMEEDING

S OCIAL SCIENCE has long been interested in the causal determinants of child outcomes. In sociology, for example, the origin-education-destination (OED) framework has offered illuminating insights into the patterns of association between parental origins and adult outcomes, and how children got there (Blau and Duncan 1967). In economics, among others, Gary Becker and Nigel Tomes (1979) have developed a formal model to examine how economic advantage is transmitted across generations.

It is important to gain insights into the causes of intergenerational transmission. While there are examples of convincing analyses of the causal determinants of child outcomes (see, for example, chapter 7, this volume), it would be very difficult, if not impossible, to assemble for multiple countries, on a comparable basis, compelling causal evidence for any of the determinants of child outcomes at various stages of their development. In this volume and in this chapter, we opt for a novel approach to assembling evidence on the intergenerational association of various child outcomes with parental socioeconomic status. These associations, or intergenerational gradients, are not to be interpreted causally. Rather, in exploring several different potential pathways through which advantage or disadvantage may be transmitted, these gradients convey information about the overall relevance of these pathways and their importance in comparative perspective.

As summarized in the introductory chapter to this volume, this research effort includes multiple studies of the parent-child socioeconomic gradient across a variety of outcome domains and child ages in ten countries. Most of the studies are explicitly comparative (including two or more countries), and are carried out by groups of researchers who have worked to make the datasets and variables as comparable as possible. The noncomparative, or single-country, studies also attempt to examine the socioeconomic gradient of particular outcomes across two or more different life stages to investigate how, for example, an expansion of child care (chapter 7, this volume) affects the socioeconomic gradient of labor market outcomes in adulthood.

Such detailed analyses are highly useful. To quantitatively summarize the gradients, obtained from a variety of statistical models and empirical approaches, is no simple task. To gain more general insights, and rather than list in detail the specific coefficient estimates from the different chapters, we asked the participating research groups to provide data in a standardized format to enable us to examine the patterns in the data more broadly.

The purpose of this chapter is to use these standardized data as a separate database to examine how the association of child outcomes with parental SES varies across domains, countries, and child's development stages in an admittedly broad, but informative, way. Specifically, we asked each team who contributed to the volume to provide us with cross-tabulations of child outcomes against a particular measure of parental socioeconomic status (SES), namely parental education.

We measure parental education by the level of educational achievement of the more highly educated parent (in the case of two-parent households; otherwise the lone parent's level) as measured on the International Standard Classification of Education (ISCED) scale.[1] We have cross-classified parental education with a given child outcome divided into four quartile groups (for continuous outcomes, such as test scores) or the levels of the outcomes themselves (for discrete outcomes). We then use those tables to estimate latent (polychoric) correlations, which measure the strength of the association in the cross-classification.[2]

Data and Methods

To examine broad patterns of intergenerational associations across different kinds of outcomes, called domains, across different ages of the child, called stages, and across countries, we have created some broad categorizations. Throughout this volume, and as shown in figure 1.2 in the introductory chapter, we have divided child development into broad stages, roughly corresponding to the birth year (ages zero through one), early childhood (ages two through six), middle childhood (ages seven through eleven), adolescence (ages twelve through seventeen), early adulthood (ages eighteen through twenty-nine), and adulthood (ages thirty-plus). We follow this convention throughout and treat each of these stages as a discrete group. We have classified the many different types of outcomes, as in many of the chapters in this volume, into

Table 2.1   **Variable Domains**

Acronym	Description
EC	Economic outcomes (various incomes, labor market position)
ED	Educational attainment (graduation, grades, final attainment)
C	Cognitive (IQ and other test scores)
SE	Socioemotional behavior (or noncognitive)
P	Physical (includes health, height, birth weight, BMI)

Source: Authors' compilation; see figure 1.2 in chapter 1.

five groups or domains: economic (EC), educational attainments (ED), cognitive (C), socioemotional behavior (often called noncognitive, SE) and physical (P). Table 2.1 summarizes the different types of outcome variables that fall into and constitute the domains we use. As an example, educational (D) attainments can include measures such as grade progression, graduation, and either college entry or college degree.

For every outcome variable the studies in this volume examine, authors have prepared a cross-classification with parental education. Although actual years of observation differ across outcomes and analyses, parental education has been measured at a point in time as close as possible to that when the earliest child outcome was measured. Continuous outcomes, such as test scores or incomes, measured such that higher values denote more favorable outcomes, are discretized into four quartile groups for the purposes of the cross-classifications. Discrete outcomes are ordered from less to more favorable. Where the data contain sampling weights, we use the weighted tables. The online appendix shows the variables, (in most cases) the outcome year, the data source, the country, the correlation, and also gives the weighted and unweighted cross-classifications along with the row and column labels.[3]

Table 2.2 presents a cross-tabulated summary of the raw data by country, life stage, and outcome domain. Although we have carefully combed the literature and datasets with our colleagues and rely on the same data used in the various chapters, coverage is somewhat spotty. This is for the most part because of data limitations, but also the nature of the domains. For instance, panel A in table 2.2 shows that we only have birth year data for Australia, Canada, Denmark, Sweden, the United Kingdom, and the United States, and, as shown in panel C, all of these data for the birth year fall into the physical domain (for example, birth weight, health). In this case, for some countries the birth year data were not available (a data limitation), but panel C highlights the fact that some outcomes will not be applicable to particular life stages (we don't expect economic outcomes for early childhood). We also have no data for the Nordic countries in early childhood, nor is our coverage of early adulthood complete. However,

Table 2.2   Raw Data

A. Countries and Stages

	0 to 1	2 to 6	7 to 11	12 to 17	18 to 29	30+
Australia	1	6	6	2	0	0
Canada	5	3	4	12	3	0
Denmark	2	0	1	2	0	3
Finland	0	0	3	0	0	3
France	0	3	4	6	3	3
Germany	0	1	1	13	13	27
Italy	0	0	1	1	8	40
Sweden	2	0	5	2	8	6
United Kingdom	3	11	28	14	2	19
United States	6	10	19	14	10	4

B. Countries and Domains

	Economic	Cognitive	Socioemotional	Education	Physical
Australia	0	6	7	0	2
Canada	0	7	6	4	10
Denmark	2	2	0	2	2
Finland	2	0	2	2	0
France	4	3	0	12	0
Germany	6	12	29	8	0
Italy	10	2	0	38	0
Sweden	3	5	4	4	7
United Kingdom	15	29	19	6	8
United States	2	20	27	4	10

C. Domains and Stages

	0 to 1	2 to 6	7 to 11	12 to 17	18 to 29	30+
Economic	0	0	0	0	4	40
Cognitive	0	14	38	27	4	3
Socioemotional	0	13	27	24	20	10
Education	0	3	3	11	11	52
Physical	19	4	4	4	8	0

Source: Authors' compilation based on data from chapter authors.

we do have reasonable coverage for several countries that are highly interesting for comparative purposes, because they are large and important countries that display widely varying patterns of mobility, namely, Canada (where we lack only the adult outcome), Germany, the United Kingdom, and the United States (see chapter 1, this volume; Corak 2004;

Björklund and Jäntti 2009). Our coverage of different domains is similarly somewhat spotty, but for the large countries with quite diverse mobility patterns, our coverage is quite good (panel B). Examining next which child development stages and outcome domains are covered (panel C), we again note that our coverage is quite reasonable.

In short, we have a large number of cross-classifications of child outcomes with parental education across numerous domains, ages, and countries. These tables are the raw data for this chapter. Several alternative approaches for analyzing the association in such cross-classified tables are available. One that is very prominent in the intergenerational mobility literature is to analyze the table using log-linear models (Agresti 2002; Fienberg 2007; Erikson and Goldthorpe 1992). These have the benefit of flexibility in that by carefully choosing the parameterization, very general patterns can be examined in the data. For our purposes, however, given the large number and highly variable character of our child outcomes, log-linear models might be too detailed to provide useful insights. Moreover, it would be hard to parameterize across tables of varying dimensions in such a way as to get for each table some reasonably easily interpretable measures of association.

We have, instead, decided to treat each pair of parental education and child outcome measures as bivariate latent variables. We then estimate the correlation coefficient of those underlying continuous latent variables—known as a polychoric correlation (Olsson 1979)—by the maximum likelihood (ML) method, assuming the underlying variables are bivariate-normally distributed. This generates a substantial number of correlation coefficients that we then examine for commonalities and differences across countries, child ages, and domains.

Our chosen approach comes at some cost. Because the bivariate normality assumption might be inappropriate, our ML estimate may be statistically suboptimal.[4] Moreover, this assumption can restrict the theoretical probabilities associated with the table. However, because it is our intention to take the first steps to gain insights into the broad patterns of intergenerational association across a wide variety of countries, outcomes, and child ages, we believe our approach has the merits of simplicity and straightforward interpretation.

Parental Education and Child Outcomes: Estimated Polychoric Correlations

We estimated the polychoric correlations using the package *polycor* (Fox 2010) in the statistical package R (Ihaka and Gentleman 1996). The full set of correlations and their estimated standard errors, along with the variable name, its description, domain, child stage, and country as well as which of the chapters it stems from can be found in the online data appendix. Of 341 tables, the estimation routine failed in 49 cases, leaving us with 292 correlations to work with.[5] As the outcome variables have been ordered to categorize increasingly good outcomes from left to right, we would in general expect the correlations to be positive. That is, better child outcomes are expected to be associated with higher parental education.

Before we explore differences across the correlations along their domain, stage, and country dimensions, we show the raw correlations. In particular, we show in figures 2.1 to 2.5 the estimated correlations one domain at a time. Each stage is shown in its own panel, and the estimated correlations from each country within that stage and domain are plotted on the rows along with their 95 percent confidence intervals. We have added the zero line to assist in distinguishing between positive and negative estimated correlations.

Given that we have tabulated more favorable outcomes to the right, it is somewhat surprising that we find a reasonable number—fifty-three in all—of negative associations in our data; that is, lower parental education is associated with better child outcomes. Some of those are found among the socioemotional outcomes, where parent's education is not typically strongly correlated with such outcomes (see, for example, chapter 3, this volume). Several also occur in Italy within the educational domain and in economic outcomes (occurring largely in early adulthood and adulthood). For the latter, it is at times hard to judge if an outcome really is more favorable. For instance, labor market participation for those under twenty-five years old tends to either denote the person is not participating in higher education—an adverse outcome—or possibly that the labor market participation is taking place alongside education, which may indicate an adverse socioeconomic position.

Some of the negative correlations may also be by chance. This is, in part, why we choose to fit regression models to the correlations to examine their broad patterns. Before we proceed to the models, however, we look more closely at the correlations.

Correlation of Outcomes

To understand the data we use in this chapter, consider the following two cross-tabulations in table 2.3 of whether a child ever attended postsecondary education or college in Canada and the United States. We use these cross-tabulations to estimate the correlations of two underlying latent variables, the parental educational achievement and college attendance of the offspring. The Canadian and U.S. correlations are estimated to be 0.347 (CI 0.291–0.404) and 0.531 (CI 0.463–0.600), respectively.[6] The U.S. correlation is thus higher in a both substantive and statistical sense than the Canadian estimate. Our regressions essentially take all such correlations and measure the extent to which differences across all of these correlations can be attributed to differences across outcome domains, child age, and, importantly, country.

Table 2.3   Ever Attended Postsecondary Education (Canada) or College (United States)

Canada (NLSCY)				United States (PSID)			
ISCED of Highest-Educated Parent	No	Yes	Row Total	ISCED of Highest-Educated Parent	No	Yes	Row Total
0–2 (low)	113	71	184	0–2 (low)	86	71	156
3–4 (med)	291	403	694	3–4 (med)	213	373	586
5b	186	296	482	5b	13	59	72
5a/6 (high)	105	450	555	5a/6 (high)	17	289	306
Column total	695	1219	1,914	Column total	329	791	1,120

Source: Authors' calculations based on data from chapter 14.

All estimated correlations—for each country, stage, and domain—are shown in figures 2.1 to 2.5 to offer a broad overview of the patterns we find. Figure 2.1 shows the estimated correlations of parental education with economic outcomes by country and by age in the two age categories, thirty-plus and eighteen through twenty-nine. We have plotted for each country all estimated correlations (the points) along with their 95 percent confidence intervals (the lines around the points). As one would expect, economic outcomes are measured mainly in early adulthood and adulthood. Although the majority of measures are for outcomes over the

Figure 2.1   Correlations by Country by Age in Domain, Economic

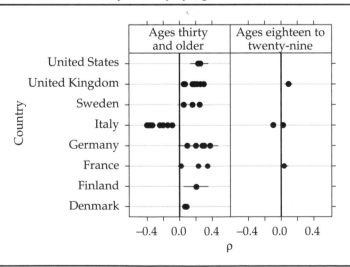

Source: Authors' calculations based on data from chapter authors.

Figure 2.2   Correlations by Country by Age in Domain, Cognitive

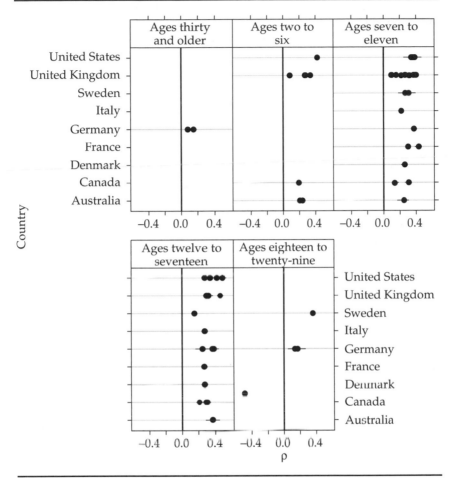

Source: Authors' calculations based on data from chapter authors.

age of thirty, we do have some observations from early adulthood. All of the negative point estimates stem from Italy, something that will later be picked up in the regressions. There is quite a bit of variation in these correlations, especially for Germany, but also for the United Kingdom. The overall visual impression is that, at least among those who are age thirty and above, countries are reasonably similar in the correlation of the underlying latent variables.

In figure 2.2, we show the estimated correlations of offspring cognitive achievement and parental education. These correlations are all estimated to be positive, have in general reasonably narrow confidence intervals, but also vary quite widely within country and stage. The overall impression is that the United States generally shows a reasonably large correlation, as do France and the United Kingdom, even if the range in the latter appears quite wide. The substantial variation for those countries for which many measurements are available suggests some caution should be exercised in interpreting the country differences for the cases in which only a few measurements are available.

In part these results speak to the issue of fanning out, mentioned in chapter 1, and most simply stated as a pattern where correlations increase as children age. From visual inspection of these estimates, we do not find strong evidence that would suggest the correlation of cognitive achievement with parental education increases as children age. We return to this question of so-called fanning out when we report regression results. It is important, however, that we also do not find support for fanning in, that is, the data do not suggest that socioeconomic disparities in outcomes diminish as children age. Such "fanning in" might be expected to occur within the cognitive domain, for instance, in a truly egalitarian school system which provided help to children of all backgrounds, such that the parental gradients were reduced by the school system.

Figure 2.3 shows the estimated correlations in the domain of socioemotional behaviors. In several instances, socioemotional behaviors are negatively associated with parental education, although most of the estimated correlations are positive. The positive correlations appear to be lower in magnitude than for cognitive outcomes, suggesting that the SES gradient is steeper for cognitive and educational outcomes (up to the oldest children's age cohort, in which only Germany is observed).

Next, figure 2.4 shows the estimated correlation of offspring and parental educational achievement. Although several point estimates—all of them from Italian data—are negative, the majority of these associations are positive and, in comparison to the other domains, large. The reason the Italian data are negative is that several of the outcomes measure formal educational enrollment or achievement in adulthood, at which point the more advantaged apparently have long since completed the higher education. The data appear to support the view that the U.S. correlations are high relative to those in other countries, suggesting more of an effect of parental SES on educational attainment in the United States, but the range of estimates (for instance for Germany) is still very large.

Finally, figure 2.5 shows our point estimates for the physical domain. We do not have very many estimates here, and, by and large, they appear relatively low compared with most other domains. Interestingly, among infants—where the correlations tend to be with birth weight and related measurements—the differences across countries appear to be quite small,

Figure 2.3   Correlations by Country by Age in Domain, Socioemotional

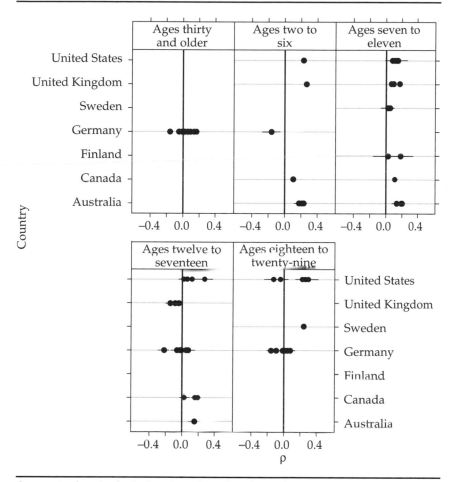

Source: Authors' calculations based on data from chapter authors.

even if the United Kingdom and the United States may have the greatest socioeconomic gradient.

These estimated correlations span a wide variety of different kinds of child outcomes, some of which are hard to classify as more or less adverse. The goal of this volume is to carefully compare gradients across countries (in the case of comparative chapters) or across other contrasts and to explain the possible social and institutional features that might influence the patterns found in each nation. Rather than discuss each estimate in detail, we fit simple linear regressions to these correlations to examine similarities and differences across the key outcome dimensions.

Figure 2.4   Correlations by Country by Age in Domain, Education

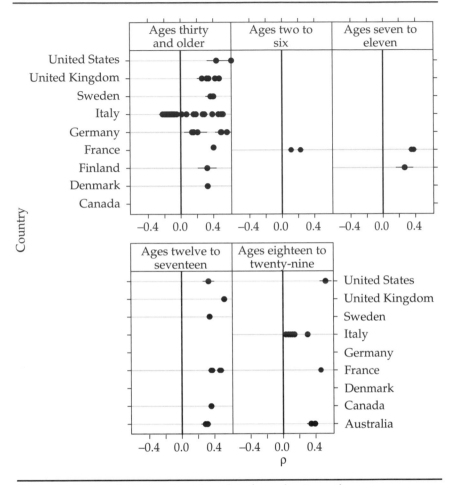

Source: Authors' calculations based on data from chapter authors.

Modeling the Correlations

To examine commonalities in estimated socioeconomic gradients, as captured by the latent correlation of various outcomes with parental education, we estimate linear regressions of the correlations against domain, stage, and country dummy variables. The regressions, whose model fit is summarized in table 2.4 and which weight each observed correlation using the inverse of its estimated standard error, allow us to capture broad patterns in the data as well as country fixed effects.[7] We include successively more information in the regressions—that is, we start out by allowing the correlations to vary by domain and by stage, but do not include country dummies (model 1). We next add country dummy

Figure 2.5   Correlations by Country by Age in Domain, Physical

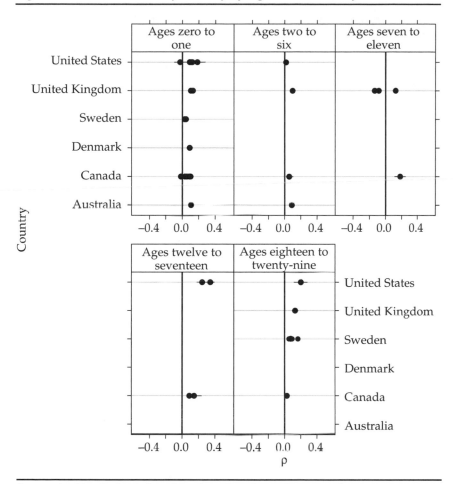

Source: Authors' calculations based on data from chapter authors.

Table 2.4   Model Comparison

	Residual Degrees of Freedom	Residual Sum of Squares	Degrees of Freedom	Sum of Squares	F-statistic	Probability (>F)
1	301.00	569.10				
2	292.00	388.82	9.00	180.28	16.42	0.00
3	280.00	350.14	12.00	38.68	2.64	0.00
4	255.00	298.89	25.00	51.25	1.68	0.03
5	228.00	278.11	27.00	20.78	0.63	0.92

Source: Authors' calculations based on data from chapter authors (see tables 2.5 and 2.6).

variables (model 2) and after that, we allow the stage coefficients to vary across domains (model 3). We then also allow the country coefficients to vary across domains (model 4). Finally, we add stage and country interactions, that is, we allow the coefficient estimates for each stage to differ across countries (model 5).

Table 2.4 shows the F-test of each broader model against the narrower. Model 4, that is, the model that includes stage and domain as well as country and domain interactions, is statistically preferred to the more parsimonious specifications, in the sense that it provides a statistically significantly better fit to the data, as measured by the improved of fit in the data, corrected for the added number of parameters, as indicated by the significance of the F-statistic. However, adding country and stage interactions in model 5, by contrast, does not improve the model fit. We therefore proceed to use model 4.

Table 2.5 shows the coefficient estimates for stage in life cycle and country for each domain based on model 4. In each of the cases, the United States is the omitted country and adult outcome (age thirty-plus) is the omitted stage. Thus, the intercept is the meta estimate of the correlation of outcomes in each domain with parental education for adult outcomes in the United States.

It is instructive to start with the relative size of these correlations across each domain in the United States. By far the highest of the latent correlations is that of the educational outcomes of children and their parents. The point estimate for the United States is 0.488. Although much lower, at 0.353, the correlation of cognitive outcome with parental education is the next strongest association. We expect that cognitive performance is highly positively correlated with educational achievement, although not perfectly so.

The correlations of parental education with physical and with socioemotional behaviors—0.113 and 0.136, respectively—are the lowest. The low association of parental education with socioemotional behaviors, in particular, is intriguing, as there is substantial evidence that what are often called noncognitive skills especially affect labor market outcomes (see, for example, chapter 3, this volume). Their low correlation with parental background probably counteracts the reasonably high correlation of parental background with offspring education and cognitive outcomes. The intergenerational gradient in the economic outcome, measured mainly as an adult outcome, but also in early adulthood (eighteen through twenty-nine), at 0.248, falls between the high educational and cognitive outcome correlations and low physical and socioemotional behavior outcomes.

The country coefficients tend to be quite imprecisely estimated, so only rarely is the difference between the United States and a particular country statistically significant. However, the relevant statistical test is if all country coefficients are zero. The F-test for deciding whether this is the case indicates that differences across countries are statistically significant in

Table 2.5 Coefficient Estimates by Domain

		Economic	Cognitive	Educational	Physical	Socioemotional
(Intercept)		0.248	0.353	0.488	0.113	0.136
		(0.134)	(0.044)	(0.164)	(0.034)	(0.049)
Country	Australia		-0.102		-0.002	-0.004
			(0.050)		(0.041)	(0.050)
	Canada	-0.171	-0.136	-0.126	-0.058	-0.013
		(0.139)	(0.049)	(0.191)	(0.043)	(0.050)
	Denmark	-0.041	-0.119	-0.131	-0.019	
		(0.209)	(0.081)	(0.182)	(0.039)	
	Finland	-0.149		-0.161		-0.086
		(0.145)		(0.422)		(0.146)
	France	-0.019	-0.045	-0.034		
		(0.158)	(0.066)	(0.173)		
	Germany		-0.095	-0.055		-0.128
			(0.058)	(0.205)		(0.044)
	Italy	-0.505	-0.142	-0.346		
		(0.137)	(0.084)	(0.165)		
	Sweden	-0.036	-0.075	-0.096	-0.061	0.149
		(0.138)	(0.063)	(0.170)	(0.042)	(0.048)
	United Kingdom	-0.059	-0.057	-0.057	-0.010	-0.089
		(0.136)	(0.042)	(0.179)	(0.044)	(0.048)

(Table continues on p. 46.)

Table 2.5 *Continued*

	Economic	Cognitive	Educational	Physical	Socioemotional
Stage					
2 to 6			-0.303	-0.024	0.095
			(0.129)	(0.032)	(0.056)
7 to 11		0.021	-0.071	-0.084	0.054
		(0.028)	(0.142)	(0.049)	(0.057)
12 to 17		0.066	-0.026	0.100	-0.048
		(0.031)	(0.068)	(0.053)	(0.044)
18 to 29	0.118	0.069	0.007	0.043	-0.040
	(0.059)	(0.061)	(0.065)	(0.030)	(0.038)
F-tests Stage	1.157[1]	1.927[3]	2.569[4]	1.892[4]	13.640[4]
	(0.290)	(0.135)	(0.047)	(0.140)	(0.000)
Country	23.721[7]	1.455[8]	4.211[8]	0.906[5]	9.251[6]
	(0.000)	(0.194)	(0.000)	(0.491)	(0.000)
N	42	70	72	38	72
k	9	12	13	10	11
σ	0.865	0.737	1.63	0.625	0.682
Adj R^2	0.795	0.0852	0.31	0.0773	0.585

Source: Authors' calculations based on data from chapter authors.

Table 2.6   Hypothesis Tests that Groups of Countries Have Zero
Coefficients, p-Values

	Economic	Cognitive	Educational	Physical	Socioemotional
Anglophone	0.67	0.03	0.78	0.49	0.15
Nordic	0.07	0.26	0.91	0.30	0.01
European	0.00	0.25	0.00	0.00	0.01

Source: Authors' calculations based on data from chapter authors.
Note: Groups of countries are Anglophone: Australia, Canada, United Kingdom; Nordic: Denmark, Finland, Sweden; European: France, Germany, Italy.

three of the five regressions—see table 2.6. The exceptions are the cognitive (C) and physical (P) outcomes where the p-values are 0.194 and 0.491, respectively. Thus, even if all country point estimates are negative for these two domains, suggesting the correlation in these cases is the highest for the United States, we cannot reject the null hypothesis that there are no country differences for these particular outcomes. Note, however, that for the cognitive domain, both Canada and Australia are significantly different from the United States, showing lower correlations.

Do Gradients Change as Children Age?

The question of whether the socioeconomic gradients of outcomes fan out as children age can be examined by looking at the stage coefficients. The evidence for fanning out in the cognitive, educational and socioemotional behavior outcomes is—at best—mixed.

Figure 2.6 shows graphically the evidence we have for, or against, fanning out across the domains (based on the coefficient estimates reported in table 2.5). First, in the economic domain, we have estimates only from eighteen through twenty-nine and thirty-plus, so these cannot be considered as evidence for or against fanning out. In the cognitive domain, there is some evidence suggesting increased association of child outcomes with parental education, in that the coefficient estimates, with quite narrow confidence intervals before young adulthood, do, indeed, increase with child age. The increase from ages seven through eleven to ages twelve through seventeen is particularly pronounced. In the educational domain, only France provides information before age twelve, so we are unable to examine fanning out before that age (and have therefore suppressed the point estimates from the figure). These coefficients also display an increasing pattern, albeit with very wide confidence intervals. The socioemotional behavior domain, by contrast, if anything shows a decline in the gradients and the physical domain shows no obvious pattern whatsoever. Thus, the strongest evidence for fanning out is to be found in the domain of cognitive achievement. This suggests that

Figure 2.6   Estimated Socioeconomic Gradients Across Stages of Development, Fitted Correlations Against Stage

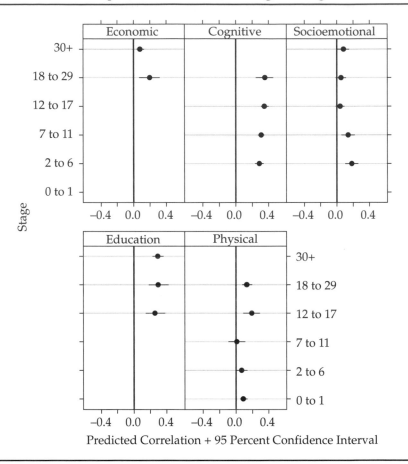

Source: Authors' calculations based on data from chapter authors.

cognitive achievement builds (or falters) as a child ages in these societies and also may be reflected in educational attainment.

Figure 2.7 shows the fitted correlations based on the estimates in table 2.5 for each country across the domains. In the case of the economic outcomes, Italy is the outlier with a large negative fitted correlation. This is driven by the fact that most Italian data points are about labor market outcomes during an age—the early twenties—when the advantaged offspring would be expected to be in higher education and where most children still reside with their parents, thus reducing the necessity of enough labor market earnings to become independent. Still, being employed at that age is not necessarily a good outcome if it comes at the expense of additional education. As for the other coun-

Figure 2.7   Estimated Socioeconomic Gradients Across Countries, Fitted Correlations Against Country

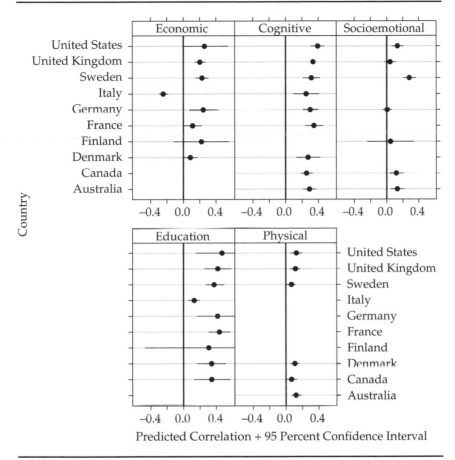

Predicted Correlation + 95 Percent Confidence Interval

Source: Authors' calculations based on data from chapter authors.

tries, the United States has the greatest gradient of economic outcomes with respect to parental socioeconomic status, as all country coefficient estimates in this domain in table 2.5 are negative.

For both cognitive and educational outcomes, the United States has the largest correlation. As noted, the statistical test for whether the country coefficients are jointly zero for the cognitive outcomes fails to reject the null hypothesis. The country differences for cognitive outcomes range from −0.045 for France to −0.142 for Italy. Although many of the point estimates are not statistically different from zero, to repeat, the U.S. correlation is significantly different from that in both Australia and Canada.

The country differences for educational outcomes are quite large, but rarely approach statistical significance. Although France has a correlation that is both substantively and statistically indistinguishable from that for the United States, it is based in part on outcomes at very young ages, and should be viewed with some caution. Germany has the next highest point estimate of 0.433, and the United Kingdom is close behind at 0.431. The largest difference is, again, for Italy with the Nordic countries in between.

For the physical domain outcomes, all point estimates are negative, suggesting a greater U.S. gradient, but, as pointed out above, the null hypothesis of no differences is not rejected. The point estimates are all quite small in magnitude, especially in comparison with the other outcome domains.

The country differences in socioemotional behaviors are the exception to the pattern that the United States has the highest socioeconomic gradient. Here the Swedish point estimate at 0.285 is well above the U.S. point estimate of 0.136. The Swedish point estimate stems from army enlistment interviews with psychologists, taken around the ages of eighteen or nineteen. The U.S. estimates, by contrast, stem from a variety of sources and stages. However, abstracting from the Swedish estimate, the differences in the gradients of socioeconomic behaviors appear small across countries and vary around a much lower intercept than outcomes in the other domains.

Finally, in table 2.6 we show the p-values for statistical tests where we have set all the country coefficients for particular groups of countries to zero (that is, a test whether the group is different from the United States). For instance, the first column shows the p-value of the hypothesis that the coefficients for Sweden, Finland, and Denmark in column EC in table 2.5 are all zero. This p-value is 0.07, insignificant by the conventional statistical significance level of 5 percent. The results suggest that France, Germany, and Italy as a group differ significantly from the United States in the economic, educational, physical and socioemotional domains. The Anglophone countries of Australia, Canada, and the United Kingdom only differ from the United States as a group significantly in the cognitive domain, and the Nordic from the United States in the socioemotional domain.

Conclusion

This chapter has taken a broad look at the association of a key measure of parental socioeconomic status, namely parental education, with children's outcomes. We measure the association by fitting latent polychoric correlations to the cross-classifications provided to us by the chapter authors of this volume. Although the estimated correlations display wide variation, we use them as the basis for discerning commonalities and differences in the data across outcome domain, child development stage, and country. Our regressions suggest important ways in which the intergenerational gradients differ, and some in which they do not, across these different dimensions.

We find large differences in the level of intergenerational association across domains; the cognitive and educational domains show the largest gradients, the physical and socioemotional behavior have the smallest, and the economic domain falls in between. The economic domain is based on outcomes at quite different and sparsely measured points in the life cycle and should be viewed with caution.

The evidence across countries mostly, but not exclusively, suggests the gradient in the United States is the steepest across the countries we study. The examination of correlations does not tell us about the causes of the steeper U.S. gradient. The results suggest, however, that the steeper U.S. gradient is established early on in a child's life. But there are variations in both the difference across countries and across domains in the U.S. lead in this respect. A cautious conclusion at this point is that the steeper U.S. gradient in adult outcomes cannot be traced back to any single stage or domain. Finally, we find mixed evidence for whether the intergenerational associations grow stronger as children age, with the cognitive outcome domain most clearly suggesting this pattern, as one might imagine given the cumulative nature of the education process.

The analyses in this chapter are intended to examine broad patterns in the data and life stages, all in a single chapter. We believe our book is unique in this respect. The remaining chapters in this volume, on whose data we have based this comparative analysis, offer many studies of the same data that exploit in greater detail the possibilities offered by cross-national comparative analysis across fewer nations, and in part by also simultaneously including multiple control variables and different decomposition techniques. The meta-analysis offered here, although broadly consistent with the findings of the individual chapters, is intended to complement rather than replace a more detailed reading of the studies we have based it on and to provide a broader framework for summing the individual effects across the wide span of nations and life stages we observe.

Notes

1. ISCED is an educational classification scheme developed by the United Nations to allow for the compilation and presentation of comparable educational statistics within and across countries. For a general description of the ISCED classification, see UNESCO 1997, and for country-specific mappings, see UNESCO 2010.
2. These estimates assume the variables are discretized versions of underlying continuous latent variables. All of the tables we use, as well as the correlations we have estimated are available in the online data appendix to this chapter.
3. The online appendix can be found at: http://www.russellsage.org/Ermisch_et_al_OnlineAppendix.pdf.
4. In particular, in case bivariate normality is violated, the standard errors of the correlation estimates are underestimated.
5. The estimation routine invariably failed because the assumed bivariate normality was too restrictive, which was most often associated with having off-diagonal elements in the cross-table being too large relative to the diagonal elements.

6. We use 95 percent confidence intervals in all cases.
7. Weighting the regressions by the inverse of the estimated standard deviation of each correlation adjusts the variance of the parameter estimate for the fact that our dependent variable is itself an estimate. We have not here followed the practice in part of this literature to model Fisher z-transformed correlations (see Goldberger 1979) but follow the procedure in Björklund, Jäntti, and Solon (2005) to model the raw correlations themselves.

References

Agresti, Alan. 2002. *Categorical Data Analysis*. Wiley Series in Probability and Statistics. New York: John Wiley & Sons.

Becker, Gary S., and Nigel Tomes. 1979. "An Equilibrium Theory of the Distribution of Income And Intergenerational Mobility." *Journal of Political Economy* 87(6): 1153–189.

Björklund, Anders, and Markus Jäntti. 2009. "Intergenerational Income Mobility and the Role of Family Background." In *The Oxford Handbook of Economic Inequality*, edited by Wiemer Salverda, Brian Nolan, and Timothy Smeeding. Oxford: Oxford University Press.

Björklund, Anders, Markus Jäntti, and Gary Solon. 2005. "Influences of Nature and Nurture on Earnings Variation: A Report on Various Sibling Types in Sweden." In *Unequal Chances: Family Background and Economic Status*, edited by Samuel Bowles, Herbert Gintis, and Melissa Osborne. Princeton, N.J.: Princeton University Press.

Blau, Peter M., and Otis Dudley Duncan. 1967. *The American Occupational Structure*. New York: John Wiley & Sons.

Corak, Miles. 2004. "Generational Income Mobility in North America and Europe: An Introduction." In *Generational Income Mobility in North America and Europe*. Cambridge: Cambridge University Press.

Erikson, Robert, and John H. Goldthorpe. 1992. *The Constant Flux: A Study of Class Mobility in Industrial Societies*. Oxford: Clarendon Press.

Fienberg, Stephen E. 2007. *The Analysis of Cross-Classified Categorical Data*. New York: Springer.

Fox, John. 2010. "Package 'Polycor' Version 0.78." CRAN Technical Report. Available at: http://cran.r-project.org/web/packages/polycor/polycor.pdf (accessed December 28, 2011).

Goldberger, Arthur S. 1979. "Heritability." *Economica* 46(184): 327–47.

Ihaka, Ross, and Robert Gentleman. 1996. "R: A Language for Data Analysis and Graphics." *Journal of Computational and Graphical Statistics* 5(3): 299–314.

Olsson, Ulf. 1979. "Maximum Likelihood Estimation of the Polychoric Correlation Coefficient." *Psychometrika* 44(4): 443–60.

UNESCO. 1997. *ISCED 1997: International Standard Classification of Education*. Montreal: UNESCO Institute for Statistics. Available at: http://www.unesco.org/education/information/nfsunesco/doc/isced_1997.htm (accessed December 28, 2011).

————. 2010. "ISCED Mappings." Available at: http://www.uis.unesco.org/ev_en.php?ID=7434_201&ID2=DO_TOPIC (accessed December 28, 2011).

Chapter 3

Socioeconomic Persistence Across Generations: Cognitive and Noncognitive Processes

CARINA MOOD, JAN O. JONSSON,

AND ERIK BIHAGEN

THE STUDY of intergenerational social mobility, or persistence, is concerned with estimating an association between the socioeconomic standing of parents and their children's standing as adults. Established associations between origin and destination statuses (measured, for example, as education, social class, or income) are often used as prime indicators of inequality of opportunity (for reviews, see Breen and Jonsson 2005; Björklund and Jäntti 2009), and many studies attempt to trace changes over time or differences between countries in such inequality (Erikson and Goldthorpe 1992, Breen 2004; Solon 2002; Bratsberg et al. 2007; Jonsson et al. 2009).

This research tradition also includes studies of the processes by which the intergenerational associations emerge—for example, to what extent various resources, characteristics, and choices intervene between the parental and filial conditions. The conventional analysis estimates the origin-destination association controlling for children's education (Duncan and Hodge 1963; Blau and Duncan 1967), and further elaborations have also included measures of IQ and academic achievement (Jencks et al. 1972; Jencks et al. 1979; Sewell and Hauser 1975), reflecting a widely held belief that the reproduction of socioeconomic advantages and disadvantages are connected with the transmission of cognitive ability, general learning capacity, and economic investments in children that take effect through the educational system. However, recent research has come to focus also on other types of characteristics, such as personality traits, quite different from the usual cognitive indicators (for example, Bowles, Gintis, and Osborne Groves 2005). Our aim in this chapter is to study the transmission of socioeconomic status—measured as the intergenerational correlation between fathers' and sons' income and educational attainment,

53

respectively—taking cognitive ability, personality traits, and physical characteristics into account. We benefit from large-scale Swedish register data that include many observations of incomes in two generations, and high-quality enlistment data on cognitive and noncognitive characteristics from extensive tests and interviews with professional psychologists.

We find that the intergenerational educational correlation (r=0.38) is mostly mediated by cognitive ability, and that personality traits and physical characteristics are of little importance. The income correlation (r=0.31) is mediated by cognitive ability too, but also by personality traits—and our analyses suggest that characteristics such as social maturity, emotional stability, and leadership capacity gain their importance directly in the labor market rather than through schooling. An interesting finding is that father's income has a persistent and non-negligible effect on sons' income despite extensive controls for other parental characteristics (such as education, social class, and occupation) and for other important mediators.

Previous Research

Research has shown sizeable intergenerational correlations for both occupations and educational credentials (Blau and Duncan 1967; Jencks et al. 1972; Jencks et al. 1979; Erikson 1987; Hauser and Mossel 1985; Sieben and de Graaf 2001; Hertz et al. 2007) as well as for cognitive ability (Black, Devereux, and Salvanes 2009; Björklund, Eriksson, and Jäntti 2010; Anger and Heineck 2010; see also chapter 16, this volume). For all these dimensions, correlations are mostly in the 0.35 to 0.5 range, with estimates as high as 0.7 when corrected for measurement error or based on sibling correlations. Estimates of intergenerational income correlations are fewer and sensitive to definitions, but appear to be of the same magnitude in the United States, but appreciably lower in the Scandinavian countries (Jäntti et al. 2006). Research has documented that children's cognitive ability and educational credentials are important mediators in the intergenerational process (Blau and Duncan 1967; Sewell and Hauser 1980; Erikson and Jonsson 1998).

When studying the origin-destination association in income or social class, controlling for children's educational attainment or cognitive ability, one typically finds a remaining association (Ishida, Müller, and Ridge 1995; Erikson and Jonsson 1998). In social class mobility analysis, using log-linear modeling of class or occupational matrices, it is clear that much of this net association depends on the inheritance of social positions, the prototypical example of which pertains to farmers and other self-employed (Ishida, Müller, and Ridge 1995). Although inheritance of physical capital is critical for these classes, and education of marginal or no importance, more subtle forms of inheritance are likely to prevail for other occupations, in the form of the transmission of occupationally relevant skills, social networks, information, and tastes (Jonsson et al. 2009). Related to this is a family of noncognitive mediators, which we call personality traits, and which have come to the fore in recent research.[1] The argument is that parents either transfer noncognitive characteristics to their offspring, or provide an environment that is conducive for instilling personality traits in children, traits that subsequently are favorable for their labor market success. Such personality traits, understood in a broad sense, range from beauty and height, over extroversion and emotional stability, to subtle social or cultural skills, such as manners and style of expression.

Although the research into noncognitive characteristics is still not much developed, a number of empirical studies have revealed that some have positive associations with labor market outcomes. This goes for personality traits such as leadership and perseverance (Jencks et al. 1979; Lindqvist and Westman 2011), emotional stability and antagonism (Mueller and Plug 2006), and being outgoing (Jackson 2006); characteristics such as motivation (Goldsmith, Veum, and Darity 2000), locus of control, and self-esteem (Heckman, Stixrud, and Urzua 2006); more structural indicators of personality, such as organization and efficiency in the home (Dunifon, Duncan, and Brooks-Gunn 2001); as well as physiological characteristics, such as testosterone level (Dabbs 1992). Closely related to sociopsychological factors are indicators of physical appearance, such as beauty, height, and obesity, all of which have been shown to explain some part of the variation in earnings (see the review by Bowles, Gintis, and Osborne 2001; for height, Persico, Postlewaite, and Silverman 2004; for obesity, Finkelstein, Ruhm, and Kosa 2005).

That various noncognitive traits are positively associated with labor market outcomes is however not in itself proof that these traits also account for the intergenerational transmission of advantage and disadvantage. The crucial issue here, of course, is whether and to what extent they are also associated with parental characteristics. The association between social origin and noncognitive traits tend to be lower than for education and cognitive ability, but less often studied. Melissa Osborne Groves (2005) summarizes earlier research and reports intergenerational correlations of personality traits (such as the big five) that mostly vary between 0.14 and 0.25. In a systematic and comprehensive review, John Loehlin (2005) estimates the average correlation across previous studies to be around 0.13, that is, close to the lower bound of that range. Greg Duncan and his colleagues (2005) find positive mother-child correlations between a broader band of traits and behaviors (such as self-esteem, shyness, and delinquent behavior). These correlations are however quite low—around 0.08 to 0.16—and markedly lower than for cognitive skills, where, for example, math and reading test scores correlate around 0.4. Silke Anger reports similar findings in chapter 16 of this volume. Moreover, these intergenerational associations tend not to be driven by general socioeconomic processes, because they remain intact even when controlling for socioeconomic factors.

A few studies have used data that include both socioeconomic measures of intergenerational persistence and personality traits, and have attempted to estimate how much of the former association the latter stand for. On U.S. data, Osborne Groves (2005) estimates that the Rotter scale of locus of control (fatalism and the like) accounts for one-tenth of the father-son earnings correlation (compare Bowles and Gintis 2002, who report a slightly lower figure for the income correlation). This is likely to be quite an imprecise estimate, however, given that the sample consists of only 195 matched father-son pairs, methodological problems aside. Jo Blanden, Paul Gregg, and Lindsey Macmillan (2007) find a nontrivial effect of noncognitive traits, particularly locus of control, accounting for 10 percent of the intergenerational association between family income and sons' earnings. In their British data, however, cognitive characteristics stand for twice as much of this association. Finally, Lalaina Hirvonen (2010), on Swedish data, estimates that 12 percent of the father-son income correlation is accounted for by personality characteristics such as persistence, social skills, and stability.

From this research, it is not clear how important personality traits are in the intergenerational mobility process—they are expected to be of some significance, albeit less so than cognitive ability. To be sure, this will no doubt depend on which trait is measured, along with differences in data, population, and methods. Previous research has suffered from several well-known problems, including small samples and cross-sectional measurement of fathers' and sons' income, which leads to lower correlations than income averaged over a longer period (for example, Corak and Heisz 1999). We will study the intergenerational transmission process using indicators of cognitive ability and personality traits, as well as physical indicators. We overcome most of the problems accruing to this type of analysis as we are able to use register data for 150,000 to 180,000 Swedish fathers and sons, and estimate the intergenerational income correlation with high precision, using twelve years of income for fathers (ages forty-four to fifty-five) and five years for sons (ages thirty-eight to forty-two).[2] From the military enlistment, at around age eighteen, we have access to a range of physical and cognitive test results for sons, as well as four different personality traits measured in personal interviews with trained psychologists.

We take as a point of departure both the intergenerational income correlation and the correlation between the highest education attained by fathers and sons, thus analyzing two commonly used and theoretically interesting facets of the intergenerational transmission of advantage and disadvantage.[3] We attempt to disentangle the intergenerational process by estimating regression models with and without mediating variables, cognitive as well as noncognitive. To give a full representation of this process within the limits of our data, we also present bivariate correlations between origin and mediators, and mediators and outcomes, respectively. Finally, we decompose the intergenerational correlation into different parts that are mediated by different characteristics of sons. We also use sons' educational attainment and occupation as mediators in our income analysis, and control for father's occupation, social class, and education. In an extension, carried out on subsamples, we also study the mediating role of leadership ability and grade point averages. In terms of the model of intergenerational transmission of advantage outlined in chapter 1, this chapter concentrates on the association between parental socioeconomic conditions (Pses) and adult outcomes (O_A), and how this association is mediated by sons' characteristics at around age eighteen (C_4).

Although models of intergenerational processes have a natural temporal order and commonly assume a causal direction—for example between social origin, education, and future labor market rewards—our analyses do not pretend to claim that the effects we report are in fact causal. Evidently, father's income and father's education will to some degree capture other aspects of the social origin. For example, father's education and income are correlated with mother's characteristics, so their coefficients will partly capture the effects of mother variables when these are not controlled for. The regression coefficients for father's income and education are thus best seen as representing social origin in general. However, we also estimate models with controls for different aspects of social origin to come closer to a net effect of father's income. We address this issue further as we go along, because the complex structure that our models entail opens for different interpretations of the results.

Data and Variables

The data we use stem from official registers and are extracted from the STAR database kept by Statistics Sweden for the Swedish Institute for Social Research. We selected all men born between 1962 and 1965, with a total population of 156,837 for the income regression and 179,696 for the education regression[4] (in an additional analysis, we also use the 1972 cohort with n=35,377). Through a unique personal multigenerational identifier, we added information on parents. In addition, we acquired data for sons from the enlistment which all Swedish men in our cohorts underwent at around age eighteen. The variables and descriptive statistics are shown in online appendix table 3A.1.[5]

Income, Education, Occupation, Class Origin

Because our point of departure is the intergenerational correlation, we begin with variables tapping father's and son's income and education.

Incomes are the average of father's yearly personal incomes at ages forty-four to fifty-five and of sons' at ages thirty-eight to forty-two, if at least six of twelve (father) and three of five (son) of these years were not missing, taking the sum of pre-tax income from business, employment, and taxable benefits. Years with zero or negative incomes and years when more than 50 percent of income was from self-employment have been coded missing for reliability reasons.[6] Incomes are z-standardized in relation to the entire income distribution among men for the year in question, and incomes above four standard deviations from the mean are top-coded, which affects .3 percent of those born 1962 to 1965, and .5 percent of their fathers.

Education is based on information on the highest out of seven levels attained from the register of the education of the population (*Utbildningsregistret;* see Statistics Sweden 2000), and then recalculated to years of education. We base this recalculation on data from the Swedish Level of Living Survey (LNU), in which respondents are asked directly about both years and level of education, using cohorts for fathers and sons, respectively, that are similar to the ones we analyze here.[7] There is a possibility that father affects son not only through level of education, but also through the field of study, and we know from previous research that there is a heterogeneity of incomes among various fields of study also at given levels (Erikson and Jonsson 1998)—medical doctors have higher income than secondary school teachers, for example. In our income regression, where we control for father's and son's education in some models, we therefore also use a set of forty-three dummy variables combining levels and field of education.

Occupation of the sons is measured by information from the wage structure statistics, which is based on information from all work organizations in the public sector and firms with more than five hundred employees in the private sector. For smaller private firms, a random selection is made. Because individuals may have several employments, we have chosen the one where the sons work most of their work hours. To maximize the number of persons with occupational information, we have in the first place chosen the occupation at the age of forty-two and then, if the information is missing, taken the occupation at the age of forty-one and so on, down to the age of thirty-seven. If there is still no occupational information, we have chosen the occupation at the age of forty-three and onward. Occupational information is available for the years 1997 through 2007.

Class origin is measured by the occupation and employment status of fathers at the approximate age of fifty, by using the censuses conducted every five years from 1960 to 1990, with the exception of 1965, when this information is lacking. Because the cohorts we follow were born in the 1960s and 1970s, most information about class origin stems from the latter censuses. The coding follows a standard classification used by Statistics Sweden (1989).[8]

Occupational prestige of the father reflects the general desirability of occupations and is measured by the so-called Treiman scale of prestige, using the algorithm provided by Harry Ganzeboom and Donald Treiman (1996). The information is gathered in the same way as for class origin.

Cognitive Ability

The enlistment tests give rise to five measures of cognitive ability, of which four are dimensions and one is an overall measure. The separate dimensions are as follows:

Logic-inductive ability (reasoning),

Verbal comprehension (synonyms),

Spatial ability (metal folding), and

Technical understanding (including knowledge about chemistry and physics).

It is often acknowledged that intelligence—a common way of denoting what we call cognitive ability—is a multidimensional and hierarchical concept (Carroll 1993). At the lowest level are a large number of specialized areas of intelligence, and at a higher level a few factors that stand out as the most influential for the highest level, the general (and latent) g-factor. The most prominent among the level-2 factors, almost inseparable from the g-factor in some studies (Gustafsson 1984), is Gf (fluid intelligence, problem solving)—which in our case is closest to the first, logic-inductive, dimension (Carlstedt and Mårdberg 1993). The second most important factor is Gc (crystallized intelligence, measuring knowledge from experience and closest to verbal ability), which lies near our second dimension (but also the first). A less fundamental but not unimportant factor is visual perception (Gv), which is captured by our third dimension, spatial ability. This dimension and technical understanding are less central to the g-factor, but represent facets of intelligence not covered by the others—though the technical dimension in the enlistment test partly reflects Gc because it is based on knowledge. All four tests are graded on a scale from 0 to 40. The overall measure of cognitive ability (Cogn) is the arithmetic sum of the four tests.

Personality Traits

During the enlistment, the conscripts go through a semi-structured interview of about twenty minutes with a trained, and often very experienced, psychologist. This personality evaluation, based mostly on behavioral questions (that is, on what the interviewee does rather than thinks), results in four dimensions (which, in turn, are based on several indicators, some mentioned within parentheses):

Social maturity (extroversion, having friends, taking responsibility, independence)

Intensity (the capacity to activate oneself without external pressure, the intensity and frequency of free-time activities)

Psychological energy (perseverance, ability to fulfill plans, to remain focused)

Emotional stability (ability to control and channel nervousness, tolerance of stress, and disposition to anxiety)

These dimensions are graded on a scale from 1 to 5, where the value 3 means that the conscript is a normally functioning eighteen-year-old male in the measured respect. The psychologist also judges the *overall psychological fitness for the military* on a Stanine scale from 1 to 9. This variable is not a direct function of the four separate variables, but rather an overall clinical assessment that stems from the different parts but reflects a separate judgment. In addition, for those who score 5 and above on the Stanine measure of general intelligence, the psychologist assesses their *leadership capacity* on a 9-point scale that is not Stanine-distributed but roughly normally distributed around a mean of 5. Although this is a separate judgment by the psychologist, it is strongly influenced by the other psychological variables and is highly correlated to them.

Physiological Characteristics

Naturally, the military put emphasis also on the physical status of the enlisted. We will use a measure of physical work capacity, estimated from a training bike test and reported on a scale from 1 to 9. In addition, we have calculated the body mass index (BMI), which is a person's weight in relation to their height (BMI=(weight in kilogram/height in centimeter squared)). We found the relation between BMI and income to be curvilinear, so the BMI variable has been transformed to a variable measuring the absolute deviation from the average. As a result, BMI and height are virtually uncorrelated, so we are able to use height as our third physiological characteristic.

Grade Point Average

Grade point average (GPA) is the average of the grades in the sixteen best subjects in the last grade of comprehensive school (ninth grade, normal age=sixteen). The variable is collected from digitalized school reports for the National Board of Education and is available on data medium from 1988, meaning that the cohort born 1972 is the first for which this informa-

Table 3.1   Correlations, Mediating Variables and Origin and
            Destination Characteristics

Origin		Mediators	Destination	
Correlation with Father's . . .		Dimension of Son's . . .	Correlation with Son's . . .	
Education	Income	Cognitive Ability	Education	Income
0.29	0.27	Logic-inductive ability	0.49	0.35
0.32	0.27	Verbal comprehension	0.50	0.32
0.25	0.21	Spatial ability	0.40	0.27
0.26	0.22	Technical understanding	0.40	0.29
0.33	0.28	Cognitive ability, total	0.53	0.36
		Personality traits		
0.21	0.20	Social maturity	0.29	0.30
0.09	0.11	Intensity	0.17	0.21
0.18	0.17	Psychological energy	0.28	0.28
0.18	0.18	Emotional stability	0.26	0.29
0.20	0.21	Overall psychological fitness	0.31	0.34
0.21	0.21	Leadership	0.31	0.34
		Physical characteristics		
0.09	0.10	Height	0.12	0.12
−0.07	−0.06	BMI-deviation	−0.09	−0.09
0.14	0.14	Physical ability	0.23	0.21

Source: Authors' calculations based on STAR register database (not publicly available).
Note: N=156,837.

tion is possible to use. Grades are teacher assigned and based on performance on various knowledge-based tests as well as course work during a
long period (that is, they build neither on ability tests, nor on final exams).

Results: Correlations

We set the stage for our multivariate analyses in the simplest fashion,
by presenting correlations between our variables. Table 3.1 demonstrates
how the different items correlate with parental characteristics and own
attainments, respectively. A more extensive correlation matrix is shown
in online appendix table 3A.2, which presents correlations also between
items within each of our three main groups (cognitive ability, personality
traits, and physical characteristics).

To begin with, the two fundamental intergenerational correlations we
will be studying are 0.38 (education)[9] and 0.31 (income).[10] Furthermore,

these two indicators are correlated with each other, higher for fathers than for sons (0.56 versus 0.40)—the difference probably comes about partly because income is measured at a more mature age for fathers, and partly because the income return to education has decreased over time. Over and above that, we can draw four conclusions from the initial correlations. First, the mediating variables are more highly correlated with outcomes than with origin characteristics, though in some cases the difference is small (table 3.1). Second, the four dimensions of cognitive ability and personality traits are highly correlated internally (online appendix table 3A.2). Third, both for fathers and sons, cognitive ability is more highly correlated with education than with income (table 3.1). Fourth, the mediating variables are correlated with each other (online appendix table 3A.2), and although these correlations are not very strong, overall cognitive ability and general psychological fitness correlate at 0.38.

Results Regressions

We now turn to OLS regressions of son's income and educational attainment, respectively, on father's income and education. In all analyses, we present standardized (beta) coefficients (these are also the basis for the decomposition that follow). We show coefficients both before and after controlling for mediating variables, which we introduce in the three blocks described.[11] Table 3.2 presents the results for son's income.

The intergenerational income effect[12] (correlation) of 0.31 means that the average income difference between two young men (aged between thirty-eight and forty-two) whose fathers' incomes were one standard deviation apart is slightly less than one-third of a standard deviation. This is obviously a significant regression to the mean over two generations but still a fairly sizeable windfall profit viewed from the filial perspective (and the inheritance of wealth, which we do not measure here, will further increase the intergenerational transmission of economic resources).

Our first task is to unravel to what extent this intergenerational income effect is due to cognitive and noncognitive characteristics of sons. Columns 2 through 4 show the inclusion of the three blocks of variables described earlier. Each of these models returns a decrease in the conditional effect of father's income, most clearly model 2, which introduces the cognitive indicators. However, the personality variables also account for a nontrivial part of the income effect, whereas the physiological indicators tend not to be of the same importance. Of the mediating variables, logical reasoning, which is the main component in the general g-factor in intelligence analysis (Kvist and Gustafsson 2008), has the strongest effect on income. Holding constant for the other indicators of cognitive performance, a one standard deviation increase in logical reasoning is associated with an income increase of 0.18 standard deviations. It is interesting

Table 3.2 OLS Regression, Son's Income on Father's Income and Mediating Variables

	1	2	3	4	5	6	7	8	9	10
Father's income	0.312	0.224	0.249	0.283	0.197	0.160	0.132	0.127	0.114	0.073
Father's education								-0.003	(-0.002)	0.009
Father's occupational prestige								0.008	0.007	-0.003
Father's class								yes	yes	yes
Father's municipality									yes	yes
Logic-inductive		0.178			0.133	0.099	0.090	0.090	0.090	0.051
Verbal		0.068			0.041	-0.008	(-0.001)	(0.000)	(0.000)	(-0.002)
Spatial		0.035			0.030	0.009	(-0.003)	(-0.003)	(-0.001)	(-0.004)
Technical		0.070			0.050	0.045	0.032	0.032	0.035	0.018
Social maturity			0.117		0.069	0.061	0.066	0.065	0.068	0.039
Intensity			0.040		0.026	0.034	0.031	0.031	0.031	0.017
Mental energy			0.056		0.062	0.050	0.051	0.051	0.052	0.041
Emotional stability			0.103		0.076	0.072	0.062	0.061	0.060	0.040
BMI deviation				-0.053	-0.027	-0.023	-0.022	-0.022	-0.020	-0.010
Height				0.054	0.035	0.034	0.031	0.030	0.028	0.019
Physical capacity				0.145	0.039	0.020	0.021	0.021	0.025	0.021
Son's education						0.216	—	—		
Son's detailed education							yes	yes	yes	yes
Son's occupation									yes	yes
R^2	0.10	0.18	0.18	0.13	0.22	0.25	0.31	0.31	0.32	0.52

Source: Authors' calculations based on STAR register database (not publicly available).
Note: Because of the large size of the data set, the precision in the regression estimates is very high and showing standard errors is not necessary. The estimates within parentheses are the only ones with a T-value less than 1.96. Beta coefficients. N=156,837. Model 10: N=102,812.

that the two dimensions closest to technical occupations—spatial ability and technical knowledge—are only modestly related to income.

In model 5, we add cognitive ability, personality characteristics, and physiological characteristics simultaneously, which in total reduces the effect of fathers' income from 0.30 to 0.19. We know from previous research that the mediating effect of cognitive performance reflects the high association between cognitive ability and educational attainment, which in turn is positively associated with occupational attainment and income. The cognitive dimension measuring logical reasoning still has the largest net effect on income of the observed characteristics, and emotional stability, social maturity and psychological energy all have rather strong effects. In model 6 and 7, we include also son's education, first as a metric variable approximating years of education (model 6) and second (model 7) as a set of forty-three dummy variables combining level and field of education. As expected, the coefficient for father's income is reduced (and more strongly so with the more detailed measure of education), meaning that part of the intergenerational income correlation is mediated through son's education. The conditional effect of son's education (in the metric specification) on income is relatively strong at 0.216. The effects of cognitive ability on income shrink, and two of them vanish entirely, because these effects are channeled through education: smarter men get higher education and (partly) therefore better incomes. Again, we should beware that the models we test are descriptive in the sense that causality is a conjecture rather than established fact. Given that this model includes many of the variables we normally do not observe (but that we often suspect influence the regression coefficients in attainment models), and given that their effects are estimated with high precision, we nevertheless believe that the effect sizes of our mediating variables contribute to our understanding of the income attainment process.

What is much less clear is whether the effect of *father's income* is causal. Some theories routinely referred to—for example, in family economics (Becker and Tomes 1986)—do argue for a causal effect of income, because parents use income to invest in children's productive assets. However, it is not obvious that father's income in itself affects son's in a modern welfare state such as Sweden where education is free. It is likely that father's income reflects some general socioeconomic standing, and may thus proxy for other mechanisms, such as occupational inheritance. To address this, and thereby come closer to a pure income effect, we introduce, in model 8, three other socioeconomic indicators used extensively in research on social mobility, namely father's education, social class, and occupational prestige. The unmediated effect of father's income on son's in model 7—which at 0.132 is small but not trivial—remains surprisingly stable. In fact, controlling for income and the set of intermediate variables, father's education, occupational prestige, and class have virtually no effects on son's income. In analyses not shown, we have also controlled for a detailed measure of father's education (forty-three dummies), father's country of origin (twenty dummies), and mother's education, and none of these variables makes any difference to the intergenerational income correlation. In model 9, we control for the municipality of origin, thus eliminating any part of the income effect that is due to father and son living in areas with similar income levels (although this is not necessarily a spurious relationship as fathers with higher incomes may relocate to areas with better income opportunities). This reduces the income effect somewhat, but a net effect of 0.114 remains. Given the comprehensive controls in model 9, also for variables that normally are assumed to represent unobserved heterogeneity in income effects, the remaining effect of father's income is remarkable.

For part of our population of sons, we can identify their occupation in our data, and when we add this variable (as dummies) in model 10 we can see, as expected, that the net income effect is substantially reduced to 0.072 (23 percent of the bivariate correlation). The number of cases is lower in model 10 because of missing cases in son's occupation variable, but the changes in coefficients are not due to the change in population. Thus, part of the intergenerational income association is due to the fact that sons from high income families more often reach more economically rewarding occupations (given both their and their fathers' educational attainment, and controlling for mediators).

In table 3.3, we turn to the intergenerational correlation in education, which, as we saw in table 3.1, is higher than that in income. In difference to our previous analysis, cognitive ability is very important for the educational correlation—especially logical reasoning and verbal ability. Both physical capacity and psychological energy, together with social maturity, predict clearly higher level of education among men, but in model 5, when all mediators are included, only three predictors stand out. These are logic-inductive ability, verbal ability, and father's education. It is not surprising to see a net effect of father's education even after extensive controls for cognitive ability, personality, and physical characteristics, because there are many potential mechanisms, including the ability to help with the school work, the ability to navigate the school system, and educational aspirations (Erikson and Jonsson 1996).

In model 6, we introduce father's income, which turns out to have a non-negligible net effect on education. This may be because economic resources affect the decision to continue to higher education, for example, by reducing the disincentive of earnings forgone, but we suspect that a part of this effect picks up unmeasured heterogeneity in the measure of father's education (for example, the differences between fields of education at given educational length). In addition, in model 7, we control for father's occupational prestige and social class origin (a series of dummies,

Table 3.3   OLS Regression, Son's Education on Father's Education and Mediating Variables

	1	2	3	4	5	6	7
Father's education	0.379	0.220	0.320	0.348	0.205	0.158	0.140
Father's income						0.091	0.077
Father's class							yes
Father's occupational prestige							0.021
Logic-inductive		0.194			0.164	0.159	0.158
Verbal		0.223			0.207	0.204	0.202
Spatial		0.091			0.088	0.088	0.088
Technical		0.030			0.021	0.021	0.021
Social maturity			0.123		0.032	0.030	0.029
Intensity			−0.006		−0.027	−0.026	−0.025
Mental energy			0.120		0.057	0.056	0.055
Emotional stability			0.074		0.025	0.022	0.022
BMI deviation				−0.043	−0.018	−0.017	−0.017
Height				0.042	(0.004)	(0.002)	(0.002)
Physical capacity				0.170	0.085	0.083	0.083
R^2	0.14	0.34	0.21	0.18	0.36	0.36	0.36

Source: Authors' calculations based on STAR register database (not publicly available).
Note: Because of the large size of the data set, the precision in the regression estimates are very high and showing standard errors is not necessary. All estimates but those in parentheses are significant at conventional levels.
Beta coefficients. N=179,696.

the effect of which we do not show, but which are available on request).[13] These variables have in general rather small effects, and are only marginally at the expense of the effects of father's education or income.

In additional analyses (not shown), we include mother's education in all models. Mother's education has a strong effect on son's education (about two-thirds of the father's effect), and because of a strong correlation between father's and mother's education ($r=0.51$), the coefficient for father's education is reduced by about 25 percent (from 0.38 to 0.28 in the first model). All other coefficients—including father's income—remain largely similar. Furthermore, the decomposition of the education correlation shows similar results for mother's education and father's.

Extensions: Leadership, Grade Point Averages

In asking what processes mediate the correlation between origin and destination, we have access also to two other potential mediators, neither of which unfortunately is available for the entire population under study. In the next section, we carry out two more sets of income regressions, the first controlling for *leadership capacity* and the second for *grade point averages*.

The Impact of Leadership Capacity

Leadership capacity is rated only for a select group of conscripts, namely those with value 5 or above (on the Stanine scale) on the general cognitive ability measure. Because of this, and because high cognitive ability is associated with other positive characteristics, we have a nonrepresentative sample of the entire group of conscripts, consisting of those with on average "better" characteristics. The leadership variable correlates 0.87 with the general personality (or psychological functioning) variable, and even though the psychological test does not determine the leadership rating, it influences it strongly. Table 3.4 replicates table 3.2 for conscripts with a leadership rating and includes additional models (6 and 7) with the leadership variable.

Generally, the coefficients for this group are somewhat weaker, which is to be expected when the group is more homogenous (the effect of father's income is, for example 0.29, versus 0.31 in the full sample). However, in model 5, where all mediators are included, the relations between the variables are very similar to the whole sample. Model 6 demonstrates that leadership capacity has a relatively strong net effect on son's income, and (not surprisingly) the net effects of the personality variables are strongly reduced. Leadership capacity appears to subsume social maturity and emotional stability most, suggesting that active, responsible, and mature eighteen-year-old men are likely to have a relatively favorable income career.

The Impact of GPA

A reasonable assumption is that the intergenerational education correlation depends on investments in children or socialization that ensure that children of resourceful parents perform well in school. Although this to some extent could be a reflection of cognitive ability, parents promote their children's school achievements in other ways as well—by affording them their own room, a computer and other technical aids, travels, and occasionally extra tutorials, for example. In school systems such as Sweden's, where teacher-assigned grades reflect much more than cognitive ability, it is likely that parents' active help with assignments and general encouragement also affect GPA. To the extent that such processes are at work, controlling for grade point averages should account for a part of the effect of father's education. In table 3.5, we test this hypothesis, in an analysis similar to the one in table 3.4 but on a sample of boys born in 1972 for whom we have GPA information.

Models 1 and 2 (both coefficients and the model fit) are quite close to the ones shown on our whole sample in table 3.4. When GPA is

Table 3.4   OLS Regression, Son's Income on Father's Income and Mediating Variables, Including Leadership Capacity

	1	2	3	4	5	6	7	8	9	10
Father's income	0.288	0.235	0.241	0.266	0.200	0.192	0.130	0.125	0.111	0.072
Father's education								(0.002)	(−0.004)	0.009
Fathers class							yes	yes	yes	yes
Father's occupational prestige								0.006	0.007	(−0.001)
Father's municipality								yes	yes	yes
Logic-inductive		0.153			0.122	0.116	0.071	0.071	0.072	0.043
Verbal		0.074			0.059	0.051	0.007	(0.006)	0.007	0.011
Spatial		0.022			0.022	0.018	(−0.004)	(−0.004)	−0.007	(−0.005)
Technical		0.058			0.043	0.041	0.020	0.020	0.022	0.014
Social maturity			0.096		0.073	0.020	0.028	0.027	0.032	0.021
Intensity			0.041		0.038	(0.000)	(0.005)	(0.006)	(0.006)	(0.004)
Mental energy			0.093		0.067	0.034	0.031	0.031	0.034	0.032
Emotional stability			0.099		0.079	0.015	0.013	0.013	0.013	0.012
BMI deviation				−0.046	−0.031	−0.028	−0.022	−0.022	−0.021	−0.010
Height				0.046	0.038	0.037	0.031	0.031	0.028	0.020
Physical capacity				0.132	0.038	0.034	0.016	0.016	0.020	0.016
Leadership capacity						0.178	0.136	0.135	0.129	0.073
Son's detailed education							yes	yes	yes	yes
Son's occupation								yes	yes	yes
R^2	0.08	0.14	0.15	0.11	0.19	0.20	0.29	0.29	0.30	0.50

Source: Authors' calculations based on STAR register database (not publicly available).
Note: Because of the large size of the data set, the precision in the regression estimates is very high and showing standard errors is not necessary. The estimates within parentheses are the only ones with a T-value less than 1.96. Only conscripts with leadership rating. Beta coefficients. N=105,031. Model 10: N=70,461.

Table 3.5   **OLS Regression, Son's Education on Father's Education and Mediating Variables, Including GPA**

	Model 1	Model 2	Model 3	Model 4	Model 5
Father's education	0.370	0.187	0.156	0.135	0.121
Father's income				0.046	0.037
Father's class					yes
Logic-inductive		0.177	0.069	0.068	0.068
Verbal		0.229	0.137	0.136	0.136
Spatial		0.064	0.027	0.027	0.027
Technical		0.030	0.017	0.017	0.017
Social maturity		0.047	0.021	0.021	0.020
Intensity		0.025	−0.025	0.025	−0.025
Mental energy		0.059	0.017	0.017	0.017
Emotional stability		0.011	0.003	0.001	0.001
BMI deviation		−0.005	0.005	0.004	0.004
Height		0.022	0.016	0.015	0.015
Physical capacity		0.082	0.045	0.044	0.044
GPA			0.372	0.369	0.368
R^2	0.13	0.36	0.42	0.42	0.43

Source: Authors' calculations based on STAR register database (not publicly available).
Note: Because of the large size of the data set, the precision in the regression estimates is very high and showing standard errors is not necessary. The estimate within parentheses is the only one with a *T*-value less than 1.96.
Only conscripts born 1972. Beta coefficients. N=35,377.

added in model 3, the model fit improves. The effect of GPA on education is the strongest in table 3.5. Most cognitive ability and personality coefficients are substantially reduced, meaning that their effects on education are to a large extent (one-half to two-thirds) transmitted through GPA. The coefficient for father's education is also somewhat reduced, so GPA also transmits an independent part of the intergenerational correlation not previously captured by the cognitive and personality variables.

Results: Decomposition

To get a clearer image of the contribution of different mediating variables to the intergenerational correlation, a common procedure is to decompose the correlation into its constituent parts, as estimated by beta coefficients from an OLS regression. Consider two OLS regressions of son's income on father's income, one bivariate (1) and one multivariate (2):

$$inc_s = \alpha + inc_p\beta_1 + \varepsilon_1 \tag{1}$$

$$inc_s = \alpha + inc_p\beta_2 + cogn_s\beta_3 + pf_s\beta_4 + fy_s\beta_5 + ed_s\beta_6 + \varepsilon_2 \qquad (2)$$

where inc_s is son's income, inc_p is father's income, $cogn_s$ is son's cognitive ability, pf_s is son's psychological functioning, fy_s is son's physiological characteristics, ed_s is son's education, α, β_1, β_2, β_3, β_4, β_5, and β_6 are (beta-standardized) parameters to be estimated, and ε_1 and ε_2 are error terms. Also, let the relevant correlations among the independent variables be labeled r_{ii} (for inc_p and $cogn_s$), r_{ip} (for inc_p and pf_s), r_{if} (for inc_p and fy_s), and r_{ie} (for inc_p and ed_s).

β_1 is the intergenerational income correlation. Because we control for variables assumed to mediate this correlation in Equation 2, we expect that $\beta_2 < \beta_1$. A decomposition estimates the relative contribution of the independent variables to β_1 according to equation (3):

$$\beta_1 = \beta_2 + r_{ii}\beta_3 + r_{ip}\beta_4 + r_{if}\beta_5 + r_{ie}\beta_6 \qquad (3)$$

Although the decomposition technique and related path-analytical methods once was standard in sociological stratification research (for example, Duncan 1966; Alwin and Hauser 1975) and have been used recently in econometric analyses (Bowles, Gintis, and Osborne Groves 2005; Blanden, Gregg, and Macmillan 2007), they rely on some strong assumptions, such as linearity and additivity. Probably more important, error terms are assumed to be uncorrelated. In equation 3, β_1 will capture not only the causal effect of father's income, but also the effect of any variable that is correlated to father's income and that affects son's income. The coefficient is thus best perceived as a proxy for the effect of social origin in a more general sense. In addition, the included variables can obviously be related to unmeasured variables that also transmit the intergenerational correlation, so the relative weights of different mediating variables could change if more variables were included. These caveats notwithstanding, in our case the problem of unobserved variables is smaller than usual because most of the prime suspects (cognitive and non-cognitive characteristics) are observed. Even if we encourage a healthy skepticism to interpreting the details of the decomposition in table 3.6, we still believe that the big picture is informative.

Turning to table 3.6, we can first note that in total, cognitive ability, personality traits, and physical characteristics account for 37 percent of the income correlation (model 1) and 46 percent of the education correlation. When adding son's education to the income regression (model 2), a total of 57 percent of the intergenerational correlation is accounted for. Cognitive ability accounts for the largest share of both correlations, but although it is by far the most important component of the education correlation (accounting for as much as 37 percent), it is just somewhat more important than personality characteristics for the income correlation (20 versus

Table 3.6 Decomposition of Intergenerational Income, and Educational Correlations

| | Full Sample, 1962–1965 | | | Born 1972 | | Excluding Low Cognitive Ability | |
| | Income | | Education | Education | | Income | |
Mediators	Model 1	Model 2		Model 1	Model 2	Model 1	Model 2
Cognitive							
Logic-inductive	0.11	0.08	0.13	0.14	0.06	0.05	0.05
Verbal	0.04	0.00	0.17	0.20	0.12	0.01	0.00
Spatial	0.02	0.00	0.06	0.04	0.02	0.00	0.00
Technical	0.03	0.02	0.01	0.02	0.01	0.01	0.01
Cognitive ability total	0.20	0.10	0.37	0.40	0.20	0.06	0.06
Personality							
Social maturity	0.04	0.04	0.02	0.03	0.01	0.04	0.02
Intensity	0.01	0.01	-0.01	-0.01	-0.01	0.01	0.00
Mental energy	0.03	0.03	0.03	0.03	0.01	0.03	0.01
Emotional stability	0.04	0.04	0.01	0.01	0.00	0.03	0.01
Personality total	0.13	0.12	0.05	0.06	0.02	0.11	0.04
Physical							
BMI deviation	0.01	0.00	0.00	0.00	0.00	0.00	0.00
Height	0.01	0.01	0.00	0.00	0.00	0.01	0.01
Physical capacity	0.02	0.01	0.03	0.04	0.02	0.01	0.01
Physical total	0.04	0.02	0.04	0.04	0.02	0.02	0.02
Son's education		0.33				0.34	0.33
Grade point average					0.34		
Leadership capacity							0.10
Remaining	0.63	0.43	0.54	0.50	0.42	0.47	0.45
Number of cases	156,837		179,696	35,377		105,031	

Source: Authors' compilation based on STAR register database (not publicly available).
Note: The total contributions of the cognitive ability, personality, and physical variables are the sums of the contributions of their constituent dimensions, though in the table there are some rounding errors.

13 percent). Predictably, part of the cognitive ability component appears to be mediated by education, but the contribution of cognitive ability to the income correlation remains large even after controlling for education. Considering that the personality and physical variables show rather modest associations with son's education (see table 3.3, model 5), it is not surprising that these variable's contribution to the income correlation in model 1 hardly changes when controlling for education in model 2.

The decomposition of the education correlation for the 1972 cohort illuminates the transmission process a bit further. Here, we can control for the GPA in the final year of compulsory school (age sixteen), which accounts for 34 percent of the correlation. Its impact was previously captured to a large extent by cognitive ability, but both GPA and cognitive ability contribute independently and strongly to the intergenerational education correlation. In a similar manner, the decomposition of the income correlation for those rated on leadership capacity reveals that this variable has a strong impact on the intergenerational correlation, which was previously captured by the personality variables. In this case, the personality characteristics contribute little to the intergenerational correlation once leadership capacity is taken into account. The interpretation of these two extensions is not evident, however, because of the close relations between the variables in question: cognitive ability and GPA may be seen as two ways of measuring one underlying intelligence dimension, and the leadership rating is to a large extent a function of the psychological variables.

In sum, the decomposition suggests a less complex process behind the education correlation than the income correlation. Father's education appears to affect son's education through cognitive ability (and unobserved variables), and only to a minor extent through observed physiological and personality characteristics. When decomposing the effect of mother's education, the results are similar (results not shown). Cognitive ability also contributes strongly to the intergenerational transmission of income, and part of this impact stems from its effect on education. However, a non-negligible proportion of the income correlation is accounted for by cognitive ability even after controlling for education, and personality traits account for a substantial share of the income correlation. The physiological characteristics analyzed here, on the other hand, do not contribute much to either of the intergenerational correlations.

We also carried out all income analyses above using son's incomes at ages thirty-three to thirty-seven, which extends the number of birth cohorts analyzed. Although most results remain the same, one interesting difference is worth noting: the mediating effect of education is more than halved when analyzing income at younger ages, due to a much weaker effect of own education on income. Obviously, the effect of education on income is lower at the onset and early parts of an individual's work-life career, which means that the ages chosen for the income analysis makes a big difference to the role ascribed to education.

Conclusions

We estimated the intergenerational correlation between father's and son's income and education, respectively, for four full cohorts of Swedish men. With several observations of income for each generation, with high-quality data, and with a large population (157,000 to 180,000), we are fairly confident that our estimates of 0.31 for income and 0.38 for education are reliable estimates, given the definitions that we use. Of course, these estimates are likely to be lower bound as measurement error is not accounted for, and may increase also with the inclusion of more information on mothers (Nordli Hansen 2010). Subsequently, we used register data on school achievement and educational attainment, in combination with data on cognitive ability and personality characteristics from enlistment at age eighteen, to study how the intergenerational correlations were mediated. Although our study does not attempt to solve issues of causality, and our decompositions of the intergenerational correlations build on some relatively strong assumptions, we believe that some of our main findings are sufficiently clear-cut to shed new light on the intergenerational transmission of advantage and disadvantage.

Ostensively, our results are complex, as we used several indicators of mediating factors, divided into three broad categories—cognitive ability, personality traits, and physical characteristics—and also a range of controls as well as mediators of different status (education and occupation). However, the main story generated by our analyses is fairly simple. Our measures of cognitive ability, personality, and physical characteristics explain 37 percent of the intergenerational income correlation and 46 percent of the intergenerational education correlation. The explained part of the intergenerational educational correlation is mainly mediated by cognitive ability (predominantly logic-inductive reasoning), and only to a small extent by personality traits. However, both cognitive ability and personality traits contribute substantially to the explained part of the intergenerational *income* correlation. Physical traits play a minor role in both cases. The intergenerational income association is partly due to the fact that sons from high-income families more often get a higher education and, given both their and their fathers' educational attainment, they reach more economically rewarding occupations. A part of the effect of cognitive ability and personality on the income correlation is due to their effects on education and occupation—that is, part of the reason that sons from high income families get higher education and high-income occupations is that they have higher cognitive ability and more "desirable" personality characteristics. However, cognitive ability and personality characteristics contribute independently to the intergenerational correlation also after controlling for education and occupation.

What is of interest here is in particular the non-negligible role played by personality traits for the intergenerational income correlation, amounting to more than 10 percent. This finding has been reported also from Britain (Blanden, Gregg, and Macmillan 2007) and from the United States (Osborne Groves 2005), although these studies used a different indicator of personality as well as more dubious income measures. Also, Hirvonen, analyzing Swedish data, finds a role for personality traits comparable to ours (2010). Our analysis adds an important additional fact to these estimates, namely that although personality traits also contribute to the intergenerational transmission of education, their contribution to the intergenerational transmission of income goes only to a small extent through education. Instead, it seems as if the personality traits mainly secure their income returns directly in the labor market.

An interesting result is that a substantial part of the intergenerational associations cannot be accounted for by the extensive set of variables we use. What processes could be behind this are of course unknown, though a part could be attributable to measurement error. It is unlikely that unmeasured aspects of cognitive ability (or intelligence) are behind, as other studies have found our four dimensions to be highly correlated with the common g-factor (Carlstedt and Mårdberg 1993). For personality traits, consensus is weaker on what personality consists of, and thus possible other traits are unobserved in our data and perhaps not highly correlated with the variables we use (an example of traits we do not observe is locus of control). It would have been natural to assume that the unaccounted intergenerational income correlation to some extent is due to the fact that father's occupation and social class position (well-known correlates with income) had ramifications for son's occupational choice and structural opportunities in the labor market, and consequently his income. However, when we controlled for father's education, occupational prestige, and social class, the conditional effect of father's income on son's decreased only marginally. Including mother's education did not lead to different conclusions, but it is likely that including other characteristics of mothers would give a fuller, albeit more complex, picture of the intergenerational process. All in all, this lingering intergenerational income effect has, as far as we know, never been shown before.

Although it can only be speculations, three different explanations for the unaccounted intergenerational income effect stand out. First, high-income fathers may have access to superior information that facilitates both the educational and income attainment of their sons. However, that the income effect remains even after controlling for fathers' education and occupation makes this explanation less likely. Second, high-income fathers may have networks that improve the chances of income raises for sons. For example, as shown in chapter 18 for Denmark and Canada, sons who get a job in the same firm as high-income fathers tend to get an income bonus, possibly through mechanisms of nepotism or favoritism. It is likely that networks could have a similar effect also through the father's acquaintances in other firms. However, a mechanism of this kind is unlikely to explain the remaining intergenerational correlation in education. Third, a sociological explanation would be coached in terms of aspirations. Notably, parents and children may want to avoid intergenerational downward mobility. This type of explanation was put forward by Raymond Boudon (1974), and elaborated by Robert Erikson and Jan Jonsson (1996). It assumes that the costs for downward mobility is higher than the benefits for upward, reflected in the utility of higher income (or education, or occupational prestige) leveling off at a certain reference point in the income (education-occupation) distribution, a point typically taken to be the parents' attainments. For example, the child of a doctor would struggle very hard to avoid ending up "only" as a nurse, whereas the child of a hospital attendant would feel relatively content in doing so. These alternative explanations are not possible to test using the data at hand, but appear important for future research.

Discussion: Possibilities for Equalization

We cannot draw firm causal conclusions from our analyses, and therefore are not in a position to say with any certainty what remedies might exist for the intergenerational inequalities we register. However, our results give us some leads in this ongoing discussion. Most of the sons' characteristics that we show to have positive effects on their education and income are generally desirable, such as logic reasoning, verbal ability, emotional stability, and social maturity. In fact, almost everyone would agree that parents' should instill such qualities in their children (compare Swift 2005; chapter 20, this volume). The same logic applies to aspirations, though we have not studied them here, but only discussed them as a possible explanation for the unobserved origin effect.

In practice, at least in the short run, the main focus for equalization must then reside with the active compensation for those children who score lower on income-generating characteristics. This could be targeted early in a child's life or focus on the educational transitions later in the school career. High-quality day care and well-functioning compulsory schools that not only center on children's cognitive and verbal abilities, but also provide room for the positive development of psychological traits, would have the potential for equalization. Whether early interventions are efficient is moot, but recent research suggests that they carry some promise (on day care, see Barnett 2008; Camilli et al. 2010; chapter 7, this volume; compare chapter 9, this volume on schools).[14] Sweden has, since our cohorts went through the school system, introduced almost completely comprehensive day care of high and equal quality, but these cohorts (born in the late 1980s and later) are still too young to study.

Behind the association between socioeconomic origin and education lies the importance of origin resources not only for school performance, but also for educational choices at given performance levels (Erikson and Rudolphi 2010). Therefore, policies are potentially effective that encourage gifted children to continue to higher levels of education, by, for example, minimizing the consequences of exclusive information and increasing the active recruitment of promising students, thus compensating low-income children for their or their parents' lower aspirations (Erikson and Jonsson 1996). A general equalization in the parental generation, in terms of incomes or economic security, may also benefit students from poorer circumstances (Erikson 1996), presumably because their perceived risks with tertiary education investments are higher.

Policy recommendations for equalizing opportunities often focus on younger ages, perhaps because institutions that can serve as vehicles of policy are concentrated to children. But our results show that a nontrivial part of the intergenerational income correlation remains even when controlling for a host of child characteristics, including their educational attainment, suggesting that inequality-generating mechanisms in the labor market are also at work. Favoritism, networks, limited information, discrimination, and sheer nepotism—excluding children from socioeconomically disadvantaged families—are probably present in most labor markets. However, given the persistent discrimination in the labor market on the basis even of visible characteristics such as ethnicity and gender, the hopes for effective intervention reducing socioeconomic origin disadvantage are slim.

In sum, our study, in addition to others in the field, has identified the structure of intergenerational persistence, but to go from there to policy recommendations would need more careful causal analysis, and, even so, reducing intergenerational transmission of advantage and disadvantage is unlikely to be achieved easily.

Notes

1. We use the term *noncognitive* to refer to characteristics not normally included in analyses of cognitive traits, notably in the measurement of cognitive ability, though we are aware that such noncognitive characteristics may also have cognitive content.
2. At the age of thirty-eight to forty-two, most have reached some kind of "income maturity" (Böhlmark and Lindquist 2006), and though income

differences between children of different income origins increase rapidly between age twenty-five and thirty-five, they have begun to level off at around age forty (Jonsson, Mood, and Bihagen 2010, fig. 3.18).

3. We have chosen to study the correlations rather than the elasticities because the former correspond more closely to the concept of inequality of opportunity, that is, they address the relative chances of achieving educational and income positions without confusing these with changes in the marginal distribution of incomes across generations.

4. The smaller sample in the income regression is due to the larger share of missing information on income than on education. Using the income regression sample for the education analysis does not change the results.

5. That these variables are measured at age eighteen, after the first important educational branching point, may cause a problem of reversed causality in the educational mobility analysis when we use them as mediators. This goes especially for cognitive ability. Men who follow the academic program at upper secondary school, for example, are likely to be more exposed to tests, literature, and teaching that promote performance on cognitive tests than those who either have left school or follow a vocational track, and therefore the correlation between education and cognitive ability could partly reflect an effect of the former on the latter. Differences in cognitive ability at age eighteen have indeed been shown to increase according to which educational track thirteen-year-olds in Sweden followed in the old school system (Härnqvist 1968). The same result is reported for IQ change between age ten and age twenty (Husén and Tuijnman 1991; see also Cliffordson and Gustafsson 2008). Our assumption here is that the major parts of the mediating variables are stable characteristics that would have taken similar values also if they had been measured before the end of comprehensive school, an assumption that is supported by results showing the correlation between child IQ and adult IQ to be around 0.9 (Husén and Tuijnman 1991; compare Jencks et al. 1979). The results in chapter 16 of this volume suggest that the intergenerational association of noncognitive traits become stronger with age, which may indicate that it is an advantage to have the measure at age eighteen rather than earlier. Online appendix can be found at: http://www.russellsage.org/Ermisch_et_al_OnlineAppendix.pdf.

6. The income correlation is slightly lower (0.289 versus 0.312) when self-employed are included in the analysis, but the substantive conclusions from the decomposition of the correlation remain the same.

7. The years of education we apply to the various levels of education, based on the Swedish standard classification, or SUN (see Statistics Sweden 2000) are as follows: level 1, short compulsory (fathers=7.2, sons=8.2); level 2, long compulsory or lower secondary, 9 to 10 years (9.7, 9.3); level 3, short-cycle upper secondary (10.6, 11.6); level 4, long upper secondary (11.7, 12.2); level 5, lower tertiary, 1 to 2 years (13.4, 14.3); level 6, degree (17.4, 16.9); level 7, master or doctorate (20.3, 21.7). Father's estimates come from men born between 1922

and 1950 interviewed in LNU 1991, and son's estimates from cohorts 1962 to 1970 interviewed in LNU 2000.

8. This classification (SEI) is close to the commonly used EGP class schema (Erikson and Goldthorpe 1992, chap. 1; differences described in Jonsson 2004). The classes are as follows: manual workers (SEI=11, 12, 21, 22), lower nonmanuals (36), lower service class (46), higher service class (56, 60), self-employed and farmers (79, 89), and a category of missing (99).

9. This correlation deviates slightly from the correlation in table 3.3, model 1, because of differences in population—men with missing income data are included in the education regression but not in the income regression and the correlation matrix.

10. An intergenerational income correlation of 0.31 is relatively high in comparison with previous estimates for Sweden, which is due to our averaging across many years of income, measuring income at thirty-eight to forty-two rather than at younger ages, studying labor income rather than disposable income, and using the metric rather than the log form of income (for a comparison of income correlations across different studies, definitions, and populations, see Mood 2010).

11. Analyses include all men that have nonmissing values on included variables, regardless of whether they have lived with their father. Excluding those who did not live with the father at age ten (about 13 percent of the analyzed population) increases the intergenerational correlation slightly but does not change the overall results.

12. In the description of the regression analyses we will for convenience use the term effect as a technical term of the beta-coefficients, but without implying that the relation is causal.

13. We have also controlled for municipality of origin in the education regression, but it affects the results only marginally.

14. The intense discussions during recent decades about child obesity and fitness—and thereby the broader issues of nutrition and exercise—make important points about children's health and well-being, and possibly about their labor market opportunities. Changes in children's physical characteristics, however, are likely to have little impact on intergenerational socioeconomic inequality.

References

Alwin, Duane F., and Robert M. Hauser. 1975. "The Decomposition of Effects in Path Analysis." *American Sociological Review* 40(1): 37–47.

Anger, Silke, and Guido Heineck. 2010. "Do Smart Parents Raise Smart Children? The Intergenerational Transmission of Cognitive Abilities." *Journal of Population Economics* 23(3): 1105–132.

Barnett, W. Steven. 2008. "Preschool Education and Its Lasting Effects: Research and Policy Implications." Working Paper. East Lansing, Mich.: Great Lakes Center for Education Research and Practice.

Becker, Gary S., and Nigel Tomes. 1986. "Human Capital and the Rise and Fall of Families." *Journal of Labor Economics* 4(3): S1–S39.

Björklund, Anders, Hederos Eriksson, Karin, and Markus Jäntti. 2010. "IQ and Family Background: Are Associations Strong or Weak?" *The B.E. Journal of Economic Analysis & Policy* 10(1): Article 2. Available at: http://www.bepress.com/bejeap/vol10/iss1/art2 (accessed December 19, 2011).

Björklund, Anders, and Markus Jäntti. 2009. "Intergenerational Income Mobility and the Role of Family Background." In *The Oxford Handbook of Economic Inequality*, edited by Wiemer Salverda, Brian Nolan, and Timothy Smeeding. Oxford: Oxford University Press.

Black, Sandra E., Paul J. Devereux, and Kjell G. Salvanes. 2009. "Like Father, Like Son? A Note on the Intergenerational Transmission of IQ Scores." *Economic Letters* 105(1): 138–40.

Blanden, Jo, Paul Gregg, and Lindsey Macmillan. 2007. "Accounting for Intergenerational Income Persistence: Noncognitive Skills, Ability, and Education." *Economic Journal* 117(519): C43–60.

Blau, Peter M., and Otis Dudley Duncan. 1967. *The American Occupational Structure*. New York: John Wiley & Sons.

Böhlmark, Anders, and Matthew J. Lindquist. 2006. "Life-Cycle Variations in the Association Between Current and Lifetime Income: Replication and Extension for Sweden." *Journal of Labor Economics* 24(4): 879–96.

Boudon, Raymond. 1974. *Education, Opportunity, and Social Inequality*. New York: John Wiley & Sons.

Bowles, Samuel, and Herbert Gintis. 2002. "The Inheritance of Inequality." *Journal of Economic Perspectives* 16(3): 3–30.

Bowles, Samuel, Herbert Gintis, and Melissa Osborne. 2001. "The Determinants of Earnings: A Behavioral Approach." *Journal of Economic Literature* 39(4): 1137–176.

Bowles, Samuel, Herbert Gintis, and Melissa Osborne Groves, eds. 2005. *Unequal Chances: Family Background and Economic Success*. Princeton, N.J.: Princeton University Press and Russell Sage Foundation.

Bratsberg, Bernt, Knut Røed, Oddbjorn Raaum, Robin Naylor, Markus Jäntti, Tor Eriksson, and Eva Österbacka. 2007. "Nonlinearities in Intergenerational Earnings Mobility: Consequences for Cross-Country Comparisons." *Economic Journal* 117(519): C72–92.

Breen, Richard, ed. 2004. *Social Mobility in Europe*. Oxford: Oxford University Press.

Breen, Richard, and Jan O. Jonsson. 2005. "Inequality of Opportunity in Comparative Perspective: Recent Research on Educational Attainment and Social Mobility." *Annual Review of Sociology* 31: 223–43.

Camilli, Gregory, Sadako Vargas, Sharon Ryan, and W. Steven Barnett. 2010. "Meta-Analysis of the Effects of Early Education Interventions on Cognitive and Social Development." *Teachers College Record* 112: 579–620.

Carlstedt, Berit, and Bertil Mårdberg. 1993. "Construct Validity of the Swedish Enlistment Battery." *Scandinavian Journal of Psychology* 34(4): 353–62.

Carroll, John B. 1993. *Human Cognitive Abilities.* Cambridge: Cambridge University Press.

Cliffordson, Christina, and Jan-Eric Gustafsson. 2008. "Effects of Age and Schooling on Intellectual Performance: Estimates Obtained from Analysis of Continuous Variation in Age and Length of Schooling." *Intelligence* 36(2): 143–52.

Corak, Miles, and Andrew Heisz. 1999. "The Intergenerational Earnings and Income Mobility of Canadian Men: Evidence from Longitudinal Income Tax Data." *Journal of Human Resources* 34(3): 504–33.

Dabbs, James M., Jr. 1992. "Testosterone and Occupational Achievement." *Social Forces* 70(3): 813–24.

Duncan, Otis Dudley. 1966. "Path Analysis: Sociological Examples." *American Journal of Sociology* 72: 1–16.

Duncan, Otis Dudley, and Robert W. Hodge. 1963. "Education and Occupational Mobility: A Regression Analysis." *American Journal of Sociology* 68(6): 629–44.

Duncan, Greg J., Ariel Kalil, Susan E. Mayer, Robin Tepper, and Monique R. Payne. 2005. "The Apple Does Not Fall Far from the Tree." In *Unequal Chances,* edited by Samuel Bowles, Herbert Gintis, and Melissa Osborne Groves. Princeton, N.J.: Princeton University Press.

Dunifon, Rachel, Greg J. Duncan, and Jeanne Brooks-Gunn. 2001. "As Ye Sweep, So Shall Ye Reap." *American Economic Review* 91(2): 150–54.

Erikson, Robert. 1987. "The Long Arm of the Origin: The Effects of Family Background on Occupational and Educational Achievement." In *Sociological Miscellany, Essays in Honour of Gunnar Boalt,* edited by Ulla Bergryd and Carl-Gunnar Janson. Stockholm: University of Stockholm.

———. 1996. "Explaining Change in Educational Inequality: Economic Security and School Reforms." In *Can Education Be Equalized?* edited by Robert Erikson and Jan O. Jonsson. Boulder, Colo.: Westview Press.

Erikson, Robert, and John H. Goldthorpe. 1992. *The Constant Flux: A Study of Class Mobility in Industrial Societies.* Oxford: Clarendon Press.

Erikson, Robert, and Jan O. Jonsson. 1996. "Explaining Class Inequality in Education: The Swedish Test Case." In *Can Education Be Equalized?* Boulder, Colo.: Westview.

———. 1998. "Social Origin as an Interest-Bearing Asset: Family Background and Labour Market Rewards Among Employees in Sweden." *Acta Sociologica* 41(1): 19–36.

Erikson, Robert, and Frida Rudolphi. 2010. "Change in Social Selection to Upper Secondary School: Primary and Secondary Effects in Sweden." *European Sociological Review* 26(3): 291–305.

Finkelstein, Eric A., Christofer J. Ruhm, and Katherine M. Kosa. 2005. "Economic Causes and Consequences of Obesity." *Annual Review of Public Health* 26(3): 239–57.

Ganzeboom, Harry B. G., and Donald J. Treiman. 1996. "Internationally Comparable Measures of Occupational Status for the 1988 International Standard Classification of Occupations." *Social Science Research* 25(3): 201–39.

Goldsmith, Arthur H., Jonathan R. Veum, and William Darity. 2000. "Motivation and Labor Market Outcomes." *Research in Labor Economics* 19: 109–46.

Gustafsson, Jan-Eric. 1984. "A Unifying Model for the Structure of Intellectual Abilities." *Intelligence* 8(3): 179–203.

Härnqvist, Kjell. 1968. "Relative Changes in Intelligence from 13 to 18." *Scandinavian Journal of Psychology* 9(1): 50–82.

Hauser, Robert M., and Peter A. Mossel. 1985. "Fraternal Resemblance in Educational Attainment and Occupational Status." *American Journal of Sociology* 91(3): 650–73.

Heckman James J., Jora Stixrud, and Sergio Urzua. 2006. "The Effects of Cognitive and Noncognitive Abilities on Labor Market Outcomes and Social Behavior." *Journal of Labor Economics* 24(3): 411–82.

Hertz, Thomas, Tamara Jayasundera, Patrizio Piraino, Sibel Selcuk, Nicole Smith, and Alina Verashchagina. 2007. "The Inheritance of Educational Inequality: Intergenerational Comparison and Fifty-Year Trends." *The B.E. Journal of Economic Analysis & Policy* 7: Article 10. Available at: http://www.bepress.com/bejeap/vol7/iss2/art10 (accessed March 7, 2012).

Hirvonen, Lalaina. 2010. *Essays in Empirical Labour Economics: Family Background, Gender and Earnings*. Ph.D. diss., Swedish Institute for Social Research, Stockholm University.

Husén, Torsten, and Albert Tuijnman. 1991. "The Contribution of Formal Schooling to the Increase of Intellectual Capital." *Educational Researcher* 20(1): 17–25.

Ishida, Hiroshi, Walter Müller, and John M. Ridge. 1995. "Class Origin, Class Destination, and Education: A Cross-National Study of Industrial Nations." *American Journal of Sociology* 101(1): 145–93.

Jackson, Michelle. 2006. "Personality Traits and Occupational Attainment." *European Sociological Review* 22(2): 187–99.

Jäntti, Markus, Bernt Bratsberg, Knut Røed, Oddbjørn Raaum, Robin Naylor, Eva Österbacka, Anders Björklund, and Tor Eriksson. 2006. "American Exceptionalism in a New Light: A Comparison of Intergenerational Earnings Mobility in the Nordic Countries, the United Kingdom and the United States." *IZA discussion paper 1938*. Bonn: Institute for the Study of Labor.

Jencks, Christopher, Susan Bartlett, Mary Corcoran, James Crouse, David Eaglesfield, Gregory Jackson, Kent McClelland, Peter Mueser, Michael Olneck, Joseph Schwartz, Sherry Ward, and Jill Williams. 1979. *Who Gets Ahead? The Determinants of Economic Success in America*. New York: Basic Books.

Jencks, Christopher, Marshall Smith, Henry Acland, Mary Jo Bane, David Cohen, Herbert Gintis, Barbara Heyns, and Stephan Michelson. 1972. *Inequality: A Reassessment of the Effect of Family and Schooling in America.* New York: Basic Books.

Jonsson, Jan O. 2004. "Equality at a Halt? Social Mobility in Sweden 1976–99." In *Social Mobility in Europe,* edited by Richard Breen. Oxford: Oxford University Press.

Jonsson, Jan O., David B. Grusky, Matthew Di Carlo, Reinhard Pollak, and Mary C. Brinton. 2009. "Micro-Class Mobility. Social Reproduction in Four Countries." *American Journal of Sociology* 114(4): 977–1036.

Jonsson, Jan O., Carina Mood, and Erik Bihagen. 2010. "Fattigdomens förändring, utbredning och dynamik (Poverty in Sweden: Recent Trends, Prevalence, and Dynamics)." In *Social Rapport 2010.* Stockholm: Socialstyrelsen.

Kvist, Ann Valentin, and Jan-Eric Gustafsson. 2008. "The Relation Between Fluid Intelligence and the General Factor as a Function of Cultural Background: A Test of Cattell's Investment Theory." *Intelligence* 36(5): 422–36.

Lindqvist, Erik, and Roine Westman. 2011. "The Labor Market Returns to Cognitive and Noncognitive Ability: Evidence from the Swedish Enlistment." *American Economic Journal: Applied Economics* 3(1): 101–28.

Loehlin, John C. 2005. "Resemblance in Personality and Attitudes Between Parents and their Children. Genetic and Environmental Contributions." In *Unequal Chances,* edited by Samuel Bowles, Herbert Gintis, and Melissa Osborne Groves. Princeton, N.J.: Princeton University Press.

Mood, Carina. 2010. "The Importance of Income Definitions for the Magnitudes and Trends in Intergenerational Income Correlation." Unpublished manuscript. Swedish Institute for Social Research.

Mueller, Gerrit, and Erik Plug. 2006. "Estimating the Effect of Personality on Male and Female Earnings." *Industrial and Labor Relations Review* 60(1): 3–22.

Nordli Hansen, Marianne. 2010. "Change in Intergenerational Economic Mobility in Norway: Conventional Versus Joint Classifications of Economic Origin." *Journal of Economic Inequality* 8(2):133–51.

Osborne Groves, Melissa. 2005. "Personality and the Intergenerational Transmission of Economic Status." In *Unequal Chances,* edited by Samuel Bowles, Herbert Gintis, and Melissa Osborne Groves. Princeton, N.J.: Princeton University Press.

Persico, Nicola, Andrew Postlewaite, and Dan Silverman. 2004. "The Effect of Adolescent Experience on Labor Market Outcomes: The Case of Height." *Journal of Political Economy* 112(5): 1019–53.

Sewell, William H., and Robert M. Hauser. 1975. *Education, Occupation, and Earnings. Achievement in the Early Career.* New York: Academic Press.

———. 1980. "The Wisconsin Longitudinal Study of Social and Psychological Factors in Aspirations and Achievements." *Research in Sociology of Education and Socialization* 1: 59–99.

Sieben Inge, and Paul M. de Graaf. 2001. "Testing the Modernization Hypothesis and the Socialist Ideology Hypothesis: A Comparative Sibling Analysis of

Educational Attainment and Occupational Status." *British Journal of Sociology* 52(3): 441–67.

Solon, Gary. 2002. "Cross-Country Differences in Intergenerational Income Mobility." *Journal of Economic Perspectives* 16(3): 59–66.

Statistics Sweden. 1989. *Yrkesklassificeringar i FoB85 enligt Nordisk yrkesklassificering (NYK) och Socioekonomisk indelning (SEI).* MIS 1989: 5. Stockholm: Statistics Sweden.

———. 2000. *Svensk utbildningsnomenklatur, SUN 2000.* MIS 2000: 1. Stockholm: Statistics Sweden.

Swift, Adam. 2005. "Justice, Luck, and the Family. The Intergenerational Transmission of Economic Advantage from a Normative Perspective." In *Unequal Chances,* edited by Samuel Bowles, Herbert Gintis, and Melissa Osborne Groves. Princeton, N.J.: Princeton University Press.

PART II

EARLY CHILDHOOD

Chapter 4

Inequality in Early Childhood Outcomes

BRUCE BRADBURY, MILES CORAK,
JANE WALDFOGEL, AND ELIZABETH WASHBROOK

T HE IMPORTANCE of the early years is now a mainstay of public policy discourse. Early investments are often claimed to frame the chances children will successfully navigate the series of transitions they must make in becoming successful and self-reliant adults. As such they have a direct bearing on the conduct of social policy in many countries.

This perspective reflects a large and growing literature from a number of different disciplines on the importance of the early years. Eric Knudsen and his colleagues (2006) offer a particularly clear and succinct summary, but just as importantly they sketch out the logic of an argument stressing the relevance for public policy. How and why early experiences have long lasting consequences has important implications, in their view, for the future productivity of society, and raises a need for public policy to invest in the development of young children from disadvantaged backgrounds. This question also relates to an important shared value: equality of opportunity, the idea that all children regardless of socioeconomic background should have the opportunity to develop their capacities to become all that they can be.

As such the focus in this chapter is on the emergence of inequality during the early years. We offer a comparative analysis of children who, at about age five, are at the onset of formal schooling, and therefore put the focus on the environment and on public policies other than the education system. We study a series of child outcomes related to readiness to learn—focusing on vocabulary development and externalizing behavior—in a comparative way across four countries: Australia, Canada, the United Kingdom, and the United States. Although family is the principle influence on child outcomes during these early years, the time and skills parents bring to bear in investing in their children are also influenced by public policies addressed to families and their interaction with labor markets. Our analysis describes the extent to which inequalities in outcomes emerge by the age of five according to parental education and income. While our estimates are not intended to be causal, our descriptive results may point toward possible policy remedies. In particular, the implications for public policy may well be different if inequality of outcomes is due solely to relatively well-advantaged families capitalizing on their resources to improve the lives of their children, than if it is due to the relatively disadvantaged raising children that fall far below the mainstream. We therefore pay particular attention to charting the gaps that emerge at both the top and the bottom of the education and income hierarchy.

Our major findings are three in number. First, significant inequalities in child capacities emerge even in these early years in all four countries, but the disparities are notably greater in the United States and the United Kingdom than in Australia, and particularly in Canada. Second, large differences in cognitive outcomes exist in all countries between children from disadvantaged backgrounds and the mainstream, and these are of similar magnitudes across countries. Differences across countries in the overall disparity between cognitive outcomes of the least and most advantaged, therefore, largely reflect variation in the degree to which children at the top of the socioeconomic status (SES) distribution out-perform those in the middle. Third, disparities in social and behavioral development are markedly smaller than in cognitive outcomes and differ from cognitive outcomes in their association with SES across countries. While the smallest SES gaps are found in Australia and Canada for both types of outcome, differences in cognitive outcomes are greatest in the United States, while differences in behavioral outcomes are greatest in the United Kingdom.

Background

By focusing on early cognitive and socioemotional development we are speaking to a literature that has highlighted the importance of both cognitive skills (such as reading and math knowledge) and other types of skills (such as social and emotional development) for adult earnings, employment, and other outcomes. As suggested this literature also argues that early experiences are important, and that interventions in early childhood can be particularly effective at reducing longer-term inequalities (Almond and Currie 2010; Carneiro and Heckman 2003; Cunha et al. 2005; Currie and Stabile 2006; Heckman and Lochner 2000; Duncan and Magnuson 2011; Smith 2009).

Our analysis is also predicated upon the idea that there is value in a cross-country comparative analysis. We focus on these four particular countries because they are often thought of as having similar types of welfare states and labor markets (Esping-Anderson 1990), and indeed

Table 4.1   Indicators of Economic and Policy Inputs

	Australia	Canada	United Kingdom	United States
Inequality (Gini coefficient, 2003–2004)	0.31	0.32	0.35	0.37
Child poverty (relative, 2005)	11.8%	15.1%	10.1%	20.6%
Per capita social expenditure on children aged under six as proportion of median working-age income				
Cash and tax breaks	9.9	NA	8.9	4.3
Child care, education, and other	8.8	NA	12.7	6.4
Public expenditure as share of total health expenditure (2005)	66.9	70.3	81.9	44.4

Source: Author's compilation based on data from Luxembourg Income Study (2010) and OECD (2009, 2011).

they often look to each other for policy models and reforms. Yet at the same time there are important and interesting differences in both outcomes and inputs.

As shown in table 4.1, each of these countries is characterized by levels of income inequality that for the most part are above the OECD average—with Gini coefficients ranging from about 0.31 and 0.32 in Australia and Canada to 0.35 and 0.37 in the United Kingdom and the United States. They also differ in their levels of social mobility in adult earnings across generations. The United States and United Kingdom are identified as among the least mobile countries; Australia and Canada are among the most mobile (Corak 2006). The countries also differ in the levels of child poverty. Child poverty rates based on a relative income threshold (50 percent of median equivalized income) are as high as 21 percent in the United States, but significantly lower at 15 percent in Canada, 12 percent in Australia, and 10 percent in the United Kingdom.

Further, there are substantial differences in expenditures and policy frameworks for families with young children, with the United States standing out as having the least generous provisions. Per capita social expenditure on children younger than six is significantly higher in Australia and the United Kingdom than in the United States (table 4.1).[1] Moreover, across the four major domains of public policy that affect families with young children—parental leave, child care, income supports, and health insurance—the United States has the weakest provisions, and if anything the gap between the United States and the other countries has widened in recent years as the other countries' policies to support families with young children have evolved and expanded.

Australia, like the United States, was one of the few countries to not offer paid parental leave at the time of our data collection (although it did offer twelve months of unpaid leave, and in 2011 introduced a system of eighteen weeks of paid leave). Child-care policies are evolving as well. Child care in Australia is provided by a combination of state, nongovernmental organizations, and private providers. Historically, there has been a split between long day care (which is subsidized by the federal government by providing child-care rebates of up to 50 percent of the fees) and preschool (which is provided by the states as part of the education system). Payment for preschool and availability differs from state to state, as does the school starting age. There is currently a policy program initiated by the Council of Australian Governments (the commonwealth and the states acting together) to develop a unified early years framework that will bring together the commonwealth and state provisions and iron out the anomalies. Overall, Australia is one of the lowest spenders in the OECD on childhood services but in contrast provides relatively generous cash transfers to parents of young children including a generous baby bonus, various family tax benefits, and other in-kind provisions. The benefit system is also relatively progressive, with many of the cash transfers being targeted at the most disadvantaged. Most Australians have access to comprehensive health care, which is mainly publicly financed. The state provides financial incentives to doctors to encourage them to provide free services to children under sixteen and to income support recipients (Healy, Evelyn, and Buddhima 2006).

Several important expansions in family policy in Canada were enacted during the 1990s, and the cohort studied here was among the first to be exposed to some of these provisions. These include the introduction of a National Child Benefit and Early Childhood Development Agreements, which involved increased financial transfers provided through the tax system targeted according to family income and the number of children, and including supplements based on the number of children younger than seven. This change significantly increased the financial support to lower income families. At the same time there was an increase of in-kind support through the development of early childhood learning and day-care facilities. These innovations also included an increase in paid parental leave through the unemployment insurance program, so that beginning in 2001 up to one year of benefits are provided for a parent of a newborn or adopted child. This includes fifteen weeks of maternity benefits to the biological mother, and a further thirty-five weeks of parental benefits that can be shared between the mother and the father. With regard to health care, in Canada all children and their families are covered by a universal health-care system. This has been a long-standing program that permits families of all socioeconomic backgrounds access to publicly provided health care. In other domains, variation in policies across the ten provinces is also considerable, with, for example, Quebec offering essentially free child care for working mothers, and Ontario currently implementing a program of full-day kindergarten beginning at age four.

The past decade in the United Kingdom has witnessed dramatic expansions in programs and supports for preschool age children (Waldfogel 2010). Parents of the cohort studied here had the right to take up to three months of unpaid parental leave, and mothers had the right to up to twenty-nine weeks of job-protected maternity leave, with eighteen weeks paid (this has since been extended to a year of job-protected maternity leave, with nine months paid). In addition, low-income families with young children in this period benefited from sizable increases in means-tested benefits as well as in the universal child allowance program. Home visiting and child-care services provided to children under age three by the Sure Start program began on a small scale in 1999, just before the birth of this cohort, and expanded progressively thereafter. And this cohort of children was the very first entitled to free universal preschool at age three (although preschool for four-year-olds had been introduced six years earlier in 1998). As in Australia and Canada, all children and their families benefit from universal health care, which is provided free at the point of service by the National Health Service.

In contrast, the United States remains one of the few advanced industrialized countries without a national policy providing a period of paid maternity leave (Waldfogel 2006). Under the Family and Medical Leave Act, qualifying employees may take up to twelve weeks of leave following a birth, but only about half of new parents are covered and eligible, the period of leave is quite short by international standards, and it is unpaid. The United States also differs from other advanced industrialized countries in having a system of early childhood care and education that relies heavily on the private market. Subsidies are provided to low-income working families, but there are not enough dollars to support all eligible families. The federal Head Start program provides preschool to disadvantaged three- and four-year-olds, but, in spite of recent expansions, does not serve all eligible children. Public prekindergarten programs serve only a small share (roughly one-sixth) of the country's four-year-olds. Thus, a child's experience of preschool remains very strongly correlated with parental resources, with the most advantaged children the most likely to participate. Moreover, the United States still does not provide universal health insurance coverage for children and their families, even after the recent expansions in Medicaid and the Children's Health Insurance Program, and the passage of health-care reform in early 2010.

Whether these inputs have bearing on the outcomes we consider is hard to tell without first documenting at what point in the life cycle significant socioeconomic gradients begin to emerge. A comparative analysis may be helpful in appreciating the role of differences in public policy choices, but is obviously a challenge because of the need for comparable data. Our analysis therefore takes advantage of rich data on specific cohorts from each of the four countries to investigate variations in the connection between parental resources and inequality in early child outcomes. Part of our contribution to the literature is, therefore, methodological. We focus attention on measures and indicators that are relatively similar across the very detailed surveys conducted in these countries, highlighting areas where future research and data development in other countries might be directed.

The most important antecedent for our work is Jane Waldfogel and Elizabeth Washbrook (2011a, 2011b) who study income-related gaps in school readiness in the United States and the United Kingdom. Some of this ground is covered by Miles Corak, Lori Curtis, and Shelley Phipps (2011), who study differences between Canada and the United States, and by Bradbury and others on disparities in Australia (Bradbury 2007; Katz and Redmond 2009; Redmond and Zhu 2009).

Although this work indicates that substantial gaps in school readiness exist in all four countries, only two explicit cross-country comparisons have been carried out, and these focused only on pairs of countries and examined different age groups and outcomes. Comparing income-related gaps in cognitive and behavioral aspects of school readiness for preschool-age children in the United States and the United Kingdom, Waldfogel and Washbrook (2011a, 2011b) found that overall the results were quite similar. Large gaps were evident in both countries between children in the bottom and middle income quintiles, and between children in the top and middle income quintiles. Another point of agreement was that differences in parenting behavior were found to be an important mediator of the gaps in both countries. But some of the Corak, Curtis, and Phipps findings (2011) would suggest that these similarities are not likely to hold in general. Their analysis of a range of cognitive, behavioral, and health outcomes for preschool- and school-age children in Canada and the United States found that income-related gaps differed across the two countries. In general, gaps in outcomes between low-income children and their more advantaged peers tended to be larger in the United States than they are in Canada, suggesting the presence of less mobility even in childhood.

Data and Measurements

Our analysis is based on the Longitudinal Study of Australian Children (LSAC), for Australia; the National Longitudinal Survey of Children and Youth (NLSCY), for Canada; the Millennium Cohort Study (MCS), for the United Kingdom; and the Early Childhood Longitudinal Study-Birth Cohort (ECLS-B), for the United States. The U.K. and U.S. studies each survey a single birth cohort, and we use both in their entirety. The Australian and Canadian studies contain multiple birth cohorts from which we select the subsets most comparable in time with the available U.K. and U.S. data. Some details of the full scope of the Australian and Canadian studies are given in the online appendix; for the rest of the chapter we describe only those cohorts used in the analysis.

These data are vast in both the breadth and depth of information they contain on children in all stages of their lives. Indeed, some of these surveys could more accurately be described as containing multiple surveys, involving separate questionnaires for parents, schools, and children. Our use of this information is very selective, and driven by the objectives of our analysis and the need for cross-country comparability. Table 4.2 provides an overview of some of the key features of each survey, with further detail provided in the appendix. Although the four datasets have many similarities, the task of developing comparable measures of outcomes and background is not simple.

We use information on more than 40,000 children across the four countries born in the first four years of the twenty-first century. All these children were age four to five when their outcomes were assessed. The samples were designed to be broadly representative of all children born in the country in the relevant time window, and who remained resident until the dates of the follow-ups. Survey weights are used in all analyses to adjust for oversampling of certain groups, geographical clustering, and nonrandom attrition. The study-specific details on survey design are discussed in the appendix.

Each of the datasets contains three waves: wave 1, when the children were one year or younger; wave 2, when they were two or three; and wave 3, when they were age four or five. Each wave contains a parent interview in which the most knowledgeable parent or caregiver—the child's biological mother in the overwhelming majority of cases—responded to detailed questions on the family's socioeconomic circumstances and the early care environment of the child. The wave 3 modules also include direct assessments of the child's cognitive ability based on several well-known psychometric instruments, parent reports of the frequency at which the child exhibited certain behaviors, and anthropomorphic measurements.[2] Hence comparable measures of both parental socioeconomic status (P) and cognitive, socioemotional, and health outcomes in early childhood (C1) can be constructed for all four countries.

The differences in child development at age four or five are related to two indicators of parental resources. Following the literature on the importance of parental education for child outcomes, the first indicator we use is the highest educational qualification attained by the primary caregiver or partner who is coresident with the child at the time of the wave 3 survey. We recode the information to the United Nations

Table 4.2 Overview of Datasets

	Australia	Canada	United Kingdom	United States
Survey name	Longitudinal Study of Australian Children Birth Cohort (LSAC)	National Longitudinal Study of Children and Youth (NLSCY)	Millennium Cohort Study (MCS)	Early Childhood Longitudinal Study Birth Cohort (ECLS-B)
Year of birth (range)	Mar. 2003 to Feb. 2004	Jan. 2000 to Dec. 2002	Sept. 2000 to Jan. 2002	Jan. 2001 to Dec. 2001
Exclusions from eligible birth cohort	Nonpermanent residents; children with the same name as deceased children; only one child per household	Children living on reserves or Crown Lands, residents of institutions, full-time members of the Canadian armed forces, and residents of some remote regions	Families ineligible for child benefit	Children born to mothers less than 15 years old; children adopted before 9 months old
Sampling frame	Medicare Australia database, clustered by postal area	Labour Force Survey using the 1994 and 2004 design	Child benefit records, clustered by electoral ward (oversamples: 3 smaller countries in U.K.; areas >30% black/Asian; areas with Child Poverty Index >75th percentile)	Registered births in the vital statistics system (oversamples: twins; low and very low birth weight babies; American Indians; Chinese; other Asian/Pacific Islanders)

Number children ever participated	5,107	8,522	19,517	10,700*
Wave 1 response rate	57% (33% refusal, 11% noncontact)	74.9%	76.7%	71.6%
Number children in wave 3	4,386	7,147	15,460	8,950*
Percentage ever participated in wave 3	85.9%	83.9%	79.2%	83.7%
Mean age in months at wave 3	57.7	58.6	62.1	53.0
Standard deviation age in months at wave 3	2.9	6.7	3.0	4.2

Source: Authors' compilation based on data from Australian Institute of Family Studies (2010), Statistics Canada (2006a), Centre for Longitudinal Studies (2010), and National Center for Education Statistics (2009).
*ECLS-B frequencies rounded to the nearest fifty in accordance with NCES reporting rules.

Educational, Scientific and Cultural Organization's (UNESCO's) International Standard Classification of Education (ISCED), a scale explicitly designed to enable cross-national comparisons. In this way it is possible to distinguish four common levels: lower secondary or less (level 2); upper secondary and postsecondary nontertiary (levels 3 and 4); first-stage tertiary, practical, technical, or occupationally specific programs (level 5B); and first-stage tertiary, theoretically based, research preparatory, or highly skilled professional programs and second-stage tertiary, advanced research qualifications (levels 5A and 6).

Table 4A.1 in the online appendix provides details of common national qualifications that fall into each category, and distributions of parental education for the full wave 3 samples analyzed in this chapter.[3] Inspection of this table alerts us to the fact that the imposition of ISCED definitions results in apparently very different education distributions across the countries. Although the proportion of families in the lowest (level 2) and highest (levels 5A and 6) categories are roughly similar in three of the four countries, the Canadian distribution is heavily skewed toward the more highly educated. In addition, the proportions of families falling into the middle two categories is complicated by the fact that level 5B qualifications are relatively more common in Canada and the United States, whereas level 3 and level 4 qualifications are the norm among the middle-educated in Australia and the United Kingdom. We judge it likely that this discrepancy is more a function of the rigidities of the ISCED classification system than evidence of higher average levels of educational attainment in North America, and for this reason we group levels 3, 4, and 5B together in a single middle-education category that covers around 50 percent of the population in three of the four countries (and 40 percent in Canada). Our analysis uses this middle group as the reference category and documents the difference in average outcomes between children in this group and those in the lowest and highest ISCED categories.

Whether the difference in education distribution matters for our discussion of the correlation between P and C1 depends on the mechanisms by which parental education acts on outcomes. If parental education has a direct effect on outcomes, then it will be appropriate to compare child outcomes within parental education groups. If, on the other hand, education acts as a mechanism for sorting parents on the basis of academic aptitude, and it is this underlying aptitude that has an impact on child outcomes, then a country that has a smaller proportion of the population in the extreme education groups would be expected to have more unequal child outcomes across education groups. Because of the possibility of this mechanism, some caution is required when comparing outcomes across education groups.

The second indicator of parental socioeconomic status is average gross household income, divided into quintile groups in our main analysis (this is thus not subject to the issues raised in the previous paragraph, but does assume that it is relative—rather than absolute—income which matters for defining groups). We derive a measure of gross nominal household income at each of the three waves, deflate to 2006 values using national price indices, and convert the amounts to U.S. dollars using OECD purchasing power parity indices (see online appendix). The square root of household size is used as the equivalence scale. These three observations of real gross equivalized household income for each family are then averaged and the survey weights are used to define nationally representative quintile boundaries.[4] The intent of the averaging is to minimize the influence of transitory fluctuations in income due to employment patterns after child birth, reporting, or other factors that may introduce measurement error into the analysis. Measurement error will have a tendency to lead to an understatement of the true relationship between child outcomes and parental resources.

In addition, the precision of the income questions posed in the parental interviews differs across the countries. We adopt a lowest common denominator approach to minimize the risk that differential measurement error affects our results. We downgrade the quality of the income data from the three more accurate surveys, so that it is comparable in quality with that of the fourth. The least detailed measure comes from the U.S. survey, in which parents are asked to give their total gross annual household income in one of thirteen bands. We calculate the percentage of U.S. families in each band, separately for single-parent and couple families, and separately for each wave. For the other countries, we then use this information on the U.S. distribution to derive a comparable measure from the more continuous income data available in each dataset. All families are then classified into one of twenty-six income–family structure groups at each wave. A representative dollar value for gross household income is assigned to each group, and it is this "lumpy" nominal measure that is used in the rest of the income variable derivation (see the online appendix for further details of how these values are assigned).

We organize our analyses by two broad outcome domains, cognitive and socioemotional. For each domain, we focus primarily on a single outcome measure that is the most comparable across the full set of four countries. We then go on to explore other outcomes that are measured consistently in fewer than four countries or that measure a more narrow subset of skills, but which provide some evidence on the robustness of our core findings (see the online appendix for details of these additional outcomes). Our focal cognitive outcomes are picture vocabulary test scores. Children's receptive vocabulary is measured in the Australian, Canadian, and American datasets with items from the Peabody Picture

Vocabulary Test (PPVT). In this assessment, the child is shown pictures on an easel and is asked to identify the picture that best represents the meaning of the word read out by the interviewer.[5] The U.K. picture vocabulary assessment—the British Ability Scales Naming Vocabulary (BAS-NV) test—differs slightly from the PPVT by requiring the child to name out loud the object shown in a single picture. Although this assesses expressive rather than receptive vocabulary, both the BAS-NV and the PPVT are well-known assessments designed to capture verbal ability and tap very similar, if not identical, abilities. For all picture vocabulary tests the sequence of items administered is routed according to the child's responses, and Item Response Theory (IRT) techniques are used to score the final pattern of responses on a single difficulty scale. The availability of the BAS-NV for the U.K. children at age three as well as age five allows some analysis of the sensitivity of vocabulary gradients to age at measurement.

Early socioemotional development has an important influence on adult socioeconomic outcomes independently of cognitive ability. Behavior problems in early to mid-childhood have been linked to range of later outcomes such as high school completion, college attendance, and the probability of arrest in early adulthood (Duncan and Magnuson 2011; Currie and Stabile 2006; McLeod and Kaiser 2004). Our core measure of socioemotional development captures two types of childhood behavior problems: hyperactivity-inattention and conduct problems. For all countries we derive a total externalizing behavior score that is the sum of ten items (five per type of behavior), each of which is scored 0, 1, or 2 by the parent respondent. The instruments used in the Australian and U.K. studies are identical: the combined hyperactivity and conduct problems subscales from the parent-report strengths and difficulties questionnaire (SDQ) (Goodman 1997). The Canadian and U.S. studies also include sets of parent-report behavior items that, although not drawn from any single well-recognized behavioral scale, are very similar to the SDQ items selected.[6] The item details are described in table 4.3. Given evidence that hyperactivity-inattention and conduct problems differ in the degree to which they are consequential for later outcomes (Duncan and Magnuson 2011), we also explore gradients in the two measures separately in supplemental analyses.

Descriptive statistics for the two key outcome variables, as they appear in the raw data, are shown in table 4.4. It is clear that the vocabulary variables are measured in units that are not comparable across countries, and moreover that have no natural interpretation. The externalizing behavior variables differ from the vocabulary variables in that they are nominally measured in the same units across countries, although it should be noted that only the Australian and U.K. behavior scores are measured using an identical instrument.

Table 4.3   Externalizing Behavior Items

Australia and United Kingdom	Canada	United States
Conduct problems		
Often has temper tantrums	When somebody accidentally hurts him, he reacts with anger and fighting	Has temper outbursts or tantrums
Fights with or bullies other children	Gets into many fights	Is physically aggressive (for example, hits, kicks, or pushes)
Can be spiteful to others	Physically attacks people	Bothers and annoys other children
Generally obedient	Bullies or is mean to others	Destroys things that belong to others
Often argumentative with adults	Kicks, bites, or hits other children	Gets angry easily
Hyperactivity or inattention		
Can stop and think before acting	Is impulsive, acts without thinking	Acts impulsively without thinking (for example, runs across the street without looking)
Sees tasks through until the end	Cannot settle on anything for more than a few moments	Keeps working until finished
Easily distracted	Is easily distracted, has trouble sticking to any activity	Has difficulty concentrating or staying on task
Restless, overactive, cannot stay still for long	Is inattentive	Pays attention well
Constantly fidgeting	Can't concentrate, can't pay attention for long	Overly active, unable to sit still

Source: Authors' compilation based on data from Australian Institute of Family Studies (2010), Statistics Canada (2006a), Centre for Longitudinal Studies (2010), and National Center for Education Statistics (2009).

Notes:

Australia and the United Kingdom:

Sources: Strengths and Difficulties Questionnaire (SDQ) administered in full.

Question: What is <child> like? Please give your answers on the basis of <child>'s behavior over the last six months.

Responses (scoring): not true (0); somewhat true (1); certainly true (2). Scoring reversed for positively phrased items.

Canada:

Sources: Items taken from multiple instruments, including Achenbach's Child Behavior Checklist (CBCL), the Ontario Child Health Study (OCHS), and the Montreal Longitudinal Survey.

Question: How often would you say that this child . . . ?

Responses (scoring): never or not true (0); sometimes or somewhat true (1); often or very true (2).

United States:

Sources: Items taken from multiple instruments, including Preschool and Kindergarten Behavior Scales—Second Edition (PKBS-2), Social Rating Scale (SRS), and ECLS-K behavioural assessment

Question: How often in the last three months have the following things occurred . . . ?

Responses (scoring): never (0); rarely (0); sometimes (1); often (2); very often (2). Scoring reversed for positively phrased items.

Table 4.4   Descriptive Statistics for Key Raw Outcome Variables

	Vocabulary				Externalizing Behavior			
	Australia	Canada	United Kingdom	United States	Australia	Canada	United Kingdom	United States
Observations	4266	6234	15168	8450*	3823	6758	13474	8900*
Mean	64.61	57.94	108.40	8.50	6.64	3.93	4.64	5.62
Standard deviation (SD)	6.38	20.00	15.88	1.99	3.33	3.14	3.36	3.86
Minimum	34.19	NA	10	4.62	0	0	0	0
Maximum	84.78	NA	170	13.63	20	20	20	20
Mean monthly increment	0.39	1.35	0.85	0.09	0.03	−0.03	−0.05	−0.02
Monthly increment/SD	0.06	0.07	0.05	0.05	0.01	−0.01	−0.02	−0.01

Source: Authors' calculations using data from Australian Institute of Family Studies (2009), Statistics Canada (2006b), University of London, Institute of Education, Centre for Longitudinal Studies (2006), and U.S. Department of Education, National Center for Education Statistics (2009).

Notes: Higher vocabulary scores denote more favorable outcomes here and throughout our analysis. Higher externalizing behavior scores denote more adverse outcomes in table 4.4 only—the sign of the standardized behavior measures are reversed in all following tables for consistency with the cognitive measures. The minimum and maximum of the Canadian vocabulary are not released by Statistics Canada. The mean monthly increment is the linear regression slope of the outcome against age in months at assessment. All statistics calculated using survey weights.

*ECLS-B frequencies rounded to the nearest fifty in accordance with NCES reporting rules.

One way to get some sense of the comparability of the measures is to examine the average increment in the test score associated with an additional one month of age. Such calculations are only approximate, because they depend on the range of children's ages at the time of the assessment (see table 4.2), and assume linear growth in test scores over that period. Nevertheless, when we express the monthly increment in the vocabulary test score (the regression coefficient on age in months) as a fraction of the overall standard deviation of the variable, we see that the average score increases by a very similar amount per month—between 5 percent and 7 percent of a standard deviation—in all four countries. This implies that 1 standard deviation of a vocabulary score is equivalent to somewhere between fourteen to twenty months of development at this age. Systematic variation with child age in the behavior scores is less than in the vocabulary scores. In three of the four countries, behavior problems appear to decrease slightly with age, but only at the rate of 1 to 2 percent of a standard deviation per month, hence age equivalents seem a less useful way to think about the magnitude of group differences in this context.[7]

To ease interpretation of our results across countries and across domains, all outcomes analyzed in the remainder of the paper are standardized with mean zero and standard deviation one using the survey weights. Raw outcome variables are adjusted for age (by taking the residuals from a regression of the outcome score on a polynomial of age) before standardization. In addition, although all the raw behavior measures are constructed such that higher scores indicate more behavior problems, we reverse the signs of the standardized variables in our analysis for consistency with the cognitive outcomes. Thus, henceforth in our analysis, higher scores refer to better socioemotional functioning.

Descriptive Statistics

The composition of the population across the four countries differs substantially. Table 4.5 shows the average demographic characteristics of all families with four- to five-year-olds by country. Table 4A.2 in the online appendix provides sample characteristics by education group for each country; table 4A.3 provides similar information by income group.

Not only are there mean differences in population characteristics across countries, differences within education and income groups are also significant. Differences in racial-ethnic group membership and immigrant status are particularly notable. For example, while the United States displays the most racial-ethnic diversity among the native-born population, Australia and Canada have the highest share of immigrant parents (with roughly one-third of children having at least one foreign-born parent). However, children with immigrant parents are much more concentrated

Table 4.5   Average Characteristics of Families with Four- to Five-Year-Old Children

	Australia (N = 4,386)	Canada (N = 6812)	United Kingdom (N = 15,460)	United States (N = 8,500)*
Low education (ISCED 2)	8.2%	6.2%	12.2%	10.4%
Middle education (ISCED 3/5B)	53.5%	39.6%	52.9%	56.6%
High education (ISCED 5A/6)	38.4%	54.2%	34.1%	33.0%
Mean household income (SD)	25,569 (15,375)	29,539 (17,983)	27,195 (19,447)	28,534 (27,604)
Single-parent household at wave 3	15.0%	14.4%	19.7%	21.8%
Mother younger than twenty at birth	4.0%	3.4%	7.6%	11.0%
Mother older than thirty at birth	50.0%	42.6%	40.8%	31.7%
Number of people under age eighteen in household at wave 3	2.51 (1.05)	2.25 (0.98)	2.40 (1.05)	2.44 (1.14)
Foreign-born parent	33.0%	31.5%	13.0%	23.4%
White (non-Hispanic for United States)	—	81.0%	86.7%	54.0%
Black (non-Hispanic for United States)	—	3.3%	2.8%	13.8%
Hispanic	—	—	—	25.1%
Asian	—	—	—	2.6%
South Asian	—	4.9%	—	—
Pakistani or Bangladeshi	—	—	4.2%	—
Indian	—	—	1.8%	—
Chinese	—	2.4%	—	—
Indigenous (Australia)–Aboriginals (Canada)	4.9%	1.9%	—	—
Mixed	—	—	3.3%	—
Race-ethnicity not otherwise coded	—	6.6%	1.2%	4.5%

Source: Authors' calculations using data from Australian Institute of Family Studies (2009), Statistics Canada (2006b), University of London, Institute of Education, Centre for Longitudinal Studies (2006), and U.S. Department of Education, National Center for Education Statistics (2009).

*ECLS-B frequencies rounded to the nearest fifty in accordance with NCES reporting rules.

in the low-education group in the United States than in other countries. Half of the low-education group in the United States is foreign-born, in contrast to roughly 30 percent in Australia and Canada and 17 percent in the United Kingdom (table 4A.2). These differences are intrinsic features of the countries in question, and it is not clear how to interpret results that adjust them away. Nevertheless, it is of interest to see how the SES gradients in various outcomes are affected by allowing intercept differences for different groups. Hence for some outcomes, we estimate SES gradients conditional on whether the child has a foreign-born parent and the country-specific set of indicators for racial-ethnic group shown in table 4.5.[8]

Differences across countries in family composition and structure are also notable. The United States (followed by the United Kingdom) has the highest share of single parents and young mothers (mothers under age twenty at the time they gave birth), and the lowest share of older mothers (over age thirty). Australia has the highest share of older mothers, and Canada has the lowest number of children in the household. These differences are particularly pronounced in the low- and middle-SES groups. To the extent that children with more parents in the home, more mature parents, and fewer competing siblings tend to receive more or higher-quality parental inputs, and to the extent these attributes are differentially distributed within SES groups across countries, these differences may help explain variation in the gaps across countries. As with the racial, ethnic, and immigrant differences, these family characteristics are an intrinsic feature of the countries, and it is not clear that our estimates should adjust for them. Nevertheless, in a descriptive sense, it is useful to know to what extent the SES gradients change if these factors are held constant. Thus, for some outcomes we estimate supplemental models where we add controls for these factors in addition to the race-ethnicity and immigrant variables described earlier.

These summary statistics also confirm the presence of greater income inequality in the United States and United Kingdom than in Australia and Canada. Although mean incomes are roughly similar across the four countries, income gaps between education groups are larger in the United States and the United Kingdom. In the United States, for example, the low education group has an average income of $9,680 versus $19,699 for the middle group and $49,613 for the top group. In contrast, for Australia the comparable figures are $16,090, $21,416, and $33,362. The distribution of the population across education groups, however, varies by country. For the same reasons as outlined with respect to child outcomes, a country with a smaller proportion of the population in extreme education groups might be expected to have more unequal incomes across groups.

Methods

The relationship between parental SES and a child outcome can be summarized in a single statistic by the correlation between the log of household income and the outcome variable. This correlation coefficient has the advantage that it makes use of the full distributions of both continuous variables. However, to gain a more nuanced picture that allows for nonlinearities and comparison of results using household income and parental education as the stratifying variables, we generate estimates from the following least squares regression (estimated separately for each country):

$$y_{ic} = \beta_{0c} + \beta_{Lc}(1|SES_{ic} = Low) + \beta_{Hc}(1|SES_{ic} = High) + \varepsilon_{ic}$$

where y_{ic} is the standardized outcome measure of child i in country c; $(1/SES_{ic} = Low)$ and $(1/SES_{ic} = High)$ are binary indicators equal to 1 if child i in country c is respectively in the low- or the high-SES group; and ε_{ic} is an uncorrelated error term. When SES_{ic} is measured by parental education Low denotes ISCED 2 and $High$ denotes ISCED 5A/6; when it is measured by parental income Low denotes the lowest quintile of average gross household income and $High$ denotes the highest quintile.

Gradients are thus measured relative to the mean outcome of children in the middle-SES reference group: ISCED 3/5B in the case of education, the middle three quintile groups in the case of income. We refer to β_{Lc} as the bottom-middle gap and β_{Hc} as the top-middle gap. A single summary measure of the inequality in child outcomes is given by $(\beta_{Hc} - \beta_{Lc})$, the difference in mean outcomes between those in the high- and low-SES groups. All outcome variables are standardized to have unit variance, and so these coefficients represent the number of standard deviations difference between the different SES groups. The appropriate survey weights are used in the calculation of all estimates and sample design features are accounted for in the calculation of confidence intervals.[9]

All four of these countries are characterized by diversity in terms of ethnic and racial identity and immigrant status. For this reason, we augment the above equation with controls for race, ethnicity, and immigrant status to examine the extent to which SES gradients are associated with demographic heterogeneity. It is often suggested in the literature that race and ethnicity play a particularly important role in distinguishing child outcomes in the United States from other countries. But we should also note that these countries have very different policies with respect to immigration selection rules. The variables used to define race and ethnicity are, of necessity, different in each country (see table 4.5), but we believe that we have been able to capture the most salient features of the within-country heterogeneity.

As discussed, a second way in which families differ across countries, and that might matter in explaining differential SES gaps, is their structure and composition. Accordingly, we estimate an additional model in which we further add controls for single parenthood, age of mother, and number of children in the household.

Results

Figure 4.1 displays the correlations between log gross household income and our two focal outcomes, with 95 percent confidence intervals shown by the range plots. On the basis of this simple statistic, the four countries appear to divide into two groups of two—Australia and Canada show similar relationships between family income and child outcomes that are markedly weaker than the correlations for the United Kingdom and the United States. In both cases, the Canadian correlation is the lowest of the four, closely followed by Australia. Among the high correlations, the United States income-vocabulary relationship is slightly stronger than that in the United Kingdom, whereas the reverse is true for the income-externalizing behavior relationship.

However, although these correlations tell us about the overall strength of the association between parental SES and child outcomes, they do not tell us where in the distribution this occurs. For this reason, we turn next to models that explicitly compare outcomes for the top group and the middle, and for the bottom group and the middle.

Figure 4.2 explores the associations of SES and vocabulary outcomes in more detail. Panel A refers to the overall country results with no controls for demographic characteristics, panel B shows the results after adding controls on racial ethnic-immigrant composition, and panel C adds further controls for family composition and mother's age at birth. The lighter bars in these figures show β_{Hc}, the mean outcome score for the top group minus the mean score for the middle group. The darker bars similarly show β_{Lc}, the bottom-middle gap, with the combined bar lengths $(\beta_{Hc} - \beta_{Lc})$, the gap between the top and bottom, summarized in parentheses alongside the relevant bars. The outcomes are all standardized measures, so that a difference of 0.50 represents a 0.5 standard deviation difference in outcomes. The figures also show approximate 95 percent confidence intervals. Note that countries can be significantly different from one another even if the confidence intervals overlap to some extent. Details of all estimates, along with pairwise t-tests of country differences, are provided in the online appendix.

Focusing first on the unconditional estimates in panel A, we see that the overall differences in vocabulary scores between the top and bottom SES groups mimic the pattern of correlations shown in figure 4.2, regardless of whether parental income or education is used as the SES

Figure 4.1   Correlation of Household Income with Key Child Outcomes

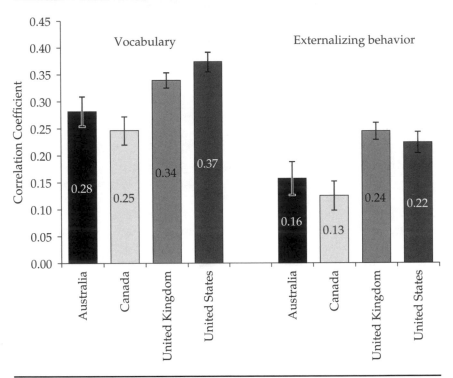

Source: Authors' calculations using data from Australian Institute of Family Studies (2009), Statistics Canada (2006b), University of London, Institute of Education, Centre for Longitudinal Studies (2006), and U.S. Department of Education, National Center for Education Statistics (2009).
Note: Range plots show 95 percent confidence intervals.

indicator. The United States shows the greatest disparities, followed by the United Kingdom and Australia, with the smallest average differences found in Canada. Pairwise *t*-tests of cross-country differences confirm that the top-bottom U.S. gradient is significantly larger than those of each of the other three countries, and also that this gradient is significantly smaller in Canada than the United Kingdom. However, we cannot reject the hypotheses of no significant differences between Australia and either Canada or the United Kingdom.

Comparison of the top-middle and bottom-middle gaps reveals that these country differences are almost entirely driven by variation at the upper part of the SES distribution. In no case is the bottom-middle income-related gap significantly different between any pair of countries,

Figure 4.2   Disparities in Vocabulary Outcomes

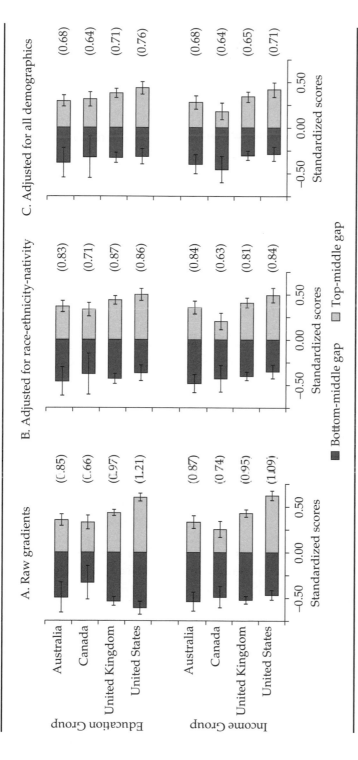

A. Raw gradients

B. Adjusted for race-ethnicity-nativity

C. Adjusted for all demographics

Education Group

	A	B	C
Australia	(0.85)	(0.83)	(0.68)
Canada	(0.66)	(0.71)	(0.64)
United Kingdom	(0.97)	(0.87)	(0.71)
United States	(1.21)	(0.86)	(0.76)

Income Group

	A	B	C
Australia	(0.87)	(0.84)	(0.68)
Canada	(0.74)	(0.63)	(0.64)
United Kingdom	(0.95)	(0.81)	(0.65)
United States	(1.09)	(0.84)	(0.71)

Standardized scores

■ Bottom-middle gap   ■ Top-middle gap

Source: Authors' calculations using data from Australian Institute of Family Studies (2009), Statistics Canada (2006b), University of London, Institute of Education, Centre for Longitudinal Studies (2006), and U.S. Department of Education, National Center for Education Statistics (2009).

Note: Numbers in parentheses are the total gap between the top and bottom groups (the sum of the darker and lighter bars). Range plots show 95 percent confidence intervals. The control variables introduced in panels B and C are listed in table 4.5.

although children from the lowest educated families in Canada (6.2 percent of the cohort) do perform significantly better in a relative sense than their counterparts in either the United Kingdom or the United States.

Differences at the top end of the distribution are much more marked. American children in the highest-education households score 0.60 of a standard deviation higher than children from the middle-education group, versus 0.43 for the United Kingdom and 0.33 to 0.35 for the other two countries. A similar pattern is seen for income, with American children in the highest-income households scoring 0.62 of a standard deviation higher than children from the middle-income group. This gap ranges from to 0.25 (Canada) to 0.33 (Australia) to 0.43 (United Kingdom) in the other countries. Again, we cannot reject the hypothesis that the top-middle gaps are equal in Australia and Canada on either measure, nor that the top-middle income gap is the same in Australia and the United Kingdom. Other than this, all country differences in the top-middle gaps, and in particular the differences between the United States and all other countries, are significant.

Panel B displays a similar set of results, but based on models that include controls for racial-ethnic diversity and immigrant status.[10] The contrast between these results and those in panel A highlights the extent to which SES gradients are associated with this heterogeneity, and in particular the extent to which the greater divergence in vocabulary scores in the United States is associated with the racial and ethnic heterogeneity in that country.

As expected, the overall lengths of the bars are generally either smaller or the same length as those in panel A (this can also be seen in online appendix table 4A.4). The portion of the SES gradients explained by these controls is particularly large for the United States. For example, after controlling for race-ethnicity and immigration status, the gap in vocabulary scores between children of middle-income and high-income parents falls by 36 percent in the United States versus 9 percent in Australia and 24 percent in the United Kingdom. After controlling for race-ethnicity and immigration status the top-middle differences between the United States and both Canada and Australia are reduced, but not eliminated. No significant differences in the any of the vocabulary gradients between the United States and the United Kingdom, however, remain in panel B. It appears that some, but not all, of the greater variation in vocabulary outcomes in the United States is associated with the divergent outcomes of children in different racial-ethnic and nativity groups within that country, but that significant differences between the United States and other countries remain.

Panel C shows the estimates from a further set of models adding a set of controls for single parent, age of mother (binary indicators for below twenty or above thirty at the time of the birth, with age twenty to thirty as the reference category), and number of children in the home. The results show that the correlation between family composition and SES contributes to the vocabulary gradients in all four countries, but does little to explain the country differences, which remain largely unchanged from panel B. Again, no differences between the United States and the United Kingdom remain, but high-SES children in the United States continue to exhibit an advantage in vocabulary that is relatively greater than for their counterparts in either Australia or Canada.

Although the vocabulary measures presented in figure 4.2 are the most comparable measures of child cognitive development across the four countries, the surveys also include a number of other cognitive scores. Figure 4.3 offers a brief look at the two cognitive domains where we have comparable data for three countries (estimates of the unconditional gradients in all supplementary outcomes are available in the online appendix). It is unfortunate that the instruments used to measure math skills differ considerably across the three countries in which they were included, and are only available for the United Kingdom at the earlier wave 2 (age three). The copying instrument was identical in the Australian and Canadian surveys, but again differs in the U.S. case. Hence we cannot draw strong conclusions from the correlations shown in figure 4.3, but the ranking of the countries under both additional measures is the same as for the vocabulary measure—the United States shows the greatest disparities in both outcomes, followed by the United Kingdom and Australia, with the lowest correlations found in the Canadian measures. Analysis of the top-middle and bottom-middle gaps (not shown here) shows that, as before, higher U.S. gradients are generally driven by greater disparities at the top of the SES distribution, although some differences in the relative position of the lowest SES groups are also discernible.

Figure 4.4 depicts in more detail the socioeconomic gradients in our most comparable measure of socioemotional functioning, externalizing behaviors. As suggested by the correlations in figure 4.1, SES-related disparities in behavioral outcomes are smaller than in cognitive outcomes in all countries. The unconditional results in panel A highlight Canada as a clear outlier in this domain, and t-tests provided in the online appendix confirm that all top-bottom and top-middle gradients—whether by income or education—are significantly smaller in Canada than all the other three countries. Assessment of the relative position of low-SES children in Canada varies depending on whether income or education is the stratifying variable—the bottom-middle income gap is not significantly different in Canada to that in any of the other countries, but children of the less-educated show smaller disparities in externalizing behavior than elsewhere.

In contrast to the results for vocabulary outcomes, the greatest disparities in behavioral outcomes are found not in the United States but in the United Kingdom. Differences between high- and middle-SES children

Figure 4.3   Correlation of Household Income with Other Cognitive Outcomes

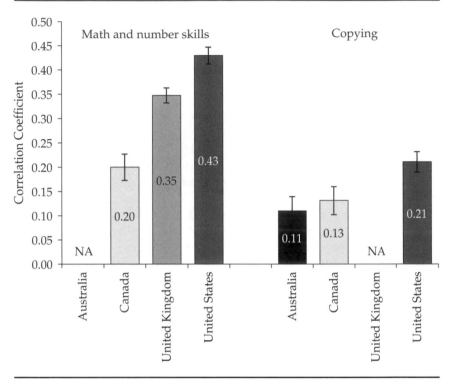

Source: Authors' calculations using data from Australian Institute of Family Studies (2009), Statistics Canada (2006b), University of London, Institute of Education, Centre for Longitudinal Studies (2006), and U.S. Department of Education, National Center for Education Statistics (2009).
Notes: Math and number skills were assessed using the Number Knowledge assessment in Canada and the ECLS-B Math assessment in the United States. The U.K. measure is the sum of four of the six Bracken School Readiness Assessment (BRSA) subscales—Numbers, Sizes, Shapes, and Comparisons—which were administered in wave 2 only when the MCS children were age three. Copying was assessed via the Copying subscale of the Who Am I assessment in Canada and Australia, and via the ECLS-B copying forms task in the United States. See the online appendix for further details.
Range plots show 95 percent confident intervals. NA indicates the measure is not available for that country.

are virtually identical in the two countries, and it is solely the relatively greater level of behavioral problems of low-SES children in the United Kingdom that is responsible for this finding.

The addition of racial-ethnic-nativity controls in panel B makes very little difference to the estimated gradients in any country, but the demographic controls added in panel C have a stronger explanatory role,

Figure 4.4   Disparities in Externalizing Behavior Problems

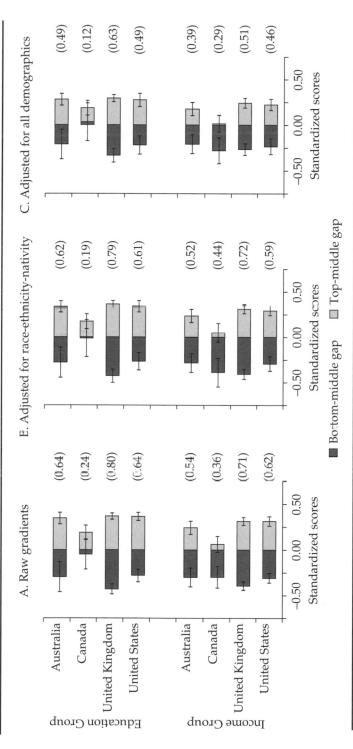

Source: Authors' calculations using data from Australian Institute of Family Studies (2009), Statistics Canada (2006b), University of London, Institute of Education, Centre for Longitudinal Studies (2006), and U.S. Department of Education, National Center for Education Statistics (2009).

Note: Numbers in parentheses are the total gap between the top and bottom groups (the sum of the darker and lighter bars).

suggesting that somewhat different mechanisms underlie the gradients in cognitive and socioemotional outcomes. The smaller behavioral gradients in Canada are not accounted for by any of the controls, but differences between the United Kingdom and both the United States and Australia become insignificant when family composition and maternal age are held constant. Additional analyses provided in the online appendix find little systematic variation across countries in the gradients of the subdomains of hyperactivity inattention and conduct problems. Low-SES children in the United Kingdom have the greatest disparities in both subdomains of all the four countries, and overall gradients are the lowest in Canada on both measures.

Implications

Although ascribing the variation in outcomes to particular policies or institutions is difficult, our results do complement other indicators of social inequality and mobility, and offer a starting point to reflect on the particular accomplishments and challenges in each country. In particular, our results indicate that, in spite of the broad similarities, young children grow up in very different contexts in these four countries.

The descriptive statistics in table 4.5 highlight the fact that the resources families are able to bring to bear, both monetary and nonmonetary, differ in an absolute sense across these countries. Although overall average income is about the same at about $26,000 to $29,000, it is distributed differently, with lower-educated parents having substantially less income in the United Kingdom, and particularly in the United States. But this reflects a number of other demographic factors that also determine the amount of time and other nonmonetary resources parents have to invest in their young children. Children raised in the bottom of the income distribution are more likely to have parents with low levels of education and mothers who tend to be younger at the child's birth, and more likely to be in a single parent household. Racial-ethnic and cultural diversity also play out across socioeconomic groups in a different way in the four countries. Australia and Canada have high proportions of children living with foreign-born parents, who are equally as likely to be found among low-income as among high-income groups. The United Kingdom has a lower proportion of second-generation immigrant children in general but again this has little relation with socioeconomic status, whereas in the United States the high proportion of children with foreign-born parents is concentrated disproportionately in the lower socioeconomic groups.

The extent of the disparities and differences across these countries is somewhat muted when account is taken of the diversity in demographic composition of the population. The outcomes look more similar when account is made of these differences, particularly between the United States and United Kingdom, where no significant differences remain. The characteristics of families in different socioeconomic groups clearly have an impact on social outcomes of the next generation, and like many other countries in the OECD these countries will increasingly face the need to cope with racial and ethnic diversity and other demographic shifts, and to integrate and foster the development of new citizens. But a host of broader issues are also associated with the support that families in challenging circumstances can rely on. As we emphasized earlier, children experience very different policy contexts across the four countries in four policy domains that determine the amount of time parents have for nonmarket activities associated with family life, as well as other material resources important for the development of children: parental leave, child care, income supports for families with young children, and health insurance. Such policies may be one dimension contributing to a much more muted socioeconomic gradient in Canada. Exploring the role of these policy contexts in early inequalities is an important challenge for future research.

Conclusion

This chapter is intended to shed light on the origins of inequality and social immobility by examining the gaps that exist in cognitive and socioemotional development in early childhood in four countries that have a good deal in common but that also display important differences. We emphasize three basic findings and also offer some thoughts about the use of cross-country comparative data.

First, our analysis of four- and five-year-olds in Australia, Canada, the United Kingdom, and the United States reveals that although gaps in readiness to learn between the children of relatively advantaged and relatively disadvantaged families are clearly evident in each country, so is variation across them. Disparities in Australia and Canada are consistently smaller on a range of outcome measures than disparities in the United States and the United Kingdom.

Second, differences in cognitive development seem to be more strongly linked to disparities in parental resources in the United States than in the other countries, with the difference driven by a particularly large advantage of high-SES children relative to those in the middle. Thus, any explanation of cross-national differences must account for why children at the top outperform children in the middle to different degrees. One hypothesis, which might be tested in future research, is that families in the middle receive less support in the United States due to the highly targeted nature of its social welfare system, and thus lag further behind those at the top. Although the very poorest in the United States are eligible for programs such as Medicaid and Head Start, these benefits are withdrawn at a much lower level of income in the United States than in Canada and the United Kingdom. High rates of full-time maternal employment, combined with a largely private child-care market in which quality is very costly, is another factor that may disadvantage middle-income children in the United States relative to those in other countries. Another possible factor is the greater disparity of incomes in the United States, with particularly high incomes for those at the top.

Third, the cross-country pattern of SES disparities in school readiness differs depending on the outcome measure considered. Social and behavioral development is less strongly linked than cognitive development to family background in all countries. In comparative terms, low-SES children in the United Kingdom have high levels of behavior problems but appear in line with other countries in terms of their deficits in cognitive outcomes. Conversely, the cognitive advantages displayed by high-SES children in the United States are not accompanied by unusually low levels of behavior problems relative to other countries.

In addition to these substantive conclusions, we also offer a call for more attention to comparable data across a larger number of OECD countries. Our analysis is descriptive, but good description is the first step to informed policy discussion and hypotheses about causal relationships. Although the data we rely on are extremely rich, they are designed to inform public policy by offering a longitudinal perspective on child development in a particular national context. This no doubt is central to an appreciation of the causal mechanisms determining outcomes, but without attention to the comparability of measures across countries, an opportunity is missed to illustrate the role of different public policies and social situations. We draw an analogy to the important role the Programme of International Student Assessment has had on discussions of schooling outcomes for fifteen-year-olds across the OECD. Now that public policy has come to fully appreciate that this variation is also rooted in disparities of outcomes during the early years, the development of a similar instrument offering comparable cross-sectional indicators over many more countries than we are able to examine here would inform the quality of future research and public discourse directed to the well-being of children.

In this chapter, we find clear evidence of differences in the correlation between socioeconomic status and child cognitive outcomes. This correlation is strongest in the United States and the United Kingdom and weakest in Australia and Canada. Although our four countries have a common heritage, their economic and social policy environments differ in many ways. Our results cannot be used to point unambiguously to any particular causal determinant, but they do suggest the importance of future research on the role specific policies might play.

Our findings are also relevant to some of the larger questions about intergenerational mobility addressed in this volume. Previous research has shown a noticeable (though admittedly not large) positive correlation between high parental inequality and high levels of parent-child immobility of adult income levels (Björklund and Jantti 2009; Corak 2006). Indeed, the U.S. experience of high inequality and high intergenerational immobility is a key data point for this cross-national correlation. It is certainly not inevitable that high inequality should imply low mobility, indeed the rhetoric advanced in unequal societies is often just the opposite. The results found here can be seen as contributing to an explanation of this relationship. The distribution of resources available to families with young children does seem to matter for their developmental outcomes—and this in turn is one part of the explanation for the broader patterns of intergenerational mobility.

This work was funded by the Russell Sage Foundation. We are also grateful for funding support from the Sutton Trust, the Australian Research Council (DP0878643), and for research assistance from Ali Akbar Ghanghro and Liana Fox. We gratefully acknowledge support from award number R01HD047215–05 and R24HD058486 from the Eunice Kennedy Shriver National Institute of Child Health & Human Development (NICHD). The content is solely the responsibility of the authors and does not necessarily represent the official views of NICHD or the National Institutes of Health.

We also acknowledge the support of Statistics Canada in facilitating access to the Canadian data through the Carelton, Ottawa, Outaouais Local Research Data Centre at the University of Ottawa and Carelton University.

This paper uses unit record data from Growing Up in Australia, the Longitudinal Study of Australian Children. The study is conducted in partnership between the Department of Families, Housing, Community Services and Indigenous Affairs (FaHCSIA), the Australian Institute of Family Studies (AIFS), and the Australian Bureau of Statistics (ABS). The findings and views reported in this paper are those of the authors and should not be attributed to FaHCSIA, AIFS, or the ABS.

Notes

1. Expenditures in the United States would be higher if they took into account tax support for employer-sponsored health insurance.

2. In some cases assessments at wave 2 are also available. We make only limited use of these measures for comparability reasons, and make it clear when we do so that the outcome in question is not taken from the default wave 3 survey.

3. The online appendix can be found at: http://www.russellsage.org/Ermisch_et_al_OnlineAppendix.pdf.

4. We use measures from one or two waves if information on all three waves is not available.

5. It should be noted, however, that different items and versions of the PPVT were used in different countries. These details are available in the online appendix at: http://www.russellsage.org/Ermisch_et_al_OnlineAppendix.pdf.

6. We are confident that although the wording of items is different across countries, collectively they capture similar emotional and behavioral concepts. A number of alternative scales are commonly used to measure child behavior problems. Two of the most widely used—the Rutter scale and the Child Behavior Checklist—have both been shown to predict high-psychiatric-risk cases with the same accuracy as the SDQ (Goodman 1997; Goodman and Scott 1999). In addition, note that differences in distribution of responses to items that vary across countries will affect our conclusions only to the extent that they differ systematically with socioeconomic status.

7. The pattern of decreasing behavior problems with age is supported by a comparison of the U.K. scores at wave 2 (age three) and wave 3 (age five) as the mean falls from 6.46 to 4.64 over this period.

8. Note that the Australian survey does not record the child's racial-ethnic background as such, so we are able only to distinguish between indigenous children and the rest. Definitions from the Canadian survey relate to the race-ethnicity of the main carer rather than the child.

9. The exception to this is that the confidence intervals for the correlation coefficient in Australia do not take account of sample design. Also, in all countries, our confidence intervals do not account for the sampling variance associated with the standardization of the dependent variables, and so are slightly too narrow.

10. An alternative approach would be to estimate a model only for the non-minority and native-born subgroup in each country. We did estimate such models as a robustness check (shown in online appendix table 4.A3) and found the results were broadly comparable to those obtained in the full sample model with controls for minority and foreign-born status. We also estimated more detailed models including controls for language spoken in the home (although the variables regarding language are not fully comparable across countries) and results were similar.

References

Almond, Douglas, and Janet Currie. 2010. "Human Capital Development Before Age Five." *NBER* Working Paper 15827. Cambridge, Mass.: National Bureau of Economic Research.

Australian Institute of Family Studies. 2009. *Longitudinal Study of Australian Children, Release 3 Confidentialised Dataset.* Melbourne: Australian Institute of Family Studies.

———. 2010. "Longitudinal Study of Australian Children Data User Guide, April 2010." Melbourne: Australian Institute of Family Studies.

Björklund, Anders, and Markus Jäntti. 2009. "Intergenerational Economic Inequality." In *The Oxford Handbook of Economic Inequality,* edited by Wiemer Salverda, Brian Nolan, and Timothy Smeeding. Oxford: Oxford University Press.

Bradbury, Bruce. 2007. "Child Outcomes and Family Socio-Economic Characteristics." *SPRC* report 9/07. Canberra: Department of Families, Community Services and Indigenous Affairs.

Carneiro, Pedro, and James Heckman. 2003. "Human Capital Policy." In *Inequality in America: What Role for Human Capital Policies?* edited by James Heckman, Alan Krueger, and Benjamin Friedman. Cambridge, Mass.: MIT Press.

Centre for Longitudinal Studies. 2010. "Millennium Cohort Study First, Second, Third, and Fourth Surveys: A Guide to the Datasets." London: Institute of Education.

Corak, Miles. 2006. "Do Poor Children Become Poor Adults? Lessons for Public Policy from a Cross Country Comparison of Generational Earnings Mobility." In *Research on Economic Inequality,* vol. 13, edited by John Creedy and Guyonne Kal. Amsterdam: Elsevier Press.

Corak, Miles, Lori Curtis, and Shelley Phipps. 2011. "Economic Mobility, Family Background, and the Well-Being of Children in the United States and Canada." In *Persistence, Privilege, and Parenting: The Comparative Study of Intergenerational Mobility,* edited by Timothy Smeeding, Robert Erikson, and Markus Jäntti. New York: Russell Sage Foundation.

Cunha, Flavio, James Heckman, Lance Lochner, and Dmitri Masterov. 2005. "Interpreting the Evidence on Life Cycle Skill Formation." In *Handbook of the Economics of Education,* edited by Eric Hanushek and Finis Welch. Amsterdam: North Holland.

Currie, Janet, and Mark Stabile. 2006. "Child Mental Health and Human Capital Accumulation: The Case of ADHD." *Journal of Health Economics* 25(6): 1094–118.

Duncan, Greg J., and Katherine Magnuson. 2011. "The Nature and Impact of Early Achievement Skills, Attention and Behavior Problems." In *Whither Opportunity? Rising Inequality, Schools, and Children's Life Chance,* edited by Greg Duncan and Richard Murnane. New York: Russell Sage Foundation.

Esping-Anderson, Gösta. 1990. *Three Worlds of Welfare Capitalism.* Princeton, N.J.: Princeton University Press.

Goodman, Robert. 1997. "The Strengths and Difficulties Questionnaire: A Research Note." *Journal of Child Psychology and Psychiatry* 38(5): 581–86.

Goodman, Robert, and Stephen Scott. 1999. "Comparing the Strengths and Difficulties Questionnaire and the Child Behavior Checklist: Is Small Beautiful?" *Journal of Abnormal Child Psychology* 27(1): 17–24.

Healy, Judith, Sharman Evelyn, and Lokuge Buddhima. 2006. *Australia: Health System Review*, vol. 8, bk. 5, *Health Systems in Transition*. Copenhagen: WHO/European Observatory on Health System and Policies.

Heckman, James J., and Lance Lochner. 2000. "Rethinking Education and Training Policy: Understanding the Sources of Skill Formation in a Modern Economy." In *Securing the Future: Investing in Children from Birth to College*, edited by Sheldon Danziger and Jane Waldfogel. New York: Russell Sage Foundation.

Katz, Ilan, and Gerry Redmond. 2009. "Family Income as a Protective Factor for Child Outcomes." In *Social Policy Review* 21, edited by Kirstein Rummery, Ian Greener, and Chris Holden. Bristol: The Policy Press.

Knudsen, Eric I., James J. Heckman, Judy L. Cameron, and Jack P. Shonkoff. 2006. "Economic, Neurobiological, and Behavioural Perspectives on Building America's Future Workforce." *Proceedings of the National Academy of Sciences* 103(27): 10155–162.

Luxembourg Income Study. 2010. "Key Figures." Available at: http://www.lisdatacenter.org/wp-content/uploads/data-key-inequality-workbook.xlsx (accessed December 2, 2011).

McLeod, Jane D., and Karen Kaiser. 2004. "Child Emotional and Behavioral Problems in Educational Attainment." *American Sociological Review* 69(5): 636–58.

National Center for Education Statistics. 2009. "Early Childhood Longitudinal Study, Birth Cohort (ECLS-B), Longitudinal 9-Month-Kindergarten 2007 Restricted-Use Data File and Electronic Codebook DVD." Washington, D.C.: Institute of Education Sciences.

Organisation for Economic Co-operation and Development (OECD). 2009. "Doing Better for Children." Paris: Organisation for Economic Co-Operation and Development.

———. 2011. "Health Data from OECD StatExtracts." Available at: http://stats.oecd.org/ (accessed December 2, 2011).

Redmond, Gerry, and Anna Zhu. 2009. "Maternity Leave and Child Outcomes." Final Report for Department of Families, Housing, Community Services and Indigenous Affairs. Sydney: Social Policy Research Centre, University of New South Wales.

Smith, James. 2009. "The Impact of Childhood Health on Adult Labor Market Outcomes." *Review of Economics and Statistics* 91(3): 478–89.

Statistics Canada. 2006a. *National Longitudinal Survey of Children and Youth: Survey Overview (Cycle 6)*. Ottawa: Statistics Canada.

———. 2006b. *National Longitudinal Survey of Children and Youth, individual level micro data*. Ottawa: Statistics Canada. Accessed at the Carelton, Ottawa, Outaouais local Research Data Centre.

University of London, Institute of Education, Centre for Longitudinal Studies. 2006. *Millennium Cohort Study: Third Survey* [computer file]. 4th Edition. Colchester, Essex: U.K. Data Archive [distributor], April 2010. SN: 5795. Available at: http://dx.doi.org/10.5255/UKDA-SN-5795-1 (accessed January 3, 2011).

U.S. Department of Education, National Center for Education Statistics. 2007. *Early Childhood Longitudinal Study, Birth Cohort (ECLS-B) Longitudinal 9-Month-Preschool Restricted-Use Data File and Electronic Codebook.* (NCES 2008-034). Washington, D.C.: NCES.

Waldfogel, Jane. 2006. *What Children Need.* Cambridge, Mass.: Harvard University Press.

———. 2011a. *Britain's War on Poverty.* New York: Russell Sage Foundation.

Waldfogel, Jane, and Elizabeth Washbrook. 2011a. "Early Years Policy." *Child Development Research* 2011: 1–12.

———. 2011b. "Income-Related Gaps in School Readiness in the United States and the United Kingdom." In *Persistence, Privilege, and Parenting: The Comparative Study of Intergenerational Mobility*, edited by Timothy Smeeding, Robert Erikson, and Markus Jäntti. New York: Russell Sage Foundation.

Chapter 5

Early Childhood Outcomes and Family Structure

JOHN ERMISCH, FRAUKE H. PETER,

AND C. KATHARINA SPIESS

VIDENCE IS substantial that child development—and accordingly, children's skills—are influenced by family characteristics, such as parental education and income and other factors that contribute to parental quality. This influence of family is especially important in the early years (see Cunha and Heckman 2007, 2009). Family-related factors contributing to parental quality seem to be particularly important, probably more important for the explanation of child outcomes than the quality of other caregiving and learning institutions, such as day-care centers or schools.[1] A large body of literature shows, for instance, that children with less-educated or poor parents do worse than their counterparts. Many studies illustrate that parental education or household income are associated with the channels through which intergenerational transmission of ability works. But other family-related indicators are important as well. This chapter focuses on the impact of changes in family structure during early childhood (age six or younger) on socioemotional development. Family change is correlated with parental socioeconomic status (SES) indicators, which we know are associated with child outcomes through aspects of parental quality. Changes in family structure early in a child's life may help to account for why indicators of socioemotional development differ by parental SES.

The goal of this chapter is to determine whether children whose mothers experience partner changes (either a separation or a new partnership) behave differently from children whose mothers always or never live with a partner during the child's early years. Usually it is assumed that the separation of parents has a negative influence on child development. From a child's perspective, however, a separation might not necessarily be negative if the parents were in conflict before the divorce. Paul Amato (2005), for instance, finds that children are affected negatively by their parent's divorce only if they did not anticipate it. Moreover, another change in the family structure, such as remarriage, might also affect child outcomes. Paula Fomby and Andrew Cherlin (2007) argue that more changes can increase the stress children face than if the mother were to remain single after a separation. Evidence indicates that family break-up early in a child's life has effects that last over time (Ermisch and Francesconi 2001; Ermisch, Francesconi, and Pevalin 2004).

Our analysis concentrates on the early years, which means we analyze short-term correlations. We focus on the early years for two reasons. First, they are arguably the most important for later outcomes (see Carneiro and Heckman 2003; Cunha and Heckman 2007). Second, the literature on family structure as an influence on child outcomes usually focuses on school-age or even older children, and so does not reveal what happens earlier. We focus on family changes and their correlation with early childhood social-behavioral outcomes, and examine whether different correlations exist depending on the parents' SES. We might find that children whose parents have a low SES are disadvantaged in two ways, first through a direct SES effect' and second through an indirect effect, in which low-SES parents are affected more by family changes than others.

Although our measurements are of short-term outcomes, evidence indicates that social-behavioral problems during childhood have longer-term implications. For instance, Jo Blanden and her colleagues (2007) show from a study of British children born in 1970 that behavior and personality traits measured at age ten, such as locus of control, application, extroversion, and self-esteem, are correlated with earnings at the age of thirty, even after controlling for cognitive abilities at ages five and ten. These are also correlated with the family income when the child is age ten and sixteen. Pedro Carneiro and his colleagues (2007) find, from a cohort of British children born in 1958, that an overall measure of noncognitive skill at age eleven is important for a number of outcomes at the age of forty-two, including educational attainment and earnings. In particular, aspects of child behavior and depression at age eleven lead to lower educational attainments and earnings later in life. To the extent that there is persistence in social-behavioral outcomes between ages five and eleven, which is likely, our findings on impacts of family changes on these outcomes at ages five and six are likely to have long-term consequences for income during adulthood.

Our main finding is that a stable family environment significantly reduces difficulties in children's social-emotional behavior during their preschool years.

Institutional and Demographic Background

Our analysis uses German and British data for children during their first five years of life, before they have entered school. As table 5.1 shows, in the first three years of a child's life, German parents can go on parental

Table 5.1   Parental Leave, Day Care, and Mother's Employment

	United Kingdom	Germany
Parental leave	Eight months	Three years
Public child-care coverage, children under age three	2%	8%
Mothers employed: youngest child under age three	49%	31%
Mothers employed: youngest child aged three to six	57%	42%

Source: Authors' calculations based on Pronzato (2009); OECD (2006)
Note: All figures refer to the years 2002 or 2003.

leave and take care of the child themselves. Most mothers and a small percentage of fathers took parental leave for the entire three-year period. Only a small percentage of children, in particular in West Germany, attend day care: 8 percent of all children below the age of three attended day care in West Germany in 2006, whereas in East Germany 40 percent did so (DJI 2007). Children spend less time with their mothers once they are three years old because most of them enter day care. In 2006, 86 percent of all children aged three to six years attended day care in West Germany and 92 percent in East Germany (DJI 2007). Most attend for fewer than six hours a day. Most children in Germany thus spend most of their time in early childhood at home. In almost all cases, it is the mother who takes care of the children and thus reduces her working hours, or stops working, at least for the period of parental leave.

In the United Kingdom, parental leave is much shorter than in Germany.[3] Public child-care coverage for children younger than three has been one of the lowest in Europe, and public coverage of preschool children age three and older is also relatively low in the United Kingdom (60 percent). Table 5.1 shows that employment is more common among United Kingdom than German mothers of young children, but part-time work is the norm for mothers of preschool children who take paid employment, and it is therefore not surprising that only about one-fifth of children aged three born between 2000 and 2001 (from the Millennium Cohort Study) ever had a child-care arrangement. Even when they did, a mother's partner or a grandparent were the most important modes of care. Private care arrangements also play a significant role in the United Kingdom

Given this clear pattern that mothers are the main caregiver—in Germany and the United Kingdom—we focus our analysis on changes in family structure analyzed from the perspective of the mother. We concentrate on separations and whether a new partner of the mothers moves into the household.

In general, family dissolution is an important factor in Germany and the United Kingdom, as table 5.2 illustrates. About half of divorces in Germany

Table 5.2   Divorce and Family Structure

	United Kingdom	Germany
Divorce rate per 1000 married couples (2008)	11	10
Divorces affecting children (2008)	50%	51%
Family structure for families with young children:	Children under five*	Children under three
Married couples	63%	75%
Cohabiting couples	21%	14%
Single-parent families	16%	11%

Source: Authors' calculations based on Statistisches Bundesamt (2009); Office of National Statistics (2010)
*Authors' calculations for Great Britain from British Household Panel Study, 2000–2007 (Institute for Social and Economic Research 2011).

and the United Kingdom affect children. Although divorce rates have decreased in both Germany and the United Kingdom in recent years,[4] rates remain high. Furthermore, more couples are having children in cohabiting unions, the dissolutions of which are not covered by official statistics. For example, in England and Wales, 30 percent of births in 2008 were to mothers in cohabiting unions, and only 55 percent were to married couples. The cohabiting unions are unstable—about one half of them break up (Ermisch and Murphy 2006).

Previous Findings for Other Countries

Numerous studies have analyzed the correlation of family structure with child outcomes (see Mahler and Winkelmann 2004; Del Bono, Ermisch, and Francesconi 2007; Francesconi, Rainer, and van der Klaauw 2008; Francesconi, Jenkins, and Siedler 2009). Some claim to find causal links and others clearly describe correlations. However, these studies often focus on a particular status, either being single or coming from a non-intact family. Most do not analyze whether changes in family structure over time determine child outcomes. But changes per se, in particular the type of change, may affect child outcomes.

Fomby's and Cherlin's study (2007) is one of the few that focuses on changes in family structure. For a sample of American children, they point out that children who experience multiple changes in family structure might be worse off than their counterparts growing up in stable families—two-parent as well as single-parent. They emphasize that the mechanisms through which instability operates can have different origins. The authors use cognitive and behavioral outcome measures, such as the Peabody Individual Achievement Test (PIAT) and the Behavior of Problems Index

(BPI). They analyze whether these child outcomes are affected by family structure changes—including a measure of the number of family structure changes. Controlling for mothers' education, and differentiating between white and African American children, Fomby and Cherlin find that the number of family structure changes are positively correlated with white children's externalizing behavior. They also report that for white children the number of transitions is negatively associated with children's cognitive test scores. However, controlling for mothers' prior characteristics attenuates the correlation between the number of family structure changes and cognitive achievement for white children. The authors do not find such associations for black children. But they find that living in a mother-only household during the first four years of childhood is correlated positively with children's externalizing behavior—for both black and white children.

Astrid Würtz-Rasmussen (2009) estimates the effect of family structure change on children's health outcomes (among other outcome measures) using administrative data from Denmark. In order to assess a possible association, she uses a difference-in-difference (DiD) model. She analyzes two periods for children that do not experience a change (control group) and for children that experience a change in their family structure (treatment group) from one period to the next. The first period ranges from birth until the age of eleven, and in this period none of the children in the sample have experienced a change. The second period is defined from age twelve until age twenty. In both periods children's health outcomes are observed. Applying the DiD, Würtz-Rasmussen concludes that children that experience multiple family structure changes after the age of six are exposed to worse health outcomes than children without family structure transitions. Another paper using Danish data estimates the effect of divorce and remarriage on socioemotional behavior of children (Andersen, Deding, and Lautsen 2007). Using the same index of socioemotional behavior as we do and a measure of the number of problems at the start of first grade as the outcome measure, the authors show that experiencing a divorce early in life leads to poorer socioemotional behavior in the short-term. Additionally, they show that if a divorce or separation is followed by a remarriage or a new partner moving into the household, the child is even worse off than just experiencing divorce as the only family change. Their outcome is measured at a slightly later stage of children's life than ours—children are seven years old and have started school. Angelo Andersen and his colleagues (2007) control for different SES variables, such as parental education, parental employment and unemployment, and parental income below a threshold.

Data and Methods

Our empirical analysis is based on data from two sources: the German Socio-Economic Panel Study (SOEP), a representative annual household panel study (for more about the SOEP, see Wagner, Frick, and Schupp

2007), and the United Kingdom Millennium Cohort Study (MCS), a representative sample of births between 2000 and 2001.[5]

German Socioeconomic Panel

In 2003, a series of questionnaires for surveying the development of children from the very beginning of their lives was implemented in the SOEP. The first of these questionnaires (M1, questionnaire for mothers of newborns) was implemented in 2003 and targeted mothers of newborn children. In 2005, a follow-up questionnaire (M2, questionnaire for mothers of infants) was implemented to be answered by mothers of children aged two to three years. The latest follow-up questionnaire (M3, questionnaire for mothers of preschoolers) was introduced in 2008 to collect data on children aged five to six years old (see Schupp et al. 2008; Siedler et al. 2009). It surveys information on the child's socioemotional behavior, health, and child care.

We use data obtained using the M3 mother-child questionnaire. To control for socioeconomic and demographic characteristics, we merge personal and household-specific data to periods after the birth of the child. With period $t = 0$ indicating the period when the child is newborn, family structure information can be observed as the "initial condition" of family composition. Period $t = 6$ indicates when the child is five to six years old and the M3 questionnaire has been filled out. The sample size for $t = 6$ is 431. Family structure and its changes over time are observed every year up to period $t = 6$.

Millennium Cohort Study (MCS)

As explained in chapter 4, the sample population for the MCS was drawn from all live births in the United Kingdom over twelve months from September 2000 in England and Wales and from December 2000 in Scotland and Northern Ireland. The survey for the first sweep occurred between June 2001 and January 2003, when children were aged about nine months, gathering information from the parents of 18,818 babies about themselves and the babies (for example, problems during pregnancy, birth weight). The second sweep took place when the children were around three years of age, and the third sweep took place during 2006, when the survey child entered primary school, at age five. Physical measurements (height and weight) and cognitive and behavioral assessments were made at ages three and five. The MCS sample is clustered geographically and disproportionately stratified to overrepresent areas with higher proportions of ethnic minorities in England, areas of high child poverty, and the three smaller countries in the United Kingdom: Wales, Scotland, and Northern Ireland. The clustered sample design and non-response at the first sweep is taken into account in all of the summary

Table 5.3   Strength and Difficulties Questionnaire

Dimensions	United Kingdom	Germany
Emotional symptoms	5 items	3 items
Conduct problems	5 items	2 items
Hyperactivity-inattention	5 items	4 items
Peer relationship problems	5 items	4 items
Pro-social behavior	5 items	4 items
Average difficulties score	7.4	10.7
based on first four dimensions	(SD=5)	(SD=6)
	(median=6.3)	(median=10.4)

Source: Authors' calculations based on the Millenium Cohort Study (Centre for Longitudinal Studies 2010) and the German Socio-Economic Panel Study (German Institute for Economic Research 2011).

measures reported in the paper, and so the statistics presented should be representative for United Kingdom births during the sampling period.[6] Family structure is observed at each of the three waves, and its changes over time are inferred from these.

Child Outcome Variable

Our primary measure of child outcomes is the *socioemotional behavior (SEB) of five- to six-year-old children,* which is based on versions of the strength and difficulties questionnaire (SDQ) proposed by Robert Goodman (1997). The SDQ is part of a self-completion module filled out mainly by mothers. It consists of statements the responses to which are: not true, somewhat true, and certainly true. As table 5.3 illustrates, the responses generate scores on five dimensions: emotional symptoms, conduct problems, hyperactivity-inattention, peer relationship problems, and prosocial behavior. As is conventional (see also chapters 4 and 6, this volume), we sum the four scores other than the last for an overall total difficulties measure at age five or six. The MSC and SOEP differ in terms of the number of items covered, as table 5.3 shows.[7] We transform the measure into standardized scores with mean zero and a standard deviation of one by adjusting for the mean and variance in each country.

Changes in Family Structure

We use maternal reports of household composition variation, as only biological mothers and not fathers of children can be identified definitively in our data sets. In the SOEP, the biological father is assumed to be the male household member observed in the household at time of birth of the child. All other male household members that are surveyed in a child's household are considered to be social fathers or new life partners of the child's mother. Any observed change in numbers or identities of the parents in a child's household from one year to the next is considered to be a family structure change. It can occur due to separation without divorce, separation with divorce or new partners moving in, being newly married or cohabiting. Thus, a family structure change in our analysis is any parental change that a child experiences. It does not necessarily have to be enforced by law by divorce or remarriage. We compare these children to their counterparts who always live with the same parents.

In the United Kingdom MCS, we observe whether the mother has a partner living with her when the child is nine months, three years, and five years. Analogous to the German data, we characterize changes in the number of "parents" in the household, but we do not directly observe changes between waves of the MCS data collection, and so we may understate family change in the United Kingdom data. In particular, we would misclassify some multiple changes in family structure as always-partnered (separation and repartnering between waves) or never-partnered (partnering and separation between waves). This may also be the case in the German data, but the annual interviews make it less common.[8] In both countries, we expect it to be relatively rare. The distribution of family changes over the first five or six years of a child's life is remarkably similar in the two countries. In both countries, 5 percent experienced one change involving the addition of a new partner for the mother; 9 percent of United Kingdom mothers had one partnership separation compared with 10 percent in Germany; and 3 percent in both countries experienced multiple changes. The main difference is the larger percentage of United Kingdom mothers who never were observed living with a partner (8 percent versus 5 percent). Thus, 75 percent of United Kingdom mothers and 77 percent of German mothers always lived with a partner throughout the first five or six years of the child's life. In both countries just under 20 percent of mothers were living as a single parent when the child was age five or six.

Figure 5.1 shows the relationship between parents' highest education (using the ISCED classification) and the probability of living with a partner throughout the first five years of the child's life. The relationship is statistically significant in both countries. Figure 5.2 shows gradients in the probability with respect to household income, with this gradient being steeper for the United Kingdom than Germany.

Results

We first present graphically the simple relationships between SDQ scores and family background, including family structure changes. Then we introduce some control variables and estimate the relationships in a multivariate setting.

Figure 5.1   Percentage Always Partnered by Parents' Highest Education

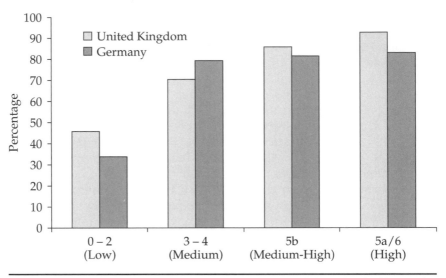

Source: Authors' calculations based on the Millenium Cohort Study (Centre for Longitudinal Studies 2010) and the German Socio-Economic Panel Study (German Institute for Economic Research 2011).

Figure 5.2   Percentage Always Partnered by Parents' Household Income Quartile

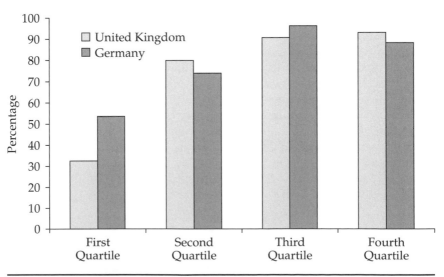

Source: Authors' calculations based on the Millenium Cohort Study (Centre for Longitudinal Studies 2010) and the German Socio-Economic Panel Study (German Institute for Economic Research 2011).

Figure 5.3   Mean of SDQ and ISCED of Highest-Educated Parent

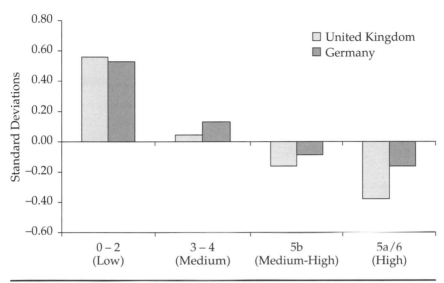

Source: Authors' calculations based on the Millenium Cohort Study (Centre for Longitudinal Studies 2010) and the German Socio-Economic Panel Study (German Institute for Economic Research 2011).

Bivariate Results: Education, Income, and Family Change Gradients

Research analyzing child development often associates child outcomes with parental education or income. Therefore we first describe education and income gradients, before we present gradients with respect to family structure changes.

There is a gradient in the standardized total difficulties score for five- to six-year-olds with respect to the highest ISCED classification of parents in both countries (see figure 5.3). It is steeper in the United Kingdom, but in both countries the lowest education group has a much higher total difficulties score (over 0.5 of a standard deviation higher). A similar pattern, but less steep gradient, can be found for parental income (see figure 5.4).

When we depict children's standardized total difficulties score in relation to the number and type of family structure experiences, the pattern in terms of children's SDQ differs somewhat between countries, but bear in mind that the standard errors of these estimates are much larger for Germany because of the small sample size (see figure 5.5). In the United Kingdom, all changes are associated with more difficulties relative to the always partnered, but the biggest score is for the never partnered. In Germany,

Figure 5.4   Mean of SDQ and Parental Income

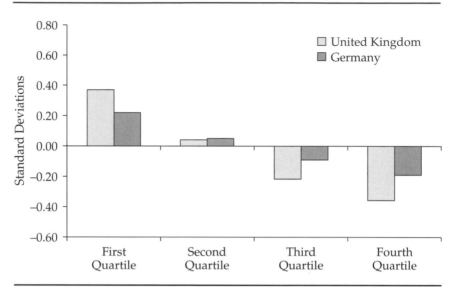

Source: Authors' calculations based on the Millenium Cohort Study (Centre for Longitudinal Studies 2010) and the German Socio-Economic Panel Study (German Institute for Economic Research 2011).

Figure 5.5   Mean of SDQ and Family Structure Changes

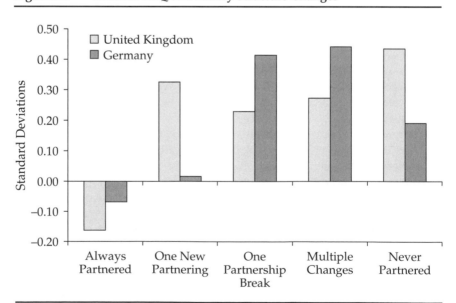

Source: Authors' calculations based on the Millenium Cohort Study (Centre for Longitudinal Studies 2010) and the German Socio-Economic Panel Study (German Institute for Economic Research 2011).

partnership breaks (including multiple changes, but excluding "one new partnering") are associated with the largest socioemotional difficulties.

Results from Multivariate Models

We now analyze how the results of our bivariate analysis change if we control for other variables. In addition to parents' highest education or household income around the time of the child's birth, our multivariate regressions control for the age of the mother, child's age in months, gender of the child, and the number of siblings. For each country, we present three models, all of which contain these four control variables. The first model includes parents' highest education as the SES variable, the second includes household income near the time of birth as an indicator of SES and the third contains both parents' highest education and income. In table 5.4, we present only the estimates for the variables of interest: the SES variables and the family change variables. Figure 5.6 compares the effects of family change between the two countries based on the third model.

Before discussing these estimates it is noteworthy that in both countries the absence of a parent when the child is aged five to six (18 to 19 percent of mothers in each country) significantly increases the child's SDQ score (by 0.16 standard deviations in the United Kingdom and 0.35 in Germany, controlling for all of the variables in model 3 other than family change; full results not shown). The family change variables allow us to explore the association between social and behavioral problems and family structure in more detail.

Table 5.4 indicates that, for the United Kingdom, social behavioral difficulties are more common for children from low-income and low-parental-education households. Controlling for SES background, difficulties are more likely to occur for children whose mother never partnered or who experienced some change in their mother's partner. In fact, relative to the always partnered there is no significant difference between the other family change variables: all raise the SDQ score by about 0.20 to 0.25 of a standard deviation. For Germany the results show significant correlations with education. The children from less educated families have higher SDQs. Controlling for SES background in the German case shows that in particular children who experienced multiple changes show significantly higher social-behavioral difficulties. We did not find evidence that the effect of family change varied among parental education groups (that is, no significant interaction effects), even with the large MCS sample.

Using parents' highest education as the SES indicator, figure 5.7 shows that adding controls for family change reduces the gradient by parental education by a moderate amount (similar results emerge if household income is the SES variable for the United Kingdom). This suggests that differences in family stability by SES account for some of the gradient in social-behavioral difficulties.

Table 5.4 Regression for SDQ Z-Score Results

	Model 1		Model 2		Model 3	
	United Kingdom	Germany	United Kingdom	Germany	United Kingdom	Germany
Parents' highest education						
ISCED 0–2 (low)	REF	REF			REF	REF
ISCED 3–4 (medium)	−0.43 (0.04)	−0.27 (0.25)			−0.39 (0.04)	−0.28 (0.26)
ISCED 5b (medium-high)	−0.55 (0.05)	−0.48 (0.26)			−0.46 (0.05)	−0.48 (0.27)
ISCED 5a/6 (high)	−0.71 (0.04)	−0.48 (0.26)			−0.60 (0.05)	−0.48 (0.27)
Household income, near birth						
First quartile (lowest)			REF	REF	REF	REF
Second quartile			−0.19 (0.03)	−0.07 (0.15)	−0.13 (0.03)	−0.05 (0.15)
Third quartile			−0.37 (0.04)	−0.10 (0.14)	−0.25 (0.04)	−0.06 (0.15)
Fourth quartile (highest)			−0.47 (0.04)	−0.13 (0.15)	−0.31 (0.04)	−0.03 (0.16)
Family structure changes						
Always partnered	REF	REF	REF	REF	REF	REF
One new partnering	0.19 (0.05)	−0.08 (0.24)	0.14 (0.05)	−0.05 (0.23)	0.09 (0.05)	−0.08 (0.24)
One partnership break	0.26 (0.04)	0.34 (0.19)	0.25 (0.04)	0.42 (0.25)	0.22 (0.04)	0.34 (0.26)
Multiple changes	0.22 (0.07)	0.43 (0.26)	0.23 (0.07)	0.39 (0.25)	0.19 (0.07)	0.41 (0.25)
Never partnered	0.30 (0.04)	0.17 (0.26)	0.24 (0.05)	0.19 (0.21)	0.17 (0.05)	0.15 (0.21)
Unweighted N	12504	424	11592	422	11592	422

Source: Authors' calculations based on the Millenium Cohort Study (Centre for Longitudinal Studies 2010) and the German Socio-Economic Panel Study (German Institute for Economic Research 2011).
Note: Standard errors in parentheses.

Figure 5.6   Effects of Family Change on SDQ, Model 3

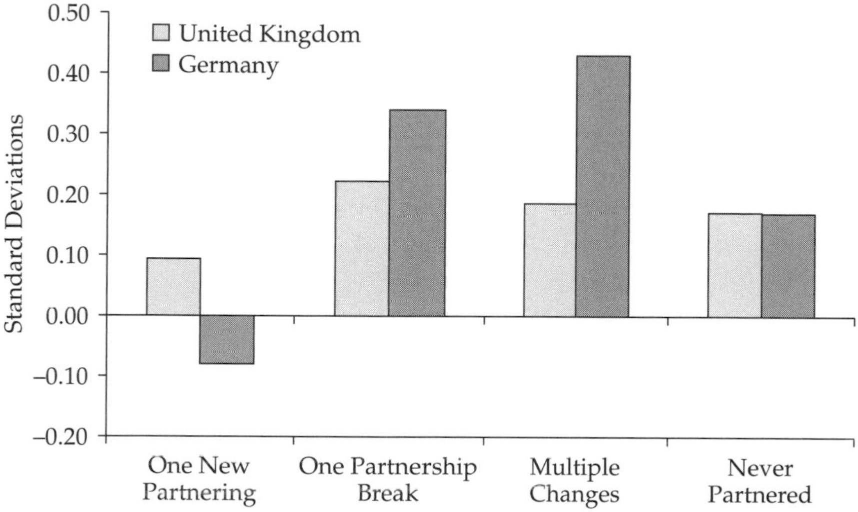

Source: Authors' calculations based on the Millenium Cohort Study (Centre for Longitudinal Studies 2010) and the German Socio-Economic Panel Study (German Institute for Economic Research 2011).

The coefficients of the control variables (not shown) indicate that social-behavioral difficulties are less common among children of older mothers, girls, children who are older at the survey, and those with fewer siblings.

Other Results from MCS

There is an issue of whether the correlations that we have found between SDQ and family change reflect any causal mechanism, or indeed whether the causation is in the other direction: mothers of children with behavioral problems are more likely to break up with their partners. We examine this issue by relating the SDQ score at age three and future family breakup.[9] The idea is that future breakup cannot 'cause' the SDQ score at age three, and so any association must reflect other factors. The estimates of the association between partnership breakup between the ages of three and five on the SDQ at age three (among children of mothers who had a partner up to and including age three) indicate a significant positive association after controlling for the other variables in model 3. The estimated coefficient of future family breakup is 0.10, which is about half the impact of one partnership break on SDQ at age five in model 3 of table 5.4. This association at age three may reflect earlier family conflict that evolves

Figure 5.7   Effects of Parents' Highest Education on SDQ Relative to Lowest Education Group

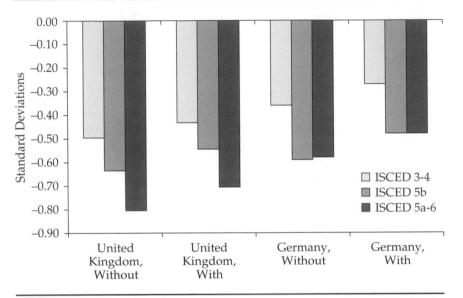

Source: Authors' calculations based on the Millenium Cohort Study (Centre for Longitudinal Studies 2010) and the German Socio-Economic Panel Study (German Institute for Economic Research 2011).
Note: Figures are with and without family change variables.

into a partnership dissolution by age five but is correlated with earlier reductions in child well-being (Potter 2010), or it may reflect persistent child- or family-specific influences on socioemotional problems that are correlated with family change.

From the MCS, we can also examine whether a child's cognitive achievements at age five are associated with family change. We find that after controlling for parents' highest education and household income (as in model 3), the family change variables are jointly insignificant. Thus, family change appears to mainly affect social and behavioral outcomes for preschool children.

Conclusions

This chapter focuses on changes in family structure taking the perspective of the mother when the children are preschoolers. Given the assumption that these changes influence parental quality, we analyze the correlation of these changes with a commonly used measure of children's socio-emotional behavior at ages five or six. Thus our analysis describes short-term outcomes. However, the described outcomes are important for further skill formation. If children are already disadvantaged in early childhood, it may be even more difficult for them to compensate for disadvantage later on.

Our analysis shows that changes in family structure are significantly correlated with the socioemotional behavior. Stable environments with respect to family structure seem to be the best for this child outcome. These results are consistent with studies for other countries as well (see for instance, Andersen, Deding, and Lautsen 2007). Using an IV-approach, they also find a relatively large effect of divorce on the socioemotional behavior of children. In addition, they find an extra negative effect on the SDQ outcome if the mother has remarried after the divorce, in which case the child has experienced two family-changes. These findings can be explained by developmental psychology research, which indicates that a disruption of family bonds is harmful in early years (see, for example, Ricks 1985; Erickson, Sroufe, and Egeland 1985). The attachment theory going back to John Bowlby (1969) indicates that the relationship between children and their primary caregiver influences later socioemotional behavior. Thus, losing an attachment figure once or twice early in life is likely to result in a drawback for children's development and disadvantages seem to emerge early.

After controlling for family changes over the first five or six years of a child's life, the gradient between an index of a child's social-emotional problems and parents' highest education is less steep, indicating that the greater likelihood of family changes among less educated parents accounts for some of the parental education gradient. Nevertheless, a substantial gradient remains.

However, our results do not identify a causal effect of family change on our child outcome measure. Thus the direction of the effect is unclear or indeed there may be no effect at all if parents have attributes that have negative impacts on their child's socioemotional behavior and also associate with family instability, although the literature suggests that family structure changes do have causal impacts on particular child outcomes.[10] If this would be the case, and if this could be confirmed by further studies, our results would underline the suggestion by others to focus much more on a stable family environment if we want to improve early skills. A stable environment is one important precondition for a successful development of today's children.

Nevertheless, for those children who experience a family change, in particular the ones from low-SES families, policy measures are needed to help them to cope with these changes. If other institutions, such as day care centers and schools, are sensitive to the needs of these children, their future prospects might be adversely affected to a smaller degree than would be the case in the absence of support. A precondition for this intervention is that teachers know about the family situation of the children in their groups and classes. Given this knowledge, they can interact with these children in a way that helps them to cope with the stress they experience due to family changes (see Potter 2010). Moreover, knowledge about the situation of families might allow day-care centers to support the parents as well, either with information on the possibilities of external help or with an internal support. Such centers would operate with a much broader approach than a classical day care center. The examples of Early Excellence Centers and the Sure Start Program in the United Kingdom or new developments in Germany through so-called Familienzentren or Eltern-Kind-Zentren might help parents and children to better handle stress due to changes in their family structure. The concept of these centers tries to bring the whole family and not only the child into focus.

Notes

1. Carneiro and Heckman summarize these results as follows: "Families are just as important, if not more important than schools in producing human capital" (2003, 75).
2. Using the term *effect* in this study with respect to our analysis is not correct in the strict sense, because we do not claim to find causal relationships. However, for simplicity's sake, we use the term.
3. Also, beyond a mother protection period of eighteen weeks leave is unpaid; the average replacement of earnings during the mother protection period is only 43 percent in the United Kingdom versus 100 percent in Germany, though the German mother protection period covers only six weeks before and eight weeks after birth.
4. In Germany, the overall divorce rate declined between 2000 and 2007, but increased slightly in 2007 and 2008. In England and Wales, it declined between 2004 and 2008. The decline is likely to be related to the rise in premarital cohabitation because the conversion of cohabiting unions to marriage tends to increase the stability of the married population—less stable unions dissolve before marriage.
5. For more information on the MCS, see http://www.cls.ioe.ac.uk/page.aspx? &sitesectionid=851&sitesectiontitle=Welcome+to+the+Millenium+Cohort+ Study (accessed March 12, 2012).
6. The analyses only include singleton births, thereby dropping the 246 sets of twins and 10 sets of triplets in the data.
7. The modified version of the strength and difficulties questionnaire (SDQ) is based on the original SDQ scale but slightly reduced on the basis of results obtained from pretest data and factor analysis.
8. To the extent such misclassification takes place, estimated differences in outcomes between children experiencing multiple changes and those whose mothers were always (never) partnered will be biased downward.

9. The correlation between SDQ scores at ages three and five is 0.62. The German data cover no earlier SDQ measures than the one we use at age five and six.

10. These attributes may even be related to genes. Terrie Moffitt reports that the tendency for children whose fathers are absent from the family to have more conduct problems is not causal and that when parents' antisocial history was controlled for, the association between father absence and children's conduct problems disappeared (2005, 543).

References

Amato, Paul R. 2005. "The Impact of Family Formation Change on the Cognitive, Social, And Emotional Well-Being of the Next Generation." *The Future of Children* 15(2): 75–96.

Andersen, Angelo R., Mette Deding, and Mette Lautsen. 2007. "How Much Does Parental Divorce Affect Children's Well-Being?" *SFI* working paper. Copenhagen: Danish National Centre for Social Research.

Blanden, Jo, Paul Gregg, and Lindsey Macmillan. 2007. "Accounting for Intergenerational Income Persistence: Noncognitive Skills, Ability and Education." *Economic Journal* 117(519): C43–C60.

Bowlby, John. 1969. *Attachment and Loss*, vol. 1, *Attachment*. London: Hogarth Press and Institute of Psychoanalysis.

Carneiro, Pedro, Claire Crawford, and Alissa Goodman. 2007. "The Impact of Early Cognitive and Noncognitive Skills on Later Outcomes." *CEE* discussion paper 0092. London: London School of Economics.

Carneiro, Pedro, and James J. Heckman. 2003. "Human Capital Policy." In *Inequality in America: What Role for Human Capital Policy?* edited by James Heckman and Alan Krueger. Cambridge, Mass.: MIT Press.

Centre for Longitudinal Studies. 2010. *Millennium Cohort Study.* London: University of London, Institute for Education / Economic and Social Research Council. Available at: http://www.cls.ioe.ac.uk (accessed January 5, 2012).

Cunha, Flavio, and James J. Heckman. 2007. "The Technology of Skill Formation." *American Economic Review* 97(1): 31–47.

———. 2009. "The Economics and Psychology of Inequality and Human Development." *NBER* working paper no. 14695. Cambridge, Mass.: National Bureau of Economic Research.

Del Bono, Emilia, John Ermisch, and Marco Francesconi. 2007. "Intrafamily Resource Allocation: A Dynamic Model of Birth Weight." *IZA* discussion paper 3704. Bonn: Institute for the Study of Labor.

Deutsches Jugendinstitut and Universität Dortmund (DJI). 2007. *Zahlenspiegel 2007: Kindertagesbetreuung im Spiegel der Statistik.* Munich: Bundesministerium für Familie, Senioren, Frauen und Jugend.

Erickson, Martha F., L. Alan Sroufe, and Byron Egeland. 1985. "The Relationship Between Quality of Attachment and Behavior Problems in Preschool in a High-

Risk Sample." In *Monographs of the Society for Research in Child Development*, vol. 50, no. 1/2, *Growing Points of Attachment Theory and Research*. Oxford: Wiley-Blackwell.

Ermisch, John, and Marco Francesconi. 2001. "Family Structure and Children's Achievements." *Journal of Population Economics* 14(2): 249–70; reprinted in *Family, Household and Work*, edited by Klaus F. Zimmermann and Michael Vogler. London: Springer Verlag, 2003.

Ermisch, John, Marco Francesconi, and David J. Pevalin. 2004. "Parental Partnership and Joblessness in Childhood and Their Influence on Young People's Outcomes." *Journal of the Royal Statistical Society* 167(1): 69–101.

Ermisch, John, and Mike Murphy. 2006. "Changing Household and Family Structures and Complex Living Arrangements." In ESRC seminar series *Mapping the Policy Landscape*. London: Economic and Social Research Council.

Fomby, Paula, and Andrew J. Cherlin. 2007. "Family Instability and Child Well-Being." *American Sociology Review* 72(2): 181–204.

Francesconi, Marco, Stephen P. Jenkins, and Thomas Siedler. 2009. "Childhood Family Structure and Schooling Outcomes: Evidence for Germany." *Journal of Population Economics* 23(3): 1201–231.

Francesconi, Marco, Helmut Rainer, and Wilbert van der Klaauw. 2008. "Unintended Consequences of Welfare Reforms: The Case of Divorced Parents." *IZA* discussion paper no. 3891. Bonn: Institute for the Study of Labor.

German Institute for Economic Research. 2011. *The German Socio-Economic Panel Study.* Berlin: German Institute for Economic Research (DIW, Duetsches Institut fur Wirtschaftsforschung). Available at: http://www.diw.de/en/soep (accessed January 5, 2012).

Goodman, Robert. 1997. "The Strengths and Difficulties Questionnaire: A Research Note." *Journal of Child Psychology and Psychiatry* 38(5): 581–86.

Institute for Social and Economic Research. 2011. *British Household Panel Study.* Colchester, U.K.: University of Essex. Available at: http://www.iser.essex.ac.uk/bhps (accessed January 5, 2012).

Mahler, Philippe, and Rainer Winkelmann. 2004. "Single Motherhood and (Un) Equal Educational Opportunities: Evidence for Germany." *IZA* discussion paper no. 1391. Bonn: Institute for the Study of Labor.

Moffitt, Terrie. 2005. "The New Look of Behavioral Genetics in Development Psychopathology: Gene Environment Interplay in Anti-Social Behaviors." *Psychological Bulletin* 131(4): 533–54.

Organisation for Economic Co-Operation and Development (OECD). 2006. *OECD Family Database.* Paris: OECD.

Office of National Statistics. 2010. *Marriage and Divorce Statistics.* London: Office of National Statistics.

Potter, Daniel. 2010. "Psychosocial Well-Being and the Relationship Between Divorce and Children's Academic Achievement." *Journal of Marriage and Family* 72(4): 933–46.

Pronzato, Chiara D. 2009. "Return to Work After Childbirth: Does Parental Leave Matter in Europe?" *Review of Economics of the Household* 7(4): 341–60.

Ricks, Margaret H. 1985. "The Social Transmission of Parental Behavior: Attachment Across Generations." In *Monographs of the Society for Research in Child Development*, vol. 50, no. 1/2, *Growing Points of Attachment Theory and Research*. Oxford: Wiley-Blackwell.

Schupp, Jürgen, Sabrina Herrmann, Peter Jaensch, and Frieder R. Lang. 2008. "Erfassung kognitiver Leistungspotentiale Erwachsener im Sozio-oekonomischen Panel (SOEP)." Data Documentation 32. Berlin: Deutsches Institut für Wirtschaftsforschung.

Siedler, Thomas, Jürgen Schupp, C. Katharina Spiess, and Gert G. Wagner. 2009. "The German Socio-Economic Panel (SOEP) as Reference Data Set." In *Schmollers Jahrbuch* (European Data Watch Section) 129(2):367–74.

Statistisches Bundesamt. 2009. "Zahl der Ehescheidungen stieg 2008 wieder an." Pressemitteilung nr. 251 vom 8. Juli 2009. Wiesbaden: Statistisches Bundesamt Deutschland.

Wagner, Gert G., Joachim R. Frick, and Jürgen Schupp. 2007. "The German Socio-Economic Panel Study (SOEP): Scope, Evolution, and Enhancements." In *Schmollers Jahrbuch* 127(1): 139–69.

Würtz-Rasmussen, Astrid. 2009. "Family Structure Changes and Children's Health, Behavior and Educational Outcomes." Department of Economics working paper no. 09–15. Aarhus, Denmark: Aarhus University School of Business.

Chapter 6

Family Background and Child Outcomes

JO BLANDEN, ILAN KATZ, AND

GERRY REDMOND

THIS VOLUME is concerned with understanding international variations in the intergenerational transmission of economic status. It has become increasingly clear that intergenerational inequality starts young; differences in very early development set the stage for inequalities by family background that last a lifetime. In this chapter, we use data from the United Kingdom and Australia to explore the relationship between parental education and indicators of children's development over ages three to nine (that is, the transition from C1 to C2).

We structure our analysis around the following questions:

How persistent are early differences in cognitive and social and emotional development?

Are development scores in both nations equally influenced by parental education?

Is there convergence or divergence in the outcomes of children from different backgrounds as they move into middle childhood? Is this similar in both nations?

What is the connection between parental education and persistent weak or strong performance in cognitive, social, and emotional development in the two countries?

Are the trajectories of initially good or poor performers influenced by their parents' education?

By taking a longitudinal as well as a comparative approach, this chapter moves toward a better explanation of how policies in different countries influence the contribution of early childhood to social immobility. As in chapter 4, this volume, we find a strong association between parental education and children's performance in the cognitive and socioemotional domains. These differences emerge early, but in contrast to findings from some other studies (Feinstein 2003; Carneiro and Heckman 2005), do not appear to expand as children age. Of the two nations we study, it seems that parental education has a more substantial effect on children's development in the United Kingdom. In addition, parental education also affects children's trajectories; for the United Kingdom, there is evidence that even for children who started with similar scores, those with lower-educated parents have relatively lower levels of achievement or well-being by age seven, but such effects are less evident for Australia. Similarly, British children who start off with low levels of well-being are more likely to persist in this situation than their equivalents in Australia.

There are a number of possible drivers of the differences between the two countries, including differences in early education policies and programs, differences in the effects of school on children's well-being, and differences in the return to children on parents' educational attainment. We speculate on the most likely explanations in our conclusions.

Background

Numerous studies have pointed to the importance of family background and parental characteristics, including income, education, and social status, in significantly influencing children's developmental outcomes from an early age (Heckman, Stixrud, and Urzua 2006; Feinstein 2003).

However, the mechanisms by which family background affects children's well-being and their longer-term outcomes are complex, operating through a number of interacting proximal and distal mediating processes (Conger and Donnellan 2007). Scholars have argued that differences in the emotional and behavioral development of children from different backgrounds emerge at very early ages (Carneiro and Heckman 2005; Feinstein 2003; Ermisch 2008). John Ermisch (2008) shows steep gradients for cognitive and behavioral assessments, with three-year- old children in high-income families in the United Kingdom having higher cognitive assessments and fewer behavioral problems than children in low-income families. He further argues that these differences are apparent throughout the income range and not only between the lowest-income groups and the rest, a point Ilan Katz and Gerry Redmond (2009) echo in their analysis of Australian data. Jo Blanden and Stephen Machin (2010) find that the impact of family background on cognitive, social, and emotional scores is substantial at ages three and five in the United Kingdom's Millennium Cohort, and that the magnitudes of these gaps appear to be fairly constant when compared to previous cohorts going back as far as those born in the mid-1980s. Similarly, Redmond and his colleagues (in press) find that the gaps between children from different socioeconomic backgrounds have remained stable since the early 1980s.

The implications of these findings are demonstrated by James Heckman, Jora Stixrud, and Sergio Urzua (2006), who show that gaps in cognitive ability and noncognitive skills in early childhood matter for wages at age thirty, both because those with high ability get more education, and because even among those with the same education level, those with higher ability tend to earn more. These cognitive and noncognitive characteristics were also shown to be related to later employment, likelihood of smoking, involvement in crime, and early motherhood.

Leon Feinstein, using the 1970 British Cohort Study, also finds that inequalities in very early outcomes are, in part, responsible for long-lasting differences in life chances associated with family background (2003). However, his finding that parent educational achievement is the major determinant of children's cognitive developmental trajectories has recently been criticized by John Jerrim and Anna Vignoles (2011) on a number of statistical grounds, not least that the trajectories he shows—where children with low socioeconomic status (SES) and high measured cognitive ability at twenty-two months are shown to be overtaken in their cognitive development at age five by high-SES children with low measured cognitive ability at twenty-two months—are an artifact of regression to the mean. Jerrim and Vignoles argue that the effect of regression to the mean is likely to be exacerbated for groups of high-performing children of low-SES parents and low-performing children of high-SES parents, because the initial scores on which these groups are selected are likely to be especially far from their long-term average (Jerrim and Vignoles 2011). This critique does not question that there is a strong relationship between family socioeconomic status and children's outcomes, but does question whether existing evidence can show this relationship growing stronger as children get older. In this context, despite considerable differences between countries in relation to the importance of family background on children's outcomes (OECD 2008a), little is known about how developmental trajectories from the early years to adulthood are influenced by different national contexts and how social policy influences intergenerational mobility in different countries.

Many factors are shown to contribute to intergenerational transmission of advantage and disadvantage. However, in her study of Organisation for Economic Co-Operation and Development (OECD) countries, Anna Cristina d'Addio shows that parental education is by far the most important background characteristic (2007), and it is for this reason that we use parental education as the measure of family socioeconomic advantage and disadvantage in this paper.

The United Kingdom and Australia

The United Kingdom and Australia offer an interesting contrast for studying social mobility. The two countries are very closely related, both culturally and structurally, and there is a large exchange of population between the two, especially in the form of migration from the United Kingdom to Australia. The education systems also have a number of common features, including relatively underdeveloped early childhood education sectors, large nongovernment sectors at both primary and secondary levels, and an orientation toward measuring school performance in terms of numerical indicators. Many of the two countries' social policies are modeled on each other, including a range of policies for early years' provision, welfare to work, industrial relations, and family support. Although both countries have been classified as supporting liberal welfare regimes (Esping-Andersen 1990) and both have relatively high levels of income inequality (OECD 2008a), they have both increased overall public expenditure on the early years (as a percentage of GDP) in recent years to considerably higher levels of expenditure than the OECD average (OECD 2008b).

Nonetheless, the literature on adult intergenerational mobility has tended to portray Australia as having a relatively higher degree of intergenerational mobility than the United Kingdom (Leigh 2007; OECD 2008a). Analysis of the PISA international tests also shows that there is greater overall inequality in outcomes for adolescents in the United Kingdom compared with Australia and that parental SES matters more for outcomes in the United Kingdom (Redmond 2009).

With regards to policy on early childhood education and care, perhaps the most important difference between the two countries has been the greater emphasis in the United Kingdom on services as opposed to cash benefits for families with children in their early years. The United Kingdom, especially since the late 1990s, has greatly expanded early childhood services that target disadvantaged children in particular. This is reflected in the considerably higher level of expenditure on services aimed at families with children in the United Kingdom in comparison with Australia, which has tended to focus more on increasing cash payments for families with children. The United Kingdom has also had an explicit policy of eradicating child poverty by 2020.

This is confirmed by OECD analysis showing the public expenditure on services for OECD countries in 2003 (OECD 2007b). The United Kingdom was just at the OECD average of 0.6 percent of GDP, whereas in Australia expenditure was around 0.4 percent of GDP, about two-thirds of that. Policy has changed considerably in both countries, and these numbers indicate the situation when these cohorts were in their infancy.

Nevertheless overall expenditure on family benefits (as a percentage of GDP) was very similar for the two countries, both spending virtually identical proportions of GDP, and both having considerably higher levels of expenditure than the OECD average in 2003 (OECD 2007a).

The main question this chapter seeks to address is whether the difference between the two countries in the relationship between parents' socioeconomic status and children's early developmental outcomes is significant, and whether this relationship diminishes or increases over the child's early life course. This comparative approach is aimed at improving our understanding of how early developmental trajectories contribute to differences in the intergenerational transmission of advantage and disadvantage in different national contexts, with the ultimate goal of identifying those policies that appear to be most effective at improving social mobility.

Data

The data we use for the United Kingdom is the Millennium Cohort Study (MCS), which examines the progress of children born in 2000 and 2001 and provides information on their cognitive, social, and emotional development at ages three, five, and seven. This is paired with the Longitudinal Study of Australian Children (LSAC) data for Australia, which tracks a sample of children born in 1999 and 2000 and provides information on development at ages four to five, six to seven, and eight to nine.

Survey Structure

The MCS began with a survey of babies age nine months in 2002 and 2003 and has continued with data collection at three years, five years, and very recently, seven years. The sample population for the study was drawn from all live births in the United Kingdom over twelve months from September 2000 in England and Wales and December 2000 in Scotland and Northern Ireland. The sample was selected from a random sample of electoral wards, disproportionately stratified to ensure adequate representation of all four U.K. countries, deprived areas, and areas with high concentrations of black and Asian families. Child Benefit records were used to select and locate respondents.

Of around 27,000 initially selected into the sample, 18,553 successful interviews were carried out at MCS 1 (around nine months). MCS 2 at age three attempted to follow up all of these families plus some additional respondents who lived in the target wards at the time of MCS 1 but who were not contacted at that time. Response rates at MCS 2 and 3 (age five) were 80 percent of the target sample, falling to around 70 percent at MCS 4 (age seven). Families with twins and triplets meant that the number of children in the MCS was greater than the number of families interviewed. In this analysis, we restrict the sample to single children and the first child listed in twin and triplet groups. To reflect the oversampling of ethnic minorities and disadvantaged groups, longitudinal weights are used in all analyses.

The MCS surveys primarily focus on questioning the main respondent (generally the mother) and finding out about the family's education, health, economic situation, and community. There are also questions about parenting behaviors and mother-reported child assessments. We use mother reports of the child's socioemotional behaviors in this study. The cognitive assessments we use are carried out directly by the interviewer. The MCS also questions the mother's partner, and in later waves the child's teacher and older siblings (for more information on the survey, see Hansen 2010).

The LSAC was launched in 2004, with detailed information collected from responding families every two years. Three waves of data have been collected so far. Data from two separate samples of children and their families are being collected, the first age one year or less in 2003 and 2004 (the B cohort), and the second ages four to five years in 2003 and 2004 (the K cohort). The sampling frame for the two age cohorts was taken from the Medicare Australia enrolment and activity databases held by the Health Insurance Commission. This analysis uses the K cohort.

In general, response rates among K cohort parents were relatively low. Of the original sample of 10,275 four- to five-year-old children selected from the Medicare enrolments database, 4,983 were successfully recruited to the study, giving an overall response rate of 48 percent. Reasons for nonresponse included database mismatches, (3 percent), noncontacts (14 percent), and refusals (35 percent) (Soloff et al. 2006). Nonetheless, Carol Soloff and her colleagues argue that nonresponse is not seriously biased and that the final reweighted sample is representative of the cohort of Australian children born in 1999 or 2000 (2006).

The LSAC sample for this chapter comprises families who responded at each wave and when the mother was the primary respondent at each wave. This gives a working sample size of 3,972 for the present analysis. Although sample attrition is not random and families from lower socioeconomic backgrounds are more likely to drop out than other families, this attrition is at least partially compensated for with longitudinal and cross-sectional weights, which are used in the present analysis. Unlike in the MCS, disadvantaged groups were not oversampled in the LSAC. Therefore, we might suspect that the Australian data may be poorer than the U.K. data at capturing children with low-SES parents. Comparison with other Australian data sources, however, suggests that the LSAC is representative of lower-income families with young children (Mullan and Redmond 2011).

In the first three waves of the LSAC, most information about the household and about the child is collected in face-to-face interviews with the mother. Secondary carers are also interviewed, as are parents living apart from the child, where they are successfully contacted. The child's teacher in child-care centers (at wave 1) and school (at waves 2 and 3) are also asked to participate in interviews about the child. For parents and teachers, interviews consist of a mixture of face-to-face interviews and self-completion questionnaires. Interviews in all three waves with the primary carer form the raw material for most of the analysis in this report, most particularly the responses to the strengths and difficulties questionnaire (Goodman 1997). As in the MCS, the tests we use to create our composite cognitive score are performed directly on the child by the interviewer.

Child Development Variables

We follow Feinstein in using a composite score derived from principal components analyses of all the cognitive achievement tests at each age as our measure of cognitive outcomes (2003).[1] However, we recognize issues with this approach that a high degree of random error is likely in these tests, especially those carried out on very young children (see Jerrim and Vignoles 2011); but also, that error is likely to higher among low-SES children with high initial scores and high-SES children with low initial scores, and that error, even across different tests, may be correlated. These points need to be taken into account in the interpretation of results. The tests included at each wave in the two surveys are listed in table 6.1. A short description of each test is given in online appendix table 6A.1; all are administered directly to the child by the interviewer.[2] Principal components analysis provides us with an indicator of latent cognitive ability for each wave and each dataset; this enables us to rank children.

Table 6.1 also reports basic statistics from the principal components analysis: eigenvalues for the first components, and the proportion of total variance in the original variables that the first component captures (which is calculated as the eigenvalue divided by the number of variables in the principal components analysis). The table shows that the first components at ages three and five in the United Kingdom capture more of the total variance of cognitive scores than the first component at age seven in the United Kingdom, or at any age in Australia. Most notable is that in neither country does the proportion of variance captured increase as the child grows older. This suggests, in contrast to Feinstein's expectation, that the latent composite cognitive score that we use in the remainder of this analysis is no more representative of children's real level of cognitive development at older ages than it is at younger ages. This is important for the interpretation of our findings. In our analysis, we use standardized scores, with mean zero and standard deviation one in each nation.

Table 6.1   First Component Scores from Cognitive Development Outcomes

United Kingdom	Eigenvalue	Proportion Total Variance	Australia	Eigenvalue	Proportion Total Variance
Age three (BAS vocabulary and Bracken School Readiness)	1.5863	0.7928			
Age five (BAS vocabulary, BAS picture similarity, and BAS pattern construction)	2.1008	0.7003	Ages 4 to 5 (PPVT & Who Am I?)	1.2797	0.6398
Age seven (BAS word reading, BAS pattern construction, and number skills)	1.7881	0.5960	Ages 6 to 7 (PPVT and matrix reasoning)	1.2722	0.6361
			Ages 8 to 9 (PPVT and matrix reasoning)	1.3472	0.6736

Source: Authors' calculation based on the Longitudinal Study of Australian Children (Australian Institute of Family Studies 2010) and the Millenium Cohort Study (Hansen 2010).
Note: BAS = British Ability Scale; PPVT = Peabody Picture Vocabulary Test.

In both the MCS and LSAC, social and emotional outcomes are measured using the strengths and difficulties questionnaire (SDQ), developed as a screening tool for detecting mental health problems in children age three to sixteen years old (Goodman 1997). It consists of a questionnaire with twenty-five positive and negative attributes, each answered on a three-point scale: not true, somewhat true, certainly true (Goodman 1997; Muris, Meesters, and van den Berg 2003). We use the twenty negative attributes scale consisting of five items each from the following four scales: emotional problems, conduct problems, hyperactivity-inattentive, and peer relationship problems. We sum the responses to these items to form a total difficulties scale. The SDQ can be administered directly to children as well as to parents and teachers who respond with respect to a particular child. In this study, parental responses are used to calculate the total difficulties score. Again, scores are standardized for the main body of the analysis.[3]

Parental Education Variables

We base our categorization of parental education around the International Standard Classification of Education (ISCED) definition, following the same definitions as chapter 2. Low education families are defined as those for whom the highest educational qualification of parents in the first wave is below good general certificates of secondary education (GCSEs) in the United Kingdom (the target for school leavers). In Australia, low-education families are defined as those where neither the mother nor the father, if living with the child, completed secondary education, and neither had any postschool qualifications such as diplomas or certificates. In both countries, high-education families are defined as those where the mother or father has a tertiary qualification (bachelor degree or higher). Education frequencies for the two nations (shown in terms of ISCED codes), and the three categories into which they are aggregated for the purposes of this study, are shown in online appendix table 6A.3. In the United Kingdom, 19 percent of the sample children fall into the low-education category compared with 12 percent in Australia. In the United Kingdom, 37 percent of the sample are defined as having high education, as are 34 percent in Australia. Families who fit into neither of these definitions are categorized as having medium levels of education.

To use an observation in our analyses, it is necessary to have information on the selected outcome in all three waves of the data. To check the impact of this sample selection, we also show the parental education distribution for children who meet this restriction. It is clear that for the United Kingdom we lose about 20 percent of the sample due to missing information on outcomes, and it appears that this skews the sample slightly toward those with better-educated parents. In Australia, the losses due to missing values are smaller (around 12 percent), but are once again focused on the low-educated parents. It seems likely that the higher item response rate is connected to the lower overall response rate observed for Australia.

Results

In this section, we present the results of the various analyses we have undertaken to compare disparities in outcomes for children from the two countries under study; the mean impact of parental education on children's cognitive and socioemotional outcomes; persistence of disparities as children develop; and the trajectories of children from different backgrounds in the two countries.

Figure 6.1   Transition Matrices in Composite Cognitive Test Scores

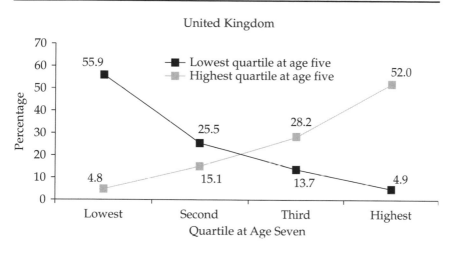

United Kingdom

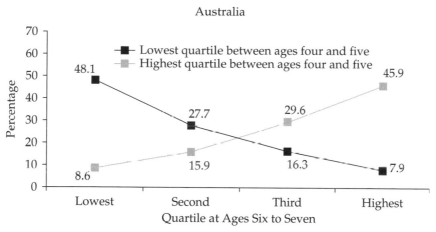

Australia

Source: Authors' calculation based on the Longitudinal Study of Australian Children (Australian Institute of Family Studies 2010) and the Millenium Cohort Study (Hansen 2010).

Stability of Outcomes

Before exploring the role of parental education, we first consider the persistence of test scores across the waves in both nations. Feinstein speculates that scores are more likely to be stable at later ages (2003), so we must take the difference in ages into account when making comparisons; here we limit the analysis to the two waves with common ages in both nations. Figures 6.1 and 6.2 show a pictorial version of transition matrices

Figure 6.2   Transition Matrices in SDQ

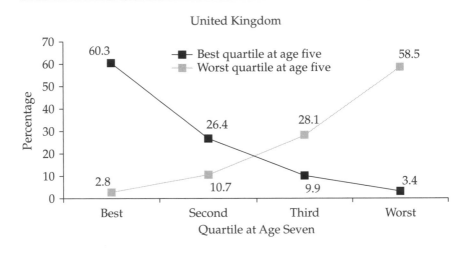

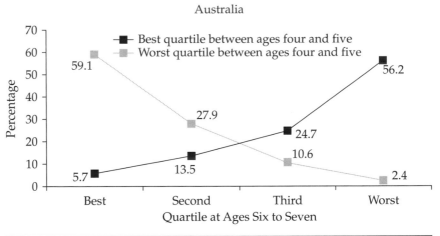

Source: Authors' calculations, adapted from Feinstein and Bynner (2004).
Note: Figure shows the quartile in which children's developmental scores fall in both the United Kingdom and Australia at around age seven, given the quartile into which their developmental score falls at age five. In the case of cognitive test scores, the best scores are highest, and in the case of the SDQ, the best scores are lowest (representing fewer behaviour difficulties). The tables show patterns in both tests, in the two countries, are similar. In all cases, about half (minimum 46 percent) or more children in the best or the worst quartile at age five are in the same quartile at age seven. In all cases too, relatively few observations move from the best to the worst quartile, or from the worst to the best quartile between ages five and seven (maximum 8.6 percent).

between quartiles at ages four to five and five to seven (Australia) and ages five and seven (United Kingdom), that is, the outcome quartile at the older age for children who were in the lowest and highest outcome quartiles at the younger age.

The figure highlights the difference between the performance at ages six to seven years of those who are high performers at ages four to five (the black line) and those who were low performers (the gray line). As we would expect, a relationship between performance at the two ages is clear, around half of children who were in the bottom or top quartile at ages four to five are in the same quartile at ages six to seven, and less than 10 percent move all the way up or down the quartile ranking. The evidence from the cognitive scores shows slightly stronger persistence in the United Kingdom than in Australia, but this is less evident in the social and emotional domain. Persistence in the quartile of total difficulties score is stronger than in the cognitive test scores. This likely reflects that the survey instrument for the social and emotional domain was the same in each wave.[4]

Mean Impacts of Parental Education on Test Scores

Figure 6.3 presents the mean cognitive and social and emotional outcomes by age and parental education. As we would expect, the cognitive scores are higher for those with highly educated parents whereas the reverse is true for the total difficulties score (that is, children of highly educated parents have fewer behavior problems). The figure shows that there is more inequality by parental background for the United Kingdom than Australia, in line with the results from chapter 4 of this volume. The difference is found in the outcomes of the children of less-educated parents. In the United Kingdom, mean scores for less-educated parents in the cognitive domain are significantly lower than those for Australia in all years, whereas mean scores in the social and emotional domain are higher.

We are also interested in the evolution of inequality as children age. One of the headline findings from Feinstein (2003) was the fanning-out and growth in inequality by socioeconomic status as children age. Even though, as noted, Feinstein's findings have been subject to critical comment, it is useful to replicate his analysis because the question he asks is important: does the influence of socioeconomic status on developmental outcomes increase as children get older? There is no consistent evidence of this phenomenon here. If anything, evidence for the United Kingdom indicates a convergence in outcomes between ages three and five and only a slight fanning out between five and seven, after most U.K. children enter primary school. There is no evidence for a fanning-out associated with school entry in Australia because children are entering school around the first wave, and the trajectory is fairly flat from there on. In other words, the evidence presented here suggests that disparities in children's developmental

Figure 6.3   Mean Cognitive Scores and Social and Emotional Difficulties

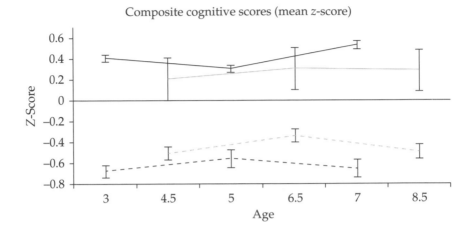

Composite cognitive scores (mean z-score)

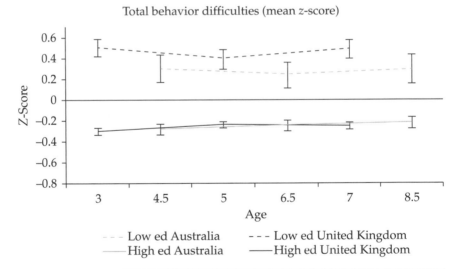

Total behavior difficulties (mean z-score)

- - - Low ed Australia   - - - Low ed United Kingdom
——High ed Australia   ——High ed United Kingdom

Source: Authors' calculations, adapted from Feinstein and Bynner (2004).
Note: Average cognitive scores (left graph) and behavior difficulties scores (right graph) for children whose parents have low and high levels of education at ages three, five, and seven years (United Kingdom) and at four to five, six to seven, and eight to nine (Australia). Scores are in z-scores, with mean 0 and standard deviation of 1, to allow easier comparison across countries and graphs. Trends in average scores for children of highly educated parents are shown by the continuous lines, and for less-educated parents by the dashed lines, with trends for the United Kingdom in black and for Australia in gray. Vertical lines represent 95 percent confidence intervals for each of the point estimates (that is, the true population value is likely to fall within these confidence intervals in 95 samples of every 100 drawn from this population).

outcomes that are evident at ages seven or eight in the two countries are quite similar to those that are evident at ages three or four.

Association of Parental Education with Persistence

We are also interested in considering those who have persistently poor or good scores over three waves of the studies. In the United States, it is persistence of low levels of child well-being, rather than problems at particular points in a child's development, that is most strongly correlated with poor outcomes later in life (Kowaleski-Jones and Duncan 1999).

Poor outcomes are defined here as the bottom quartile of the composite test score measure and the top quartile of difficulties while good outcomes are defined as the other extreme 25 percent. Persistence means remaining in that quartile at all three waves. A review of the overall levels of persistence shows that slightly more children have persistently low cognitive scores in the United Kingdom compared with Australia (almost 9 percent versus 7 percent), but that the proportion of children with persistently high difficulties is very similar across the two nations (8 percent). We might expect ex ante to find more persistence among the Australian children because their outcomes are measured at a later age (see online appendix table 6A.5).

Figure 6.4 demonstrates the particularly strong relationship between parental education and persistence in the United Kingdom. Although the proportion of children with persistently low cognitive scores is only 2 percentage points higher in the United Kingdom overall, there are 10 percentage points more children in this category in the United Kingdom if we restrict the sample to those with low-educated parents. Persistently low cognitive scores are substantially more closely associated with low parental education in the United Kingdom than in Australia. Persistently good cognitive scores are also more closely associated with higher parental education levels, but differences in this dimension between the United Kingdom and Australia are not as large. Similar patterns are observed for persistence in the behavior difficulties scores in figure 6.5.

Interaction of Initial Performance and Parental Education

The next set of analyses attempts to more directly replicate those of Feinstein (2003). Feinstein's analysis involved selecting children into groups depending on their parental socioeconomic status (SES) and performance in cognitive test scores at age twenty-two months, and then tracking their relative performance in cognitive test scores up to age ten (Feinstein did not study the social and emotional domain). Feinstein's results showed children with poor early performance and high parental SES quickly catching up with those with good early performance and

Figure 6.4   Persistence in Composite Cognitive Scores

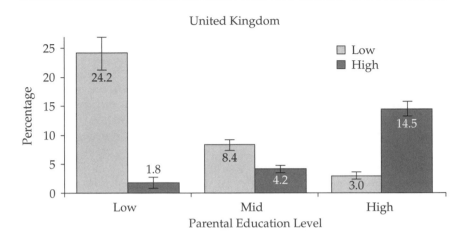

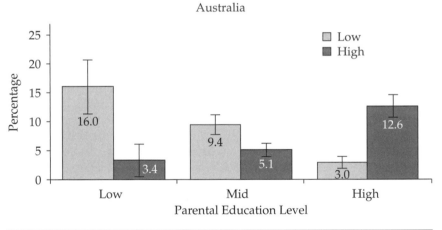

Source: Authors' calculation based on the Longitudinal Study of Australian Children (Australian Institute of Family Studies 2010) and the Millenium Cohort Study (Hansen 2010).

low SES; in other words, SES dominated initial measured ability in determining children's developmental trajectories. Our aim here is to examine whether we observe the same patterns as Feinstein, or whether we can draw any conclusions about the stability of results over time in the U.K. and Australian data. Figures 6.6 and 6.7 show the trajectories for different groups of children as categorized by parental education and performance in the first available sweep (age three for the MCS and ages four to five for the LSAC). As noted above, the method used to derive data in figure 6.6 closely replicates Feinstein's method (although the actual tests are

Figure 6.5   Persistence in Behavior Difficulties

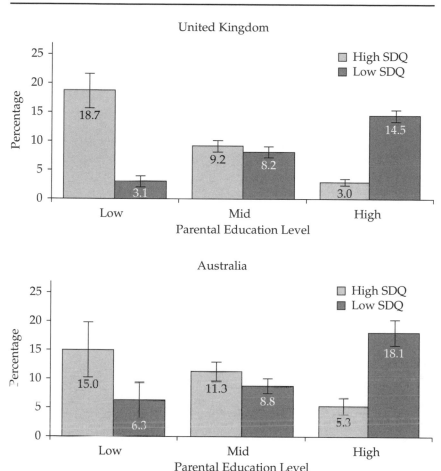

Source: Authors' calculations based on the Longitudinal Study of Australian Children (Australian Institute of Family Studies 2010) and the Millenium Cohort Study (Hansen 2010).

different). This is not the case with figure 6.7, however, because Feinstein does not look at social and emotional development, and because data are derived from a single composite score representing behavioral difficulties as reported by the mother.

The results in both figures confirm the influence of parents' education on children's development in both countries, but not on their trajectories. Figure 6.6 shows that in both the United Kingdom and Australia, regression to the mean effects between waves 1 and 2, as discussed above in relation to Feinstein's analysis, are striking. Few further effects are found

Figure 6.6   Trajectory of Composite Test Scores

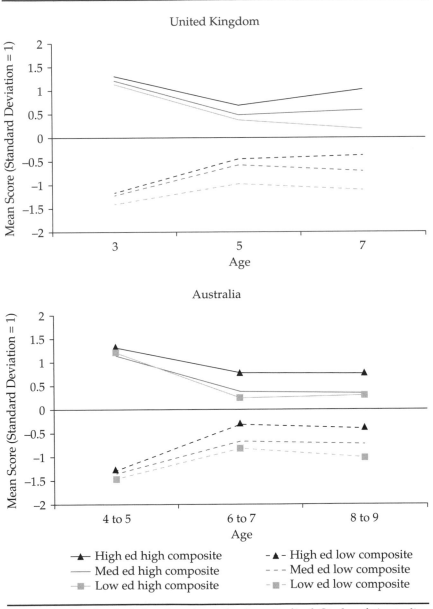

Source: Authors' calculation based on the Longitudinal Study of Australian Children (Australian Institute of Family Studies 2010) and the Millenium Cohort Study (Hansen 2010).
Note: The sample sizes for the six groups (in the same order as the legend) are as follows. U.K.: 1426, 1059, 106, 492, 1386, 720; Australia: 468, 412, 45, 203, 452, 111.

between waves 2 and 3; however, it is worth noting a slight fanning out in trajectories for children in the United Kingdom with high initial test scores. Given that the method used here is similar to Feinstein's, it might be expected, ceteris paribus, that the pattern of regression to the mean after wave 2 might also be similar. In this analysis, however, there appears to be little regression to the mean effects after wave 2. This suggests the possibility that a key finding of Feinstein—the continuing decline in scores after wave 2 for low-SES children with high initial scores, and the continuing improvement in scores for high-SES children with low initial scores, may have some foundation. Although exploring this possibility is beyond the scope of this chapter, it warrants closer attention.

The pattern for trajectories in behavioral problems (figure 6.7) is similar in both the United Kingdom and Australia to patterns observed in cognitive development. However, regression to the mean effects between waves 1 and 2 for the different parent SES groups is virtually indistinguishable. This suggests that regression to the mean effects may be due to randomness in the measurement of children's behavioral difficulties at wave 1, but that most of this randomness has been accounted for by wave 2. This finding is potentially at odds with the suggestion by Jerrim and Vignoles (2011) that error in tests performed at repeated intervals by the same person (as is the case with the SDQ, which is completed in both countries by the mother in all waves) might be correlated, and therefore a cause of continuing regression to the mean after wave 2. Again, this suggests that further work is needed on trajectories in children's development and regression to the mean effects over several waves of longitudinal data.

Conclusions

In both nations studied, we find a large and continuing association between children's developmental outcomes and parental levels of education. Our findings with respect to persistence in outcomes are perhaps the most robust. In both countries, children from low-socioeconomic-status backgrounds are more likely to have persistently poor developmental scores (in cognitive and in social and emotional domains) than children from middle- or high-socioeconomic-status backgrounds. However, inequalities between children of low and high socioeconomic status are significantly greater in the United Kingdom than in Australia. The second major finding is that, on the whole, the pattern of fanning out identified by Feinstein in his analysis is not evident either in the United Kingdom or in Australia. We find that average differences between children whose parents have different educational outcomes tend to remain fairly constant over time, in both the cognitive and socioemotional domains. In other words, the considerable differences in outcomes by socioeconomic background that we find in this analysis appear to be already in place by age

Figure 6.7   Trajectory of Behavior Problems

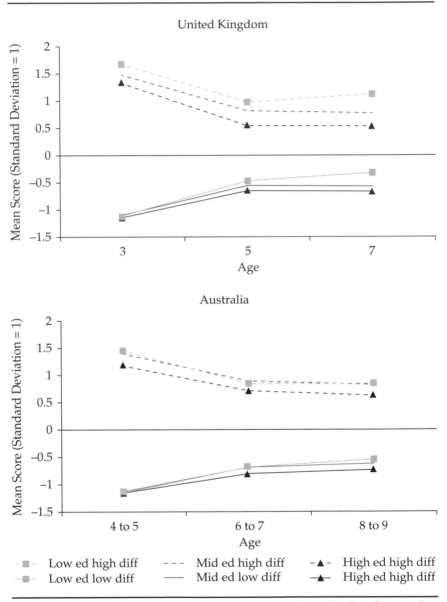

Source: Authors' calculation based on the Longitudinal Study of Australian Children (Australian Institute of Family Studies 2010) and the Millenium Cohort Study (Hansen 2010).
Note: The sample sizes for the six groups (in the same order as the legend) are as follows. U.K.: 416, 142, 1125, 1154, 443, 1318; Australia: 100, 438, 214, 46, 396, 525.

three or four. This finding suggests that further research is needed on the starting points of socioeconomic inequalities in children's developmental outcomes. And since the findings presented here are somewhat different to those of Feinstein (2003) even though methods used are similar, they suggest the need for further work, complementing recent research by Jerrim and Vignoles (2011) to distinguish children's true developmental trajectories from regression to the mean effects.

In summary, our main substantive finding relates to the consistent pattern of greater inequality driven by parental education in the United Kingdom than in Australia, with the biggest difference being the poorer relative performance of children in the United Kingdom with the lowest parental education. This finding lines up with other international comparisons of intergenerational mobility, which tend to show that there is less equality and less social mobility in the United Kingdom than in Australia (OECD 2008a). It demonstrates the possibility that at least some of the difference in mobility can be explained by differences in children's early years' experiences in the two countries.

Our findings are perhaps surprising from a policy perspective. As we mention above, the United Kingdom has implemented a raft of policies and programs aimed at children over the past decade, and in 1999 the U.K. government adopted an explicit policy target of eliminating child poverty (as did Australia in the 1980s; the goal has not been fully attained in either country). In contrast, Australia is only now implementing such landmark programs as paid parental leave, Sure Start, the national curriculum, and school league tables. Although Australia has substantially increased investment in the early years since the early 1990s, it has relied mainly on means-tested cash transfers to parents as the mainstay of its early years' policies. Both Australia and the United Kingdom are laggards in terms of investment in early childhood education in comparison with Scandinavian countries and France. The United Kingdom invests more than Australia in early childhood services (Katz and Redmond 2009). However, in the mid-2000s, Australia was investing more in families with children *in total* than was the United Kingdom (Bradshaw, Holmes, and Redmond 2011).

It is possible that the United Kingdom performs more poorly in spite of its more targeted policy interventions because social and economic inequalities have traditionally been higher in the United Kingdom than in Australia, and because these inequalities in children's development are fundamentally resistant to policy manipulation. The differences between children from different backgrounds appear to be remarkably stable over time in both countries despite substantial changes in social policies (Blanden and Machin 2010; Leigh 2007; Redmond et al., in press), which may indicate that the most likely explanation for the differences in outcomes in the two countries lies not in the specifics of their policies, but in broader societal and economic structures. An alternative explanation is one of timing; the targeted reforms carried out in the United Kingdom have not yet had a chance to impact on the particular cohorts under study (for a more favorable picture showing narrowing gaps among school leavers, see Gregg and Macmillan 2010).

Indeed, a key difference between the two nations is the higher level of cross-sectional inequality in the United Kingdom. We could infer that the negative influence of high inequality has more of an effect on the United Kingdom than the recent policy focus on the early years. Some evidence indicates greater social segregation in schools in the United Kingdom than in Australia (Jenkins, Micklewright, and Schnepf 2008), but we must bear in mind that only 20 percent of the variation in U.K. children's PISA scores can be explained by differences between schools (OECD 2002, table A7.1).

Clearly a great deal of research remains to be done in this area. One limitation of this chapter is its focus on two domains: cognitive and socio-emotional. Our data appear to indicate that parental education may have a greater impact in the cognitive than the socioemotional domains, but this hypothesis needs to be examined in more detail. It would also be important to focus on other domains, particularly physical health. In addition, this is a comparison of two countries, so it is difficult to contextualize the differences between them. In chapter 4 of this volume, for example, Bruce Bradbury and his colleagues, using a cross-sectional analysis, found that Australia and the United Kingdom and Canada are comparatively similar in outcomes, and that the United States was the outlier, with much higher levels of inequality.

Although these findings are consistent with the overall body of research on inequality in the United Kingdom and Australia, we can only speculate here on the reasons for these differences. To obtain more confident policy recommendations we would need to examine in more detail the demographic, policy, and cultural differences between the two countries, and also look much more closely at mediating mechanisms between socioeconomic status and child outcomes.

Notes

1. Initially, it was our intention to use vocabulary scores at all waves in the LSAC (measured by the Peabody Picture Vocabulary Test) and the vocabulary assessments given to the MCS children at three and five, combined with a word reading test administered at seven. However, analysis revealed that combining the vocabulary and reading scores for the United Kingdom does not generate a consistent series, because the correlation between the scores from the two tests was very low.

2. The online appendix is available at: http://www.russellsage.org/Ermisch_et_al_OnlineAppendix.pdf.

3. Because the SDQ is measured using the same instrument in both countries, we can also compare the absolute values of the total difficulties score across countries, with results provided in online appendix table 6A.2. In summary, Australian children have a higher difficulties score on average. Differences across countries should be interpreted with care, however, because they could reflect cultural differences regarding expectations of children (Marzocchi et al. 2004).

4. Online appendix table 6A.4 shows the correlations between the standardized scores across different ages for both nations. The correlation between outcomes at different ages is roughly .5, and higher in the socioemotional dimension than among the cognitive scores. There is more stability at later ages, so figures for Australia are higher.

References

Australian Institute of Family Studies. 2010. *Growing Up in Australia: The Longitudinal Study of Australian Children Data User Guide.* Melbourne: Australian Institute of Family Studies.

Blanden, Jo, and Stephen Machin. 2010. "Intergenerational Inequality in Early Years Assessments." In *Children of the 21st Century,* edited by Shirley Dex, Kirstine Hansen, and Heather Joshi. Bristol, U.K.: Policy Press.

Bradshaw, Jonathan, John Holmes, and Gerry Redmond. 2011. "A Comparative Analysis of Generational Equity in the Australian and UK Welfare States." Presented at the SPRC Workshop on the Well-Being of Children in Australia, University of New South Wales. Sydney (April 6–7, 2011).

Carneiro, Pedro, and James Heckman. 2005. "Human Capital Policy." In *Inequality in America: What Role for Human Capital Policies?,* edited by James Heckman and Alan Krueger. Cambridge, Mass: MIT Press.

Conger, Rand D., and M. Brent Donnellan. 2007. "An Interactionist Perspective on the Socioeconomic Context of Human Development." *Annual Review of Psychology* 58(1): 175–99.

d'Addio, Anna Cristina. 2007. "Intergenerational Transmission of Disadvantage: Mobility or Immobility Across Generations?" *Social, Employment and Migration* working paper 52. Paris: OECD, Directorate for Employment, Labour and Social Affairs. Available at: http://www.oecd.org/dataoecd/27/28/38335410.pdf (accessed December 20, 2011).

Ermisch, John. 2008. "Origins of Social Immobility and Inequality: Parenting and Early Child Development." *National Institute Economic Review* 205(1): 62–71.

Esping-Andersen, Gösta. 1990. *The Three Worlds of Welfare Capitalism.* Cambridge: Polity Press.

Feinstein, Leon. 2003. "Inequality in the Early Cognitive Development of British Cohort Children in the 1970 Cohort." *Economica* 70(1): 73–77.

Feinstein, Leon, and John Bynner. 2004. "The Importance of Cognitive Development in Middle Childhood for Adulthood Socioeconomic Status, Mental Health, and Problem Behavior." *Child Development* 75(5): 1329–39.

Goodman, Robert. 1997. "The Strengths and Difficulties Questionnaire: A Research Note." *Journal of Child Psychology and Psychiatry* 38(5): 581–86.

Gregg, Paul, and Lindsey Macmillan. 2010. "Family Income, Education and Cognitive Ability in the Next Generation: Exploring Income Gradients in Education and Test Scores for Current Cohorts of Youth." *Longitudinal and Life Course Studies* 1(3): 259–80.

Hansen, Kirstine. 2010. *Millennium Cohort Study First, Second, Third and Fourth Surveys: A Guide to the Datasets,* 5th ed. London: Centre for Longitudinal Studies.

Heckman, James J., Jora Stixrud, and Sergio Urzua. 2006. "The Effects of Cognitive and Noncognitive Abilities on Labor Market Outcomes and Social Behavior." *Journal of Labor Economics* 24(3): 411–82.

Jenkins, Stephen P., John Micklewright, and Sylke Schnepf. 2008. "Social Segregation in Secondary Schools: How Does England Compare with Other Countries?" *Oxford Review of Education* 34(1): 21–37.

Jerrim, John, and Anna Vignoles. 2011. "The Use (and Misuse) of Statistics in Understanding Social Mobility: Regression to the Mean and the Cognitive Development of High Ability Children from Disadvantaged Homes." *DoQSS Working Paper* 11–01. London: University of London, Institute of Education, Department of Quantitative Social Science. Available at: http://repec.ioe. ac.uk/REPEc/pdf/qsswp1101.pdf (accessed June 14, 2011).

Katz, Ilan, and Gerry Redmond. 2009. "Family Income as a Protective Factor for Child Outcomes." In *Social Policy Review 21: Analysis and Debate in Social Policy, 2009,* edited by Kirsten Rummery, Ian Greener, and Chris Holden. Bristol, U.K.: Policy Press.

Kowaleski-Jones, Lori, and Greg Duncan. 1999. "The Structure of Achievement and Behavior Across Middle Childhood." *Child Development* 70(4): 930–43.

Leigh, Andrew. 2007. "Intergenerational Mobility in Australia." *The B.E. Journal of Economic Analysis & Policy* 7(2): Article 6. Available at: http://www.bepress.com/ bejeap/vol7/iss2/art6. doi: 10.2202/1935-1682.1781 (accessed June 14, 2011).

Marzocchi, Gian Marco, Christiane Capron, Mario Di Pietro, Enric Duran Tauleria, Michel Duyme, Alessandra Frigerio, Maria Filomena Gaspar, Helena Hamilton, Gérard Pithon, Alexandra Simões, and Carine Thérond. 2004. "The Use of the Strengths and Difficulties Questionnaire (SDQ) in Southern European Countries." *European Child & Adolescent Psychiatry* 13(suppl. 2) (July): 40–46.

Mullan, Killian, and Gerry Redmond. 2011. "Validating Income in the Longitudinal Study of Australian Children (LSAC)." Report prepared for the Australian Government Department of Families, Housing, Community Services and Indigenous Affairs. Sydney: Social Policy Research Centre.

Muris, Peter, Cor Meesters, and Frank van den Berg. 2003. "The Strengths and Difficulties Questionnaire (SDQ): Further Evidence For Its Reliability and Validity in a Community Sample of Dutch Children and Adolescents." *European Child & Adolescent Psychiatry* 12(1): 1–8.

Organisation for Economic Co-Operation and Development (OECD). 2002. *Education at a Glance.* Paris: Organisation for Economic Co-Operation and Development.

———. 2007a. "PF1: Public Spending on Family Benefits." OECD Family Database. Paris: Organisation for Economic Co-Operation and Development. Available at: http://www.oecd.org/dataoecd/55/58/38968865.xls (accessed June 20, 2011).

———. 2007b. "PF10: Public Spending on Childcare and Early Education." OECD Family Database. Paris: Organisation for Economic Co-Operation and Development. Available at: http://www.oecd.org/dataoecd/44/20/38954032.xls (accessed June 20, 2011).

———. 2008a. "Growing Unequal? Income Distribution and Poverty in OECD Countries." Paris: Organisation for Economic Co-Operation and Development.

———. 2008b. OECD Family Database. Paris: Organisation for Economic Co-Operation and Development., Directorate for Employment, Labour and Social Affairs. Available at: http://www.oecd.org/els/social/family/data base (accessed June 19, 2011).

Redmond, Gerry. 2009. "What Can Data on Educational Outcomes Reveal Regarding Australian Children's Right to Develop to their Fullest Potential." *Economic and Labour Relations Review* 20(1): 35–58.

Redmond, Gerry, Bina Gubhaju, Diana Smart, and Ilan Katz. In press. "Intergenerational Mobility in Australia: How Do Vulnerable Kids Fare?" Canberra: Australian Government Department of Families, Housing, Community Services and Indigenous Affairs, Social Policy Research Centre, University of New South Wales.

Soloff, Carol, David Lawrence, Sebastian Misson, and Robert Johnstone. 2006. "The Longitudinal Study of Australian Children: Wave 1 Weighting and Non-Response." *LSAC* technical paper 3. Melbourne: Australian Institute of Family Studies. Available at: http://www.aifs.gov.au/growingup/pubs/techpapers/tp3.pdf (accessed June 9, 2011).

Chapter 7

Early Schooling and
Later Outcomes

CHRISTELLE DUMAS AND ARNAUD LEFRANC

E DUCATIONAL POLICY is usually seen as the means *par excellence* to
foster equality of opportunity and reduce the intergenerational
transmission of inequality. Among the various policy instruments,
pre-primary schooling programs have recently received considerable
attention, notably among economists (Cunha, Heckman, and Lochner
2006). The arguments in favor of such programs are twofold. First, family background shapes inequality of individual success very early in the
life cycle, as shown, for instance, in chapter 4 of this volume. Second, the
likely existence of dynamic complementarities in the process of human
capital accumulation strongly enhances the efficiency of interventions
that occur very early in the process of skill acquisition. Indeed, preschool
programs are often thought to be able to compensate for the detrimental
influence of a disadvantaged family background, as has been argued in
the educational policy debate since at least Plato's *Republic*.

Evidence on the effect of early education programs for schooling and
labor market outcomes is much more recent and indeed rather limited.
Much has been learned recently on the effect of intensive and comprehensive intervention programs targeted at groups facing obvious learning
impediments. But despite renewed political interest in these programs
worldwide, much less is known about the impact of large-scale universal
preschooling programs. The objective of this chapter is to provide evidence on the impact of these programs on educational and labor market
outcomes in the case of France.

France offers an interesting case for assessing the impact of universal
preschool programs. Preschool education programs in France take the
form of a universal, public, free, full-fledged schooling program, with
warranted access from the age of three and possible access from age
two. Very few countries offer early childhood programs with such extensive scope, with the notable exceptions of Denmark, which is studied in

chapter 8 of this volume, and the Scandinavian countries. Furthermore, the French early childhood program strongly emphasizes child education, much more than child care, contrary to what is often found in other countries, including Denmark.

Nowadays in France, virtually all children are enrolled in preschool at the age of three and a significant share are already enrolled at the age of two. Given the current situation of full participation at the age of three, it is only possible to evaluate, from contemporary data, the effect of early preschool enrollment at the age of two, as in Jean-Paul Caille (2001) and Dominique Goux and Eric Maurin (2008). But the marginal effect of extending access to preschool by one more year, from enrollment at age three to age two, may presumably differ from the effect of extending preschool from age four to age three, which is probably closer to the policy changes that most developed countries may think of introducing. Despite an old tradition in the promotion of preschool education, the current situation of universal access mostly results from the take-up of enrollment that occurred in the 1960s and 1970s. During this period, the enrollment rate for three-year-olds rose, according to official statistics, from around 35 percent to more than 90 percent. In this chapter, we exploit this rise in enrollment to assess the impact of preschool participation.

Our main analysis estimates the impact of the time spent in preschool on a variety of short- and long-term educational and labor market outcomes. We rely on individual data covering cohorts born between the 1950s and the 1970s that provide a measure of the duration of preschool participation as well as a wealth of information on individual subsequent outcomes. We focus on assessing the impact of the age of preschool enrollment on the educational success measured by three main variables: grade repetition throughout the individual school career, test scores in secondary school, and final educational attainment. We also examine the long-term effect of preschool enrollment by measuring its impact on wages earned when adult. Given our concern for the potential impact of preschool at reducing the intergenerational transmission of socioeconomic inequality, we also estimate heterogeneous effects of preschool by family background to test for whether preschool enrollment helps in compensating for poorer family socioeconomic resources.

Because preschool participation is voluntary, it may be endogenous with respect to unobserved family characteristics that have an independent influence on individual outcomes. The direction of the resulting bias will of course depend on the type of selection. In the case of France, preschool participation was for a long time concentrated on the urban lower class, which suggests potential underestimation of the effect of preschool. We deal with selection in preschool participation in two ways. First, we rely on a control strategy that uses information on family socioeconomic status as well as school fixed-effects to capture heterogeneity in individual background. Second, we implement an instrumental variables-estimation strategy that exploits regional variation in access to preschool.

Our main findings indicate that preschool has significant and lasting positive effects and helps children succeed better in school and improve their labor market prospects. Furthermore, the benefit of preschool attendance seems to vary across social groups and is higher for children from middle and lower social groups. Consequently, preschool helps equalize opportunities across social groups and reduce the intergenerational transmission of economic advantage by helping children from worse-off socioeconomic environment catch up with their better-off classmates.

Preschool in France: Institutional Arrangement and History

Since the 1960s, France has developed the provision of preschool education within the context of a universal-access, publicly organized, free of charge schooling system.

Institutional Arrangement

Pre-elementary education in France is offered nationally within *école maternelle* (maternal school) to children between two and five years old, before they enter elementary school at the age of six. In contrast to elementary school attendance, which is compulsory, participation to pre-elementary school is voluntary.[1] Access to preschool is granted by law to all children who have reached the age of three and is in most cases free of tuition fees. Currently almost all French children attend preschool from the age of three onwards.

Preschool in France is centrally administered by the Ministry of Education and is to a very large extent offered within public schools.[2] The stated objective of école maternelle is to help children reach autonomy and acquire knowledge and skills in order to promote their readiness for elementary school.[3] To reach these goals, preschool follows a standardized and integrated curriculum, for a duration of three years. According to the official presentation, the curriculum emphasizes language acquisition, socialization to group interactions, psychomotor development, and the promotion of individual creativity and attitude towards learning.

In many ways, instruction in preschools takes place in conditions that are similar to primary education instruction. Preschool teachers are national civil servants and receive the same level of training as primary school teachers, typically a bachelor's degree level. As a consequence, preschool teachers are significantly more skilled than the average early-child-care personnel. Annual instruction time is also substantial and amounts to 864 hours, that is, six hours per day, four days a week, thirty-six weeks per year. Average

Table 7.1   Preschool Enrollment Rates

Enrollment rate at:	1969 Birth Cohort		1972 Birth Cohort		1978 Birth Cohort	
	DEPP 1980 Report	Official Statistics	DEPP 1978 Report	Official Statistics	DEPP 1989 Report	Official Statistics
Two years old	16%	25%	13%	25%	16%	35%
Three years old	54	73	61	73	69	90
Four years old	82	85	87	95	89	100

Source: Authors' compilation based on DEPP panels and official registry data (Ministère de l'éducation nationale, various years).

class size is around twenty-five children. The annual cost per pupil of pre-elementary education is €4,970, against €5,440 for primary education.[4]

Attendance at école maternelle is possible from the age of two. At present, the enrollment rate at the age of two is around 25 percent. Enrollment at the age of two depends on the availability of vacant places, and priority is given to three-year olds. The development of preschool capacity aimed at enrolling two-year-olds has been targeted at disadvantaged areas, be it for poor socioeconomic environment or geographic seclusion.

Apart from the preschool program, the public provision of early child care is much more limited and rests to a large extent on family care. For instance, 67 percent of children below the age of three are primarily taken care of by one of their parents or a relative during the day. Among children attending preschool, 84 percent are taken care of by one of their parents or a relative on Wednesdays when preschools do not operate (Ananian and Robert-Bobée 2009). Consequently, preschool education is the main alternative to family-based child care.

Participation and Historical Trends

Enrollment rates in preschools, by age and year, are presented in table 7.1. Current participation in preschool in France is very high by international standards, and almost all children age three and older attend preschool. This results from the gradual generalization of preschool enrollment between the 1960s and the 1980s.

Preschool education in France is well established. École maternelle was created in 1882, by the same law that introduced free and compulsory primary education. From the origin, it fell within the scope of intervention of the ministry of education. Its objective was to offer child care and education to working-class children and remedy the negative consequences of a deprived family environment, for intellectual and moral development. During this period, the social recruitment of preschools was selective originally and mostly concentrated among urban lower-class children. It stayed so until the 1950s.

The expansion of preschool participation occurred mainly in the 1960s and 1970s. The enrollment rates rise from 35 percent of the children age three and 65 percent of children age four, in 1960, to, respectively, 90 percent and 100 percent in 1980. By the beginning of the 1990s, virtually all children in their third year attended preschool. Historically, this expansion occurred through a general rise in preschool enrollment across all social groups and geographical areas (Prost 1981).

During the same period, the enrollment of two-year-old children also rises markedly from 10 percent to 35 percent. To some extent, this extension reflects the low provision of public child-care services. Of course, two-year-olds benefit from special programs. In principle, the instruction time for two-year-olds is similar to what it is for older children, though part of that time is devoted to rest in afternoon. Sometimes very young children can also be welcomed in specific classes.[5] As discussed, very early enrollment in preschool is concentrated heavily on disadvantaged groups. Recently, the enrollment has fallen to about 25 percent under the joint influence of the recent demographic boom of the early 2000s and the rise in the supply of day-care facilities.

Prior Research

An abundant literature has documented the largely positive impact of targeted early intervention programs (for a survey, see Barnett 1992). But whether lessons can be drawn from these targeted experiments regarding possible benefits of universal access preschool programs, such as école maternelle, is highly unlikely for at least two reasons. First, targeted interventions are usually more intensive than universal access programs. Second, model interventions are usually targeted at subpopulations whose responsiveness to the program may be unrepresentative. There are, however, relatively few evaluations of the impact of universal access preschool programs. Existing studies typically face two main challenges. The first, as in any nonexperimental setting, is the possible endogeneity of preschool enrollment vis-à-vis other family determinants of child achievement. The second is the restricted time span that often prevents assessment of the long-term impact of preschool enrollment.

For the United States, the analysis has focused mainly on the impact of kindergarten and prekindergarten programs. Because these programs are targeted at children ages four to five years old, they correspond to educational interventions that occur later than the typical maternal school enrollment in France. Katherine Magnuson, Christopher Ruhm, and Jane

Waldfogel (2007) evaluate the short-term impact of prekindergarten enrollment on primary school readiness using a control strategy. They show that preschool enrollment is positively associated with reading and mathematics readiness at the time of entry into first grade, once family characteristics are taken into account. This result is confirmed by William Gormley and Ted Gayer (2005) and by Maria Fitzpatrick (2008). Furthermore, both studies indicate a larger impact for children from disadvantaged or minority backgrounds. However, the results of Magnuson and her colleagues (2007) also suggest that prekindergarten tends to be associated with behavioral problems and that the positive academic impact may quickly dissipate. Elizabeth Cascio (2009) uses census data to examine the long-term impact of the adoption of universal kindergarten by several U.S. states in the 1960s and the 1970s. She finds no effect of kindergarten enrollment on long-term labor market outcomes. As for educational outcomes, the only positive influence of kindergarten is on the probability of dropping out of high school. Furthermore, her estimates indicate that only white children benefit from kindergarten. The lack of effect for black children may reflect the substitution of kindergarten for higher intensity programs such as Head Start. Last, Todd Elder and Darren Lubotsky (2009) provide related evidence on the negative effect of delayed entrance into kindergarten on children's attainment.

Several papers have documented the impact of preschool enrollment in a variety of other countries. Estimates obtained for developing countries indicate large and lasting effects of preschool enrollment. Samuel Berlinski, Sebastian Galiani, and Paul Gertler (2009) find that one year of preschool raises third grade test scores by about one-fourth of a standard deviation. Berlinski, Galiani, and Manacorda (2008) suggest that the effect of preschool attendance may increase as children grow older, resulting in a sizeable rise in school enrollment by age fifteen. For developed countries, several studies also find positive short- and long-term effects. Edwin Leuven and his colleagues (2010) find a positive short-term effect of early enrollment in preschool in the Netherlands but only for children from disadvantaged families.[6] Tarjei Havnes and Magne Mogstad (2009) find that the development of child care for children ages three to six that occurred in Norway in the 1970s had strong positive effects on children's educational attainment and labor market participation. For Great Britain, Alissa Goodman and Barbara Sianesi (2005) reach a similar conclusion and find significant positive effects of precompulsory education on long-term educational and labor market outcomes. Last, Philipp Bauer and Regina Riphahn (2009) study the impact of preschool extension in Swiss cantons from the perspective of educational mobility and show that the take-up of preschool enrollment fosters intergenerational educational mobility. In other terms, children from disadvantaged family backgrounds seem to benefit more from preschool enrollment.

Last, a limited number of studies have examined the impact of preschool participation in France. The focus of our study is close to that of Goux and Maurin (2008) and Caille (2001). Caille examines the effect of early preschool enrollment on primary school outcomes among children born in the early 1990s. He finds that preschool participation significantly reduces the probability of grade retention, once family characteristics are controlled for. He also indicates significant heterogeneity, with children from disadvantaged families benefiting more from preschool. Goux and Maurin examine the impact of preschool enrollment on test scores in primary school and later school dropout rate for children born in the early 1980s, using a difference-in-difference approach. In contrast to Caille, they find no significant effect of early preschool enrollment. In both cases, it should be noted that the analysis conducted in these two papers essentially amounts to estimate the effect of preschool enrollment at age two instead of age three, because the cohorts studied have an enrollment rate at age three that is close to 100 percent. In contrast, we are able to study the impact of preschool enrollment at different ages, in particular around age four, which in many respects comes closer to policy objectives discussed in most countries.

Data

This chapter makes use of several data sets. This section describes the information available in each of them, which is also summarized in table 7.2, and discusses its quality.

Data Sets

The analysis relies on two main data sources. The first is a set of panel data sets, known as the DEPP panels, that have been collected by the French Ministry of Education and follow French pupils over the course of their school years. These panels start following individuals either in primary school or in secondary school, depending on the cohort. We use three cohorts of these panels. The first two come from the secondary school panels. They sample pupils at the beginning of secondary education (sixth graders) in two years, 1980 and 1989, and follow them for about twelve years. The third cohort comes from the primary school panels. It samples pupils who were enrolled in first grade in 1978 and follows them over seven years. Each wave surveys about 21,000 individuals, but the sampling scheme varies by survey.[7] These panels include detailed information on schooling careers (grade, tracks, school identifier), together with assessments of individual achievement at various points. Most data sets include a rough description of family background.

Table 7.2   Datasets and Variables

Variables	DEPP			FQP
	1969	1972	1978	
Age of entry in preschool	x	x	x	
Duration of preschool	x	x	x	x
Repetitions in primary school	x	x	x	x
Repetitions in secondary school	x		x	x
Test scores in sixth grade			x	
High school graduation	x		x	x
Wage				x
Gender	x	x	x	x
Number of siblings	x	x	x	x
Rank among siblings	x	x	x	x
Parental occupation	x	x	x	x
Parental education			x	x
Department of birth	x	x	x	x

Source: Authors' compilation based on DEPP panels (Ministère do l'éducation nationale, various years) and FQP survey (INSEE 1993).
Note: The figures for the DEPP panels represent the year of birth cohort and not the year of the survey.

Because most children enter primary school the year they turn six and secondary school the year they turn eleven, our surveys mostly correspond to birth cohorts 1969, 1972, and 1978, although some children may also come from adjacent cohort because of delayed or anticipated school entry or grade repetition. We nevertheless refer to each of the three waves as the 1969, 1972, and 1978 cohorts. Given the timing of preschool expansion, these correspond to cohorts that exhibit large variations across individuals in the exposure to pre-primary education, as shown in figure 7.1.

Our second data set is the FQP (Formation, Qualification, Profession—that is, education, training, occupation) survey, a labor force survey collected by the French national statistical agency. The population sampled is the French population between twenty and sixty-five years old. The data focuses on three main dimensions: current labor market outcomes (employment status, job characteristics, earnings); family background; and schooling history (yearly calendar for the entire schooling period from primary to tertiary education, including detailed information on class level, tracks specialization, and class repetition). We use the 1993 wave that provides information on preschool attendance. In the analysis of the impact of preschool participation on educational and labor market outcomes, we focus on cohorts born between 1950 and 1973, which corresponds, again, to the expansion of preschool enrollment.

Figure 7.1   Variations in Exposure to Pre-Primary Education

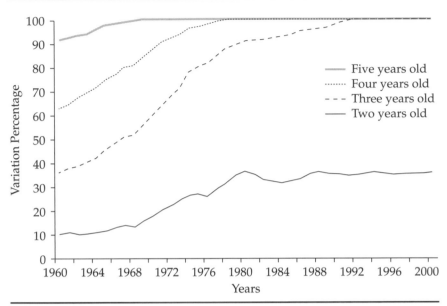

Source: Authors' calculations based on French ministry of education data (Ministère de l'éducation nationale 2001).

Preschool Participation

Both data sets provide information of the duration of exposure to preschool. It is of course crucial for our analysis to rely on accurate information regarding this variable.

The information on preschool participation varies between the two data sources. In the DEPP panels, preschool experience is reported by the principal of the school attended in the first interview year. In the primary school panel (1972 cohort), the information is usually made available to the school principal by the principal of the preschool in which the pupil was enrolled. In the secondary school panels (1969 and 1978 cohorts), school principals typically obtain this piece of information from the pupils' parents. In both cases, the information reported is the duration of preschool and the age when the pupil started attending preschool. In the FQP survey, preschool participation is reported at the time of the survey. Respondents are asked to report whether they attended preschool at all and the duration of preschool participation.

To assess the quality of our preschool participation data, in table 7.1 we compare the enrollment rates computed from the DEPP surveys with the official enrollment rates published by the ministry of education.

Figure 7.2   Distribution of Preschool Duration

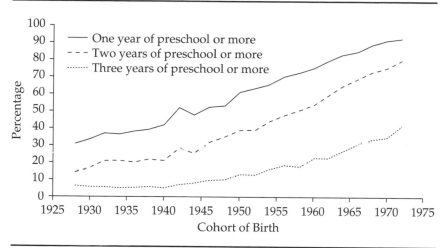

Source: Authors' calculation.

Enrollment rates computed from the 1972 cohort fall short of the official statistics by about 10 percentage points. For the secondary school panels, the gap can be larger but remains lower than 20 percentage points. In fact, official enrollment rates are notoriously overestimated.[8] This occurs for two main reasons. First, the official enrollment rates are based on the number of children registered in preschool. This number may differ from actual enrollment; children may enter after the beginning of the school year or attend part time, for example. Second, although the number of registered pupils is directly observed, the total number of children of a given age is estimated in the official statistics, which represent another source of error. As a consequence, official enrollment rates can sometimes be above 100 percent. Overall, the quality of information contained in the primary school panel is good and the information from the secondary school panels is not too far off the mark: the lower enrollment rate found in the DEPP panel, which reflects reported effective preschool experience, should not be over interpreted.

Figure 7.2 shows the distribution of preschool duration by birth cohort, computed from the FQP surveys. The survey reports markedly lower enrollment rates than the ones published in official statistics and reported in figure 7.1. For instance, among children born in 1973, 40 percent report having attended preschool for three years of more, but the official enrollment rate at the age of three (that is, 1976) for this cohort is about 80 percent. This suggests important measurement error and systematic underreporting of

Table 7.3   **Descriptive Statistics**

	DEPP Panels	FQP Survey
Number of repetitions at age eleven	0.29	.34
Number of repetitions at age sixteen	0.81	.92
Some degree (indicator)		.73
Baccalauréat or more (indicator)	0.58	.33
Monthly wage (in euros 1993)		1262.49
First grade repetition (indicator)	0.12	
Second grade repetition (indicator)	0.06	
Third grade repetition (indicator)	0.06	
Fourth grade repetition (indicator)	0.06	
Fifth grade repetition (indicator)	0.07	

Source: Authors' compilation based on DEPP panels (Ministère de l'éducation nationale, various years) and FQP surveys (INSEE 1993).

preschool participation, which is not particularly surprising given that the survey information is retrospective, collected in adulthood and relative to the early school experience. At the same time, beyond the overall underestimation of enrollment, the data establish sizeable differences across cohorts in their exposure to preschool, which suggests that, despite internal errors, the FQP records of preschool participation may be informative of actual exposure.

Educational and Labor Market Outcomes

To assess the impact of preschool enrollment on later outcomes, our data provide useful information on both schooling and labor market experience in adulthood. We consider two main schooling outcomes: the number of grade repetitions and the highest degree attained. The number of repetitions can be built using the year-by-year calendar of school enrollment and grade participation that is available in both the DEPP panels and the FQP surveys. In the main analysis, we focus on the number of repetitions at age eleven and age sixteen. Regarding the highest completed degree, we distinguish two distinct variables. The first is an indicator for having passed the baccalauréat, the qualification taken at the end of secondary education, and corresponds, especially among older cohorts, to rather high levels of education. In addition, the baccalauréat is the key qualification for university admittance. The second variable is an indicator for having passed at least one secondary education degree, whether general or vocational. As for the labor market outcomes, we focus on the monthly wage earned on the current job at the survey date.

Table 7.3 presents descriptive statistics on our main variables of interest. It emphasizes two aspects of the French educational system that should be kept in mind. The first one is the relatively high rate of grade repetition. For instance, in the FQP survey, for cohorts born between 1950 and 1973, 30 percent of the respondents report having repeated at least once before age eleven and 64 percent before age sixteen. Multiple repetitions are frequent and explain the even higher average number of years repeated reported in the table. Furthermore, repetition is a good predictor of later schooling success (or failure), which makes it an interesting outcome to study. For example, having repeated in primary school is associated with a .22 points lower rate of high school graduation and .14 log points lower annual earnings, conditional on parental characteristics (for a complementary analysis of grade repetition in other countries, see chapter 14, this volume). Second, the share of the population with a baccalauréat is relatively small with respect to many countries. In the FQP sample, only 33 percent have a baccalauréat. In the younger cohorts surveyed in the DEPP panels, about 60 percent do.

Main Results

We now turn to the analysis of the effect of preschool enrollment on later outcomes. Our objective is to assess the impact of the duration of preschool participation on these outcomes. This impact is likely to depend on the timing of intervention, given that children's responsiveness to preschool education is likely to change very quickly during early childhood. Similarly, there is no reason to expect the returns to one additional year of preschool education to be constant and independent of previous preschool enrollment. For these reasons, for each of our surveys, we regress educational and labor market outcomes on a set of dummy variables that indicate different levels of preschool participation.

The information on preschool participation varies between our two surveys. For the DEPP panel, the age of entry in preschool is available and will be used as the key explanatory variable. For the FQP survey, only the actual duration of preschool is available. In assessing the benefits of early intervention, the age of entry in preschool, rather than the duration, is probably the most relevant measure. In fact, duration may be endogenous because it depends on achievement in preschool. For instance, one benefit of early preschool enrollment may be early entry to primary school, and, similarly, a penalty of delayed enrollment may be delayed entry to primary school. However, both early and delayed primary school enrollment are rare events.

One of the problems for assessing the impact of preschool on later outcomes is that preschool participation is likely to be correlated with family characteristics that have an independent effect on individual success. Our first strategy is to control for as much information on family characteristics as possible given the information available in our survey. Of course, the validity of this strategy depends on the quality of our controls. Hence, we perform several robustness checks on subsamples of our data that provide more detailed information on family characteristics. Next, to account for possible endogeneity biases arising from omitted variable or measurement errors, we implement an instrumentation strategy based on the temporal variation within regions in access to preschool to wipe out any endogeneity attributable to household idiosyncrasies. In both cases, the results do not differ markedly from those obtained with our base specification.

Base Specification

In both surveys, we are able to control for the following characteristics: the father's occupational group (seven-level classification), family composition (number of siblings and birth rank), as well as cohort and regional fixed effects.[9] There are a number of discrepancies between DEPP and FQP specifications regarding data availability. In DEPP, we have detailed information on the exact month of entry in preschool and month of birth, so we are able to compute precisely and to control for the additional months spent in preschool. In the FQP survey, we also have detailed information on mother's education and therefore control for it. Regional variation is taken into account using the *département* of birth in FQP and school regional district in DEPP. Départements correspond to a geographical and administrative division. There are twenty-six school regional districts and ninety-five départements in metropolitan France.

Table 7.4, panel A, shows the effect of entering preschool at age two or four, rather than at age three, on later schooling outcomes. The effect of earlier enrollment in preschool is always positive. Delaying preschool enrollment by one year leads to a higher occurrence of repetitions: the increase is 0.09 year of delay at age eleven and 0.11 at age sixteen. This represents between one-fourth and one-third of mean repetition at these ages. The 1978 cohort also provides individual test scores at the entry into sixth grade and shows that delayed preschool enrollment leads to test scores that are 0.10 of a standard deviation lower. Last, children with late enrollment also have a lower probability of graduating from high school (–4 percentage points). All in all, this indicates that the effects of preschool participation are long lasting.

Panel B provides comparable estimates of preschool effects using the FQP data set. It can be seen that staying one more year in preschool reduces repetitions, increases the probability of leaving school with a secondary degree (+2 percentage points), and increases wage earnings when adult by 3 percent. However, the estimates are slightly lower than what is obtained in panel A. These lower values could reflect the incidence of an attenuation bias arising from measurement error in the FQP data, as documented in the previous section.

Table 7.4   Effect of Preschool in Base Specification

	Number of Repetitions at Eleven	Test Score in Sixth Grade	Number of Repetitions at Sixteen	Some Degree	Graduate from High School	Monthly Wage
Panel A. DEPP: effect of age of entry						
Age two at entry	−0.0938***	0.0672**	−0.142***		0.0287***	
	(0.0094)	(0.0266)	(0.0157)		(0.0101)	
Age three at entry	REF					
Age four at entry	0.0843***	−0.105***	0.106***		−0.0405***	
	(0.0071)	(0.0241)	(0.0125)		(0.0079)	
Observations	51255	9607	29079		29581	
Model	OLS	OLS	OLS		probit	
Panel B. FQP: effect of preschool duration						
Less than one year of preschool	REF					
Two years of preschool	−0.0366**		−0.0663***	0.0196*	−0.0106	0.0298**
	(0.0145)		(0.0239)	(0.0109)	(0.0134)	(0.0141)
Three years of preschool	−0.0680***		−0.0988***	0.0431***	0.0270*	0.0460***
	(0.0165)		(0.0271)	(0.0121)	(0.0153)	(0.0161)
Observations	8672		8672	8750	8761	5843
Model	OLS		OLS	probit	probit	OLS

Source: Authors' calculations based on DEPP panels (Ministère de l'éducation nationale, various years) and FQP survey (INSEE 1993).
Note: Coefficients reported are marginal effects and standard errors in parentheses. Panel A: Interpretation of the first coefficient: starting preschool at age two rather than age three decreases the number of repetitions at age eleven by 0.0938. Panel B: Interpretation of the first coefficient: staying in preschool two years rather than one decreases the number of repetitions at age eleven by 0.0366. Control variables include: father's occupational group, number of siblings, rank among them, and cohorts fixed effects; school districts fixed effects are included in panel A, a birth département fixed effects and education of the parents are included in panel E.
***$p < .01$; **$p < .05$; *$p < .10$

Last, in the case of DEPP, the table seems consistent with a linear effect of preschool duration on later outcomes. For instance, in panel A, the coefficients on the dummies for enrollment at two and at four are often comparable in absolute value. We proceed with a linear specification for the remainder of the chapter.

Additional Controls and Fixed-Effects Estimation

One limitation of these estimates is that they rely on a rather coarse description of family background. As a consequence, the association between preschool duration and individual outcomes discussed so far may partly reflect the confounding influence of unmeasured family characteristics. This is especially true for the DEPP panels where the major conditioning variable available in all waves is father's occupation. In this section, we perform two robustness checks using subsamples of our data. First, we add information on parents' education and then school fixed effects. Results are presented in table 7.5.

Parental education is a likely source of bias because parents' education might affect both their preferences regarding preschool and their child's later outcomes. Parental education is available for DEPP 1989, and we therefore restrict the analysis to this subsample to check that the results are robust to the inclusion of this additional variable. It turns out that this barely changes anything, given that we were already controlling for parental occupation. The decrease in the estimate is notable only for test scores (see change from column 1 to 2 in table 7.5). This suggests that little household heterogeneity to control for remains in these estimations.

Other variables are likely to jointly affect early schooling decisions and later schooling outcomes. These may include unobservable aspects of the family background or the broader socioeconomic environment as well as the quality of schooling infrastructures. In the 1980 DEPP panel, sampled children were clustered at the level of the school they attended in sixth grade, which depends on their residence at that time.[10] Controlling for school fixed effects is therefore a good way to control for most of the heterogeneity in the child's socioeconomic environment and for most of the heterogeneity in the quantity and quality of school supply the child faces. This will lead to unbiased estimates of the effect of preschool, under the assumption that preschool enrollment is exogenous within catchment areas. In table 7.6, we therefore compare column 4, with schools fixed effects, to column 3, without fixed effects but on the same subsample. Results indicate that controlling for schools effects leads to a systematic increase in the preschool effect. This suggests that a negative correlation between preschool openings and the socioeconomic environment, which is consistent with the evidence that preschools were at first intended for worse-off urban workers' children. As a consequence, neglecting this for

Table 7.5 Effect of Preschool: Robustness Checks

Dependent variable	Subsample (1)	With Parental Education (2)	Subsample (3)	With Schools Effects (4)	Subsample (5)	Instrumentation (6)
Test score at age eleven	-0.0700***	-0.0544***				
	(0.0108)	(0.0105)				
Repetitions at age eleven	0.123***	0.114***	0.0548***	0.0681***	0.0951***	0.00615
	(0.00427)	(0.00424)	(0.00540)	(0.00618)	(0.00335)	(0.0239)
Repetitions at age sixteen	0.112***	0.0998***	0.0815***	0.102***	0.0974***	0.0764*
	(0.00740)	(0.00723)	(0.00881)	(0.0102)	(0.00566)	(0.0446)
High school graduation	-0.0268***	-0.0224***	-0.0417***	-0.0430***	-0.0413***	-0.148**
	(0.00441)	(0.00439)	(0.00425)	(0.00491)	(0.00356)	(0.0698)
Parental education	No	Yes	No	Yes	No	Yes
Schools fixed effects				Yes		Yes
Instrumentation						Yes
Birth cohorts	78 (and 72)	78 (and 72)	69	69	59 (and 72)	69 (and 72)

Source: Authors' calculations based on DEPP panels (Ministère de l'éducation nationale, various years).

Notes: The effect of preschool is assumed to be linear in the age of entry. Coefficients reported are marginal effects of starting one year later, standard errors in parentheses. Interpretation: entering preschool one year later decreases test score by 0.07 of a standard deviation without controlling for parental education and by 0.0544 of a standard deviation when controlling for it. Control variables include: father's occupational group, number of siblings, rank among them, cohorts fixed effects, and school districts fixed effects. Column (2) adds parental education and has to be compared to column (1), which is on the same sample. Column (4) adds schools fixed effects and has to be compared with column (3). Column (6) instruments for age of entry in preschool and has to be compared with column (5). All models are OLS except for high school graduation, estimated by a probit. The number of observations for column (2) ranges from 9607 for the tests to 32867 for repetitions at age eleven; the number of observations in column (4) ranges from 13132 for repetitions at 16 to 18563 for repetitions at age eleven; the number of observations in column (6) ranges from 6799 for repetitions at 16 to 21710 for repetitions at age eleven.

***p < .01; **p < .05; *p < .10

Table 7.6   Dynamics: Effect of Preschool on Probability of Repeating
Each Grade

	First Grade	Second Grade	Third Grade	Fourth Grade	Fifth Grade
Age of entry in preschool	0.0248*** (0.00156)	0.00750*** (0.00116)	0.00729*** (0.00115)	0.00727*** (0.00123)	0.00559*** (0.00130)

Source: Authors' calculations based on DEPP panels (Ministère de l'éducation nationale, various years).
Notes: Coefficients reported are marginal effects of starting one year later, standard errors in parentheses. Interpretation: entering one year later in preschool increases by 2.48 percentage points the probability of repeating first grade of primary school. Control variables include: father's occupational group, number of siblings, rank among them, cohorts fixed effects, and school districts fixed effects. All models are probits.
***$p < .01$; **$p < .05$; *$p < .10$

the other waves means that we estimate only a lower bound of the impact of preschool on later outcomes. Classical measurement error is another reason we expect our estimate to be a lower bound.

Instrumental Variable Estimation

Last, we check that when instrumenting preschool attendance, we find consistent results. Our identification strategy relies on the variation in access to preschool during the 1970s within regions. Municipalities have benefitted from openings of preschool classes during the 1960s and 1970s at different rates, and this translated into different preschool participation at the municipal level and also at the level of the départements. Controlling for cohort and school district, we instrument age of entry in preschool by the average age of entry in a given département for a given cohort. The assumption is therefore that temporal variation within départements in average access to preschool is not related to temporal variation in schooling or labor market outcomes beside any effect preschool may have on these outcomes. Given the massive increase in preschool supply that occurred in the 1960s and 1970s, we expect that the variation is mainly supply-side driven: the number of public preschool classes increased from 19,641 in 1958, to 31,880 in 1968, and 51,830 in 1976. However, we can not rule out that changes in the population objectives (in particular, with respect to children's schooling as well as female labor supply) could also have occurred in this same period. Results are provided in column 6 of table 7.5. Estimates tend to be lower than those obtained in the base specification (see column 5), but we identify significant and positive effects of preschool and we systematically fail to reject exogeneity,[11] which is consistent with the view that access to preschool has increased regardless of child, parent, school, and environment characteristics.

Complementary Results

Beyond the estimation of the mean impact of preschool enrollment, two additional questions may arise. The first pertains to the dynamics of the impact of preschool enrollment. To some extent, previous research suggests that the effect of preschool participation may be short lived. This view is not supported by our estimates. But when the effects are persistent, the persistence needs to be further investigated. Does preschool provide a one-shot advantage very early during the school year or does it make children more likely to succeed at each subsequent step of their schooling career, and even beyond, in the labor market?

The second question consists in understanding who benefits the most from preschool. Does preschool affect success independently of family background? Does it mostly help remedy the negative impact of a disadvantaged family environment and primarily benefit the most disadvantaged children? In a context where the intergenerational transmission of inequalities tends to widen when progressing through education levels, it is important to understand whether a public policy such as universal preschool can really help disadvantaged children catch up with better-off children. Figure 7.3 summarizes the evolution of odds ratios between children from better-off and worse-off families at different stages of their school careers. The light grey bars evaluate the mobility at the lowest end of the parental education distribution, and the dark grey bars provide the same figures for the upper end of the distribution. It appears that the intergenerational transmission of inequality increases through education levels but much more for the upper end of the distribution: children who will manage to join the elite come from the elite. If one compares the life chances using odds ratios, it appears that the probability that a child from an advantaged background graduates from high school and at the same time, a child from a disadvantaged background fails, is six times as large as the probability of the opposite situation, where the advantaged child fails and the disadvantaged one succeeds. The odds ratio was only about four (which is really high) for determining whether they entered early in primary school.

Dynamics of Preschool Advantage

To assess the dynamics of the effect of preschool participation, we first focus on the timing of grade repetition in primary schools. The reason for focusing on primary school is that information is available in all waves of the DEPP panels. Table 7.6 provides the marginal effects of entering preschool one

Figure 7.3   Odds Ratios Between Children Through Education Levels

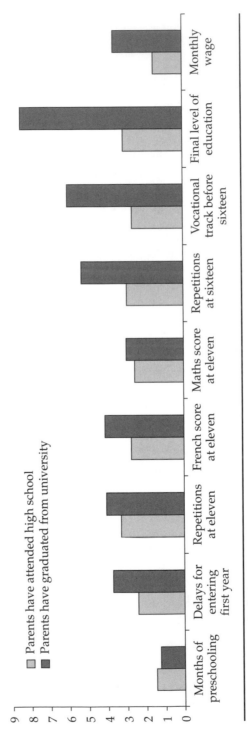

Source: Authors' calculations.

Table 7.7   Dynamics: Effect of Preschool on Monthly Wage

	Monthly Wage	
Less than one year of preschool	REF	
Two years of preschool	0.0298**	0.0321**
	(0.0141)	(0.0130)
Three years of preschool	0.0460***	0.0361**
	(0.0161)	(0.0149)
Education level	no	yes

Source: Authors' calculations based on FQP survey (INSEE 1993).
Notes: Coefficients are marginal effects. Standard errors in parentheses. Interpretation: having attended preschool for two years rather than one increases by 2.98 percent one's monthly wage.
***$p < .01$; **$p < .05$; *$p < .10$

year later on the probability of repeating each grade. We see that the largest effect occurs for the first grade: one more year of preschool reduces by 2 percentage points the probability of repeating first grade. However, even if the effect is approximately half as much for higher grades, it persists and is significantly different from zero. Preschool seems to help individuals not only when they are very young but also later on.

The persistence of preschool enrollment effects is best illustrated by our results on the positive impact of preschool exposure on subsequent wages. The channel through which preschool affects labor market needs to be investigated. The question is whether all the effect runs through higher educational attainment or whether an independent residual effect remains once educational outcomes have been taken into account. Table 7.7 compares estimates of the impact of preschool on monthly wage without controlling for final level of education (column 1) and with such a control (column 2). It is striking to see that even though the coefficient for three years of preschool decreases a bit, the order of magnitude of the effect remains the same. Preschool has an effect on wage earnings in addition to the effect it has through education. This could reflect the acquisition of noncognitive skills that are rewarded on the labor market (for a deeper discussion on the returns to noncognitive skills in the labor market, see chapter 3, this volume).

Heterogeneity in the Effect of Preschool

To assess the heterogeneity in the effect of preschool, we interact our measures of preschool participation with characteristics of the family background. We distinguish three social groups on the basis of the father's occupation: children of farmers or manual workers; children of nonmanual workers, lower-grade professionals, and artisans; and children of

Table 7.8   Descriptive Statistics by Socioeconomic Group

	Socioeconomic Group 1	Socioeconomic Group 2	Socioeconomic Group 3
Number of repetitions at age eleven	0.44	0.22	−0.01
Number of repetitions at age sixteen	1.03	0.78	0.33
Test score (roughly at age eleven)	5.11	5.51	5.96
Some degree (indicator)	0.64	0.83	0.93
Baccalauréat or more (indicator)	0.46	0.61	0.85
Monthly wage (in euros 1993)	1,153.94	1,340.69	1,633.66

Source: Authors' calculations based on DEPP panels (Ministère de l'éducation nationale, various years) and FQP survey (INSEE 1993).

higher-grade professionals. Table 7.8 shows that indeed children's schooling outcomes vary by socioeconomic group. Table 7.9 provides estimates for preschool interacted with these dummies. Our main explanatory variable is age of entry for the DEPP data and whether the child attended preschool for two years at least for the FQP data. The reference category is the second social group. As a consequence, the coefficient for the preschool variable measures the effect of preschool for children in the second group, and the interacted variables give the differential effect when the child belongs to another social group.

The results indicate significant heterogeneity in the effect of preschool exposure. The children of higher-grade professionals systematically get lower returns to preschool than the reference category—that is, the children of non-manual workers, lower-grade professionals, and artisans. In fact, the global effect of preschool for the children of higher-grade professionals is not significantly different from zero. The exception is for test scores, where all groups benefit from preschool in the same way. Manual workers' and farmers' children gain as much as the reference category from preschool: in most of the specifications, the coefficient in the second line is not significantly different from zero. As a consequence, preschool is an intervention that tends to close the gap between children from lower and upper social groups and therefore plays a role in reducing intergenerational transmission of inequalities.

To get a grasp of the inequality reduction effect of preschool, it may be useful to compare for each subgroup the impact of preschool attendance with the overall advantage or disadvantage of each category in

Table 7.9 Heterogenous Effects

Panel A. DEPP: age of entry

	First Grade	Second Grade	Third Grade	Fourth Grade	Fifth Grade	Test Score	High School Graduation
Age of entry	0.0208***	0.0067***	0.0061***	0.0068***	0.0062***	−0.0754***	−0.0399***
	(0.0028)	(0.0017)	(0.0017)	(0.0018)	(0.0018)	(0.0168)	(0.0039)
Age of entry × socioeconomic group 1	−0.0040	−0.0025	−0.0011	−0.0043	−0.0069***	0.00855	0.0093
	(0.0037)	(0.0027)	(0.0026)	(0.0030)	(0.0032)	(0.0230)	(0.0077)
Age of entry × socioeconomic group 3	−0.0249***	−0.0065**	−0.0054*	−0.0110***	−0.0049*	0.0226	0.0243***
	(0.0045)	(0.0030)	(0.0030)	(0.0035)	(0.0033)	(0.0344)	(0.0084)

Panel B. FQP: preschool duration

	Monthly Wage
At least two years	0.0457**
	(0.0204)
At least two years × socioeconomic group 1	−0.00263
	(0.0261)
At least two years × socioeconomic group 3	−0.0998**
	(0.0470)

Source: Authors' calculations based on DEPP panels (Ministère de l'éducation nationale, various years) and FQP survey (INSEE 1993).
Notes: Coefficients reported are marginal effects and standard errors in parentheses. Interpretation: entering preschool one year later increases probability to repeat first grade of primary school by 2.08 percent for children belonging to socioeconomic group (SG) 2. For children in SG 1, this effect is lower by 0.4 percent. SG equals 1 for farmers' and manuals workers' children; 2 for non-manual workers', lower-grade professionals', and artisans' children; 3 for higher-grade professionals' children.
***p < .01; **p < .05; *p < .10

terms of outcomes. Let us quantify this with some examples. Regarding the probability of repeating first grade: preschool has the same effect for children from the lower social group and for those from the middle one. As a consequence, universal preschool cannot close the gap between the two groups. However, it can be computed that an additional year of pre-school offered to children from the lower social group and not to children from the middle social group would compensate for one-third of the gap between the two groups in terms of grade retention. In addition, given that preschool does not affect outcomes of children from the better-off social group, it does reduce inequalities between groups. For instance, we compute that one year of preschool compensates children from the middle (or the lower) social group by one-third (or one-sixth) of the effect of their origin, compared with children from the higher social group. This exercise can be performed for all the variables under study. We find that the reduction in inequality between social groups of origin brought by pre-school diminishes for later schooling outcomes. For instance, one additional year of preschool compensates for one-tenth of the gap between the middle and lower social groups when it comes to the probability of graduating from high school. For wages, the positive effect of having attended preschool at least two years makes up for about one-fourth of the wage gap between the middle social group and the upper group but only 8 percent of the gap between the lower and the upper social group.

Conclusion

We find evidence that preschool has significant and lasting positive effects and helps children succeed in school and secure higher wages in the labor market. The effects on school performance are observed at different ages and through a variety of outcomes (number of repetitions, test scores, diplomas). Identification of long-lasting effects contradicts the results of Magnuson and her colleagues (2007) for the United States. More precisely, preschool does not provide a one-shot advantage but, rather, makes children more likely to succeed at each step of their schooling career and in the labor market. This suggests that this early intervention manages to affect more than just the cognitive level of the children. Unfortunately, the data do not allow us to identify what changes for the children who have attended preschool. Are they more able to concentrate? Have they developed social skills? Do they assimilate rules more easily? The answer is probably a mix of these mechanisms, but is a matter for future research to explore.

Another key result is that the effect is not quite the same between social groups: it is almost entirely driven by children from middle and lower social classes; those from upper social groups gain hardly anything from preschool, but do not suffer from it either.[12]

These results tend to confirm that early interventions can foster both equity and efficiency: preschool prepares children for primary schooling but also promotes equal opportunity by helping children from a disadvantaged socioeconomic environment catch up with their more affluent classmates. By comparison, an analysis of intergenerational transmission of inequalities in France shows that trajectories from children with different socioeconomic backgrounds tend to diverge. This suggests that, when progressing through education levels, school is less and less able to compensate for the inequalities in background that the children face. An equalizing intervention later in the life cycle is therefore likely to be more expensive and would not benefit the children for as long as preschool does. In the end, preschool extension may have contributed to the fall in earnings inequality observed in France over the last few decades, although one could also object that the universal scope of preschool programs in France may also have diverted resources from the least privileged children. This connection should be investigated in further research.

We are grateful to Jean-Paul Caille for his help in accessing and using the DEPP panel data and to Gisèle Rousseau and Jocelyne Sourget for useful discussions. This research received financial support from the Russell Sage Foundation and from the French National Research Agency under the grant TRANSINEQ (ANR-08-JCJC-0098-01).

Notes

1. Elementary school attendance is compulsory from the beginning of the academic year that starts in the (calendar) year in which a child turns six years old.
2. Around 20 percent of children attend private preschools.
3. Bulletin officiel de l'éducation nationale, hors série no 3, juin 2008.
4. Ministère de l'éducation nationale, Repères et références statistiques, 2009.
5. These classes are denoted *très petite section* (very young section) and are added to the usual three-sections division: petite section, moyenne section, grande section (young section, middle section, old section).
6. The outcome considered is age-six test scores.
7. The 1978 primary school panel is a random sample of all children enrolled in first grade in 1978. The 1980 secondary school panel consists of a stratified sample of high schools, within which sixth graders are uniformly sampled at the rate of one-eighth. The 1989 secondary school includes all sixth graders of all high schools who were born on the fifth of any given month.
8. Oral communication with French Ministry of Education official.
9. In most of the analysis based on the DEPP data, we pool the three surveys. A cohort is defined as all children entering the survey in a given wave. We refer

to them by the most common year of birth in this cohort, that is, the year of birth of those who haven't repeated a grade.

10. The sampling scheme differs in other waves. For this reason, they could not be used in the fixed effect approach, as the number of observations per school was much smaller. See note 7.

11. The instrument is highly significant for the first stage regression, and we do not face a weak instrument issue.

12. Upper social groups benefit from preschool because the cost for child care is close to zero; from that point of view, they probably benefit even more than the other social groups from preschool since their (implicit) cost for child care is expected to be higher (they have a higher opportunity cost of time).

References

Ananian, Sévane, and Isabelle Robert-Bobée. 2009. "Modes de garde et d'accueil des enfants de moins de 6 ans en 2007." *Etudes et Résultats* 678: 1–8.

Barnett, W. Steven. 1992. "Benefits of Compensatory Preschool Education." *Journal of Human Resources* 27(2): 279–312.

Bauer, Philipp C., and Regina T. Riphahn. 2009. "Age at School Entry and Intergenerational Educational Mobility." IZA discussion paper 3977. Bonn: Institute for the Study of Labor.

Berlinski, Samuel, Sebastian Galiani, and Paul Gertler. 2009. "The Effect of Pre-Primary Education on Primary School Performance." *Journal of Public Economics* 93(1–2): 219–34.

Berlinski, Samuel, Sebastian Galiani, and Marco Manacorda. 2008. "Giving Children a Better Start: Preschool Attendance and School-Age Profiles." *Journal of Public Economics* 92(5–6): 1416–440.

Caille, Jean-Paul. 2001. "Scolarisation à 2 ans et réussite de la carrière scolaire au début de l'école élémentaire." *Education et Formations* 60: 7–18.

Cascio, Elizabeth U. 2009. "Do Investments in Universal Early Education Pay Off? Long-Term Effects of Introducing Kindergartens into Public Schools." *NBER* working paper 14951. Cambridge, Mass.: National Bureau of Economic Research.

Cunha, Flavio, James J. Heckman, and Lance Lochner. 2006. "Interpreting the Evidence on Life Cycle Skill Formation." In *Handbook of the Economics of Education*, vol. 1. Philadelphia: Elsevier.

Elder, Todd E., and Darren H. Lubotsky. 2009. "Kindergarten Entrance Age and Children's Achievement: Impacts of State Policies, Family Background, and Peers." *Journal of Human Resources* 44(3): 641–83.

Fitzpatrick, Maria D. 2008. "Starting School at Four: The Effect of Universal Pre-Kindergarten on Children's Academic Achievement." *The B.E. Journal of Economic Analysis and Policy* 8(1): 46.

Goodman, Alissa, and Barbara Sianesi. 2005. "Early Education and Children's Outcomes: Low Long Do the Impacts Last?" *Fiscal Studies* 26(4): 513–48.

Gormley, William T., and Ted Gayer. 2005. "Promoting School Readiness in Oklahoma: An Evaluation of Tulsa's Pre-K Program." *Journal of Human Resources* 40(3): 533–58.

Goux, Dominique, and Eric Maurin. 2008. "Preschool Enrollment, Mother's Participation in the Labor Market and Children's Subsequent Outcomes." Unpublished manuscript.

Havnes, Tarjei, and Magne Mogstad. 2009. "No Child Left Behind: Universal Child Care and Children's Long-Run Outcomes." *IZA* discussion paper 4561. Bonn: Institute for the Study of Labor.

Institut National de la Statistiques et des Etudes Economiques (INSEE). 1993. Formation, Qualification, Profession (FQP) data, 1993. Paris: INSEE. Information available at: http://www.insee.fr (accessed December 30, 2011).

Leuven, Edwin, Mikael Lindahl, Hessel Oosterbeek, and Dinand Webbink. 2010. "Expanding Schooling Opportunities for 4-Year-Olds." *Economics of Education Review* 29(3): 319–28.

Magnuson, Katherine A., Christopher Ruhm, and Jane Waldfogel. 2007. "Does Prekindergarten Improve School Preparation and Performance?" *Economics of Education Review* 26(1): 33–51.

Ministère de l'éducation nationale. 2001. *L'état de l'école*. Paris: DEPP/Département de la valorisation et de l'édition.

———. Various years. *DEPP panels 1978, 1980, 1989*. Direction de l'évaluation, de la prospective, et de la performance (DEPP). Paris: DEPP/Ministère de l'Éducation Nationale, de la Jeunesse, et de la Vie Associative. Information available at: http://www.education.gouv.fr/cid1180/direction de-l-evaluation-de-la-prospective-et-de-la-performance.html (accessed December 30, 2011).

Prost, Antoine. 1981. *Histoire de l'enseignement et de l'éducation. IV Depuis 1930*. Paris: Perrin.

Chapter 8

Intergenerational Transmission and Day Care

PAUL BINGLEY AND

NIELS WESTERGÅRD-NIELSEN

IN NORTH AMERICA and Europe since the 1980s, a growing proportion of children younger than six have been in nonparental care while their parents are at work. By 2006, the majority (52.6 percent) of children below six in OECD countries were in formal care or preschool (OECD 2010). This is a huge shift in how children spend many hours of most days during their formative years. It will affect intergenerational mobility depending on the pattern of substitution between modes of care and the distribution of changes in care quality. For some countries, the first generation of children involved in this expansion has now completed schooling and entered the labor market. Denmark has had one of the most comprehensive systems of publicly provided day care for decades. In this chapter, we describe the relationship between the expansion of publicly provided child care in Denmark and the intergenerational transmission of schooling and earnings.

Denmark is especially informative for several reasons. It has probably the lowest intergenerational income elasticity in the world (Björklund and Jäntti 2009), public provision of care for the under-sixes is the most comprehensive (76.9 percent in 2006), expensive ($4,940 per child in 2006) and highly prioritized (1.2 percent of GDP in 2005) (OECD 2010), and coverage has a long and well-documented history. Two generations of Danes have now been exposed to the institutionalization of childhood from early ages. This may seem like a national experiment without a control, but by virtue of differential municipal organization of preschool care, there is a wealth of historical variation from which we can learn. Day care plays a very important role in Danish society.[1] Most Danes spend most days during their formative years in day care. Yet the effects of day care are largely unknown. This chapter describes the contribution of expansion of day-care provision to intergenerational mobility.

Day care is often cited as being one of the main engines of high intergenerational mobility. Pedro Carneiro and James Heckman (2003) propose a theoretical framework of learning-begets-learning to interpret the observed high returns to targeted early childhood interventions (for a reinterpretation of the most influential experimental findings, see Andersen 2007). Gösta Esping-Andersen (2008) argues that maternal employment reduces child poverty risk and, in combination with substitution to high quality nonparental care, can diminish reproduction of inequality. In Denmark, current provision is now population-wide, but there has been an enormous variation in development of provision over time across municipalities. It is this differential regional expansion that we will relate to changes in intergenerational transmission for children growing up at different times in different parts of the country.

Three recent studies are closest to ours in terms of topic and design, though with different focus. They all look at day care or preschool in a quasi-experimental (differences-in-differences) framework, but focus on the causal effect on child outcomes of day care or preschool per se. Our focus is the extent to which day care might moderate correlations between parent and child outcomes. Michael Baker, Jonathan Gruber, and Kevin Milligan (2008) analyze the phased introduction of the Quebec Family Policy, a heavily subsidized $5-a-day day-care program in Quebec for children age four in 1997 down to those age one and younger in 2000. Other Canadian provinces were not part of the program, and the Canadian National Longitudinal Survey of Children and Youth 1994–2003 is used to compare outcomes for children younger than four years before and after in Quebec with the rest of Canada. They find uniformly negative short-run effects on maternal reports of child behavior and health, in terms of increased anxiety, aggression, illness, and poorer motor skills. Although these short-run outcomes may miss unmeasured long-run positives and partially reflect adjustment costs of rapidly introducing such an extensive program, it is remarkable that they are so consistently and significantly negative.

Tarjei Havnes and Magne Mogstad (2009) analyze the 1976 to 1979 Norwegian expansion in publicly provided day care for children ages three to six. The expansion was differential between municipalities and administrative register data for children born between 1967 and 1976 on outcomes at ages thirty to thirty-three are compared for those growing up in high- versus low-expansion day-care regions. They find uniformly large and positive effects on long-run outcomes, in terms of length of schooling, employment, earnings (especially for women), and reduced welfare dependency. These positive findings are in stark contrast to those for Canada. Apart from differences in place and time and time horizon of the analyses, an important reconciling factor is likely alternative mode of care. Most Canadian mothers reentered the labor market, whereas most Norwegian mothers were already employed, and substitution from parental or informal nonparental care probably differed accordingly.

In chapter 7 of this volume, Christelle Dumas and Arnaud Lefranc consider the 1971 to 1982 French expansion of publicly provided preschool for children ages two to four. The expansion differed between departments and both survey and administrative data for the 1969, 1972, and 1978 birth cohorts on educational attainment and wages are compared for those who did and did not attend preschool. Recall data on attendance is instrumented by the provision of local preschool. Dumas and Lefranc find significant positive effects of preschool attendance on both educational attainment and wages. Interactions with paternal occupation show that the effect is primarily felt in families with low socioeconomic status.

The importance of alternative care in driving results is evident and obvious because day care is about who is caring for the children. Evaluating care depends on substituting between alternatives. However, both the Canadian and Norwegian studies address this indirectly through maternal labor supply response to subsidized public provision. In analyzing Norwegian and French regional day care and preschool roll-out, the maintained assumption is that maternal demand does not determine which municipalities provide day care and when. The Danish data we have access to does not, at present, have enough identifying information to pursue the causal effects of day-care exposure. Although we do not look at maternal labor supply response to day-care expansion, the context of alternative forms of child care are likely closer to the Norwegian than the Canadian and French cases (for a long time series of day-care provision and female labor supply, see Statistics Denmark 2001).

To preview our results, intergenerational correlations are moderated only slightly (insignificantly downward) by including a simple measure of local day-care provision—municipal places per child. Interactions with municipal day-care density are positive and modest across parental schooling distribution, but mostly insignificant across parental earnings distribution. Density of day-care provision is correlated with longer daughter schooling for mothers with least schooling in nonrural areas, and with longer son schooling for mothers with intermediate schooling in urban areas. Father-daughter correlation interactions are similar to mother-daughter. However, father-son correlation interactions are largely insignificant. We conclude that (our simple measure of) municipal day-care provision contributes little to the high level of intergenerational mobility.

Institutional Background

Public provision of child care in Denmark has a long tradition (see Enoksen 1997). The first kindergartens were developed in line with the ideas of German pedagogue Friedrich Fröbel. In the beginning, efforts were all privately organized, but in 1919 the government began subsidizing existing kindergartens, albeit to a small extent. A 1933 reform increased the subsidy. Still, growth was slow. By 1940, nurseries had been established for 1,100 children and kindergartens for 11,000, a tiny fraction of Denmark's child population. Until around 1950, the major purpose of subsidies was to assist "those parents who had to leave their homes to earn a living," and accordingly the institutions, to maintain their subsidy, were required to have two-thirds of enrolled children from poor households. Thus there was clearly a social purpose to publicly subsidized child care. The political foundation for day-care expansion was laid, but bad business cycles in the 1950s delayed implementation. In the 1960s, demand for female labor increased with the economic upswing, which spurred the growth and expansion of institutions.

The training and education of personnel in child-care institutions improved over these years, but no formal educational requirements existed. By the early 1950s, however, regulations were enacted. Various existing private educations became organized and financed by the state. The duration of education was later extended to three years. Each institution should have a certain minimum proportion of educated personnel but could also employ untrained helpers.

The laws regulating and subsidizing child-care institutions were changed several times. By 1965, the shift from social institutions to pedagogical institutions was almost complete. The state covered all housing costs and 40 percent of running costs, municipalities 30 percent, and parents the remaining 30 percent. After 1976, responsibility for organization and public funding was transferred to municipalities, and the growth in the number of institutions and places took off.

A private alternative to institutions has always existed: licensed carers opening their homes for two to five children. Most of those arrangements were organized and quality-assured by the municipality, and most carers were municipality employees. No formal educational requirements for licensed carers were in place.

Subsidies were organized such that municipalities were given incentives to save on day-care costs, especially from 1976. The choice was between licensed care and the more expensive institutions that also provided a qualitatively different type of care. The result was that municipalities with other budgetary priorities had fewer institutions than their counterparts where pedagogical concerns dominated. The division was largely political but also urban versus rural. Over time, institutions with educated personnel have become more and more the norm.

Data Description

The Statistics Denmark day-care institution register begins in 1976, and we use this through 1989 to capture relevant exposure for birth cohorts 1976 through 1983 for ages zero through six. Figure 8.1 illustrates

Figure 8.1   Day-Care Expansion

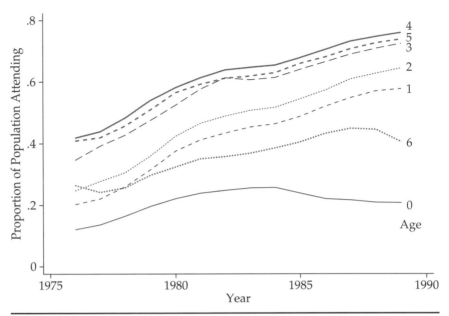

Source: Authors' calculations based on administrative register data documented in Statistics Denmark (2011b) and described in Statistics Denmark (1990).

the expansion of day care by child age between 1976 and 1989. Figures are proportion of children in day care by age and year. For ages one through five, aggregate expansions were roughly parallel by age, the youngest experiencing a threefold increase and the oldest a doubling of coverage. Half of the expansion took place in the first five years. Coverage increased dramatically for one-year-olds, from 20 percent in 1976 to 40 percent in 1981, and then slowed to reach 58 percent by 1989. For five-year-olds, the corresponding figures are 40, 60, and 77 percent. The exceptions are those younger than one and age six because of changing parental leave and interactions with school start, respectively.

The large aggregate expansions presented in figure 8.1 cover a wide variety of regional experience. Figure 8.2 illustrates the variance of the expansion over time by considering the 25 and 75 percentile municipalities of the day-care density distribution in each year. Variance in coverage began large and expanded, especially for nursery (ages two and younger). For nursery (kindergarten), the interquartile range was 12 percent (18 percent) in 1976, increasing to 18 percent (24 percent) in 1981, and ending the period

Figure 8.2   Day-Care Coverage

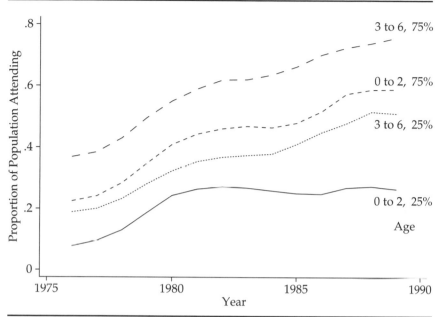

Source: Authors' calculations based on administrative register data documented in Statistics Denmark (2011b) and described in Statistics Denmark (1990).

at 32 percent (26 percent) in 1989. It is clear from figure 8.2 that the expansion was different across the country, and indeed the variance between municipalities increased markedly.

Our data spans this period of growth in level and dispersion of day-care provision with birth cohorts 1976 through 1983 with ages zero through six. We distinguish between outcomes for boys and girls throughout the chapter. Gender differences in patterns of intergenerational transmission have long been recognized (Black and Devereux 2010), and stronger day-care effects for girls have been found (Havnes and Mogstad 2009). We also distinguish between municipalities according to urbanicity (thirds of the distribution). For a given density of provision, access to care is likely to be more costly in the countryside, and alternative (extended family) modes of care are likely to be available to a different extent. Separating regions according to urbanicity allows day-care density to be interpreted differently according to costs of care and likely crowd-out, at the expense of reduced between-municipality variation.

Tables 8.1 and 8.2 present descriptive statistics for outcomes and covariates of interest in the analysis. Table 8.1 shows means and standard

Table 8.1   Descriptive Statistics

Covariate	Female Rural		Female Semi		Female Urban		Male Rural		Male Semi		Male Urban	
Mother school years	11.25	(2.74)	11.53	(2.74)	11.50	(2.72)	11.25	(2.73)	11.52	(2.73)	11.50	(2.72)
Father school years	11.94	(3.06)	12.27	(3.00)	12.29	(2.94)	11.95	(3.05)	12.27	(2.97)	12.30	(2.94)
Offspring school years	12.99	(2.05)	12.98	(2.11)	12.77	(2.16)	12.85	(2.06)	12.81	(2.13)	12.64	(2.19)
Parents earnings (DKK)	557646	(279845)	613586	(300538)	608623	(295177)	554054	(276794)	611408	(298433)	607182	(294276)
Offspring earnings (DKK)	159781	(111603)	159237	(115535)	145781	(113214)	223973	(141049)	215712	(144000)	199349	(142029)
DD	0.230	(0.118)	0.364	(0.157)	0.442	(0.129)	0.230	(0.118)	0.364	(0.158)	0.442	(0.128)
	65334	201	55148	59	50652	15	69212	201	57689	59	53698	15

Source: Authors' calculations based on administrative register data documented in Statistics Denmark (2011a) and described in Leth-Sorensen (1993).

Notes: Offspring schooling is measured in 2006.

Parental schooling is measured when child is age eight.

Offspring earnings are measured in 2006.

Parents' earnings are means of mother plus father while child is seven through sixteen reflated to 2006 DKK.

DD indicates the number of day-care places by municipality per child age six or younger.

Standard deviations in parentheses.

Table 8.2   Correlation Matrix

	DD	School Offspring	School Mother	School Father	Earnings Offspring	Earnings Parents
DD	1.000	−0.083	0.103	0.100	−0.098	0.171
Offspring school	−0.083	1.000	0.245	0.205	0.268	0.233
Mother school	0.103	0.245	1.000	0.365	−0.019	0.369
Father school	0.100	0.205	0.365	1.000	−0.008	0.352
Offspring earnings	−0.098	0.268	−0.019	−0.008	1.000	0.054
Parents earnings	0.171	0.233	0.369	0.352	0.054	1.000

Source: Authors' calculations based on administrative register data documented in Statistics Denmark (2011a) and described in Leth-Sørensen (1993).
Note: DD indcates day-care density.

deviations for our population of 188,431 girls and 199,384 boys distributed across 275 municipalities. Parents living in urban or semi-urban municipalities (when their child is eight) have about 0.25 years more schooling and 10 percent higher earnings (when the child is seven through sixteen) than parents living in rural areas. However, there is a slight penalty of 0.2 years of schooling and 10 percent of earnings (in 2006) for offspring living in an urban municipality at age eight compared with those living rural or semi-urban. Offspring earnings have a relatively high variance because in 2006, at ages twenty-three through thirty, they have not all completed full-time schooling and entered career jobs. Earnings variance and age of observation have important implications for measuring intergenerational correlations, to which we will return when interpreting our estimates (for a discussion of life-cycle bias in estimation of intergenerational income mobility, see Björklund and Jäntti 2009). Day-care density (DD) is higher in more urban municipalities, but standard deviations of the density indicate substantial remaining variation.

Table 8.2 shows raw correlations between outcomes and covariates of interest. Day-care density is negatively correlated with all offspring outcomes and positively correlated with parental schooling and earnings. Intergenerational correlations are conventionally positive: 0.24 mother's schooling, 0.21 father's schooling, and 0.05 for earnings. Earnings correlations are small regardless of whether we consider up to ten years of parental earnings. There is little flexibility for child earnings because they are still so early if indeed they have begun their labor market career. Earnings correlations should increase if more years for older offspring were considered.

Estimation Results and Discussion

Ordinary least squares (OLS) regression models are run separately for dependent variables child log earning and years of completed schooling by child gender and urbanicity. Explanatory variables of interest are parental earnings and schooling, day-care density, and its interaction with parental earnings and schooling. Other controls are dummies for (seven) years of birth and (275) municipalities of residence at birth. Ours is essentially a difference-in-differences approach in which we aim to identify an intention to treat effect (similar to Baker, Gruber, and Milligan 2008; Havnes and Mogstad 2009). Christelle Dumas and Arnaud Lefranc (chapter 7, this volume) instrument individual preschool attendance to identify an effect of treatment on the treated. Our estimates could be scaled up by dividing by the proportion attending to obtain a similar treatment on treated measure. However, in our case it is not clear what the treatment would be in terms of substitution between maternal and other forms of care (for a similar argument for Canada, see Baker, Gruber, and Mulligan 2008).

Table 8.3 presents estimates from six regressions for years of completed schooling. The relationship between both longer maternal and paternal schooling and longer offspring schooling is clear and positive. Interaction terms between dummies for low maternal schooling and day-care density are positive, which means offspring of short-schooling mothers benefit from day-care exposure in terms of increased length of schooling. Interactions of paternal schooling with DD differ by offspring gender, benefiting the schooling of urban girls with short-schooling fathers and associated with shorter schooling for urban boys of long-schooling fathers. In alternative specifications excluding DD and DD interaction terms, coefficients on parental schooling dummies were quantitatively similar to those presented here.[2] There is no obvious general pattern of interactions by urbanicity and child gender as might have been expected because of differential proximity and alternative modes of care along these dimensions. Intergenerational transmission of schooling appears to be only moderated slightly by the inclusion of our measures of day-care availability. The most consistent result is for longer schooling with day care for children of low-schooling mothers.

Table 8.4 presents estimates from six regressions for child log earnings.[3] There is a clear positive relationship between parental earnings and offspring earnings. Interaction terms between dummies for parental earnings quartile and day-care density are largely negative for low earnings and positive for high. This is consistent with high-potential-earnings families' offspring benefiting most from day-care provision because of the associated greater family income gain from working. However, intergenerational earnings correlations are poorly determined. R-squared goodness-of-fit

Table 8.3 Parent and Offspring Schooling and Day-Care Density

Covariate	Female Rural	Female Semi	Female Urban	Male Rural	Male Semi	Male Urban
Mother school= 7–11	−1.0128 (0.0784)	−1.3075 (0.0940)	−1.5317 (0.1426)	−0.9911 (0.0798)	−0.9086 (0.0967)	−0.9853 (0.1472)
Mother school= 12–14	−0.3417 (0.0777)	−0.6090 (0.0931)	−0.5609 (0.1410)	−0.4315 (0.0790)	−0.3102 (0.0958)	−0.2487 (0.1453)
Mother school= 16–18	0.0815 (0.0935)	−0.0243 (0.1160)	0.2435 (0.1757)	0.0157 (0.0956)	0.1608 (0.1173)	0.1934 (0.1821)
DD*mother school= 7–11	0.2743 (0.2863)	0.6304 (0.2304)	0.8813 (0.3065)	0.7933 (0.2943)	0.2928 (0.2337)	0.2089 (0.3154)
DD*mother school= 12–14	0.1215 (0.2792)	0.5871 (0.2254)	0.4102 (0.3019)	0.5183 (0.2868)	0.1509 (0.2288)	−0.1402 (0.3099)
DD*mother school= 16–18	0.1425 (0.3282)	0.3799 (0.2742)	−0.1442 (0.3737)	0.2467 (0.3407)	0.0350 (0.2766)	−0.2026 (0.3854)
Father school= 7–11	−0.9186 (0.0900)	−1.1410 (0.1126)	−1.6681 (0.1515)	−0.7903 (0.0906)	−0.8526 (0.1123)	−1.0213 (0.1558)
Father school= 12–14	−0.4997 (0.0865)	−0.6889 (0.1082)	−0.9359 (0.1435)	−0.3277 (0.0870)	−0.3541 (0.1079)	−0.4748 (0.1476)
Father school= 16–18	0.0789 (0.1015)	−0.0941 (0.1264)	0.0399 (0.1745)	0.0271 (0.1027)	0.2322 (0.1280)	0.5678 (0.1795)
DD*father school= 7–11	0.2924 (0.3093)	0.3331 (0.2654)	1.4008 (0.3325)	−0.0336 (0.3129)	−0.1722 (0.2653)	−0.0368 (0.3419)
DD*father school= 12–14	0.2239 (0.2900)	0.3904 (0.2518)	1.1136 (0.3152)	−0.1882 (0.2930)	−0.2521 (0.2518)	−0.0006 (0.3238)
DD*father school= 16–18	0.2797 (0.3345)	0.3732 (0.2901)	0.3501 (0.3750)	0.0289 (0.3432)	−0.3514 (0.2927)	−0.9979 (0.3849)
DD	−0.5032 (0.4437)	−0.0477 (0.4328)	−2.0843 (0.7034)	−0.6956 (0.4568)	−0.4423 (0.4379)	1.7938 (0.7169)
Intercept	14.7518 (0.1174)	14.8577 (0.1587)	15.3981 (0.2823)	14.4381 (0.1192)	14.4619 (0.1605)	13.5401 (0.2882)
R^2 within overall	0.1532 0.1546	0.1705 0.1613	0.1812 0.1853	0.0978 0.0990	0.1176 0.1126	0.1236 0.1043
Number of observations, number of municipalities	65334 201	55148 59	50652 15	69212 201	57689 59	53698 15

Source: Authors' calculations based on administrative register data documented in Statistics Denmark (2011a, 2011b) and described in Leth-Sørensen (1993) and Statistics Denmark (1990).

Note: Dependent variable is years of completed schooling in 2006.
Parental schooling are measured when child is age eight. Reference schooling is fifteen years.
DD indicates the number of day-care places by municipality per child age six or younger.
Also included are year of birth and municipality dummies.

Table 8.4   Parent and Offspring Earnings and Day-Care Density

Covariate	Female Rural	Female Semi	Female Urban	Male Rural	Male Semi	Male Urban
Quartile= 1 (low)	-0.4009 (0.0902)	-0.6588 (0.1130)	-1.4008 (0.1806)	-0.5542 (0.0825)	-0.5511 (0.1039)	-0.5931 (0.1647)
Quartile= 2	-0.2725 (0.0914)	-0.4756 (0.1132)	-0.5719 (0.1813)	-0.0953 (0.0834)	-0.0898 (0.1034)	-0.0808 (0.1639)
Quartile= 4 (high)	-0.0803 (0.0942)	-0.0501 (0.1173)	0.0350 (0.1734)	-0.3268 (0.0871)	-0.2134 (0.1083)	-0.1402 (0.1589)
DD*quartile= 1 (low)	-0.9183 (0.3655)	-1.0665 (0.2973)	0.4103 (0.3928)	0.2337 (0.3351)	-0.4008 (0.2731)	-0.8801 (0.3592)
DD*quartile= 2	0.0982 (0.3669)	0.1626 (0.3005)	0.3154 (0.4033)	0.2768 (0.3351)	-0.2532 (0.2737)	-0.2000 (0.3644)
DD*quartile= 4 (high)	0.1410 (0.3400)	0.0443 (0.2850)	0.0617 (0.3760)	0.6047 (0.3158)	0.3070 (0.2624)	-0.0179 (0.3436)
DD	0.6211 (0.5742)	0.3526 (0.6407)	-0.1640 (1.2234)	-0.0097 (0.5250)	0.0628 (0.5925)	1.4705 (1.1144)
Intercept 1	10.9819 (0.1218)	11.0050 (0.2017)	10.8910 (0.4606)	11.5747 (0.1113)	11.5338 (0.1865)	10.8264 (0.4200)
R^2 within overall	0.0078 0.0081	0.0153 0.0154	0.0181 0.0183	0.0060 0.0053	0.0098 0.0093	0.0142 0.0100
Number of observations, number of municipalities	65334 201	55148 59	50652 15	69212 201	57689 59	53698 15

Source: Authors' calculations based on administrative register data documented in Statistics Denmark (2011a, 2011b) and described in Leth-Sørensen (1993) and Statistics Denmark (1990).

Notes: Dependent variable is child annual log labor earnings in 2006.
Parents' earnings are means of mother plus father while child is age seven through sixteen reflated. Reference quartile is #3.
DD indicates the number of day-care places by municipality per child age six or younger.
Also included are year of birth and municipality dummies.

measures are 1.8 percent at best in table 8.4 compared with 18.1 percent in table 8.3 for schooling. This is largely due to the single-year observation of offspring earnings and it being so early in the working life, that it is very unlikely to reflect a measure of permanent lifetime earnings more commonly sought for intergenerational earnings and income mobility measurement. Our correlations are likely downward biased and lacking in precision in the light of our not taking account of this, and should be regarded as lower bounds for these outcomes.

Summary and Conclusion

We describe the relationship between the intergenerational transmission of schooling and earnings and the expansion of day care. We use administrative data for all children born in Denmark between 1976 and 1983, and we correlate parental schooling when the offspring is eight and earnings when the child is ages seven to sixteen with offspring schooling and earnings, respectively, in 2006. Intergenerational correlations are moderated only slightly by inclusion of a simple measure of local day-care provision–municipal places per child of each age six and younger. We find some significant interactions with day-care provision. Child schooling is especially benefited by day care for children of mothers with low schooling. Child earnings are higher when day-care coverage increases for high-earning parents.

The most important result in this chapter is the finding of a significant and positive relationship between local day care and offspring outcomes seventeen to thirty years later. We also find that day care does not have any significant effect on the education level of children with higher-educated mothers or fathers. Interactions of day-care provision with low maternal schooling is associated with longer offspring schooling. Similarly, high parental earnings are associated with higher earnings among children who have been attending day care.

Our study has several limitations. Day-care density at the municipal level is quite a crude measure of day-care availability, especially in rural areas. More detailed proximity to care institution information would increase relevance and the precision of estimates. Our long-run outcomes are measured at age twenty-three, where there may still be transitions from schooling and into career occupations. Earlier day-care institutional records would allow analysis of earlier birth cohorts, and more recent outcome measures would overcome this limitation. Administrative data does not indicate which alternative types of care are available. However, whether publicly provided care draws children from parental (maternal) care at home or informal care likely has important consequences for its relative impact. Measuring associated changes in maternal labor supply, as others have done, is a feasible but indirect approach.

We acknowledge with appreciation comments on earlier drafts of this chapter from Paul Gregg, James Wilson, the editors, and other members of the Cross-National Inheritance of the Transmission of Advantage network during presentations at meetings organized by the Russell Sage Foundation in New York and London. The financial support of the Russell Sage Foundation as well as advice of Steffen Hougaard at Statistics Denmark is also acknowledged with thanks. Bingley is grateful for the financial support of the Danish Strategic Research Council through a grant to the Centre for Strategic Research in Education.

Notes

1. Throughout, we use *day care* generically to mean nursery (*vuggestue*) for ages two and younger and kindergarten (*børnehave*) for ages three through six.
2. R-squared goodness-of-fit measures were at best 1 percent higher with inclusion of DD and interactions. Results are available on request.
3. We have also considered parent and offspring annual income and different treatments of zeros. Estimates of coefficients of interest are qualitatively quite similar across specifications.

References

Anderson, Michael. 2007. "Multiple Inference and Gender Differences in the Effects of Preschool: A Reevaluation of the Abecedarian, Perry Preschool, and Early Training Projects." *Early Childhood Research Collaborative* discussion paper 109. Berkeley: University of California.

Baker, Michael, Jonathan Gruber, and Kevin Milligan. 2008. "Universal Child Care, Maternal Labor Supply and Family Well-Being." *Journal of Political Economy* 116(4): 709–45.

Björklund, Anders, and Markus Jäntti. 2009. "Intergenerational Income Mobility and the Role of Family Background." In *The Oxford Handbook of Economic Inequality*, edited by Wiemer Salverda, Brian Nolan, and Timothy M. Smeeding. Oxford: Oxford University Press.

Black, Sandra, and Paul J. Devereux. 2010. "Recent Developments in Intergenerational Mobility." *NBER* working paper 15889. Cambridge, Mass.: National Bureau of Economic Research.

Carneiro, Pedro, and James J. Heckman. 2003. "Human Capital Policy." In *Inequality in America: What Role for Human Capital Policy?* edited by James Heckman and A. Krueger. Cambridge, Mass.: MIT Press.

Enoksen, Ivan. 1997. "Folk og Fag: træk af pædagogfagets historie." Copenhagen: Forlaget Børn og Unge.

Esping-Andersen, Gösta. 2008. "Childhood Investments and Skill Formation." *International Tax and Public Finance* 15(1): 14–49.

Havnes, Tarjei, and Magne Mogstad. 2009. "No Child Left Behind: Universal Child Care and Children's Long-Run Outcomes." *IZA* discussion paper 4651. Bonn: Institute for the Study of Labor.

Leth-Sørensen, Søren. 1993. "IDA: An Integrated Database for Labour Market Research." Copenhagen: Statistics Denmark.

Organisation for Economic Co-Operation and Development (OECD). 2010. OECD Family Database. Paris: Organisation for Economic Co-Operation and Development, Directorate for Employment, Labour and Social Affairs. Available at: http://www.oecd.org/els/social/family/database (accessed January 10, 2012).

Statistics Denmark. 1990. "News from Statistics Denmark, Social Conditions, Health, and the Judiciary" (in Danish). Copenhagen: Statistics Denmark.

———. 2001. "50-års oversigten" (50-year review). Copenhagen: Statistics Denmark.

———. 2011a. "Documentation of Database Contents Integrated Database for Labour Market Research." Available at: http://www.dst.dk/en/Guide/documentation/Varedeklarationer/emnegruppe/emne.aspx?sysrid=1013 (accessed January 10, 2012).

———. 2011b. "Census Documentation–Social Conditions, Health and the Judiciary, Day Care" (in Danish). Available at: http://www.dst.dk/Statistik/dokumentation/Varedeklarationer/emnegruppe/emne.aspx?sysrid=101399 (accessed January 10, 2012).

PART III

MIDDLE CHILDHOOD
TO ADOLESCENCE

Chapter 9

Child Skills and Behaviors in Intergenerational Inequality

GREG J. DUNCAN, LARS BERGMAN,
KATHRYN DUCKWORTH, KATJA KOKKO,
ANNA-LIISA LYYRA, MOLLY METZGER,
LEA PULKKINEN, AND SHARON SIMONTON

T HE DEGREE to which grown children mimic the socioeconomic accomplishments of their parents differs markedly from one country to another. Using parent-child correlations in completed schooling as a measure of intergenerational persistence of socioeconomic status, Thomas Hertz and his colleagues (2007) find that correlations range from an average of 0.39 in Western Europe and the United States to 0.60 in Latin America. Correlations differ even among countries within general regions in the Hertz study: equality-oriented Nordic countries within Western Europe posted correlations that average 0.34, and the non-Nordic averaged 0.41.

In a structurally rigid society, parents may be able to play a direct role in securing their children's careers, whereas schools may reinforce parent actions through, for example, legacy admissions to elite colleges (Karabel 2005). In a more competitive society, the process is likely to be indirect, where higher-status parents attempt to ensure that their children acquire the kinds of skills and behaviors that boost their chances of gaining access to good schools and securing jobs similar in status to those of their parents.

Under what conditions can parents succeed in passing their socioeconomic advantages on to their children by boosting their children's job-related skills and behaviors? In equal opportunity societies, institutions and other policies boost the skills and behaviors of low-socioeconomic-status (SES) children in ways that fully offset the skill and behavioral advantages imparted by parent efforts. Unequal opportunity societies—those allowing school and neighborhood quality to reinforce family advantage and disadvantage—should see growing skill and behavior gaps between high- and low-SES children across childhood, adolescence, and early adulthood—and substantial intergenerational inequality.

This chapter focuses on the indirect skill- and behavior-based process of intergenerational inequality using five data sets from four countries: the United Kingdom, the United States, Sweden, and Finland. All of our data sets provide representative samples of children drawn from national or large community populations; measure the completed schooling of parents and children; and, most important, measure an assortment of important skills and behaviors in both middle childhood (ages seven and ten) and adolescence (age thirteen through sixteen).

Our key objective is to estimate cross-country differences in the extent to which child skills and behaviors account for intergenerational correlations in the completed schooling of parents and their grown children. The mediational role of children's skills and behaviors is, in turn, a product of two factors: how strongly parent SES determines children's skills and behaviors and the importance of children's skills and behaviors for their adult attainments. Both factors need to be at work if skills and behaviors are to play an important mediational role.

With regard to the path running from parent SES to child skills and behaviors, we are most interested in whether links are reinforced or weakened as children grow older. Work focused on child health has shown that family SES becomes increasingly predictive of a child's overall health status with age (Case, Lubotsky, and Paxson 2002). The steepening SES health gradient appears to be caused by low-SES parent inability to prevent conditions such as asthma from translating into poor general health later in childhood.

Turning from health to child skills and behaviors, we might expect that school systems that reinforce family SES advantages or disadvantages would cause parent SES to explain more and more of the variation in children's skills and behaviors as the children move through their school years. Accordingly, in a relatively stratified society such as the one into which the 1958 British cohort was born, we might expect that the links between parent background and child skills and behavior would indeed become stronger as children grow older. In contrast, because they provide more material supports to disadvantaged families, the more egalitarian societies in Sweden and Finland might be expected to show weakening links as children grow older. Because our studies provide measures of skills and behaviors in both middle childhood and adolescence, we are able to estimate whether SES gradients increase or decrease with age.

Taken together, our results show more cross-country similarities than differences, and what differences we did find did not conform readily to Nordic versus English-speaking or any other country classification. Achievement test gradients grew as children transitioned from middle childhood to adolescence in English-speaking countries but were fairly constant in Sweden (achievement data were not available in our Finnish data set).

Figure 9.1   Model of Skills and Behaviors in the Transmission of Socioeconomic Status

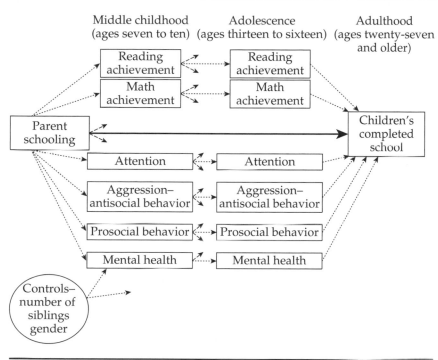

Source: Authors' figure.

In associations between children's skills and behaviors and their eventual completed schooling, virtually all of the studies showed that concrete reading and, especially, adolescent math achievement skills, were consistently stronger predictors of attainment than were any of the problem behaviors we measured. The key descriptive question driving our inquiry concerned the importance of childhood and adolescent skills and behaviors in accounting for intergenerational inequality. Across all of our data, we find that childhood and adolescent skills and behaviors account for between one-third and one-half of the intergenerational correlations in the completed schooling of parents and children.

Conceptual Framework

Our descriptive model of the role of child skills and behaviors in transmitting SES across generations is shown in figure 9.1. SES in both generations is measured by years of completed schooling. We expect children's eventual completed schooling to be a product of both skills and behaviors developed in middle childhood (between ages seven and ten in our empirical work) and adolescence (ages thirteen through sixteen). Although the ages of subjects do vary within these two stages across our data sets, the heterogeneity of developmental processes within each of these two stages is dwarfed by developmental differences between middle childhood and adolescence.

Instead of using the *cognitive* and *noncognitive* dichotomy found in much of the social science literature, we find *achievement, attention, anti- or prosocial behavior*, and *mental health* to be productive ways of categorizing the general domains of children's school-related functioning (Duncan and Magnuson 2011). By *achievement*, we mean concrete academic skills. *Attention* refers to the ability to control impulses and focus on tasks. Chief among the possible list of problem behaviors are antisocial behavior and aggression.

Middle-childhood skills and behaviors are a product of genetic endowments affecting early cognition, temperament, and health, and of the positive and negative early environmental experiences associated with socioeconomic status and parental actions and choices. None of these influences is depicted in figure 9.1, because, to accomplish our descriptive purposes, we do not attempt to model these complex processes and instead use parent schooling as our sole measure of socioeconomic status.

Figure 9.1 draws many of its elements from the Wisconsin Model of status attainment that links children's eventual socioeconomic status to the educational and occupational attainments of their parents (for example, Sewell, Haller, and Portes 1969). The child's academic performance and, in some formulations of the model, motivation and effort play important mediational roles, but so do aspirations, expectations, and socialization by parents, teachers, and peers.

Middle Childhood Skills and Behaviors and Adult Achievement

Reading and Math Achievement   Research on how children acquire reading and math skills indicates that specific early academic skills serve as the foundation for later learning. But it also suggests that more general cognitive skills, particularly oral language and conceptual ability, may be increasingly important for later mastery of more complex reading and mathematical tasks (NICHD Early Child Care Research Network 2005; Snow, Burns, and Griffin 1998; Whitehurst and Lonigan 1998; Baroody 2003). The relative stability of children's academic achievement throughout childhood and adolescence (Pungello et al. 1996) suggests that early academic skills may be strong predictors of later educational attainment.

Direct evidence on the association between early skills and later educational attainment is rare. Doris Entwisle, Karl Alexander, and Linda Olson (2007) examined the Baltimore Beginning School Study (BSS) data—one of the data sets used in our empirical work. Their analysis found that, after controls for family characteristics and students' first grade marks, a composite of first-grade reading and math test scores did not significantly predict educational attainment at age twenty or twenty-one.

More predictive are early indications that children have persistent deficits in some of these skills and behaviors. In particular, children with persistently low mathematics achievement and persistently high levels of antisocial behavior across elementary school were 10 to 13 percentage points less likely to graduate high school and about 25 points less likely to attend college than children who never have these problems (Duncan and Magnuson 2011). In contrast, persistent reading and attention problems were not predictive of these attainment outcomes.

Attention Problems   Because they increase the time children are engaged and participating in academic endeavors, attention-related skills such as task persistence and self-regulation should predict children's achievement and school outcomes. Consistent evidence suggests that the ability to control and sustain attention as well as participate in classroom activities predicts achievement test scores and grades during preschool and elementary school, even when children's academic ability is held constant (Currie and Stabile 2007; Duncan et al. 2007; Raver et al. 2005).

Whether attention problems are also linked with lower levels of eventual educational attainment is a question that has received less scrutiny. Frank Vitaro and his colleagues (2005) found that attention problems at age six predicted later high school noncompletion among a Quebec community-based sample. These analyses held constant children's aggression, but could not control for differences in early academic skills. Janet Currie and Mark Stabile (2007) take a more comprehensive look at links between hyperactivity and later schooling success, using nationally representative data on four- to eleven-year-olds from both the United States and Canada as well as both OLS and sibling fixed-effects models. Although they find consistent linkages to achievement scores, grade retention, and special-education placement, they fail to find associations between early hyperactivity and a measure of completed schooling (being in school between ages sixteen and nineteen).

Antisocial Behavior Problems   Children's problem behaviors, particularly externalizing or antisocial behavior, are expected to affect both individual learning and later attainment. Problem behavior may lead to child-teacher conflict, disciplinary actions, and social exclusion (Newcomb, Bukowski, and Pattee 1993), and as a result may adversely affect achievement (Pianta and Stuhlman 2004). The Finnish Longitudinal Study of Personality and Social Development (JYLS), a third data set used in this chapter, shows that early aggression precedes adolescent school maladjustment, which further precedes labor market problems (Kokko and Pulkkinen 2000).

Despite these theoretical justifications, empirical evidence linking problem behaviors to school outcomes is mixed. Among young children, examining externalizing problems separately from attention issues has clarified the role of each in achievement, suggesting that attention is more predictive of later achievement than more general problem behaviors (Hinshaw 1992; Duncan et al. 2007). On the other hand, several studies have found that early behavior problems are linked to subsequent educational attainment, although these studies tend to involve selective samples and few covariates to control for possible confounding factors (Ensminger and Slusarcick 1992; McLeod and Kaiser 2004). For example, based on their analysis of a New Zealand sample, David Ferguson and John Horwood (1998) find that third-grade conduct problems were predictive of high school dropout. Other studies yield less conclusive support for links between early behavior problems and later attainment. Currie and Stabile (2007) find mixed evidence for links between antisocial behaviors between ages four and eleven and school enrollment between ages sixteen and nineteen.

Internalizing Behavior Problems   Children's emotional negativity and inability to control expressions of sadness, joy, and other emotions can lead to social withdrawal, anxiety, and other behaviors commonly termed internalizing behavior problems (Eisenberg, Sadovsky, and Spinrad 2005; Posner and Rothbart 2000). These depressive behaviors are often measured by questions that ask how frequently children appear to be in a sad or irritable mood, and whether they demonstrate low self-esteem or low energy. Anxiety captures a set of factors including children's fears of separation from caregivers, obsessive-compulsive behavior, and social reticence. Socially withdrawn behavior refers to a child's social anxiety and avoidance of social interactions.

Depressive symptoms and anxiety may reduce children's engagement in classroom group learning activities (Fantuzzo et al. 2003). Evidence of this negative effect of problem behavior on achievement, however, is mixed, with correlational evidence pointing to a detrimental effect, but more controlled models yielding smaller associations or none at all (Brock et al. 2009), at least for males (Pulkkinen, Ohranen, and Tolvanen 1999).

Leon Feinstein (2000) used data from the British Cohort Study (BCS)—the fourth of our five data sets—to investigate the relationship between abilities developed by age ten and economic and educational outcomes in adulthood (measured at age twenty-six). As is the case with much of the U.K. literature, educational attainment was measured in terms of highest qualifications gained and relevant completed schooling outcomes. The analysis included age-ten measures of school achievement, attention, antisocial and prosocial behaviors, internalizing problem behavior, as well as locus of control and self-esteem, in addition to the measures we adopt in our chapter. Feinstein's results highlight the particular role of attentiveness in the production of human capital outcomes in adulthood.

Jo Blanden, Paul Gregg, and Lindsey Macmillan (2006) estimate models of the intergenerational correlation in income rather than education based on both the BCS and British National Child Development Survey (NCDS) data sets. In the BCS, they find that, taken alone, a collection of noncognitive measures taken at ages five, ten, and sixteen account for about 20 percent of the intergenerational correlation, whereas a collection of cognitive test scores taken at ages five and ten accounts for 30 percent of that correlation. When both are included in the same regression, their respective shares of variance are 11 percent and 21 percent. Among the individual measures in their combined regression, an age-ten math test was best able to account for the intergenerational correlation, followed by an age five figure-copying test of motor control and an age-ten test of "application" (concentration and perseverance). The collection of noncognitive skills in the NCDS is much less strongly associated with parent SES than in the BCS.

Adolescent Skills and Behaviors

Turning from middle childhood to adolescence, most work linking adolescent skills and behaviors to later attainment has concentrated on cognitive skills. Richard Murnane, John Willett, and Frank Levy (1995), for example, show links between the mathematics tests scores of two cohorts of high school seniors and their wages at age twenty-four. Looking at National Longitudinal Survey of Youth (NLSY) participants who were fifteen- to eighteen-year-olds when they took an armed forces qualifying test, Derek Neal and William Johnson (1996) found strong links between test scores and earnings measured a decade later.

Secondary school measurement of pre-adult skills is also a common feature of attempts to relate labor market outcomes to combinations of cognitive and so-called noncognitive skills. James Heckman and Yona Rubinstein (2001) establish the importance of adolescent behavioral profiles in understanding why GED holders earn so much less than high school graduates despite having virtually identical distributions of cognitive test scores. Heckman, Sergio Urzua, and Jora Stixtud (2006) show the remarkable power of a scale combining adolescent self-esteem and sense of personal effectiveness for explaining later earnings in NLSY data.

Despite the findings of these adolescent-based skill studies, they raise a vital question: to what extent is the apparent predictive power of adolescent skills and behaviors a mere reflection of fundamental skills determined much earlier in life? If skill trajectories are relatively rigid products of genetic factors, children's self-selection into classroom behavior, study habits, and peer-group interactions, or school structures such as tracking, then interventions during adolescence may be too late to produce lasting improvement.

In most developmental theories, notions of developmental continuity have rightly taken center stage (Schulenberg, Maggs, and O'Malley 2003). In general, problems may accumulate, with difficulties in childhood leading to difficulties in adolescence and adulthood (Masten et al. 2005). Likewise, doing well can set the stage for continuing to do well. In short, continuity of adaptation tends to prevail across the life course. Flavio Cunha and his colleagues (2005) provide a production-function interpretation in which early development of positive skills increases the payoff to subsequent investments such as K–12 education. David Magnusson's (1998) developmental model of this process emphasizes how individuals can transform their environmental experiences by differentially selecting, interpreting, and attaching meaning to their experiences.

The idea that early skills matter the most is the foundation of social policies such as enriched preschool experiences (Knudsen et al. 2006). Getting it right by middle childhood is presumed to maximize the benefit to the individual and society as the individual matures. According to this view, adolescence, by itself, may not matter that much; childhood functioning contributes directly to adolescent functioning, which in turn contributes directly to adulthood functioning, so that adolescent functioning is simply an intermediate step between childhood and adulthood functioning. We are able to test explicitly for the relative importance of middle childhood versus adolescent skills and behaviors in all five of our data sets.

Skill Levels and Gradients Across Countries   Although cross-national student achievement studies such as Program of International Student Assessment (PISA) began well after the children in our data sets secured their schooling, they provide some useful national benchmarks for skill levels and gradients and school inequalities. We draw our data from the first PISA study, which sampled fifteen-year-old students in 2000 (OECD 2001). Because their 1985 births were a decade or more after the births of the children in our data sets, the school conditions and relationships they paint may have been quite different from school conditions and relationships for the children in our cohorts.

The first column of table 9.1 show country average scores on the reading literacy test (patterns for mathematics literacy are quite similar). On average, Finnish students outscored U.S. students by close to 0.5 standard deviation, and students from the United Kingdom and Sweden fell between them. The dispersion of test scores is considerably greater in the

Table 9.1   Cross-Country Differences in Reading Literacy Among
Fifteen-Year-Olds

	Mean Scores	5th/95th Percentile Scores	Slope of SES Gradient	Between-School Variation
United States	504	320/660	48	.35
United Kingdom	523	352/682	49	.22
Sweden	516	354/658	36	.09
Finland	546	390/681	30	.11

Source: Authors' compilation based on data from OECD (2001).
Notes: The standard deviation of reading literacy scores are 100.
Slope is the score difference on the test associated with a one standard deviation change in the PISA SES scale.
Between-school variation is expressed as a fraction of average variation across all OECD countries.

United States than in other countries—U.S. students at the 5th percentile of the test score distribution are 0.7 standard deviations below their Finnish counterparts, while high-achieving (at the 95th percentile) U.S. students are only 0.2 standard deviations below their Finnish counterparts. As before, students from the United Kingdom and Sweden are between the United States and Finland.

One of our interests is in estimating associations between the socioeconomic circumstances of children and their school performance. PISA measures SES with a collection of indicators of economic, social, and cultural status.[1] The third column of table 9.1 presents the slopes of the SES gradients for children's reading literacy achievement scores. The entry for the United States means that a 1.0 standard deviation in parent SES is associated with a 48-point (roughly 0.5 standard deviation) gain in the reading test score. Gradient slopes are virtually identical in the United Kingdom as in the United States but considerably lower in Sweden and, especially, Finland, where a 1 standard deviation increase in SES is associated with a 30-point increase in test score.[2]

What role might schools play in ameliorating or reinforcing these SES differences? The fourth column in table 9.1 shows that, in the United States, 35 percent of the variation in student test score arises between schools. This is higher than in the United Kingdom (22 percent) and much higher than in either Sweden (9 percent) or Finland (11 percent).

Across our four countries, then, Finland and the United States stake out the extremes in the level and dispersion of achievement skills of fifteen-year-olds, and in the slopes of SES gradients. SES skills gradients are as large in the United Kingdom as in the United States, but U.K. student outcomes are better. Sweden nearly matches Finland in the flatness of its SES–test score gradients, but not in the achievement levels of its students.

Data and Procedures

The five data sets we use are the U.S. Baltimore Beginning School Study, the Finnish Jyväskylä Longitudinal Study of Personality and Social Development, the Swedish Study of Individual Development and Adaptation (IDA), the British National Child Development Survey (1958 birth cohort), and the British Cohort Study (1970 birth cohort).

Table 9.2 summarizes key characteristics of these data sets. All are drawn from either national populations or diverse communities. The BSS sampling universe is the population of students in Baltimore public schools. The city of Jyväskylä is located in central Finland, some 170 miles north of Helsinki. Its population was 128,245 in 2009. Its large university has generated many cutting-edge educational initiatives. The Swedish IDA sample is drawn from students in Örebro, which is located in central Sweden, roughly equidistant from Stockholm, Gothenburg, and Oslo. Its 2005 population was 98,237, making it the seventh-largest city in Sweden. The two British cohort studies are full national samples of their respective birth cohorts.

A potential worry is of bias owing to the limited variability in our three community data sets. Our choices were dictated by the fact that there are no nationally representative data sets in the United States, Sweden, and Finland with measures of skills and behaviors in middle childhood and adolescence as well as measures of completed schooling taken in adulthood. Comparisons conducted by study staff show that the demographic characteristics of the Finnish sample at ages forty-two and fifty compare favorably with national statistics compiled by Statistics Finland. Although children living in Baltimore are hardly representative of U.S. children, Baltimore public schools at the time (1982) were more racially diverse than they are now; 45 percent of the first graders in the sample are white.

Begun in a halcyon era of public and school cooperation with survey researchers, all the initial wave response rates are in excess of 95 percent, though response rates in subsequent waves are lower and raise some concerns of potential nonresponse bias. The response rates of other relevant waves listed in table 9.2 use the first wave sample as a base.

Completed Schooling of Child   All studies provide measures of the child's eventual completed schooling that are drawn from interviews taken at age twenty-eight or later. Although the structure of primary, secondary, and tertiary schooling differs across countries, conversion tables enable us to code years of completed schooling from the International Standard Classification of Education (ISCED) codes for the various education levels across our countries (UNESCO 2006). The continuous nature of years

Table 9.2 Study Characteristics

Study	Population	Sample	Sample Size and Response Rate	
			First Wave	Other Relevant Waves
U.S. BSS	First graders in Baltimore public schools in 1982	Twelve students selected at random from each classroom	First grade: 838 (97%)	Age 7/8: 545–667 (65–80%) Age 14/15: 412–668 (49–80%) Age 27/28: 660 (79%)
Finnish JYLS	Second grade classrooms in Jyväskylä, Finland, in 1968	All students in twelve randomly selected classrooms	Age 8: 369 (100%)	Age 14: 356 (96%) Age 27: 321 (87%) Age 36: 311 (85%) Age 42: 285 (79%) Age 50: 268 (75%)
Swedish IDA	All third grade students in Örebro, Sweden, in 1965	100% sampling rate	Third grade (age 10): 958 (93%)	Age 13: 90% Age 15: 87% Age 16: 83% Age 43 for females (84%); Age 48 for males (75%) *(Table continues on p. 218.)*

Table 9.2 *Continued*

Study	Population	Sample	Sample Size and Response Rate	
			First Wave	Other Relevant Waves
British NCDS	British births in one March 1958 week	100% sampling rate	Birth: 17,416 (98%)	Age 7: 15,051 (86%) Age 16: 13,917 (80%) Age 33: 10,986 (63%) Age 42: 10,979 (63%) Age 46: 9,175 (53%)
British BCS	British births in one April 1970 week	100% sampling rate	Birth: 17,287 (97%)	Age 10: 14,350 (83%) Age 16: 11,206 (65%) Age 30: 10,833 (63%) Age 34: 9,316 (54%) Age 38: Release April/May 2010

Source: Authors' compilation based on data from U.S. BSS (Alexander and Entwisle 2003); JYLS (Pulkkinen 2006); IDA (Magnusson 1988); NCDS and BCS (Bynner et al. 2002).
Note: JYLS response rate excludes deceased study participants from the demoninators.

of completed schooling provides many analytical advantages. Our key dependent variable, then, is years of formal schooling that the child had completed by well into adulthood. As shown in online appendix table 9A.1, children averaged between twelve and fourteen years of completing schooling, with higher averages in the English-speaking countries than in the Nordic countries.[3]

Age-Seven-Through-Ten Skill and Behavior Measures   Comparability of age-seven-through-ten and thirteen-through-sixteen skill and behavior measures varies somewhat by domain (online appendix table 9A.2). In our empirical work, all of these skills and behavior measures are standardized using whole-sample means and standard deviations.

Four of the five studies provide both reading and math achievement test scores; the Finnish study contains only a teacher report of a general achievement composite. All five studies include teacher reports of items that reflect attention problems. With regard to antisocial behavior-aggression, four provide teacher reports and one provides parent reports. Only three studies provide middle-childhood measures of prosocial behavior. The four studies with measures of anxiety or internalizing behavior problems draw their measures from teacher reports.

Age-Thirteen-Through-Sixteen Skill and Behavior Measures   For the most part, age-thirteen-through-age-sixteen measures parallel those drawn from ages seven through ten (online appendix table 9A.3). In antisocial behavior, all five studies draw measures from teacher reports. All five studies provide measures of social skills.

Parental Schooling and Other Controls   We use parental schooling as our sole measure of parent SES. All studies provide measures of years of completed schooling for the parent as reported by the parent in the BSS and British studies and the grown children in the Swedish and Finnish studies. As with children's eventual completed schooling, we use ISCED conversion tables to code equivalent years of schooling from reports of type of completed education. As shown in online appendix table 9A.1, parent schooling averages were higher in the United States and United Kingdom than in the two Nordic countries.

We use a minimal set of additional background measures: child's sex, number of siblings and, where available, age when outcome was measured, race-ethnicity, and birth weight. Because we do not control for other dimensions of socioeconomic status (for example, income, family structure), the associations we estimate between parent and child education and between parent education and child skills are just that—associations that almost certainly overstate causal effects.

Figure 9.2   **Parent-Child Education Correlations and Coefficients**

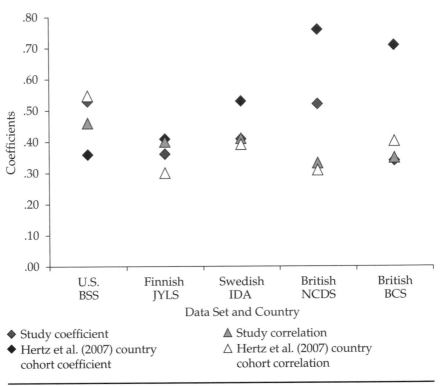

◆ Study coefficient   ▲ Study correlation
◆ Hertz et al. (2007) country   △ Hertz et al. (2007) country
   cohort coefficient   cohort correlation

Source: Authors' calculations and data from U.S. BSS (Alexander and Entwisle 2003); JYLS (Pulkkinen 2006); IDA (Magnusson 1988); NCDS and BCS (Bynner et al. 2002); and Hertz et al. (2007).

Results

In looking at the results, we begin with descriptive statistics and then move on to our regression results.

Correlations and Coefficients

We begin by presenting estimates of simple correlations and regression coefficients relating children's and parents' completed schooling. (These are labeled study correlations and coefficients in figure 9.2). Coefficients come from simple regressions of child schooling on parent schooling and can be interpreted as the fraction of a year by which a child's eventual completed schooling increases with every one-year increase in parental schooling.[4] Correlations provide a complementary measure of inter-generational associations by showing the fraction of a standard deviation increase in child schooling associated with a one standard deviation increase in parental schooling.[5]

Figure 9.2 also shows estimates of correlations and coefficients taken from the Hertz et al. study (2007), which are based on nationally representative sources of data. Because the Hertz data span a number of birth cohorts, we drew data as closely as possible to the birth years represented by our five study samples.

Looking first at correlations (the triangle markers in figure 9.1), Hertz and his colleagues find higher correlations (that is, less intergenerational mobility) in the United States relative to both the United Kingdom and our two Nordic countries. This is also true for correlations estimated from our five studies, although the differences are not as large as in the Hertz et al. study (2007).

In contrast, the Hertz et al. (2007) coefficient estimates of immobility are much higher in the United Kingdom than in any of the other countries. Despite being drawn from community rather than national samples, the Swedish and Finnish study estimates are remarkably close to their Hertz and colleague counterparts, whereas the estimates from the two British cohort studies are much lower. We have no ready explanation for the U.K. differences but note that our two nationally representative birth cohort studies are based on considerably larger sample sizes than the Hertz et al. estimates.

Skill and Behavior Gradients

How different are the SES skill and behavior gradients across countries, and do these gradients weaken or strengthen with age? As explained earlier, weakening associations are consistent with the hypothesis that school, peer, and neighborhood influences provide equalizing opportunities for children from different SES backgrounds, whereas increasing associations suggest increasing social stratification.

Our estimates of SES gradients come from a series of regressions in which each age-seven-through-ten and thirteen-through-sixteen skill and behavior measure is regressed on parent schooling, child gender, age, number of siblings, and—if available—child race-ethnicity and birth weight.[6] Because we standardize all of our skill and behavior measures to have unitary standard deviations, the resulting coefficients on parent education can be interpreted as the fraction of a standard deviation increase in a given skill or behavior associated with a one-year increase in parent schooling. Given the problems with age-sixteen data from the BCS (see online appendix), results from those data are not included in this analysis.

Coefficient estimates are plotted in figure 9.3. The first column of lines is based on the Baltimore BSS. The left point on the first line segment

Figure 9.3   Child Skill and Behavior Associations with Parent Education

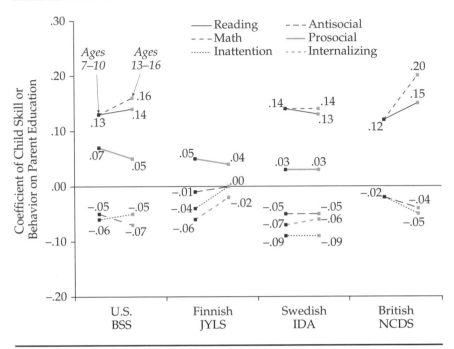

Source: Authors' calculations and data from U.S. BSS (Alexander and Entwisle 2003); JYLS (Pulkkinen 2006); IDA (Magnusson 1988); NCDS and BCS (Bynner et al. 2002).

(ages seven through ten) has a value of 0.13 and shows the slope of the SES gradient for BSS seven- and eight-year-olds: additional years of parent education are associated with about one-eighth of a standard deviation higher math scores.[7] (The coefficient on parent education in the child reading skill regression is also 0.13 and has an analogous interpretation.) A 0.13 coefficient is far from trivial. Having parents with college as opposed to high school degrees is associated with more than 0.05 standard deviation in test scores—a gap that is two-thirds as large as the black-white math gap in U.S. elementary schools (Duncan and Magnuson 2011).

The top line in the BSS column shows that the coefficient on parent schooling in predicting child math scores increased from 0.13 to 0.16 between middle childhood and adolescence, suggesting a steeper gradient and perhaps greater stratification in adolescence than middle childhood. The increase for reading scores (from 0.13 to 0.14) was smaller, but the behaviors showed a mixed pattern, the SES–antisocial coefficients becoming more negative (from –0.05 to –0.07) but those for both prosocial behavior and attention problems falling in absolute value. So, although achievement skill gradients appear to increase slightly with age in the Baltimore data, behavior gradients show a mixed pattern of small changes. More recent and nationally representative U.S. data presented in chapter 10 of this volume present a broadly similar picture: generally increasing academic skills gaps between ages seven and fourteen (although some possible equalization before age seven) and a more mixed pattern for behavior.

Ignoring slopes for the moment, a look at the general height of the test score data across the data sets suggests that almost all gradient values fall into the 0.10 to 0.20 range across the three countries where test scores are available.[8] There is little indication that Swedish gradients are flatter than gradients in the United States or United Kingdom.

Turning to the changes in gradient slopes between middle childhood and adolescence, it appears that the British NCDS patterns are quite consistent with increasing stratification with age (all of the coefficients increase in absolute value). In the NCDS achievement skills, the gradient slope increases are quite large—from 0.12 to 0.20 between ages ten and sixteen in math, and from 0.12 to 0.15 in reading.[9] Achievement gradients also increase in the BSS data, although not as much as with the NCDS. Swedish data show essentially constant coefficients across time. Although the Finnish JYLS did not provide measures of reading and math achievement, it did measure all of the behaviors of interest. Figure 9.3 shows small and falling SES gradient slopes for all of these behaviors.

Skills and Behaviors as Predictors

The top panel of table 9.3 (labeled Regression 1) shows the power of age-seven-through-age-ten skills and behaviors to predict children's years of completed schooling. Each column comes from a single regression in which completed schooling is regressed on the full set of listed skills and behaviors, plus parent education and child gender, age, number of siblings, and—where available—child race-ethnicity and birth weight. The bottom panel repeats these regressions using skill and behavior variables measured when the children were between ages thirteen and sixteen. The rightmost column presents a simple average of the coefficients in a given row.

Looking first at the averages in the top panel, it appears that middle childhood reading and, especially, math scores are most predictive of completed schooling. The 0.47 entry for math indicates that standard deviation increases in age-seven-through-ten math scores are associated, when averaged across the studies, with about one-half year of additional schooling. Looking across the math and reading rows, we see that the

Table 9.3   Coefficients and Standard Errors from Separate Regressions of Child's Completed Schooling

	U.S. BSS	Finnish JYLS	Swedish IDA	British NCDS	British BCS	Simple Average
Regression 1: middle childhood (ages seven to ten)						
Reading	0.33	—	0.33*	0.48*	0.31*	0.36
	(0.18)		(0.09)	(0.02)	(0.07)	
Math	0.57*	—	0.39*	0.42*	0.51*	0.47
	(0.16)		(0.10)	(0.03)	(0.07)	
School success	—	0.74*	—	—	—	
		(0.16)				
Attention problems	−0.08	0.00	−0.09	−0.11*	−0.27*	−0.11
	(0.15)	(0.16)	(0.09)	(0.03)	(0.08)	
Antisocial	0.07	−0.21	−0.13	−0.24*	−0.06	−0.11
	(0.14)	(0.15)	(0.08)	(0.03)	(0.05)	
Prosocial	0.29	0.28	0.06	—	−0.10	0.13
	(0.16)	(0.17)	(0.07)		(0.06)	
Anxiety-internalizing	0.23	−0.10	−0.14*	—	0.02	0.00
	(0.15)	(0.16)	(0.06)		(0.06)	
R^2	0.34	0.33	0.32	0.24	0.26	
Regression 2: adolescent (ages thirteen to sixteen)						
Reading	−0.00	—	0.23	0.46*	0.43*	0.28
	(0.16)		(0.12)	(0.03)	(0.06)	
Math	1.18*	—	0.55*	0.81*	0.78*	0.83
	(0.16)		(0.12)	(0.03)	(0.05)	
School success	—	1.64*	—	—	—	
		(0.14)				
Attention problems	0.36*	0.10	−0.30*	−0.11*	−0.17*	−0.02
	(0.18)	(0.16)	(0.11)	(0.03)	(0.07)	
Antisocial	−0.48*	0.19	−0.02	−0.14*	−0.09	−0.11
	(0.19)	(0.14)	(0.11)	(0.03)	(0.07)	
Prosocial	0.28*	0.06	0.09	0.10*	—	0.13
	(0.12)	(0.13)	(0.06)	(0.03)		
Anxiety-internalizing	−0.11	0.13	−0.15*	−0.04	−0.01	−0.03
	(0.13)	(0.13)	(0.07)	(0.03)	(0.05)	
R^2	0.40	0.47	0.38	0.34	0.31	
Observations	838	356	1026	11979	3677/3629	

Source: Authors' calculations and data from U.S. BSS (Alexander and Entwisle 2003); JYLS (Pulkkinen 2006); IDA (Magnusson 1988); NCDS and BCS (Bynner et al. 2002).
Notes: Control variables in all regressions include child's sex, number of siblings, age when outcome was measured, race-ethnicity, and, where available, birth weight. Standard errors in parentheses.
*$p < .05$

math and reading coefficients are positive and statistically significant in all four of the studies in which math and reading achievement was measured.

Average coefficients are smaller and patterns of individual coefficients less consistent in the various attention and behavior measures. The negative associations for attention and antisocial behaviors are most consistent, both averaging –0.11. Prosocial behavior is measured in four studies and has a substantial coefficient in two of the four.

The bottom panel shows that the patterns are generally repeated when the skills and behavior are measured between ages thirteen and sixteen. The math coefficients now average 0.83 and are uniformly much larger than coefficients on reading and the behavior measures. As with middle childhood, the adolescent measures of antisocial behavior generally have negative coefficients, whereas measures of prosocial behaviors all have positive coefficients. One anomalous result is the positive coefficients for adolescent attention problems in the Baltimore BSS.[10]

To gauge the relative predictive power of the middle childhood and adolescent skills and behaviors, we included both sets of measures, plus parent education and other background controls, in the same regression. Results, reported in table 9.4, show that adolescent skills are generally more powerful predictors of educational attainment than middle childhood skills. (One way of thinking about this is that adolescent skills and behaviors account for much of the association between middle childhood skills and behaviors and completed schooling observed in the top panel of table 9.3.) As in the bottom panel of table 9.3, adolescent math skills dominate, and average coefficient is 0.74.

Accounting for Inequality with Skills and Behaviors

Turning to one of the key questions of this chapter—whether child skills and behavior account for intergenerational SES correlations—figure 9.4 shows what fraction of the parent-child schooling correlation can be accounted for by middle childhood and adolescent skills and behaviors. The first bar (for example, with a height of 25 percent in the Baltimore BSS) shows that the intergenerational correlation between parent and child schooling is reduced by 25 percent when our collection of middle childhood skills and behaviors is added to the model.[11] The second bar (40 percent in the BSS) shows that the intergenerational correlation between parent and child schooling is reduced by 40 percent when that study's collection of adolescent skills and behaviors is added to the model. The third bar (also 40 percent in the BSS) shows the percentage of correlation accounted for by both sets of middle childhood and adolescent skill and behavior measures.

Table 9.4   Coefficients and Standard Errors from Regressions of Child's Completed Schooling

	U.S. BSS	Finnish JYLS	Swedish IDA	British NCDS	British BCS	Simple average
Middle childhood (ages seven to ten) skills-behaviors						
Reading	0.09	—	−0.08	0.17*	0.12	0.08
	(0.21)		(0.11)	(0.02)	(0.07)	
Math	0.01	—	0.01	0.18*	0.26*	0.12
	(0.16)		(0.15)	(0.02)	(0.06)	
School success	—	0.19	—	—	—	
		(0.15)				
Attention problems	−0.11	−0.01	0.09	−0.01	−0.14	−0.04
	(0.14)	(0.15)	(0.10)	(0.02)	(0.08)	
Antisocial	0.11	−0.02	−0.08	−0.12*	−0.02	−0.03
	(0.143	(0.14)	(0.08)	(0.03)	(0.05)	
Prosocial	0.17	0.34*	−0.04	—	−0.07	0.10
	(0.13)	(0.15)	(0.07)		(0.06)	
Anxiety-internalizing	0.20	−0.07	−0.08	—	0.00	0.01
	(0.15)	(0.14)	(0.08)		(0.06)	
Adolescent (ages thirteen to sixteen) skills-behaviors						
Reading	−0.07	—	0.29*	0.39*	0.35*	0.24
	(0.22)		(0.13)	(0.03)	(0.06)	
Math	1.11*	—	0.56*	0.70*	0.58*	0.74
	(0.17)		(0.16)	(0.03)	(0.05)	
School success	—	1.52*	—	—	—	
		(0.15)				
Attention problems	0.33*	0.05	−0.32*	−0.11*	−0.15*	−0.05
	(0.17)	(0.16)	(0.11)	(0.03)	(0.08)	
Antisocial	−0.44*	0.19	0.00	−0.14*	−0.09	−0.10
	(0.22)	(0.14)	(0.11)	(0.03)	(0.06)	
Prosocial	0.28*	−0.03	0.11	0.09*	—	0.11
	(0.12)	(0.13)	(0.07)	(0.03)		
Anxiety-internalizing	−0.14	0.23	−0.13	−0.03	−0.02	−0.02
	(0.15)	(0.13)	(0.08)	(0.03)	(0.05)	
R^2	0.41	0.49	0.38	0.35	0.33	
Observations	838	356	1026	11979	3629	

Source: Authors' calculations and data from U.S. BSS (Alexander and Entwisle 2003); JYLS (Pulkkinen 2006); IDA (Magnusson 1988); NCDS and BCS (Bynner et al. 2002).

Notes: Control variables in all regressions include child's sex, number of siblings, age when outcome was measured, and, where available, race/ethnicity and birth weight.

*$p < .05$

Figure 9.4   Intergenerational Correlation in Education

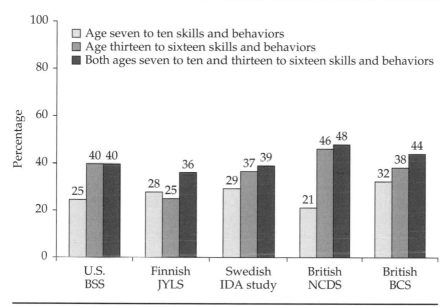

Source: Authors' calculations and data from U.S. BSS (Alexander and Entwisle 2003); JYLS (Pulkkinen 2006); IDA (Magnusson 1988); NCDS and BCS (Bynner et al. 2002).

The patterns are broadly similar across the five data sets. Middle childhood skills account for 21 percent to 32 percent of the intergenerational correlations. Adolescent skills account for significantly more than that in four of the five data sets.[12] And the combination of middle childhood and adolescent skills usually adds relatively little to the set of adolescent measures taken alone.[13] If anything, skills and behaviors appear to account for somewhat less of the intergenerational schooling correlations in the Nordic than English-speaking countries in our study.

Based on a much larger sample, chapter 3 of this volume provides a useful point of comparison for the adolescent measurements in our Swedish data. It finds that a collection of IQ and personality characteristics assessed at the point of military enlistment account for 46 percent of the correlation in completed schooling between fathers and sons. The counterpart figure for the Swedish IDA for adolescent skills and behaviors is 37 percent. As Carina Mood and her colleagues point out in chapter 3, their late-adolescence point of assessment may, in reverse causation, artificially inflate the explanatory power of their IQ and personality variables. Moreover, their powerful measures of cognitive ability are likely picking more of a genetic component than our measures of concrete achievement skills.

Extensions

To establish the robustness of our results, we engaged in a number of extensions of our basic analyses.

Does IQ Account for the Math Achievement Effect?   The strong relative predictive power of math achievement in both middle childhood and adolescence raises the question of whether the math achievement effect is really just a more general effect of cognitive ability. In adolescent math skills, the regressions presented in table 9.4 are most revealing, as they show that adolescent math skills strongly predict completed schooling even when prior math test scores are included in the regression.

With the two British data sets, it is possible to include measures of cognitive ability in the regression analyses reported in table 9.3. In the NCDS, the coefficients on age-seven reading and math scores in the top panel of table 9.3 are 0.48 and 0.42, respectively. The addition of scores from an age-seven copying test and a Draw-A-Man test reduces these two coefficients modestly—to 0.43 and 0.36. Adding an age-eleven measure of nonverbal IQ lowers the coefficients of these two age-seven measures to 0.29 and 0.25 (in all cases, standard errors are in the 0.02 to 0.03 range). Thus, even with the addition of cognitive scores taken four years after the measurement of math achievement, the math scores retain more than half of their explanatory power.[14] In age-sixteen reading and math, controls for all of these ability measures plus age-seven reading and math scores produce reading and math coefficients of 0.35 and 0.61, respectively.

In the BCS, the coefficients on age-seven reading and math scores in the top panel of table 9.3 are 0.31 and 0.51, respectively. The addition of scores from an age-five human figure drawing, a copying test, and a vocabulary assessment reduces these two coefficients to 0.27 and 0.46. In age-sixteen reading and math, controls for all of these ability measures plus age-ten IQ, plus age-seven reading and math scores produce reading and math coefficients of 0.35 and 0.58, respectively. As with the NCDS, the addition of ability controls still leaves quite substantial reading and, especially, math coefficients.

In the Swedish IDA data, the coefficients on age-ten reading and math in the top panel of table 9.3 are 0.33 and 0.39, respectively. The addition of an IQ composite score—the mean across two tests each of verbal, inductive, and spatial reasoning at age ten (α=0.80 across all six tests)—reduces the reading and math coefficients to 0.12 and 0.29. In age-thirteen reading and math, controlling for the age-ten IQ test score decreases reading and math associations from 0.23 and 0.55 to 0.20 and 0.52, respectively. So again, adolescent reading and math scores provide robust predictors of educational attainment, although in the IDA case the predictive power of middle-childhood reading scores is reduced substantially by the IQ controls. All in all, however, the academic skill measures in all three data sets remain significant predictors of completed schooling even in the presence of extensive controls for cognitive ability.

Summary

Our analyses have focused on the role of child skills and behaviors in intergenerational inequality in four countries: the United Kingdom, the United States, Sweden, and Finland. Across our five data sets and four countries, similarities were more striking than differences, and what differences we did find did not conform readily to Nordic versus English-speaking or any other country classification.

In skill and behavior gradients—essentially correlations between parent schooling levels and children's skill levels and behaviors—we generally found steeper gradients favoring higher-SES children in reading and math test scores than with behavior problems involving inattention, antisocial behavior, or mental health. Achievement test gradients grew as children transitioned from middle childhood to adolescence in two cases from our English-speaking countries (the Baltimore BSS and the U.K. NCDS). Gradients were fairly constant in Sweden. Finnish data did not include math and reading achievement; gradients for attention and behavior measures were small and falling with age. Whether the homogenous Finnish population and egalitarian-minded school system accounts for its unique status is an important but unanswered question.

In associations between children's skills and behaviors and their eventual completed schooling, virtually all of the studies showed that concrete reading and, especially, math achievement skills were consistently stronger predictors of attainment than were any of the problem behaviors we measured. This was true both in skills and behaviors measured in middle childhood and in adolescence.

Worries by adolescence researchers that the apparent predictive power of adolescent-based measures of skills and behaviors are mere reflections of more fundamental, earlier skills and behavior appear unwarranted. Adolescent skills and behaviors add a great deal to the explanation of variation in completed schooling over and above middle childhood skills in all five of the data sets we used.

The key descriptive question driving our inquiry concerned the importance of childhood and adolescent skills and behaviors in accounting for intergenerational inequality. Across all of our data, we find that childhood and adolescent skills and behaviors account for between one-third and one-half of the intergenerational correlations in the completed schooling of parents and children.

Looking across countries, Finland conformed more closely than Sweden to the Nordic ideal of promoting equality of opportunity. Finnish parent and child schooling levels were only weakly correlated, and children's SES-based skills and behavior gradients were modest and, if anything, decreased in slope as children advanced through school. Skills still mattered for children's completed schooling in Finland, but that they differed relatively little by SES appeared to weaken links between the accomplishments of parents and children.

Notes

1. This is described as follows: "The PISA Index of economic, social and cultural status was created on the basis of the following variables: the International Socio-Economic Index of Occupational Status . . . the highest level of education of the student's parents, converted into years of schooling. . . . the PISA index of family wealth, the index of home educational resources and the index of possessions related to the 'Classical' culture in the family home. . . . The ISEI represents the first principle component of the factors described above. The index has been constructed such that its mean is 0 and its standard deviation is 1" (OECD 2001, 221).

2. In chapter 11 of this volume, John Jerrim and John Micklewright also use PISA data to investigate SES gradients in reading scores. Using books in the home as their SES measure and 2002 PISA data, they find the steepest gradients for fifteen-year-olds in the United States and the flattest gradients for fifteen-year-olds in Sweden (data for Finland are not available). England's gradients are usually closer to those of the United States than of Sweden. The bulk of their chapter is focused on changes in gradient slopes between ages ten and fifteen, and they are unable to secure robust cross-country results.

3. In levels of schooling such as a university degree that may take varying numbers of years to complete, we took the normal completion time. See the note about schooling for the Finnish data in the online appendix, available at: http://www.russellsage.org/Ermisch_et_al_OnlineAppendix.pdf.

4. The regressions also control for child sex, age, number of siblings, and—if available—race-ethnicity and birth weight. The addition of these controls had little effect on the estimated schooling coefficients.

5. Ignoring the small adjustments for background controls, the correlation equals the coefficient multiplied by the ratio of the standard deviations of parent to child completed schooling.

6. As with the parent-child coefficients, results were quite similar when these regressions included only the parent schooling measure.

7. The standard error for this coefficient is 0.01, so the 0.13 is highly significant in a statistical sense. For the entire set of BSS coefficients, standard errors

ranged from 0.01 to 0.02. For the British NCDS, the standard errors are around 0.01, whereas all of the IDA and JLYS standard errors are in the 0.02 to 0.03 range.

8. Finnish data provide a teacher-reported measure of general achievement at age eight and a school-records-based GPA at age fourteen. Slopes of these measures by parent education are 0.10 and 0.06, respectively, but their obvious differences from reading and math achievement led us to not include them in figure 9.3.

9. Chapter 6 in this volume examines British gradients between ages three and seven and fails to find clear patterns.

10. The BSS results proved somewhat sensitive to which measures were included in the regression models. The simple correlation between adolescent attention problems and adolescent reading scores was –0.22. The math correlation was –0.25.

11. These regressions also include child gender, age, number of siblings, and—when available—race-ethnicity and birth weight.

12. To say that adolescent skills and behaviors add to the ability of middle childhood skills and behaviors to account for intergenerational correlations does not necessarily imply that SES-biased gradients in these skills and behaviors are fanning out over time. Figure 9.3 addresses the fanning-out issue more directly, and shows that parent education accounts for an increasing amount of the variation in academic skills in the U.S. and U.K. data sets, but more mixed patterns, particularly for behaviors, in those of Finland and Sweden.

13. One point of comparison is with the BCS, for which both sets of predictors account for 44 percent of the intergenerational schooling correlation Blanden, Gregg, and MacMillan (2006) find that their larger collection of cognitive and noncognitive skills up to age sixteen accounts for only 32 percent of the intergeneration income correlation.

14. The coefficients on aggression and attention problems fall from –0.24 and –0.11 to –0.20 and –0.07, with standard errors of 0.03.

References

Alexander. Karl, and Doris Entwisle. 2003. *The Beginning School Study, 1982–2002*. 01293Murray Research Archive [Distributor] V2 [Version]. Information available at: http://dvn.iq.harvard.edu/dvn/dv/mra/faces/study/StudyPage.xhtml?globalId=hdl:1902.1/ (accessed February 27, 2012).

Baroody, Arthur J. 2003. "The Development of Adaptive Expertise and Flexibility: The Integration of Conceptual and Procedural Knowledge." In *The Development of Arithmetic Concepts and Skills: Constructing Adaptive Expertise Studies*, edited by Arthur J. Baroody and Ann Dowker. Mahwah, N.J.: Lawrence Erlbaum.

Blanden, Jo, Paul Gregg, and Lindsey Macmillan. 2006. "Accounting for Intergenerational Income Persistence: Noncognitive Skills, Ability and Education." *CEE* discussion papers 0073. London: London School of Economics.

Bynner John, Neville Butler, Elsa Ferri, Peter Shepherd, and Kate Smith. 2002. *The Design and Conduct of the 1999–2000 Surveys of the National Child Development Study and the 1970 British Birth Cohort Study. U.K. Data Archive.* CLS Cohort Studies Working Paper 1. London: Centre for Longitudinal Studies, Instititute of Education.

Brock, Laura, Sara E. Rimm-Kaufman, Lori Nathanson, and Kevin J. Grimm. 2009. "The Contributions of Hot and Cool Executive Function to Children's Academic Achievement, Learning-Related Behaviors, and Engagement in Kindergarten." *Early Childhood Research Quarterly* 24: 337–49.

Case, Anne, Darren Lubotsky, and Christine Paxson. 2002. "Economic Status and Health in Childhood: Origins of the Gradient." *American Economic Review* 92(5): 1308–334.

Cunha, Flavio, James Heckman, Lance Lochner, and Dimitri Masterov. 2005. "Interpreting the Evidence on Life Cycle Skill Formation." In *Handbook of the Economics of Education,* edited by Eric Hanushek and Finis Welch. Oxford: North Holland.

Currie, Janet, and Mark Stabile. 2007. "Child Mental Health and Human Capital Accumulation: The Case of ADHD." *Journal of Health Economics* 25(6): 1094–118

Duncan, Greg J., Chantelle Dowsett, Amy Classens, Katherine Magnuson, Aletha Huston, Pamela Klebanov, Linda Pagani, Leon Feinstein, Mimi Engel, Jeanne Brooks-Gunn, Holly Sexton, Kathryn Duckworth, and Christa Japel. 2007. "School Readiness and Later Achievement." *Developmental Psychology* 43(6): 1428–446.

Duncan, Greg J., and Katherine Magnuson. 2011. "The Nature and Impact of Early Achievement Skills, Attention Skills, and Behavior Problems." In *Whither Opportunity: Rising Inequality, Schools, and Children's Life Chances,* edited by Greg Duncan and Richard J. Murnane. New York: Russell Sage Foundation.

Eisenberg, Nancy, Adrian Sadovsky, and Tracy L. Spinrad. 2005. "Associations of Emotion-Related Regulation with Language Skills, Emotion Knowledge, and Academic Outcomes." *New Directions for Child and Adolescent Development* 2005(109): 109–18.

Ensminger, Margaret E., and Anita L. Slusarcick. 1992. "Paths to High School Graduation or Dropout: A Longitudinal Study of a First-Grade Cohort." *Sociology of Education* 65(2): 95–113.

Entwisle, Doris R., Karl L. Alexander, and Linda S. Olson. 2007. "Early Schooling: The Handicap of Being Poor and Male." *Sociology of Education* 80(2): 114–38.

Fantuzzo, John, Rebecca Bulotsky, Paul McDermott, Samuel Mosca, and Megan N. Lutz. 2003. "A Multivariate Analysis of Emotional and Behavioral Adjustment and Preschool Educational Outcomes." *School Psychology Review* 32(2): 185–203.

Feinstein, Leon. 2000. "The Relative Economic Importance of Academic, Psychological and Behavioural Attributes Developed in Childhood." *CEP* discussion paper 0443. London: London School of Economics.

Fergusson, David M., and L. John Horwood. 1998. "Early Conduct Problems and Later Life Opportunities." *The Journal of Child Psychology and Psychiatry and Allied Disciplines* 39(8): 1097–108.

Heckman James, and Yona Rubinstein. 2001. "The Importance of Noncognitive Skills: Lessons from the GED Testing Program." *American Economic Review* 91(2): 145–49.

Heckman, James, Sergio Urzua, and Jora Stixtud. 2006. "The Effects of Cognitive and Noncognitive Abilities on Labor Market Outcomes and Social Behavior." *Journal of Labor Economics* 24(3): 411–82.

Hertz, Thomas, Tamara Jayasundera, Patrizio Piraino, Sibel Selcuk, Nicole Smith, and Alina Verashchagina. 2007. "The Inheritance of Educational Inequality: International Comparisons and Fifty-Year Trends." *The B.E. Journal of Economic Analysis and Policy* 7(2): Article 10.

Hinshaw, Stephen P. 1992. "Externalizing Behavior Problems and Academic Underachievement in Childhood and Adolescence: Causal Relationships and Underlying Mechanisms." *Psychological Bulletin* 111(1): 127–55.

Karabel, Jerome. 2005. *The Chosen: The Hidden History of Admission and Exclusion at Harvard, Yale and Princeton.* New York: Houghton Mifflin.

Knudsen, Eric I., James Heckman, Judy Cameron, and Jack Shonkoff. 2006. "Economic, Neurobiological, and Behavioral Perspectives on Building America's Future Workforce." *Proceedings of the National Academy of Science* 103(27): 10155–162.

Kokko, Katja, and Lea Pulkkinen. 2000. "Aggression in Childhood and Long-Term Unemployment in Adulthood: A Cycle of Maladaptation and Some Protective Factors." *Developmental Psychology* 36(4): 463–72.

Magnusson, David. 1988. *Individual Development from an Interactional Perspective: A Longitudinal Study (Paths Through Life,* vol. 1). Hillside, N.J.: Lawrence Erlbaum Associates, Inc.

——. 1998. "Back to the Phenomena: Theory, Methods, and Statistics in Psychological Research." *European Journal of Personality* 6(1): 1–14.

Masten, Ann, Glenn I. Roisman, Jeffrey D. Long, Keith B. Burt, Jelena Obradovic, Jennifer R. Riley, Kristen Boelcke-Stennes, and Auke Tellegen. 2005. "Developmental Cascades: Linking Academic Achievement and Externalizing and Internalizing Symptoms Over 20 Years." *Developmental Psychology* 41(5): 733–46.

McLeod, Jane D., and Karen Kaiser. 2004. "Childhood Emotional and Behavioral Problems in Educational Attainment." *American Sociological Review* 69(5): 636–58.

Murnane, Richard, John Willett, and Frank Levy. 1995. "The Growing Importance of Cognitive Skills in Wage Determination." *Review of Economics and Statistics* 77(2): 251–66.

Neal, Derek, and William Johnson. 1996. "The Role of Premarket Factors in Black-White Wage Differences." *Journal of Political Economy* 104(5): 869–95.

Newcomb, Andrew F., William M. Bukowski, and Linda Pattee. 1993. "Children's Peer Relations: A Meta-Analytical Review of Popular, Rejected, Neglected, Controversial, and Average Sociometric Status." *Psychological Bulletin* 113(1): 99–128.

NICHD Early Child Care Research Network. 2005. "Pathways to Reading: The Role of Oral Language in the Transition to Reading." *Developmental Psychology* 41(2): 428–42.

Organisation for Economic Co-Operation and Development (OECD). 2001. *Knowledge and Skills for Life: First Results from the OECD Program of International Student Assessment (PISA) 2000*. Paris: Organisation for Economic Co-Operation and Development.

Pianta, Robert, and Megan Stuhlman. 2004. "Teacher-Child Relationships and Children's Success in the First Years of School." *School Psychology Review* 33(3): 444–58.

Posner, Michael, and Mary K. Rothbart. 2000. "Developing Mechanisms of Self-Regulation." *Development and Psychopathology* 12(3): 427–41.

Pulkkinen Lea. 2006. *The Jyva "Skyla" Longitudinal Study of Personality and Social Development (JYLS)*. In *Socioemotional Development and Health From Adolescence to Adulthood*, edited by Lea Pulkkinen, Jaakko Kaprio, and Richard Rose. New York: Cambridge University Press. Information available at: https://www.jyu.fi/ytk/laitokset/psykologia/en/research/jyls (accessed March 6, 2012).

Pulkkinen, Lea, Minna Ohranen, and Asko Tolvanen. 1999. "Personality Antecedents of Career Orientation and Stability Among Women Compared to Men." *Journal of Vocational Behavior* 54(1): 37–58.

Pungello, Elizabeth P., Janis B. Kupersmidt, Margaret R. Burchinal, and Charlotte Patterson. 1996. "Environmental Risk Factors and Children's Achievement from Middle Childhood to Adolescence." *Developmental Psychology* 32(4): 755–67.

Raver, C. Cybele, Radiah Smith-Donald, Tiffany Hayes, and Stephanie M. Jones. 2005. "Self-Regulation Across Differing Risk and Sociocultural Contexts: Preliminary Findings from the Chicago School Readiness Project." Paper presented at the biennial meeting of the Society for Research in Child Development. Atlanta, Georgia (April 10, 2005).

Schulenberg, John E., Jennifer. L. Maggs, and Patrick M. O'Malley. 2003. "How and Why the Understanding of Developmental Continuity and Discontinuity Is Important: The Sample Case of Long-Term Consequences of Adolescent Substance Use." In *Handbook of the Life Course*, edited by J. T. Mortimer and M. J. Shanahan. New York: Plenum Publishers.

Sewell, William H., Archibald O. Haller, and Alejandro Portes. 1969. "The Educational and Early Occupational Attainment Process." *American Sociological Review* 34(1): 82–92.

Shepherd, Peter M. 1985. *The National Child Development Study. An Introduction to the Background to the Study and the Methods of Data Collection*. Working Paper No. 1. London: Social Statistics Research Unit, City University.

Snow, Catherine E., Marie S. Burns, and Peg Griffin, eds. 1998. *Preventing Reading Difficulties in Young Children*. Washington, D.C.: National Academy Press.

UNESCO. 2006. *International Standard Classification of Education 2006*. Montreal: UNESCO Institute for Statistics.

Vitaro, Frank, Mara Brendengen, Simon Larose, and Richard E. Tremblay. 2005. "Kindergarten Disruptive Behaviors, Protective Factors, and Educational Achievement by Early Adulthood." *Journal of Educational Psychology* 97(4): 617–29.

Whitehurst, Grover J., and Christopher J. Lonigan. 1998. "Child Development and Emergent Literacy." *Child Development* 69(3): 848–72.

Chapter 10

SES Gradients in Skills During the School Years

KATHERINE MAGNUSON, JANE WALDFOGEL,

AND ELIZABETH WASHBROOK

THE FOCUS of this study is the development of socioeconomic status (SES) gradients in skills between the ages of four and fourteen in the United States and England, two countries characterized by high levels of income inequality and low levels of intergenerational mobility. Prior research provides ample evidence that sizable disparities in school readiness between children from more or less advantaged families are present at school entry in both these countries (Lee and Burkam 2002; Duncan and Magnuson 2011; Magnuson and Waldfogel 2005; Waldfogel and Washbrook 2009a, 2009b).

In this study, we address the question of whether these early SES gradients in skills widen, hold constant, or diminish as children move through the school years. Answering this question is important because if we are to tackle the high levels of income inequality and low levels of mobility that exist in these two countries, it is essential to know the extent to which schools are playing an equalizing or a disequalizing role.

We recognize that factors outside schools (factors related to families, neighborhoods, and peers, as well as labor markets and social welfare policies) may contribute to widening or narrowing differentials during the school years. Nevertheless, to the extent that schools are equalizing, we would expect these skill gradients to narrow as children move through school; conversely, if schools act to magnify inequalities in early skills, we would expect to see a widening of gradients. If school systems in some countries are more equalizing than others, then the development of gradients may vary across countries. John Jerrim and John Micklewright provide some evidence in chapter 11 of this volume that this is the case, finding that gradients widen, particularly at the top of the distribution, between fourth grade and eighth grade (roughly ages ten and fourteen) in both the United States and England and that they tend to widen less in some other countries (such as Canada and Germany).[1]

Gradients could also vary within countries if some parts of the school system are more equalizing than others. For example, in England, children tend to attend more equal schools at the primary level, when most attend their local school, than at the secondary level, when complex admissions processes and large differences in school quality increase the stakes to admission to the right school.[2] Research in England has confirmed that affluent parents are more likely to send their children to a secondary school outside their local area and that when they do so, it is likely to be of higher quality (Burgess and Briggs 2006; Burgess et al. 2006). Thus, we might expect gradients in England to widen more during the secondary school years (after age eleven) than they do during the primary years. In chapter 12 of this volume, John Ermisch and Emilia Del Bono provide evidence of this pattern and argue that it is a function of the sorting of children into secondary schools.

Relatively little empirical evidence describes the development of such SES disparities in academic skills and behavior in either of our countries. In the United States, research on racial and ethnic test score gaps suggests that the black-white test score gap at school entry is about half of the size of the eventual high school gap (Jencks and Phillips 1998; Magnuson and Waldfogel 2008). However, less attention has been given to understanding the development of SES gradients. Pedro Carneiro and James Heckman (2003) analyze reading and math scores for children age six to twelve from the National Longitudinal Survey of Youth (NLSY) by family income quartile and find that large gradients exist at age six and widen somewhat through age twelve. Analyses of children from the Early Childhood Longitudinal Study—Kindergarten Cohort (the data set we use here) find that children from families with more risk factors (defined as income below poverty, primary home language not English, parent with less than high school education, and single-parent family) make less progress in the number of questions answered correctly on reading and math assessments between kindergarten and third grade (Rathbun, West, and Germino-Hausken 2004), suggesting that SES gradients widen over that period, but results after third grade have not been reported. A much smaller study found that SES gaps in cognitive outcomes either narrowed or held constant over the first year or two of school (Stipek and Ryan 1997).

Two recent studies in England examine SES gradients in cognitive outcomes during the school years. A report for the National Equality Panel finds that gaps in cognitive outcomes between SES groups (whether defined by income or parental education) widen both between ages seven and eleven and ages eleven and fourteen, before narrowing slightly between ages fourteen and sixteen (Goodman, Sibieta, and Washbrook 2009). A report for the Joseph Rowntree Foundation reports similar findings. Both studies used the children from the Avon Longitudinal Study of Parents and Children (ALSPAC) for their analysis of children ages seven to eleven (the same data set we analyze in this chapter) and the Longitudinal Study of Young People in England for older children (Goodman and Gregg 2010).

In this chapter, we provide new evidence on the gradients across the two countries taking advantage of detailed data on both parental SES and child outcomes. Consistent with the approach taken by the CRITA project, our primary measure of parental SES is parental education (measured as the highest education of either parent in the home), but we also present results by family income. With regard to child outcomes, our primary focus is on academic achievement skills as measured by children's scores on tests of reading and math, but we also conducted supplementary analyses of children's behavior.

Data Sources and Measures

Our data for the United States come from the Early Childhood Longitudinal Study-Kindergarten Cohort (ECLS-K), which follows a nationally representative sample of 21,409 children from their start in primary (elementary) school in the fall of 1998. Children were typically age five at school entry and thus most of the children in this cohort were born in 1993. Parental caregivers were interviewed, and a rich array of child and family information was collected. In addition, reading and math assessments were administered by research staff, and teachers rated children's skill proficiencies and behavior across a variety of dimensions. Six waves of data collection have been completed, with the most recent wave of data collected in 2007 when most children were age fourteen.

Our data for England come from the Avon Longitudinal Survey of Parents and Children, which follows a cohort of 13,988 children born in the county of Avon (in the south-west of England) in 1991 and 1992. ALSPAC aimed to recruit all the pregnant women in a given time window in a single geographical region. The study surveys and assesses mothers and their children frequently, using postal questionnaires, hands-on clinics, and a variety of other instruments. Information about children's reading and math skills come from the National Pupil Database (NPD), an administrative data set matched to ALSPAC, which provides information about achievement assessments administered periodically to all children in English state schools. It is important that although we use the term *England*, our data are drawn from a single county in the southwest of England. However, although not a nationally representative survey, ALSPAC covers a diverse area and has been shown to be broadly representative of the English population (Golding et al. 2001).[3]

Table 10.1 provides a summary of the main features of the national education systems in our two countries. In both countries, the school year traditionally begins in September after the summer recess. In England, children's progression is based strictly on age, whereas in the United States it is possible for children to repeat or skip grades on the basis of academic performance.

The starting age for compulsory schooling and the major transition points between levels of schooling differ across the two countries. Compulsory schooling in the United States typically begins at age five when children enter kindergarten, and elementary schooling spans the subsequent five years, beginning with first grade at age six and ending with fifth grade at age eleven.[4] Middle school then spans the next three years (sixth to eighth grades), the transition to high school occurring at the start of ninth grade when most children are age fourteen.

Compulsory schooling begins a year earlier in England, with children entering reception year at age four. Primary schooling is typically provided within a single institution for seven years, each grade being referred to as numerical year. A distinction is made between *infants*—the three years from age four to age seven—and *juniors*—the four years from age seven to age eleven. The key transition occurs when children begin secondary school, entering year seven at age eleven. Unlike in the United States, there is generally no distinction between middle and high school, and the vast majority of English children remain in the same institution from age eleven until the end of compulsory schooling at age sixteen.[5]

Reading and Math Achievement Outcomes

Our analysis of U.S. children's reading and math skills uses data from all six waves of the ECLS-K, as shown in table 10.1. The assessments were created for the ECLS-K by a team of experts, with some items adapted from existing instruments. The reading test assessed knowledge of letters and word recognition, beginning and ending sounds, vocabulary, and passage comprehension. The math test evaluated understanding of numbers, geometry, and spatial relations. Reported reliabilities for the tests were quite high for all assessments (National Center for Education Statistics 2001). These tests assess children's performance using Item Response Theory (IRT) methods, which use a small set of items to route children to a second set of items that differ in their difficulty. The resulting IRT scores represent the number of items the children would answer correctly if they had taken the entire battery of test items.

Our England measures of reading and math achievement differ in a number of dimensions from the U.S. outcome measures. Key stage (KS) assessments of reading and math skills are compulsory for all pupils in English state schools at ages seven (KS1), eleven (KS2), and fourteen (KS3).[6] Tests are designed to assess whether children have learned the material expected

Table 10.1   Outcome Assessment in Context of Typical Compulsory Schooling System

Age at End of School Year	United States		England	
	Level-Grade	Date of Assessment	Level-Grade	Date of Assessment
Four to five	**Preschool** Prekindergarten*		**Primary school (infants)** Reception	EA: Fall 1998–1997 (4.5)
Five to six	Kindergarten*	Fall 1998 (5.7), Spring 1999 (6.2)	Year 1	
Six to seven	**Elementary school** Grade 1	Spring 2000 (7.2)	Year 2	KS1: Spring 1998–2000 (7.2)
Seven to eight	Grade 2		**Primary school (juniors)** Year 3	
Eight to nine	Grade 3	Spring 2002 (9.2)	Year 4	
Nine to ten	Grade 4		Year 5	
Ten to eleven	Grade 5	Spring 2004 (11.2)	Year 6	KS2: Spring 2002–2004 (11.2)
Eleven to twelve	**Middle school** Grade 6		**Secondary school** Year 7	
Twelve to thirteen	Grade 7		Year 8	
Thirteen to fourteen	Grade 8	Spring 2004 (14.2)	Year 9	KS3: Spring 2005–2007 (14.2)
Fourteen to fifteen	**High school** Grade 9		Year 10	
Fifteen to sixteen	Grade 10		Year 11	

Source: Authors' calculations based on data from ECLS-K (U.S. Department of Education 2009) and ALSPAC (University of Bristol 2009).
*Prekindergarten is not compulsory in the United States, and kindergarten is compulsory only in some states, although nearly all age-eligible children attend kindergarten even in states where it is not mandatory.
EA = Entry Assessment; KS1 = Key Stage 1; KS2 = Key Stage 2; KS3 = Key Stage 3.

by their age or grade and are scored on a scale from 0 to 7.[7] In addition, information from a teacher-rated entry assessment (EA) of reading and math skills is available on the ALSPAC children at the time of school entry, just before the age of five, although these measures are not strictly comparable with the key stage scores. The ALSPAC children entered school in three different cohorts, starting in 1995, 1996, or 1997 depending on their dates of birth.[8] As each achievement assessment is administered in specific school year, collection of the measures took place over three calendar years, as shown in table 10.1.

Raw Versus Standardized Scores

One important consideration for our analysis is whether to use raw or standardized scores, particularly for the measures of academic achievement. Each measurement approach has limitations. Studies indicate that children's academic achievement skills typically demonstrate increasing variance over the course of development. Put another way, the absolute difference in skills between low- and high-achieving children tends to increase as children grow, as evident by increasing standard deviations around mean test scores. Although there may be increasing divergence in absolute levels of skills, standardized test scores remove such variation by equating standard deviations (or variance) across time points, which in turn remove the increasing variance we are interested in documenting. At the same time, however, raw scores reflect the number of questions children have answered correctly or the number of skills they demonstrate proficiency in, which is determined in large part by the specificity of test construction (rather than skill levels), and thus are difficult to interpret because a one-unit change may have different meanings at different points on the scale (Reardon 2007). As a practical result of this non-uniform interval metric, in the ECLS-K gains may seem greater at the higher end of the scale because there are disproportionately more items that discriminate between higher levels of skills (Reardon 2007). In addition, it is difficult to construct meaningful measures that are based on the same metric from early childhood to adolescence, so frequently standardization is necessary to compare scores over time. An advantage of the ECLS-K data is that, for the most, part raw scores are measured on a common scale over time so that we are able to contrast gradients using the two methods.[9]

For these reasons, we balance the strengths and limitations of each approach by analyzing both raw and standardized scores and interpreting both with appropriate caution. All standardized scores are normalized to have a mean of 0 and a standard deviation of 1, and thus regression coefficients can be interpreted as effect sizes that can be compared across different outcomes.

Missing Data

Another important consideration for our analysis is how to handle missing data. As is always the case with longitudinal data, there is attrition in both samples over time. In the U.S. data set, of the 13,278 children who are present, have data on parental education, and are assessed in reading in the fall of kindergarten, only 6,759 have complete data at all assessment points for the reading test score.[10] In the England data set, of the 13,988 children in the core ALSPAC cohort, only 9,209 have complete key stage test score data, indicating that they attended a state school at seven, eleven, and fourteen.

If this attrition were random, simply analyzing complete cases (that is, those that are present, with no missing data, at all time points) would not yield biased estimates. But, the attrition in the England achievement sample is certainly nonrandom, reflecting the mechanism of school selection because children who move to independent fee-paying schools are missing achievement data since children in such schools do not take Key Stage tests. Likewise, attrition from the U.S. ECLS-K sample is also nonrandom by design in that only a portion of children who move schools are followed by the study, creating a pattern of greater missing data among disadvantaged groups. For this reason, we elected instead to use multiple imputation to replace missing data. We do not impute data for children who were never assessed or only assessed once in a given domain (with the exception that we do impute key stage data for English children who ever attended a state school), and we omit U.S. students who were not deemed proficient in English (and were therefore not tested in reading) in kindergarten.[11]

We implemented multiple imputation using the user-written ICE command in Stata (Royston 2009). For the ECLS-K and the ALSPAC, we created five data sets and analyzed them using the MICOMBINE Stata command (Royston 2009).[12]

After multiple imputation, the U.S. sample size is 15,654 for reading and 15,648 for math. The England sample size is 12,986 for reading and math (implying that 1,002 children, or 7.2 percent of the original birth cohort, had never attended an English state school by age fourteen). Descriptive statistics for each of the national samples by education and by income are available in online appendix 10A.[13]

Methodology

We document the distributions of children's academic scores by two indicators of parental resources defined as comparably as possible across the two countries.

The first indicator we use is the highest level of education attained by a parent or parent's spouse or partner in the home. This is measured at the first wave, when children were approximately age five, in the ECLS-K and during pregnancy in ALSPAC. The levels of educational qualifications are quite different in the two countries. To create some consistency, we categorize parents' education using the ISCED categories, which have been specifically developed by UNESCO to harmonize education categorization across countries. Using this system, those with less than a high school education in the United States are categorized as low-educated (ISCED 2), those with a high school diploma or GED are low-middle (ISCED 3 to 4), those with an associate's degree are high-middle (ISCED 5B), and those with a bachelor's degree or more education are high-educated (ISCED 5A and 6). For England, having only GCSEs D-F maps onto low-educated (ISCED-2), GCSEs A-C or A-levels map onto low-middle (ISCED 3 to 4), other qualifications map onto high-middle (ISCED 5B), and a first degree or more education maps onto high-educated (ISCED 5A and 6).

This classification results in similar shares of children with low-educated parents in the reading and math samples across the two countries (7 percent in the United States and 11 percent in England), but somewhat different shares with highly educated parents (34 percent in the United States versus 19 percent in England).[14] Proportions in the low-middle versus high-middle education categories also differ, but these differences within the middle two categories are not of great concern because our main interest is in the divergence (or convergence) of children's skills and behavior at the bottom and at the top of the distributions.

Our second indicator of family SES is family income. The ECLS-K collects information about total annual household income in the second wave of data collection (age 6.2). In ALSPAC, weekly net household income is collected slightly earlier when the children are thirty-three and forty-seven months old and the information is much less specific than in the ECLS-K. We average the two available measures to create the most accurate household income measure possible, but recognize that as it is likely to be of poorer quality than the U.S. measure we will tend to underestimate the income gradients in the ALSPAC cohort.[15] In both data sets, families are categorized into income quintiles, quintile 1 representing the poorest fifth and quintile 5 the richest. This measure, based only on the ranking of families within each country by income, has the advantage that it is largely insensitive to differences in the definition of income across the data sets.

Categorizing families by their income quintile by definition creates five equally sized groups. Our parental education categories, in contrast, result in unequal groupings, which distinguish the bottom tenth, the top 20 to 30 percent, and the roughly 60 to 70 percent in the middle two categories. Therefore, we would not expect parental education gradients to be the same as family income gradients. In addition, the use of parental education as a stratifying mechanism, rather than family income, results in different characteristics of families within groups. In the United States, for example, 28 percent of children in the lowest parental education group are Hispanic, compared with only 16 percent in the lowest income quintile. Similarly, single-parent families make up 58 percent of the lowest income quintile group, but represent only 46 percent of the lowest parental education group. Ethnic differences are less marked in the ALSPAC cohort, where only 5 percent of the sample is nonwhite, but again single-parent families are a greater fraction of the low-income group (40 percent) than of the low-education group (26 percent). Note also that although the lowest parental education group is much smaller than the lowest income group in both countries, it does not signify more extreme economic disadvantage. Average incomes are twice as high among the (smaller) low-education group than the (larger) low-income group in the United States, and 50 percent higher in England.

Our analysis of gradients relies on regression models that estimate the mean child outcomes in each parental education group, or family income quintile, at the various age points in each of our countries. For ease of comparability across countries, we characterize the timing of each assessment according to the mean age of sample children at the time of assessment, using whole years when referring to ages in the text (as in normal parlance), but using year to one decimal place when plotting figures so that distances between points accurately reflect the number of months that have passed. Our main interest is whether the gaps between these mean scores—SES gradients—that are apparent at the earliest assessment point widen, narrow, or remain constant as children move through the school years

Results: Development of the Gradients in Achievement Skills

Figures 10.1 and 10.2 display the development of mean reading and math raw (unstandardized) scores in the U.S. sample, by parental education group and by family income quintile. Detailed regression results treating the lowest SES category as the reference group are presented in tables 10.2 and 10.3. Results for reading scores at each age by the four ISCED categories of parental education show that the gaps between the groups are relatively flat between fall (age 5.7) and spring of kindergarten (age 6.2) but widen thereafter. In particular, it appears that the group with highly educated parents pulls away from the others over time, and that children with the least-educated parents lose ground. Detailed regression results indicate that children of the highly educated parents score 10 points higher than children of the least-educated parents at age five,

Figure 10.1   Mean U.S. Raw Scores

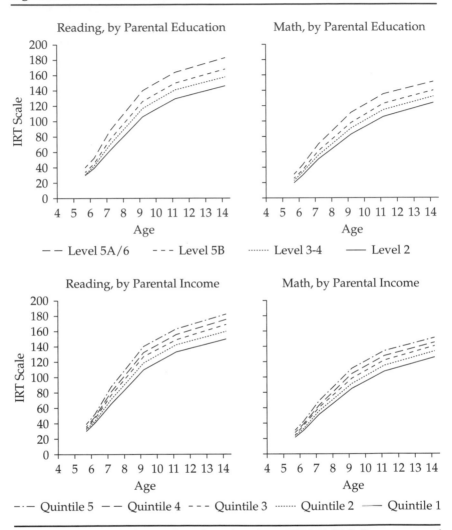

Source: Authors' calculations based on data from ECLS-K (U.S. Department of Education 2009).

and this gap increases significantly to 37 points by age fourteen. By age fourteen, children with the least-educated parents have mean reading scores that are about the same as the mean reading scores that children with highly educated parents had at age nine.

A similar pattern is evident for trends in mean math scores by parental education group, all groups making gains over time but the children of

Figure 10.2   Mean U.S. Standardized Scores

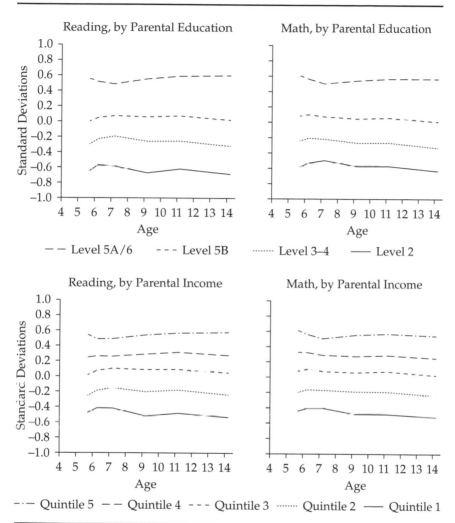

Source: Authors' calculations based on data from ECLS-K (U.S. Department of Education 2009).

the most highly educated making larger gains. In this case, the performance of the children of the least-educated does not lag as much, their mean scores at age fourteen on par with those that the middle groups earned at age eleven. Nevertheless, by age fourteen, the gap between the children of the most- and least-educated parents has significantly widened to 27.5 points, versus 10 points at age five.

Table 10.2   U.S. Achievement Outcomes, Reading IRTs

Education	KF (5.7)	KS (6.2)	1S (7.2)	3S (9.2)	5S (11.2)	8S (14.2)
A. Parental Education						
Level 3	2.48**	3.36**	7.92**	11.27**	10.79**	12.36**
	(0.33)	(0.46)	(0.80)	(0.89)	(0.89)	(0.89)
Level 5B	4.93**	6.61**	13.98**	20.24**	19.73**	22.35**
	(0.33)	(0.45)	(0.80)	(0.89)	(0.93)	(1.02)
Level 5A6	10.15**	13.08**	25.71**	35.19**	33.50**	36.99**
	(0.33)	(0.45)	(0.79)	(0.89)	(0.97)	(0.98)
Constant	29.71**	39.30**	62.81**	105.98**	129.76**	145.81**
	(0.29)	(0.41)	(0.72)	(0.81)	(0.86)	(0.87)
Observations	15654	15654	15654	15654	15654	15654
R^2	0.12	0.10	0.12	0.16	0.16	0.17
B. Family Income						
Quintile 2	1.68**	2.41**	5.40**	8.57**	8.57**	9.76**
	(0.28)	(0.38)	(0.67)	(0.87)	(0.95)	(0.90)
Quintile 3	3.79**	5.34**	11.45**	16.66**	16.10**	18.90**
	(0.26)	(0.35)	(0.62)	(0.72)	(0.71)	(0.75)
Quintile 4	5.95**	7.60**	15.30**	22.80**	22.21**	25.27**
	(0.26)	(0.36)	(0.60)	(0.74)	(0.77)	(0.74)
Quintile 5	8.93**	11.15**	21.85**	30.36**	28.89**	32.27**
	(0.27)	(0.36)	(0.64)	(0.71)	(0.79)	(0.77)
Constant	30.92**	40.95**	66.33**	110.36**	133.88**	150.12**
	(0.20)	(0.27)	(0.47)	(0.57)	(0.59)	(0.62)
Observations	15654	15654	15654	15654	15654	15654
R^2	0.10	0.08	0.10	0.14	0.14	0.16

Source: Authors' calculations based on data from ECLS-K (U.S. Department of Education 2009).
Notes: Standard errors in parentheses. Reference groups are level 2 for parental education, quintile 1 for income. KS = kindergarten spring; 1S = first grade spring; 3S = third grade spring; 5S = fifth grade spring; 8S = eighth grade spring.
**$p < 0.01$, *$p < 0.05$

Patterns of IRT test scores by income quintile also display widening gradients. Again, gaps open up after age six. For example, the gaps between the children with the most highly educated parents and those with the lowest-educated parents grow by twenty-three questions for reading and fifteen questions in math. A striking feature of the income graphs, for both reading and math, is the relative monotonicity of the gradient between income groups at each age. It is not that the top or bottom income quintiles pull away while the three middle quintiles stay together. Rather, the patterns are suggestive of linear effects of income group, despite mean dollar incomes in the higher quintiles being many times higher than those in the lower quintiles (see online appendix 10A).

Table 10.3 U.S. Achievement Outcomes, Math IRTs

	KF (5.7)	KS (6.2)	1S (7.2)	3S (9.2)	5S (11.2)	8S (14.2)
A. Parental Education						
Level 3	2.53**	3.40**	4.86**	7.74**	8.16**	8.12**
	(0.29)	(0.39)	(0.59)	(0.86)	(0.84)	(0.90)
Level 5B	5.08**	6.67**	9.85**	15.46**	16.63**	16.11**
	(0.28)	(0.38)	(0.57)	(0.79)	(0.80)	(0.77)
Level 5A6	10.16**	12.85**	18.84**	28.25**	29.12**	27.46**
	(0.28)	(0.38)	(0.58)	(0.82)	(0.85)	(0.90)
Constant	20.86**	29.67**	51.23**	82.67**	105.92**	123.70**
	(0.26)	(0.35)	(0.53)	(0.75)	(0.77)	(0.79)
Observations	15648	15648	15648	15648	15648	15648
R^2	0.14	0.13	0.12	0.14	0.15	0.16
B. Family Income						
Quintile 2	1.91**	2.57**	4.13**	7.25**	7.95**	7.42**
	(0.25)	(0.33)	(0.51)	(0.75)	(0.73)	(0.84)
Quintile 3	4.12**	5.60**	8.53**	13.54**	14.86**	13.89**
	(0.23)	(0.30)	(0.46)	(0.62)	(0.68)	(0.60)
Quintile 4	6.26**	8.22**	12.50**	18.83**	20.05**	18.93**
	(0.22)	(0.30)	(0.47)	(0.64)	(0.67)	(0.63)
Quintile 5	9.29**	11.45**	17.17**	25.92**	26.91**	24.69**
	(0.23)	(0.29)	(0.45)	(0.63)	(0.69)	(0.66)
Constant	21.87**	30.98**	52.82**	85.01**	108.16**	126.26**
	(0.17)	(0.23)	(0.35)	(0.49)	(0.55)	(0.53)
Observations	15648	15648	15648	15648	15648	15648
R^2	0.13	0.11	0.11	0.13	0.13	0.14

Source: Authors' calculations based on data from ECLS-K (U.S. Department of Education 2009).
Notes: Standard errors in parentheses. Reference groups are level 2 for parental education, quintile 1 for income. KS = kindergarten spring; 1S = first grade spring; 3S = third grade spring; 5S = fifth grade spring; 8S = eighth grade spring.
**$p < 0.01$, *$p < 0.05$

Figure 10.2 (and tables 10.4 and 10.5) present results for the standardized scores for reading and math in the U.S. sample. Again, trends in mean scores for each education or income group are shown (here with dashed lines indicating 95 percent confidence intervals). Focusing on the top education group, there is evidence of some convergence with the lower SES groups through age seven, but trends indicate that test scores between these groups diverge in the later years. Because these changes are small and offset each other, the gaps between the two groups at age fourteen (effect size of 1.3 standard deviation for reading, 1.2 for math) are statistically about the same magnitude as they were at age five (1.2 for both reading and math).

Table 10.4   U.S. Achievement Outcomes, Reading *T*-Scores

Education	KF (5.7)	KS (6.2)	1S (7.2)	3S (9.2)	5S (11.2)	8S (14.2)
A. Parental Education						
Level 3	0.35**	0.34**	0.39**	0.41**	0.36**	0.36**
	(0.03)	(0.03)	(0.03)	(0.03)	(0.03)	(0.04)
Level 5B	0.64**	0.62**	0.66**	0.72**	0.69**	0.70**
	(0.03)	(0.03)	(0.03)	(0.03)	(0.03)	(0.04)
Level 5A6	1.20**	1.08**	1.08**	1.22**	1.21**	1.28**
	(0.03)	(0.03)	(0.03)	(0.03)	(0.03)	(0.04)
Constant	−0.64**	−0.56**	−0.58**	−0.66**	−0.62**	−0.68**
	(0.03)	(0.03)	(0.03)	(0.03)	(0.03)	(0.03)
Observations	15654	15654	15654	15654	15654	15654
R^2	0.15	0.12	0.12	0.15	0.16	0.18
B. Family Income						
Quintile 2	0.22**	0.23**	0.27**	0.32**	0.30**	0.29**
	(0.03)	(0.03)	(0.03)	(0.03)	(0.03)	(0.03)
Quintile 3	0.49**	0.49**	0.52**	0.60**	0.57**	0.58**
	(0.02)	(0.02)	(0.02)	(0.03)	(0.03)	(0.03)
Quintile 4	0.73**	0.67**	0.68**	0.81**	0.79**	0.81**
	(0.02)	(0.02)	(0.02)	(0.03)	(0.03)	(0.03)
Quintile 5	1.04**	0.91**	0.91**	1.06**	1.05**	1.12**
	(0.02)	(0.02)	(0.02)	(0.03)	(0.03)	(0.03)
Constant	−0.48**	−0.41**	−0.42**	−0.51**	−0.48**	−0.53**
	(0.02)	(0.02)	(0.02)	(0.02)	(0.02)	(0.02)
Observations	15654	15654	15654	15654	15654	15654
R^2	0.13	0.10	0.11	0.14	0.14	0.15

Source: Authors' calculations based on data from ECLS-K (U.S. Department of Education 2009).
Notes: Standard errors in parentheses. *T*-scores have 0 means and 1 standard deviation. Reference groups are level 2 for education and quintile 1 for income. KS = kindergarten spring; 1S = first grade spring; 3S = third grade spring; 5S = fifth grade spring; 8S = eighth grade spring.
**p < 0.01, *p < 0.05

Results for income quintiles are more suggestive of gap-widening for reading, but not for math. With respect to reading, the advantage of the middle quintile relative to the bottom quintile grows from 0.49 to 0.58 standard deviations between age five and age fourteen (effect size of 0.09), while the advantage for the top quintile relative to the bottom grows from 1.04 to 1.12 standard deviations (effect size of 0.08).

As discussed earlier, in interpreting these results, we must recall that standardized scores by construction suppress the growth in variation in scores that occurs over time. In spite of this, the standardized results are consistent with the raw score results in suggesting that the evolution

Table 10.5   U.S. Achievement Outcomes, Math T-Scores

	KF (5.7)	KS (6.2)	1S (7.2)	3S (9.2)	5S (11.2)	8S (14.2)
A. Parental Education						
Level 3	0.35**	0.33**	0.28**	0.31**	0.30**	0.30**
	(0.03)	(0.03)	(0.03)	(0.03)	(0.03)	(0.04)
Level 5B	0.67**	0.63**	0.57**	0.62**	0.63**	0.65**
	(0.03)	(0.03)	(0.03)	(0.03)	(0.03)	(0.03)
Level 5A6	1.19**	1.11**	0.99**	1.12**	1.14**	1.20**
	(0.03)	(0.03)	(0.03)	(0.03)	(0.03)	(0.03)
Constant	−0.58**	−0.53**	−0.49**	−0.57**	−0.57**	−0.63**
	(0.03)	(0.03)	(0.03)	(0.03)	(0.03)	(0.03)
Observations	15648	15648	15648	15648	15648	15648
R^2	0.15	0.14	0.12	0.14	0.15	0.17
B. Family Income						
Quintile 2	0.25**	0.24**	0.24**	0.29**	0.29**	0.28**
	(0.03)	(0.03)	(0.03)	(0.03)	(0.03)	(0.03)
Quintile 3	0.52**	0.52**	0.48**	0.54**	0.55**	0.54**
	(0.02)	(0.02)	(0.02)	(0.03)	(0.03)	(0.03)
Quintile 4	0.77**	0.74**	0.69**	0.76**	0.76**	0.77**
	(0.02)	(0.02)	(0.02)	(0.02)	(0.03)	(0.03)
Quintile 5	1.06**	0.97**	0.91**	1.03**	1.05**	1.06**
	(0.02)	(0.02)	(0.02)	(0.02)	(0.03)	(0.03)
Constant	−0.44**	−0.40**	−0.40**	−0.48**	−0.48**	−0.52**
	(0.02)	(0.02)	(0.02)	(0.02)	(0.02)	(0.02)
Observations	15648	15648	15648	15648	15648	15648
R^2	0.14	0.12	0.11	0.13	0.14	0.14

Source: Authors' calculations based on data from ECLS-K (U.S. Department of Education 2009).
Notes: Standard errors in parentheses. *T*-scores have 0 means and 1 standard deviation. Reference groups are level 2 for education and quintile 1 for income. KS = kindergarten spring; 1S = first grade spring; 3S = third grade spring; 5S = fifth grade spring; 8S = eighth grade spring.
**$p < 0.01$, *$p < 0.05$

of gradients may be different during kindergarten, and possibly up to age seven, than in later years. In particular, both sets of results suggest that gradients may narrow or hold constant during the first year or two of school, but widen thereafter. Nevertheless, the two approaches differ quite a bit in the extent to which such gaps may widen in the later years. Taking the number of questions answered correctly as the metric, the widening in test scores after age six seems to be clear across income and education groups for both reading and math. However, taking standardized (relative) achievement as the metric, after age six the gap only widens to about the same size it was at school entry, but not any further. The

Figure 10.3   Mean England Raw Scores

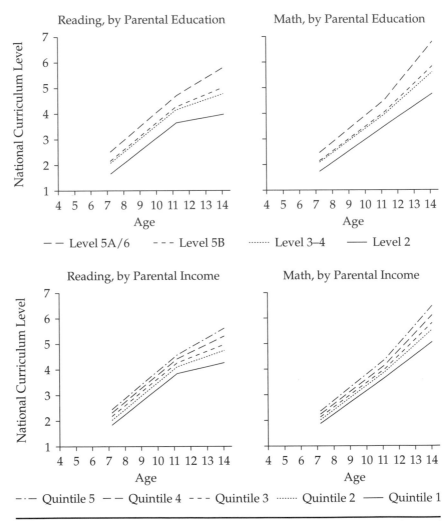

Source: Authors' calculations based on data from ALSPAC (University of Bristol 2009).

finding regarding early convergence in academic achievement, although small, is quite robust across achievement measures and different measures of parental SES.

Figures 10.3 and 10.4 (and tables 10.6, 10.7, 10.8, and 10.9) provide the achievement skills results for the England sample. Results for the raw key stage test scores, shown in figure 10.3, show gaps widening

Figure 10.4   Mean England Standardized Scores

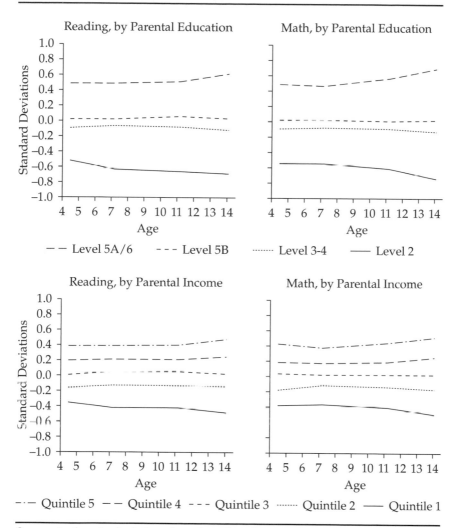

Source: Authors' calculations based on data from ALSPAC (University of Bristol 2009).

between age seven and fourteen, slowly between seven and eleven and then much faster between age eleven and fourteen, as children at the top pull away and children at the bottom make lesser gains than those in the middle. By age fourteen, children of the most educated parents have reading achievement 1.85 levels higher and math scores two levels higher (on a scale from 0 to 7) than children of the least educated, up

Table 10.6   England Achievement Outcomes, Reading Raw Variables

	EA (4.5)	KS1 (7.2)	KS2 (11.2)	KS3 (14.1)
A. Parental Education				
Level 3		0.43**	0.50**	0.81**
		(0.03)	(0.03)	(0.07)
Level 5B		0.50**	0.62**	1.03**
		(0.03)	(0.03)	(0.06)
Level 5A6		0.85**	1.01**	1.85**
		(0.04)	(0.03)	(0.06)
Constant		1.67**	3.66**	3.99**
		(0.03)	(0.03)	(0.06)
Observations		12,986	12,986	12,986
R^2		0.10	0.10	0.13
B. Family Income				
Quintile 2		0.22**	0.26**	0.48**
		(0.02)	(0.03)	(0.06)
Quintile 3		0.36**	0.40**	0.72**
		(0.03)	(0.03)	(0.05)
Quintile 4		0.49**	0.55**	1.04**
		(0.02)	(0.03)	(0.05)
Quintile 5		0.62**	0.71**	1.35**
		(0.03)	(0.03)	(0.06)
Constant		1.82**	3.87**	4.27**
		(0.02)	(0.02)	(0.04)
Observations		12,986	12,986	12,986
R^2		0.08	0.08	0.10

Source: Authors' calculations based on data from ALSPAC (University of Bristol 2009).
Notes: Standard errors in parentheses. Reference groups are level 2 for education and quintile 1 for income. EA = **Entry Assessment;** KS1 = Key Stage 1; KS2 = Key Stage 2; KS3 = Key Stage 3.
**$p < 0.01$, *$p < 0.05$

from advantages of 0.85 and 0.7 levels at age seven. (As mentioned earlier, key stage assessments are not available before age seven.) This pattern is seen for both reading and math and for both parental education and family income groups.

The results for standardized scores (figure 10.4) tell a slightly different story. Here we can follow children from age four, making use of the teacher's assessment at school entry. Results for reading indicate that children from the bottom group (whether defined in terms of parental education or income) lose ground between age four and seven. Reading gradients then hold relatively constant between age seven and eleven, but the top and bottom groups then pull away between age eleven and age fourteen.

Table 10.7   England Achievement Outcomes, Math Raw Variables

	EA (4.5)	KS1 (7.2)	KS2 (11.2)	KS3 (14.1)
A. Parental Education				
Level 3		0.32**	0.45**	0.86**
		(0.03)	(0.03)	(0.05)
Level 5B		0.40**	0.54**	1.07**
		(0.03)	(0.03)	(0.05)
Level 5A6		0.70**	1.00**	2.02**
		(0.03)	(0.03)	(0.05)
Constant		1.74**	3.51**	4.75**
		(0.02)	(0.03)	(0.04)
Observations		12,986	12,986	12,986
R^2		0.08	0.10	0.16
B. Family Income				
Quintile 2		0.17**	0.23**	0.46**
		(0.03)	(0.04)	(0.06)
Quintile 3		0.26**	0.37**	0.74**
		(0.02)	(0.03)	(0.05)
Quintile 4		0.37**	0.51**	1.05**
		(0.02)	(0.03)	(0.05)
Quintile 5		0.51**	0.72**	1.44**
		(0.03)	(0.03)	(0.05)
Constant		1.87**	3.69**	5.08**
		(0.02)	(0.02)	(0.04)
Observations		12,986	12,986	12,986
R^2		0.06	0.08	0.12

Source: Authors' calculations based on data from ASLPAC (University of Bristol 2009).
Notes: Standard errors in parentheses. Reference groups are level 2 for education and quintile 1 for income. EA = Entry Assessment; KS1 = Key Stage 1; KS2 = Key Stage 2; KS3 = Key Stage 3.
**$p < 0.01$, *$p < 0.05$

By age fourteen, the gap between children of the most highly educated parents and the least educated is 1.3 standard deviations, up from 1.0 at age five. Over the same period, the gap in reading scores between the middle- and bottom-income quintile groups grows from 0.36 to 0.51 standard deviations, and that between the top- and bottom-income quintile group from 0.74 to 0.95. Results for math differ in that gaps hold constant between age four and seven but widen thereafter, as children at the bottom lose ground and those at the top pull away, gradients becoming especially steep between age eleven and fourteen. By age fourteen, the gap between children of the most highly educated parents and the least educated is 1.5 standard deviations, up from 1.0 at age four. Over the

Table 10.8 **England Achievement Outcomes, Reading Standardized Variables**

	EA (4.5)	KS1 (7.2)	KS2 (11.2)	KS3 (14.1)
A. Parental Education				
Level 3	0.43**	0.56**	0.58**	0.57**
	(0.04)	(0.04)	(0.03)	(0.05)
Level 5B	0.54**	0.66**	0.72**	0.72**
	(0.04)	(0.04)	(0.04)	(0.05)
Level 5A6	1.01**	1.12**	1.18**	1.30**
	(0.04)	(0.05)	(0.04)	(0.04)
Constant	−0.51**	−0.63**	−0.66**	−0.68**
	(0.04)	(0.04)	(0.03)	(0.04)
Observations	12,986	12,986	12,986	12,986
R^2	0.08	0.10	0.10	0.13
B. Family Income				
Quintile 2	0.20**	0.29**	0.30**	0.34**
	(0.05)	(0.03)	(0.04)	(0.04)
Quintile 3	0.36**	0.47**	0.47**	0.51**
	(0.03)	(0.03)	(0.03)	(0.03)
Quintile 4	0.55**	0.64**	0.64**	0.73**
	(0.05)	(0.03)	(0.04)	(0.03)
Quintile 5	0.74**	0.82**	0.83**	0.95**
	(0.05)	(0.04)	(0.03)	(0.04)
Constant	−0.35**	−0.42**	−0.42**	−0.48**
	(0.03)	(0.02)	(0.02)	(0.03)
Observations	12,986	12,986	12,986	12,986
R^2	0.06	0.08	0.08	0.10

Source: Authors' calculations based on data from ALSPAC (University of Bristol 2009).
Notes: Standard errors in parentheses. Standardized scores have mean 0 and 1 standard deviation. Reference groups are level 2 for education and quintile 1 for income. EA = Entry Assessment; KS1 = Key Stage 1; KS2 = Key Stage 2; KS3 = Key Stage 3.
$**p < 0.01, *p < 0.05$

same period, the gap in reading scores between the middle- and bottom-income quintile groups grows from 0.41 to 0.52 standard deviations, and that between the top and bottom from 0.80 to 1.0.

Although specific results differ depending on whether raw or standardized scores are used, a clear take-away finding from the England data is that gradients tend to widen more after age eleven than before. This finding is consistent with what we might expect given the more unequal distribution of children across secondary schools and primary schools. It is noteworthy that this result is found only for England, and not the United States.

Table 10.9   **England Achievement Outcomes, Math Standardized Variables**

	EA (4.5)	KS1 (7.2)	KS2 (11.2)	KS3 (14.1)
A. Parental Education				
Level 3	0.46**	0.47**	0.52**	0.61**
	(0.04)	(0.04)	(0.04)	(0.04)
Level 5B	0.56**	0.58**	0.63**	0.75**
	(0.04)	(0.04)	(0.04)	(0.04)
Level 5A6	1.03**	1.02**	1.18**	1.42**
	(0.05)	(0.04)	(0.04)	(0.04)
Constant	−0.54**	−0.55**	−0.61**	−0.73**
	(0.04)	(0.03)	(0.03)	(0.03)
Observations	12,986	12,986	12,986	12,986
R^2	0.09	0.08	0.11	0.16
B. Family Income				
Quintile 2	0.20**	0.25**	0.27**	0.33**
	(0.04)	(0.04)	(0.04)	(0.04)
Quintile 3	0.41**	0.38**	0.43**	0.52**
	(0.03)	(0.03)	(0.03)	(0.04)
Quintile 4	0.57**	0.54**	0.60**	0.74**
	(0.04)	(0.03)	(0.03)	(0.03)
Quintile 5	0.80**	0.74**	0.84**	1.02**
	(0.04)	(0.04)	(0.03)	(0.04)
Constant	−0.37**	−0.36**	−0.40**	−0.49**
	(0.02)	(0.02)	(0.02)	(0.03)
Observations	12,986	12,986	12,986	12,986
R^2	0.07	0.06	0.08	0.12

Source: Authors' calculations based on data from ALSPAC (University of Bristol 2009).
Notes: Standard errors in parentheses. Standardized scores have mean 0 and 1 standard deviation. Reference groups are level 2 for education and quintile 1 for income. EA = Entry Assessment; KS1 = Key Stage 1; KS2 = Key Stage 2; KS3 = Key Stage 3.
**$p < 0.01$, *$p < 0.05$

Results: Development of the Gradients in Socioemotional Development

The ECLS-K and ALSPAC both contain information about children's behavior at several points over the course of childhood. Unfortunately, these data cover a shorter period than the achievement data (five to eleven in the United States and six to thirteen in England) and, more important, are much less comparable across countries. In the United States, the measures are based on teacher reports, whereas in England they are based on parent reports. Such reports typically differ, both because parents (or teachers) may be subjective reporters of a child's behavior but also because parents observe their children in different settings than teachers do.

In supplementary analyses (available in online appendix 10B), we conducted a parallel analysis of the development of gradients in two behavior measures—externalizing or aggressive behaviors and internalizing behaviors associated with symptoms of depression and anxiety. To summarize our results, we find SES gaps in behavior outcomes that, though significant, are markedly smaller than those in achievement outcomes and that show no systematic pattern of widening or narrowing over time.

For example, the U.S. gap in externalizing behavior scores between the lowest- and the highest-educated groups is 0.25 standard deviations at age five, compared with a difference of 1.2 standard deviations at the same age in reading achievement. This difference widens to 0.53 standard deviations by age nine but then falls back to 0.47 by age eleven. The pattern of modest educational gaps that widen until age nine and then contract again is repeated in the internalizing problems scale, with differences of 0.29 standard deviations at age five, 0.44 at age nine, and 0.32 at age eleven. Differences by education in the England parent report measures are comparable in magnitude and are broadly constant over time. The gap in externalizing problems between lowest- and highest-educated groups is 0.44 standard deviations at age six and 0.48 at thirteen, and the comparable gaps in internalizing problems are 0.09 and 0.21.

Minor differences in these patterns emerge when we use raw rather than standardized scores, and when differences are calculated between income rather than education groups. Full details are provided in the online appendix.

Conclusion

Our results shed new light on the evolution of SES gradients in cognitive and socioemotional skills over the school years, across two countries that have high levels of inequality and low levels of mobility. Our findings confirm that large and meaningful gaps in both cognitive skills and behaviors are already apparent at school entry. In England, gaps widen during the later school years regardless of how achievement is measured, a finding consistent with the results of chapters 11 and 12 this volume. In the United States, how test scores are measured matters much more in whether one concludes that gaps widen in the later years.

As noted earlier, we recognize that factors outside of school may contribute to equalization. To the extent that such factors differ across countries, we can not attribute all cross-country differences to the influence of schools. Nevertheless, the differential development of the gradients in academic skills during the school years across these two countries is striking and may point to a role for school policies.

The results in the United States, particularly those for reading, are sensitive to whether one focuses on raw scores or on standardized scores. As noted earlier, each approach has limitations. The U.S. results for reading and math provide some evidence of equalization during the first two years of schooling, but such gains are lost in the later years. Both patterns are consistent with U.S. schools teaching basic skills in kindergarten and first grade, but then moving on to more advanced skills in third and fourth grade. However, whether the later school years are characterized by larger gaps than found at school entry depends on whether emphasis is placed on raw scores or standardized scores. T-scores suggest that SES groups' relative position in the child skill distribution is largely the same at school entry as it is in eighth grade. Yet, the difference in the number of questions that children in the highest SES grouping can answer correctly, compared to the lowest SES grouping, grows substantially during the school years. To the extent that answering more questions correctly is a rough proxy for the amount and types of skills students have, we might interpret this as indicating diverging levels of skills or skill proficiencies.

The England results, in contrast, provide consistent evidence that achievement gaps widen more in secondary school (after age eleven) than they do in primary school (up to age eleven). This may seem surprising, given that the vast majority of English pupils attend non-fee-paying state secondary schools that are forbidden under the School Admissions Code of Practice from selecting intake on the basis of ability or aptitude.[16] However, secondary schools vary widely in quality and academic orientation, and the practice of covert selection, whereby affluent parents exploit residential location or the ability to navigate a complex admissions system, is well documented (Smithers and Robinson 2010; Burgess and Briggs 2006; Jenkins, Micklewright, and Schnepf 2007). Our results, which are supported by the analysis of Ermisch and Del Bono in chapter 12 of this volume, suggest that such sorting is disequalizing, increasing the gradients present when children left primary school, and to a greater extent than occurs in the United States.

Although results also differ by country with regard to gradients in socioemotional development, here we hesitate to draw strong conclusions given the differences in measurement across the two countries. Rather, we see our results as providing some preliminary findings to be explored in further research. Two apparent regularities are that socioeconomic gaps in behavior outcomes are smaller than in achievement outcomes, and that they do not appear to widen or narrow systematically over the course of childhood.

Although our findings regarding widening gradients in academic skills are discouraging, we would like to end on an optimistic note. Our findings also provide some hints that school practices and policies can be equalizing. Something is occurring to narrow gaps in the first few years in primary school in the United States, and English primary schools appear to be doing a better job than secondary schools in that country at holding gaps in check. This study cannot identify why gaps do not diverge in the early school years, and more work should be done to understand which school experiences and policies reduce the inequalities with which children arrive at school and produce students who stand a better chance at social mobility.

We gratefully acknowledge funding from the Russell Sage Foundation's CRITA project. Waldfogel and Washbrook also gratefully acknowledge funding from the Sutton Trust. We also thank YouGeon Lee for excellent research assistance with the ECLS-K data.

Notes

1. As the authors discuss, specific country rankings vary depending on which measure of SES is used.
2. Increasing selection occurs in the context of a dramatic concentration of pupils in schools in secondary education. In 2010, the ratio of state-maintained primary schools to state-maintained secondary schools in England was roughly 5 to 1 (calculated from figures in DCSF 2010, table 2A).
3. There are considerable differences in the education systems of Wales, Scotland, and Northern Ireland, so our analysis cannot be generalized to children in those regions of the United Kingdom.
4. Note, however, that 79 percent of the ECLS-K sample attended some form of preschool before entering compulsory schooling.
5. A small number of English education authorities operate a three-tier system with an intermediate middle level from age nine to age thirteen.
6. Other subjects (such as science) are tested at some ages, but we focus only on reading and math here.
7. Expected levels are level 2 at key stage 1 (age seven); level 4 at key stage 2 (age eleven), and level 5 at key stage 3 (age fourteen).
8. In chapter 12 of this volume, John Ermisch and Emilia Del Bono analyze KS2 and KS3 scores and also KS4 scores (age sixteen) for a nationally representative cohort that started Reception slightly earlier, in 1993.
9. The exception is that achievement outcomes for the England children age four (entry assessment) are measured on a different scale to the later outcomes. For this reason, we present results for entry assessment in standardized form only.
10. The specific number of complete cases varies by domain and by measure of parental SES.

11. Even after imputation, we may be underestimating gradients. In England, we are not able to include children who always attended independent schools. Moreover, the imputation assumes that children who left state school and attended independent school had test score growth comparable to similar children who remained in state school and have observable test scores; this ignores the possibility that children who attend private schools may make greater learning gains. In the United States, the exclusion of children who are not proficient in English in kindergarten likely affects the composition of the low parental education and low income groups more than others and, if those children have lower scores subsequently, may lead us to understate gaps between those groups and others.

12. In results not shown, we repeated all our analyses using the complete case samples. As expected, we found that results differed for England, gradients tending to widen less at the top of the distribution in the complete case data than in the multiply imputed data, implying the differential movement of high-performing children from more advantaged families to the independent school sector. In the United States, results for the complete case data and multiply imputed data were broadly similar, but where differences were seen, again these tended to indicate less widening of gradients in the complete case data than in the multiply imputed data.

13. The online appendix can be found at: http://www.russellsage.org/Ermisch_et_al_OnlineAppendix.pdf.

14. The proportion of children in the England sample with highly educated parents would be even lower (13.5 percent) if we used complete case data because children who were not present in state school for all assessments would be excluded.

15. Respondents were asked to place their income in one of five bands at each survey wave, giving ten possible combinations in total. In order to define five equal-sized groups that can be compared with the U.S. sample, we use national data on the disposable incomes of families with children under five from the Family Expenditure survey (1993 to 1998) to assign a representative median value in pounds to each band. We then deflate to 1995 values using the annual RPI and take the average of the two measures. Quintiles are defined over the imputed data set for all 13,988 children in the core ALSPAC cohort.

16. A small number of state-funded grammar schools (accounting for around 5 percent of state school pupils) select pupils with high academic ability on the basis of a test at age eleven. In addition, oversubscribed schools may select up to 10 percent of their intake on the basis of aptitude in a specialist area, although very few schools use this criteria in practice (West, Barham, and Hind 2009).

References

Burgess, Simon, and Adam Briggs. 2006. "School Assignment, School Choice, and Social Mobility." *Centre for Market and Public Organization* working paper 06/157. Bristol: Bristol University.

Burgess, Simon, Adam Briggs, Brendan McConnell, and Helen Slater. 2006. "School Choice in England: Background Facts." *Centre for Market and Public Organization* working paper 06/159. Bristol: Bristol University.

Carneiro, Pedro, and James Heckman. 2003. "Human Capital Policy." In *Inequality in America: What Role for Human Capital Policies?* edited by James Heckman, Alan Krueger, and Benjamin Friedman. Cambridge, Mass.: MIT Press.

Duncan, Greg J., and Katherine Magnuson. 2011. "The Nature and Impact of Early Achievement Skills, Attention, and Behavior Problems." In *Whither Opportunity?*, edited by Greg J. Duncan and Richard J. Murnane. New York: Russell Sage Foundation.

Golding, Jean, Marcus Pembrey, Richard Jones, and the ALSPAC Study Team. 2001. "ALSPAC—The Avon Longitudinal Study of Parents and Children I. Study Methodology." *Paediatric and Perinatal Epidemiology* 15(1): 74–87.

Goodman, Alissa, and Paul Gregg, eds. 2010. *Poorer Children's Educational Attainment: How Important Are Attitudes and Behaviour?* York: Joseph Rowntree Foundation.

Goodman, Alissa, Luke Sibieta, and Elizabeth Washbrook. 2009. "Inequalities in Educational Outcomes Among Children Aged 3 to 16." Report for the National Equality Panel, September 2009. London: Home Office.

Jencks, Christopher, and Meredith Phillips, eds. 1998. *The Black-White Test Score Gap*. Washington, D.C.: Brookings Institution.

Jenkins, Stephen P., John Micklewright, and Sylke V. Schnepf. 2007. "Social Segregation in Secondary Schools: How Does England Compare with Other Countries?" *Oxford Review of Education* 34(1): 21–37.

Lee, Valerie, and David Burkam. 2002. *Inequality at the Starting Gate: Social Background Differences in Achievement as Children Begin School*. Washington, D.C.: Economic Policy Institute.

Magnuson, Katherine, and Jane Waldfogel. 2005. "Child Care, Early Education, and Racial/Ethnic Test Score Gaps at the Beginning of School." *The Future of Children* 15(1): 169–96.

———, eds. 2008. *Steady Gains and Stalled Progress: Inequality and the Black-White Test Score Gap*. New York: Russell Sage Foundation.

National Center for Education Statistics. 2001. *User's Manual for the ECLS-K Base Year Public-Use Dataset*. Washington, D.C.: U.S. Department of Education.

Rathbun, Amy, Jerry West, and Elvira Germino-Hausken. 2004. *From Kindergarten Through Third Grade: Children's Beginning School Experiences*. Washington, D.C.: U.S. Department of Education, National Center for Education Statistics.

Reardon, Sean. 2007. "Thirteen Ways to Look at the Black-White Test Score Gap." Unpublished manuscript. Stanford University.

Royston, Patrick. 2009. "Multiple Imputation of Missing Values: Further Update of ICE, with an Emphasis on Categorical Variables." *Stata Journal* 9(3): 466–77.

Smithers, Alan, and Pamela Robinson. 2010. "Worlds Apart: Social Variation Among Schools." London: Sutton Trust.

Stipek, Deborah, and Rosaleen Ryan. 1997. "Economically Disadvantaged Preschoolers: Ready to Learn but Further to Go." *Developmental Psychology* 33(4): 711–23.

University of Bristol, Department of Social Medicine. 2009. *Avon Longitudinal Study of Parents and Children* (ALSPAC). Data files prepared for grant number RES-060-23-0011. Information available at: http://www.bristol.ac.uk/alspac (accessed December 30, 2011).

U.S. Department of Education, National Center for Education Statistics. 2009. *Early Childhood Longitudinal Study, Kindergarten Class of 1998–1999 (ECLS-K) Kindergarten Through Eighth Grade Full Sample Public-Use Data and Documentation* (DVD). NCES 2009-005. Washington: U.S. Department of Education, NCES.

Waldfogel, Jane, and Elizabeth Washbrook. 2009. "Early Years Policy." London: Sutton Trust.

———. 2011. "Income-Related Gaps in School Readiness in the United States and United Kingdom." In *Persistence, Privilege, and Parenting: The Comparative Study of International Mobility*, edited by Timothy Smeeding, Robert Erikson, and Markus Jäntti. New York: Russell Sage Foundation.

West, Anne, Eleanor Barham, and Audrey Hind. 2009. *Secondary School Admissions in England: Policy and Practice*. London: Research and Information on State Education Trust.

Chapter 11

Children's Cognitive Ability and Changes over Age in the Socioeconomic Gradient

JOHN JERRIM AND JOHN MICKLEWRIGHT

THERE HAS long been interest in how differences in child outcomes that are associated with parental background may grow as childhood progresses. Parents from higher socioeconomic backgrounds with better levels of education and higher incomes may invest more time and goods into their children.[1] The resulting differences in outcomes, it is argued, emerge early at the preschool level and then are reinforced in childhood and the teenage years, despite the potential equalizing effect of compulsory education. The differences may be further compounded on entry to tertiary education and beyond into adult life. Various authors have produced evidence showing this pattern. Leon Feinstein (2003) considered cognitive ability of British children at two points during the preschool years and at ages five and ten. The difference in average percentile ranks between children from high and low socioeconomic status, defined on the basis of parental occupation, widened from around 13 points at just under two years to nearly 30 points at age ten. Alissa Goodman, Luke Sibieta, and Elizabeth Washbook (2009) use more recent data to look at differences for English children, showing these to grow for much of childhood. In the United States, James Heckman (2008) reports differences in average percentile rank in math tests between children from the bottom and top family income quartiles, rising from about 14 points at age six to 23 points at age twelve.

Other chapters in this volume provide further evidence for one or more countries. Our contribution is to compare the socioeconomic gradient in children's cognitive ability at two ages for almost all the countries covered by other chapter authors: the United States, Canada, England, Scotland, Italy, France, Germany, Denmark, and Sweden. Our measures of cognitive ability are from reading tests at age ten shortly before the end of primary schooling and at fifteen when all children are still in compulsory secondary schooling. We do not have panel data like the authors just cited, so we are not considering the change in socioeconomic gradient for the same children. But, at each of the two ages, the data sources we use are specifically intended to allow comparison across countries since they are cross-national surveys with common sample designs and survey instruments. And, on the face of it, the two surveys have some socioeconomic background variables in common, thus allowing the type of comparisons across two points during childhood that we wish to make.

We first consider how large the gradients are at the two ages and whether they differ significantly across countries. We then measure the changes in the gradients across the two ages within each country. Do they steepen and is the change significantly greater in some countries than in others? If the changes with age do differ across countries, we want to comment on why that may be, and especially whether the changes seem related to institutions that kick in between the two ages. One example of such institutional change is the sorting of children into different types of secondary school by ability level, known as tracking. This takes place to varying degrees in a number of European countries, most notably Germany, where the implications in terms of subsequent possibilities of entering higher education are most extreme.

This approach can be thought of as a difference-in-differences analysis of the impact of institutions. Imagine if one were to compare across countries the socioeconomic gradients in test scores at just one age, say fifteen, with the extent of tracking in each country. The unobservable societal factors that lead countries to use tracking may also steepen socioeconomic gradients in scores. The apparent effect of tracking seen when comparing countries could therefore be due to those unobservable factors. The difference-in differences approach controls for this by comparing the change in gradients between two ages with the change in institutions operating at these ages.

We are not the first people to think of this strategy: Andreas Ammermueller (2005) and Fabian Waldinger (2007) use some of the same data sources with similar objectives. However, the differences between these studies and our own are important. We should also acknowledge the work of Eric Hanushek and Ludger Wößmann (2006), who related the change in institutions between ages to the change in the variance of test scores, rather than to the change in the covariance of scores with socioeconomic background, which is our focus. We consider the results of these studies later in the chapter.

Survey Data

We want to compare socioeconomic gradients in reading ability in two surveys, the Progress in International Reading Literacy Study (PIRLS) for ten-year-olds, and the Programme of International Student Assessment

(PISA) for fifteen-year-olds. We use PIRLS data for 2001 and PISA data for 2003.[2] The exception is for Denmark, where we use PIRLS data for 2006, when the next round of the survey was conducted, as there are no Danish data for 2001. Sample size in PIRLS for our nine countries ranges from around 2,700 for Scotland to 8,200 for Canada, with a median of about 3,500. For PISA, the extremes are again Scotland at 2,700 and Italy at 11,600, with a median of about 4,500. The Canadian sample in PIRLS refers to the provinces of Ontario and Quebec only, and we therefore restrict the PISA sample for Canada to this basis as well (this is about a quarter of the total Canadian sample). Both PIRLS and PISA have two-stage designs in which schools and then pupils within schools are sampled. In PIRLS, a whole class is selected at random, whereas in PISA a fixed number of pupils, thirty-five, are sampled randomly within the school. We allow for this clustering in design in all our estimates of standard errors.

The first issue is the two surveys' assessment of reading ability. It is not clear how they really differ in approach. PISA emphasizes measurement of skills that can be applied in real-life situations. The PIRLS organizers argue that the approaches in the two surveys are similar, both being based on "an expanded notion of literacy" (Campbell et al. 2001, 85). We assume that the reading tests are sufficiently comparable for our purposes.[3] Among our nine countries, the mean scores at the two ages have low positive correlation and the standard deviations have low negative correlation ($r = +0.19$ and -0.29, respectively).[4] England, the United States, and Scotland (in that order) have the highest variance at age ten, and Germany, the United States, and Italy at age fifteen.

The measures of reading scores have a metric that appears superficially comparable across the surveys as scores are scaled in both PIRLS and PISA by the survey organizers to have a mean across all participating countries of 500 and a standard deviation of 100. But the pool of participating countries differs across the surveys. We transform the scores into a metric that is comparable between the surveys: national z-scores. That is, in each survey we adjust an individual's reading test score by subtracting the country mean and dividing by the country standard deviation. Note that it is the national mean and standard deviation that are used in this standardization: we strip out differences in the variance of scores across countries at each age. We then assess the extent to which socioeconomic background is associated with score dispersion, where the extent of this dispersion is standardized to be the same everywhere.

The alternative is to leave these differences in national variances in the data, by adjusting the raw scores in each survey by the mean and standard deviation in the pooled sample of the nine countries we study (each country's data are given an equal weight in the calculation of the pooled statistics). With this international metric at each age, the standard deviation for Germany rises by a quarter between ages ten and fifteen, and that for Italy by a tenth, whereas those for England and Scotland fall by about a tenth and fifth respectively. We return to consider this alternative metric later in the chapter.

The choice of socioeconomic background variables is a major issue. We need measures that are comparable across the two surveys. There seem to be only two candidates: the number of books in the home and parental education.[5] Parental education would normally be our first choice given the importance of human capital explanations of earnings, occupation, and incomes, and the ability to link the analysis to an extensive existing literature on intergenerational transmission of educational advantage. However, it poses two problems. First, parental education is missing for large numbers of children in PIRLS, in which information on this variable is collected through questionnaires administered to parents. No parental questionnaires were issued in the United States (true of both the 2001 and 2006 survey rounds). Parental education is missing for about half of children in England and a third in Scotland and Germany, due mainly to no parental questionnaire being completed (again true in 2006). The data are not missing at random. In each case, average reading scores for children with missing parental data are, roughly speaking, about a third of a national standard deviation below the national mean. The missing data problem for parental education is much less in PISA (information was collected from the children) but where it occurs the test scores are also very different on average—between a half and one standard deviation below the mean. Second, we have concerns about the comparability of the data across countries and surveys. In both PIRLS and PISA, information on parental education is coded into levels of the International Standard Classification of Education (ISCED). This should provide a comparable variable but, as we explain later, we have some doubts.

We are drawn therefore to the number of books in the home. This is a standard background variable in international surveys of children's cognitive ability, including the well-known Trends in Maths and Science Study (TIMSS) as well as PIRLS and PISA. It has been used prominently by a variety of authors, for example, Andreas Ammermueller and Jörn-Steffen Pischke (2009), and Gabriela Schütz, Heinrich Ursprung, and Ludger Wößmann (2008), as well as in the work by Ammermueller (2005) and Waldinger (2007) that we referred to in the chapter introduction. Results on the association of test scores and books in the home are drawn on in leading review articles by Stephen Machin (2009) and Eric Hanushek and Ludger Wößmann (2011). Schütz and her colleagues give a spirited defense of the use of this variable as a measure of socioeconomic background compared to parental education, and are echoed by Hanushek and Wößmann. They contend that a large number of books indicates a home environment that encourages academic effort and that it is a reasonable proxy of both the social and the economic background of the parents, arguments also made by Mariah Evans and her colleagues (2010). Schütz and colleagues point to the far lower missing data problem in the international surveys for books in the home than for parental education, express concern over the true comparability across countries of the ISCED measure of education, and argue that books in the home is a "considerably stronger" (2008, 286) predictor of student performance. They also compare the books variable in PIRLS with a household income variable, which is available for a few countries. They interpret their results as supporting the validity of cross-country comparisons that use books in the home as an indicator of socioeconomic background.

Information on books in the home is requested of the child in both PIRLS and PISA so the lack of a completed parental questionnaire does not generate missing values. On average across our nine countries, 97 percent of children respond to the question concerned. With the exception of an additional category at the top of the range in PISA, the variable has the same categories in the particular PIRLS and PISA survey rounds that we use.[6] On the face of it, therefore, books in the home as reported by the child looks to be an attractive option. For the moment we take this variable at face value but we then return to reconsider its validity. To trail our findings: we are less sanguine than previous authors.

We begin by taking the child's report of books in the home as our sole measure of socioeconomic background. We then compare the information on books collected from children with that collected from parents, before investigating the robustness of the results to using in addition some of the information on parental education.

Books in the Home and Test Scores

The books variable has five categories, ranging from ten or fewer books to more than 200 (see figure 11.1).[7] Excluding missing values, the proportion of the PIRLS sample in the lowest category ranges from 3 percent (Sweden) to 15 percent (Italy), and in PISA from 5 percent (Sweden) to 13 percent (Italy). The figures for the top category are much higher, ranging from 13 percent (Italy) to 33 percent (Sweden), and in PISA from 21 percent (France) to 36 percent (Sweden).

Figure 11.1 plots mean reading test scores at each age, in national z-scores, against the books variable categories. The data are presented as line graphs in order to fit all the information on the page, but the distortion of the horizontal scale should be noted—neither graph implies anything near a linear relationship between the actual number of books and the test scores. Three features stand out. First, the variation in mean scores within each country at each age is large. Children reporting only ten or fewer books in the home have reading scores on average about

Figure 11.1   Average Reading Ability by Categories of Books in Home Reported by Child

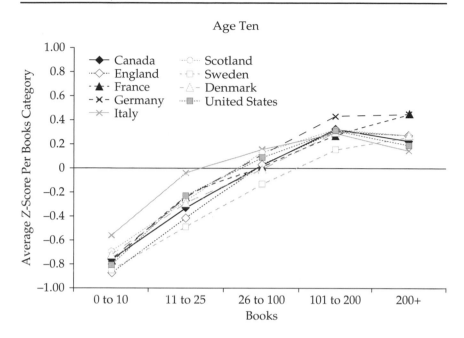

Age Ten

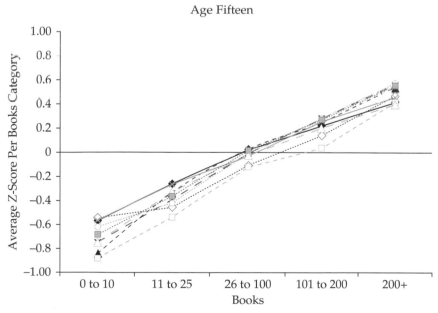

Age Fifteen

Source: Authors' calculations based on data from the Programme for International Student Assessment 2003 (OECD 2005) and the Progress in International Reading Literacy Study 2001 (Mullis et al. 2003).
Note: Reading ability measured in national z-scores.

0.75 of a standard deviation below the national mean in both surveys; those reporting 200 or more books are on average around 0.3 (PIRLS) or 0.4 (PISA) standard deviations above the mean. Second, as these figures illustrate, the rise in scores with the number of books appears in general to be greater at age fifteen. The prima facie evidence therefore suggests a steepening in the socioeconomic gradient. Third, and perhaps most striking, the steeper profile at fifteen seems to result from a strengthening in the association of books in the home with reading scores at the top of the books distribution, a finding not uncovered in previous studies. Mean reading scores for ten-year-olds typically fall slightly between the categories of 100 to 200 and more than 200 books. But the same is clearly not true for the fifteen-year-olds. The suggestion is that, between ages ten and fifteen, the children from the most advantaged backgrounds pull away, and that this appears to be the case in all nine countries. Fourth, and following from this, the similarities in the patterns across countries appear at first sight more obvious than the differences.

We now investigate these patterns in more detail in a simple regression framework (model 1). For each country, we estimate two regressions, one for each age group, in which the dependent variable is the test score (measured in national z-scores) and the explanatory variables are as follows:

- books categories (dummies, base eleven to twenty-five)
- language spoken at home is not that of the test (dummy)
- interactions of the books and language dummies
- age (in months)
- gender (dummy, base male)

The regression model therefore contains only very limited controls. (We also include dummies for missing values for books in the home, language spoken at home, and interactions of missing language with the books dummies.) We take the base for the books dummies as eleven to twenty-five books in preference to the bottom category of ten or fewer books because the latter is very sparsely populated in some countries and may not provide the most useful contrast with the quite well populated top category. Table 11.1 reports for each age group the estimated coefficients on the dummy for the top category of books, more than 200, together with the difference between the estimates (age fifteen coefficient minus age ten coefficient), which is the basis for the ordering of the countries. An online appendix to accompany this chapter gives the full results of each regression model.

In line with figure 11.1, the average reading test score of children reporting more than 200 books in the home differs from that in the base category of eleven to twenty-five books by between 0.25 and 0.75 of a national standard deviation at age ten (average 0.54). In all countries, this difference is larger

Table 11.1   **Differences in Predicted Reading Ability for Eleven to Twenty-Five and More than 200 Books in Home**

	Age Ten		Age Fifteen		Change in Difference	
Country	Difference	S.E.	Difference	S.E.	Amount	S.E.
Canada	0.575	0.062	0.691	0.065	0.116	0.090
Denmark	0.519	0.067	0.729	0.056	0.210	0.088
Germany	0.656	0.047	0.867	0.054	0.211	0.072
Sweden	0.631	0.058	0.849	0.064	0.218	0.086
England	0.703	0.056	0.929	0.066	0.225	0.087
France	0.599	0.056	0.841	0.063	0.242	0.085
Scotland	0.594	0.073	0.970	0.058	0.377	0.093
United States	0.412	0.075	0.870	0.051	0.459	0.091
Italy	0.208	0.067	0.675	0.069	0.467	0.096
Average	0.544		0.825		0.281	

Source: Authors' calculations based on data from the Programme for International Student Assessment 2003 (OECD 2005) and the Progress in International Reading Literacy Study 2001 (Mullis et al. 2003).
Note: S.E. stands for the standard error of the difference. Results are based on an OLS regression using dummy variables indicating the number of books in the home. The specification is described in more detail in the text (model 1). Reading ability is measured in national z-scores. Books are reported by children at both ages.

at age fifteen (average 0.82), indicating a rise in the socioeconomic gradient when measured in this way. In all but Canada, the change between ages ten and fifteen is by over 0.2 of a standard deviation—not insubstantial—and is significantly different from zero at the 5 percent level or better (*t*-statistics vary from 2.4 to 5.0). In three countries the differences are about 0.4 of a standard deviation. Although this represents a substantial variation across countries, the hypothesis that the increase is the same in Italy or the United States at one end of the range and Denmark and Germany at the other can only just be rejected at the 5 percent level.[8] Finally, reflecting figure 11.1, the increase in socioeconomic gradient between ages ten and fifteen is driven almost entirely by the steepening between the top two categories of books.

Doubts Over the Child's Reporting of Books in the Home

The number of books in the home reported by the child is a standard measure of socioeconomic background collected in international surveys. Despite the arguments that have been made in its favor, we feel some unease with this variable, especially over its reporting by young children. Children who respond to PIRLS and PISA fill in self-completion questionnaires about their home background. The fifteen-year-olds in PISA are told "there are usually about 40 books per meter of shelving" before being asked to tick one box indicating the number of books in their home. The ten-year-olds in PIRLS are given more guidance. A description in words and a diagram accompanies each category of books. For example, twenty-six to one hundred books is described as "enough to fill one bookcase" and the diagram shows a full bookcase with four shelves (eleven to twenty-five books is described as enough to fill one shelf). Despite this guidance, the potential for measurement error seems obvious.

In particular, our interest focuses on the reporting of the top two categories of books in PIRLS. We have noted that it is the lack of difference in average reading test scores between these two groups, shown clearly in figure 11.1, that drives the conclusion from table 11.1 that the gradient of test scores with books in the home rises between ages ten and fifteen.

We investigate the validity of the children's reports in PIRLS in two ways. First, when a parental questionnaire was completed, we can compare the report by the child with information given by the parents because the latter were also asked to report the number of books in the home. We have noted the major problem with missing data from the parental interview in PIRLS in some countries: no data for the United States and very large numbers missing in England, Scotland, and Germany. But when information from both child and parents are present, a comparison can be made. Children and parents are asked slightly different questions: the children are asked not to include "your school books" and parents are asked to exclude children's books and are then asked a separate question about these books. The same categories of books are given in the parental and child questionnaires. We compare the distribution of books reported by children and parents, restricting attention for the latter to the question excluding children's books. We pool data for the eight countries for which there is any parental data. There is a reasonable degree of agreement between the two variables but it is far from complete. In 40 percent of cases where the child reported more than 200 books, the parent indicated a lower category. Where the child reported 100 to 200 books, the parent reported the same category in only a quarter of cases; roughly equal numbers reported more than 200 and reported a lower category. The rank correlation coefficient for the two variables is only 0.49. Figures for individual countries vary from 0.39 for Scotland to 0.54 for France.

We then calculate average reading test scores for the children at age ten in each category of books as reported by the parents—see the series for parent reports in figure 11.2, which shows averages across countries. The graph also gives the averages in each category reported by the children, restricting the analysis to the same children for whom there is information

Figure 11.2   Average Reading Ability at Age Ten by Categories of Books in Home

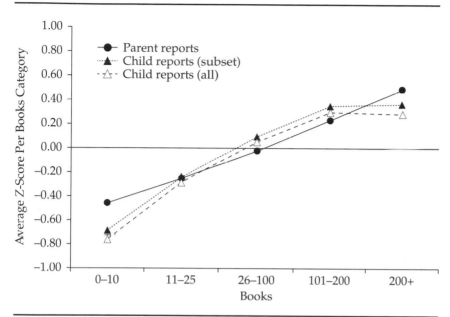

Source: Authors' calculations based on data from the Progress in International Reading Literacy Study 2001 (Mullis et al. 2003).
Notes: Reading ability is measured in national z-scores. Unweighted averages of figures for each country excluding the United States. The solid line for children refers to those children with parents who also report books at home. The dotted line refers to all children including those with no data on books at home reported by the parents.

on books reported by the parents, for example, only about half of children in the United Kingdom. This is the series, "child reports (subset)." For comparison, we also show the figures for all children, including those for whom there are no parental reports of books: "child reports (all)." The contrast in pattern between the parent and child reports is striking. There is no flattening out or decline in average scores between 100 and 200 books and more than 200 books in the parents' reports, and average child test scores in the lowest category of books reported by the parents is substantially above that for children in the lowest category of their own reports.

Our second validity check is to compare the children's reports of books to the parents' reports of household income, which are available for certain countries in PIRLS. Is income significantly higher on average in households where more than 200 books are reported than for households in the 100-to-200-books category? Among our nine countries, there are income data in PIRLS for Canada, England, Germany, and Sweden. The measurement of household income is certainly not ideal. The information is collected in banded form with a single question on all forms of income to one parent, typically the mother. This method of collection is likely to result in substantial measurement error (Micklewright and Schnepf 2010). There is also considerable item non-response. The income levels indicated by each band differ from country to country, and we estimate for each country a censored regression model of (log) income on dummies for each category of books (we use ordinal probit for Canada, where we have been unable to establish the boundaries of the income bands). We estimate two models, one using the child's report of books and one using the parent's report. In all four countries, we easily reject the null of no difference in average income between the top two books categories when using the parent's report. But we fail to reject the null at the 5 percent level in England and Canada when using the child's report, and in both Germany and Sweden the estimated difference in income between the two categories is substantially reduced compared with results with the parent's report (from 18 percent to 9 percent and from 19 percent to 12 percent respectively). We view this as further evidence that the children's reporting of books in PIRLS toward the top of the distribution may be prone to error, calling into question the apparent flattening out in average test scores that drives the results for change over age in table 11.1.[9]

We then estimate the regressions for test scores at ages ten and fifteen using the parents' reports of books rather than the children's reports, including dummy variables for missing values where parental reports are missing. This is model 2. Another change is that we enter the variable for the parents' reports as a continuous variable, rather than as a series of dummies. This imposes the constraint that the marginal increase in the reading test score is constant between each level. The levels represent greatly varying ranges of book numbers, so this is quite different from assuming that the marginal increase in score with a given number of books is constant, which the data show clearly not to be the case. The constraint imposed is suggested by the pooled sample average test scores for PIRLS in figure 11.2 (parent reports), and by the figures for PISA in figure 11.1. We test the constraint formally. In no country for PIRLS do we reject the null of a constant marginal effect at the 5 percent level. In PISA, we do reject at this level in Sweden, Denmark, and France but figure 11.1 does not suggest that we do the data a great disservice. We again include the controls present in model 1, for example, language in the home. A dummy variable is included for missing parental reports of books in the home in PIRLS: in England, Scotland, and Germany we have around one-third to one-half of the sample with no parental information on books.

Table 11.2 reports the key result from these regressions, the estimated coefficient for each country on the categorical books variable at each age, ten and fifteen, and its change between the two ages. There are results for

Table 11.2   Predicted Reading Ability on Increase in Books in Home

Country	Age Ten		Age Fifteen		Change in Difference	
	Difference	S.E.	Difference	S.E.	Amount	S.E.
Italy	0.741	0.048	0.726	0.057	−0.015	0.072
Germany	0.774	0.039	0.837	0.045	0.063	0.057
France	0.777	0.048	0.885	0.051	0.111	0.069
Canada	0.555	0.051	0.690	0.048	0.135	0.069
Sweden	0.618	0.057	0.786	0.039	0.168	0.069
Denmark	0.558	0.045	0.771	0.045	0.213	0.063
England	0.606	0.069	0.837	0.051	0.231	0.087
Scotland	0.672	0.069	0.924	0.042	0.252	0.078
United States	—	—	0.854	0.013	—	—
Average	0.663		0.807		0.145	

Source: Authors' calculations based on data from the Programme for International Student Assessment 2003 (OECD 2005) and the Progress in International Reading Literacy Study 2001 (Mullis et al. 2003).
Note: The average at age fifteen does not include the difference for the United States. S.E. stands for the standard error of the difference. Results based on an OLS regression using a continuous variable with five values indicating numbers of books in the home. The specification is described in more detail in the text (model 2). Reading ability is measured in national z-scores. Books reported by parents at age ten and children at age fifteen.

the United States only at age fifteen. To aid comparison with table 11.1, we have multiplied the coefficients and their standard errors by three, thus showing the estimated increase in score with a three category change in the books variable. In some cases, there are marked changes from table 11.1. Italy moves from having the largest change in gradient between the two ages in table 11.1 to having the smallest in table 11.2—a change essentially of zero. In only four of the eight countries is the change significantly different from zero, and the average change is substantially lower than in table 11.1. Germany, the classic case of tracking by ability at secondary age, is one of the countries where the change is insignificant. Germany has one of the steeper gradients at age ten, significantly greater than that in Canada, Sweden, Denmark, and England. But at age fifteen, the gradient in Germany is not exceptionally steep. It should be remembered that we have removed from the data the differences in the national variances in reading scores at each age, a point that we will return to later and one that is particularly relevant for Germany. England and Scotland show the largest changes in the gradient in table 11.2 between the two ages, about 0.25 of a national standard deviation.

Using Information on Parental Education

We now turn to the other measure of socioeconomic background available at both ten and fifteen: parental education. In principle, the data are comparable across PIRLS and PISA as well as across countries within each survey. Information for each parent on the highest level of education attained is recorded in both surveys with the ISCED classification, albeit with some small differences in aggregation of the detailed categories. The information is obtained from parents in PIRLS and from children in PISA. This means that at age ten there is no parental education recorded for the United States and a major missing data problem for several other countries. Among the latter, missing data are much more common for children with lower reading scores. When present, we take whichever value of parental education is higher, the father's or the mother's.

The distribution of children across categories of parental education displays some large differences between the two surveys. For example, the share of the low education group, ISCED 0–2 (compulsory education only or initial vocational education), is much higher in England, Scotland, and France in PIRLS than in PISA.[10] In England and Scotland, this is despite the substantial nonresponse to the parental questionnaire being more common in PIRLS for children with lower reading scores, which should have the opposite effect. One possibility is that the difference may reflect the reporting of the information in PIRLS by the parents and in PISA by the children, with the fifteen-year-old children of lower-educated parents overestimating their parents' education. Another possibility is that the translation of national educational systems into ISCED categories differs between PIRLS and PISA. Hilary Steedman and Steven McIntosh report that "there is disagreement between international organisations about the allocation of different education and training outcomes to the categories of the ISCED scale" and go on to use the United Kingdom as an example (2001, footnote 3).

We therefore include information on parental education into regressions of the reading test scores with some caution. We adopt a conservative approach, using just one dummy variable for a highly educated parent: those in ISCED levels 5A and 6 (university or college education). This is model 3. The rest of the specification is as for model 2, except that we interact the language dummies with the parental education dummy rather than the books categories. As for parental reports of books in the home, we have a substantial fraction of the sample at age ten with no information on parental education in England, Scotland, and Germany, and must again exclude the United States from the age-ten regressions. The parental education dummy has a powerful and well-determined effect in the regressions: holding constant books in the home and the other

Table 11.3   Predicted Reading Ability on Increase in Books and Change in Parent Education

Country	Age Ten		Age Fifteen		Change in Difference	
	Difference	S.E.	Difference	S.E.	Amount	S.E.
Canada	0.863	0.057	0.807	0.055	−0.056	0.079
Sweden	0.845	0.062	0.791	0.047	−0.054	0.078
Italy	0.927	0.056	0.919	0.070	−0.008	0.089
France	0.977	0.054	1.003	0.061	0.026	0.081
Germany	0.950	0.048	0.998	0.050	0.048	0.069
Denmark	0.762	0.061	0.907	0.056	0.145	0.083
Scotland	0.860	0.084	1.055	0.053	0.195	0.100
England	0.860	0.087	1.085	0.057	0.225	0.104
United States	—	—	0.999	0.046	—	—
Average	0.881		0.946		0.065	

Source: Authors' calculations based on data from the Programme for International Student Assessment 2003 (OECD 2005) and the Progress in International Reading Literacy Study 2001 (Mullis et al. 2003).
Note: The average at age fifteen does not include the difference for the United States. S.E. stands for the standard error of this difference. Results based on an OLS regression using a continuous variable with five values indicating numbers of books in the home and a dummy variable for at least one parent having college or university education. The specification is described in more detail in the text (model 3). Reading ability is measured in national z-scores. Books reported by parents at age ten and children at age fifteen.

controls, tests scores for children with at least one college- or university-educated parent averages 0.35 of a national standard deviation higher at age ten across the eight countries and 0.26 higher at age fifteen. These figures are roughly double that for one category of the books variable at age ten and equal to it at age fifteen. In this rather narrow sense, parental education is more important than books at age ten and as important at age fifteen.

We use the regression results to predict at each age the difference in reading scores associated with an increase in books in the home of three categories plus a change in parental education from neither parent having university or college-level education (ISCED 5A/6) to having at least one parent educated at this level (see table 11.3). The differences average 0.88 of a national standard deviation at age ten and only a little higher, 0.95, at age fifteen. In only two countries, Scotland and England, is the change in the difference between the two ages as much as 0.2 of a standard

Figure 11.3   How Inclusion of Parental Education Alters Results

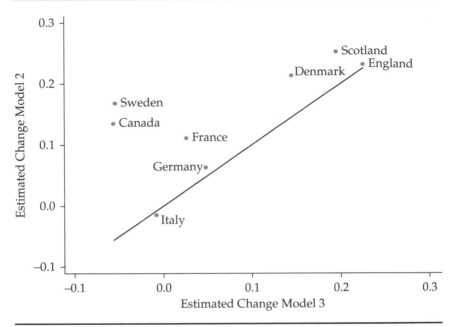

Source: Authors' calculations based on data from the Programme for International Student Assessment 2003 (OECD 2005) and the Progress in International Reading Literacy Study 2001 (Mullis et al. 2003).
Note: The graph plots the Change in Difference figures from table 11.2 and table 11.3 on the vertical and horizontal axis respectively.

deviation, and in neither country is this change very well determined. The change is small, whether positive or negative, and insignificant (less than a standard error) in five countries.

Figure 11.3 plots the change figures from tables 11.2 and 11.3 against one another. Including parental education, albeit in a very limited way, produces a substantial difference in the picture for Canada and Sweden, but similar or very similar results for several other countries.

Summary

Taking together tables 11.1 through 11.3, based on our three different regression models, what have we found? First, using *child reports of books in the home* alone as the measure of socioeconomic background, there are statistically significant increases in gradients between ages ten and fifteen in all countries except Canada (table 11.1). In these eight countries, the rise in test scores when moving from a low category (eleven to twenty-five books) to the top category (two hundred or more) increases between the two ages by between about 0.2 and 0.5 of a national standard deviation. This range is quite large but the standard errors around the figures are such as to preclude most firm statements about the variation across countries.

Second, when switching to *parent reports of books in the home* at age ten (and living with the large number of missing values in some countries), the picture is somewhat less clear (table 11.2). Moving from the same low category of books to the top category, and now constraining the marginal change in score across categories to be constant, leads to smaller increases in the gradients than before.

Third, adding a second measure of socioeconomic background, information on *parental college or university completion* (for which there is also a substantial missing value problem), has little effect on the results for most countries but reduces again the number of countries for which the increase in the apparent effect of socioeconomic background is positive and significant (table 11.3).

As far as individual countries are concerned, it is not always easy to summarize. Across the three sets of results, there is little evidence of a significant rise in socioeconomic gradient for Canada (barely significant at the 5 percent level in table 11.2 only), not much evidence for a rise in Germany (statistically significant in table 11.1 only) or in Italy (strongly significant rise in table 11.1 only), significant rises in each table of results for England and Scotland (caution is needed in tables 11.2 and 11.3 given the extent of missing data) and, rather less obviously, Denmark. The absence of a clear and sharp rise in Germany, with its system of secondary school tracking by ability, is notable.

All our results have been obtained using test scores that have been transformed into national z-scores. We have removed from the data the differences across countries in the national variances at each age. How would our results change if we left those differences in the data, and used the alternative approach we mentioned, of adjusting the recorded scores in PIRLS and PISA by the mean and standard deviation at each age in the pooled sample of the nine countries that we study? With this international metric, the mean score is equal to 0 and the standard deviation is equal to 1 in the pooled sample at each age. But the means and standard deviations at each age vary across countries.

We noted earlier that using this international metric for reading scores at each age, the standard deviation for Germany rises considerably between ages ten and fifteen but falls for England and Scotland. To be clear, the reading tests at ages ten and fifteen are different tests, so these changes in dispersion are not measured with a single absolute metric for reading ability that is the same at the two ages. The changes in the standard deviations imply only that, relative to other countries, the dispersion of scores in Germany is higher at age fifteen than it is at age ten, but lower in England and Scotland.

Figure 11.4   How Switch in Reading Score Metric Alters Results

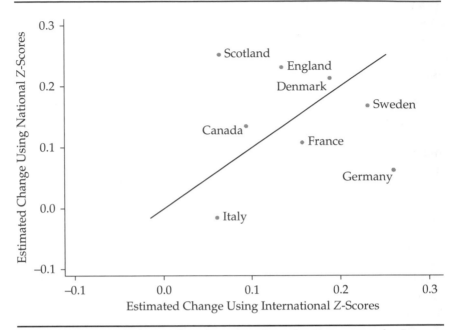

Source: Authors' calculations based on data from the Programme for International Student Assessment 2003 (OECD 2005) and the Progress in International
Reading Literacy Study 2001 (Mullis et al. 2003).
Notes: The graph plots the change in difference figures from table 11.2 on the
vertical axis. These figures are based on model 2 and use reading scores
measured in national z-scores. The horizontal axis provides analogous results in
terms of international z-scores. The 45 degree line shows where there is no difference in results.

To recover key results for scores based on this international metric
at each age is simple. For a given country, we need only to multiply
our regression slope coefficients, estimated with data transformed into
national z-scores, by the country's standard deviation in the data re-scaled
using the international metric at the age in question. Figure 11.4 shows
how use of this alternative metric changes the picture obtained of change
in socioeconomic gradient between ages ten and fifteen. The vertical axis
measures the changes shown in table 11.2, based on national z-scores. The
horizontal axis measures changes using the international metric. The rise
in score dispersion for Germany using the international metric between
ages ten and fifteen has the effect of substantially increasing the change
in the socioeconomic gradient. On the other hand, the fall in dispersion
for England and Scotland between the two ages has the effect of damp-
ening the change in gradient. Which is the more appropriate measure, a

national or an international z-score transformation? Arguments can be made both ways. Our results in tables 11.1 through 11.3 based on national z-scores focus on the relationship between socioeconomic background and scores when score dispersion is set to be the same in each country at each age.

Comparison with Other Results

We mentioned work of other authors who have used the international surveys PIRLS, PISA, and TIMSS to try to shed light on the role of institutions in determining how the inequality of children's learning achievement changes with age. How do their results compare with ours?

In a widely cited paper, Hanushek and Wößmann (2006) used published results from all three surveys to argue that early tracking of children into different types of schools by level of ability increases inequality in achievement. They focused on the change in the variance of test scores between primary and secondary schooling, rather than on the covariance of scores with socioeconomic characteristics. They noted, however, that "one channel for increasing inequality is re-enforcing the effects of family background" and argued that this would be a valuable direction for further research.[11]

Subsequent authors have taken up this challenge. Ammermueller (2005) used data on reading scores from PIRLS 2001 for ten-year-olds and PISA data for 2000 for fifteen-year-olds to estimate regression models that are similar to ours for fourteen countries, including six covered in our study. The main family background variables were the children's reports of books in the home (in both surveys), parental education, and parental attitudes to their children's schooling. The substantial problem of missing data, especially in parental education and attitudes at age ten, was carefully documented and was addressed by imputing values.[12] Ammermueller concludes that the impact of family background increases between primary and secondary education "in almost all countries" and that social origin becomes more important with age in countries with "a differentiated schooling system with various school types and a large private school sector" (2006, 27). Among other differences from Ammermueller's study, we have not included the parental attitude variables in our analysis because we wish to capture the full association of test scores with socioeconomic background, including that coming through attitudes to education. Nor does it seem to us that the attitude variables are comparable across the surveys.

Waldinger (2007) questions the earlier studies, arguing that his results "cast serious doubt" on conclusions that tracking increases the importance of family background on learning achievement. He uses data from PIRLS, PISA, and TIMSS and reports that "slight changes" in the measurement of the extent of tracking, in choice of samples, and in specification of regression models "renders the [earlier authors'] results . . . insignificant" (6). Two notable differences between Waldinger's analysis and Ammermueller's, which Waldinger does not highlight, are that Waldinger uses the parental reports on books in the home in PIRLS rather than the child reports (the large problem of missing values is not mentioned) but does not use information on parental attitudes to education. Like is not being compared with like. A similar conclusion of a lack of robustness and no apparent effect of tracking on inequality in achievement is reached by Maciej Jakubowski (2010). He focuses on a reexamination of the Hanushek and Wößmann, study, using the survey microdata to define samples that he argues are more comparable than those used to generate the published figures which formed the basis of the earlier analysis.

Our own analysis has looked at a smaller set of countries than any of these other authors. We have used data from PIRLS and PISA but not TIMSS. The focus has also been rather different, as we have concentrated on the measurement of socioeconomic background rather than on measures of institutions such as the degree and strength of tracking by ability. We have transformed the score data into a different metric. That said, we think our results are more in line with the questioning stance of Waldinger and of Jakubowski than with the earlier results of Hanushek and Wößmann and of Ammermueller.

Conclusions

We have considered socioeconomic gradients in reading scores at ages ten and fifteen for most of the countries considered in other chapters of this book. In all countries, we find large differences in reading scores at both ages between children of low and high socioeconomic positions. We used measures of reading scores standardized to have the same dispersion in all countries at each age. The results we have obtained are not very robust to changes in the specification of the simple regression models that we use to explore the socioeconomic gradients. Among the nine countries we consider, we vary from concluding that there are significant increases in the gradient between ages ten and fifteen in eight of them to just two.

In this situation, it is clearly difficult to draw any conclusions that might inform policy. Some earlier authors, who have conducted similar cross-country analyses to ours, have concluded that their results reflect differences between countries in the policy of tracking students into different secondary schools according to ability level. Specifically, they suggest that this leads to a strengthening in the socioeconomic gradient of test scores between primary and secondary school ages. Our own results do not support this conclusion.

We have been limited in the measures of family background available to us, given our need for measures that are comparable across the age-ten and age-fifteen surveys that we have analyzed. Each survey alone provides a number of measures, but the common set is very small—essentially books in the home and parental education—and we have emphasized problems with these variables. The international surveys of children's achievement require good measures of socioeconomic status, and preferably measures that are in common, if the data are to be used to provide good estimates of how the socioeconomic gradient varies across countries and across childhood.

Notes

1. Robert Haveman and Barbara Wolfe (1995) provide a simple framework for considering these investments. Their framework underlines that the apparent effect of parental education and income in part reflects unobserved ability inherited by children. See also the review in Anders Björklund and Kjell Savanes (2011).

2. PIRLS assessed children in the upper of the two grades with the most nine-year-olds at the time of testing. This corresponds to the fourth grade and an average age of just over ten years for most of our countries. PISA assesses fifteen-year-olds regardless of their grade. PISA also measures ability in math and science. Reading was a "minor" subject in 2003, implying less question time devoted to testing, but we nevertheless choose this year so as to maximize comparability of socioeconomic measures between PISA and PIRLS.

3. In both surveys, children's answers to the reading test questions are summarized by the survey organizers into a score using an item-response model. The intuition is that true reading ability is unobserved, and must be estimated from the answers to the test. Five plausible values are generated for each individual, each estimating the individual's true proficiency. Except where indicated, we estimate parameters (means, standard deviations, or regression coefficients) and their standard errors with each plausible value and then average the five estimates. We also use survey weights. The 2003 PISA data contain plausible values of reading scores for all responding children but there is some question in our minds over whether all children actually took the assessment in reading, given its status as a minor subject that year, or whether the recorded scores for some children are just estimates from the item response model. We have checked results for the subsample of children we are fairly sure took the reading test, and the results are similar to those obtained with the whole sample.

4. Giorgina Brown and her colleagues (2007) provide more systematic comparison of central tendency and dispersion of scores in PIRLS, PISA, TIMSS, and the International Adult Literacy Survey (IALS).

5. There are also variables measuring migrant status and language spoken in the home that seem comparable, but we see these (and use the latter) as control variables and not measures of socioeconomic background as such. Both surveys contain measures of parental occupation but our assessment is that the coding systems are not comparable for our purposes.

6. By contrast, the categories differ somewhat in PISA in 2000, when reading was the major subject under investigation, which is why we do not follow Ammermueller (2005) in using the data from this survey round.

7. There is an additional closed-interval category at the top of the distribution in PISA, 201 to 500 books, which we combine with the 500+ category.

8. Were we to take the sparsely populated zero-to-ten books category as the base, the rises in gradient between the two ages would appear smaller, this group being further adrift at age ten from the eleven-to-twenty-five category than at age fifteen.

9. There are income data reported by parents in the PISA survey round for Germany in 2006 when parental questionnaires were introduced for a small number of countries. We estimated a censored regression model for the data and found a substantially steeper gradient with children's reports of books in the home than in the PIRLS data for 2001.

10. Taking only those children for whom there is information on parental education recorded, the PIRLS shares are higher by around 30 percentage points in England, 20 points in France, and 15 points in Scotland. The differences between the distributions for PIRLS 2001 and PISA 2000 are documented in Ammermueller (2005, table A3).

11. Consider the following simple model for achievement, A, as a function of family socioeconomic background, S, and unobserved factors, u: $A = \alpha + \beta.S + u$. The model implies that $var(A) = \beta^2.var(S) + var(u)$. One driver for the change in inequality of achievement, measured by $var(A)$, is a change in the slope coefficient β. The OLS estimate of β is equal to $cov(A,S)/var(S)$.

12. Notes 2 and 6 describe differences between the PISA rounds for 2000 and 2003, the year we use. It is unclear how the analysis of the PISA 2000 data dealt with the differences in books categories from PIRLS 2001. The test score data do not appear to have been restandardized to allow for the difference in the pool of countries participating in each survey.

References

Ammermueller, Andreas. 2005. "Educational Opportunities and the Role of Institutions." Research Memoranda 004. Maastricht, the Netherlands: ROA, Research Centre for Education and the Labour Market.

Ammermueller, Andreas, and Jörn-Steffen Pischke. 2009. "Peer Effects in European Primary Schools: Evidence from the Progress in International Reading Literacy Study." *Journal of Labor Economics* 27(3): 315–48.

Björklund, Anders, and Kjell G. Savanes. 2011. "Education and Family Background: Mechanisms and Policies." In *Handbook of the Economics of Education*, vol. 3, edited by Eric A. Hanushek, Stephen Machin, and Ludger Woesmann. Amsterdam: North Holland.

Brown, Giorgina, John Micklewright, Sylke Schnepf, and Robert Waldmann. 2007. "International Surveys of Educational Achievement: How Robust Are the Findings?" *Journal of the Royal Statistical Society: Series A* 170(3): 623–46.

Campbell, Jay, Dana Kelly, Ina Mullis, Michael Martin, and Marian Sainsbury. 2001. *Framework and Specifications for PIRLS Assessment 2001*, 2d ed. Chestnut Hill, Mass.: Boston College.

Evans, Mariah, Jonathan Kelley, Joanna Sikora, and Donald Treiman. 2010. "Family Scholarly Culture and Educational Success: Books and Schooling in 27 Nations." *Research in Social Stratification and Mobility* 28(2): 171–97.

Feinstein, Leon. 2003. "Inequality in the Early Cognitive Development of British Children in the 1970 Cohort." *Economica* 70(1): 73–97.

Goodman, Alissa, Luke Sibieta, and Elizabeth Washbook. 2009. "Inequalities in Educational Outcomes Among Children Aged 3 to 16." Report for the National Equality Panel. London: Home Office.

Hanushek, Eric A., and Ludger Wößmann. 2006. "Does Educational Tracking Affect Performance and Inequality? Differences in Differences Evidence Across Countries." *Economic Journal* 116(510): C63–C76.

———. 2011. "The Economics of International Differences in Educational Achievement." In *Handbook of the Economics of Education*, vol. 3, edited by Eric A. Hanushek, Stephen Machin, and Ludger Woesmann. Amsterdam: North Holland.

Haveman, Robert, and Barbara Wolfe. 1995. "The Determinants of Children's Attainments: A Review of Methods and Findings." *Journal of Economic Literature* 33(4): 1829–878.

Heckman, James J. 2008. "Schools, Skills, and Synapses." *IZA* discussion paper 3515. Bonn: Institute for the Study of Labor.

Jakubowski, Maciej. 2010. "Institutional Tracking and Achievement Growth: Exploring Difference-in-Differences Approach to PIRLS, TIMSS and PISA Data." In *Quality and Inequality of Education: Cross-National Perspectives*. New York: Springer.

Machin, Stephen. 2009. "Inequality and Education." In *The Oxford Handbook of Economic Inequality*, edited by Wiemer Salverda, Brian Nolan, and Timothy M. Smeeding. Oxford: Oxford University Press.

Micklewright, John, and Sylke Schnepf. 2010. "How Reliable Are Income Data Collected with a Single Question?" *Journal of the Royal Statistical Society: Series A* 173(2): 409–29.

Mullis, Ina V. S., Michael O. Martin, Eugenia J. Gonzalez, and Ann M. Kennedy. 2003. "PIRLS 2001 International Report." Report for the International Association for the Evaluation of Educational Achievement. Chestnut Hill, Mass.: Boston College.

Organisation for Economic Co-Operation and Development (OECD). 2001. *Knowledge and Skills for Life: First Results from OECD Programme of International Student Assessment (PISA) 2000.* Paris: Organisation for Economic Co-Operation and Development.

———. 2005. "PISA 2003 Technical Report." Paris: Organisation for Economic Co-Operation and Development.

Schütz, Gabriela, Heinrich Ursprung, and Ludger Wößmann. 2008. "Education Policy and Equality of Opportunity." *Kyklos* 61(2): 279–308.

Steedman, Hilary, and Steven McIntosh. 2001. "Measuring Low Skills in Europe: How Useful Is the ISCED Framework?" *Oxford Economic Papers* 53(3): 564–81.

Waldinger, Fabian. 2007. "Does Ability Tracking Exacerbate the Role of Family Background for Students' Test Scores?" Unpublished manuscript. London School of Economics.

Chapter 12

Inequality in Achievements During Adolescence

JOHN ERMISCH AND EMILIA DEL BONO

T HE MAIN aim of the chapter is to measure differences in mobility-relevant skills and outcomes by parental socioeconomic status (SES) among English children during adolescence and to compare the association between these skills and parents' SES across a number of other countries. It uses the Longitudinal Study of Young People in England (LSYPE), which samples children born between 1989 and 1990 and links their survey data to their achievement results in the education system's national standardized tests. It measures achievements at ages eleven (end of primary schooling), fourteen, and sixteen (end of compulsory schooling). In particular, we address the following question: do differences by parents' SES narrow, widen, or stay the same as children move through secondary school? In addition to the cross-sectional relationship between parental SES and achievement at each age, we use the LSYPE data to undertake longitudinal analyses of the trajectories of achievement for individual children. That is, to what extent do some children move up or down the distribution in test scores as they progress through secondary school, and how are these trajectories related to parents' SES?

The national standardized tests (called key stage results) are administered to all pupils by schools and are related to the national curriculum. They are used to provide information about how children are doing in school and how schools are performing. As school results may serve as a signal as well as an indicator of cognitive proficiency, they may be more strongly related to subsequent labor market outcomes than cognitive test scores administered in surveys.

We find that there is a steep gradient in children's achievement during adolescence with respect to parents' highest education. In England, the answer to our main question is that the gradient becomes steeper between the end of primary school and part-way through secondary school and then stabilizes, the steepening being consistent with analyses of other

English data (chapters 10 and 11 in this volume). It appears to be related to the sorting of children into secondary schools, with more educated parents sending their children to better-quality schools, but there remains a parental education gradient within schools. We also find that children of better-educated parents are more likely to improve their relative position during the first three years of secondary school. In the United States, the parental education gradient when the child's age is around fourteen is similar if not steeper than in England. In contrast, children's achievements in test scores at fifteen are less strongly related to parents' highest education in Canada and Australia.

Differences by Parent Education in England

The LSYPE, which began in early 2004, interviewed about 16,000 English children born between 1989 and 1990, and followed them for the next six years. It is, therefore, the most up-to-date information on children during their adolescence, and is linked to administrative data from the National Pupil Database.[1] This resource provides the education system's key stage (KS) achievement results in national standardized tests for pupils in the state education system (about 93 percent of pupils), starting with KS2 results at age eleven and continuing with KS results at ages fourteen (KS3) and sixteen (KS4).

The LSYPE sample was selected using a multistage stratified random sampling procedure. The first stage sample was taken at the school level using a sampling frame stratified by region, results, gender, and local education authority. The second stage sampled pupils from the rolls of the selected schools, taking an average of thirty-two pupils per school. The sample was boosted for deprivation factors at the school level and for ethnicity at the pupil level to ensure an adequate representation of relevant subpopulations (for more detail, see U.K. Data Archive 2010, 9–13; for information on the complex weighting procedure, see 49–67).

Our main parental SES variable for cross-country comparison purposes is the highest of the two parents' education (in the case of one-parent families, the education of the co-resident parent). Education is coded using the International Standard Classification of Education (ISCED). We distinguish four groups: low (ISCED 0–2; no qualifications or below level 1 qualifications in England), medium (ISCED 3–4; A-level, general certificate of secondary education or level 1 qualifications in England), medium-high (ISCED 5b; higher education below degree level), and high (ISCED 5a-6; degree level or higher). The distribution of parents' education in the first wave of the LSYPE (when the child was about fourteen) is given in table 12.1.

The KS test results are expressed in terms of a child's position in the achievement distribution, either in terms of standard deviations from the mean or the proportion of children in each quartile for the overall KS

Table 12.1   Distribution of Parents' Highest Education, Child Age About Fourteen

Parent's Highest ISCED	Percentage*
0–2 (low)	15.6
3–4 (medium)	52.9
5b (medium-high)	15.7
5a/6 (high)	15.8
Total unweighted N	14,319

Source: Authors' calculations based on data from the Longitudinal Study of Young People in England (U.K. Data Archive 2010).
*Using sample weights; weighted N = 13,944.

score (using sample weights). Figure 12.1 illustrates the results by showing the proportions in the top KS quartile by parents' education.[2] The gradient by parents' education is clear and steep, children of more educated parents being more likely to be in the top quartile and (not shown) less likely to be in the bottom quartile. It appears that the gradient becomes steeper when moving from age eleven to age fourteen, particularly the advantage of the top parental education group.

To provide a wider childhood context for cognitive development during adolescence we use the English sample of the U.K. Millennium Cohort

Figure 12.1   Proportion of Children in Top Quartile of Test Score Distribution by Parents' Highest Education

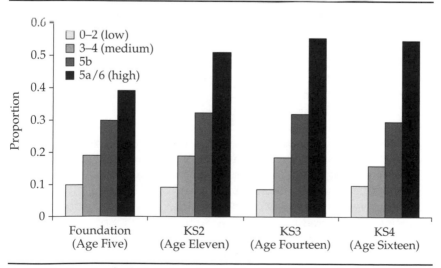

Source: Authors' calculations based on data from the Longitudinal Study of Young People in England (U.K. Data Archive 2010).

Study (MCS) to establish the size of the differences in children's cognitive ability by parents' SES before they start school, at age five. As described in more detail in chapters 4, 5, and 6 of this volume, the English sample for the MCS was drawn from all live births over twelve months from September 1, 2000. The third sweep of the study took place during 2006, when the survey child was age five, and this is the main source of information used here.

An outcome at age five comparable to the KS outcomes is the overall results from the foundation stage profile, which provides a baseline assessment on entry to primary school. The foundation stage was introduced in September 2000 as a statutory stage of the national curriculum for England alongside key stage 1 through 4 national tests. The profile summarizes young children's achievements at the end of the foundation stage (after various forms of early years' education) and provides important information for parents and first-year teachers. It assesses personal, social, and emotional development; communication, language and literacy; mathematical development; knowledge and understanding of the world; physical development; and creative development. As part of the third sweep of the MCS, teachers completed the foundation stage profiles on five-year-old children participating in the MCS (for previous use of these data, see Hansen 2011). Figure 12.1 shows a strong gradient in foundation stage outcomes by parents' education, although it is less steep than at age eleven (the end of primary school). On the other hand, the foundation stage profile is steeper than at eleven if we focus on the proportion in the bottom quartile (not shown). We cannot be sure whether the age differences reflect changes in cognitive achievement differentials between the 1989 to 1990 and 2000 cohorts, or whether the differentials are indeed different before children start primary school, or both.[3]

Another way to illustrate the association between parents' education and childhood outcomes is to calculate odds ratios. With four education categories and outcomes indicated by four quartiles, there are nine such ratios, which are illustrated in table 12.2, panel A, for KS3 results. For instance, the odds-ratio in the middle of the table is the ratio of odds of scoring in the top two quartiles relative to the bottom two quartiles for children with parents having some higher education (ISCED 5–6) to the odds of scoring in the top two quartiles for children with parents who did not have any higher education (ISCED 0–4). It is equal to 3.715; that is, the odds of scoring in the top two quartiles are 3.7 times larger for children of the better-educated parents. Because the logarithm of the odds-ratio has an approximately normal distribution (for example, see Bland and Altman 2000),[4] it is more convenient to work with. The log-odds-ratio is 1.312 for the middle odds ratio. Table 12.2, panel B, shows the other eight log-odds ratios.

Table 12.2   Key Stage 3 Results, Child Age About Fourteen

Parent's Highest ISCED	Q1 Versus Q2–4	Q1–2 Versus Q3–4	Q1–3 Versus Q4
A. Odds ratios			
ISCED 3–6 versus ISCED 0–2	3.653	3.694	4.139
ISCED 5–6 versus ISCED 0–4	4.033	3.715	4.020
ISCED 5a/6 versus ISCED 0–5b	6.003	5.341	5.249
B. Log-odds ratios			
ISCED 3–6 versus ISCED 0–2	1.295	1.307	1.420
ISCED 5–6 versus ISCED 0–4	1.395	1.312	1.391
ISCED 5a/6 versus ISCED 0–5b	1.792	1.675	1.658

Source: Authors' calculations based on data from the Longitudinal Study of Young People in England (U.K. Data Archive 2010).

As a measure of the global log-odds ratio, we calculate a simple average of the nine log-odds ratios, for example, 1.472 for those in table 12.2, panel B (see also Cox, Jackson, and Lu 2009). These are reported in figure 12.2 for a series of childhood outcomes along with the middle log odds ratio. We now also include the MCS cognitive tests because other studies in the book use similar tests to examine the association with family background. The global and middle log-odds ratios for the cognitive tests are almost identical to that for the foundation stage results. There are small increases in the log-odds ratios from age five to age eleven (keeping in mind that these are from different cohorts) and a bigger one from age eleven to age fourteen after which it stabilizes. There is no evidence that the log-odds ratios associated with parents' highest education were different between boys and girls.

We test whether the increase in the association between parents' education and KS outcome from age eleven to age fourteen is statistically significant. To determine this, we form a panel of the KS quartile group outcomes for the three key stages (KS2, KS3, and KS4) based on the first wave LSYPE sample (using the measure of parents' education at that wave),[5] and then run nine logistic regressions corresponding to different cells in a table like panel B of table 12.2. The outcome variable in each is being in the higher of the two attainment categories (for example, the top two quartile groups versus the bottom two). In addition to the parents' highest education contrast

Figure 12.2   Log-Odds Ratio Associated with Parents' Highest Education

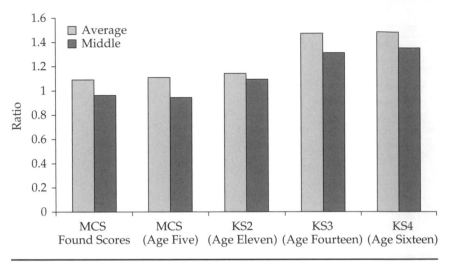

Source: Authors' calculations based on data from the Longitudinal Study of Young People in England (U.K. Data Archive 2010).

(for example, ISCED 3–6 versus ISCED 0–2), the regression contains indicators for the KS (KS2 is the reference category) and interaction of these with the parents' highest education contrast. For each of these logistic regressions, the interaction term for KS3 and the parents' highest education contrast is positive and statistically significant.[6] With two exceptions, there is no significant change in the impact of parents' higher education between KS3 and KS4. In other words, there appears to be an increase in the steepness of the gradient with respect to parents' highest education between KS2 and KS3, after which the gradient stabilizes, as was suggested by figure 12.1.

In sum, our cross-section analysis suggests a widening of the gaps in cognitive achievement by parents' highest education between ages eleven and fourteen, stabilizing after that. Before exploring what lies behind the widening of the gaps in England, it is important to establish how strong the association between parental education and children's achievement is from a cross-country perspective. In other words, is the inequality in school outcomes experienced by English children at age fourteen high or low by international standards?

Differences in Other Countries

Here we briefly examine inequality in school grades or standardized test scores in relation to parents' highest education for Germany, Australia, Canada, the United States, France, and Sweden. English children age fourteen from the LSYPE are compared with French children age eleven, American children age thirteen through sixteen, German children age seventeen, Australian and Canadian children age fifteen, and Swedish children age sixteen. The overall KS3 results are taken as the achievement measure for England.

The data for the United States comes from the Child Development Supplement of the Panel Study of Income Dynamics for a sample of children who were age twelve or younger in 1997, and reinterviewed in 2002 and 2007 (chapter 14, this volume). Here we focus on children age thirteen through sixteen during this period. There are three test outcomes. Letter word score and passage comprehension are both standardized verbal-reading scores; and applied problem scores is a math score. The scores are from the Woodcock-Johnson test. The combined achievement score is taken to be a weighted average of the three tests giving weights of one-fourth each to the two verbal-reading tests and one-half to the math test. The German data comes from the German Socio-Economic Panel. The achievement measure is the overall IQ test score from three domains: verbal skills, numerical skills, and abstract reasoning (chapter 16, this volume). Adolescents age seventeen between 2006 and 2008 are the sample. For both Australia and Canada, the sample is of fifteen-year-olds and the achievement measure is the average of reading and math scores. The Australian data are from the 1998 Longitudinal Survey of Australian Youth, and the data for Canada are from Youth in Transition Survey in 2000 (chapter 14, this volume). The Swedish achievement measure is the average percentile rank of the grades they received in biology, physics, chemistry, technology, geography, history, religion, social studies, and Swedish at the end of compulsory school (grade 9 at age sixteen), for a 35 percent random sample of the cohort born in Sweden in 1973. These come from administrative data and are linked to population register data (see chapter 17 this volume). The French data are from the DEPP panel (chapter 7 this volume). It is a sample of children at the beginning of lower secondary school, at about the age of eleven. The achievement measure is the average of their scores in French and math (on a 20-point scale). There are no sample weights available, and as these children are younger may not be as comparable.

Table 12.3 shows the marginal distributions of parents' highest education and sample sizes. There are quite large differences between the countries in parents' highest educational levels, England having the least educated parents on average (France is lower but there are no sample weights), and Australia appearing to have the most educated, at least according to the ISECD classifications used.

To explore the differences in the association with parents' highest education in a simple way, table 12.4 shows the middle log-odds ratio of the matrix of the nine log-odds ratios (that is, the log-odds ratio for the

Table 12.3   Weighted Distribution of Parents' Highest Education, Percentages

Parent's Highest ISCED	England[a]	Germany[b]	Australia[c]	United States[d]	Canada[c]	France[e,f]	Sweden[g]
0–2 (low)	15.6	8.5	11.7	14.7	7.4	32.4	17.9
3–4 (medium)	52.9	56.6	32.3	46.1	31.1	46.2	64.3
5b (medium-high)	15.7	9.0	15.0	8.0	33.2	8.9	
5a/6 (high)	15.8	25.9	41.0	31.2	28.4	12.5	17.8
Total unweighted N	14,319	659	9,573	1,585	13,785	8,743	99,888

Source: Authors' calculations based on data from the Longitudinal Study of Young People in England (U.K. Data Archive 2010).
[a]Age fourteen
[b]Age seventeen
[c]Age fifteen
[d]Age thirteen to sixteen
[e]Age eleven
[f]Unweighted data
[g]Age sixteen, levels 5a and 5b combined

Table 12.4 Log-Odds Ratio for Middle Ratio

	Australia	England	Germany	United States	Canada	France	Sweden
Log-odds ratio	0.759	1.312	1.157	1.524	0.830	1.360	1.338
Standard error	0.042	0.039	0.171	0.111	0.036	0.067	0.014
Difference in log-odds versus England	−0.553	0.000	−0.156	0.212	−0.482	0.048	0.025
Standard error of difference	0.057		0.176	0.118	0.053	0.078	0.042
T-statistic for difference	−9.62		−0.89	1.80	−9.06	0.61	0.60

Source: Authors' calculations based on data from other chapters, this volume.

Table 12.5   Changes in Key Stage Quartiles

Quartile, Previous Stage	Q1 Next Stage	Q2 Next Stage	Q3 Next Stage	Q4 Next Stage
A. Between KS2 and 3 results (ages eleven to fourteen)				
Q1	0.783	0.207	0.009	0
Q2	0.184	0.550	0.252	0.013
Q3	0.029	0.225	0.542	0.204
Q4	0.002	0.023	0.193	0.783
B. Between KS3 and 4 results (ages fourteen to sixteen)				
Q1	0.765	0.206	0.027	0.003
Q2	0.219	0.534	0.227	0.019
Q3	0.034	0.264	0.502	0.201
Q4	0.009	0.018	0.208	0.764

Source: Authors' calculations based on data from the Longitudinal Study of Young People in England (U.K. Data Archive 2010).
Notes: Panel A: unweighted N = 13,725, weighted N = 13,476. Panel B: unweighted N = 14,073, weighted N = 13,652.

top half versus the bottom half of the distribution in achievement for ISCED 5–6 rather than ISCED 0–4; this is the one with the lowest standard error). The first row shows the log-odds ratio and the second its standard error. The remainder of the table shows differences between each country and England in this middle log-odds ratio, their standard errors, and the *t*-statistic for the difference. England's log-odds ratio is significantly larger than that in Australia and Canada, but not significantly smaller than that in the United States (at the 0.05 level), which is the highest among the seven countries.[7]

The achievement tests are of course different in the seven countries, but the difference in the strength of the association between the log-odds ratio in either Australia or Canada and that in the other five countries is so large that is appears likely that it reflects more than differences in the tests. The relatively high ratio for the United States may reflect the existence of local education funding there, which more strongly relates expenditures on education to local incomes, and the analysis in chapter 10 of this volume suggests that there may be a widening of American socioeconomic differentials in cognitive outcomes before secondary school level, in contrast to England.

Dynamic Changes by Parents' Highest Education in England

The correlation between KS scores at successive stages is high: correlation coefficients of 0.88 between KS2 and KS3 and 0.81 between KS3 and KS4. Table 12.5 shows that movements of more than one quartile between key

Table 12.6   Dynamic Regressions

Parent's Highest ISCED	KS3 Coefficient	KS4 Coefficient
3–4 (medium)	0.06 (0.01)	−0.04 (0.01)
5b (medium-high)	0.18 (0.01)	0.00 (0.02)
5a/6 (high)	0.33 (0.01)	0.04 (0.02)
Female	0.05 (0.01)	0.16 (0.01)
Lagged standardized KS score	0.835 (0.004)	0.797 (0.005)
N	13725	14319
R^2	0.795	0.659

Source: Authors' calculations based on data from the Longitudinal Study of Young People in England (U.K. Data Archive 2010).
Note: Standard errors in parentheses.

stages are rare, and the largest persistence in quartile position is at the top and bottom.

To investigate how changes in standardized KS test results between key stages are related to parents' education, we use simple regressions including lagged standardized KS scores. It should be noted that these regressions are purely descriptive. If we were, for instance, aiming to estimate a value-added model of test scores (for example, Todd and Wolpin 2003, 2007), then the parameter estimates are likely to be inconsistent because of persistence in unobserved factors affecting KS results. In particular, the coefficient on the lagged KS results is likely to be biased upwards. The results of this analysis are shown in table 12.6. Between KS2 and KS3, children of parents' with higher education are more likely to improve their position in the KS score distribution. For example, children of degree-educated parents have overall KS3 scores one-third of a standard deviation higher than children of parents from the lowest education group after controlling for their KS2 results. At KS4, however, parents' education has only a small association with test results conditional on KS3 results.[8]

In sum, it appears that an important contribution to a steeper parents' education profile at age eleven compared with age fourteen is the larger chance of improvement in KS results for adolescents with better-educated parents.

Other Family Background Influences

A number of other family background factors are correlated with parents' educational attainments and may also influence (or be associated with) the child's schooling achievements. In particular, the LSYPE data indicates that the children of better-educated parents are less likely to live in a single-parent family, have fewer siblings, tend to have an older mother, and were heavier at birth. They are also more likely to have attended nursery school and have attended fewer schools before the age of fourteen. Household income was higher and financial difficulties were less likely to be reported among better-educated parents.

We investigate whether these other factors are associated with student achievement and examine how taking them into account affects the achievement gradient with respect to parents' highest education. A problem we must address in undertaking this analysis is missing data for some of these variables for a substantial proportion of the sample. It is most acute for household income: only about three-fifths of the sample responded to questions on income at age fourteen.[9] To address this issue, we assign mean values for the missing value of the two continuous variables, form dichotomous variables indicating whether there was a missing response corresponding to each of these variables, and include these variables in the multivariate model.[10]

The multivariate model we use is an ordinary least squares regression with the standardized overall KS score as the dependent variable. The baseline or small model contains only parents' highest education and the child's sex. The next model includes in addition a set of variables representing family composition at age fourteen and characteristics of the child and mother at the child's birth. These are whether there is only one parent in the household (at age fourteen), whether the child is the first-born child (that is, has no older siblings), the number of older siblings, the number of younger siblings, the child's birth weight, the age of the child's mother when he or she was born, and whether the mother was a single mother when the child was born. In addition, we include indicators for missing responses for each of these variables. The gradient with respect to parents' highest education is less steep after controlling for these variables, but it remains substantial. The third model adds controls for whether the child attended nursery school and the number of schools attended before the age of fourteen; the fourth model—the large model—adds quartiles of the household income distribution. Although the additional variables in these last two models are all significantly associated with the child's KS results, the gradient with parents' highest education changes very little after the second model. It is the introduction of the family composition and at-birth variables that reduces the gradient, and it changes very little with the introduction of the school history and income variables.

Figure 12.3 shows the gradients in terms of standard deviation increases relative to the lowest education category for the small and large models. The parental education gradient is steeper at KS3 than KS2, as we would expect from the earlier analysis. There is some compression at KS4, but less apparent in the large model because including the other family background variables makes the gradient much shallower at every key stage than in the small model.

Figure 12.3   **Parents' Education Gradients Relative to Lowest Education Group**

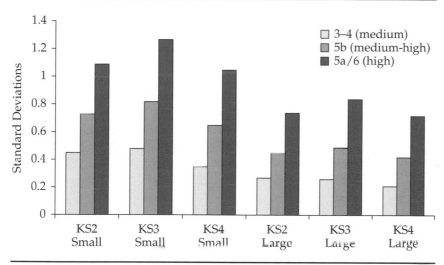

Source: Authors' calculations based on data from the Longitudinal Study of Young People in England (U.K. Data Archive 2010).

Table 12.7 shows the parameter estimates for the large model, which includes all of the mentioned variables.[11] A number of features are worth noting. First, girls do better than boys and their advantage increases as they age, and children of older mothers do better and their advantage is larger at later key stages. Having been born to a single mother is a large disadvantage with respect to key stage results, and this disadvantage increases as the child proceeds through secondary school. The disadvantage of being from a single-parent household at age fourteen is significant only at KS4. Other factors have a more stable influence over these ages. Having more siblings, particularly older ones, is associated with lower KS achievement, as is attending more schools up to the age of fourteen. Being a first child, being heavier at birth, and attending nursery school is associated with better secondary school achievement outcomes, although the advantage of higher birth weight declines, and is substantially lower at KS4.[12]

There is a gradient in KS outcomes with respect to household income (at age fourteen), but it is not as strong as the parents' education gradient. For instance, at KS4 children whose parents have a degree or higher have a 0.9 standard deviation higher KS score than those of the lowest education group, whereas being from a family in the top household income quartile is associated with a score 0.3 standard deviations higher than those of the bottom-income quartile. Nevertheless, both sorts of parental

Table 12.7   Regression for Standardized Key Stage Results

	KS2 (Age Eleven) Coefficient	KS3 (Age Fourteen) Coefficient	KS4 (Age Sixteen) Coefficient
Parent's highest education			
ISCED 0–2 (low)	Ref.	Ref.	Ref.
ISCED 3–4 (medium)	0.348 (0.030)	0.330 (0.027)	0.339 (0.030)
ISCED 5b (medium-high)	0.544 (0.035)	0.584 (0.033)	0.579 (0.035)
ISCED 5a/6 (high)	0.849 (0.034)	0.964 (0.033)	0.902 (0.034)
Girl	0.090 (0.017)	0.134 (0.017)	0.245 (0.017)
Single-parent household (age 14)	0.002 (0.025)	−0.041 (0.023)	−0.189 (0.025)
First-born child	0.145 (0.027)	0.166 (0.025)	0.160 (0.026)
Number of older siblings (age fourteen)	−0.091 (0.012)	−0.103 (0.011)	−0.108 (0.013)
Number of younger siblings (age fourteen)	−0.028 (0.010)	−0.024 (0.009)	−0.021 (0.010)
Mother's age at child's birth			
Under twenty	Ref.	Ref.	Ref.
Twenty to twenty-four	0.200 (0.042)	0.211 (0.037)	0.280 (0.041)
Twenty-five to twenty-nine	0.380 (0.042)	0.424 (0.038)	0.519 (0.041)
Thirty to thirty-four	0.479 (0.045)	0.562 (0.041)	0.656 (0.044)
Thirty-five or older	0.582 (0.051)	0.692 (0.047)	0.787 (0.050)
Child's birth weight	0.135 (0.016)	0.124 (0.015)	0.076 (0.015)
Mother single parent at birth	−0.132 (0.025)	−0.168 (0.024)	−0.228 (0.026)
Child went to nursery school	0.100 (0.024)	0.123 (0.023)	0.104 (0.025)
Number of schools attended (by age fourteen)	−0.063 (0.012)	−0.036 (0.011)	−0.089 (0.012)
Household income quartile (age fourteen)			
Bottom	Ref.	Ref.	Ref.
Second quartile	0.071 (0.028)	0.077 (0.026)	0.097 (0.028)
Third quartile	0.145 (0.029)	0.144 (0.028)	0.137 (0.030)
Top quartile	0.291 (0.0030)	0.356 (0.0030)	0.303 (0.029)
Unweighted N	14,090	14,319	14,803
R^2	0.201	0.264	0.275

Source: Authors' calculations based on data from the Longitudinal Study of Young People in England (U.K. Data Archive 2010).
Notes: Robust standard errors in parentheses.
*Using sample weights from wave 1 (age fourteen). Equations also contain dichotomous variables for missing values on each of the variables other than parents' highest education and sex.

advantage—education and income—matter for achievements in school among adolescents.

How do these family background variables alter dynamic regressions like those in table 12.6? The coefficients on parental education are about half their size in table 12.6, but the coefficient on the lagged KS result is very similar. We again conclude that the parents' education significantly increases the chances of improvement between KS2 and KS3 but has little effect on changes between KS3 and KS4.

School Quality and the SES Gradient

One way these parental advantages may work is through putting their children into better schools, particularly at the secondary school level. Although this includes private schools, only about 7 percent of pupils are in such schools. A better school would be one with better teachers and other educational resources, and if there are peer effects it would also be one with better students. The English state school system operating when the parents of the LSYPE cohort were choosing secondary schools can be described as a mixture of neighborhood schooling (attend local school) and choice-based schooling. Although pupils do not need to go to their nearest school (less than half do so), distance between school and home is part of the admission criteria used by most schools and local education authorities, with those living nearest given priority.[13] Thus location is a key factor in admissions.

Defining a good school as one among the top third in terms of the percentage of pupils with five A*-C GCSE grades, Simon Burgess and his colleagues (2006) find that 44 percent of poor parents (those whose children are eligible for free school meals) have a good school amongst their nearest three schools compared with 61 percent for the remainder of parents. Thus, better-off parents reside at locations in which schools are better. For the majority of parents who are homeowners, access to better schools would likely come at a cost in terms of paying higher house prices. For parents housed in the social sector, their movement is restricted and they may find it difficult to find social housing in the areas with good access to better schools. Social sector tenants are on average poorer than homeowners.

Given location, better-off parents are also less likely to send their children to the local school if it is of poorer quality (measured by the percentage of pupils with five A*-C GCSE grades). In contrast, among poor parents there is little relationship between the quality of the local school and attendance there. Furthermore, although pupils who are not poor and do not attend their local school attend a better rather than a lower quality school by a ratio of two to one, pupils with poor parents who do not go to their local school are just as likely to attend better schools

Table 12.8   School Effects: Orthogonal Decomposition

		Controls	
	Sex	Sex and Parents' Highest Education	All Family Factors and Covariates*
A. Proportion of residual variance attributable to schools			
Key stage 2	0.247	0.183	0.158
Key stage 3	0.318	0.217	0.134
B. School variances			
KS2: between school variance	0.251	0.162	0.130
Percentage reduction in school variance relative to first column		35.3	48.4
KS3: between school variance	0.339	0.187	0.099
Percentage reduction in school variance relative to first column		44.9	70.9

Source: Authors' calculations based on data from the Longitudinal Study of Young People in England (U.K. Data Archive 2010).
Note: *Covariates as in table 12.7.

as worse ones (Burgess et al. 2006). Overall, though, it is location near a good school that mainly drives the tendency for poorer children to attend poorer quality schools (Burgess and Briggs 2006).

Orthogonal Decomposition

We exploit the link between the LSYPE individual data and the schools the children attended at each key stage and the LSYPE multistage stratified sampling scheme. The stratification by school permits identification of the variance of a latent school effect influencing individual achievement. More specifically, key stage attainment in terms of the total score for individual i attending school j (y_{ij}) is assumed to be given by $y_{ij} = X_{ij}\beta + S_j + \varepsilon_{ij}$, where X_{ij} is a set of individual (for example, sex) and family variables (for example, parents' education); S_j is a school effect assumed to be uncorrelated with X_{ij} and the individual effect ε_{ij}. That is, we perform an *orthogonal decomposition* of family background and school effects. We estimate the parameters β and the variances of the school and individual effects, the so-called between and within school variances, respectively.[14]

We focus on a comparison of KS2 and KS3 because we observe a large increase in the association between parents' highest education and school achievement between these two stages. Panel A of table 12.8 shows that the proportion of the residual variance attributable to schools (between schools variance) rises as pupils move from primary school (age eleven) to secondary school (age fourteen) when we control only for the pupil's gender. But when we control for all of the family background factors used in table 12.7, there is no longer an increase in the contribution of schools to the residual variance between KS2 and KS3; there is indeed a small decline. In other words, the stronger contribution of school effects to the variance in outcomes at KS3 than KS2 was attributable to the association of family background with the quality of school attended.

Panel B shows the same idea in a different way. The key stage total score variables are transformed to have unit variance at each stage. The first column indicates that the variance of the school effect is larger at KS3 than at KS2, but it is reduced by 71 percent when we include all the family background controls. The KS3 school variance net of these controls is actually smaller than at KS2.

We infer from this statistical exercise that the school effect is more strongly related to family background at KS3 than at KS2. That is, children with family backgrounds more favorable to school achievement end up in better schools in terms of achievement, and so once we control for family background the contribution of schools to the variance in outcomes is smaller.[15]

Fixed School Effects

Our main exercise is to compare the coefficients of family background variables in ordinary regressions for achievement at key stage levels (analogous to table 12.7) with regressions that allow for a fixed effect for each school (within school regressions). In other words, we estimate the regression $y_{ij} = X_{ij}\beta + S_j + \varepsilon_{ij}$, where S_j is now a fixed effect that may be correlated with the family background variables (X_{ij}).

The left side of figure 12.4 shows the coefficients (in terms of standard deviations) associated with parents' highest education from the large model in table 12.7 for KS2 and KS3 (but for the sample for which we can match them to schools). The right side of figure 12.4 shows these same coefficients from a model allowing for a fixed school effect.[16] It is clear that there is very little change in the parental education gradient between KS2 and KS3 when we control for school.[17] This comes about because the school fixed effect is less strongly associated with family background at KS2 than KS3 (the estimated correlation between $X_{ij}\beta$ and S_j is 0.12 at KS2 compared with 0.29 at KS3). In other words, there is more sorting into good schools according to family background at secondary than at primary school.[18] There may be concern that the estimation of the contribution of the school effect to the residual variance can vary across key stages because of the size of within-school samples, which is much smaller at KS2 than KS3 (2.7 pupils per school at KS2 compared with 20.8 at KS3).

Figure 12.4   Parents' Education Gradient Relative to Lowest Education Group

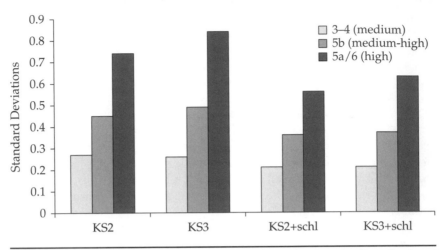

Source: Authors' calculations based on data from the Longitudinal Study of Young People in England (U.K. Data Archive 2010).

But figure 12.4 shows that even at KS2 the fixed effects are able to capture quite a lot of unobserved heterogeneity, and the fixed effect estimates of the family background influences are nevertheless consistent regardless of the size of the within-school samples.

We conclude that sorting into better quality secondary schools plays an important role in the increase in the parental education gradient between KS2 and KS3. Nevertheless, for a given level of school quality a substantial gradient in children's achievement with respect to parents' education remains. It is worth pointing out that the fixed effect estimates of the impacts of parental background condition on existing school fixed effects. These may change if the system of sorting children into schools changes. For example, suppose there are two schools, and currently high-education parents send their children to school A and low-education parents send their children to school B. If there are positive peer effects on learning and children of better-educated parents perform better, then the school effect for school A will be increased relative to that of school B because of the peer effects. Now suppose there is a random allocation of children to the two schools, then, all else equal, the school effect will decline in school A relative to that in B.

Including a school fixed effect in the dynamic models of table 12.6 leads to smaller parental education coefficients at KS3, but larger ones at KS4. At both stages, parents' education has significant positive effects on KS outcomes conditional on school and on previous KS results. Similar

Figure 12.5   **Parents' Education Gradient, Odds of Attending University at Age Nineteen Relative to Lowest Education Group**

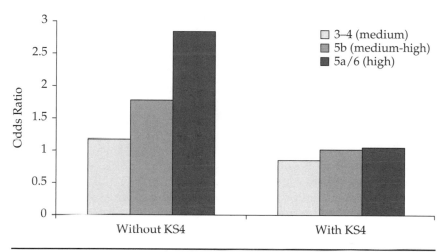

Source: Authors' calculations based on data from the Longitudinal Study of Young People in England (U.K. Data Archive 2010).

patterns emerge when we also control for the other family background variables in table 12.7. Of course, as noted earlier, the approach of adding lagged KS results does not necessarily provide consistent parameter estimates of a dynamic relationship.

Do achievements at secondary school have long-term consequences? We can examine this in a limited way be considering how controlling for school achievements at the end of compulsory education at age sixteen affects the influence of family background on the odds of going to university (over four-fifths of English entrants complete university). The sixth wave of the LSYPE provides information on whether or not a young person is attending university around the age of nineteen. On the left side of figure 12.5, we present the gradient in the odds ratio with respect to parents' education from a fixed effects' conditional logit regression (controlling only for student's age, sex, and school effects).[19] On the right side, we also control for previous achievements at KS4 in the regression. Virtually no relationship between university enrollment and parental education remains. This means that association of parental education with university enrollment works solely through its influence on the child's performance in secondary school up to age sixteen. Given the impact of university education on people's subsequent incomes, there indeed appear to be long-term consequences of secondary school achievement.

Conclusions

The gradient with respect to parents' education in children's achievement during adolescence in a number of countries is relatively steep. Of the seven countries examined, it appears to be highest in the United States, followed by a group of four large European countries consisting of England, Germany, France, and Sweden. Australia and Canada have the shallowest gradients. In England, the gradient becomes steeper between the end of primary school (age eleven) and part-way through secondary school and then stabilizes. It appears that an important contribution to a steeper parents' education profile at age fourteen compared with age eleven is the larger chances of improvement in school test results for adolescents with better-educated parents.

The widening of the parental education gap in pupil performance after primary school appears to be related to the sorting of children into secondary schools. Better-educated parents have their children in better-quality schools, and the association between school quality and parental background is stronger at secondary school than primary school. The sorting is primarily achieved by living in areas with good access to better schools. In light of local education funding and economic sorting into neighborhoods in the United States, this interpretation may also be consistent with the relatively steep parental education gradient in cognitive test scores in the United States. Katherine Magnuson and her colleagues suggest in chapter 10 of this volume that the U.S. gap in test scores by parental education may widen earlier in school.

Nevertheless, at least in England, a gradient with respect to parents' education remains for children going to the same school, and part of it appears to be related to differences in cognitive achievement before children start school. Other family background factors, such as being born into a single-parent family and household income, are also related to English children's achievements in school. These associations indicate better performance for more advantaged children, but the gradient with respect to parents' highest education remains after controlling for these factors. Achievements in secondary school are found to have important consequences for university enrollment in England.

How can policy reduce inequality in school achievements related to parental background? Our analysis suggests that a more equal access to good schools could make some contribution, but as long as there is large variation in school quality it would be limited, because more affluent parents can afford to locate closer to better schools. A reduction in the variance of school quality through a leveling up of quality could make a large contribution, but it is not clear how this can be achieved, particularly if there are peer effects on school performance. Finding the resources and methods to achieve a small school quality variance is a considerable challenge. Other sources of inequality in achievement emerge before children start school, as chapters 4 through 8 of this volume indicate.

Notes

1. For information on the linking mechanism, see U.K. Data Archive 2010, 49. The match rate is 97 percent. Later we discuss the extent to which matching is related to key variables (see note 11).

2. At KS4, we use the capped score, based on each pupil's eight best grades, as recommended by George Leckie and Harvey Goldstein (2009). The uncapped score is related to how many GCSE examinations a pupil takes, and it can be higher merely because they take many examinations. For 22 percent of the young people in our sample, assignment of quartiles is different when based on the uncapped KS4 score.

3. In fact, the quartile performance in cognitive tests administered as part of the MCS in relation to parents' education is almost identical to that shown in figure 12.1 for the foundation stage profile. There are three cognitive tests at age five administered in the MCS. Factor analysis indicates that these load onto one cognitive factor, and we express each child's factor score in terms of his quartile in the factor score distribution.

4. The standard error of the log odds ratio is estimated by the square root of the sum of the reciprocals of the frequencies of the four cells of a table used to calculate the particular odds ratio.

5. The KS results are available for the wave 1 sample even if they subsequently dropped from the survey, as long as they remain in the state education system. Thus, the pooled sample is the wave 1 sample times three.

6. The standard errors for these tests take into account sample design (weights) and are clustered on each young person's identification number, thereby taking into account correlation within people over time.

7. Table 12.4 only refers to one of the nine log-odds ratios. For example, in terms of differences between England and the United States, only four of the nine are significantly larger in the United States. In contrast, for seven of the nine log-odds ratios it is significantly larger in England than in Canada. In the case of a comparison of Canada and Australia, four of the nine log-odds ratio are significantly larger in Canada, but that does not include the middle one (t-value=1.27).

8. This is consistent with what Haroon Chowdry, Claire Crawford, and Alissa Goodman (2009) found in relation to family income and children's educational achievements.

9. Nonresponse on household income is significantly larger for the lowest education group—30 percent compared with 22, 20, and 23 percent for the other three education groups.

10. Although this approach is not problematic for the dichotomous variables, which account for most of the explanatory variables, it can be for the continuous

ones, namely birth weight and number of schools. For these variables, the approach produces biased estimates, although the size of the bias is small if the covariances of these with the other variables are small and if the differences between the means of these variables in the missing and nonmissing samples are small.

11. Note that differences in sample sizes across key stages reflect ability to match KS results from the National Pupil Database to the LSYPE. Subject to this matching issue, sample size does not change across the key stages. The prevalence of missing KS information varies significantly with parents' highest education, but not in any clear way; the patterns are neither monotonic nor consistent across key stages.

12. Missing information on household income and mother's age at the child's birth is significantly associated with better KS outcomes, whereas missing information on the number of schools attended, the child's birth weight, and whether or not the mother was single when the child was born, is associated with poorer outcomes.

13. In the cohort beginning secondary school at the same time as the LSYPE sample, half of secondary school pupils traveled more than 1.7 kilometers to school; nearly 30 percent did not attend one of their three nearest schools (Burgess et al. 2006).

14. At KS2, the number of students per school in our sample ranges from one to twenty-two, averaging 2.7; at KS3, from one to forty-six, averaging 20.8; and at KS4, from one to forty-seven, averaging 15.1. The larger average at KS3 reflects the fact that the first stage (school level) sample was selected at that time. Because many primary schools feed into one secondary school, the average numbers per school in our sample is bound to be much smaller at KS2.

15. For example, the raw data indicates that, compared with parents in the lowest education category (ISCED 0-2), parents with a degree have their children in schools (at KS3) in which the percentages who achieve level five or higher in math, English, and science (averaged over the three subjects and over 2003 and 2004) is 19 percentage points higher. The chance that the child is in a school with a selective admissions policy also increases with parents' education.

16. The parental education gradient at KS4 taking into account a fixed school effect is similar to that at KS3, the only significant difference being a smaller advantage of having parents in the top education group (0.56 versus 0.63).

17. The picture is the same if we restrict the family background variables to parents' highest education only, although of course the levels of the impacts of parents' education on the log-odds ratios are higher in this case.

18. With the fixed effect estimates, the proportion of residual variance at each key stage attributable to schools remains similar across the specifications analogous to those in table 12.8; for KS2 it is about .45, for KS3 about .3, and for KS4 about .5.

19. The school fixed-effects do not in fact affect the association between attending university and parental education.

References

Bland, J. Martin, and Douglas G. Altman. 2000. "The Odds Ratio." *British Medical Journal* 320(7247): 1468.

Burgess, Simon, and Adam Briggs. 2006. "School Assignment, School Choice, and Social Mobility." *Centre for Market and Public Organisation* working paper 06/157. Bristol: Bristol University.

Burgess, Simon, Adam Briggs, Brendan McConnell, and Helen Slater. 2006. "School Choice in England: Background Facts." *Centre for Market and Public Organisation* working paper 06/159. Bristol: Bristol University.

Chowdry, Haroon, Claire Crawford, and Alissa Goodman. 2009. "Drivers and Barriers to Educational Success: Evidence from the Longitudinal Study of Young People in England." Research Report DCSF-RR102. London: Department for Schools, Children, and Families.

Cox, David R., Michele Jackson, and Shiwei Lu. 2009. "On Square Ordinal Contingency Tables: A Comparison of Social Class and Income Mobility for the Same Individuals." *Journal of the Royal Statistical Society Series A* 172(2): 483–93.

Hansen, Kirstine. 2011. "Teacher Assessments in the First Year of School." In *Children of the 21st Century*, vol. 2, *The First Five Years*, edited by Kirstine Hansen, Heather Joshi, and Shirley Dex. Bristol: Policy Press.

Leckie, George, and Harvey Goldstein. 2009. "The Limitations of Using League Tables to Inform School Choice." *Journal of the Royal Statistical Society Series A* 172(4): 835–51.

Todd, Petra E., and Kenneth I. Wolpin. 2003. "On the Specification and Estimation of the Production Function for Cognitive Achievement." *Economic Journal* 113(485): F3–F33.

———. 2007. "The Production of Cognitive Achievement in Children: Home, School and Racial Test Score Gaps." *Journal of Human Capital* 1(1): 91–136.

U.K. Data Archive. 2010. *LSYPE User Guide to the Datasets: Wave One to Wave Six*, Study 5545. Colchester, U.K.: University of Essex.

PART IV

LATE ADOLESCENCE AND BEYOND

Chapter 13

School Tracking and Intergenerational Transmission of Education

MASSIMILIANO BRATTI, LORENZO CAPPELLARI,
OLAF GROH-SAMBERG, AND HENNING LOHMANN

I N STUDIES of intergenerational mobility that attempt to describe its mechanisms and explain cross-national differences, the interplay between parental background and specific features of educational systems has been shown to play a critical role in determining individual educational outcomes. Here, the early selection of children into different educational tracks that lead to distinct and stratified labor market chances has been posited as one potentially important factor in the persistence of educational inequality. The main argument is that early educational choices are more likely to reflect parental background than the abilities and talents of the children.

In this chapter, we study two countries (Germany and Italy) with relatively early tracking (at ages ten and fourteen, respectively) into different types of secondary schools with specific educational curricula—typically either academically or vocationally oriented. Therefore, the tracking we refer to is not the ability tracking widely practiced in countries like the United States, where children are grouped, based on their abilities, into different classes within a homogeneous system of secondary education (*streamlining*). The educational systems we study in this chapter are similar in some respects to the tripartite system that existed in England up to the early 1980s, which included an academically oriented track (grammar schools), a technical track (technical schools), and a lower track (modern schools). One difference is that in the United Kingdom the technical track was also intended for students who wanted to go on to pursue high-level technical professions in science or engineering, whereas in Italy and Germany students can enter these professions only by following the academic track and studying at a university. Moreover, in the United Kingdom, selection into the academic track was conditional on performance in standardized tests, whereas in Germany and Italy track placement is based on teachers' evaluations or is subject to parental choice, or both.

Our focus here is on the interplay between parental influences on individual outcomes and the tracked structure of secondary schools. From this perspective, some interesting questions emerge. What impact does parental background have on children's enrollment in the various tracks? Are parents capable of influencing the educational trajectories of their offspring after the initial choice has been made? Finally, and related to this, does the interplay between school tracking and parental background amplify or mitigate the effect of individual ability? These are important questions. If, for example, the findings show that parental background has no further influence on educational outcomes after the choice of school track, this would suggest that policies affecting selection into tracks are key factors in reducing intergenerational inequality.

We provide answers to these questions using survey data for Germany and Italy. To contribute to the understanding of intergenerational inequality, we provide a cross-national perspective on the intergenerational transmission of education in the central and final stages of educational development, focusing on choices made from the end of primary (Germany) or lower secondary (Italy) education up to college enrollment. With reference to the conceptual framework underlying this volume, we focus on the following stages of development: C2/C3 (defined by the age at initial track choice, which differs between Germany and Italy) and C4.

We find that parental background is key in determining student selection into tracks. We show that school tracks do not necessarily lock students to a particular path, and that parents can play a role in shaping student mobility across tracks after initial enrollment. Even within school tracks, we find evidence of significant social gradients in student achievement that differ by student ability. In the academic track, for example, low-ability students with highly educated parents are less likely to repeat grades or switch to lower tracks than students with similar ability levels but less-educated parents. This is particularly true in Italy. We attribute the cross-country differences to the different institutional rules that govern track choice and the different structure of tertiary education in Germany than in Italy.

Literature Review

Despite ongoing educational expansion and school reforms in the OECD countries, inequality of educational opportunity between children from different social backgrounds still persists. Whereas inequality between genders and between urban and rural regions seems to be declining, the relative odds of attaining certain educational degrees, conditional on parental education, have remained almost stable over time (see Shavit and Blossfeld 1993; Shavit, Yaish, and Bar-Haim 2007; Pfeffer 2008).[1] This has spurred the search for explanations of this persistent inequality and for the mechanisms behind the intergenerational transmission of education. Most of the existing explanations focus either on the effects of parents on school choice (see Boudon 1974; Breen and Goldthorpe 1997; Erikson and Jonsson 1996) or on institutional effects (see, for example, Coleman 1966). In line with our research question, we focus in the following on recent findings on the effects of tracking on educational inequality, and on the rich literature addressing the impacts of parental background on educational careers.

Tracking

Secondary school tracking is a hotly debated issue. In Germany up to 1970, early school tracking was commonly justified based on the assumption of different levels of student ability that call for correspondingly stratified curricula and school levels. Since the 1970s, the assumption of fixed individual abilities has been criticized and gradually replaced by the idea of merit selection based on individual achievements and, thus, fostering mobility within the educational system. The case in Italy is similar.

Early tracking has been criticized for increasing inequality in secondary education, thus violating the merit-based selection of pupils. Negative impacts of tracking on equality of opportunity have been argued to operate through various channels, for example, classroom and peer effects, the attraction of more able and motivated teachers to more academic tracks, and differences in school curricula and resource endowments. On the other hand, early school tracking has been advocated based on the idea that a differentiated supply of education may increase efficiency. This controversy has led to the frequently cited assumption of an equity-efficiency trade off. However, this assumption has been seriously called into question by the recent evidence provided by international student assessment data (see Wößmann 2007).[2]

Initially, comparative analysis based on the OECD Program for International Student Assessment (PISA) 2000 did not yield a systematic effect of tracking on the magnitude of the social gradient (Baumert et al. 2001). Yet more recent studies seem to point in the opposite direction (see Hanushek and Wößmann 2006; Schütz, Ursprung, and Wößmann 2005; Wößmann 2007). Eric Hanushek and Ludger Wößmann (2006) provide evidence that tracking increases inequality in educational achievements. They also show that tracking negatively affects levels of achievement across the whole distribution of test results. Giorgio Brunello and Daniele Checchi (2007) find that tracking reinforces family effects on educational attainment and labor market outcomes. However, chapter 11 in this volume uses a similar cross-country approach based on PISA and PIRLS (Progress in International Reading Literacy Study) data, and finds evidence for Germany that is consistent with the idea that tracking plays a limited role

in the social gradients of student achievement. Moreover, the causal interpretation of the correlations found between early tracking and inequality in competencies has been called into question by Fabian Waldinger
(2007). Indeed, using a slightly different research strategy on PIRLS data,
Waldinger finds no significant effect of tracking on inequality of test results
once the pretracking inequality in reading results is controlled for.

In a paper closely related to the analyses in this chapter, Daniele Checchi
and Luca Flabbi (2007) use PISA data to show that although parental background has the predominant effect on track choice in Italy, in Germany student ability appears to exert a larger effect. They conclude that the Italian
system is more prone to inefficient allocation than the German one, low-
ability students from privileged family backgrounds standing good chances
of entering the academic school tracks.[3] However, because the PISA data on
competencies are collected at the age of fifteen, and because the measures
of reading and math literacy are sensitive to effects of schooling that might
differ across tracks, they cannot tell us the initial inequality of ability that
may have existed before tracking took place, nor do they allow us to assess
the ongoing impact of parents on track changes and school achievement. In
an attempt to overcome some of these limitations, we consider a larger set
of educational outcomes in a longitudinal perspective.

Parental School Choice

Effects of parental background on school choice have been studied
extensively. In his seminal work, Raymond Boudon (1974) distinguishes
between primary and secondary effects of social origin on educational
decisions. Primary effects reflect the differences in abilities and competencies between children of different origins. These inequalities emerge
from different styles of parenting and family support, and translate into
unequal educational outcomes. However, educational decisions are
also driven by the expected costs of further educational achievements,
subjective estimates of the success probability, and, most important, the
expected utility from obtaining a certain educational degree (see Erikson
and Jonsson 1996; Breen and Goldthorpe 1997). Central to these explanations is the motive of *status maintenance,* in particular the desire to avoid
downward mobility and the aversion against risky decisions such as
moving up the educational hierarchy rather than choosing a more secure
educational track. Explanations of this risk-averse pattern of educational
decisions in lower social strata cite the uncertainty and lack of intimate
knowledge of the institutions of higher education and their corresponding academic labor markets, the tendency to underestimate the success
probabilities and abilities, and a general resistance against higher education and academia. In addition, arguments are compelling for leaving
the educational system with intermediate (vocational) certificates that

already guarantee status maintenance at an early stage of life. Of course, direct and indirect (opportunity) costs may also support such a decision, at least from a medium-term perspective. Despite the difficulty in testing the Boudon model empirically (see Stocké 2007), the literature suggests that secondary effects on school decisions that are mediated by low educational aspirations, expected utility, and estimated success probability play the crucial role in explaining the persistent inequality in education.

Still, fairly little is known about how these effects are shaped by institutional settings and how they occur and develop across the early educational career.[4] A common argument is that the effects of parental background—and secondary effects on school choice in particular—are stronger on earlier transitions in the child's life. Empirical studies following the work of Robert Mare (1980, 1981) have confirmed a regular pattern of declining effects of parental background on subsequent educational transitions, the so-called waning patterns effect. Several explanations have been proposed to explain this pattern. The life-course hypothesis states that later educational decisions tend to reflect the child's abilities and experiences and thus show a lower degree of parental (secondary) effects.[5]

However, another more mechanical explanation of this pattern refers to the dynamic selection bias inherent in the Mare model of educational decision-making, which posits that the highest educational degrees are the result of previous, nested educational transitions (Shavit and Blossfeld 1993). In this model, at each stage only a positively selected population is at risk of later transitions. Given this positive selection on unobserved characteristics like motivation and ability, the impact of parental background on later transitions should decline automatically.

Both the Mare model and the dynamic selection interpretation have been seriously called into question by Stephen Cameron and James Heckman (1998). They argue that the waning effect is sensitive to the choice of logit specifications to analyze educational transitions. They show that using alternative statistical models would lead to different conclusions. Moreover, they question the use of logits in terms of the underlying behavioral assumptions, which are inconsistent with the forward-looking decision-making process, which, they claim, drives educational choices. In addition, they develop models of dynamic selection leading to conclusions that contradict waning patterns (for a response to this criticism, see Lucas 2001; Breen and Jonsson 2000).[6]

Institutions

We now briefly describe the Italian and the German educational systems (Schneider 2008, Barone and Schizzerotto 2008). Both systems are characterized by a selection of students into different tracks at a relatively early age. However, apart from this similarity, the two systems differ in a number of important respects, such as the exact age at which tracking takes place, the process of selection into the tracks, the orientation of the tracks, and the system of postsecondary education. In Italy, kindergartens are available at the primary level for children aged three to five and are not compulsory. Primary education starts at age six and lasts for five years. Lower secondary education starts at age eleven and lasts for three years. At the end of lower secondary education, normally age thirteen, students have to decide which type of upper secondary school track they wish to enroll in. Compulsory education normally lasts nine years, and therefore, students must enroll in the first year of upper secondary education. At the end of lower secondary schooling, students have to pass a final exam. Although the grades in this exam should give students and their parents useful information for the choice of upper secondary school track, students and families have complete freedom of choice. We can distinguish five types of tracks in upper secondary education, all of which grant access to university conditional on having completed a five-year course of study and having passed the centralized secondary school final exit exam.[7] Cross-track mobility is allowed on a case-by-case basis. Upper secondary education at licei lasts five years, provides general education, and is meant to prepare students for entering tertiary education (the university system). The curriculum of istituti tecnici lasts five years and provides technical education, mainly meant to prepare students for white-collar jobs. The istituti professionali lasts three to five years and provides vocational education meant for skilled blue-collar careers. The two remaining tracks are meant to train students for being primary teachers (scuole magistrali) or visual artists (istituti artistici). Although some heterogeneity in the structure of these tracks is evident, in the present study, we only consider students having successfully completed five years of secondary education, who therefore all qualify for university enrollment. In recent years, university entry has become a frequent choice after finishing school. In 2007, 53 percent of all upper secondary graduates entered university, but only 14 percent of the population age twenty-five to sixty-four hold a tertiary degree (OECD 2009, 39, 48). The direct costs of tertiary education in public institutions are below the OECD average (2005: $6,385 per year; OECD 2009, 166). The share of students in private universities is low.

Like in Italy, compulsory education in Germany starts with primary school at age six. Preprimary education is not compulsory. Primary school lasts four years, in a minority of federal states six years. In the following description, we assume that primary school ends after fourth grade. Thus, lower secondary education starts usually at the age of ten. Selection into different tracks takes place earlier than in Italy because there are different types of lower secondary schools. Usually, teachers recommend a type of school at the end of primary school.[8] Even though the recommendation is not binding in most federal states during our observation period, it provides a strong signal for the pupils and their parents as to which school to choose. In theory, the schools available to them are oriented toward manual, nonmanual, or academic training, which represents a horizontal differentiation. But there is no doubt that the hierarchy, in terms of expected achievement and the prestige of these different types of schools, is more important. The Hauptschule (low track) usually lasts five years (in some federal states six years) and is oriented toward manual vocational training. Graduation from a Hauptschule does not entitle the student to enter higher secondary or university education. The Realschule (intermediate track) is also oriented toward vocational training but traditionally less towards manual occupations and lasts six years. Conditional on high achievement at the end of the Realschule, students may choose to continue secondary schooling at the Gymnasium or similar academic-track school to earn university entry qualifications. The Gymnasium (highest track) is oriented toward academic education. To graduate from Gymnasium, students must pass the Abitur exam, which they take after nine—in some federal states only eight—years of secondary education. All students who pass the Abitur are eligible to study at the university level. Although comprehensive secondary schools or a prolongation of primary school have been introduced since the late 1960s, the three-track system described here is still the general rule in Germany. Only in some federal states a larger percentage of students do attend comprehensive schools (Gesamtschulen, less than ten percent of all secondary schools in Germany). There are also schools with alternative pedagogical concepts (for example, Waldorf schools) and special education schools. Therefore, in addition to the three main types of schools, we include "other schools" as a fourth residual category in our analyses. In general, variation is considerable in the institutional regulations of secondary schools across the sixteen federal states in Germany, and between the western and eastern parts of Germany in particular. However, the main features as depicted above are rather similar. We also control for federal states to account for regional idiosyncrasies.[9]

In contrast to Italy, Germany has a formalized postsecondary vocational training system that is often attractive to students who decide to leave the academic track (Mayer, Müller, and Pollak 2007; Becker and Hecken 2009). A substantial minority of the latter choose vocational training (mainly for nonmanual occupations, for example, in the financial sector). As a consequence, Germany's university entry rate for upper secondary graduates is only 34 percent and well below the OECD average (OECD 2009, 48).[10] Assuming a dropout rate of 20 to 25 percent (Autorengruppe Bildungsberichterstattung 2010, 297), the percentage of university graduates will not be much higher than the current rate of 26 percent among thirty-five- to forty-four-year-olds.

In broad terms, the differences between Germany and Italy can be summarized as follows. Germany has a more rigid tracking system because tracking takes place earlier and the secondary school tracks are more clearly stratified in terms of eligibility for university enrollment and labor market chances. In addition, with its vocational training system, Germany offers a formalized postsecondary education geared to graduates from the lower tracks. However, in contrast to what one would expect, a study comparing Germany and Italy based on PISA data finds that parental effects on secondary school track are greater in Italy than in Germany (Checchi and Flabbi 2007). The authors argue that this is due to the more efficient and ability-orientated tracking in Germany, where teacher recommendations play a crucial role, whereas in Italy, secondary school choice is left completely to the parents, and thus is more open to parental background effects.

Despite these differences, school tracks are associated with substantial differences in labor market returns in both countries. For example, in Italy, female (male) students from the academic track enjoy an hourly wage differential of 27 percent (32 percent) relative to students in the vocational track. Clearly, part of this advantage arises from the fact that the academic track is a gateway to university degrees: keeping the level of educational attainment constant (with a dummy for holding a university degree), the differentials narrow considerably, but still remain positive and statistically significant, 12 percent and 17 percent.[11]

Data and Methods

In this chapter, we go beyond the existing literature by widening the scope of the educational outcomes considered, and by systematically comparing results for Germany and Italy. Although we do not focus on inequality or achievement levels in terms of ability and competencies, we use indicators of school achievement (grades, teacher recommendations, grade repetition) in addition to educational track choice and certificates obtained. We analyze the initial selection into secondary school tracks and the transitions from secondary to vocational or university education. Moreover, exploiting the longitudinal (Germany) and retrospective (Italy) nature of our data, we also focus on transitions that take place during secondary school, thus allowing for complex educational career paths up to university enrollment, and, for Italy, also including university dropout. To account for educational path dependency, we control for previous transitions and consider indicators of past achievements. These indicators cannot strictly serve as controls for abilities, and thus primary effects, but they allow us to assess the potential impact of past abilities and competencies.

Data

Our analyses for Italy are based on its survey on employment and educational outcomes of high-school graduates (*Indagine sui percorsi di studio e di lavoro dei diplomati*) administered by the National Statistical Institute (ISTAT). This is an ongoing cross-sectional survey conducted every three years since 1998. The survey targets individuals who graduated from upper secondary school three years before the survey year. Available survey years are 1998, 2001, 2004, and 2007, which therefore cover students who graduated from upper secondary school in 1995, 1998, 2001, and 2004. The sample is a two-stage stratified sample. In the first stage, schools are sampled by region, school track, and size of the graduating class. In the second stage, individuals are sampled from each school sampled in the first stage. The data constitute a representative sample (approximately 6 percent) of the target population. Interviews are based on computer-assisted telephone (CAT) interviews.

For Germany, we use the German Socio-Economic Panel Study (SOEP), a household panel survey that started in 1984 in West Germany (see Wagner, Frick, and Schupp 2007). The East German sample was drawn in 1990. The survey is carried out annually. The main mode is face-to-face interviewing (both paper and pencil and computer-assisted personal interviews). Each household member age seventeen and over completes a personal questionnaire. In addition, one person per household completes a household questionnaire. A number of questions from the household questionnaire refer to children living in the household and enrolled in educational institutions. This information is used to reconstruct educational choices at the end of primary school. Additionally, we merged information on school performance collected in the so-called youth questionnaire (for a similar approach, see Francesconi, Jenkins, and Siedler 2010). The youth questionnaire is primarily directed at first-time respondents (age seventeen) from sampled households and contains retrospective questions on achievement in school.

To observe students' choices and educational outcomes between the end of primary school and entry to university, we need an observation window that starts at age nine. We decided to define the end of the observation window as age twenty-three despite the fact that a certain percentage of individuals enter the university later. We use two samples for the main analyses: a sample that covers the period up to age seventeen for the analysis of track choices and early school outcomes (birth cohorts 1984 through 1991, n=1,300) and a sample of persons aged seventeen to twenty-three for the analysis of postsecondary transitions (birth cohorts 1982 through 1985, n=452). For the latter sample, we also have retrospective information about teachers' recommendations at the end of primary school.

Descriptive statistics for the Italian and German samples are reported in table 13.1. We use the International Standard Classification of Education (ISCED), collapsed into three categories of higher education

Table 13.1   Descriptive Statistics

Italian Sample		German Sample	
Number of observations			
Total	88393	Total:	1598
By years			
1995	26.2		
1998	25.6		
2001	24.3		
2004	23.9		
Gender			
Female	52.3	Female	51.5
Parental education			
ISCED 0–2	44.6	ISCED 0–2	8.9
ISCED 3	41.4	ISCED 3	62.5
ISCED 4–6	14.0	ISCED 4–6	28.6
Achievements at end of primary school (exam results, recommendation)			
Final grades, grade 8 = pass	28.7	Hauptschule (low)	17.2
Final grades, grade 8 = fair	28.9	Realschule (intermediate)	29.8
Final grades, grade 8 = good	21.3	Gymnasium (high)	35.1
Final grades, grade 8 = excellent	21.1	Other	17.8
Track choice			
Istituto professionale	14.9	Hauptschule (low)	26.3
Istituto tecnico	41.4	Realschule (intermediate)	28.6
Liceo	32.5	Gymnasium (high)	30.4
Teachers' school	8.1	Other	14.7
Art school	3.2		
Secondary school achievements			
Changed track (up)	2.1	Changed track (up)	18.6
Changed track (down)	4.9	Changed track (down)	10.1
Repeated grades	22.5	Repeated grades	17.7
Exam results grade 13 (out of 100)=60–69	33.6	Grades, age seventeen, 4.51–6	2.1
Exam results grade 13 (out of 100)= 70–79	28.3	Grades, age seventeen, 3.51–4.5	21.9
Exam results grade 13 (out of 100)= 80–89	18.8	Grades, age seventeen, 2.51–3.5	50.8
Exam results grade 13 (out of 100)= 90–100	19.4	Grades, age seventeen, 1.51–2.5	23.0
		Grades, age seventeen, ≤1.5	2.2

Table 13.1   *Continued*

Italian Sample		German Sample	
Postsecondary education			
Enrolled at university	58.0	Enrolled in vocational	59.9
		Enrolled at university	34.2
Dropped out of university	13.5		

Source: Authors' calculations based on data from ISTAT (various years) and SOEP (2009).
Notes: Figures for Germany are based on both samples if applicable.

(ISCED levels 4–6), intermediate education (ISCED level 3), and lower education (ISCED levels 0–2). There are noteworthy cross-country differences in parental education, the distribution for Germany having higher percentages of intermediate and high levels of parental education than Italy, a fact that resembles evidence from international comparisons of educational attainment in adult populations (see OECD 2009, 29). The distribution of track choices is similar in the two countries in terms of the academic track, while in Italy the percentage of students in the vocational (low) track is about half that in Germany. The degree of cross-track mobility is much higher in Germany than in Italy. One reason is the strict vertical hierarchy of the tracks in Germany, which provides a widely acknowledged option to change tracks to adapt to their academic achievements or learning outcomes. Furthermore, some students in Germany continue with a higher track after graduating in a lower track (for example, moving on to complete academic-track Gymnasium after successfully completing the intermediate-track Realschule). In Italy, on the other hand, a larger percentage of students repeat grades. The percentage of students enrolling in university studies is similar in the two countries.

Methods

We investigate the processes determining student outcomes and their relationships with parental background using econometric models. Because the variables of interest represent individual choices (such as school track choice and university enrollment) or outcomes of a qualitative or discrete nature (such as teachers' recommendations of school track or final examination results), we use models for limited dependent variables that are binary, ordered, or multinomial. Throughout the chapter, we use logit-type models, in which estimated coefficients can be read as the percentage change in the odds.

Our objective is to quantify the associations between parental background (in terms of education), student outcomes, and the interactions between parental background and school tracking in affecting outcomes. The outcomes were selected with the aim of following student progressions from the years preceding track choice up to the choice to enroll in university studies. For Italy, we investigate the following student outcomes:

- final exam results at the end of the eighth grade (that is, before choosing an upper secondary school track)
- the choice of upper secondary school track
- indicators of achievement in upper secondary school, for example, grade repetitions and track changes
- final exam results at the end of upper secondary school (grade 13)
- university enrollment
- university dropout

For Germany, we investigate the following student outcomes:

- teachers' recommendations at the end of primary school
- the choice of lower secondary school track
- indicators of achievement in upper secondary school, for example, grade repetition or track changes
- grades reported at age seventeen or final exam grades at the end of lower secondary school (if completed by age seventeen)[12]
- enrollment in university studies or vocational training

For each outcome investigated, we estimate several versions of the models. Each version includes time, gender, and regional controls. The baseline version only includes controls for parental background. This will enable estimation of the overall (gross) impact of parental education on student outcomes. Next, we augment the specification by including indicators of lagged student achievement when available, and estimate conditional social gradients (net effects). We are thus also able to assess the degree of persistence in achievement and, at the same time, to observe how estimated coefficients associated with parental background change relative to the baseline model, which should provide information about the extent of net (as opposed to gross) intergenerational associations. The last specification also adds the interactions between parental background and school tracks, allowing us to assess the extent to which parental education affects student outcomes even within groups defined homogeneously in terms of school choices. For the sake of brevity, coefficients referring to interactions are reported in the online appendix to this chapter.[13]

Table 13.2   Outcomes Preceding Selection into Tracks

	Exam Results at the End of Eighth Grade (Base = Pass)		
A. Italy	Fair	Good	Excellent
Parental education (base=ISCED 0–2)			
ISCED3	0.306***	0.596***	0.925***
	(0.029)	(0.033)	(0.036)
ISCED 4–6	0.751***	1.411***	2.153***
	(0.053)	(0.053)	(0.053)
Observations		83541	
Pseudo R^2		0.041	

	Teachers' Recommendations at End of Primary School (Base = Low)		
B. Germany	Intermediate	High	Other
Parental education (base=ISCED 0–2)			
ISCED3	0.770**	1.946***	0.461
	(0.375)	(0.506)	(0.481)
ISCED 4–6	1.510***	3.512***	0.993*
	(0.457)	(0.556)	(0.583)
Observations		1300	
Pseudo R^2		0.103	

Source: Authors' calculations based on data from ISTAT (various years) and SOEP (2009).
Notes: Multinomial logit estimates. Asymptotically robust standard errors in parentheses.
Regressions include gender, region, and year dummies and use survey weights.
P-value = 0.0000 for each model.
* $p < .10$, ** $p < .5$, *** $p < .01$

Results

Our empirical analyses cover educational outcomes during childhood and adolescence in Italy and Germany. This includes outcomes before initial track choice, initial track choice, grade repetition, and track mobility during secondary school, student achievement at the end of secondary school, and enrollment in post-secondary education.

Outcomes Before Initial Track Choice

Table 13.2 presents the results of our econometric analysis, in which we investigate the role of parental education in student outcomes at the end of the nontracked segment of the educational system. For Germany (panel B), outcomes are measured by the school track recommended by teachers, whereas in Italy we use the eighth-grade final exam results (panel A). For a common specification for the two countries, we use a multinomial logit model. Coefficients, therefore, can be interpreted as the percentage change in the odds of being in a certain category, rather than in the base category.

For Italy, parental education appears to be very strongly associated with student outcomes at the end of eighth grade. Having parents whose maximum educational level is the highest in our categorization of the ISCED scales is associated with an odds of reporting the mark *fair* rather than *pass* that is 75 percent larger compared with that of parents with low education. If we consider the odds of obtaining an *excellent* rather than a *pass*, the corresponding increase associated with highest parental education is 215 percent.

Also in Germany, we find a strong impact of parental education on student outcomes at the end of primary school. Having at least one highly educated parent (ISCED 4–6) increases the odds of obtaining a recommendation for the intermediate track rather than the low track by 151 percent. The increase is even more pronounced (+351 percent) for recommendations for the academic track. At the end of primary education, social gradients of school achievement seem to be somewhat larger for Germany than for Italy. When interpreting these results, we have to keep in mind that teachers' recommendations in Germany reflect not only the student's academic achievement in primary school but also the teacher's estimation of the student's *future academic achievement potential* in a given track. Evidence is broad that the variation by parental background in the likelihood of obtaining a high-track recommendation is only partly explained by differences in ability (primary effects). Studies that control for ability show that children with parents with higher education are more likely to obtain a recommendation for the highest track (see Ditton, Krüsken, and Schauenberg 2005). Hence, analyzing abilities at the end of primary school would probably result in less pronounced differences by parental education in Germany that are broadly comparable to those found for Italy.[14]

Overall, this evidence shows a strong association between parental education and student outcomes at the end of primary education. Parents appear to be able to affect children's outcomes before tracking takes place, and in an institutional context in which primary and lower secondary education are mainly public and of homogeneous quality. These correlations could reflect correlations among parents' and children's ability levels or be the product of better educational inputs provided by more educated parents; our data does not enable us to distinguish between the two hypotheses. In Germany, initial inequalities in abilities at the end of primary education seem to be somewhat larger than in Italy.

Initial Track Choice

In table 13.3, we begin analyzing the central issue in this chapter, the choice of school track and its relationship with parental education. In each country, we adopt a multinomial logit specification that corresponds to a random utility model.

Let us start by considering model 1. For Italy, parental education shows a strong association with the choice of the track in ninth grade. High parental education increases the odds of choosing the technical track by 112 percent. The figure becomes 385 percent if we consider enrollment in the academic track (liceo). Similarly strong associations can be observed for the *teacher's school* track. The German results also show evidence of a strong association between parental education and track choice, especially when the highest ISCED level and the academic track are considered.

Moving to the second step of the analysis of track choice, past achievement indicators (model 2) show even stronger coefficients: in Italy, the percentage change in the odds of choosing the istituto tecnico is 235 comparing students with the highest and lowest levels of academic achievement in eighth grade, whereas the percentage change amounts at 479 for enrollment in the liceo, illustrating that these schools tend to attract students from the upper tail of the ability distribution. Curiously enough, the inclusion of lagged achievement indicators induces only a very minor reduction in the impacts of parental background. This is somewhat surprising, given the strong associations between family background and pre-track student achievement, but the results are consistent with the Italian system, where tracking is not rigid and the exam results at the end of eighth grade are not binding for students' and parents' choices. For Germany, including students' past academic achievement leads to a more substantial reduction in the coefficients of parental education. This is what one would expect given that teacher recommendations are more binding for track choice in Germany (as compared here with eighth-grade exam results in Italy), and past achievements are likely to mediate a larger fraction of parental influences on track choice. Also in Germany, past achievement variables are highly significant and have large coefficients. The association is strongest between high-track recommendations and choosing the highest track.

Including interactions in model 3 provides further insights on track choice. In Italy, the estimated coefficients for the interaction terms are mostly not statistically significant, but we can observe significant effects for the interactions between the highest level of parental education and intermediate levels of student achievement on the choice of enrolling in the academic track. Although comparatively small (with respect to the main effects to which they refer), these interaction effects are negative, meaning that students with highly educated parents and intermediate

Table 13.3   Choice of School Track

| | A. Italy (Base = Vocational Education); Number of Observations = 85937 | | | | | | | | |
| | Technical Education | | | Academic-Oriented Education | | | Teachers' School | | |
	Model 1	Model 2	Model 3	Model 1	Model 2	Model 3	Model 1	Model 2	Model 3
Parental education (base=ISCED 0–2)									
ISCED 3	0.581***	0.512***	0.574***	1.617***	1.465***	1.616***	0.798***	0.756***	0.558***
	(0.028)	(0.030)	(0.044)	(0.033)	(0.038)	(0.089)	(0.050)	(0.052)	(0.095)
ISCED 4–6	1.120***	0.994***	1.004***	3.852***	3.562***	3.855***	2.055***	1.927***	1.576***
	(0.068)	(0.071)	(0.102)	(0.064)	(0.072)	(0.120)	(0.093)	(0.096)	(0.171)
Final grades, grade 8 (base=pass)									
Fair		0.925***	0.969***		1.609***	1.748***		0.823***	0.720***
		(0.031)	(0.040)		(0.047)	(0.087)		(0.059)	(0.081)
Good		1.757***	1.783***		3.351***	3.526***		1.649***	1.564***
		(0.046)	(0.056)		(0.056)	(0.091)		(0.073)	(0.099)
Excellent		2.345***	2.414***		4.793***	4.977***		2.267***	2.003***
		(0.068)	(0.088)		(0.073)	(0.109)		(0.090)	(0.126)
Pseudo R^2	0.111	0.194	0.195	0.111	0.194	0.195	0.111	0.194	0.195

B. Germany (Base = Low); Number of Observations = 1300

	Intermediate			High			Other		
	Model 1	Model 2	Model 3	Model 1	Model 2	Model 3	Model 1	Model 2	Model 3
Parental education (base=ISCED 0–2)									
ISCED 3	0.592*	0.270	0.262	1.580***	0.504	0.474	−0.081	−0.306	−0.323
	(0.345)	(0.367)	(0.363)	(0.551)	(0.542)	(0.561)	(0.464)	(0.468)	(0.470)
ISCED 4–6	1.313***	0.871*	0.886	3.332***	1.889***	4.092***	0.761	0.307	0.736
	(0.423)	(0.449)	(0.744)	(0.588)	(0.595)	(1.548)	(0.562)	(0.595)	(0.874)
Teachers' recommendation (base=low)									
Intermediate		2.417***	2.333***		3.510***	4.588***		1.143***	1.282***
		(0.309)	(0.329)		(0.850)	(1.073)		(0.392)	(0.427)
High		1.978***	2.089***		7.093***	8.260***		1.618***	1.591***
		(0.391)	(0.454)		(0.852)	(1.081)		(0.475)	(0.572)
Other		0.731**	0.904*^		2.572***	3.433***		0.929**	1.003**
		(0.358)	(0.376)		(0.864)	(1.114)		(0.451)	(0.473)
Pseudo R^2	0.134	0.356	0.360	0.134	0.356	0.360	0.134	0.356	0.360

Source: Authors' calculations based on data from ISTAT (various years) and SOEP (2009).

Notes: For Italy, results for art schools not shown. Multinomial logit estimates. Asymptotically robust errors in parentheses. Regressions include gender, region, and year dummies and use survey weights. P-value $= 0.0000$ for each model. Model 3 contains interaction effects as described in the text (reported in online appendix).

* $p < .10$, ** $p < .5$, *** $p < .01$

past academic achievement have a lower chance of enrolling into the academic oriented track than students with equally educated parents, but located in the lowest or highest tails of the past achievement distribution. This can be interpreted as an indication that choices for students with low academic achievement are made mostly on the basis of parental tastes, such that highly educated parents send even lower-achieving children to academic-track schools. This is confirmed by the impact of parental education on the odds of enrolling in the academic track being higher in column 3 (where it refers to lower-achieving students) than in column 2 (where it refers to the whole sample). As student achievement goes up, student tastes in education may affect their choice of track more strongly, giving students with intermediate achievement and highly educated parents a lower probability of enrolling in the academic track. Results show that many of these students go into the teachers' school track. The preference of children from highly educated parents for teachers' school is stratified by academic achievement.

In the German case, we do not find significant interaction effects that would support the same conclusion, but we do see an increased likelihood for children with highly educated parents to choose the highest school track, even if teachers recommend the lowest track (comparing models 3 and 2). Moreover, evidence from other studies suggests that this may indeed be the case. Highly educated parents are more likely to choose the highest track even if their children did not receive this recommendation (Lohmann and Groh-Samberg 2010). We also find large negative interaction effects, which indicate that having a high-track recommendation is less important for the choice of the highest track if at least one parent is highly educated. Yet the effects are not statistically significant by conventional standards.

Overall, our results suggest that parental choices may induce educational mismatch for low achievers from highly educated parents entering academic track. Evidence suggests that these effects might be somewhat more pronounced in Italy than in Germany. Although the gross impact of parental education on track choice appears to be similar in Germany and Italy, after controlling for some achievement measures, it turns out that the effects of parental education remain almost unchanged in Italy but decline in Germany, indicating that the sorting process in Germany rests to at least some extent on the children's ability.

Grade Repetition and Track Mobility During Secondary School

In tables 13.4 and 13.5, we look at the determinants of success in the chosen school track. We start by studying the determinants of grade repetition. The first column of table 13.4 shows that, in Italy, parental education

Table 13.4 Achievement During Secondary School, Italy

	Repeated Grades			Changed to Higher Track			Changed to Lower Track		
	Model 1	Model 2	Model 3	Model 1	Model 2	Model 3	Model 1	Model 2	Model 3
Parental education (base=ISCED 0–2)									
ISCED 3	-0.155***	-0.0188	0.0524	-0.335***	-0.0429	-0.114	-0.128**	-0.424***	-0.242***
	(0.027)	(0.030)	(0.054)	(0.104)	(0.109)	(0.157)	(0.053)	(0.059)	(0.075)
ISCED 4–6	-0.657***	-0.293***	0.195	0.111	0.708***	0.708***	-0.347***	-1.018***	-0.716***
	(0.044)	(0.051)	(0.149)	(0.162)	(0.168)	(0.247)	(0.076)	(0.086)	(0.189)
Final grades, grade 8 (base=pass)									
Fair		-0.851***	-0.853***		-0.362***	-0.363***		-0.876***	-0.882***
		(0.032)	(0.032)		(0.126)	(0.126)		(0.064)	(0.064)
Good		-1.818***	-1.822***		-0.137	-0.141		-1.691***	-1.699***
		(0.046)	(0.046)		(0.169)	(0.170)		(0.080)	(0.080)
Excellent		-3.019***	-3.021***		-0.090	-0.095		-2.707***	-2.713***
		(0.068)	(0.068)		(0.202)	(0.202)		(0.105)	(0.105)
School track (base=vocational)									
Technical		0.706***	0.727***		-1.791***	-1.812***			
		(0.034)	(0.042)		(0.114)	(0.150)			
Academic oriented		0.911***	1.044***					2.344***	2.506***
		(0.046)	(0.068)					(0.061)	(0.084)
Teachers' school		0.423***	0.495***		-2.357***	-2.765***		1.073***	1.124***
		(0.067)	(0.087)		(0.236)	(0.341)		(0.105)	(0.138)
Observations	85956	83522	83522	66095	64150	64150	62790	61055	61055
Pseudo R²	0.040	0.148	0.148	0.018	0.107	0.107	0.005	0.134	0.135

Source: Authors' calculations based on data from ISTAT (various years) and SOEP (2009).

Notes: For Italy, results for art schools not shown. Logit estimates. Asymptotically robust standard errors in parentheses. Regressions include gender, region, and year dummies and use survey weights. *P*-value = 0.0000 for each model. Model 3 contains interaction effects as described in the text (reported in online appendix).

* *p* < .10, ** *p* < .5, *** *p* < .01

exerts a relevant gross impact on grade repetition.[15] Subsequent columns highlight the channels through which this effect operates. Lagged achievement and choices, included in the second column, constitute one obvious channel. Students with the highest academic achievement levels in eighth grade have over 300 percent lower odds of grade repetition in secondary school than students with the lowest achievement levels. On the other hand, conditional on achievements, grade repetition is the highest in the academic track, which may require more effort. Inclusion of these mediating factors reduces the effects directly associated with background. However, in the third column, we can see that the protective effect of parental education against grade repetition works only for children who have highly educated parents and are enrolled in the academic track or, to a lesser extent, in technical schools. This might occur in several ways. Educated parents may help students overcome learning difficulties or understand challenging material (either by helping personally or by hiring tutors); they may influence students' expectations about the effort required for studying challenging subjects such as Greek, Latin, or math, thereby avoiding discouragement or loss of motivation that may lead to grade repetition; or teachers may have a bias in favor of students from better family backgrounds.

The analysis of grade repetition in Germany (table 13.5) yields somewhat different results. Parental education has no clear influence. This is a further indication that the process of student sorting across tracks is likely to be based more on academic achievement in Germany than in Italy. Indeed, a better match between individual abilities and the ability level required by the different tracks should reduce parents' opportunities to affect the student's academic achievement within the chosen track (for example, hiring tutors). As expected, students with a high recommendation at the end of primary school are less likely to repeat grades during secondary school (up to age seventeen). However, the model with interaction effects indicates that students with highly educated parents are less likely to repeat grades if they have not chosen the highest (most demanding) track. Grade repetition may be the result of a lack of support by parents, but also of too ambitious a track choice. While the former is on average more strongly associated with low parental education, the latter is more common among highly educated parents. Furthermore, downward mobility to less demanding tracks is an alternative to grade repetition. Our data do not allow for a separation of such mechanisms.

The next set of results for Italy (from the fourth to the sixth column in table 13.4) refer to the probability of changing track during high school and moving to a higher track—that is, closer to the academic track in terms of curriculum. Using this criterion, school tracks can be ordered from lowest to highest as: vocational, technical, art school, teachers' school, academic. Students initially enrolled in the liceo (for whom no upward

Table 13.5   Achievement During Secondary School, Germany

	Repeated Grades			Changed to Higher Track			Changed to Lower Track		
	Model 1	Model 2	Model 3	Model 1	Model 2	Model 3	Model 1	Model 2	Model 3
Parental education (base=ISCED 0–2)									
ISCED 3	0.037	0.138	0.107	1.433***	1.711***	1.710***	-0.345	-0.162	-0.167
	(0.427)	(0.444)	(0.438)	(0.410)	(0.509)	(0.517)	(0.604)	(0.814)	(0.817)
ISCED 4–6	-0.317	-0.099	0.956	2.408***	3.150***	3.164***	-1.298*	-1.160	-1.226
	(0.482)	(0.519)	(0.727)	(0.485)	(0.631)	(0.671)	(0.699)	(0.906)	(0.962)
Teachers' recommendation (base=low)									
Intermediate		0.071	0.080		2.493***	2.494***		-2.580***	-2.592***
		(0.324)	(0.317)		(0.450)	(0.449)		(0.519)	(0.516)
High		-0.700*	-0.722*		3.981***	3.981***		-3.418***	-3.432***
		(0.384)	(0.391)		(0.670)	(0.669)		(0.628)	(0.633)
Other		-0.032	-0.086		1.841***	1.841***		-1.854**	-1.853**
		(0.373)	(0.358)		(0.497)	(0.498)		(0.754)	(0.753)
School track (base=low)									
Intermediate		-0.101	0.199		-3.443***	-3.437***		-1.388***	-1.432***
		(0.325)	(0.324)		(0.412)	(0.451)		(0.399)	(0.454)
High		0.063	0.175						
		(0.402)	(0.429)						
Other		-0.329	-0.110						
		(0.384)	(0.423)						
Observations	1300	1300	1300	667	667	667	752	752	752
Pseudo R^2	0.034	0.047	0.059	0.100	0.334	0.334	0.093	0.175	0.175

Source: Authors' calculations based on data from ISTAT (various years) and SOEP (2009).

Notes: For Italy, results for art schools not shown. Logit estimates. Asymptotically robust standard errors in parentheses. Regressions include gender, region, and year dummies and use survey weights. *P*-value = 0.0000 for each model. Model 3 contains interaction effects as described in the text (reported in online appendix).

* $p < .10$, ** $p < .5$, *** $p < .01$

movement is possible) have been excluded from the analysis. Results show a significant role of family background in affecting mobility across tracks. In particular, once controls for the track of origin are included in the specification (fifth column) we see that pupils from highly educated parents have 70 percent higher odds of moving up than students from parents with low education. In the model without controls for the initial track (fourth column), the effect is counteracted by parental education's shifting initial choices toward higher tracks, from which upward mobility is lower by construction. Results in the sixth column stress that parental education is beneficial especially for pupils in the lowest track. Interestingly, student achievement does not appear to exert much impact on upward track mobility. A possible explanation for these results is that the higher freedom of choice that the Italian system leaves to families in terms of track choice is also reflected in the social gradient observed for track changes, and the low importance of student achievement. It could be that families are mainly interested in ensuring their progeny a certain status rather than in matching their children's abilities with the most suitable school track.

The last outcome considered in table 13.4 is downward track mobility; as for upward mobility, we exclude students not at risk of experiencing the event, in this case students who initially enrolled in the vocational track. Considering the basic specification with only parental background, a significant effect can be detected for parental education: highly educated parents are associated with odds of downward mobility that are 35 percent lower than for parents with low education. Including controls for achievement and the initial track (eighth column) magnifies these effects: students from highly educated families tend to select into tracks with a higher chance of downward mobility (by construction), which counteracts the effects of parental education. Controlling for the initial track keeps this opposing influence constant. Achievement, on the other hand, reduces downward mobility. Finally, in the ninth column, we include interactions between parental education and the track initially chosen. The results show that educated parents can avoid downward mobility especially for children enrolled in the academic track.

As in Italy, upward and downward mobility in Germany are clearly structured by parental education, previous educational choices, and academic achievement.[16] Columns 4 to 6 of table 13.5 show that children with highly educated parents are much more likely to move to a higher track during secondary school. Compared to children with less educated parents, the odds of moving up increases by 240 percent in the group with a high ISCED level (4–6). The differences are even more pronounced if prior choices and achievements are included in the model, underscoring the finding that parental background drives track choices, independent of abilities or even counteracting influences. The analysis of downward mobility (columns 7 through 9) points in the same direction. Children with highly educated parents are less likely to move to lower tracks. The same applies to children who received high recommendations at the end of primary school.

Taken together, the results provide strong evidence that the inequality of access to the higher tracks after primary school depending on parental education is not weakened over the course of subsequent educational decisions. In contrast, the analysis of intertrack mobility shows that groups that are already more likely to enter higher tracks are also more likely to move up, and the others more likely to move down (see also Jacob and Tieben 2009). Thus, the impact of parental background on children's school success would be underestimated if one looked only at the initial track choice. The sorting of students from different backgrounds into the corresponding tracks, independent of their abilities, continues to take place also after initial track choice. Despite social gradients observed in cross-track mobility for both countries, it is important to keep in mind the very low percentage of students changing track in Italy compared with Germany (table 13.1). This might also be an indication that parents in Germany are more interested in matching children's abilities with track-specific requirements, and that they respond to new information about their children's abilities by influencing them to change track. By contrast, in Italy track choice appears to be based mainly on parents' preferences, which makes parents more likely to stick to their initial choice and increases the likelihood of grade repetition.

Student Achievement at the End of Secondary School

In table 13.6, we investigate the determinants of student achievement at the end of secondary school. For Italy, the measure of achievement is final exam results in grade 13. Results show that both parental background and individual ability (measured by lagged school achievement) are significantly associated with student achievement. Considering the model that controls only for parental background (column 1), we observe that high parental education increases the odds of receiving better grades. The estimated effect can be compared with the impact of background at the earlier stage observable in the data, that is, in eighth grade. Rerunning the regressions for exam results in eighth grade using an ordered logit, the same specification used in table 13.6, the coefficient associated with the highest parental educational class becomes 1.37, almost double that obtained in table 13.6. This finding confirms the idea that parental influences decline as individuals move through the educational system. However, such a conclusion should be drawn with caution, both because the measures used to quantify achievement are not strictly comparable between the two grades, and logit specifications suffer from the shortcomings that

Table 13.6   Achievement at End of School Track

Italy, Age 18

	Model 1	Model 2	Model 3
Parental education (base=ISCED 0–2)			
ISCED 3	0.284***	0.126***	0.0738**
	(0.020)	(0.022)	(0.036)
ISCED 4–6	0.839***	0.475***	0.188*
	(0.030)	(0.034)	(0.106)
Final grades, grade 8 (base=pass)			
Fair		0.695***	0.696***
		(0.026)	(0.026)
Good		1.438***	1.440***
		(0.032)	(0.032)
Excellent		2.693***	2.694***
		(0.038)	(0.038)
Repeated grades		-0.922***	-0.921***
		(0.026)	(0.026)
School track (base=vocational)			
Technical		-0.338***	-0.361***
		(0.025)	(0.031)
Academic-oriented		-0.742***	-0.774***
		(0.033)	(0.049)
Teachers' school		-0.514***	-0.624***
		(0.045)	(0.067)
Observations	85956	83518	83518
Pseudo R^2	0.024	0.123	0.123

Germany, Age 17

	Model 1	Model 2	Model 3
Parental education (base=ISCED 0–2)			
ISCED 3	0.281	0.108	0.066
	(0.301)	(0.325)	(0.328)
ISCED 4-6	0.218	-0.238	-0.232
	(0.328)	(0.351)	(0.570)
Teachers' recommendation (base=low)			
Intermediate		0.848***	0.828***
		(0.261)	(0.260)
High		1.431***	1.412***
		(0.313)	(0.311)
Other		0.276	0.298
		(0.294)	(0.297)
Repeated grades		-1.292***	-1.279***
		(0.230)	(0.232)
School track (base=low)			
Intermediate		-0.333	-0.277
		(0.230)	(0.240)
High		-0.332	-0.243
		(0.297)	(0.331)
Other		-0.345	-0.587
		(0.417)	(0.477)
Observations	1300	1300	1300
Pseudo R^2	0.028	0.079	0.082

Source: Authors' calculations based on data from ISTAT (various years) and SOEP (2009).
Notes: For Italy, results for art schools not shown. Ordered logit estimates. Asymptotically robust standard errors in parentheses. Regressions include gender, region, and year dummies and use survey weights. *P*-value = 0.0000 for each model. Model 3 contains interaction effects as described in the text (reported in online appendix).
* $p < .10$, ** $p < .5$, *** $p < .01$

Cameron and Heckman (1998) discuss. As expected, exam results in grade 13 strongly depend on lagged educational achievement in terms of exam results in eighth grade and grade repetition, a finding that clearly illustrates the strong persistence in student achievement. But even after controlling for lagged achievement, parental education still exerts an impact on exam results in grade 13 in Italy. Interaction effects with school track at graduation show that highly educated parents are still able to positively influence their children's achievement at this stage, in particular in the academic track and teacher school.

For Germany, we use exam results at age seventeen or at the point of the graduation if it took place earlier. We do not find any association between exam results and parental education, only an impact of prior achievement. Students who obtained a high recommendation at the end of primary school are more likely to have good exam results. Students who repeated grades in secondary school are less likely to have good exam results. Again, this finding is in line with the overall picture obtained when considering grade repetitions and changes of track: a more ability-based choice of track, like the German one, reduces parents' capability to affect current educational achievement within a track over and above the effect mediated by past achievement.

University Enrollment

Finally, in tables 13.7 and 13.8, we look at educational transitions into tertiary education, namely university enrollment rates, university dropout rates (for Italy only), and enrollment in postsecondary vocational training (for Germany only). Looking at Italy first (table 13.7), a strong impact of parental education is evident in each case. Even when including measures of ability or educational success and school tracks (columns 2 and 5), one can see that high parental education increases the odds of enrollment by 157 percent and reduces the odds of dropping out by 58 percent. The associations with student achievement (measured in terms of exam results in grades 8 and 13) and school track at graduation are also very strong and significant.

In contrast to Italy, attending university in Germany is not the only way to obtain formal postsecondary qualifications. Vocational training is a crucial part of the educational system and the standard choice of school leavers from other than the academic track. Theoretically, school leavers from the lower tracks can also attend university if they upgrade their qualifications. Therefore, in the following analysis, we assume that individuals who were placed in the lower tracks at age seventeen are "at risk" of university entrance. This allows us to carry out an analysis with the full sample, considering three different postsecondary options: no further training, vocational training, or university entrance.

Table 13.7   Transition to Third Level of Education or Training, Italy

	University Enrollment			University Dropout		
	Model 1	Model 2	Model 3	Model 1	Model 2	Model 3
Parental education (base=ISCED 0–2)						
ISCED 3	1.048***	0.704***	0.545***	−0.333***	−0.0828*	0.0267
	(0.024)	(0.029)	(0.049)	(0.044)	(0.048)	(0.097)
ISCED 4–6	2.655***	1.577***	1.344***	−1.241***	−0.580***	−0.520***
	(0.048)	(0.057)	(0.112)	(0.071)	(0.077)	(0.183)
Final grades, grade 8 (base=pass)						
Fair		0.173***	0.176***		−0.172***	−0.172***
		(0.034)	(0.034)		(0.058)	(0.058)
Good		0.359***	0.364***		−0.180***	−0.185***
		(0.042)	(0.042)		(0.067)	(0.067)
Excellent		0.523***	0.526***		−0.374***	−0.377***
		(0.054)	(0.055)		(0.086)	(0.086)
Repeated grades		−0.396***	−0.396***		0.387***	0.382***
		(0.034)	(0.034)		(0.056)	(0.056)

School track (base=vocational)

Technical	0.871***	0.780***		−0.574***	−0.563***
	(0.052)	(0.041)		(0.060)	(0.079)
Academic-oriented	3.495***	3.429***		−1.932***	−1.805***
	(0.056)	(0.083)		(0.078)	(0.112)
Teachers' school	1.652***	1.498***		−1.072***	−0.880***
	(0.054)	(0.072)		(0.099)	(0.139)
Exam results, grade 13 (base=60–69)					
70 to 79	0.634***	0.636***		−0.493***	−0.492***
	(0.034)	(0.034)		(0.056)	(0.055)
80 to 89	1.050***	1.050***		−0.808***	−0.804***
	(0.040)	(0.040)		(0.064)	(0.064)
90 to 100	1.650***	1.658***		−1.377***	−1.370***
	(0.048)	(0.048)		(0.071)	(0.071)
Observations	85947	83509	43076	42057	42057
Pseudo R^2	0.114	0.338	0.046	0.152	0.152

Source: Authors' calculations based on data from ISTAT (various years) and SOEP (2009).
Notes: Logit estimates. Asymptotically robust standard errors in parentheses. Regressions include gender, region, and year dummies and use survey weights. Results for art school not shown. Model 3 contains interaction effects as described in the text (reported in online appendix).
* $p < .10$, ** $p < .5$, *** $p < .01$

Table 13.8   Transition into the Third Level of Education or Training, Germany

	Entry into Vocational Training		Entry into University	
	Model 1	Model 2	Model 1	Model 2
Parental education (base=ISCED 0–2)				
ISCED 3	1.706**	1.930**	1.678*	1.747*
	(0.841)	(0.873)	(0.918)	(0.926)
ISCED 4–6	2.560***	2.416***	4.478***	3.257***
	(0.938)	(0.928)	(0.997)	(0.993)
Repeated grades		−0.238		−0.567
		(0.622)		(0.756)
Grades, age seventeen (base=pass)				
Results=fair		1.111*		1.934**
		(0.669)		(0.773)
Results=good		0.439		1.766**
		(0.747)		(0.827)
Teachers' recommendation (base=low)				
Intermediate		0.347		0.194
		(1.029)		(1.160)
High		0.448		0.686
		(1.160)		(1.278)
Other		−0.917		−1.439
		(0.691)		(0.955)
School track (base=low)				
Intermediate		2.095**		5.435***
		(1.006)		(1.595)
High		0.467		5.884***
		(0.958)		(1.575)
Other		−0.036		3.946***
		(0.878)		(1.472)
Observations	452	452	452	452
Pseudo R^2	0.146	0.369	0.146	0.369

Source: Authors' calculations based on data from ISTAT (various years) and SOEP (2009).
Notes: Multinomial logit estimates. Asymptotically robust standard errors in parentheses. Regressions include gender, region, and year dummies and use survey weights. Results for art school not shown.
* $p < .10$, ** $p < .5$, *** $p < .01$

The first and third columns (model 1) of table 13.8 show that postsecondary choices are strongly associated with parental education. The differences by parental education are most pronounced for the likelihood of entry into university. Taking into account previous track choice and achievement indicators reduces the relevance of parental education (columns 2 and 4; model 2).[17] Still, parental education is highly relevant, particularly for the choice to attend university. Also, taking into account exam results and attending the highest track at age seventeen provide additional insight into the explanation of the differences in postsecondary choices.

Conclusion

We have investigated how the structure of the educational system, namely the features of school tracking (age and mode) in secondary schools, is associated with the intergenerational transmission of educational advantage. We have studied two countries (Italy and Germany), both characterized by early tracking in secondary schools, though the details of the two systems are rather different in terms of age at tracking, barriers to track entry, and type of credentials generated by school tracks in each country, all features that make the German system somewhat less flexible, in terms of the role of parental choice, than Italy. Also, another key cross-country difference is the presence in Germany of postsecondary vocational training, which may affect the choice of school tracks.

The drivers of track choice are similar in the two countries in terms of the gross effect of parental education. However, when we also take into account the effects of mediating factors—such as indicators of achievement collected at earlier stages of the educational career—the German data display a much larger attenuation of parental effects than the Italian data. Also, in Italy, we find evidence that parental education favors the allocation of lower-ability students to academic tracks. These differences could partly be explained by rules for accessing school tracks, whereas in Italy parental tastes play a greater role than in Germany in the absence of formal recommendations from schools.

In both countries, we also find evidence that parental background affects educational outcomes even after initial track choice at the end of primary school (in terms of grade repetition, track changes, final exam results, and college enrollment), but these effects are much stronger in Italy than in Germany. For example, we find evidence that parental background and school tracks may interact in shaping the effects of ability on achievement, such that, overall, parental effects may have increasing impacts over the life course.

Consistently with our previous result on initial school track choice, intertrack mobility appears to be much higher in Germany than in Italy. This is what one would have expected given that parents in Italy are less likely than those in Germany to base their initial decisions on information about their children's ability, but tend to enroll their children in certain tracks in search of a certain social status. Hence, in Italy, parents are unlikely to change school track even if their children turn out to be mismatched in terms of ability with respect to the track initially chosen, and as a consequence grade repetitions are likely to be more frequent. By contrast, in Germany parents seem to react to new information on children's ability by changing school track, which along with a more ability-driven initial choice of school track makes grade repetitions less frequent.

Overall, our results support the view that parental education is a key factor in sorting students across school tracks, which in turn are important in determining subsequent outcomes. These effects appear stronger in Italy than in Germany, and differences in educational systems may help explain these findings. More than the age at tracking, the absence of formal recommendations for access to tracks is an obvious factor strengthening parental influences (see also Checchi and Flabbi 2007). But differences in the tertiary education system may be important as well. The absence of postsecondary vocational training in Italy may encourage educated parents of low-ability students to enroll them in the academic track (leading to university enrollment), due to a lack of postsecondary education or training alternatives that suit their children's ability.

This also suggests that tracked educational systems that do not sort students effectively may have two negative effects: they increase costs for both students and the society as a whole, in terms of lost years of schooling (and potential work) due to grade repetitions, and they reduce equality of opportunity in educational outcomes by favoring individuals from wealthier backgrounds, thereby reducing intergenerational mobility.

Notes

1. In a recent paper, Richard Breen et al. (2009) find evidence for a decline in educational inequality in Germany and other European countries, with Italy being an exception and showing no clear trend over time.
2. From another perspective, Fabian Pfeffer (2008) also finds significant negative effects of early tracking on the degree of dependency of educational attainment on parental education.
3. Daniele Checchi and Luca Flabbi (2007) regard track allocation as efficient when it is based on ability and not on other factors such as parental background.
4. There exists an extensive literature comparing the various educational transitions in different countries. Taking a cohort perspective and looking at the German school system, Karl Mayer, Walter Müller, and Reinhard Pollak (2007) show that though inequalities in the odds of obtaining the *Abitur* (highest secondary track) have decreased over time, the conditional inequalities at the transition to university have increased. A similar pattern was found by Yossi Shavit and Karin Westerbeek (1998) for Italy. In the present paper, we do not address cohort or trend changes.
5. With regard to abilities, chapter 6 of this volume finds that average outcomes of children from different backgrounds are fairly constant over time. However, the discussion of a potential fanning out is only partly related

to the life-cycle hypothesis, which mainly addresses the waning impact of secondary effects.

6. Because most of our analysis is focused on the interplay between individual characteristics and parental background in shaping educational outcomes at a given level of attainment, rather than on waning effects per se, we adopt logit specifications that provide readily interpretable estimates in terms of percentage changes in the odds.

7. The content of this exam is track-specific, that is, students enrolled in the same track take the same exam.

8. These recommendations are not based on standardized tests but on pupil's grades in the last year of primary school and on an evaluation of the chances of success in a given track.

9. Because of sample size, we are not able to explore differences in educational behavior between East and West Germany or federal states. We also had to collapse neighboring federal states if sample sizes were too low and if institutional differences were not too strong, ending up with nine regions. However, we did not collapse federal states from East and West Germany.

10. As in Italy, the direct costs of tertiary education are below OECD average (OECD 2009, 166). Until 2007, there were no tuition fees for first-time students in public universities (average duration of study). Since 2007, a number of federal states have introduced tuition fees of up to €1,000 per year.

11. Estimates for Italy are derived from the 2008 wave of the Bank of Italy Survey on Households Income and Wealth (SHIW) considering a sample of employees between twenty-one and sixty years of age, using log wage regressions that control for labor market experience and regional effects.

12. In contrast to Italy, where final grades from grade thirteen are based on a central test, there are no nationwide exams in Germany. Grades are highly heterogeneous across federal states and school tracks.

13. The online appendix can be found at: http://www.russellsage.org/Ermisch_et_al_OnlineAppendix.pdf.

14. Because students do not always receive a recommendation, and sometimes receive one that is fairly unspecific (for example, "not unconditionally fit for the highest track"), we have a residual group of respondents with "other recommendations." Because this represents a rather heterogeneous group that may also capture cases that simply did not report their recommendation, we refrain from interpreting the results in detail. One of the main reasons we include this category is that we would otherwise lose a number of cases for the subsequent steps of the analysis.

15. Similarly significant effects of parental background on grade repetition for Canada and the United States are reported in chapter 14 of this volume.

16. Students initially enrolled in the highest track have been excluded from the analysis of upward mobility; students initially enrolled in the lowest track from the analysis of downward mobility.

17. Given this additional option, the group of graduates who do not enter into any kind of postsecondary education is much smaller. Therefore, the reference group in Germany is more selective than in Italy, which partly explains the differences in the size of the coefficients. Furthermore, we do not present a model with interactions between parental education and prior track due to the small number of cases in some cells.

References

Autorengruppe Bildungsberichterstattung. 2010. *Bildung in Deutschland 2010.* Bielefeld, Ger.: Bertelsmann.

Barone, Carlo, and Antonio Schizzerotto. 2008. "The Application of the ISCED-97 to Italy." In *The International Standard Classification of Education (ISCED-97): An Evaluation of Content and Criterion Validity for 15 European Countries,* edited by Silke L. Schneider. Mannheim: Mannheim Centre for European Social Research.

Baumert, Jürgen, Eckard Klieme, Michael Neubrand, Manfred Prenzel, Ulrich Schiefele, Wolfgang Schneider, Petra Stanat, Klaus-Jürgen Tilmann, and Manfred Weiß, eds. 2001. *PISA 2000. Basiskompetenzen von Schülerinnen und Schülern im internationalen Vergleich.* Opladen Ger.: Leske und Budrich.

Becker, Rolf, and Anna E. Hecken. 2009. "Why Are Working-Class Children Diverted from Universities? An Empirical Assessment of the Diversion Thesis." *European Sociological Review* 25(2): 233–50.

Boudon, Raymond. 1974. *Education, Opportunity, and Social Inequality. Changing Prospects in Western Society.* New York: Wiley-Interscience.

Breen, Richard, and John H. Goldthorpe. 1997. "Explaining Educational Differentials: Towards a Formal Rational Action Theory." *Rationality and Society* 9(3): 275–305.

Breen, Richard, and Jan O. Jonsson. 2000. "Analyzing Educational Careers: A Multinomial Transition Model." *American Sociological Review* 65(5): 754–72.

Breen, Richard, Ruud Luijkx, Walter Müller, and Reinhard Pollak. 2009. "Nonpersistent Inequality in Educational Attainment: Evidence from Eight European Countries." *American Journal of Sociology* 114(5): 1475–521.

Brunello, Giorgio, and Daniele Checchi. 2007. "Does School Tracking Affect Equality of Opportunity? New International Evidence." *Economic Policy* 22(52): 781–861.

Cameron, Stephen V., and James J. Heckman. 1998. "Life Cycle Schooling and Dynamic Selection Bias: Models and Evidence for Five Cohorts of American Males." *Journal of Political Economy* 106(2): 262–333.

Checchi, Daniele, and Luca Flabbi. 2007. "Intergenerational Mobility and Schooling Decisions in Germany and Italy: The Impact of Secondary School Tracks." *IZA* discussion paper 2876. Bonn: Institute for the Study of Labor.

Coleman, James S. 1966. "Equality of Educational Opportunity: Summary Report." Washington: U.S. Department of Health, Education, and Welfare, Office of Education.

Ditton, Hartmut, Jan Krüsken, and Magdalena Schauenberg. 2005. "Bildungsungleichheit—der Beitrag von Familie und Schule." *Zeitschrift für Erziehungswissenschaft* 8(2): 285–304.

Erikson, Robert, and Jan O. Jonsson. 1996. "Explaining Class Inequality in Education: The Swedish Test Case." In *Can Education Be Equalized? The Swedish Case in Comparative Perspective*, edited by Robert Erikson and Jan O. Jonsson. Boulder, Colo.: Westview.

Francesconi, Marco, Stephen P. Jenkins, and Thomas Siedler. 2010. "Childhood Family Structure and Schooling Outcomes: Evidence for Germany." *Journal of Population Economics* 23(3): 1201–231.

Hanushek, Eric A., and Ludger Wößmann. 2006. "Does Educational Tracking Affect Performance and Inequality? Differences-in-Differences Evidence Across Countries." *Economic Journal* 116(510): C63–C76.

ISTAT. Various years. *Indagine sui percorsi di studio e lavoro dei diplomati (Survey on Employment and Educational Outcomes of High-School Graduates), 1998–2007.* Rome: Italian National Institute of Statistics (ISTAT).

Jacob, Marita, and Nicole Tieben. 2009. "Social Selectivity of Track Mobility in Secondary Schools." *European Societies* 11(5): 747–73.

Lohmann, Henning, and Olaf Groh-Samberg. 2010. "Akzeptanz von Grundschulempfehlungen und Auswirkungen auf den weiteren Bildungsverlauf." *Zeitschrift für Soziologie* 39(6): 470–92.

Lucas, Samuel R. 2001. "Effectively Maintained Inequality: Education Transitions, Track Mobility, and Social Background Effects." *American Journal of Sociology* 106(6): 1642–690.

Mare, Robert D. 1980. "Social Background and School Continuation Decisions." *Journal of the American Statistical Association* 75(370): 295–305.

———. 1981. "Change and Stability in Educational Stratification." *American Sociological Review* 46(1). 72–87.

Mayer, Karl Ulrich, Walter Müller, and Reinhard Pollak. 2007. "Germany: Institutional Change and Inequalities of Access in Higher Education." In *Stratification in Higher Education: A Comparative Study*, edited by Yossi Shavit, Richard Arum, and Adam Gamoran. Palo Alto, Calif.: Stanford University Press.

Organisation for Economic Co-Operation and Development (OECD). 2009. *Education at a Glance.* Paris: Organisation for Economic Co-Operation and Development.

Pfeffer, Fabian T. 2008. "Persistent Inequality in Educational Attainment and Its Institutional Context." *European Sociological Review* 24(5): 543–65.

Schneider, Silke. 2008. "Applying the ISCED-97 to the German Educational Qualifications." In *The International Standard Classification of Education (ISCED-97): An Evaluation of Content and Criterion Validity for 15 European Countries*, edited by Silke Schneider. Mannheim: Mannheim Centre for European Social Research.

Schütz, Gabriela, Heinrich W. Ursprung, and Ludger Wößmann. 2005. "Education Policy and Equality of Opportunity." *CESifo* working paper 1518. Munich: Ifo Group for Economic Reseach.

Shavit, Yossi, and Hans-Peter Blossfeld, eds. 1993. *Persistent Inequality; Changing Educational Attainment in Thirteen Countries.* Boulder, Colo: Westview Press.

Shavit, Yossi, and Karin Westerbeek. 1998. "Educational Stratification in Italy: Reforms, Expansion, and Equality of Opportunity." *European Sociological Review* 14(1): 33–47.

Shavit, Yossi, Meir Yaish, and Eyal Bar-Haim. 2007. "The Persistence of Persistent Inequality." In *From Origin to Destination. Trends and Mechanisms in Social Stratification Research,* edited by Stefani Scherer, Reinhard Pollak, Gunnar Otte, and Markus Gangl. Frankfurt/New York: Campus.

SOEP. 2009. *Socio-Economic Panel v.25, Data for Years 1984–2009.* Berlin: DIW.

Stocké, Volker. 2007. "Explaining Educational Decision and Effects of Families' Social Class Position: An Empirical Test of the Breen-Goldthorpe Model of Educational Attainment." *European Sociological Review* 23(4): 505–19.

Wagner, Gert G., Joachim R. Frick, and Jürgen Schupp. 2007. "The German Socio-Economic Panel Study (SOEP): Scope, Evolution, and Enhancements." *Schmollers Jahrbuch* 127(1): 139–70.

Waldinger, Fabian. 2007. "Does Ability Tracking Exacerbate the Role of Family Background for Students' Test Scores?" Unpublished paper, London School of Economics.

Wößmann, Ludger. 2007. "Fundamental Determinants of School Efficiency and Equity: German States as a Microcosm for OECD Countries." *IZA* discussion paper 2880. Bonn: Institute for the Study of Labor.

Chapter 14

Child Development
and Social Mobility

ROBERT HAVEMAN, PATRIZIO PIRAINO,

TIMOTHY SMEEDING, AND KATHRYN WILSON

IN THIS chapter, we track and compare the mechanisms through which parental resources and choices affect offspring childhood attainments in two neighboring countries—the United States and Canada—and, in turn, how these childhood attainments impact early adult outcomes of the same offspring. By examining multiple outcomes across different stages of childhood development, we are able to see how parental income is related to offspring achievement and at what ages the effect of parental income is most strongly felt in both countries.

Early efforts to relate parental characteristics to children's attainments within single countries were limited in the range of parental characteristics and children's attainments that were studied, and in the duration of the longitudinal data sets used (see Haveman and Wolfe 1994; Duncan and Brooks-Gunn 1997). Since these early efforts, few systematic studies of this complex transmission process using long-duration longitudinal data sets have been undertaken. Because of the severe data requirements for making reliable cross-national comparisons of this sort, studies that attempt to nest estimates of parent-child linkages in the broader context of overall social mobility patterns or that systematically study these patterns across nations are even more rare (see also Black and Devereux 2010). All such efforts also confront the difficulty of demonstrating causal relationships.

Several studies find that children's educational achievement is positively correlated with their parents' education or with other indicators of their parents' socioeconomic status (see, for example, Björklund and Salvanes 2010). Substantial recent literature speculates that varying institutions and policies (for example, national spending on early child care or education, or the extent of public health insurance coverage) affect measured levels of social mobility. For example, in their review of intergenerational mobility research, Sandra Black and Paul Devereux (2010) suggest limited evidence indicating that higher national levels of public spending on education are positively related to measures of social mobility. We hope to contribute to this discussion by comparing two countries that, despite being very similar in many ways, have very different levels of social mobility.

We use comparable long-duration longitudinal data consistent in parental-child characteristics and ages across the two countries. In particular, we compare the linkages between parental status (primarily income) and a variety offspring skills-attainment at different ages in the two countries, and draw inferences from these comparisons regarding relative levels of social mobility between the nations. We also reveal changes in these levels as the cohorts age.

We find that parental income has a stronger relationship with childhood health problems and test scores in the United States than in Canada. In addition, in both countries, the effect of parental income increases as the child ages (a fanning out of the effect) but more so in Canada. However, the effect of parental income on the probability of enrolling in college is very similar between the two countries. Furthermore, although in both countries about one-third of the effect of parental income on college attendance is through the earlier childhood outcomes (for example, a child from a higher-income family is likely to have higher test scores, which increase the probability of attending college), there is still a large, independent effect of family income on college attendance.

This pattern—evidence of greater fanning out in Canada than in the United States in outcomes observed through adolescence, but similar patterns of marginal income effects in the two countries in the young adulthood outcome of college-going—is puzzling. In the summary and conclusion, we discuss potential explanations as well as implications of our results.

Background: United States and Canada

The United States and Canada are close neighbors, sharing a border and a similar culture. They are large trading partners and economically and socially intertwined (see Corak 2010). They are both large-scale immigrant countries, though with different patterns in the human capital characteristics and origins of the immigrant populations. The two nations also have quite different cultural traditions and norms for child rearing, work supports and family leave, labor market institutions, and policies involving early childhood education, schooling, health care, and income support. For example, Canada has paid child and family leave, whereas the United States generally does not (Gornick and Meyers 2004). Similarly, Canadians spend more time with their children than American parents do (Gauthier, Smeeding, and Furstenberg 2004). Educational attainment and school outcome scores

Figure 14.1   Trends in Inequality (Gini Coefficient)

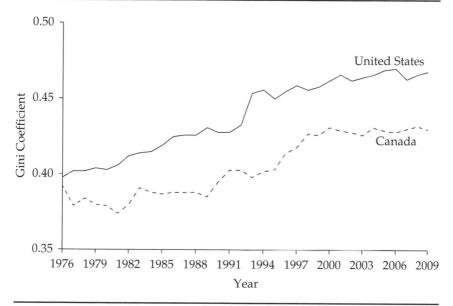

Source: Authors' calculations based on data from Brandolini and Smeeding (2009, figure 4.2).

are also higher in Canada (OECD 2009).[1] Finally, life expectancy is greater in Canada than in the United States (Thomas and Torrey 2008).

Although both the United States and Canada have relatively high levels of inequality amongst rich countries, the trends in inequality have diverged substantially over the period covered by our data (see figure 14.1). Canada experienced a smaller increase in earnings inequality than the United States did in the 1980s, in part because of the strength of Canadian unions, which have twice the participation rate of those in the United States. Moreover, because the supply of skilled workers in Canada increased in response to rising demand in the 1980s relative to the United States, skill premium is lower in Canada than the United States, implying a smaller increase in Canadian earnings equality over this period (Gottschalk and Joyce 1998; Brandolini and Smeeding 2009).[2] The unknown relative effects of these similarities and differences make it difficult to predict the likely patterns of linkages between parent economic position and children's outcomes in the two countries.

In the 1990s, David Card and Richard Freeman (1993) studied differences and similarities between Canada and the United States, and documented the importance of what may seem to be "small differences." Their work suggests that Canada's social safety net was more generous than that in the

United States, and that this contributed to the markedly lower Canadian poverty rates (and inequality) in the 1980s. These trends have continued.[3] Card and Freeman also noted that Canada's unemployment rates were persistently greater than those in the United States, in part because of differences in measuring unemployment. These and comparable disparities need to be considered in assessing the parent-child linkages we present here.

Comparisons of social mobility in the United States and Canada are based on the correlation between fathers' and sons' earnings, or earnings-income mobility: the higher the correlation (or elasticity), the higher the persistence and the lower the mobility. Existing research suggests that the degree of U.S. intergenerational income persistence is substantially larger than in Canada, indeed almost twice as large (see Blanden 2009; Björklund and Jäntti 2008; Corak 2010).[4] Comparing patterns of linkages between parental attainments and life-cycle offspring health and educational accomplishments between the United States and Canada should provide insight into the transmission mechanisms that help constitute the intergenerational mobility process in these two nations.

Data Sources

We use longitudinal data that are consistent across the two countries in parental-child characteristics and ages. For both countries, we examine the effect of parental social status on child outcomes at each of four periods in the children's life cycle: birth (C0), elementary school years (C2), middle childhood (C3), and early adulthood (C4).[5] In our estimation, we control for earlier outcomes in estimating effects on middle and late outcomes.

For the U.S. component of this study, we use the Child Development Supplement (CDS) of the Michigan Panel Study of Income Dynamics (PSID). The PSID is a nationally representative sample of families in the United States with an oversample of low-income families.[6] The PSID contains annually collected data for 1968 through 1997 and biannual data for 1999 through 2007.

The CDS component of this study sampled all PSID families with children age twelve or younger during the calendar year of 1997. Up to two children per family were selected. These children were interviewed in 1997, 2002–2003, 2005, and 2007. For those members of the CDS who reached age eighteen, a new study, called Transition into Adulthood, collected additional data in 2005 and 2007. Therefore, information on the parents of the CDS children is available in the PSID since 1968, and detailed information on the children is available in the CDS for 1997, 2002–2003, 2005, and 2007.

For the Canadian component of our study, we primarily use the National Longitudinal Survey of Children and Youth (NLSCY). The NLSCY began in 1994 and has been conducted biannually since then, with the last cycle conducted in 2006 and 2007. We use data from the original cohort, representing all children who were eleven years old or younger in 1994. These children were from ages twelve to twenty-three at cycle 7.

Although our basic estimates for Canada rely on the NLSCY, some of the descriptive results presented in this section are based on the Youth in Transition Survey (YITS). The YITS enables us to examine the relationship between parental resources and middle and later child outcomes, taking advantage of larger sample sizes.[7]

Parental Variables

We use parental income as the primary measure of parental social status. Family income is defined as the sum of income of each adult in the family unit.[8] Income is measured on a per capita basis, and adjusted to account for economies of scale associated with families of different sizes.[9] (We also describe supplementary results using parental educational attainment.)

The NLSCY and the YITS contain an adult questionnaire where the person most knowledgeable (PMK) in the household is identified and interviewed. The PSID contains an adult questionnaire on which questions on income are asked every year, and in select years an education history is created. Both data sets have information for both parents on total household income and highest educational attainment. In online appendix table 14A.1, we summarize both the Canadian and the U.S. data sets in more detail.[10]

Child Outcome Variables

We measure the effect of parental income on early, middle, and late childhood outcomes. We focus on those outcomes which have been shown to have a direct impact on a child's future socioeconomic success. For both the U.S. and Canadian data sets, we define four offspring life stages, and within each stage measure specific offspring attainments:

- *Birth Year* (first months of life) (C0)
  Birth weight
  Gestational age
  Child's physical health (as reported by the parents)
- *Middle Childhood* (seven to eleven years old) (C2)
  Behavioral scales
  Standardized test scores measuring math skills
  Child's physical health (as reported by the parents)
- *Adolescence* (twelve to seventeen years old) (C3)
  Grade repetition
  Standardized test scores measuring math and reading skills

Table 14.1   Probability of a Positive Outcome

	Canada			United States		
	Low SES	High SES	Gap	Low SES	High SES	Gap
C0 outcomes (birth)						
Birth weight greater than 2.5 kilograms	93.0	95.7	2.7	93.6	97.6	4.0
Good health at birth	95.7	96.6	0.9	89.0	95.0	6.0
Not born four or more weeks early	89.0	91.3	2.3	93.1	96.7	3.6
C3 outcomes (ages twelve to seventeen)						
Never repeat a grade	83.9	95.0	11.1	78.3	95.7	17.4
Nonsmoking	82.1	87.1	5.0	88.1	92.6	4.5
Health	79.4	92.0	12.6	52.5	76.1	23.6
C4 outcomes (ages eighteen to twenty-three)						
Postsecondary Enrollment	65.3	84.4	19.1	44.8	92.6	47.8
Health	65.5	71.3	5.8	55.0	72.2	17.2

Source: Authors' calculations based on the CDS of the Panel Study of Income Dynamics (Institute for Social Research 2009), National Longitudinal Survey of Children and Youth (Statistics Canada 2008), and the Youth in Transition Survey (Statistics Canada 2007).

Health (both self-reported and reported by parents)
Behavioral scales
Risky behaviors (smoking, drinking, and drugs)
- *Early adulthood* (eighteen to twenty-three years old) (C4)
Postsecondary enrollment
Health (self-reported)

Overview of Parental Income–Children's Attainment Relationships

Table 14.1 presents an overview of the probability of having a positive result on each of eight offspring variables spanning three stages of life for both the United States and Canada. The table shows the percentage of offspring with a positive outcome whose parents are in the bottom and top family income quartiles. Three panels are shown in the table. The first panel indicates measures of well-being at birth (C0); the second panel shows measures of attainments during adolescence (C3: age fifteen for Canada and ages twelve through seventeen for the United States); and the third panel shows attainments during early adulthood (C4). These results show simple correlations with no controls. They suggest a larger effect of parental income on both health and educational attainment in the United States than in Canada.

Table 14.2   Probability of Being in the Top Quartile of Test Scores

	Canada			United States		
	Low SES	High SES	Gap	Low SES	High SES	Gap
Reading score A (letter word)	16.7	34.1	17.4	12.4	41.6	29.2
Reading score B (passage comprehension)	16.7	34.1	17.4	7.8	41.2	33.4
Math score	18.1	32.6	14.5	8.5	43.0	34.5

Source: Authors' calculations based on the CDS of the Panel Study of Income Dynamics (Institute for Social Research 2009) and Youth in Transition Survey (Statistics Canada 2007).

For all three measures of well-being at birth (C0), there are advantages for offspring from higher-income families in both countries, but these differences are fairly small and similar between the countries. We note, however, some differences in the health-at-birth outcome: U.S. children display larger parental income gaps than Canadian children.[11]

For the attainment indicators during adolescence (C3, second panel), the United States appears to have a larger high-low income disparity in repeating a grade and health. On the other hand, there is little difference in the probability of smoking between the two countries.

In the third panel, the pattern of cross-country health disparities is continued into early adulthood (C4, ages eighteen through twenty-three). We also note that the probability of having any postsecondary education varies dramatically between offspring from families with high and low incomes for both countries, with the gap being larger in the United States.

In table 14.2, we examine three sets of continuous test score variables measured during adolescence (C3) and show the probability of a positive outcome (being in the top quartile of test scores).[12] U.S. children from high-income families are two to five times more likely to be in the top test score quartile than are children from low-income families. Again, the disparity is smaller in Canada.

We now turn to regression analysis to enable us to better isolate the effect of parental income on offspring attainments; in addition, we examine the sequential pattern of effects as offspring age.

Regression Estimation Results

In our estimation, we use standard multivariate techniques, including ordinary least squares and probit analysis (for categorical outcome variables). Offspring health, education, and behavioral outcomes are dependent variables, and parental economic status (primarily parental income, but also parental education) is the independent variable of interest:

$$C_{ti} = \alpha + \beta P_i + \lambda X_i + \varepsilon_i$$

where C_{ti} is the child's outcome at time t, P_i is the parental family income variable, X_i is a vector of control variables (that is, child's gender and age, parental age), and ε_i is an error term. This estimation approach is standard in this literature, and has been used by Jo Blanden and colleagues (2010), Robert Haveman and colleagues (1997), and in several studies included in Duncan and Brooks-Gunn (1997).

We are interested in the signs and statistical significance of the estimated βs. The magnitude of the coefficients are shown as marginal effects.

In models estimating the correlates of older children's outcomes, we also control for attainments earlier in life. This estimation procedure allows us to examine the effects of parental income on older attainments controlling for attainments at younger ages, and thereby provides evidence on the marginal impact of parental income as children age. These estimates also enable us to obtain indirect evidence on whether attainment gaps increase (or fan out) with offspring age, or decrease (or converge) with child age.[13]

To examine the relationship between family income and outcomes across childhood and adolescence, we primarily focus on five variables: low birth weight, a measure of externalizing behavior problems, standardized math scores, poor health, and college attendance. The externalizing behavior and math scores have been standardized to have a mean of 0 and a standard deviation of 1.

Although longitudinal, the data sets for each country do not include enough years of observation to cover the entire period from birth to college attendance for a given cohort. Therefore, we use two cohorts from each data set. For younger offspring (ages sixteen and younger—life stages C0, C2, and C3), we use a younger cohort of the data (cohort A). For older offspring (ages seven to twenty-three—life stages C2, C3, and C4), we also use a second cohort of the data (cohort B).[14] Table 14.3 describes the samples used in our estimation.

Results for Adolescents (C3)

Table 14.4 presents regression results for the younger sample (cohort A). We show the effect of family income on three outcomes at C3 (externalizing behavior [a component of the Behavior Problems Index, or BPI] in panel A, math scores in panel B, and poor health in panel C), both independently and controlling for prior levels of these same variables as well as for low birth weight.

Table 14.3   Longitudinal Samples Used in Regression Analysis

	United States					Canada			
	Cohort A (N = 661)		Cohort B (N = 561)			Cohort A (N = 3,123)		Cohort B (N = 1,001)	
Year	Age	Life Stage	Age	Life Stage	Year	Age	Life Stage	Age	Life Stage
Various	0	C0	NA	NA	1994	0–3	C0	7–11	C2
1997	3–6	NA	8–11	C2	1998	4–7	NA	11–15	C3
2002	8–11	C2	13–16	C3	2002	8–11	C2	15–19	NA
2007	13–16	C3	18–21	C4	2006	12–15	C3	19–23	C4

Source: Authors' calculations based on the CDS of the Panel Study of Income Dynamics (Institute for Social Research 2009) and the National Longitudinal Survey of Children and Youth (Statistics Canada 2008).

Panel A presents estimates for the effect of family income on standardized values of externalizing behavior at C3.[15] The coefficient on income is of similar magnitude in the two countries when no prior life stage variables are included. When prior levels of externalizing behavior are included, there is a larger negative income effect for Canada than for the United States (−0.13 versus −0.00) measured in standard deviation units.

Although this value is significant only for Canada, the cross-country difference between the two coefficients is statistically insignificant at the 5 percent level. This result appears to be due to the relatively small effect of BPI at C2 on BPI at C3 in Canada relative to the United States (for example, 0.22 for BPI at C2 for Canada versus 0.56 for the United States). This difference may be related to the fact that the Canadian behavioral index is based on self-completed questions at C3 rather than on parental reports at C2.

Panel B shows estimates of the effect of family income on math scores. The simple effect of family income on C3 math scores in the United States is 0.56, which is larger than that for Canada (0.34); the difference between the two coefficients is statistically significant at the 1 percent level. When earlier math scores are included, the coefficient on income in the C3 estimation falls to 0.13 for the United States. Most of the effect of family income on math scores in the United States appears to occur earlier in childhood, with the earlier scores having a large effect of 0.69. In contrast, in Canada about two-thirds of the effect of parental income on math scores remains when earlier test scores are included in the model (the coefficient falls from 0.34 to 0.27). Moreover, earlier math scores have a smaller effect on later scores, with a marginal effect of 0.56 (compared with 0.69 for the United States).

Table 14.4 Effect of Family Income on Childhood Outcomes at C3

A. Standardized Behavioral Problems Scores

	United States			Canada		
	BPI at C3	BPI at C3	BPI at C3	BPI at C3	BPI at C3	BPI at C3
Ln(income)	−0.1872*	−0.1887*	−0.0046	−0.1774*	−0.1753*	−0.1321*
	(0.0546)	(0.0547)	(0.0434)	(0.0570)	(0.0573)	(0.0561)
C0 low birth weight		−0.0599	−0.0561		−0.0692	−0.0943
		(0.1437)	(0.1116)		(0.1035)	(0.0977)
C2 behavior scores			0.6419*			0.2208*
			(0.0309)			(0.0310)
R^2	0.0382	0.0385	0.4210	0.0212	0.0215	0.0666

B. Standardized Math Scores

	United States			Canada		
	Math at C3	Math at C3	Math at C3	Math at C3	Math at C3	Math at C3
Ln(income)	0.5643*	0.5537*	0.1275*	0.3420*	0.3393*	0.2681*
	(0.0504)	(0.0501)	(0.0403)	(0.0512)	(0.0509)	(0.0439)
C0 low birth weight		−0.4265*	−0.1366		−0.0880	−0.1434
		(0.1316)	(0.0961)		(0.1139)	(0.0871)
C2 math scores			0.6909*			0.5574*
			(0.0284)			(0.0298)
R^2	0.2122	0.2246	0.5936	0.2955	0.2959	0.4555

C. Poor Health

	United States			Canada		
	Health at C3	Health at C3	Health at C3	Health at C3	Health at C3	Health at C3
Ln(income)	−0.0394*	−0.0394*	−0.0362	−0.0089*	−0.0090*	−0.0080
	(0.0196)	(0.0197)	(0.0197)	(0.0045)	(0.0046)	(0.0049)
C0 low birth weight		−0.0041	−0.0069		0.0061	0.0063
		(0.0450)	(0.0497)		(0.0042)	(0.0040)
C2 poor health			0.0738			0.0587*
			(0.0995)			(0.0547)
Pseudo R^2	0.0241	0.0241	0.0270	0.0669	0.0692	0.0801

Source: Authors' calculations based on the CDS of the Parel Study of Income Dynamics (Institute for Social Research 2009) and the National Longitudinal Survey of Children and Youth (Statistics Canada 2008).
Note: Standard errors in parentheses.

This positive marginal effect of family income suggests that there is some fanning out in both countries (parental income affects test scores in later childhood even after controlling for the effect on test scores in early childhood). For the United States, much of the large effect of parental income on math scores occurs at younger ages, with a smaller marginal effect (less fanning out later) than in Canada.[16]

Panel C reports the effect of family income on the probability of poor health at C3. When there is no control for previous health outcomes, the effect of parental income is negative and statistically significant in both countries. Although the uncontrolled effect in the United States is more than four times larger than in Canada (−0.039 versus −0.009), the high standard errors result in this difference being statistically insignificant.

When we control for previous health status, the negative effect of family income on health at C3 remains, but is not statistically significant. The magnitude of the effect and the cross-country difference are not affected.[17]

Results for Probability of Postsecondary Schooling in Early Adulthood with Controls for C2 Attainments

In table 14.5, we analyze the effect of family income on the probability of attending a postsecondary education institution in early adulthood (C4) using a sequential model that includes the C2 and C3 for prior behavior problems (panel A), math scores (panel B), and health problems (panel C).

As column 1 in each panel shows, the uncontrolled effect of family income on the probability of attending college is similar in the United States (0.27) and Canada (0.24). The three panels of table 14.3 show that, in both countries, prior behavior problems (BPI) are negatively associated with the probability of attending college, and prior math scores are positively associated with attending college; poor health does not have a statistically significant effect on college attendance in either country.

For example, panel B of table 14.5 shows that, for the United States, the simple relationship between family income and college attendance (0.271) falls to .209 when math scores at C2 are included in the model; clearly, part of the effect of income on college attendance is through these early test scores. When math scores for ages twelve through sixteen (C3) are included in the estimation, the effect of income falls to 0.189. When math scores at both C2 and C3 are included, we estimate that the coefficient of later math skills (at C3) on college attendance is greater than the coefficient on math scores at C2. We conclude that, for the United States, about one-third of the effect of income on college attendance is associated with higher math scores reported earlier in offspring life cycles.

Table 14.5   Effect of Family Income on College Attendance at C4

	United States			Canada		
	Attend College	Attend College	Attend College	Attend College	Attend College	Attend College
A. With and without controlling for childhood externalizing behavior in C2						
Ln(income)	0.2711*	0.2489*	0.2456*	0.2357*	0.2199*	0.2176*
	(0.0386)	(0.0321)	(0.0381)	(0.0377)	(0.0380)	(0.0388)
C2 behavior		−0.0875*	−0.0510*		−0.0990*	−0.0916*
		(0.0217)	(0.0257)		(0.0253)	(0.0258)
C3 behavior			−0.0697*			−0.0313*
			(0.0269)			(0.0212)
Pseudo R^2	0.1991	0.2397	0.2592	0.1010	0.1381	0.1414
B. With and without controlling for math scores in C2						
Ln(income)	0.2711*	0.2093*	0.1894*	0.2357*	0.2320*	0.2133*
	(0.0386)	(0.0384)	(0.0407)	(0.0377)	(0.0407)	(0.0419)
C2 math scores		0.1102'	0.0575*		0.1433*	0.0801
		(0.0228)	(0.0293)		(0.0371)	(0.0422)
C3 math scores			0.0836*			0.1190*
			(0.0389)			(0.0351)
Pseudo R^2	0.1991	0.2498	0.2682	0.1010	0.1342	0.1581
C. With and without controlling for poor health in C2						
Ln(income)	0.2711*	0.2697*	0.2726*	0.2357*	0.2330*	0.2298*
	(0.0386)	(0.0388)	(0.0389)	(0.0377)	(0.0378)	(0.0405)
C2 poor health		−0.0511	−0.0104		0.1954	0.1506
		(0.1726)	(0.1446)		(0.1556)	(0.1562)
C3 poor health			−0.2117			0.1669
			(0.1461)			(0.1676)
Pseudo R^2	0.1991	0.1995	0.2067	0.1010	0.1024	0.1034

Source: Authors' calculations based on the CDS of the Panel Study of Income Dynamics (Institute for Social Research 2009) and National Longitudinal Survey of Children and Youth (Statistics Canada 2008).
Notes: C2 is ages seven to eleven, C3 is ages twelve to seventeen, and C4 is ages eighteen to twenty-three.
Standard errors in parentheses.

For Canada, the simple relationship between family income and college attendance (0.236) falls to 0.213 when earlier math scores are included in the model. Although the controlled effect of family income is similar for the United States and Canada, prior math scores are not as closely related to family income in Canada, hence the marginal effect of parental income falls less. It is reasonable to suggest that the effect of parental background on earlier educational performance is less than in the United States.

Controls for Multiple C2 and C3 Attainments

In table 14.6, we present additional results on the impact of family income on the probability of attending a postsecondary institution by estimating a series of probit models with controls for multiple intervening childhood variables. Panel A shows marginal effects for the United States, and panel B marginal effects for Canada.

The striking result from table 14.6 is the similarity of the effect of family income on the probability of attending college. As shown above, the uncontrolled coefficient is 0.271 in the United States and 0.236 for Canada; it is statistically significant in both countries. Table 14.6 further shows a remarkable similarity in the coefficients on family income when controls for several C2 and C3 variables are included in the estimation. We are unable to reject the hypothesis that the income coefficient is the same in the two countries in any of the model specifications.

Table 14.6   Effect of Family Income on the Probability of College Attendance (C4)

A. United States					
Ln income	0.2712*	0.1844*	0.1667*	0.1790*	0.1642*
	(0.0386)	(0.0379)	(0.0376)	(0.0390)	(0.0384)
Math at C2		0.1006*	0.0464	0.0883*	0.0447
		(0.0228)	(0.0273)	(0.0221)	(0.0268)
BPI at C2		−0.0806*	−0.0530*	−0.0752*	−0.0492*
		(0.0209)	(0.0244)	(0.0221)	(0.0249)
Bad health at C2		−0.0104	−0.0172	−0.0192	−0.0274
		(0.1432)	(0.1389)	(0.1505)	(0.1484)
Excellent health at C2		0.0463	0.0254	0.0438	0.0220
		(0.0442)	(0.0410)	(0.0434)	(0.0407)
Math at C3			0.0835*		0.0724*
			(0.0373)		(0.0349)
BPI at C3			−0.05340*		−0.0515*
			(0.02230)		(0.0236)
Bad health at C3			−0.0907		−0.0664
			(0.1274)		(0.1313)
Excellent health at C3			0.0499		0.0652
			(0.0411)		(0.0382)
Repeat at C3				−0.2528*	−0.2051*
				(0.1053)	(0.1062)
Drink at C3				0.0218	0.0264
				(0.0526)	(0.0503)
Pot at C3				−0.0328	−0.0144
				(0.0618)	(0.0572)
Pseudo R^2	0.1991	0.2879	0.3285	0.3083	0.3426

Table 14.6   *Continued*

B. Canada

Ln income	0.2357*	0.2187*	0.1875*	0.1692*	0.1404*
	(0.0377)	(0.0403)	(0.0421)	(0.0433)	(0.0434)
Math at C2		0.1228*	0.0589	0.1292*	0.0673
		(0.0347)	(0.0391)	(0.0386)	(0.0439)
BPI at C2		−0.0843*	−0.0774*	−0.0903*	−0.0886*
		(0.0250)	(0.0262)	(0.0272)	(0.0285)
Bad health at C2		−0.2628	−0.2033	−0.4239*	−0.3586*
		(0.1598)	(0.1837)	(0.1656)	(0.1876)
Excellent health at C2		0.0334	−0.0811	0.0743	−0.1129*
		(0.0464)	(0.0483)	(0.0482)	(0.0509)
Math at C3			0.1197*		0.1066*
			(0.0323)		(0.0337)
BPI at C3			−0.0091		0.0099
			(0.0211)		(0.0248)
Bad health at C3			−0.0498		−0.2240
			(0.1547)		(0.2284)
Excellent health at C3			0.1066*		0.0863
			(0.0484)		(0.0539)
Repeat at C3				−0.5662*	−0.5498*
				(0.1383)	(0.1653)
Drink at C3				−0.1359*	−0.1379*
				(0.0562)	(0.0551)
Pot at C3				−0.0623	−0.0682
				(0.0776)	(0.0798)
Pseudo R^2	0.1010	0.1626	0.1936	0.2094	0.2354

Source: Authors' calculations based on the CDS of the Panel Study of Income Dynamics (Institute for Social Research 2009) and National Longitudinal Survey of Children and Youth (Statistics Canada 2008).
Notes: C2 is ages seven to eleven, C3 is ages twelve to seventeen, and C4 is ages eighteen to twenty-three.
Standard errors in parentheses.

Part of the effect of parental income is on the earlier outcomes (such as math scores and behavior problems), and these earlier outcomes impact the college attendance probability. However, in both countries, the effect of income has a significant impact even when these earlier outcomes are included, indicating a positive effect of income beyond outcomes early in life.

Possible Nonlinear Effects

Panel A of table 14.7 presents probit model estimates that explore the possible nonlinear effect of family income on postsecondary attendance.

The results show the effect of family income on the probability of college attendance at different points of the income distribution, and reveal important patterns for both countries. The (negative) effect of family income is more important at the bottom of the income distribution for the United States. Having parental income in the bottom quintile reduces the probability of attending college by 0.28 in the United States, but has a statistically insignificant effect in Canada. When earlier life stage variables are included, the income effect in the United States is still large and significant (0.16), but negligible and statistically insignificant in Canada. For two of the three model specifications (columns 1 and 3), the cross-country difference between the coefficients on the bottom income quartile dummy is statistically significant.

At the top of the income distribution, the effect of family income appears to be larger in Canada than in the United States. However, the difference in effects between the two countries is not statistically significant at the 5 percent level.

In panel B of table 14.7, we substitute parental education for parental income as the indicator of economic status. We define parental education level as the attainment of the more educated parent and follow the convention used in this volume (see chapter 1) to create four education categories: low (ISCED 0–2), medium (ISCED 3–4), medium-high (ISCED 5b), and high (ISCED 5a/6). The reference category in panel B is medium.

The effects of parental education on the probability of attending college are very similar for the two countries for the low and medium-high categories, and for neither category is the difference in the coefficients statistically significantly different across the countries. The coefficients differ more for the high parental education category, and the effect is greater in the United States than in Canada. However, the cross-country difference is only significant at the 10 percent level in columns 1 and 3, but insignificant in column 2.

In summary, table 14.7 shows that low parental income has a quantitatively large negative effect on college attendance in the United States, but not in Canada, but low parental education seems to have about the same quantitative effect in both countries. This divergence may be due to the fact that the income distribution in Canada is more compressed than that of the United States. Hence, children born at the bottom of the Canadian income distribution tend to have parents with higher levels of education (relative to the Canadian average) than children at the bottom of the income distribution in the United States (relative to its average). For example, in Canada about 15 percent of parents in the bottom income quartile have ISCED scores in the low and medium categories, and in the United States about 23 percent have such low educational attainment.[18]

Table 14.7 Effects of Family Income on Probability of College Attendance (C4), Further Results

	United States			Canada		
	Model with only SES	Model with SES and C2 Variables	Model with SES, C2, and C3 Variables	Model with only SES	Model with SES and C2 Variables	Model with SES, C2, and C3 Variables
A. Nonlinear effects of income						
Income in bottom quintile	-0.2808*	-0.1866*	-0.1580*	-0.0613	-0.0375	0.0138
	(0.0655)	(0.0631)	(0.0628)	(0.0533)	(0.0503)	(0.0557)
Income in top quintile	0.1942*	0.1164	0.0886	0.2414*	0.2517*	0.1973*
	(0.0485)	(0.0607)	(0.0615)	(0.0457)	(0.0419)	(0.0462)
Pseudo R^2	0.1391	0.2573	0.3149	0.0978	0.1708	0.2428
B. Parental education (comparison group is ISCED 3 or 4)						
ISCED 0–2	-0.2162*	-0.1745	-0.1487*	-0.2395	-0.1581	-0.1982
	(0.1102)	(0.0952)	(0.0991)	(0.1332)	(0.1384)	(0.1476)
ISCED 5b	0.1491*	0.1056*	0.0861*	0.0922	0.0976*	0.0537
	(0.0405)	(0.0413)	(0.0440)	(0.0505)	(0.0480)	(0.0565)
ISCED 5a or 6	0.2877*	0.2091*	0.2010*	0.1633*	0.1707*	0.0710*
	(0.0403)	(0.0454)	(0.0397)	(0.0570)	(0.0523)	(0.0622)
Pseudo R^2	0.1761	0.2895	0.3501	0.0774	0.1449	0.2285

Source: Authors' calculations based on the CDS of the Panel Study of Income Dynamics (Institute for Social Research 2009) and National Longitudinal Survey of Children and Youth (Statistics Canada 2008).

Notes: C2 is ages seven to eleven, C3 is ages twelve to seventeen, and C4 is ages eighteen to twenty-three. The control variables include all of the variables in table 14.6 but use different measures of parental SES. The first and second columns of table 14.7 correspond to the first and second columns of table 14.6; the last column in table 14.7 corresponds to the last column in table 14.6. Standard errors in parentheses.

Summary and Conclusions

Our estimates suggest that the simple relationship between parental income and offspring health problems and test scores is higher in the United States than in Canada. In addition, we estimated a sequential model (in which prior offspring attainments are controlled in measuring the relationship between income and later attainments) that allows us to assess how much of the intergenerational association at a given age is accounted for by the parental income effect on earlier outcomes. Results from this estimation suggest that in both countries family income has significant marginal effects on offspring behavior problems and test scores through adolescence and these intergenerational impacts fan out as children pass from early childhood into adolescence. The impact tends to be at younger ages in the United States, and thus, though the overall relationship is larger in the United States than Canada, there is somewhat more fanning out in Canada. The possibly greater fanning out of the relationship between family income and behavior problems and test scores through adolescence is also consistent with the weaker relationship between income and early-in-life outcomes in Canada relative to the United States (see chapter 4, this volume).

Just as the simple relationship between parental income and the probability of college-going in young adulthood is positive in both Canada and the United States, the income coefficient on college-going is also similar. When prior behavior problems and test scores are controlled for in a sequential model of college-going, we find that they have significant (and expected) relationships to later-in-life college enrollment. We conclude that part of the effect of parental income on later college-going is through these earlier math scores and behavior problems. Nevertheless, the marginal effect of parental income on the probability of college-going remains positive for both countries, again suggesting some fanning out. However, unlike results for health problems and test scores through adolescence, these marginal effects of family income on college-going do not appear larger for the United States than for Canada.

This pattern—evidence of greater marginal effect of income in the United States relative to Canada in outcomes observed through adolescence, but similar patterns of marginal income effects in the two countries in the young adulthood outcome of college-going—is puzzling, particularly in light of the higher income mobility in Canada relative to the United States.

The findings are consistent with many of the results from Peter Burton, Shelley Phipps, and Lihui Zhang (2010), who analyze inequality in child outcomes in Canada and the United States. In particular, they note bigger gaps in math scores between rich and poor children in the United States than in Canada. Moreover, they also find no significant differences across

Figure 14.2   Adults with Associate Degree or Higher

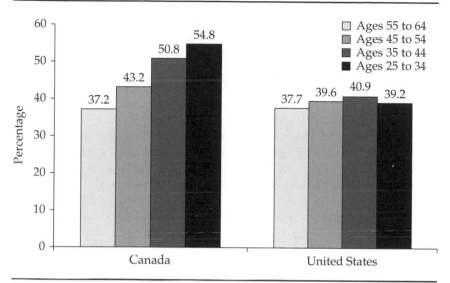

Source: Authors' calculations based on data from OECD (2008).

the two countries in the rich-poor child gap in the probability of entering postsecondary education.[19]

Our results can also be compared with those in chapter 4 in this volume. That study presents differences in child outcomes across four nations (including the United States and Canada) before formal schooling. In these comparisons, the family income and education gradients at young ages are smaller in Canada than in the other countries analyzed, including the United States, Australia, and England. But though the gaps as well as the slopes are smaller in Canada, differences are still substantial in cognitive and sociobehavioral (noncognitive) outcomes that vary by SES both in Canada and in the United States before the stages of the life course that we study.

One possible explanation for the puzzling pattern in all of these studies suggests the answer may lie not in college attendance but in college completion. Enrolling in college is not the same as graduating from college, and data from the OECD points to a larger widening of overall tertiary degree achievements (such as graduating or earning a certificate) between the United States and Canada across recent cohorts. Using data from 2008, figure 14.2 suggests that in the United States and Canada, 37 to 38 percent of the age fifty-five to sixty-four cohort had a postsecondary degree. However, 39 percent of the age twenty-five to thirty-four cohort did in United States, versus 55 percent in Canada—a 13 to 14 point difference.

The attainment level in the United States across these cohorts increased by only 1.5 percent, whereas in Canada it increased by 17.5 percentage points.

There are many reasons for these different patterns. In part, the average quality of the Canadian primary and secondary school system seems to be superior to that in the United States, with higher average performance and lower variance across the SES scale (Bishop 1997; Hanushek and Wößmann 2006). This difference in lower school experiences in the United States may also be manifest in the larger numbers of tertiary students who go on beyond high school but fail to graduate (Fitzpatrick and Turner 2008; Bound, Lovenheim, and Turner 2010). Efforts in the United States to expand college access through policies such as expanded community colleges (see Cohen 2008) may result in similar effects of income on beginning college attendance in the United States and Canada even if income has a larger effect on childhood outcomes in the United States. However, given that income affects college completion rates for those who attend college (see Haveman and Wilson 2007), just increasing college access may not be enough to increase social mobility.

Finally, some of the difference may be due to differences in immigration policy across the countries; Canada admits many more highly qualified immigrants than the United States does. Indeed, in estimating the patterns shown in this chapter, excluding immigrants for Canada, we found an increase of about 5 to 8 percent in the effect of family income on children outcomes.[20] These larger effects suggest that the lower Canadian SES gradients may be partly due to higher social mobility among second-generation immigrants.

On the basis of our estimates, we offer a few comments on the relative effectiveness of efforts in Canada and the United States to promote mobility at various levels of individual development. Given Canada's relatively low correlations between parental income and children's health at the preschool level, we would do well to learn more about the sorts of parental behaviors or early childhood public investments that are being made in Canada relative to the United States. Could these actions lead to smaller relative attainment gaps later in life between rich and poor in Canada compared with the United States (see also chapter 4, this volume)?

Our results suggest that within-country differences do not diminish but may fan out depending on the measure of attainment and parental SES used. The results between the countries are, however, remarkably similar in some of the outcomes analyzed here from adolescence to college attendance. However, these average results conceal differences across the distribution, with children in low-income families facing a greater college attendance penalty in the United States. It appears that the cumulative intergenerational effects of college graduation in Canada further increase the fraction attaining a degree (figure 14.2) compared with the United States.

In sum, despite substantial differences in social mobility between the United States and Canada (especially for offspring younger than middle and high school ages), we have only limited insight into the reasons for these differences. Our study takes its place along with other research efforts seeking to understand these patterns (see Milligan and Stabile 2011; Belley, Frenette, and Lochner 2011).

Notes

1. School outcomes are from the Program for International Student Assessment (PISA), a project of the OECD that consisted of standardized tests in reading, mathematics, and science.

2. According to figure 14.1, inequality was advancing just a bit faster in the United States than in Canada from 1990 to the early 2000s when children are observed (see the cohort description in the data section). But their parents' incomes became much more unequal in the United States in the early 1980s.

3. Luxembourg Income Study data on comparable poverty rates (http://www. lisproject.org/key-figures/key-figures.htm; accessed December 16, 2011) show that Canadian child poverty (income less than half the median disposable income) rose from 15.3 to 16.6 percent from 1981 to 2004, but from 20.0 to 23.5 in the United States from 1979 to 2004.

4. The relatively high level of parent-child socioeconomic persistence in the United States is confirmed by Tom Hertz and his colleagues (2007), who study fifty-year trends in the intergenerational persistence of educational attainment for a sample of forty-two nations around the globe.

5. We were unable to construct comparable variables between the countries for early childhood, ages one through six, C1 (but see chapter 4 of this volume for a C1 comparison).

6. The sample includes the Survey of Economic Opportunity component and is appropriately weighted to account for this oversample of disadvantaged families (for more information on sample weights, see Gouskova et al. 2008).

7. Descriptive results on math and reading scores and on postsecondary enrollment presented in this section are based on the Reading Cohort from YITS. This consisted of youth age fifteen in 2000. For this cohort, the survey was developed in conjunction with the Program for International Student Assessment, a project of the OECD that consisted of standardized tests in reading, mathematics, and science.

8. Family income includes income from all sources, including taxable income and transfer income. The income measure does not take into account taxes paid, and thus is pretax, post-transfer income. This is different from the measure of income used in many of the other chapters of this volume.

9. Family income is divided by the square root of family size (that is, the number of family members). This is a standard approach to obtaining equivalency among living units.

10. The online appendix can be found at: http://www.russellsage.org/Ermisch_ et_al_OnlineAppendix.pdf.
11. This is consistent with the findings in chapter 4 of this volume.
12. There are two reading scores presented in the PSID, a letter word score and a passage comprehension score. These are each compared to the one standard-ized reading score in the Canadian data.
13. A different approach to analyze the fanning out question involves separate regressions on the same child outcome at various ages. This is the approach used in other chapters in this volume. In what follows, we present only the results from our sequential model, but note, when discussing evidence on fanning out, their consistency with the results obtained from the alternative approach.
14. The Canadian samples for the longitudinal analysis are based solely on the NLSCY data.
15. All income coefficients should be interpreted as the effect of a log point increase in family income. This is equivalent to an increase of about 170 percent in dollar value.
16. This finding is supported by estimates (not shown) obtained from separate regressions on the same outcomes at different child ages. Although the parental income effect in the United States stays more or less constant as children age, the income coefficient increases in the Canadian sample.
17. We also estimated the family income effect on three additional outcomes in adolescence: repeating a grade, drinking, and marijuana use. In both coun-tries, the family income coefficient was statistically significant only on the probability of repeating a grade. The results showed a substantial similarity in the coefficients across the two countries, with statistically insignificant cross-country differences for the most part. These additional results are available from the authors on request.
18. The Canadian sample has only about 40 percent of parents in the lowest two educational groups (ISCED low and ISCED medium), compared with more than 60 percent for the United States. Canada has about 5 percent of parents in the lowest ISCED category, and the United States about 8 percent.
19. Their analysis is based on the same Canadian data, but uses a different data source (NLSY) for the United States.
20. These additional results are available on request from the authors. The main findings of the paper are robust to the exclusion of immigrants.

References

Belley, Philippe, Marc Frenette, and Lance Lochner. 2011. "Post-Secondary Attendance by Parental Income in the U.S. and Canada: What Role For Financial Aid Policy?" *NBER* working paper 17218. Cambridge, Mass.: National Bureau for Economic Research.

Bishop, John H. 1997. "The Effect of National Standards and Curriculum Based Exams on Achievement." *American Economic Review* 87(2): 260–64.

Björklund, Anders, and Markus Jäntti 2008. "Intergenerational Income Mobility and the Role of Family Background." In *The Oxford Handbook of Economic Inequality,* edited by Wiemer Salverda, Brian Nolan, and Timothy M. Smeeding. Oxford: Oxford University Press.

Björklund, Anders, and Kjell G. Salvanes. 2010. "Education and Family Background: Mechanisms and Policies" *IZA* discussion paper 5002. Bonn: Institute for the Study of Labor.

Black, Sandra, and Paul J. Devereux. 2010. "Recent Developments in Inter-generational Mobility" *NBER* working paper 15889. Cambridge, Mass.: National Bureau for Economic Research.

Blanden, Jo. 2009. "How Much Can We Learn from International Comparison of Social Mobility?" *CEE* discussion paper 111. London: London School of Economics.

Blanden, Jo, Kathryn Wilson, Robert Haveman, and Timothy M. Smeeding. 2010. "Comparative Mobility Across Generations: US and UK." Paper presented to the RSF, PEW, SOFI, IRP research conference. Madison, Wisc. (September 21, 2009).

Bound, John, Michael Lovenheim, and Sarah Turner. 2010. "Why Have College Completion Rates Declined: Marginal Students or Marginal College?" *American Economic Journal: Applied Economics* 2(3): 129–57.

Brandolini, Andrea, and Timothy M. Smeeding. 2009. "Income Inequality in Richer and OECD Countries." In *The Oxford Handbook of Economic Inequality,* edited by Wiemer Salverda, Brian Nolan, and Timothy M. Smeeding. Oxford: Oxford University Press.

Burton, Peter, Shelley Phipps, and Lihui Zhang. 2010. "From Parent to Child: Emerging Inequality in Outcomes." Paper prepared for the 31st General Conference of the International Association for Research in Income and Wealth. Paris (November 22–23, 2010).

Card, David, and Richard B. Freeman, eds. 1993. *Small Differences that Matter: Labor Markets and Income Maintenance in Canada and the United States.* Chicago: University of Chicago Press.

Cohen, Arthur M. 2008. *The American Community College.* San Francisco: Jossey-Bass.

Corak, Miles. 2010. "Chasing the Same Dream, Climbing Different Ladders: Economic Mobility in the United States and Canada." Pew Economic Mobility Project, Washington, D.C. Available at: http://www.economicmobility.org/assets/pdfs/PEW_EMP_US-CANADA.pdf (accessed June 27, 2010).

Duncan, Greg J., and Jeanne Brooks-Gunn, eds. 1997. *Consequences of Growing Up Poor.* New York: Russell Sage Foundation.

Fitzpatrick, Maria, and Sarah Turner. 2008. "Blurring the Boundary: Changes in the Transition from College Participation to Adulthood." In *The Economics of the Transition to Adulthood,* edited by Sheldon Danziger and Cecilia Rouse. New York: Russell Sage Foundation.

Gauthier, Anne H., Timothy M. Smeeding, and Frank F. Furstenberg Jr. 2004. "Are Parents Investing Less Time in Children? Trends in Selected Industrialized Countries." *Population and Development Review* 30(4): 647–71.

Gornick, Janet C., and Marcia K. Meyers. 2004. "Helping America's Working Parents: What Can We Learn from Europe and Canada?" New America Foundation Issue Brief (November). Available at: http://www.newamerica.net/files/nafmigration/Doc_File_2059_1.pdf (accessed June 27, 2010).

Gottschalk, Peter, and Mary Joyce. 1998. "Cross-National Differences in the Rise in Earnings Inequality: Market and Institutional Factors." *The Review of Economics and Statistics* 80(4): 489–502.

Gouskova, Elena, Steven Heeringa, Katherine McGonagle, Robert Schoeni, and Frank Stafford. 2008. "Panel Study of Income Dynamics Revised Longitudinal Weights 2007." PSID technical report #08-05. Ann Arbor: University of Michigan. Available at: http://psidonline.isr.umich.edu/Publications/Papers/tsp/2008–05_PSID_Revised_Longitudinal_Weights_1993-2005%20.pdf (accessed June 27, 2010).

Hanushek, Eric, and Ludiger Wößmann. 2006. "Does Educational Tracking Affect Performance and Inequality? Differences-in-Differences Evidence Across Countries." *Economic Journal* 116(510): C63–C76.

Haveman, Robert, and Kathryn Wilson. 2007. "Access, Matriculation, and Graduation." In *Economic Inequality and Higher Education*, edited by Stacy Dickert-Conlin and Ross Rubenstein. New York: Russell Sage Foundation.

Haveman, Robert, Kathryn Wilson, and Barbara Wolfe. 1997. "Childhood Poverty and Adolescent Schooling and Fertility Outcomes: Reduced-Form and Structural Estimates." In *Consequences of Growing Up Poor*, edited by Greg J. Duncan and Jeanne Brooks-Gunn. New York: Russell Sage Foundation.

Haveman, Robert, and Barbara Wolfe. 1994. *Succeeding Generations: On the Effects of Investments in Children*. New York: Russell Sage Foundation.

Hertz, Thomas, Tamara Jayasundera, Patrizio Piraino, Sibel Selcuk, Nicole Smith, and Alina Verashchagina. 2007. "The Inheritance of Educational Inequality: International Comparisons and Fifty-Year Trends." *The B.E. Journal of Economic Analysis & Policy* 7(2): Article 10. Available at: http://www.bepress.com/bejeap/vol7/iss2/art10 (accessed June 27, 2010).

Institute for Social Research, Survey Research Center [producer and distributor]. 2009. *Panel Study of Income Dynamics, public use dataset*. Ann Arbor: University of Michigan. Available at http://simba.isr.umich.edu/data/data.aspx (accessed November 23, 2009)

Milligan, Kevin, and Mark Stabile. 2011. "Do Child Tax Benefits Affect the Well-Being of Children? Evidence from Canadian Child Benefit Expansions." *American Economic Journal: Economic Policy* 3(August): 175–205. Available at: http://www.aeaweb.org/articles.php?doi=10.1257/pol.3.3.175 (accessed June 27, 2010).

Organisation for Economic Co-Operation and Development (OECD). 2008. *Education at a Glance*. Paris: Organisation for Economic Co-Operation and

Development. Available at: http://www.oecd.org/document/9/0,3746,en_2649_
39263238_41266761_1_1_1_1,00.html (accessed November 28, 2011).

———. 2009. *Education at a Glance.* Paris: Organisation for Economic Co-Operation
and Development. Available at: http://www.oecd.org/document/24/0,3746
,en_2649_39263238_43586328_1_1_1_1,00.html (accessed November 28, 2011).

Statistics Canada. 2007. *Youth in Transition Survey (YITS),* 2000–2005 [Restricted use
datafiles]. Access can be requested at: www.statcan.gc.ca (accessed June 27, 2010).

———. 2008. *National Longitudinal Survey of Children and Youth (NLSCY), 1993–
2007* [Restricted use datafiles]. Access can be requested at: www.statcan.gc.ca
(accessed June 27, 2010).

Thomas, David M., and Barbara Boyle Torrey. 2008. *Canada and the United States:
Differences that Count,* 3d ed. Toronto: University of Toronto Press.

Chapter 15

Reform of Higher Education and Social Gradients

MASSIMILIANO BRATTI AND

LORENZO CAPPELLARI

T HE FIRST decade of the new millennium has been a period of profound changes in several European countries' higher education (HE) systems. In seven government meetings (Paris 1998; Bologna 1999; Prague 2001; Berlin 2003; Bergen 2005; London 2007; Leuven 2009), many European countries set the main principles for the development of an integrated and coherent European Higher Education Area (EHEA).[1] The main changes, envisaged to promote labor mobility among member countries, involved harmonizing the structure of university programs, as well as introducing a credit system to facilitate mutual recognition of degrees across countries and higher education institutions (HEIs). We refer to this process as the Bologna process, named after the place where agreements to build an EHEA were first formalized, the University of Bologna, with the signing in 1999 of the Bologna declaration by ministers of education from twenty-nine European countries.

Italy was among the first to change its HE system according to the Bologna guidelines. In particular, a binary single-tier structure, in which students could enroll into either long (laurea) or short (diploma universitario) degrees was abandoned in favor of a unitary two-tier system in 2001. Before 2001, the Italian higher education system was based on a binary single-tier structure, in which students could enroll into either long (four to six years, laurea) or short (two years, diploma universitario) courses in a selected number of fields. Short courses, however, were not a popular choice: for example, among the high school graduates of 1998, only 11 percent opted for the two-year degrees. Long courses can be considered by far the most common form of university education under the old system. In the new HE system, students first enroll in a three-year cycle (laurea breve, the so-called first-level courses approximately equivalent to undergraduate studies in the United States) and then, after

370

graduation from the first tier, can continue university studies to pursue a second two-year degree (laurea magistrale, the second-level courses, that is, master's). The new structure is often referred to as the 3+2 system. The reform affected the vast majority of fields of study, with the exception of some college majors that maintained a unitary structure with four-year to six-year durations (single-cycle degrees, lauree magistrali a ciclo unico).[2] This restructuring of university degrees implied, among other things, a shortening of undergraduate studies in many college majors, such as engineering (from five to three years) and economics (from four to three years) just to take two examples.

One of the goals of the 3+2 reform was to ensure a larger diffusion of HE among the population. This was particularly important for Italy, which, before the reform, lagged in terms of number of university graduates, university dropout rates, and actual length of university studies; it was common for Italian students to complete undergraduate studies in their late twenties. Another long-standing issue of Italian higher education used to be a slow college-to-work transition. The articulation of university studies in two tiers was considered a way of facilitating the match between labor supply and demand and speeding up the transition.

Recent research has shown that the reform achieved some of these objectives. Lorenzo Cappellari and Claudio Lucifora (2009) showed that the reform increased participation in HE, but left dropout rates essentially unaffected; on the other hand, Giorgio Di Pietro and Andrea Cutillo (2008) report significant reductions in university dropout due to the reform. Empirical analyses also show that the reform had a differential effect on individuals with different family backgrounds and mostly benefitted able individuals coming from poorer socioeconomic backgrounds. Unfortunately, not all objectives were achieved. Indeed, preliminary evidence also showed that, contrary to expectations, more than two-thirds of university graduates were continuing in the second tier (Cammelli 2006), and employers were still complaining about the lack of practical knowledge of the new university graduates. In short, it is fair to say the reform has increased the equality of opportunities in undergraduate university education. We focus here on a different, related, but relatively unexplored issue: whether the 3+2 reform also had a role in equalizing the education and labor market outcomes of individuals once they have overcome the first threshold of enrolling in HE and the second threshold of completing their undergraduate studies. In particular, we investigate whether— provided that it increased equality of educational opportunities in university enrollments—the reform also had an impact on the social advantage of some groups in the labor market for university graduates. This is likely to be a hot topic for Italy, a country characterized by low levels of intergenerational mobility (Checchi, Ichino, and Rustichini 1999; Checchi 2010), where the potential for policy reforms to increase mobility is accordingly high, and in which until recently parental background had a very important role despite the expansion of the HE system (see Checchi, Fiorio, and Leonardi 2008; Checchi and Flabbi 2007); but it is also likely to be of interest to the many countries that only recently implemented or are about to implement the Bologna process.

We consider four outcomes of university graduates: the degree final grade, enrollment in postgraduate studies, wages, and satisfaction with wages, where the last two outcomes are conditional on employment. Our objective is to assess whether social gradients in educational and employment outcomes persist after the introduction of the 3+2 reform, and to give an idea of the magnitude of the advantage given by parental socioeconomic status. Our analysis shows that the main effect of the university reform was to increase the inequality in the access to postgraduate education by family background, increasing the advantage of individuals with better-educated parents; this in turn also had an effect on postuniversity outcomes, as short degrees generally command lower wage premia in the labor market.

Italian Education System

Italy has a tracked upper secondary school system (see chapter 13, this volume). Students must be in education at least until age fifteen. At the age of fourteen, students must choose among three broad tracks: academic, technical, or vocational. University entry is not selective, except for a few majors (such as medicine and dentistry, for instance), and all individuals who completed five years of upper secondary education and obtained a diploma by passing the central exit examination (Esame di Stato) are entitled to enroll in HE.

The reform of university studies became effective at the start of the 2001–2002 academic year throughout the country. Students already enrolled could opt to switch to the new regime, and we will control for those who did switch in our analyses.

The timing and implementation of the reform means that students treated with the two regimes can only be compared in a before-after fashion: the absence of any, say, regional variation in the implementation of the reform across the country prevents the use of difference-in-difference type of evaluations. However, it is important to stress that the data used for the analyses in this chapter allow observation of students from the pre- and postreform regimes entering the labor market in the same year, thus ensuring that the effects we estimate are not driven by differential business cycles, one of the main shortcomings of before-after comparisons.

One of the main reasons the reform may have affected educational choices is the reduction from four to three in the years of education required to earn an undergraduate degree. A reduction in the length of undergraduate studies is likely to reduce both upfront and nonpecuniary costs of studying, benefiting therefore poor and low-ability students, increasing equal opportunities in the access to undergraduate education. The Bologna reform also implied a complex restructuring of university curricula, and the toughest exams of the old degrees were often moved to the new second level degrees. The reform has also granted universities a large autonomy in terms of setting their educational supply. Universities can decide the names of the degree courses as well as their curricula, which have to meet standard requirements set at the national level. This also produced a large increase in the number of courses supplied by HEIs, although partly explained by the degrees' splitting. Last but not least, the reform also introduced a system of university credits. The credit system should ease the mutual recognition of credits by HEIs and make it easier for students to change degree course or institution. Credits represent the total course workload (including class time, self-study, and complementary activities) and are obtained once a student has passed the course assessment (exam). Each credit should correspond to twenty-five hours of total activities, and the full-time workload for one academic year is sixty credits. As a consequence, the study material for some courses has been reduced according to the new guidelines, determining a simplification (in terms of student workload) of some exams. As in the old system, students who fail can take several re-sit exams during the year, they can also re-sit the exam if they passed but are not satisfied with the grades obtained, and they can re-enroll even if they did not pass any exam during an academic year. These features have often been blamed for the long time Italian students, compared with their European peers, take to complete a university education (the so-called fuori corso phenomenon). As for other aspects, to the best of our knowledge, there is no generalized evidence on the fact that teachers may have changed their teaching methods and styles after the reform, though case-study evidence suggests that grade inflation may have increased (Bratti, Broccolini, and Staffolani 2010).

There are reasons to believe that, beside university enrollments and dropouts, the reform may also have affected the performance of university graduates, and that these effects may depend on parental background. First, we may expect lower returns to shorter undergraduate degrees following the switch to a mass university system. This may happen through several channels: a relative supply effect between short-degree and long-degree university graduates in case they are imperfect substitutes in the labor market;[3] a reduction in the signaling value of undergraduate education; changes in the ability distribution of university graduates searching for a job; or a lower stock of human capital. To some extent, parental background may shield new graduates from wage penalties (say through informal labor market networks), so that a steepening in the social gradient associated with wages may emerge after the reform.

Second, the introduction of a second tier of university studies has expanded the set of postgraduate studies available to Italian students, with a likely increase in the average probability of continuing in postgraduate studies due to the higher variety of degrees. A priori, however, it is not clear how this average increase is distributed by parental background, and one possibility is that the factors that pre-reform operated at the undergraduate level are still effective at the postgraduate level after the reform. Moreover, as we have seen, the reform also split unified curricula into two levels characterized by increasing levels of difficulty. Hence, although academic requirements may have been lowered in first level degrees, the same could not have happened in second level degrees. To put it differently, the expansion of higher education and the equality of educational opportunities in undergraduate education may not automatically translate into higher equality in the second tier of HE and, as a consequence, in the labor market. This phenomenon has for instance been already observed in other countries, such as, for instance, the U.K. (Blanden and Machin 2004), where the expansion of HE mainly benefitted relatively wealthy individuals. Clearly, wage effects and postgraduate enrollment are not independent, so that, ultimately, the direction and extent of changes in the social gradient is a matter of empirical assessment.

The Literature

At least three streams of literature are worth mentioning for the purpose of the analysis in this chapter. The first concerns similar HE reforms reducing the length of undergraduate degrees that were implemented in other countries to comply with the Bologna process. The second relates to the effect of the Italian 3+2 reform on individual outcomes before obtaining a degree, such as college enrollment and dropout. The third and last stream pertains to the existence and magnitude of a social gradient in tertiary education and labor market outcomes in Italy.

We were able to find only one study evaluating the effect of HE reforms reducing the length of undergraduate studies in European countries other than Italy. Ana Rute Cardoso and her colleagues (2008) investigate the consequences of the Bologna process in Portugal on the demand for higher education. The study exploits the fact that universities had the choice to implement the reform and restructure academic programs in the 2005–2006 academic year, or to postpone it up to two years. They show that degree courses whose curricula were modified in order to comply with the new principles recorded an increase in demand. This positive association is found to be stronger in those institutions taking the lead in the reform process, which the authors interpret as a signaling (of quality) effect.

The literature on the consequences of the 3+2 reform in Italy is richer. Di Pietro and Cutillo (2008) use Italian National Statistical Institute's (ISTAT) survey data on high school leavers and show a reduction in dropout rates after the reform; Beatrice D'Hombres (2007) comes to the same conclusion using the same data and different econometric strategies. Cappellari and Lucifora (2009) use the same survey to investigate the effect of the reform on the probability of enrolling in HE. They use a before-after strategy and show that the reform significantly increased the probability of going to college and that this effect was stronger for individuals with good upper secondary schooling results but poor family background. Hence, the reform led to more equality of opportunities at entry into HE. Although these studies show that the reform achieved the objectives of widening participation into HE and of reducing dropout rates, they do not investigate the channels through which these effects took place. Massimiliano Bratti, Chiara Broccolini, and Stefano Staffolani (2010) use a case study for the faculty of economics of a university located in the center of Italy and show that the reform reduced student workloads and raised student outcomes measured in terms of the average marks obtained in first-year exams and the number of exam attempts failed. The authors also show that despite this effect being consistent with both an increase in universities' efficiency and a reduction in HE standards after the reform, several pieces of evidence point to the latter explanation.

The literature that investigates the social gradients in tertiary education and labor market outcomes in Italy is also quite rich. Several studies report positive correlations between family background and various forms of university achievement. Individuals with a good family background (for example, with college-educated parents) are more likely to enroll in HE, less likely to drop out from university, and more likely to hold a university degree (see among others Checchi, Ichino, and Rustichini 1999; Checchi and Flabbi 2007; Checchi, Fiorio, and Leonardi 2008). A social gradient exists despite the Italian HE system being highly subsidized (Perotti 2002) and the policies that were implemented to improve access to HE during the 1990s, when a very high number of new degrees and university campuses were created (see Bratti, Checchi, and de Blasio 2008). Various explanations have been put forward for the strong correlation between parents' and children's education, especially for HE, including the existence in Italy of early tracking (Brunello and Checchi 2007; Checchi and Flabbi 2007), which reinforces social advantage (see chapter 13, this volume), and the *parking lot hypothesis,* according to which individuals from poor backgrounds often enroll in HE while continuing to look for a job, and their enrollment and dropout choices are more sensitive to the status of the labor market (Dornbusch and Giavazzi 2000; Di Pietro 2006).

The social gradient is not limited to tertiary education but extends also to labor market outcomes. Graduates with good family backgrounds are more likely to experience better outcomes when it comes to entering the labor market. Luigi Biggeri, Matilde Bini, and Leonardo Grilli (2001) show that individuals with highly educated parents have faster university-to-work transitions. Di Pietro and Cutillo (2006) find that university graduates with parents with prestigious jobs earn higher wages, and Manuel Bagüès and his colleagues (2008) show that graduates with more educated parents also enjoy wage premia.

In general, in Italy there are no data on performance in standardized tests that can be included as controls for innate ability, and indicators of secondary school track choice and grades must be considered instead. Therefore, the causal interpretation of the effect of family background generally rests on these variables being sufficient controls for university graduates' ability. When this is not the case, there might be different explanations for this social gradient observed in employment outcomes. It might reflect graduates' *unobserved ability* not captured by the secondary schooling variables, degree, final grade, or other *observed ability* controls normally included in empirical studies; or it might act as a proxy of the graduate's social network, helping her to find a good job. This latter explanation is the "true" causal effect that researchers aim to identify, although recent empirical work does not seem to support this second interpretation (see Pellizzari 2010; Sylos-Labini 2004).

Data

Since 1992, ISTAT has collected data every three years on the education and employment outcomes of Italian university graduates through a graduate employment survey (indagine campionaria sull'inserimento professionale dei laureati, or the GES). The target population is formed by university graduates of a given year, and a stratified sample from that population is interviewed three years after graduation. GES gathers information on university graduates' family background (parents' education and occupation), secondary education (school track, secondary school final grade), undergraduate university education (major, degree, final grade, institution attended, completion time), postgraduate education (enrollment, major), and the labor market outcomes (labor force status, type of occupation, working hours, wages).

The latest available GES refers to the graduates of 2004, interviewed in 2007. For our analysis, 2004 is a special year in that university graduates from both the old and new regime obtained a degree that year. Specifically, the last cohort of students enrolling in the old regime (academic year 2000–2001) and the first cohort from the new regime (enrolling in 2001–2002) completed their studies in 2004. Therefore, we are able to observe individuals from the two groups obtaining a university degree in the same period, so that we can exclude that any difference in their postgraduation behavior is driven by differences in the business cycle, which is typically a problem with before-after comparisons.

The survey population is represented by all students of Italian universities graduating in 2004 from both the old and new system, 167,886 and 92,184 graduates, respectively. The survey sample is stratified by gender, HE institution, and type of degree course and includes 26,570 graduates from long degree courses and 20,730 from short degree courses. In the survey, short degree graduates were oversampled. However, ISTAT provides sampling weights that report the sample to population proportions (after applying the weights, 64.6 percent of the sample are long degree graduates and 35.4 percent are short degree graduates).

The final aim of our analysis is to determine whether reducing the length of undergraduate degrees increased equality in postgraduation outcomes by individual socioeconomic background. The ideal experiment would be to take two random groups in the population of high school leavers, make one of the them graduate with a short degree (the treated group), the other one with a long degree (the control group) and then compare their post-graduation outcomes. Such a research design cannot be implemented. In our data, we can observe individuals with degrees of different lengths, but because the shortening of degree length has changed the incentives to enroll in HE (see Cappellari and Lucifora 2009; Bratti, Broccolini, and Staffolani 2010), new graduates will differ in terms of background and ability from previous ones. This is very likely to be the case, as the reform increased participation in undergraduate university education by more than 10 percent in the year of the reform, from 62.3 percent of the cohort of secondary school graduates in 2000–2001 to 71.9 percent in 2001–2002 (MIUR 2006). In the empirical analysis, it is therefore crucial to control for all individual characteristics that are likely to affect self-selection into HE, which we will pursue by adding to our regression models a vast array of controls for student performance and fixed effects for field of studies and university attended.

Besides changes in the composition of the relevant population before and after the reform, a second issue with our data is due to the sampling scheme being targeted on the graduates of 2004. Therefore, graduates from the new regime (who enrolled in 2001, that is, when the new system was introduced) completed their studies within the legal duration (three years). On the other hand, students from the old regime may have not necessarily enrolled in 2000 (that is, 2004 minus the legal duration of studies in the old regime) but may in fact belong to older cohorts. To the extent that delayed completions are a function of ability, new students will be, on average, more able than old ones for reasons that have to do with the sampling framework. Hence, to perform a meaningful analysis and to compare like-with-like, we decide to drop older graduates and those who graduated with a delay with respect to the legal length. Applying these criteria, we are left with 15,824 individuals (6,554 long-degree and 9,270 short-degree graduates, corresponding to 44.2 and 55.8 percent of the weighted sample, respectively). To check the robustness of our analysis to this sample definition, we also considered an extended control group, which includes individuals from long degrees who graduated with a one-year delay. Indeed, in light of the fact that long degrees may be more difficult or that educational standards might have been reduced in short degrees (Bratti, Broccolini, and Staffolani 2010), this second definition could provide a better comparison group. In this case, the selected sample includes 20,105 individuals (10,835 long-degree and 9,270 short-degree graduates, corresponding to 53.9 and 46.1 percent of the weighted sample, respectively).[4]

We consider four university graduates' outcomes. The first is the undergraduate degree final mark, which varies between 66 and 110 cum laude (recoded to 111). The second is the probability of enrolling in postgraduate education. The third is the hourly wage (computed by dividing monthly labor income by the number of weekly working hours multiplied by 4.2), and the fourth is job satisfaction with respect to hourly wages. The last two outcomes are conditional on employment.[5] The description of the dependent and the independent variables is reported in the online appendix.[6]

Table 15.1 reports the sample means for some of the covariates used in the econometric analysis and the outcome variables distinguished by type of degree, short versus long. The table shows a remarkable variation in the university graduates' characteristics after the reform. It is clear, for instance, that graduates with short degrees have a poorer socioeconomic and academic background, and are of course younger. This is consistent with the fact that the reform increased participation in HE (Cappellari and Lucifora 2009), and suggests that to compare like-with-like is necessary to include in our empirical analysis controls for past educational performance and age, among others.

As for the outcomes we will consider, graduates with short degrees have lower final grades, earn lower hourly wages, are much more likely to continue in HE, and are more satisfied with their wages.

The differences between long and short degrees generally fall when the second definition of the control group is considered, although they remain statistically significant.

Econometric Strategy

To assess how the social gradient changed with the university reform, we estimate the following model of university graduates' outcomes:

$$y_i = \alpha_0 + \alpha_1 FAMILY_i + \alpha_2 SHORT_i + \alpha_3(FAMILY_i * SHORT_i) + x_i'\beta + \varepsilon_i \quad (1)$$

Table 15.1   Means and Difference in Means of Selected Variables by Length of Degree

Variable	Control Group: Long Degrees in Time			Control Group: Long Degrees with One Year of Delay at Maximum	
	Long	Short		Long	
	A	B	A-B	C	C-B
Selected independent variables					
Socioeconomic status					
HISCED 1–2	0.224	0.274	−0.051***	0.240	−0.035***
HISCED 3–4	0.412	0.453	−0.041***	0.420	−0.033***
HISCED 5–6	0.365	0.272	0.092***	0.340	0.068***
Secondary school type					
Scientific lyceum	0.469	0.424	0.046***	0.443	0.019*
Classical lyceum	0.223	0.154	0.070***	0.222	0.068***
Language lyceum	0.050	0.048	0.002	0.050	0.002
Art school	0.011	0.013	−0.001	0.014	0.001
Pedagogic school	0.070	0.076	−0.006	0.073	−0.004
Technical school	0.161	0.250	−0.089***	0.185	−0.065***
Vocational school	0.015	0.036	−0.021***	0.014	−0.022***
Secondary school final grade	51.413	51.140	0.273	50.837	−0.303**
Gender (men)					
Women	0.665	0.600	0.065***	0.643	0.043***
Age (twenty-four or younger)					
Twenty-five to twenty-nine	0.524	0.174	0.350***	0.661	0.487***
Outcome variables					
Degree final grade (66–111)	105.487	103.665	1.822***	104.579	0.914***
Log hourly wage	2.072	2.039	0.034***	2.065	0.026***
Fraction enrolled in PG education	0.415	0.704	−0.289***	0.389	−0.315***
Job satisfaction about wage (1–4)	2.655	2.732	−0.078***	2.635	−0.097***

Source: Authors' calculations based on data from ISTAT (2007).
Notes: Means and significance levels are computed using ISTAT sampling weights. The sample using the first control group includes 15,824 observations (6,554 graduates with long degrees and 9,270 with short degrees), the one using the second control group 20,105 observations (10,835 graduates with long degrees and 9,270 with short degrees). For the first sample the weighted proportion of short-degree graduates is 55.76 percent and for the second sample 40.92 percent.
*p < .10, **p < .05, ***p < .01

where y_i is the university graduates' outcome, $FAMILY_i$ is the measure of family background we are interested in, $SHORT_i$ is a dichotomous indicator that takes on value one for individuals enrolled in short degrees and zero otherwise, x_i is a vector of individual characteristics, and ε_i is a classical error term. The list of controls includes age, gender, secondary school track, secondary school final grade, interaction between secondary school track and grade, parental HISCED, a dummy for individuals initially enrolled in the old system having switched to the new one, a dummy for working while studying, college, and major fixed effects. According to the specific outcome variables considered, other controls were also included. The full list is specified in the footnotes to the tables reporting the results (see tables 15.2, 15.3, and 15.4).

We are interested in assessing the differences in the social gradient between long and short degrees, which are captured by the $FAMILY_i{}^*SHORT_i$ interaction terms. We do not attribute to these coefficients a causal interpretation, though. The observed correlations between family background and the outcomes may either reflect some other unobserved individual trait such as innate ability or they may capture a true causal relationship (for example, educated parents may help students with their homework, buy better educational inputs or help them find good jobs). We are mainly interested here in assessing robust statistical correlations, and our main concern is to avoid that the differences in the social gradient between the two different types of degrees is capturing the effect of some other unobservable characteristic systematically differing between individuals enrolled in long and short degrees. To put it briefly, we want the difference in the effect of social gradients by long and short degrees to be driven only by degree length. For this reason, it is important to control for all characteristics that may covary with both length of studies and outcomes, thereby inducing spurious correlation if omitted. In this respect, some important factors appear to be family background, proxied by parental education (the highest education between parents, codified using the International Standard Classification of Education, or ISCED), gender and academic ability, proxied by the school track, final secondary school grade, and their interaction. So, our main identifying assumption is that, conditional on the covariates we included, the degree length is not capturing any other systematic difference between individuals enrolled in long and short degrees that also interacts with family background leading to better (or worse) graduates' educational or labor market outcomes. In short, conditional on the covariates, graduates from the two regimes are the same except for the length of their degrees, and a short degree shows what would be the social gradient for an individual enrolled in a long degree had he chosen the shorter degree.

To increase the credibility of this assumption, we also estimated specifications including college major and HEIs fixed effects. There are two main reasons to include these fixed effects. The first is that, as we said, the reduction in degree length was not the same in all majors. Hence, the reform is likely to have changed also the college major mix among graduates, especially by socioeconomic background. Also the distribution of graduates across HEIs may have changed, in case some institutions expanded their offer especially of short degrees. Controlling for both college major and HEIs is also important as—regardless of degree length—educational standards and labor market outcomes are likely to systematically differ both among college majors (Ballarino and Bratti 2009; Buonanno and Pozzoli 2009) and among HEIs (Brunello and Cappellari 2008; Bagüès, Sylos-Labini, and Zinovyeva 2009; Di Pietro and Cutillo 2006), which in turn are likely to be correlated with family background.

When both college major and HEIs fixed effects are included in the analysis, we will be investigating the differences in the social gradients between long and short degrees' graduates *in the same college major* and *from the same HE institution*. This increases the likelihood of comparing like with like but at the same time in this way we will estimate the *net effect of family background*.[7]

Results and Discussion

In this section, we describe the main results of the empirical analysis related to the four outcome variables we consider. To assess the robustness of our results to potential *omitted variables bias*, we often estimate several specifications, progressively saturating the models. In each table, we present two sets of results, one for the narrower comparison group of long-degree individuals graduating in time, and the other for the broader comparison group, including also individuals graduating with one-year delay.

University Degree Final Grade

In the GES 2004, university degree final grade is observed in interval form for grades below 100 (≤ 79, 80–89, 90–94, 95–99) and continuously above this threshold. For the cases in which the grade is observed in interval form, we simply imputed the central value in the interval and used OLS.[8]

Parental background is measured by the maximum educational level between father and mother measured with the ISCED scale, a variable we call HISCED. Table 15A.1 in the online appendix shows that the social gradient is not differentiated between short and long degrees. A possible interpretation of these results is that high socioeconomic status individuals may have better connections in the labor market and find good jobs regardless of degree performance (and degree length)— that is, they may have lower economic returns to effort.

Probability of Enrolling in Postgraduate Studies

Postgraduate education differs for long and short degrees. For individuals graduating from long degrees, postgraduate education essentially coincided with Ph.D. programs, because first degrees were approximately equivalent to a foreign master's degree. Because the reform introduced a totally new study course, the two-year second tier, it is natural to expect this widening of the supply of postgraduate education to exert a positive effect on the probability of postgraduate enrollment, for example by meeting the needs of individuals who desire some postgraduate education, but without facing the burden of enrolling in a Ph.D.

Although the overall positive effect of the reform is expected, less obvious is whether continuation rates differ among individuals with different family backgrounds, conditional on holding the same type of degree. Did the reform increase postgraduate education for all university graduates? Or were these increases unevenly distributed by social class? Answering these questions will indicate the extent to which inequalities of opportunities were actually reduced by the reform or whether they were simply shifted upward in the education ladder.

Table 15.2 reports the coefficients from a logit model for the continuation probability, in which the dependent variable takes on value one in case the individual continued in postgraduate education and zero otherwise. Logit coefficients on dummy variables multiplied by 100 can be interpreted as the discrete change in the log-odds (that is, an approximation of the odds' percentage change) determined by switching on the characteristics represented by the dummy. As we said, the positive effect of short degrees on the probability to continue was largely expected. The most interesting result is that the positive effect associated with the reform increases with the level of parental education. For men, the relative advantage involves only the highest class (HISCED 5–6), whereas for women both the medium (HISCED 3–4) and the highest class are more likely to continue in postgraduate education after short degrees. The magnitude of the effect is large, and the coefficients are precisely estimated. When the first definition of the control group is adopted, men (women) with HISCED 5–6 and short degrees have 51.3 (89) percent higher odds than those with the same level of parental education but with long degrees (columns 5 and 6). For women, individuals with HISCED 3–4 and short degrees also have an advantage over those with long degrees and equal family background. Results are very similar when the second definition of the control group is used and robust to adding control variables. Hence, overall we find that social gradients are higher in short degrees, or, said differently, that the 3+2 reform increased social gradients as to the likelihood of enrolling in postgraduate education. This

Table 15.2   Probability to Continue in Postgraduate Education

| | Control Group: Long Degrees in Time | | | | | | Control Group: Long Degrees with One Year of Delay at Maximum | | | | | |
| | All | | | | Men | Women | All | | | | Men | Women |
	1	2	3	4	5	6	7	8	9	10	11	12
Short degree (SD)	1.637***	1.075***	1.406***	1.548***	2.128***	1.269***	1.679***	1.240***	1.482***	1.611***	2.227***	1.333***
	(0.074)	(0.107)	(0.110)	(0.193)	(0.234)	(0.202)	(0.063)	(0.090)	(0.094)	(0.188)	(0.245)	(0.172)
HISCED 3–4	0.148**	-0.208*	-0.143	-0.113	0.201	-0.295*	0.154**	-0.055	-0.027	0.003	0.351***	-0.163*
	(0.068)	(0.124)	(0.122)	(0.102)	(0.192)	(0.157)	(0.060)	(0.087)	(0.087)	(0.069)	(0.131)	(0.087)
HISCED 5–6	0.484***	-0.037	0.168	0.218*	0.238	0.160	0.482***	0.170*	0.294***	0.347***	0.363***	0.365***
	(0.080)	(0.122)	(0.124)	(0.128)	(0.160)	(0.156)	(0.070)	(0.092)	(0.094)	(0.082)	(0.112)	(0.095)
Degree final grades	0.021***	0.021***	0.027***	0.025***	0.034***	0.021***	0.032***	0.032***	0.031***	0.028***	0.032***	0.026***
	(0.004)	(0.004)	(0.005)	(0.004)	(0.005)	(0.007)	(0.004)	(0.004)	(0.004)	(0.003)	(0.005)	(0.006)
HISCED 3–4 * SD		0.600***	0.466***	0.441***	0.175	0.578***		0.473***	0.377***	0.359***	0.069	0.455***
		(0.140)	(0.140)	(0.123)	(0.251)	(0.175)		(0.110)	(0.111)	(0.092)	(0.187)	(0.119)
HISCED 5–6 * SD		1.092***	0.796***	0.743***	0.513**	0.890***		0.925***	0.727***	0.683***	0.472**	0.718***
		(0.145)	(0.148)	(0.158)	(0.217)	(0.189)		(0.122)	(0.125)	(0.125)	(0.194)	(0.143)
Majors fixed effects			yes	yes	yes	yes			yes	yes	yes	yes
Institutions fixed effects				yes	yes	yes				yes	yes	yes
Pseudo R^2	0.151	0.156	0.198	0.213	0.288	0.193	0.144	0.147	0.183	0.196	0.269	0.174
Number of observations	15,824	15,824	15,824	15,809	6,586	9,207	20,105	20,105	20,105	20,086	8,533	11,540

Source: Authors' calculations based on data from ISTAT (2007).

Notes: The dependent variable is a dummy indicator that takes value one if an individual is enrolled in postgraduate education and zero otherwise. All models are estimated with logit, and the table reports logit coefficients. Estimates use probability weights. Heteroskedasticity robust standard errors in parentheses. Errors are clustered by HEIs in the model using HEIs fixed effects. The sample includes only individuals who found their current work after university graduation. The models also include controls for age, gender (except the gender specific regressions), secondary school track, upper secondary school final grade, grade by track interactions, and dummies for working while studying and being a switcher (to the new system). Job characteristics are two dummies for part-time (versus full-time) and temporary (versus permanent) jobs, respectively. See the online appendix for a detailed description of the variables.

*p < .10, **p < .05, ***p < .01

is both an interesting and surprising result as, like we already said, after the reform the first level of postgraduate education available (second tier degree) implies a lower workload than a doctorate or the other levels of postgraduate degrees available to graduates with long degrees.

Wages Conditional on Employment

Labor incomes are observed in banded form, with monthly income categories increasing by €10 up to €2,000 per month, then by €100 above this threshold. Considering the very large number of income categories (181), we treated the variable as continuous and applied OLS. Following most of the literature estimating earnings equations, we used the logarithmic transformation of hourly wages as the dependent variable. Because we do not have convincing exclusion restrictions to estimate a sample selection model, we simply run an analysis conditional on employment. This is likely to be a problem especially for females, for whom labor force participation is not universal, although less in our case than in others because we consider university-educated women, who generally exhibit high attachment to the labor market. To focus on a homogenous sample, in estimating earnings equations we only considered individuals who found their current job after graduation, and excluded those who started the current job while still in education.

Table 15.3 shows a negative wage premium for short degrees. In the pooled sample, this amounts to 7.1 percent when using the first control group and to 6.5 percent when the second control group is used, in our preferred specifications controlling for major and HEIs fixed effects (columns 5 and 12, respectively). However, from the gender specific estimates in columns 6–7 and 13–14 it is clear that short degrees penalize men more, for whom negative premia are –12 percent or –9.3 percent according to the specific control group adopted. By contrast, for women short degrees negative wage premia are statistically insignificant or significant only at the 10 percent level, when the first and the second definition of the control group is used, respectively. As we said earlier, different justifications can be given for this lower return to short degrees, it might come from a relative supply effect, an education signaling effect, the lower ability of new graduates, or just the lower human capital content of short degrees.[9] However, that there are gender differences in the returns to short degrees is not easy to reconcile with any of these explanations, because the expansion of HE especially benefitted women who are now becoming increasingly more educated than men. One possible explanation for this finding is that for women the lower human capital content of short degrees is more than compensated by the preference of employers for younger (short degrees) over older (long degrees) female graduates, which in the light of the increasing age at first birth may ensure a

Table 15.3 Log Hourly Wages

	Control Group: Long Degrees in Time							Control Group: Long Degrees with One Year of Delay at Maximum						
	All					Men	Women	All					Men	Women
	1	2	3	4	5	6	7	8	9	10	11	12	13	14
Short degree (SD)	−0.033***	−0.005	−0.076***	−0.074**	−0.071*	−0.120***	−0.052	−0.023*	0.005	−0.073***	−0.066**	−0.065**	−0.093**	−0.055*
	(0.012)	(0.022)	(0.022)	(0.034)	(0.034)	(0.045)	(0.035)	(0.012)	(0.019)	(0.020)	(0.032)	(0.032)	(0.046)	(0.030)
HISCED 3–4	0.005	0.016	0.010	0.007	0.009	−0.061	0.036	0.002	0.008	0.007	0.006	0.008	−0.029	0.022
	(0.013)	(0.026)	(0.025)	(0.029)	(0.029)	(0.046)	(0.030)	(0.013)	(0.021)	(0.020)	(0.025)	(0.025)	(0.038)	(0.026)
HISCED 5–6	−0.013	0.023	0.012	0.008	0.013	−0.001	0.012	−0.010	0.017	0.012	0.013	0.017	0.001	0.023
	(0.014)	(0.025)	(0.025)	(0.027)	(0.027)	(0.043)	(0.036)	(0.014)	(0.021)	(0.020)	(0.019)	(0.018)	(0.037)	(0.022)
Degree final grade	0.002***	0.002**	0.001	0.001	0.001	0.001	0.001	0.002**	0.002**	0.001	0.000	0.000	0.001	0.001
	(0.001)	(0.001)	(0.001)	(0.001)	(0.001)	(0.001)	(0.002)	(0.001)	(0.001)	(0.001)	(0.001)	(0.001)	(0.001)	(0.001)
HISCED 3–4 * SD		−0.018	0.006	0.009	0.006	0.099*	−0.033		−0.015	0.006	0.005	0.002	0.067	−0.024
		(0.029)	(0.028)	(0.036)	(0.036)	(0.054)	(0.038)		(0.024)	(0.023)	(0.031)	(0.032)	(0.046)	(0.034)
HISCED 5–6 * SD		−0.069**	−0.015	−0.014	−0.016	−0.001	−0.015		−0.075***	−0.022	−0.028	−0.029	−0.004	−0.038
		(0.028)	(0.028)	(0.034)	(0.034)	(0.046)	(0.042)		(0.025)	(0.024)	(0.029)	(0.030)	(0.040)	(0.031)
Majors fixed effects			yes	yes	yes	yes	yes			yes	yes	yes	yes	yes
Institutions fixed effects				yes	yes	yes	yes				yes	yes	yes	yes
Job characteristics					yes							yes		
R^2	0.075	0.076	0.151	0.170	0.186	0.197	0.182	0.057	0.059	0.117	0.136	0.157	0.156	0.152
Number of observations	7,724	7,724	7,724	7,719	7,719	3,177	4,542	10,142	10,142	10,142	10,135	10,135	4,403	5,732

Source: Authors' calculations based on data from ISTAT (2007).

Notes: The dependent variable is log hourly wage in 2007 euros. All models are estimated with OLS. Estimates use probability weights. Heteroskedasticity robust standard errors in parentheses. Errors are clustered by HEIs in the model using HEIs fixed effects. The sample includes only individuals who found their current job after university graduation. The models also include controls for age, gender (except the gender specific regressions), secondary school track, upper secondary school final grade, grade by track interactions, dummies for working while studying and being a switcher (to the new system), and region where the individual works. Job characteristics are two dummies for part-time (versus full-time) and temporary (versus permanent) jobs, respectively. See the online appendix for a detailed description of the variables.

*p < .10, **p < .05, ***p < .01

longer period of stable labor market attachment before experiencing the job interruptions related to childbearing. An alternative interpretation is that female university graduates are likely to be employed mainly in high level white-collar jobs, for which a three-year university degree may be considered as a sufficient educational title, whereas the same title may not be considered enough to enter more remunerative top managerial or professional (and traditionally male) occupations, thus being more penalizing in terms of wage for men. In other words, the differential effect of the reform may stem from gender discrimination in the graduates' labor market and glass ceiling. For this reason, we estimated specifications 6 and 7, adding the occupational qualification of university graduates, but did not find any noticeable change in the estimates of the short degree negative wage premium. These gender differences in the wage effects of the reform are somewhat surprising and would surely deserve further investigation.

In general, conditional on the other covariates there is no social gradient in the return to a degree, short nor long. This does not, of course, rule out the possibility that poor family background graduates could be overrepresented in short degrees, a fact that will be investigated below. It is anyway useful to stress that our analysis refers to early labor market outcomes. We cannot exclude that a high socioeconomic status may help university graduates enter jobs with steeper earnings profiles or enhance their career opportunities.

Worker's Wage Satisfaction Conditional on Employment

Table 15A.2 in the online appendix reports the coefficients of an ordered logit for job satisfaction regarding earnings. The results show a positive effect on satisfaction for graduates in short degrees in the pooled sample, which is, however, not robust to splitting the sample by gender. No significant social gradient emerges. Interestingly, graduates from shorter degrees are more satisfied with their salaries despite being paid less than their counterparts graduating from longer degrees, suggesting that the new graduates may have lower expectations about their job, or at least about their pay.

Discussion

The overall picture provided by the foregoing analysis seems to be that of an educational system which grants equal opportunities in the labor market to individuals, conditional on the type of degree achieved. However, as we already said, conditioning on the type of degree, short versus long, may mask all the effects of socioeconomic status on the labor market outcomes that are mediated by the type of degree. Indeed, we already

Table 15.4   **Probability of Switching to a Short Degree**

	Long Degrees in Time			Long Degrees with One Year of Delay at Maximum		
	All	Men	Women	All	Men	Women
HISCED 3–4	−0.044	0.007	−0.086	−0.035	0.064	−0.106
	(0.093)	(0.136)	(0.123)	(0.084)	(0.125)	(0.112)
HISCED 5–6	−0.447***	−0.352**	−0.526***	−0.423***	−0.362**	−0.477***
	(0.111)	(0.155)	(0.151)	(0.103)	(0.148)	(0.142)
Pseudo R^2	0.086	0.103	0.077	0.087	0.106	0.078
Number of observations	8,547	3,467	5,080	12,828	5,415	7,413

Source: Authors' calculations based on data from ISTAT (2007).
Notes: The dependent variable is a dummy variable taking on value one if an individual enrolled in the old system switched to a short degree and zero otherwise. All models are estimated with logit, and the table reports the logit coefficients. Estimates use probability weights. Heteroskedasticity robust standard errors in parentheses. The models also include controls for age, gender (except the gender specific regressions), secondary school track, upper secondary school final grade, grade by track interactions, and a dummy for working while studying. See the online appendix for a detailed description of the variables.
*$p < .10$, **$p < .05$, ***$p < .01$

saw that short degrees produce significant negative wage premia compared with long degrees, which may also explain why individuals from privileged backgrounds who obtained a short degree tend to enroll in the second tier. In particular, although the 3+2 reform reduced the time needed to obtain an undergraduate degree, it increased the time needed to acquire an educational title comparable to the old laurea (masters' level) generally by one year. Hence, credit constraints are more likely to be binding for poor background individuals now than in the past, and opportunity costs are also likely higher, when deciding to enroll in programs providing a M.A. level of education.

As a way of providing further evidence that this is likely the case, we exploit one institutional feature of the reform to understand who would choose to enroll in short (rather than long) degrees if the educational system offered both types of degrees simultaneously. As discussed, individuals enrolling in the old system in the years immediately before the reform were offered the alternative to switch to the new system, that is, to shorter degrees that were not available at the time of their enrollment.[10] Therefore we can estimate a model of the probability to switch from long to short degree courses for those graduates who enrolled in HE before the reform was in place. Table 15.4 shows the estimates of a logit model under which the dependent variable takes on value one if the student made the switch to the new system and zero otherwise, with the estimation sample restricted to students enrolling in the old system. Results clearly indicate that individuals with the highest socioeconomic status (HISCED 5–6) were less likely to switch to the new system, their odds are 35.2 lower for men, and 53.6 lower for women, than individuals with parental HISCED 1–2, who are in turn not statistically different from individuals with HISCED 3–4. Our findings suggest that individuals from the low and medium classes did prefer shorter degree programs and when the new option was introduced they largely took advantage of it. This result is in line with previous evidence, for instance, that provided by Denis Rochat and Jean Luc De Meulemeester (2001), who find that low social class individuals generally enroll in short technical courses.

Concluding Remarks

Previous research showed that the 3+2 reform increased participation into HE of individuals from less wealthy family backgrounds, by increasing university enrolment and reducing dropout. Does this mean that the reform was a step further toward equal opportunities in postgraduate education and in the labor market?

Our results indicate that the social gradient in the transitions to postgraduate education was increased by the reform. At the same time, our analysis shows a substantial wage gap between university graduates with long and short degrees in favor of the former, but without evidence of any social gradient, or changes in it. Curiously enough, this wage penalty is larger for men. Thus, poor family background individuals are more likely to enter the labor market immediately after completion of the first tier of university education, when the wage returns to college education are lower compared with the past. One issue to be addressed by future research is the extent to which these lower returns may act as a disincentive for university enrollment of students from poor background, thereby partially counteracting the immediate egalitarian effect of the reform on college enrollment choices.

Additionally, when investigating satisfaction with pay, we found that new graduates are happier with their wages more than their older counterparts, which, considering the wage penalty discussed above, may be the result of lower expectations about the returns to education.

What is the overall balance of the 3+2 reform? It is probably too early to express an informed judgment about the reform. Previous research showed that the shortening of undergraduate studies had an important role in increasing access to HE by individuals coming from less privileged family backgrounds, increasing this way equal opportunities in education. This chapter shows that this step toward mass undergraduate HE reduced the wage of the new cohorts of university graduates, and increased social inequality in the access to postgraduate education. There are therefore concerns that equal opportunities in HE may not necessarily translate into equal opportunities in the labor market. However, the recent literature on the nonmarket returns to HE suggests that the long-term effects of the HE expansion (reduction of crime, increase in health and in political participation, and so on) may go well beyond the market outcomes analyzed in this chapter, and the positive effects of the reform could be much more substantial than those that are immediately evident.

Notes

1. Signatory countries were as follows: from 1999: Austria, Belgium, Bulgaria, the Czech Republic, Denmark, Estonia, Finland, France, Germany, Greece, Hungary, Iceland, Ireland, Italy, Latvia, Lithuania, Luxembourg, Malta, the Netherlands, Norway, Poland, Portugal, Romania, Slovakia, Slovenia, Spain, Sweden, Switzerland, United Kingdom; from 2001: Croatia, Cyprus, Liechtenstein, Turkey; from 2003: Albania, Andorra, Bosnia and Herzegovina, the Holy See, Russia, Serbia, Republic of Macedonia; from 2005: Armenia, Azerbaijan, Georgia, Moldova, and Ukraine; from May 2007: Montenegro.

2. These are often degrees necessary to enter regulated professions whose exercise requires passing a qualification exam, such as the Medical professions. The complete list of single-cycle degrees is as follows: medicine and surgery (six years), dentistry (five years), veterinary (five years), pharmacy and industrial pharmacy (five years), architecture (five years), construction engineering (five years), teaching (four years). The degree in law was converted to a single-cycle structure as of 2003.

3. As the number of short-degree graduates increases, graduates with the old long degrees become relatively scarcer and their relative price increases, in case they possess different competences, which cannot be easily replaced by those of the new graduates.

4. We also run sensitivity checks using as controls: individuals with long degrees with a two-year delay at maximum and individuals with long degrees with a three-year delay at maximum. The results for enrollment in postgraduate studies, log wages, and wage satisfaction are unaffected, as far as the social gradients are concerned. The analysis of the graduation final mark shows a statistically significant premium for HISCED 5-6 and short degrees reflecting the fact that grades are generally inversely related to time of graduation (that is, actual degree length), which is much longer for pre-reform graduates by construction with these alternative sample definitions.

5. We also considered as an outcome the probability of being in employment. However, three years from graduation, most graduates participating in the labor market are employed (86.57 percent). Logit analysis of the probability of being employed generally did not show any social gradient both for graduates with long degrees and with short degrees.

6. The online appendix can be found at http://www.russellsage.org/Ermisch_ et_al_OnlineAppendix.pdf.

7. Due to small cell sizes, we could not include HEIs (sixty-seven) by college major (sixteen) interactions— that is, we do not allow HEIs to have differential effects on graduates' outcomes by college major. Moreover, the specification in equation 1 assumes that the effect of family background is the same across college majors and HEIs. In general, both college major and HEIs can be considered as *confounding factors* when assessing the effect of short degrees, but also as *mediating factors,* as the choice of specific majors or HEIs may be affected by socioeconomic status. An analysis of the effect of family background on college major and HEIs is beyond the scope of this chapter, and in any case, because we only have data on graduates, only analyses conditional on university graduation would be possible with our data.

8. We also used *interval regression* to estimate the model (see Stewart 1983). However, in the specifications including HEIs fixed effects, we failed to obtain standard errors for some of the coefficients. This is likely to be due to the small number of individuals sampled from some institutions. For this reason, we had to switch to OLS. Although this naïve procedure is known not to give consistent estimates, a comparison between OLS and interval regression estimates of the model with college major fixed effects shows only minor differences. This is likely to be the case as for the large majority of individuals we observe the grade precisely and not in interval form. This leads us to conclude that estimating the model with OLS is not particularly harmful in our specific case.

9. Moreover, the increase in the probability of postgraduate studies for graduates in short degrees could imply that short-degree graduates are relatively less able, and wage differences may reflect unobserved ability differences. However, we maintain that secondary school type and its interaction with the upper secondary school final mark, which are included in the wage equation, are good proxies of individual abilities in the Italian context. For instance, Massimiliano Bratti, Daniele Checchi, and Antonio Filippin (2007) found strong differences in OECD Programme for International Student Assessment (PISA) mathematical literacy scores across upper secondary school tracks.

10. Observations referring to these individuals have been used in the regression analyses of the paper, while including a dummy variable for switchers in the relevant conditioning sets. We also estimated the same models excluding switchers altogether. Also in this case, no significant social gradient emerges in the degree final grade and log hourly wage, though, as expected, because low socioeconomic status individuals are overrepresented among switchers, there is a decline in the social gradient in the probability of postgraduate studies for graduates of short degrees; the social gradient turns out to be statistically significant at conventional levels only for women. These additional results are available from the authors on request.

References

Bagüès, Manuel, Mauro Sylos-Labini, and Natalia Zinovyeva. 2008. "Differential Grading Standards and University Funding: Evidence from Italy." *CESifo Economic Studies* 54(2): 149–76.

Ballarino, Gabriele, and Massimiliano Bratti. 2009. "Field of Study and University Graduates' Early Employment Outcomes in Italy During 1995–2004." *Labour* 23(3): 421–57.

Biggeri, Luigi, Matilde Bini, and Leonardo Grilli. 2001. "The Transition from University to Work: A Multilevel Approach to the Analysis of the Time to Obtain the First Job." *Journal of the Royal Statistical Society. Series A (Statistics in Society)* 164(2): 293–305.

Blanden, Jo, and Stephen Machin. 2004. "Educational Inequality and the Expansion of U.K. Higher Education." *Scottish Journal of Political Economy* 51(2): 230–49.

Bratti, Massimiliano, Chiara Broccolini, and Stefano Staffolani. 2010. "Higher Education Reform, Student Time Allocation and Academic Performance in Italy: Evidence from a Faculty of Economics." *Rivista Italiana degli Economisti* 15(2): 275–304.

Bratti, Massimiliano, Daniele Checchi, and Guido de Blasio. 2008. "Does the Expansion of Higher Education Increase the Equality of Educational Opportunities? Evidence from Italy." *Labour* 22(s1): 53–88.

Bratti, Massimiliano, Daniele Checchi, and Antonio Filippin. 2007. "Geographical Differences in Italian Students' Mathematical Competencies: Evidence from PISA 2003." *Giornale degli Economisti e Annali di Economia* 66(3): 299–333.

Brunello, Giorgio, and Lorenzo Cappellari. 2008. "The Labour Market Effects of Alma Mater: Evidence from Italy." *Economics of Education Review* 27(5): 564–74.

Brunello, Giorgio, and Daniele Checchi. 2007. "Does School Tracking Affect Equality of Opportunity? New International Evidence." *Economic Policy* 22(October): 781–861.

Buonanno, Paolo, and Dario Pozzoli. 2009. "Early Labour Market Returns to College Subject." *Labour* 23(4): 559–88.

Cappellari, Lorenzo, and Claudio Lucifora. 2009. "The Bologna Process and College Enrollment Decisions." *Labour Economics* 16(6): 638–47.

Cammelli, Andrea. 2006. "La qualità del capitale umano dell'università. Caratteristiche e performance dei laureati 2004." In *L'università in transizione: Laureati vecchi e nuovi alla luce della riforma*, edited by Consorzio Interuniversitario Almalaurea. Bologna: Il Mulino.

Cardoso, Ana Rute, Miguel Portela, Sá Carla, and Fernando Alexandre. 2008. "Demand for Higher Education Programs: The Impact of the Bologna Process." *CESIfo Economic Studies* 54(2): 229–47.

Checchi, Daniele, ed. 2010. *Immobilità diffusa. Perché la mobilità intergenerazionale è così bassa in Italia*. Bologna: Il Mulino.

Checchi, Daniele, Carlo Fiorio, and Marco Leonardi. 2008. "Intergenerational Persistence in Educational Attainment in Italy." *IZA* discussion paper 3622. Bonn: Institute for the Study of Labor.

Checchi, Daniele, and Luca Flabbi. 2007. "Intergenerational Mobility and Schooling Decisions in Germany and Italy: The Impact of Secondary School Tracks." *IZA* discussion paper 2876. Bonn: Institute for the Study of Labor.

Checchi, Daniele, Andrea Ichino, and Aldo Rustichini. 1999. "More Equal but Less Mobile? Education Financing and Intergenerational Mobility in Italy and in the United States." *Journal of Public Economics* 74(3): 351–93.

D'Hombres, Beatrice. 2007. "The Impact of University Reforms on Dropout Rates and Students' Status: Evidence from Italy." *JRC* scientific and technical report. Brussels: European Commission.

Di Pietro, Giorgio. 2006. "Regional Labour Market Conditions and University Dropout Rates: Evidence from Italy." *Regional Studies* 40(6): 617–30.

Di Pietro, Giorgio, and Andrea Cutillo. 2006. "University Quality and Labour Market Outcomes in Italy." *Labour* 20(1): 37–62.

———. 2008. "Degree Flexibility and University Drop-out: The Italian Experience." *Economics of Education Review* 27(5): 546–55.

Dornbusch, Rudi, and Francesca Giavazzi. 2000. "Italy Must Abandon Its University Populism." *International Herald Tribune,* September 14.

ISTAT. 2007. *Inserimento professionale dei laureate—Indagine 2007* (Graduate Employment Survey [GES]). Available at: http://www.istat.it/it/archivio/6993 (accessed December 21, 2011).

MIUR. 2006. "Settimo rapporto sullo stato del sistema universitario." Rome: Ministero dell'università e della ricerca.

Pellizzari, Michele. 2010. "Do Friends and Relatives Really Help in Getting a Good Job?" *The Industrial and Labor Relations Review* 63(3): 494–510.

Perotti, Roberto. 2002. "The Italian University System: Rules vs. Incentives." Unpublished manuscript. European University Institute, Florence.

Rochat, Denis, and Jean-Luc De Meulemeester. 2001. "Rational Choice under Unequal Constraints: The Example of Belgian Higher Education." *Economics of Education Review* 20(1): 15–26.

Stewart, Mark. 1983. "On Least Squares Estimation When the Dependent Variable Is Grouped." *Review of Economic Studies* 50(4): 737–53.

Sylos-Labini, Mauro. 2004. "Social Networks and Wages: It Is All About Connections!" *LEM* working paper 2004/10. Pisa: Scuola Superiore Sant'Anna di Studi Universitari e di Perfezionamento.

Chapter 16

Intergenerational Transmission of Cognitive and Noncognitive Skills

SILKE ANGER

For the last few decades, societies in most developed countries have been characterized by rising economic inequality. Social science research has generated cross-national evidence that this rising inequality is closely related to less social mobility across generations. Literature has mainly focused on intergenerational income mobility and education mobility as the two benchmarks against which differences between the socioeconomic status of parents and their children are measured. However, although the intergenerational correlation of economic status is well known, it is much less clear what drives these correlation patterns. To develop policy measures that aim to enhance intergenerational mobility and reduce inequality in the long term, it is crucial that we understand how economic disadvantage is transmitted from parents to children. One potential factor that may help explain how socioeconomic status is linked across generations is skills and their transmission from parents to children. Both cognitive and noncognitive skills have been found to be important predictors of economic and social success. Cognitive skills refer to various dimensions of intelligence, such as an individual's verbal fluency or ability to solve new problems, whereas noncognitive skills comprise personality traits, such as openness to experience or emotional stability.[1] Cognitive and noncognitive skills have been shown to play a substantial role in educational achievement (for example, Heckman and Vytlacil 2001) and income (for example, Hanushek and Wößmann 2008). Thus, a significant transmission of intelligence or personal traits from parents to their children could play a major role in determining the intergenerational correlation of socioeconomic status. A small body of economic literature has investigated whether the intergenerational correlation of economic status is driven by cognitive and noncognitive skills (for example, Blanden, Gregg, and Macmillan 2007; chapter 3, this volume), but very few data sets provide information on the abilities and economic outcomes of both parents and their children.

This chapter discusses the transmission of cognitive and noncognitive skills from parents to their children during adolescence and young adulthood. Using representative data from the German Socio-Economic Panel Study (SOEP), the study compares the impact of parental skills on children's skill outcomes with the effects of parental background and childhood environment, which can account, to some extent, for early life conditions that are critical to individuals' cognitive and noncognitive development (Ermisch 2008). The focus of this chapter is on the determinants of children's intelligence and personal traits as potential mediating variables in intergenerational education and earnings transmission.[2] The intergenerational correlations of skills are analyzed for children of two age groups: adolescents about age seventeen and young adults between eighteen and twenty-nine.[3] The German school system means that some adolescents may already have finished secondary school at age seventeen with the most basic school leaving certificate (Hauptschule) or with no certificate. However, the majority of young people are still enrolled in either an intermediate secondary school (Realschule) or an academic one (Gymnasium) or in a vocational school (Berufsschule). In contrast, young adults between the ages of eighteen and twenty-nine have mostly finished secondary school with some kind of certificate and eventually pursue or have completed tertiary education, or have dropped out with no qualification. Hence, in this age group, children are mainly in the labor market or enrolled at a university, though some may have started a family and, thus, are not part of the labor force.

The SOEP enables us to distinguish between fathers and mothers, and sons and daughters. This means that we can account for possible gender differences in IQ and personality transmission and compute overall transmission effects from both parents.[4] Furthermore, we can analyze whether intergenerational skill transmission occurs differently according to the type of skill. With respect to cognitive skills, the data allow us to distinguish between fluid intelligence (coding speed, abstract reasoning) and crystallized intelligence (verbal and numerical skills). Noncognitive skills are measures of the five factor model (openness, conscientiousness, extraversion, agreeableness, neuroticism) and locus of control.

Finally, the intergenerational correlation patterns in Germany will be compared with previous findings for other countries with different institutional frameworks. With respect to IQ transmission, this analysis can be compared with two recent Scandinavian studies by Sandra Black, Paul Devereux, and Kjell Salvanes (2009) for Norway, and by Anders Björklund, Karin Hederos Eriksson, and Markus Jäntti (2010) for Sweden. These studies use a largely comparable framework for analyzing the various channels between parental resources and the attainment of cognitive skills. Although their data sets are based on matched administrative registers, census data, and military records, and thus only available for fathers and their sons, a subsample of males from the SOEP can be used to match the samples of these studies. With respect to the transmission of personal traits, the results will be compared with findings from Susan Mayer and her colleagues (2004) and Greg Duncan and his colleagues (2005), who examine the relationship between maternal personality traits and the skills of their sons and daughters using the National Longitudinal Survey of Youth (NLSY). Further, the reviews of existing studies on intergenerational correlations of noncognitive skills provided by Melissa Osborne Groves (2005) and John Loehlin (2005) will be drawn on for comparison.

Existing literature considers two main channels for the transmission of cognitive and noncognitive skills between generations. On the one hand, skills may be transmitted from parents to their biological children by the inheritance of genes (nature). On the other hand, the transmission may work through a productivity effect of parental skills (nurture). For example, more able parents are more likely to be able to afford high quality child care, housing in areas with access to high quality schools, and bear the costs of private lessons and tertiary education. They may also enhance the skills of their children by employing favorable parenting styles and by promoting good health conditions for their offspring. Unfortunately, the SOEP data do not allow us to clearly distinguish nature and nurture effects. Findings from recent research on income and educational mobility suggest the importance of both nature and nurture (Björklund, Jäntti, and Solon 2007). Moreover, Flavio Cunha and James Heckman (2007) point out that the assumed separability of nature and nurture is obsolete as the mechanisms interact in more complex ways.

Research on Intergenerational Skill Transmission

Existing economic literature on intergenerational mobility concentrates predominantly on education (for example, Hertz et al. 2007) and income mobility (for example, Solon 1999). In modern societies, years of schooling completed by parents and their children's schooling have been found to be correlated between 0.14 and 0.45 (Mulligan 1999). Kenneth Couch and Thomas Dunn (1997) report a father-son correlation of 0.25 for Germany, but, most likely, underestimate the true correlation because their estimates are based on a sample of relatively young children. Intergenerational correlations of earnings have an even wider range, from about 0.10 to 0.55 (Solon 1999). Thorsten Vogel (2006) estimates an intergenerational earnings elasticity of 0.24 in Germany and of 0.34 for a comparable sample in the United States.

There is far less research on the underlying causes of these intergenerational correlations, but ongoing research aims at disentangling the causal mechanisms (Black and Devereux 2011). Skills could serve as an intergenerational transmission mechanism as both cognitive skills and noncognitive skills have been found to be important predictors for economic and social success (for example, Cameron and Heckman 1993; Heckman, Stixrud, and Urzua 2006; Anger and Heineck 2010b, Heineck and Anger 2010). The crucial question as to whether the intergenerational transmission of cognitive abilities or personality may explain the persistence of socioeconomic status across generations is examined in chapter 3 of this volume. The authors use register data from Sweden to decompose father-son education and income correlations into different mediating characteristics of the children. They find that the intergenerational income effect can be explained to 20 percent out of 63 percent by the son's cognitive skills and to a somewhat lesser extent by noncognitive traits. However, cognitive abilities are much more important for education and account for 37 percent out of 46 percent of the transmission between fathers and sons. Additional evidence that cognitive and noncognitive skills serve as one of the causal channels of intergenerational transmission of economic status has been provided by Samuel Bowles and Herbert Gintis (2002), Melissa Osborne Groves (2005), and Jo Blanden and colleagues (2007).

Although economic research on skill formation is rather scarce, the determinants of cognitive and noncognitive skills and intergenerational correlations have been analyzed by psychologists for decades. IQ correlations between parents and their children were found to be in the range between 0.42 and 0.72 (Bouchard and McGue 1981; Devlin, Daniels, and Roeder 1997; Plomin et al. 2000). However, the data sets used by most psychological studies are based on a small number of observations or lack representativeness. One of the first economic studies by Mark Agee and Thomas Crocker (2002) reports a positive association between mean parental IQ and their child's cognitive outcome using U.S. data. Using the British National Child Development Study (NCDS), Sarah Brown, Steven McIntosh, and Karl Taylor (2009) find a positive link between the literacy and numeracy abilities possessed by parents in their childhoods and their children's performance in reading and mathematics. Their results support the importance of parenting style for the transmission of literacy skills, while genetic effects seem to be the driving force behind the transmission of numeracy skills. Measures of reading performance and numerical skills during adolescence can also be found in the National Longitudinal Survey of Youth (NLSY), which Greg Duncan and his colleagues (2005) use to show positive mother-child correlations for both reading and mathematics skills.

Two recent Scandinavian studies investigate the relationship between the cognitive skills of fathers and sons using IQ test scores from large-scale nationally representative data sets: Sandra Black, Paul Devereux, and Kjell Salvanes (2009) use composite IQ test scores conducted at age eighteen and find a strong intergenerational transmission of IQ scores for fathers and their sons in Norway. Björklund (2010) find similar intergenerational IQ correlations for Sweden. Finding sibling correlations to be close to one half, they conclude that 50 percent of the variation in IQ can be attributed to family and community background factors. Finally, in a previous study, Silke Anger and Guido Heineck (2010a) report intergenerational correlations for sons and daughters in Germany that were stronger than those for Scandinavia. Their estimates are based, however, on a sample of older children age up to sixty-four at the time of skill measurement. In contrast, this chapter focuses on the intergenerational correlation of skills between parents and their children during adolescence and young adulthood to obtain results that are suitable for cross-national comparisons. In addition, adolescents observed in this study conduct an IQ test more elaborate than that of Anger and Heineck.

Another strand of research (predominantly psychological) provides evidence of the intergenerational correlation of noncognitive skills which has been found to be substantially lower than the correlation of cognitive skills. In his review of psychological studies on parent-offspring correlations of personality traits and attitudes, Loehlin (2005) concludes that parents and their children do not resemble each other very much. He reports intergenerational correlations of personality measures, including the Big Five, of about 0.10 to 0.15 for young adult children. Somewhat stronger intergenerational correlations of personality traits are reported by Osborne Groves (2005) in her overview of previous research estimates. Mayer and her colleagues (2004) find only weak mother-daughter correlations for personal traits and behaviors measured during adolescence based on the NLSY, and that these correlations are barely affected by family socioeconomic status. Using the same data set and a supplementary study conducted in Maryland, Greg Duncan and his colleagues (2005) report that parents mainly pass on their specific rather than their general skills. Furthermore, they confirm that "neither socioeconomic status nor parenting behaviors appear very important to the intergenerational transmission process" (26). Instead, their results are consistent with an important genetic component in the intergenerational correlation of personality attributes.

Data and Methodology

The analysis presented in this chapter is based on data from the German Socio-Economic Panel Study (SOEP) for the years 2005 through 2008. The SOEP is a representative household panel survey (Wagner, Frick, and Schupp 2007) and described in greater detail in the online appendix.[5] The intergenerational transmission of skills will be analyzed separately for adolescent children age around seventeen and for young adult children age eighteen to twenty-nine as the available skill measures differ for both groups. The family background and childhood environment variables used in this study are the potential determinants of cognitive and noncognitive skills other than parental IQ or parental personality. In particular, the analysis considers parental education, which is based on the ISCED classification (low education: 0–2, medium education: 3–4, higher education: 5–6). Further controls include family size (number of brothers and sisters), a dummy for being the first-born child, a dummy for having been raised by a single parent, a dummy for good self-rated health status, and a set of childhood area dummies: childhood in a rural area, town, city, where childhood in an urban area serves as a reference category. The individual's childhood environment may partially capture socioeconomic conditions (for example, health-care infrastructure, educational provision) that may be critical to cognitive and noncognitive development. To complement the aforementioned, this study uses the individual's body height (at the time the skills were measured) as an indicator of health and nutritional conditions in early childhood development. The key variables in this project are personality measures and measures of cognitive skills, both of which are available for adult respondents and for adolescents.

Skill Measures for Parents and Adult Children

Information on cognitive skills was collected from adult respondents (age eighteen and older) in 2006 and comprises test scores from a word fluency test and a symbol correspondence test. Both tests correspond to different modules of the Wechsler Adult Intelligence Scale (WAIS) and produce outcomes that are relatively well correlated with test scores from more comprehensive and well-established intelligence tests (Lang et al. 2007).[6] The symbol correspondence test is conceptually related to the mechanics of cognition or fluid intelligence and comprises general abilities. The word fluency test is conceptually related to the pragmatics of cognition or crystallized intelligence. It consists of the fulfillment of specific tasks that improve with knowledge and skills acquired in the past. While verbal fluency is based on learning, speed of cognition is related to an individual's innate abilities (Cattell 1987). In addition, a measure of general intelligence is generated by averaging the two types of ability test scores.[7] The overall sample of young adult offspring with IQ measures, for whom at least one parent with valid information on IQ test scores can be identified, consists of 446 sons and daughters ages eighteen to twenty-nine.[8]

Measures of personality for adult respondents (age eighteen and older) are available for 2005 (Dehne and Schupp 2007). They include self-rated measures that were related to the five factor model (McCrae and Costa 1999) and make up the five basic psychological dimensions—openness to experience, conscientiousness, extraversion, agreeableness, neuroticism (Big Five)—as well as measures of locus of control. The sample consists of 2,228 adult children with noncognitive skill measures who can be linked to their parents with valid information on personality traits.

Skill Measures for Adolescent Children

Cognitive skills were measured for adolescents at age seventeen in the years 2006, 2007, and 2008. The somewhat more complex intelligence tests are modified versions of the I-S-T 2000-Test (Solga et al. 2005) and cover the following domains: verbal skills, numerical skills, and abstract reasoning. An integrated index of verbal and numerical skills provides an adequate assessment of the adolescent's crystallized intelligence, that is, skills that improve with knowledge acquired in the past, whereas abstract reasoning is related to fluid intelligence and thus comprises largely innate abilities.

Adolescents' personality measures (at age seventeen) are also available in the years 2006, 2007, and 2008. These measures relate to the five factor model containing the same dimensions as for adults, and measures of locus of control. To analyze intergenerational skill transmission, intelligence test scores and personality indicators of adolescent respondents from 2006 to 2008 are linked to the parental skill measures that were available in 2005 and 2006. This selection leaves us with 280 adolescents for whom information on their own cognitive skills and their parents' IQ is available. In addition, 1,184 parent-child pairs with personality measures for both generations can be identified.

Methodology

To avoid spurious effects of age on test outcomes age-standardized scores for all cognitive ability tests are used. These are generated by calculating the scores' standardized values for every year along the age distribution. The study also uses age-standardized scores from the dimension-specific questions on the five factor model and locus of control to net out age effects in self-rated personality.[9] Summary statistics of all variables are provided in online appendix table 16A.1.

In the following section, children's test scores are regressed on parental test scores, family background, childhood environment variables, and a gender dummy using ordinary least squares (OLS) regressions. Intergenerational skill transmissions are estimated using different subsamples for both age groups. First, the regressions will be based on all children for whom either maternal or paternal test scores are available to maximize the number of observations. Whenever the test scores of both parents are available, the averages of the mother's and father's test scores are used. Second, in additional regressions only father-son relationships will be considered to compare the results with findings from recent Scandinavian studies (Black et al. 2009; Björklund, Eriksson, and Jäntti 2010) that are based on males only. Although the interdependence of cognitive abilities and personal traits could play a role in the process of skill transmission, this analysis investigates only the intergenerational transmission of the same skill. This approach is supported by the findings of Anne Case and Lawrence Katz (1991) and Duncan and his colleagues (2005), suggesting that parents' specific skills primarily determine the same but not other skills of their children. Whether interdependencies between different types of skills indeed do only play a minor role in intergenerational skill transmission in the German data is left for future research.

Results

The following tables present intergenerational associations in cognitive and noncognitive skills for children of two age groups: adolescents and young adults. Table 16.1 summarizes the results of the most basic specification: children's test scores are regressed on the main independent variable of interest, the test scores of the parents, without including further control variables. The first column of each table displays parent-child correlations for all children of an age group for whom either maternal or paternal test scores are available, and the samples in the second column are restricted to sons for whom separate effects of paternal skills will be measured for comparison with previous studies.

Adolescents

The results reported in table 16.1 demonstrate an intergenerational transmission of both cognitive and noncognitive skills for the whole sample of adolescents (column 1). The positive correlations between parental and children's test scores range between 0.13 and 0.24 for cognitive skills and between 0.12 and 0.22 for noncognitive skills, and all estimated coefficients, except for fluid intelligence, are statistically significant at the 1 percent level. The strongest link between parental and children's skills is shown for external locus of control and for general intelligence: a 1-point increase in the age-standardized test score of parents is associated with a 0.22-point increase in their children's external locus of control and with a 0.24-point increase in their children's general intelligence test scores. This corresponds to two and a half right answers (of sixty) in the IQ test. However, the variation is very small with an adjusted R-squared of at

Table 16.1   Transmission of Cognitive and Noncognitive Skills

	Adolescent Children		Young Adult Children	
	All	Sons	All	Sons
Cognitive skills				
Fluid intelligence				
Test score parents	0.134*	—	0.522***	—
	(0.070)	—	(0.044)	—
Test score father	—	0.028	—	0.388***
	—	(0.129)	—	(0.077)
Adjusted R^2	0.009	0.011	0.240	0.150
Crystallized intelligence				
Test score parents	0.180***	—	0.531***	—
	(0.065)	—	(0.044)	—
Test score father	—	0.214**	—	0.421***
	—	(0.099)	—	(0.072)
Adjusted R^2	0.023	0.038	0.246	0.192
General intelligence				
Test score parents	0.237***	—	0.556***	—
	(0.070)	—	(0.043)	—
Test score father	—	0.203*	—	0.424***
	—	(0.111)	—	(0.076)
Adjusted R^2	0.036	0.026	0.281	0.185
Noncognitive skills				
Openness				
Test score parents	0.173***	—	0.245***	—
	(0.025)	—	(0.017)	—
Test score father	—	0.166***	—	0.310***
	—	(0.043)	—	(0.032)
Adjusted R^2	0.038	0.026	0.083	0.093
Conscientiousness				
Test score parents	0.146***	—	0.226***	—
	(0.024)	—	(0.017)	—
Test score father	—	0.159***	—	0.245***
	—	(0.042)	—	(0.031)
Adjusted R^2	0.030	0.024	0.068	0.061
Extraversion				
Test score parents	0.168***	—	0.193***	—
	(0.026)	—	(0.019)	—
Test score father	—	0.140***	—	0.201***
	—	(0.043)	—	(0.033)
Adjusted R^2	0.034	0.018	0.043	0.037

(Table continues on p. 402.)

Table 16.1   *Continued*

	Adolescent Children		Young Adult Children	
	All	Sons	All	Sons
Agreeableness				
Test score parents	0.163***	—	0.224***	—
	(0.025)	—	(0.017)	—
Test score father	—	0.146***	—	0.206***
	—	(0.041)	—	(0.031)
Adjusted R^2	0.034	0.021	0.070	0.045
Neuroticism				
Test score parents	0.147***	—	0.206***	—
	(0.025)	—	(0.018)	—
Test score father	—	0.162***	—	0.209***
	—	(0.045)	—	(0.034)
Adjusted R^2	0.028	0.022	0.055	0.039
LOC: internal				
Test score parents	0.116***	—	0.214***	—
	(0.023)	—	(0.017)	—
Test score father	—	0.085**	—	0.191***
	—	(0.042)	—	(0.032)
Adjusted R^2	0.021	0.006	0.065	0.036
LOC: external				
Test score parents	0.220***	—	0.265***	—
	(0.022)	—	(0.016)	—
Test score father	—	0.215***	—	0.282***
	—	(0.040)	—	(0.031)
Adjusted R^2	0.075	0.050	0.107	0.085
Number of observations (cognitive skills)	280	90	446	141
Number of observations (noncognitive skills)	1184	518	2228	892

Source: Author's calculations based on data from SOEP version 26, years 2005 to 2008 (SOEP 2010).

Notes: Dependent variables: age-standardized scores of the child's skill measures. The first three dependent variables include cognitive skill measures (fluid intelligence, crystallized intelligence, general intelligence); the other dependent variables comprise noncognitive skill measures (Big Five, locus of control).

"Test score parents" refers to the average of parents' age-standardized test scores when test scores for both parents are available.

Fluid intelligence refers to the coding speed of young adult children and parents (symbol correspondence test) and to the abstract reasoning of adolescent children (matrix test). Crystallized intelligence refers to the word fluency of young adult children and parents (animal-naming task) and to the verbal and numerical skills of adolescent children (word analogies, arithmetic operations). General intelligence combines fluid and crystallized intelligence measures.

Standard errors in parentheses.

*** $p < 0.01$, ** $p < 0.05$, * $p < 0.1$

most 7.5 percent. Compared with earlier findings based on similar data, these coefficients are not even half the size of the ones found in Anger and Heineck (2010a) for children in middle and late adulthood who participated in different IQ tests.

To compare the results with previous studies on father-son-correlations, this chapter examines the role of fathers for their sons using the relatively small sample of male adolescents (column 2). The exclusion of daughters and mothers leads to an insignificant transmission effect for fluid intelligence, but slightly increases the intergenerational correlation of crystallized intelligence to 0.21. Noncognitive skills of sons seem to be largely correlated with their fathers' personality traits. In particular, fathers play an important role in the intergenerational transmission of external locus of control. However, the correlations tend to be slightly stronger when taking into account both mothers' and fathers' skills for the sample of all children.

In sum, the intergenerational transmission effects for adolescent children are not found to be overwhelmingly large. However, the estimates of noncognitive skill transmissions are somewhat bigger than the ones Loehlin reports in his review of psychological studies (2005). For instance, the reviewed studies revealed parent-offspring correlations of the Big Five measures of between 0.09 and 0.17.

Young Adults

Table 16.1 also presents the estimates for intergenerational correlations of skills between parents and their young adult children (columns 3 and 4). It is striking that the transmission of skills, and in particular of cognitive skills, is much stronger for this older age group of children. Similarly, the explained variance is much higher than in the estimates for the younger age group, with an adjusted R-squared of up to 0.28 in the regression of general cognitive skills for all children (column 3). The parent-child correlation is as high as 0.56 for general intelligence, and between 0.19 and 0.27 for personality traits with highly significant coefficients. The transmission effects of noncognitive skills, therefore, correspond to the intergenerational correlation of personality traits of between 0.14 and 0.29, which Osborne Groves reports in her overview of previous studies (2005). The parent-child correlations of cognitive skills in this study are even higher than the ones found in Anger and Heineck (2010a) based on the same data set for a sample that includes children at older ages. However, they are in line with the correlations summarized in studies by Bouchard and McGue (1981) from a sample of familial studies of IQ where an average correlation of 0.5 between parents and their offspring is reported.

Even in the clearly smaller sample, where effects from fathers on the cognitive and noncognitive skills of their sons are calculated for cross-national comparison of the results with father-son-correlations of previous studies, almost all of the paternal test scores are large in both size and statistical significance (column 4). For coding speed, the transmission effect is clearly less when compared with the full sample, but both the crystallized and general intelligence of fathers and sons are still correlated with a coefficient of 0.42. In contrast to cognitive skills, the exclusion of daughters and maternal skills significantly increases the coefficients of the parental test scores for some of the personality traits. In particular, fathers' openness, conscientiousness, and external locus of control seem to play an important role for the noncognitive skills of their sons.

The question arises as to why the intergenerational correlations of skills are so much stronger for young adult children than for adolescent children. In the case of cognitive skills, this discrepancy may be partially explained by the different IQ tests conducted with adults and adolescents. While young adult children and their parents participate in exactly the same ultra-short IQ tests, the intelligence tests for adolescent children are more complex and may measure slightly different facets of cognition. Although both intelligence tests produce measures of fluid and crystallized intelligence, the fit between the two measures is unlikely to be perfect, and the discrepancy may be traced back in part to measurement error.[10]

However, this argument does not apply to the measures of noncognitive skills, which have also been shown to be transmitted more strongly from parents to adult children than to adolescent children. Both adult and adolescent respondents have rated their personality traits based on an identical set of questions using exactly the same scales. One possible explanation is that the personality of children is not fully developed during adolescence and may still be quite malleable. This argument is supported by Paul Costa and Robert McCrae (1994), who suggest that personality traits are stable from middle adulthood. It could, therefore, be the case that adolescents' personal traits do not bear a strong resemblance to their parents' noncognitive traits but change during young adulthood in such a way that the intergenerational correlation for young adults increases in size. However, it could be the case that the convergence between children's and parental skills during young adulthood is due to parents being affected by their children.[11] Both explanations could also account for the stronger correlation between parental cognitive performance and their children's IQ at older ages.

The intergenerational correlations of cognitive skills (0.52 to 0.56) and noncognitive skills (0.19 to 0.27) revealed for young adults compare to the father-son correlation in schooling of 0.25 for Germany that Couch and Dunn (1997) report based on a sample of young adult children. Thus, though the transmission of personality traits seems to be comparable in size to the education transmission, the transmission effect is clearly stronger for cognitive skills than for schooling. Similarly, the estimated skill transmission effects for personality traits are of similar size and the transmission effects for intelligence twice as large when compared with the intergenerational earnings elasticity of 0.24 in Germany reported by Thorsten Vogel (2006).

Family Background and Childhood Environment

The intergenerational correlation between parents' and their children's skills in the basic specifications could be driven by third variables because family characteristics during childhood or other factors could affect skill formation. The rich data set available allows the inclusion of additional variables in the regression to control for family background, childhood environment, and child's health status. In unreported regressions, the study uses richer specifications controlling for gender, physical strength (height, health status), family background (single parent, first-born child, number of brothers, number of sisters), and childhood environment (childhood area dummies).[12] Interestingly, this variation increases only slightly, and the coefficients of parents' test scores are barely affected by the inclusion of the control variables.[13] This is in line with the results from the U.K. study by Sarah Brown and her colleagues (2009), which finds a robust transmission effect for reading and mathematics test scores, independent of additional controls.

However, factors other than parental skills seem to play an important role. For adolescents, for whom the parent-child correlation of cognitive skills is not found to be very high, good health condition plays a major role in determining intelligence test scores. Being healthy is also an important determinant of locus of control, agreeableness, and emotional stability. Furthermore, being raised by a single parent considerably lowers crystallized intelligence, general intelligence, and internal locus of control. For young adults, for whom parental cognitive skills were a much better predictor of IQ test scores, the number of brothers was the only other determinant of measured intelligence. Although affecting cognitive skills negatively, the number of brothers had a positive influence on personality measures. In contrast, personality traits were adversely affected by the single-parent variable. Again, health status emerged as an important factor of all noncognitive skills except openness. Test scores on the internal locus of control and emotional stability of a young adult significantly benefit from the child's good health.

Parental Education and Skill Formation

So far, this analysis has not taken into account parental socioeconomic status, which is widely considered to be the most important family background variable. Socioeconomic resources could be one of the channels through which skills are transmitted from parents to their children (for example, Duncan et al. 2005). As skills are rewarded on the labor market, more able parents have more resources to afford high-quality child care, housing in areas with access to high-quality schools, and bear the costs of private lessons and tertiary education, which, combined, may benefit children's skills. Moreover, educated parents may provide a favorable home environment and also enhance the skills of their children by employing favorable parenting styles and promoting good health conditions for their offspring. The socioeconomic status of the family may, therefore, act as an important mediator in the intergenerational transmission of intelligence and personality traits. The role of parental socioeconomic status in children's skill formation will be examined by linking children's skill outcomes to their parents' education, which is available for fathers and mothers in the sample. A first impression on the relationship between parental schooling and children's skills is presented in figure 16.1, which displays adolescents and young adults' average intelligence test scores by parental highest education. In both domains of the IQ test is a clear SES gradient in the cognitive skills of adolescents, because children of higher educated parents perform better in the cognitive tests. This finding holds regardless of the type of school, that is, when the current school type of a child is taken into account (not displayed). The association is clearly weaker for the older cohort, but young adult children with highly educated parents also perform better, particularly in the verbal fluency test.[14]

Noncognitive skills show a less clear SES gradient, even for adolescents. Average scores on the personality scales by parental highest education are displayed in online appendix figure 16A.1. If there is any difference at all, adolescent children's conscientiousness and agreeableness—but also their neuroticism—increase with higher parental education, and extraversion and external locus of control decrease. In contrast, young adult children's openness and extraversion slightly increase with parental education, and also their agreeableness and neuroticism. A weaker link between parental SES (as measured by education and income) and personality, versus between parental SES and IQ, is also shown for Sweden in chapter 3 of this volume.

Next, the link between parental education and skill outcomes is analyzed in a regression-adjusted framework. First, children's intelligence and personality test scores are regressed on dummies for the highest parental educational degrees (medium and high education, with low education being the reference group). Second, parental test scores are included in these regressions to measure the relative importance of these characteristics. Table 16.2 reports results for the relationship between the parental education and cognitive skills of adolescent children (panel A) and of young adult children (panel B). As the results of the first three columns (without IQ transmission effects) show, the association between parents' education and the intelligence of their adolescent children is

Figure 16.1   Children's IQ Test Scores According to Parental Education

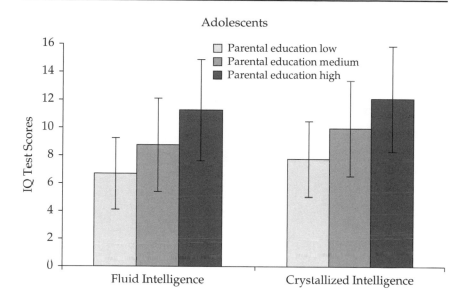

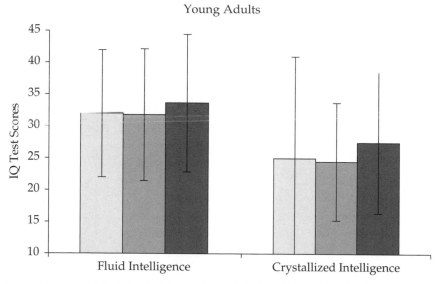

Source: Author's calculations based on SOEP version 26, years 2006 to 2008 (SOEP 2010).
Note: The IQ test for adolescents consists of sixty individual tasks and allow for a total time of twenty-seven minutes. The IQ test for young adults includes two ultra-short tests lasting ninety seconds each (see online appendix).

Table 16.2   Parental Education and Cognitive Skills of Adolescents and Young Adults

	Fluid Intelligence	Crystallized Intelligence	General Intelligence	Fluid Intelligence	Crystallized Intelligence	General Intelligence
Adolescents						
Medium-educated parents	0.444*	0.628***	0.643***	0.404*	0.563**	0.568**
	(0.227)	(0.223)	(0.227)	(0.227)	(0.222)	(0.226)
Highly educated parents	1.013***	1.198***	1.289***	0.956***	1.069***	1.127***
	(0.233)	(0.229)	(0.233)	(0.234)	(0.232)	(0.235)
Test score parents	—	—	—	0.127**	0.145**	0.191***
	—	—	—	(0.062)	(0.060)	(0.063)
Constant	-0.691***	-0.839***	-0.928***	-0.633***	-0.744***	-0.795***
	(0.216)	(0.212)	(0.216)	(0.216)	(0.212)	(0.216)
Adjusted R^2	0.091	0.109	0.127	0.098	0.122	0.146
Observations	280	280	280	280	280	280
Young adults						
Medium-educated parents	0.137	-0.071	-0.016	-0.094	-0.122	-0.184
	(0.210)	(0.212)	(0.212)	(0.186)	(0.184)	(0.182)
Highly educated parents	0.361*	0.093	0.233	0.003	-0.157	-0.130
	(0.214)	(0.216)	(0.216)	(0.191)	(0.188)	(0.187)
Test score parents	—	—	—	0.517***	0.536***	0.555***
	—	—	—	(0.045)	(0.045)	(0.044)
Constant	-0.175	0.005	-0.059	0.103	0.110	0.171
	(0.200)	(0.203)	(0.203)	(0.178)	(0.176)	(0.174)
Adjusted R^2	0.010	0.002	0.010	0.238	0.243	0.280
Observations	446	446	446	446	446	446

Source: Author's calculations based on SOEP version 26, years 2005 to 2008 (SOEP 2010).

Notes: Dependent variable: age-standardized scores of the child's skill measure.

"Test score parents" refers to the average of parents' age-standardized test scores when test scores for both parents are available.

Reference group: low-educated parents

Fluid intelligence refers to the coding speed of parents and young adult children (symbol correspondence test) and to the abstract reasoning of adolescents (matrix test). Crystallized intelligence refers to the word fluency of parents and young adults (animal-naming task) and to the verbal and numerical skills of adolescents (word analogies, arithmetic operations). General intelligence combines fluid and crystallized intelligence measures.

Standard errors in parentheses.

*** $p < 0.01$, ** $p < 0.05$, * $p < 0.1$

strong. This is in line with the Swedish study in chapter 3 of this volume, which reports a correlation between fathers' schooling and their sons' IQ of 0.32. Table 16.2 shows that parents' higher education is most strongly correlated with general cognitive skills and more important for crystallized than for fluid intelligence. However, even for fluid intelligence, having a highly educated parent is associated with a 1-point increase in the child's intelligence, which corresponds to more than three answers (of twenty) in the corresponding IQ test. The association between parental education and children's cognitive skills is, however, much weaker for older children (panel B). Only coding speed (fluid intelligence) is significantly affected by parents' higher education.

As displayed in the last three columns in panel A, including parental test scores only slightly changes the effect of parental education on adolescents' cognitive skills. Parents' higher education still has a significant impact on all three skill outcomes. However, despite including the obviously important parental education, parental test scores still matter for the cognitive skills of their children. Compared with the raw regressions in table 16.1, the coefficients of crystallized and general intelligence were reduced in size and significance, whereas there is only a small change in the transmission of fluid intelligence. Thus, both parents' education and their skills seem to matter independently for the intelligence of their adolescent children. In contrast, the last three columns in panel B show that parental education has no effect on the test scores of their young adult children, and the IQ transmission effect is virtually unchanged for this age group when compared with the raw regressions in table 16.1. This is in line with previous findings of Anger and Heineck (2010a) for older children. Overall, although parents' educational background affects the skills of adolescent children, it seems to play only a minor role as mediator in the intergenerational transmission of intelligence. This supports findings of Brown and her colleagues (2009) for a sample of somewhat younger children in the United Kingdom. They rule out the possibility that the intergenerational effect of parents' test scores occurs through their impact on parents' income or educational attainment.

Estimates of the link between parental schooling and children's non-cognitive outcomes are displayed in table 16.3 (adolescent children) and table 16.4 (young adult children). As shown in panel A (without parental personality traits) in both tables, parents' higher education reduces both adolescent and adult children's external locus of control. For adolescent children, having parents with average education does not seem to matter for skill formation compared with having less-educated parents, whereas young adult children whose parents have an average education score higher on openness. Young adult children with highly educated parents are more extroverted, but rate themselves, like those whose parents have

Table 16.3   Parental Education and Noncognitive Skills of Adolescent Children

	Internal LOC	External LOC	Openness	Conscientiousness	Extraversion	Agreeableness	Neuroticism
A.							
Medium-educated parents	-0.185	-0.0733	-0.049	0.014	-0.203	0.084	0.145
	(0.126)	(0.127)	(0.128)	(0.128)	(0.127)	(0.128)	(0.128)
Highly educated parents	0.007	-0.420***	0.158	-0.048	-0.130	0.082	0.018
	(0.128)	(0.130)	(0.130)	(0.130)	(0.129)	(0.131)	(0.130)
Constant	0.115	0.217*	-0.012	0.023	0.181	-0.078	-0.093
	(0.120)	(0.122)	(0.122)	(0.122)	(0.121)	(0.123)	(0.122)
Adjusted R^2	0.008	0.028	0.008	0.001	0.001	0.001	0.003
B.							
Medium-educated parents	-0.226*	0.060	-0.121	-0.021	-0.238*	0.057	0.151
	(0.124)	(0.123)	(0.126)	(0.126)	(0.125)	(0.126)	(0.126)
Highly educated parents	-0.048	-0.157	0.036	-0.056	-0.164	0.057	0.066
	(0.127)	(0.127)	(0.129)	(0.128)	(0.127)	(0.128)	(0.129)
Test score parents	0.131***	0.217***	0.173***	0.157***	0.168***	0.185***	0.144***
	(0.021)	(0.021)	(0.023)	(0.023)	(0.024)	(0.023)	(0.024)
Constant	0.156	0.025	0.074	0.040	0.207*	-0.075	-0.113
	(0.119)	(0.119)	(0.120)	(0.120)	(0.119)	(0.120)	(0.121)
Adjusted R^2	0.036	0.101	0.048	0.032	0.035	0.044	0.029
Observations	1184	1184	1184	1184	1184	1184	1184

Source: Author's calculations based on SOEP version 26, years 2005 to 2008 (SOEP 2010).
Notes: Dependent variable: age-standardized scores of the child's skill measure.
"Test score parents" refers to the average of parents' age-standardized test scores when test scores for both parents are available.
Reference group: low-educated parent.

Table 16.4 Parental Education and Noncognitive Skills of Young Adult Children

	Internal LOC	External LOC	Openness	Conscientiousness	Extraversion	Agreeableness	Neuroticism
A.							
Medium-educated parents	-0.267**	-0.072	0.281**	0.200	0.171	-0.017	-0.036
	(0.129)	(0.128)	(0.132)	(0.132)	(0.134)	(0.133)	(0.132)
Highly educated parents	-0.274**	-0.238*	0.422***	0.084	0.231*	-0.062	-0.048
	(0.130)	(0.129)	(0.133)	(0.133)	(0.134)	(0.133)	(0.133)
Constant	0.263**	0.105	-0.317**	-0.166	-0.189	0.033	0.026
	(0.126)	(0.125)	(0.129)	(0.129)	(0.130)	(0.129)	(0.129)
Adjusted R^2	0.001	0.007	0.007	0.003	0.001	0.001	0.001
B.							
Medium-educated parents	-0.262**	0.051	0.197	0.196	0.180	-0.012	-0.083
	(0.124)	(0.125)	(0.127)	(0.127)	(0.131)	(0.128)	(0.129)
Highly educated parents	-0.279**	-0.050	0.254**	0.122	0.236*	-0.056	-0.054
	(0.124)	(0.126)	(0.128)	(0.128)	(0.132)	(0.129)	(0.129)
Test score parents	0.236***	0.208***	0.233***	0.224***	0.188***	0.220***	0.204***
	(0.017)	(0.017)	(0.018)	(0.018)	(0.019)	(0.017)	(0.018)
Constant	0.257**	-0.043	-0.196	-0.187	-0.209	0.012	0.058
	(0.121)	(0.122)	(0.124)	(0.124)	(0.128)	(0.125)	(0.125)
Adjusted R^2	0.085	0.070	0.080	0.070	0.041	0.067	0.053
Observations	2228	2228	2228	2228	2228	2228	2228

Source: Author's calculations based on SOEP version 26, years 2006 to 2008 (SOEP 2010).
Notes: Dependent variable: age-standardized scores of the child's skill measure.
"Test score parents" refers to the average of parents' age-standardized test scores when test scores for both parents are available.
Reference group: low-educated parents.
Standard errors in parentheses.
*** $p < 0.01$, ** $p < 0.05$, * $p < 0.1$

an average education, as having a lower internal locus of control than those from a lower-class background.

The lower panels in tables 16.3 and 16.4 (panel B) include parental personality traits, and show that parental education is still significantly related to some of the child's noncognitive skills. Children with educated parents have a lower internal locus of control, independent of their age group, whereas the stage of the life course seems to matter for extraversion. Adolescents with a middle-class background are less extroverted than their counterparts with a higher or lower educational background (table 16.3), whereas older children are more extroverted if they have highly educated parents (table 16.4). Despite the inclusion of parental personality traits, young adults from highly educated families are still significantly more open. The most remarkable finding is, however, that, compared with the raw regressions in table 16.1, the effects that parental noncognitive skills exert on the traits of their children is virtually identical when controlling for parental education. With the exception of external locus of control of young adults, the transmission effects are of the same size, or even slightly higher, when educational background is included. This is in line with findings of Duncan and his colleagues (2005), who point out that the intergenerational correlations of noncognitive skills are robust to the inclusion of family income. Thus, for both adolescents and young adults, parental schooling plays no role as mediator in the intergenerational transmission of personal traits.

Overall, the socioeconomic status of the family, as measured by parental education, does not seem to play a mediating role in the intergenerational transmission of intelligence and personality traits.

Cross-National Comparisons

The intergenerational transmission effects of cognitive and noncognitive skills revealed above can be contrasted with findings from previous studies on countries with different institutional frameworks (table 16.5). First, this chapter looks at comparisons of intergenerational IQ transmissions. To do this, the results for the father-son pairs are used to compare the findings directly with the recent studies on Norway (Black, Devereux, and Salvanes 2009) and Sweden (Björklund, Eriksson, and Jäntti 2010), which both use general intelligence measures of cognitive skills. In both Scandinavian studies, a 1-point increase in the father's ability is associated with an increase in the son's ability of about one-third.[15] The IQ transmission from fathers to adolescent sons revealed for Germany is only 0.20 for general intelligence and, therefore, considerably smaller than for Norway and Sweden. However, adolescents are slightly younger than the sons in the Scandinavian samples. In addition, as explained, the intergenerational correlations of cognitive skills may be understated for the sample of

Table 16.5   Cross-National Comparison of Intergenerational Skill Transmission, Correlation Coefficients

	Germany		Norway	Sweden	United States	United Kingdom
	Adolescent Children	Young Adult Children	Young Adult Children	Young Adult Children	Young-Adolescent Children	Young-Adolescent Children
General intelligence						
Father-son	0.20	0.42	0.38	0.35	—	—
Parent-child	0.24	—	—	—	0.31	—
Crystallized intelligence						
Mother-daughter	0.19 (0.09)	—	—	—	0.22–0.24	—
Mother-son	0.19 (0.09)	—	—	—	0.15–0.20	—
Parent-child	0.24	—	—	—	—	0.08–0.25
Personality traits						
Mother-daughter	0.14–0.32	—	—	—	0.07–0.10	—
Mother-son	0.13–0.22	—	—	—	insign.	—
Locus of control						
Mother-daughter	0.14 (internal) 0.32 (external)	—	—	—	0.07 (mastery)	—
Mother-son	0.14 (internal) 0.22 (external)	—	—	—	insign.	—

Sources: [Germany] Author's calculations based on data from SOEP (2010); Author's compilation of data from [Norway] Black, Devereux, and Salvanes (2009), [Sweden] Björklund, Eriksson, and Jäntti (2010), [United States] Agee and Crocker (2002), Mayer et al. (2004), Duncan et al. (2005), and [United Kingdom] Brown, McIntosh, and Taylor (2009).

adolescents as children, and their parents do not participate in the same intelligence test. Thus, the IQ correlations between parents and their young adult children, who participate in exactly the same ultra-short IQ tests are preferable. The estimates for the group of young adults show a coefficient of 0.42 for general intelligence, and, therefore, the transmission effect for Germany is comparable to the Nordic countries.[16] This may be somewhat surprising as the intergenerational income elasticity in Germany is higher than in Norway and Sweden (Björklund and Jäntti 2009). Thus, intergenerational correlations in cognitive skills do not seem to account for the discrepancy in social mobility between Germany and Scandinavian countries.

Intergenerational correlations of cognitive skills revealed for adolescent children seem to be of a similar size to the United States. The transmission effects reported by Mayer et al. (2004) and Duncan et al. (2005) based on reading and mathematical skills are slightly below one-quarter for pairs of mothers and daughters, and somewhat lower for mother-son pairs. Estimates from, so far, unreported regressions for the German sample of adolescent children, which disregard effects of the father, show similar findings for crystallized intelligence. In contrast, Agee and Crocker (2002) use full-scale intelligence tests and find a 1-point increase in general parental IQ to be associated with an increase in their child's IQ of almost one-third. This transmission effect is higher than the parent-child correlation for adolescent children in Germany. However, direct comparisons are difficult, because the U.S. study is based on a sample of young children of about six years old.

Similarly, Brown and her colleagues (2009) use a sample of younger children with an average age of nine years to analyze the intergenerational transmission of reading and mathematical skills in the United Kingdom. They report transmission effects of 0.25 for reading performance and 0.08 for numeracy skills, both of which correspond to crystallized intelligence in the current study. Thus, the corresponding transmission effect for the German sample of adolescent children (0.24) is presumably higher than the average of the two skill types found for the United Kingdom. However, their measures of cognitive skills clearly differ from those used in the current study for Germany.

With respect to noncognitive skills, the results for the sample of adolescent children are slightly higher than those found in psychological studies (Loehlin 2005) and roughly compare to the studies reviewed by Osborne Groves (2005). Intergenerational correlations of noncognitive skills revealed for the United States seem to be considerably smaller than those found for Germany. Duncan et al. (2005) report coefficients of the maternal transmission effect of between 0.07 and 0.10 for daughters' personality traits and mostly statistically insignificant coefficients for sons. In contrast, additional regressions for the German adolescent sample, in which father's noncognitive skills are excluded, reveal effects of between 0.14 and 0.32 for daughters and 0.13 and 0.22 for sons. All mother-child correlations are, therefore, stronger than those found for the United States. However, Duncan et al. (2005) use different measures of personality traits: self-esteem, depression, shyness, and the Pearlin mastery scale. Only the latter can be used for direct comparison with the German data, as the mastery scale roughly corresponds to the locus of control measure. Whereas mastery is transmitted at a rate of only 0.07 from mothers to daughters in the United States (and is insignificant for sons), the mother-daughter correlation of internal locus of control is 0.14 (sons: 0.14), and even 0.32 (sons: 0.22) for external locus of control in Germany, and, despite the relatively small sample sizes, always highly statistically significant.

Conclusion and Policy Implications

This chapter provided estimates of intergenerational transmissions of cognitive and noncognitive skills from parents to their children during adolescence and young adulthood using representative data from the German SOEP. Although for both age groups, intelligence and personal traits were found to be transmitted from parents to their children, discrepancies with respect to the age group and the type of skill are large. The intergenerational transmission effect was found to be relatively small for adolescent children, with correlations between 0.12 and 0.24, whereas the parent-child correlation in the sample of adult children was between 0.19 and 0.27 for noncognitive skills, and up to 0.56 for cognitive skills.

Thus it seems that the skill gradient increases with the age of the child. One explanation may be that adolescent children who are largely still in school are strongly influenced by their teachers and peers but less by their parents. Another explanation could be that institutions in Germany enhance skill inequalities by placing students with a lower skill level on lower academic tracks.[17] However, in the absence of cross-national comparisons for both age groups, it is difficult to judge whether the German education system or labor market institutions play any role in determining this increase in the gradient.

Cognitive skills were shown to increase with parental education, and these differences hold regardless of the school type. However, when parents' educational degrees are included in the regressions, the skill transmission effects are virtually unchanged. This suggests that the socioeconomic status of the family does not play a mediating role in the intergenerational transmission of intelligence and personality traits. Similarly, the effect of parental IQ and personality on children's skills barely changes when other control variables for family background and childhood environment are included. However, some of the individual and family characteristics do seem to play a role in children's skill formation.

In particular, good health seems to be important, whereas skills seem to suffer if a child is raised by a single parent.

In a cross-country comparison, intergenerational correlations of cognitive skills in Germany are roughly the same or slightly stronger than those found by previous studies for other countries with different institutional settings. Thus, characteristics of the German education system, such as early school tracking, do not seem to affect the strength of the intergenerational link of intelligence. It is also quite unlikely that intergenerational correlations of cognitive skills can account for the greater inequality persistence in Germany relative to the Scandinavian countries. This conclusion is supported by the finding that Germany has similar, or even higher, transmission effects than in the United States and the United Kingdom which both have a lower education level and income mobility than Germany.

Moreover, noncognitive skills seem to be transmitted across generations more strongly in Germany than in the United States. One tentative explanation may be a lower prevalence of child care for children under the age of three and lower childhood education in Germany, which may strengthen the link between parental personality traits and children's skills, because these are known to be largely shaped in early childhood. Furthermore, the intergenerational correlation of noncognitive skills may be stronger in countries with early school tracking, such as Germany, as initial skill differences between students with different family backgrounds may be reinforced. However, family background does not play a different role in the intergenerational skill transmission in Germany and the comparison countries analyzed by previous studies. On the whole, neither cognitive nor noncognitive skill transmission seems to be able to explain cross-country differences in socioeconomic mobility.

This study points to intergenerational persistence in cognitive and noncognitive disadvantage in Germany, which is similar in size to the countries with higher social mobility, and similar or even stronger to the countries with lower social mobility. One explanation that may reconcile these findings could be that the transmission of skills feeds differently into the process of intergenerational education or income transmission in the different countries. This underlines the necessity to examine the link between skill transmission, educational mobility, and earnings persistence in Germany. This will only be possible, however, when future waves of the SOEP data become available, allowing us to measure children's earnings at reasonable points in their life cycle. Thus, the full answer to the question as to how socioeconomic status is transmitted across generations in Germany is left for future research.

Overall, this study suggests that noncognitive skills are not as strongly transmitted as cognitive skills, but are at least as important for economic success, as empirical evidence has shown. Thus, there seems to be more room for external (nonparental) influences in the formation of personal traits. Therefore, it should be more promising for policymakers to focus on shaping children's noncognitive skills to promote intergenerational mobility. This could be achieved by focusing on the provision of high-quality child care to children from disadvantaged families, by teaching and developing noncognitive skills in class, and by providing educational support through nurseries and teachers for families with low socioeconomic backgrounds.

I gratefully acknowledge funding from the Russell Sage Foundation. I would like to thank the editors—in particular, John Ermisch—and Paul Gregg, Thomas Siedler, and participants of the CRITA meeting in New York and London for their helpful comments. My thanks also go to Antje Brümmerstädt for her excellent research assistance and to Joachim R. Frick, who initiated this project.

Notes

1. The term *noncognitive skills* is used here to distinguish these skills from typical intelligence measures. However, this does not mean that personal traits do not have any cognitive content.

2. Unfortunately, the impact of these mediating variables on children's economic outcomes cannot be investigated with the available data set because most of the children are still too young for us to observe final educational qualifications and earnings at reasonable points in time of their life cycle.

3. The advantage of the latter is that, by measuring test scores at adult age, one can observe respondents with completed (secondary) school qualifications and, thus, reduce feedback effects from cognitive and noncognitive skills on education. Furthermore, personality traits are considered as far more stable at adult age than during childhood or adolescence (Costa and McCrae 1994).

4. Due to limited space, the analysis in this chapter is restricted to overall transmission and father-son transmission effects (for differential effects of fathers and mothers on their sons and daughters, see Anger and Heineck 2010a).

5. The online appendix can be found at: http://www.russellsage.org/Ermisch_et_al_OnlineAppendix.pdf.

6. Frieder Lang and his colleagues (2007) carry out reliability analyses and find test–retest coefficients of 0.7 for both the word fluency test and the symbol correspondence test.

7. This approach has also been used in the intergenerational mobility literature to account for measurement error (for example, Zimmerman 1992). Using average test scores is expected to reduce the error-in-variable bias by diminishing the random component of measured test scores. Furthermore,

average test scores could be interpreted as an extract of a general ability type, which captures both coding speed and verbal fluency.

8. The severe reduction in sample size raises the issue of the representativeness of the data, in that there might be selection problems with respect to intergenerational associations of interest. However, despite the restrictions on the sample, selection does not seem to be a major problem for the interpretation of the results (see Anger and Heineck 2010a).

9. Whereas Costa and McCrae (1994) suggest that personality traits are stable from age thirty, recent research by Sanjay Srivastava and his colleagues (2003) show that an individual's personality traits may also be affected in early and middle adulthood.

10. This explanation is supported by unreported regressions for a very small sample of young adults (age twenty and younger), which reveal intergenerational correlations of similar results to older adults (age twenty-nine and younger).

11. Although the main direction of intergenerational transmission channels is presumably from parents to their children, there is evidence from the psychology literature that children influence their parents' values and behavior (for example, Ge et al. 1996). Because the SOEP provides contemporaneous measures and not parental skill measures when parents were young, the influence from children to their parents cannot be ruled out in this study.

12. Results are available from the author on request.

13. The association between parental education and children's skills are analyzed separately.

14. There is also a gradient in parents' test scores with respect to their own education. Results are available from the author on request.

15. These effects compare to the intergenerational education transmission for Sweden of 0.38 and income transmission effect of 0.30 reported in chapter 3, this volume.

16. The restriction of the German sample to younger adults in order to reach a sample average age closer to the ones for Norway and Sweden (eighteen) slightly reduces the coefficients and precision of the estimates and generates transmission effects of identical size to those in the Scandinavian countries.

17. The relevant distributional policy at this stage of young adulthood includes means-tested student loans, and until recently, only marginal financial contributions for tertiary education. The funding of universities and students has, nevertheless, been shown to benefit the families with a high socioeconomic background more.

References

Agee, Mark D., and Thomas D. Crocker. 2002. "Parents' Discount Rate and the Intergenerational Transmission of Cognitive Skills." *Economica* 69(273): 143–54.

Anger, Silke, and Guido Heineck. 2010a. "Do Smart Parents Raise Smart Children? The Intergenerational Transmission of Cognitive Abilities." *Journal of Population Economics* 23(3): 1105–132.

————. 2010b. "Cognitive Abilities and Earnings: First Evidence for Germany." *Applied Economics Letters* 17(7): 699–702.

Björklund, Anders, Karin Hederos Eriksson, and Markus Jäntti. 2010. "IQ and Family Background: Are Associations Strong or Weak?" *The B.E. Journal of Economic Analysis & Policy* 10(1): Article 2. Available at: http://www.bepress.com/bejeap/vol10/iss1/art2 (accessed December 28, 2011).

Björklund, Anders M., and Markus Jäntti. 2009. "Intergenerational Income Mobility and the Role of Family Background." In *The Oxford Handbook of Economic Inequality,* edited by Wiemer Salverda, Brian Nolan, and Timothy M. Smeeding. Oxford: Oxford University Press.

Björklund, Anders, Markus Jäntti, and Gary Solon. 2007. "Nature and Nurture in the Intergenerational Transmission of Socioeconomic Status: Evidence from Swedish Children and Their Biological and Rearing Parents." *The B.E. Journal of Economic Analysis & Policy* 7(2): Article 4. Available at: http://www.bepress.com/bejeap/vol7/iss2/art4 (accessed December 28, 2011).

Black, Sandra E., and Paul J. Devereux. 2011. "Recent Developments in Intergenerational Mobility." In *Handbook of Labor Economics*, vol. 4B, edited by Orley Ashenfelter and David Card. Amsterdam: Elsevier.

Black, Sandra E., Paul J. Devereux, and Kjell G. Salvanes. 2009. "Like Father, Like Son? A Note on the Intergenerational Transmission of IQ Scores." *Economics Letters* 105(1): 138–40.

Blanden, Jo, Paul Gregg, and Lindsey Macmillan. 2007. "Accounting for Intergenerational Income Persistence: Noncognitive Skills, Ability and Education." *Economic Journal* 117(519): C43–C60.

Bouchard, Thomas J., and Matthew McGue. 1981. "Familial Studies of Intelligence: A Review." *Science* 212(4498): 1055–59.

Bowles, Samuel, and Herbert Gintis. 2002. "The Inheritance of Inequality." *Journal of Economic Perspectives* 16(1): 3–30.

Brown, Sarah, Steven McIntosh, and Karl B. Taylor. 2009. "Following in Your Parents' Footsteps? Empirical Analysis of Matched Parent-Offspring Test Scores." *IZA discussion paper 3986.* Bonn: Institute for the Study of Labor.

Cameron, Stephen V., and James J. Heckman. 1993. "Nonequivalence of High School Equivalents." *Journal of Labor Economics* 11(1): 1–47.

Case, Anne, and Lawrence F. Katz. 1991. "The Company You Keep: The Effects of Family and Neighborhood on Disadvantaged Youth." *NBER* working paper 3705. Cambridge, Mass.: National Bureau of Economic Research.

Cattell, Raymond B. 1987. "Intelligence: Its Structure, Growth, and Action." New York: Elsevier Science.

Costa, Paul T., Jr., and Robert R. McCrae. 1994. "Set Like Plaster: Evidence for the Stability of Adult Personality." In *Can Personality Change?* edited by Todd F. Heatherton and Joel L. Weinberger. Washington, D.C.: American Psychological Association.

Couch, Kenneth A., and Thomas A. Dunn. 1997. "Intergenerational Correlations in Labor Market Status: A Comparison of the United States and Germany." *Journal of Human Resources* 32(1): 210–32.

Cunha, Flavio, and James J. Heckman. 2007. "The Technology of Skill Formation." *American Economic Review* 97(1): 31–47.

Dehne, Max, and Jürgen Schupp. 2007. "Persönlichkeitsmerkmale im Soziooekonomischen Panel (SOEP)—Konzept, Umsetzung und empirische Eigenschaften." *DIW* research notes 26. Berlin: German Institute for Economic Research.

Devlin, Bernie, Michael Daniels, and Kathryn Roeder. 1997. "The Heritability of IQ." *Nature* 388(6641): 468–71.

Duncan, Greg, Ariel Kalil, Susan E. Mayer, Robin Tepper, and Monique R. Payne. 2005. "The Apple Does Not Fall Far from the Tree." In *Unequal Chances: Family Background and Economic Success*, edited by Samuel Bowles, Herbert Gintis, and Melissa Osborne Groves. New York: Russell Sage Foundation / Princeton, N.J.: Princeton University Press.

Ermisch, John. 2008. "Origins of Social Immobility and Inequality: Parenting and Early Child Development." *National Institute Economic Review* 205(1): 62–71.

Ge, Xiaojia, Rand D. Conger, Remi J. Cadoret, Jenae M. Neiderhiser, William Yates, Edward Troughton, and Mark A. Stewart. 1996. "The Developmental Interface Between Nature and Nurture: A Mutual Influence Model of Child Antisocial Behavior and Parent Behaviors." *Developmental Psychology* 32(4): 574–89.

Hanushek, Erik A., and Ludger Wößmann. 2008. "The Role of Cognitive Skills in Economic Development." *Journal of Economic Literature* 46(3): 607–68.

Heckman, James J., and Edward Vytlacil. 2001. "Identifying the Role of Cognitive Ability in Explaining the Level of and Change in the Return to Schooling." *Review of Economics and Statistics* 83(1): 1–12.

Heckman, James J., Jora Stixrud, and Sergio Urzua. 2006. "The Effects of Cognitive and Noncognitive Abilities on Labor Market Outcomes and Social Behavior." *Journal of Labor Economics* 24(3): 411–82.

Heineck, Guido, and Silke Anger. 2010. "The Returns to Cognitive Abilities and Personality Traits in Germany." *Labour Economics* 17(3): 535–46.

Hertz, Thomas, Tamara Jayasundera, Patrizio Piraino, Sibel Selcuk, Nicole Smith, and Alina Verashchagina. 2007. "The Inheritance of Educational Inequality: International Comparisons and Fifty-Year Trends." *The B.E. Journal of Economic Analysis & Policy* 7(2): Article 10. Available at: http://www.bepress.com/bejeap/vol7/iss2/art10 (accessed December 29, 2011).

Lang, Frieder R., David Weiss, Andreas Stocker, and Bernhard von Rosenbladt. 2007. "Assessing Cognitive Capacities in Computer-Assisted Survey Research: Two Ultra-Short Tests of Intellectual Ability in the German Socio-Economic Panel." *Schmollers Jahrbuch* 127(1): 183–92.

Loehlin, John C. 2005. "Resemblance in Personality and Attitudes Between Parents and their Children. Genetic and Environmental Contributions." In *Unequal Chances*, edited by Samuel Bowles, Herbert Gintis, and Melissa Osborne Groves. Princeton, N.J.: Princeton University Press.

Mayer, Susan E., Greg J. Duncan, and Ariel Kalil. 2004. "Like Mother, Like Daughter? SES and the Intergenerational Correlation of Traits, Behaviors and

Attitudes." *Harris School of Public Policy Studies* working paper 0415. Chicago: University of Chicago.

McCrae, Robert R., and Paul T. Costa Jr. 1999. "A Five-Factor Theory of Personality." In *Handbook of Personality: Theory and Research,* edited by Lawrence A. Pervin and John P. Oliver. New York: Guilford.

Mulligan, Casey B., 1999. "Galton vs. Human Capital Approaches to Inheritance." *Journal of Political Economy* 107(6): 184–224.

Osborne Groves, Melissa. 2005. "How Important Is Your Personality? Labor Market Returns to Personality for Women in the U.S. and U.K." *Journal of Economic Psychology* 26(2005): 827–41.

Plomin, Robert, John C. DeFries, Gerald McClearn, and Peter McGuffin. 2000. *Behavioral Genetics,* 4th ed. New York: W. H. Freeman.

SOEP. 2010. *Socio-Economic Panel Study, Version 26, Data for Years 1984–2009.* Berlin: German Institute for Economic Research (DIW Berlin). Available at: http://www.diw.de/en/soep/ (accessed December 28, 2011).

Solga, Heike, Elsbeth Stern, Bernhard von Rosenbladt, Jürgen Schupp, and Gert G. Wagner. 2005. "The Measurement and Importance of General Reasoning Potentials in Schools and Labor Markets: Pre-Test Report." *DIW* research notes 10. Berlin: German Institute for Economic Research.

Solon, Gary. 1999. "Intergenerational Mobility in the Labor Market." In *Handbook of Labor Economics,* vol. 3, edited by Orley C. Ashenfelter, and David Card. Amsterdam: Elsevier Science.

Srivastava, Sanjay, John O. Oliver, Samuel D. Gosling, and Jeff Potter. 2003. "Development of Personality in Early and Middle Adulthood: Set Like Plaster or Persistent Change?" *Journal of Personality and Social Psychology* 85(5): 1041 53.

Vogel, Thorsten. 2006. "Reassessing Intergenerational Mobility in Germany and the United States: The Impact of Differences in Lifecycle Earnings Patterns." *SFB* 649 discussion paper 2006-055. Berlin: Humboldt University.

Wagner, Gert G., Joachim R. Frick, and Jürgen Schupp. 2007. "The German Socio-Economic Panel Study (SOEP). Scope, Evolution and Enhancements." *Schmollers Jahrbuch* 127(1): 139–69.

Zimmerman, David J. 1992. "Regression Toward Mediocrity in Economic Stature." *American Economic Review* 82(3): 409–29.

Chapter 17

Parental Education Gradients in Sweden

ANDERS BJÖRKLUND, MARKUS JÄNTTI,

AND MARTIN NYBOM

R ESEARCH INTO the intergenerational persistence of economic advantage that has emerged since the early 1990s has revealed several striking cross-national differences. Whether measured in earnings or income, the United States has, to the initial surprise of many observers, turned out to have the strongest intergenerational transmission of economic position among developed countries, whereas the Nordic countries have turned out to be relatively high-mobility countries (for example, Björklund and Jäntti 2009). Estimates for the United Kingdom are more mixed, but generally reveal lower mobility than in the Nordic countries (for alternative cross-national surveys of intergenerational income and earnings estimates, see Solon 2002; Corak 2006; Jäntti et al. 2006; Björklund and Jäntti 2009; Blanden, in press).

The rich tradition of comparative mobility research in sociology has examined mobility in occupation and in education across countries (see, for example, Erikson and Goldthorpe 1992; Breen 2004). The stylized findings in this literature is that Sweden tends to have a fair amount of mobility compared to other nations, including the United Kingdom Recently, Thomas Hertz and his colleagues (2007) examined the intergenerational association of educational achievement in a large number of countries and many time periods, and reported results that are more or less consistent with those noted above for earnings and income.

In this study, we are primarily interested in studying how offspring adult outcomes, measured in terms of both final education and earnings, vary with parental education, and in particular, if the patterns of association are different in Sweden and the United Kingdom and what those differences might reveal about processes of intergenerational transmission. What we want to examine is whether the differences in the socioeconomic gradient we observe in adulthood emerge early in life. Our contribution is to try to uncover how and at what stage differences in the parent-child socioeconomic gradient between Sweden and the United Kingdom come about. We do so by examining how important parental education is to different outcomes, measured in different phases of the offspring's life. Do these differentials show up very early in life, so that parental background matters more for early childhood characteristics such as health and school performance in one country? Or do the country differences emerge mainly when the offspring generation reaches the labor market?

For the United Kingdom and Sweden, the countries in this study, the regression coefficients in the Hertz et al. study (2007) for the child's educational outcome on parental years of schooling, averaged across time and cohorts, are 0.71 and 0.58, respectively, whereas the correlation coefficients are 0.31 and 0.40. Thus, whether the United Kingdom is considered to have more or less educational persistence than Sweden depends on whether the distributions are standardized. Rather than work with years of education, we rely on a discrete classification of educational achievement that allows for rich patterns of association between the child outcome and parental education.

We use the British Birth Cohort Study of children born in 1970 and Swedish register data of children born in 1973 to explore the gradient in parental education for birth weight, grades at the end of compulsory school at age sixteen, height at ages sixteen through eighteen, final educational attainment, and long-term income during adulthood.[1] We begin our analysis with the last, that is, by presenting comparable estimates of the socioeconomic gradient in offspring adult income for the two countries. We then explore whether these differentials show up earlier in the life cycle measured in terms of birth weight, height, school performance, and in final educational attainment, or only when the offspring reaches the labor market.

Literature Review

In this section, we briefly review recent research on how the child outcomes we are interested in are related to parental socioeconomic background

Birth Weight

A large recent literature has shown that birth weight in general, and low birth weight in particular, is related to parental socioeconomic status (Currie 2009). There are several reasons to expect such an association. The quality of the nutritional intake during pregnancy is one obvious candidate explanation. Higher socioeconomic parents may also be better informed about health-related hazards that affect the growth of the fetus. Such mechanisms have come to be known as the "fetal origin hypothesis" (Barker 1995). In addition, one can expect that biological mechanisms (genetic inheritance) cause a relationship between parental socioeconomic status and birth weight. The country's health-care system might very well have an impact on how strong these mechanisms are. A more compensatory system for care of pregnant mothers, for example, may attenuate both the nature and nurture aspect of these relationships.

Birth weight, in turn, has been shown to predict several later and adult outcomes. The literature Currie surveyed is full of examples showing that birth weight predicts outcomes related to health, including mortality, but also cognitive and noncognitive (or socioemotional) skills and thus also labor market performance. These relationships may show up because of the specific health problems that are related to low birth weight. However, it is also possible that low birth weight has direct effects on the acquisition of skills. Parents' reactions to the conditions related to the underlying health problems are also likely to affect the impact of early health problems on subsequent acquisition of skills. The same applies to the systems of health care and schooling in the country.

Much of the recent literature focuses on the issue of whether the associations between parental socioeconomic status and birth weight and between birth weight and adult outcomes are causal. For our purposes, the causality of these associations is not a major concern. We treat this variable as an indicator of several traits that are related to parental socioeconomic status and own performance later in life. Our research question is cross-national—we ask whether parental socioeconomic status, as measured by their education, is more important for this set of traits in one country than in another, and whether this set of traits is a stronger predictor of adult outcomes in one country than another.

Height During Adolescence

As explained, we have access to data on height measured at ages sixteen, eighteen, and thirty. Obviously, these height measures reflect the cumulative growth up to these ages. This means that the same combined genetic and environmental factors contributing to birth weight also affect our height measures. But our height measures are also sensitive to a number of environmental conditions experienced during childhood. In their thorough survey of height determinants, Anne Case and Christina Paxson (2008) emphasize that the period from birth to age three is considered as the postnatal period that is most critical to height. Nutritional needs are greatest at this point in life, as is sensitivity to infections of different types. Such factors are, of course, likely to be related to family background, and the magnitude of those associations may differ across countries.

Case and Paxson (2008) also emphasize that conditions during childhood affect the timing of children's growth. The timing of the typical pubertal growth spurt has been found to be sensitive to the child's health conditions and therefore also to parental background. Case and Paxson demonstrate that the growth spurt comes earlier for children with a favorable socioeconomic background. Thus, at some stages during adolescence, the pubertal growth spurt tends to magnify associations between height and parental socioeconomic status. Although we compare height at age sixteen for the United Kingdom and age eighteen for Sweden—the first ages at which we have data—sensitivity analysis using height at age thirty for the United Kingdom suggests that this does not affect our results.

The bivariate correlation between height and earnings is quite strong. Case and Paxson (2008) report that the U.S. PSID data reveal that the difference of four inches in men's height between the 25th and the 75th percentiles is associated with an expected earnings differential of 9.2 percent. Furthermore, they observe this association throughout the whole height distribution. Petter Lundborg and his colleagues (2009), using the same Swedish data source as we do, find somewhat weaker bivariate associations.

Case and Paxson (2008) and Lundborg, Nystedt, and Rooth (2009) have contributed to an interesting recent literature on the mechanisms behind the bivariate height-earnings association. Indeed, the candidate mechanisms include such individual and external factors as self-esteem, social dominance, and discrimination. It might also be that height captures omitted variables such as cognitive and noncognitive skills and physical strength. Case and Paxson find, using U.S. and U.K. data, that most of the height-earnings association is eliminated when cognitive skills are controlled for, whereas Lundborg, Nystedt, and Rooth find that physical strength is a more important underlying factor. Just as for birth weight, it is not critical for our purposes whether height is important per se or because it is an indicator of several underlying productivity traits.

Grades at Age Sixteen, or at the End of Compulsory School

Grades reflect school performance at the end of compulsory school before major choices concerning further education, such as its level, fields, or subjects are made. The literature on school success and parental background is vast, suggesting that high-SES parents are in a position to make better choices for their children (see, for example, Betts and Morell 1999). We would expect to see a reasonably steep parental SES background gradient in this variable in both countries.

Final Education Around Age Thirty-Two

From the perspective of intergenerational mobility, it is important to stress that final education captures performance in school as measured by our grade variable and the set of choices to pursue further education after the completion of compulsory schooling. A large literature in sociology has shown that family background has a strong influence on both school performance (primary social origin effects) and school choices (secondary social origin effects) (see, for example, Erikson et al. 2005). But we should stress that this variable reflects both performance and choices (primary and secondary effects in sociology).

Data

Let us now turn to the data, which were gathered from the British Cohort Study and various sources compiled by Statistics Sweden.

Sources and Sample Restrictions

The British Cohort Study surveyed all children born in England, Scotland, and Wales in one particular week in April 1970. The BCS is a very rich data set with surveys performed right after birth with repeat surveys at ages five, ten, sixteen, twenty-six, thirty, and thirty-four. The first sweep covered the births and families of just under 17,200 babies. In the two last sweeps, the number of observations fell to 11,200 (in 2000) and 9,600 (in 2004). With each sweep, the scope of enquiry has broadened from a mainly medical focus at birth, to encompass physical and educational development during the childhood years, and most recently on economic and labor market outcomes as adults.

For Sweden, we have access to register data from various sources, which have been merged by Statistics Sweden using the country's unique personal identifier. For intergenerational research purposes this is a very flexible data source. In this study, we use the available information to mimic the U.K. data as closely as possible. We restrict our sample to those born in Sweden in 1973, the first cohort for which birth-weight data on newborns in Sweden are available. The data are based on a 35 percent random sample of the population from Statistics Sweden's multigenerational register. The multigenerational register also identifies the biological parents of the children, and we add these parents to our data set. In the next step, we merge this data set of children and parents with a number of other data sets to obtain the variables we are most interested in studying.

We use the Swedish censuses from 1975, 1980, and 1985 to identify the child's rearing parents in the fall of these years. We obtain birth weight information from the National Board of Health and Welfare (Socialstyrelsen). Statistics Sweden's register of graduation from compulsory school at age sixteen (Årskurs-9 registret) provides data on grades for the whole population. We get data on height from the compulsory military-enlistment tests (administered by the National Service Administration in Sweden, Pliktverket); as a consequence, these particular data are only available for men (all other data are available for both men and women). For both parents and offspring, we collect data on education from Statistics Sweden's education register that covers the whole population. Finally, data on income and earnings are collected from Statistics Sweden registers, which in turn stem from compulsory reports from Swedish employers to the tax authorities.

Key Variables

Some key variables in our data are parental education, offspring earnings, birth weight, grades and test scores, height, and final earnings, which we look at in this section.

Parental Education   We apply the International Standard Classification of Education (ISCED) developed by UNESCO to order educational attainment into five hierarchical categories (UNESCO 2006).[2] For the British parental generation, educational data are drawn from the BCS waves in 1980 and 1986, when the parents were, on average, in their early forties. For Sweden, we use the educational register from 1970 and 1990 to measure education, choosing the higher education as our preferred measure of parental education. The sample is conditioned on the offspring's age, that is, there are no age differences in this generation between the countries. For the parents, however, systematic age differences might bias the estimates differentially due to measurement error in, for example, permanent income or final education. To take this into account, we control for parental age in the estimations. As with the data in chapter 2 of this volume, we use the level of education of the more highly educated parent as our measure of parental socioeconomic status.

Offspring Earnings   The BCS includes offspring labor earnings for ages thirty and thirty-four. From the Swedish tax register, we can extract information on labor income (Swedish arbetsinkomst) for the same ages. For the United Kingdom, both income and earnings information refers to weekly data at the time of the interview, whereas the Swedish data include annual measures of income and earnings. Although it does not affect our estimates, we divide Swedish income and earnings by fifty-two to show comparable weekly data in our descriptive tables.

The earnings measures we use are far from ideal, largely because we only have two observations for the offspring. Despite this limitation, a strength of the earnings variables is that they are measured close to ages in which we avoid the problem of a life-cycle bias (see Grawe 2006; Haider and Solon 2006; Böhlmark and Lindquist 2006).

Birth Weight   For the BCS, the birth weight data stem from the initial sweep of data and refer to the hospital's report of the birth weight, measured in grams. For the Swedish data, the birth weight variable is obtained from the hospital reports as obtained through the National Board of Health and Welfare's registers. In both cases, the variables refer to birth weight immediately following birth. In some specifications, we also use as an outcome variable *low birth weight*, defined as having a birth weight of less than 2,500 grams.

Grades and Test Scores   Comparing grades across countries is not unproblematic, to say the least. To include grades on a roughly comparable basis, we transform each grade of selected subjects of every person into a percentile rank, and then measure grades by taking the average percentile rank across all subjects.

For the United Kingdom, we use the grades in the two systems of secondary education qualifications in the United Kingdom—the O-level and the CSE—examinations in the following subjects: English language, English literature, mathematics, science, physics, chemistry, biology, history, geography, French, German, and business studies. Not all students take these qualifications, and many take only a few. If a student has not taken an exam in a subject, we treat that missing grade as being lower still than fail.

We have spliced together the O-levels and CSE in the following way:

O level A

O level B

O level C/CSE 1

O level D/CSE 2

O level E/CSE 3

CSE 4

CSE 5

Fail

Missing

We construct the variable *grade* in the following way. We invert the scale so that higher grades get coded higher. We then assign to each person for each subject listed above the percentile that corresponds to the tabulated percentile rank at the grade received (or failed or missing, as appropriate). We take the average percentile across subjects as the measure of a person's grade.

For Sweden, we use the grade at the end of compulsory schooling (that is, grade nine at age sixteen) in biology, physics, chemistry, technology, geography, history, religion, social studies, and Swedish. Because these subjects are taken by all students, we do not have a substantial missing numbers problem. Next, we tabulate the distribution of grades for each subject and assign to each person the percentile rank of the grade received if the person wrote the exam in the subject. If a person did not, we assign the percentile associated with the fraction missing on that subject. We then take the average of a person's percentile across all subjects as our measure of their grade. This procedure has been used before, for example, by Anders Björklund, Mikael Lindahl, and Krister Sund (2003), who studied the importance of family background in school performance in Sweden across time.

We have experimented with variations of these procedures, and though the exact estimates vary, the qualitative conclusions we reach do not. However, the results with respect to the parental socioeconomic background gradient in grades are likely the least comparable for the simple reason that the schooling institutions in Sweden and the United Kingdom are quite different.

Height   The U.K. data stem from a professional medical examination of the respondents to the BCS. For Sweden, we obtain information on height from data collected at the military enlistment that is compulsory for all Swedish men. Thus we cannot carry out this particular analysis for women. Most men do these tests at age eighteen. Because we measure height at different ages in the two countries, we standardize the variable when we use it as a dependent variable in our regressions.

Final Education   Because educational systems often differ across countries, it is not as straightforward how to use such data in cross-country studies as it is, for example, to use data on income and earnings. As noted earlier, we use the ISCED classification of education collapsed into five categories. The Swedish data come from Statistics Sweden's education register (Utbildningsregistret); the British data are from BCS and are thus self-reported. For the offspring generation, the BCS waves of 2000 and 2004 are used, and thus final education is measured at ages thirty and thirty-four for the U.K. sample. For the offspring in the Swedish sample, we use data on final education from 2003 and 2008, that is, when the subjects were about thirty and thirty-five years old. In both the United Kingdom and Sweden, we use the higher of the two reports of education.

Analysis

We now proceed to compare the gradient of different child outcomes with respect to parental education. We regress the outcome variables of interest—*earnings, birth weight, grades, height,* and *educational attainment*—on parental age and parental education. All regressions are run separately for men and women, and in each case, our interest is centered on the question of whether the gradient in education in the outcome differs between Sweden and the United Kingdom. The full regression results and descriptive statistics for the data in each regression are reported in the online appendix tables 17A.1 to 17A.8.[3]

To establish that our child outcomes are relevant for adult living standards, we first show regression results in tables 17.1 and 17.2 that

Table 17.1   Parental Education, Age, and All Intervening Variables, with Height

		Men-Sweden	Men-United Kingdom	Women-United Kingdom
(Intercept)		4.770	6.198	3.584
		(0.204)	(0.618)	(0.858)
avggrade		0.503	0.570	1.026
		(0.015)	(0.136)	(0.191)
avgparage		0.024	−0.020	0.067
		(0.006)	(0.029)	(0.039)
birthweight		0.000	0.000	−0.000
		(0.000)	(0.000)	(0.000)
avgparage^2/10		−0.003	0.002	−0.008
		(0.001)	(0.003)	(0.005)
ISCEDkid (omitted: 1)	2	0.681	0.224	0.262
		(0.166)	(0.087)	(0.172)
	3	0.785	0.291	0.428
		(0.166)	(0.086)	(0.172)
	4	0.761	0.378	0.548
		(0.166)	(0.096)	(0.180)
	5	0.793	0.515	0.853
		(0.166)	(0.087)	(0.172)
ISCEDpar (omitted: 1)	2	−0.002	0.177	0.117
		(0.012)	(0.071)	(0.099)
	3	0.007	0.011	−0.030
		(0.009)	(0.042)	(0.059)
	4	0.028	0.033	−0.072
		(0.011)	(0.056)	(0.079)
	5	0.032	0.109	0.000
		(0.011)	(0.047)	(0.065)
lowbw		−0.031	−0.027	0.021
		(0.017)	(0.079)	(0.115)
zheight		0.024	0.035	0.065
		(0.003)	(0.017)	(0.022)
N		43620	1255	1371
k		15	15	15
σ		0.524	0.536	0.782
Adjusted R^2		0.0558	0.135	0.161

Source: Authors' calculations based on data from the 1970 British Cohort Study (Centre for Longitudinal Studies, various years) and Statistics Sweden (2010).
Note: Standard errors in parentheses.

Table 17.2   Parental Education, Age and All Intervening Variables, Without Height

		Men-Sweden	Men-United Kingdom	Women-Sweden	Women-United Kingdom
(Intercept)		4.666	6.206	4.466	4.488
		(0.179)	(0.468)	(0.272)	(0.633)
avggrade		0.514	0.506	0.452	0.839
		(0.014)	(0.107)	(0.013)	(0.140)
avgparage		0.030	−0.017	0.031	0.019
		(0.006)	(0.023)	(0.005)	(0.030)
birthweight		0.015	0.049	0.007	0.011
		(0.005)	(0.026)	(0.005)	(0.038)
avgparage^2/10		−0.004	0.002	−0.003	−0.002
		(0.001)	(0.003)	(0.001)	(0.004)
ISCEDkid (omitted: 1)	2	0.575	0.206	0.407	0.215
		(0.137)	(0.060)	(0.246)	(0.112)
	3	0.694	0.289	0.539	0.424
		(0.137)	(0.060)	(0.246)	(0.112)
	4	0.673	0.393	0.480	0.576
		(0.137)	(0.069)	(0.246)	(0.120)
	5	0.708	0.515	0.585	0.853
		(0.137)	(0.061)	(0.246)	(0.112)
ISCEDpar (omitted: 1)	2	0.003	0.116	0.047	0.089
		(0.012)	(0.051)	(0.012)	(0.073)
	3	0.016	0.002	0.040	0.047
		(0.009)	(0.033)	(0.009)	(0.043)
	4	0.034	0.049	0.058	0.007
		(0.011)	(0.044)	(0.010)	(0.059)
	5	0.033	0.102	0.109	0.100
		(0.011)	(0.037)	(0.010)	(0.049)
lowbw		−0.028	0.038	−0.012	−0.003
		(0.016)	(0.064)	(0.014)	(0.084)
N		46925	2226	42938	2365
k		14	14	14	14
σ		0.53	0.56	0.491	0.778
Adjusted R^2		0.0566	0.12	0.0657	0.165

Source: Authors' calculations based on data from the 1970s British Cohort Study (Centre for Longitudinal Studies, various years) and Statistics Sweden (2010). *Note:* Standard error in parentheses.

Figure 17.1   Offspring Earnings on Parental Education

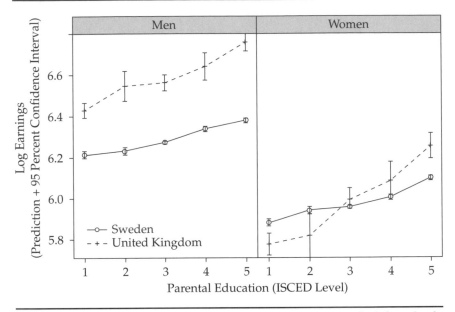

Source: Authors' calculations based on data from the 1970 British Cohort Study (Centre for Longitudinal Studies, various years) and Statistics Sweden (2010). *Note:* Gradient with respect to education level of parent.

regress the offspring's adult earnings on all child outcome variables. All the coefficient estimates, except birth weight, are statistically significant. However, this analysis is not our main object of interest. What we want is to compare the parental education gradient of each of the outcomes across countries.

We report the results graphically in figures 17.1 to 17.6, based on regressions reported in online appendix tables 17A.3 to 17A.8. Each of the figures shows the fitted gradient of the outcome variable with respect to parental education in Sweden and the United Kingdom, separately for men and women, along with the 95 percent confidence intervals of the fit. The graphs show both differences in the level of the outcome variable and the slope, that is, the gradient.

Figure 17.1 shows the gradient in log weekly earnings against parental education. Although the level of this variable is higher for British than Swedish men (left panel), its gradient is clearly greater in the United Kingdom. The null hypothesis that the coefficient vectors are the same is firmly rejected and, with one exception, every move up the parental education levels is steeper in the United Kingdom than in Sweden (the exception being moving from ISCED 2 to 3—high school only

Figure 17.2   Birth Weight on Parental Education

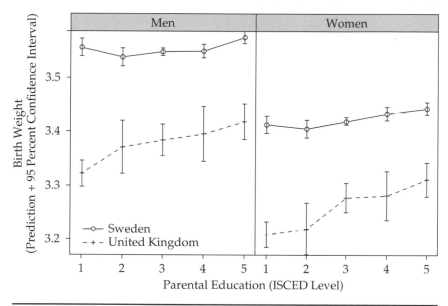

Source: Authors' calculations based on data from the 1970 British Cohort Study (Centre for Longitudinal Studies, various years) and Statistics Sweden (2010).
Note: Gradient with respect to education level of parent.

to vocational training; where Sweden takes a greater step, see online appendix table 17A.3). The difference is particularly pronounced at the top, that is, on moving from ISCED level 4 to 5 (technical college or short university to university degree). In Sweden, this is associated with a less steep increase in earnings than moving from ISCED level 3 to 4, whereas in the United Kingdom, the increase is steeper at the top than in the middle categories. The difference between the levels of log earnings of women is less dramatic, but the U.K. parental education gradient is substantially steeper.

We next examine the gradient in birth weight (figure 17.2). The parental education gradient in birth weight in the United Kingdom, though quite imprecisely measured, is still positive for both men and women. The difference between a low- and a high-parental-education baby is on average about 100 grams for both boys and girls. The gradient in Sweden, by contrast, is at most about 40 grams on average. The expected birth weight of Swedish children exceeds that of U.K. children at all education levels. For low birth weight (figure 17.3), the results are qualitatively similar in that there is a gradient in the United Kingdom, but it is very imprecisely measured, and there is essentially no gradient in Sweden.

Figure 17.3   Low Birth Weight on Parental Education

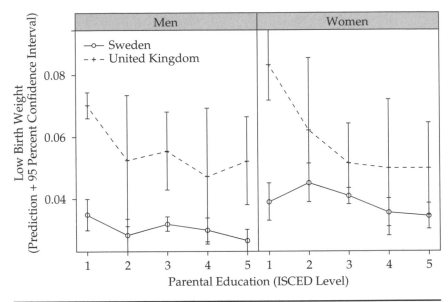

Source: Authors' calculations based on data from the 1970 British Cohort Study (Centre for Longitudinal Studies, various years) and Statistics Sweden (2010).
Note: Gradient with respect to education level of parent.

The incidence of low birth weights is at all levels of parental education lower in Sweden than in the United Kingdom.

Next, we show the estimated parental education gradient in grades (figure 17.4). Despite some differences, one is struck by the remarkable similarity of the gradients across countries. Girls have higher grades than boys in both countries, but the gradients are roughly as steep for both genders. The main difference between the two countries is that in the United Kingdom, children of the least educated parents (level 1) fare marginally better than the next lowest, whereas in Sweden, the gradient is monotonic. On the other hand, the increase in grades on moving from low to medium education (level 2 to 3) in the United Kingdom is much steeper than in Sweden. Conversely, moving from level 3 to 4 implies an increase in grades that is distinctly steeper in Sweden than in the United Kingdom.

Moving from school achievement, measured in terms of grades, to physical height, we see more dissimilarity (figure 17.5). We should recall that in Sweden, height is measured at military enlistment at age eighteen, whereas in the United Kingdom, it is measured at age sixteen. Thus, the difference in expected height between Swedish and U.K. young men is in

Figure 17.4   Average Grade on Parental Education

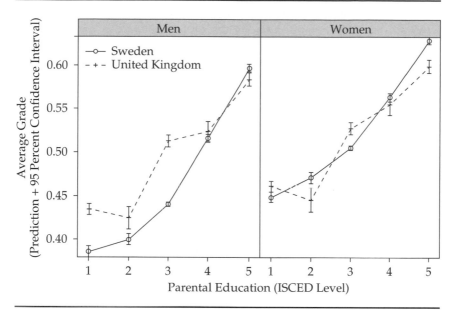

Source: Authors' calculations based on data from the 1970 British Cohort Study (Centre for Longitudinal Studies, various years) and Statistics Sweden (2010).
Note: Gradient with respect to education level of parent.

Figure 17.5   Height on Parental Education

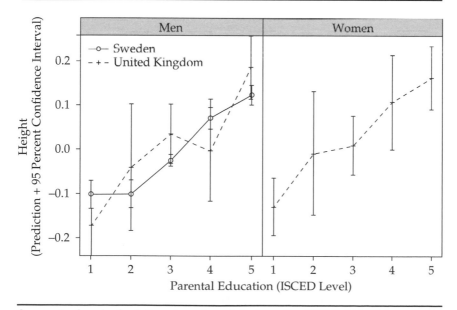

Source: Authors' calculations based on data from the 1970 British Cohort Study (Centre for Longitudinal Studies, various years) and Statistics Sweden (2010).
Note: Gradient with respect to education level of parent (height is standardized to mean 0, standard deviation 1).

part accounted for by the two-year age difference. Moreover, there may be a socioeconomic gradient to growth after age sixteen, so the difference in gradient must be viewed with caution.[4] We regress height standardized to have zero mean and unit variance on parental education.

The socioeconomic gradient of Swedish men is quite modest, albeit very precisely measured, spanning less than a 2-centimeter difference between children of the lowest- and the highest-educated parents. The difference in the United Kingdom, by contrast, exceeds 3 centimeters for men (for women the difference is smaller).

Finally, we examine socioeconomic gradients in final education. Figure 17.6 shows how the predicted probability of a child achieving each of the five education levels. Each column shows the probability that a man (upper panel) or a woman (lower panel) attains a particular level of education for each level of parental education. For example, the upper right panel (men, level 5) shows how the probability of having the highest education level varies with parental education in Sweden and the United Kingdom. In both cases, the probability of attaining a high education increases steeply with parental education, from about 0.2 and 0.1 for children of less-educated parents to about 0.60 and 0.55 for children of higher-educated parents in the United Kingdom and Sweden, respectively.

There is virtually no difference in the probability, nor how it declines as parental education increases, of a child having the lowest education level between the two countries. The probability that a child has only a level 2 education (high school) is higher in the United Kingdom than in Sweden for both men and women, and declines more steeply as parental education increases. The likelihood that a child has education level 3 (vocational training), in contrast, is much higher for Swedish less-educated parents than their United Kingdom counterparts. The Swedish probability also declines much more rapidly as parental education increases. There is less of a difference in achieving level 4 education (technical college or short university), although the gradient is a little steeper for Swedish than for British men. Finally, the likelihood that a child achieves the highest education level (university degree) is in fact higher in the United Kingdom than in Sweden, especially for men, at all levels of parental education. The probabilities converge toward higher parental education, suggesting that the increase in the likelihood across parental education is steeper in Sweden than in the United Kingdom.

Discussion and Concluding Comments

Our results suggest, first, that all the child outcomes measured before adulthood, with the exception of birth weight are statistically significantly related to the earnings of Swedish and U.K. men and women in

Figure 17.6   Child Education on Parental Education

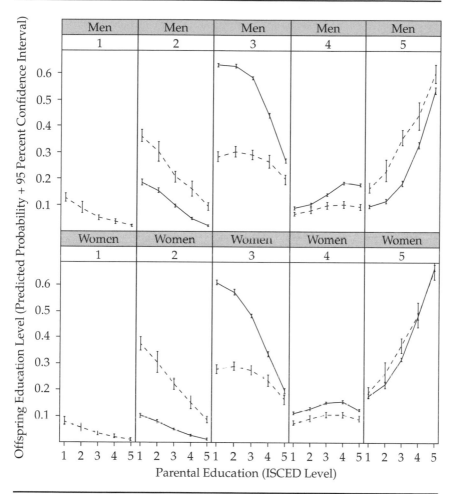

Source: Authors' calculations based on data from the 1970 British Cohort Study (Centre for Longitudinal Studies, various years) and Statistics Sweden (2010). *Note:* Gradient of probability of different child education outcomes with respect to education level of parent.

adulthood measured in a multiple regression that includes all outcomes at the same time. We make no claims of causality for that regression, only that the conditional expectation of earnings depends in a statistical sense on these variables.

When we examine the parental education gradient in each of these childhood and early adulthood variables, we compare the expected outcome across parental education levels. We find that, in general, the gradients are steeper in the United Kingdom than in Sweden, and that the differences are more pronounced among men than among women. In all cases save birth weight, the coefficient estimates for Sweden and the United Kingdom are different also in the sense of statistical significance as measured by F-tests. An interesting, albeit complex exception, is that of final education, where U.K. men in particular have a steeper gradient of low education than those in Sweden, but Swedish men have steep gradients of both medium (vocational) training and of university education.

However, despite the (at least in part) greater parental education gradient in final education, the earnings of Swedish men and women do not vary as steeply with parental education as those of their U.K. counterparts. There is little gradient in physical characteristics (birth weight, height) and remarkable similarity in grades at the end of compulsory schooling in the two countries. This suggests that the lower socioeconomic gradient in Swedish earnings may be related to how labor markets function upon entry into economic adulthood. In particular, our results are consistent with the economic returns to education and other child achievements being lower in Sweden than in the United Kingdom.

Notes

1. Swedish data on birth weight is available for cohorts starting in 1973. Of the British cohort studies, the BCS is thus closest in time to the cohorts we can study using Swedish data.
2. We do not distinguish between category 4A, which prepares for higher education, and 4B, which consists of educations that prepare directly for labor market entry. We lump all level four programs into a single category (for the U.K. BCS education coding, see Blanden, Gregg, and MacMillan 2007; for Sweden, see Björklund, Jäntti, and Lindquist 2009).
3. The online appendix can be found at: http://www.russellsage.org/Ermisch_et_al_OnlineAppendix.pdf.
4. Sensitivity analysis of U.K. height at age thirty suggests the results are robust with respect to this difference, however. Note that as the Swedish data stem from military enlistment that is not compulsory for women, we have no results for Swedish women here.

References

Barker, David J. 1995. "Fetal Origins of Coronary Heart Disease." *British Medical Journal* 311(6998): 171–74.

Betts, Julian R., and Darlene Morell. 1999. "The Determinants of Undergraduate Grade Point Average: The Relative Importance of Family Background, High School Resources, and Peer Group Effects." *Journal of Human Resources* 34(2): 268–93.

Björklund, Anders, and Markus Jäntti. 2009. "Intergenerational Income Mobility and the Role of Family Background." In *The Oxford Handbook of Economic Inequality,* edited by Wiemer Salverda, Brian Nolan, and Timothy Smeeding. Oxford: Oxford University Press.

Björklund, Anders, Markus Jäntti, and Matthew J. Lindquist. 2009. "Family Background and Income During the Rise of the Welfare State: Brother Correlations in Income for Swedish Men Born 1932–1968." *Journal of Public Economics* 93(5–6): 671–80. doi:10.1016/j.jpubeco.2009.02.006.

Björklund, Anders, Mikael Lindal, and Krister Sund. 2003. "Family Background and School Performance During a Turbulent Era of School Reforms." *Swedish Economic Policy Review* 10(2): 111–36.

Blanden, Jo. In press. "Cross-Country Rankings in Intergenerational Mobility: A Comparison of Approaches from Economics and Sociology." *Journal of Economic Surveys.* DOI: 10.1111/j.1467-6419.2011.00690.x.

Blanden, Jo, Paul Gregg, and Lindsey Macmillan. 2007. "Accounting for Intergenerational Income Persistence: Noncognitive Skills, Ability and Education." *Economic Journal* 117(519): C72–C92.

Breen, Richard, ed. 2004. *Social Mobility in Europe.* Oxford: Oxford University Press.

Böhlmark, Anders, and Matthew J. Lindquist. 2006. "Life-Cycle Variations in the Association Between Current and Lifetime Income: Replication and Extension for Sweden." *Journal of Labor Economics* 24(4): 879–96.

Case, Anne, and Christina Paxson. 2008. "Stature and Status: Height, Ability, and Labor Market Outcomes." *Journal of Political Economy* 116(3): 499–532.

Centre for Longitudinal Studies. Various years. *British Cohort Study 1970.* London: Institute of Education.

Corak, Miles. 2006. "Do Poor Children Become Poor Adults? Lessons for Public Policy from a Cross Country Comparison of Generational Earnings Mobility." *Research on Economic Inequality,* vol. 13, edited by John Creedy and Guyonne Kalb. Amsterdam: Elsevier.

Currie, Janet. 2009. "Healthy, Wealthy, and Wise: Socioeconomic Status, Poor Health in Childhood, and Human Capital Development." *Journal of Economic Literature* 47(1): 87–122.

Erikson, Robert, and John H. Goldthorpe. 1992. *The Constant Flux: A Study of Class Mobility in Industrial Societies.* Oxford: Clarendon Press.

Erikson, Robert, John H. Goldthorpe, Michelle Jackson, Meir Yaish, and D. R. Cox. 2005. "On Class Differentials in Educational Attainment." *Proceedings of the National Academy of Sciences* 102(27): 9730–733.

Grawe, Nathan D. 2006. "Life Cycle Bias in Estimates of Intergenerational Earnings Persistence." *Labour Economics* 13(5): 519–664.

Haider, Steven, and Gary Solon. 2006. "Life-Cycle Variation in the Association Between Current and Lifetime Earnings." *American Economic Review* 96(4): 1308–320.

Hertz, Thomas, Tamara Jayasundera, Patrizio Piraino, Sibel Selcuk, Nicole Smith, and Alina Verashchagina. 2007. "The Inheritance of Educational Inequality: International Comparisons and Fifty-Year Trends." *The B.E. Journal of Economic Analysis and Policy* 7(2): Article 10. Available at: http://www.bepress.com/bejeap/vol7/iss2/art10 (accessed September 5, 2011).

Jäntti, Markus, Bernt Bratsberg, Knut Røed, Oddbjørn Raaum, Robin Naylor, Eva Österbacka, Anders Björklund, and Tor Eriksson. 2006. "American Exceptionalism in a New Light: A Comparison of Intergenerational Earnings Mobility in the Nordic Countries, the United Kingdom and the United States." *IZA* discussion paper 1938. Bonn: Institute for the Study of Labor.

Lundborg, Petter, Paul Nystedt, and Dan-Olof Rooth. 2009. "The Height Premium in Earnings: The Role of Physical Capacity and Cognitive and Non-Cognitive Skills." *IZA* discussion paper 4266. Bonn: Institute for the Study of Labor. Available at: http://ftp.iza.org/dp4266.pdf (accessed September 5, 2011).

Solon, Gary M. 2002. "Cross-Country Differences in Intergenerational Earnings Mobility." *Journal of Economic Perspectives* 16(3): 59–66.

Statistics Sweden. 2010. [Register data from multiple sources, linked through the multigenerational register.] Örebro, Sweden: Statistics Sweden.

UNESCO. 2006. *ISCED 1997: International Standard Classification of Education*, re-edition. Paris: UNESCO Institute for Statistics.

Chapter 18

Equality of Opportunity and Intergenerational Transmission of Employers

PAUL BINGLEY, MILES CORAK,

AND NIELS WESTERGÅRD-NIELSEN

A S THE motivating theme of this book makes clear, children must advance through a whole series of transitions at different points in their lives, which to varying degrees may all have a bearing on their ultimate labor market success as adults. This chapter addresses the relationship between parental income and the labor market outcomes of teenagers and young adults. This gradient refers to the relationship between family circumstances during adolescence and early adult outcomes. This is an important transition in a child's life because it relates directly to some of the issues John Roemer (2004) addressed in his concern over the relationship between measures of generational mobility, equality of opportunity, and the appropriate role for public policy.

To perhaps overly simplify his argument, a strong gradient in incomes across the generations could reflect genetic and other hereditary endowments associated with the early years. The transmission of family values, preferences, and other inherent characteristics, like motivation, may permit parents who are relatively well advantaged to raise children who in turn go on to be relatively advantaged adults. If these characteristics are valued by labor markets over time, there will also be a correlation in the earnings of the two generations. Different societies will draw the line between family and the state in different ways, so the correlation in incomes across the generations would not necessarily be viewed as indicating inequality of opportunities. In other words, if hereditary endowments associated with the very nature of families and how they raise their children are driving the correlation in adult outcomes, then the case for public policy intervention—assuming it is effective—would involve a cost in terms of liberty and autonomy that may or may not be acceptable.

At the other extreme, a strong correlation in parent-child incomes could also reflect other investments later in life, particularly the role of networks or direct control in the hiring process that influence the opportunities for employment in the labor market. The children of relatively well-advantaged parents could benefit by getting jobs—either temporary jobs that facilitate the transition from schooling to work, or career jobs that determine their permanent income—by relying on the contacts and information their parents may share with them, or for that matter through the direct or indirect control parents may have in the hiring process of their employers. This perspective puts the emphasis on how social and labor market institutions function and interact with family background to determine adult outcomes. For example, Roemer points out that if nepotism is the source of the cross-generational income-income gradient, many citizens of the OECD countries may not see this as reflecting equal opportunities, and there may be a stronger consensus on the role for government intervention.

The objective of this chapter is to inform a discussion of this sort. More specifically, we document the extent of the intergenerational transmission of employers, and in a descriptive way relate it to the transmission of earnings in two relatively mobile countries: Canada and Denmark. To be precise, we study the degree to which sons—both during their teen years as they are making the transition from full-time schooling to full-time employment, and during their young adult years once they have established themselves in what will arguably be their career jobs—work for the same employer as their fathers. Our choice of these two countries is certainly driven by the availability of data with sufficient and appropriate detail, but is also important in a substantive sense because it is generally accepted that they are among the most mobile countries when comparisons are made of earnings intergenerationally. The elasticity of father-son earnings is about 0.2 or even less in both countries, compared with 0.4 to 0.6 in countries such as the United States, the United Kingdom, and France (Corak 2006). Yet, at the same time, they are very different in the structure of their labor markets, Denmark being geographically much smaller and less diverse. However, Denmark also has high equality of earnings and incomes and a high degree of intergenerational mobility. Despite high unionization rates, the degree of employee turnover and general flexibility suggests that the Danish labor market has more in common with North America than with continental Europe. Denmark is among those countries with the lowest returns to schooling (Harmon, Walker, and Westergård-Nielsen 2001). Canada is less equal in cross-sectional outcomes, less unionized, and has a higher return to human capital. As such, we feel that this comparison may have broader relevance, and suggest avenues for future research among a wider set of countries. If the intergenerational transmission of employers is significant in these countries, and if it is strongly related to generational earnings mobility, then even relatively low correlations in intergenerational earnings may be cause for concern, and by implication raise the need for closer examination of the underlying reasons for higher correlations in other countries.

Our major finding is that the intergenerational transmission of employers is both very significant and very similar across these two countries. It is a common aspect of how families and labor markets interact: about 30 to 40 percent of the young men we study have at some point been employed with a firm that also employed their fathers. This reflects the first jobs these individuals obtain during their teen years. As such, our analysis notes that parents continue to invest and influence outcomes for their children well into the teenage and young adult years. In addition, we find that about 4 to about 6 percent of the cohorts we study have their main job in adulthood at an employer who provided their fathers with a main job some fifteen years earlier. We also find that these patterns are positively associated with paternal earnings and to remarkably similar degree across the two countries, rising distinctly and sharply at the very top of the earnings distribution. Finally, we document that these patterns have implications for the intergenerational transmission of earnings. Upward mobility of teenagers raised in a low-income household has little to do with inheriting an employer from the father, but the preservation of high-income status is strongly related to this tendency. The results from a series of quantile regressions suggest that the inheritance of employers cuts against this notion of equality of opportunity in the sense that Roemer has used the term.

Definitions and Nature of the Data

With respect to the framework offered in chapter 1 of this volume, our analysis focuses on parental investments at the latter point in the child's teen years, in particular the teen years associated with secondary schooling (age fifteen to eighteen) and the early adult years associated with the transition to the labor market or to higher education (age nineteen to twenty-two). For our purposes, adult outcomes are measured at about the age of thirty or a little later.

These definitions reflect in part the characteristics of our administrative data, but also the particular type of parental investment on which we focus. During the teen years, children are beginning to interact with the labor market, finding their first jobs, and developing a work ethic, yet many are still completing their education. During their early twenties, some have made a permanent transition to the labor market, others are continuing their education, but in most cases occupational choices are beginning to crystallize.

There is a sense that our data may be unique, but our hope is that their development will spur similar research in other countries. They permit us to examine the extent to which children are employed at the same firm as their fathers, and the consequences this has for long-run labor market outcomes in adulthood. An observation of employment in the same firm as the father is taken as an indicator that parents have a network on which children can rely in their job search, that they are employed with firms that have hiring rules favoring the children of employees, or that they have some control over the hiring process. All these resources can benefit the child in making the transition to the labor market, and may also have long-term implications by translating any given level of education into employment with a particular firm.

Our analysis relies on information that in principle represents the entire population of particular cohorts of young men in both countries. For Canada, we base the analysis on about 70,000 individuals who come close to representing the population of a cohort of men born in 1963. These individuals are followed to age thirty-three. These administrative data, which are based on income tax returns, are linked to their fathers and mothers. Just as important, the data also contain identifiers on up to four firms per year for the fathers and sons from the time the child was fifteen to thirty-three. Miles Corak and Patrizio Piraino use the same data, and some of the Canadian information reported here is drawn from their studies (2010, 2011).

These data are based on individual income tax returns that have been grouped into families. Our sample is drawn from 1.9 million men who are linked to their fathers—not necessarily biological fathers—if they filed an income tax return between 1982 and 1986 while still living at home. From this data, we select the cohort born in 1963, the oldest cohort of sons available to us. To remain in the analytical sample, the father must have positive earnings in each of the five years the son was fifteen to nineteen years old. Sons must have positive earnings in each of three years, 1994 to 1996. If either the father or the son reports no earnings over these time horizons, the pair is not included in the analysis. This would imply that, for example, those who are self-employed, and never report any earnings over the five- and three-year horizons, are not part of the analysis. As mentioned, the sample size is about 71,000 observations, representing 84,000 individuals when appropriately weighted.[1] Fathers are on average forty-seven years old when their earnings are calculated.

For Denmark, the data are more extensive. They come from the administrative sources in existence since 1980, and contain information on all individuals and employers and the length of time they are matched. We construct the data to permit a focus on the same age cohort as the Canadian, but information on younger and older cohorts up to their early forties is also available. The sample size is just under 195,000.

The Danish register data cover the entire population of about 5 million people, but our analysis takes 515,986 sons from the 1965 to 1976 birth cohorts as its starting point. The link between fathers and sons requires that they live at the same address together at one point after 1965. On this basis, we identify 402,027 father-son pairs. Of these, 274,296 have an identifiable main employer, and 198,718 fathers report positive earnings in each of the five years when the son was between fifteen and nineteen. We use the earnings of sons when they are thirty years old. Danes finish higher education relatively late, so for many, thirty is the beginning of their full-time careers.

In both countries, the analysis refers to employment in the private sector only. The only exception is that municipal governments are included for Canada. Otherwise, the observation that both father and son work for the government—in Canada either the federal or one of the provincial governments—is not coded as a match. This is because the employer identifier for the government captures all possible jobs in all possible regions, many of which will have nothing to do with direct parental influence. This said, the findings should be interpreted as an understatement of the true extent to which employers are transmitted cross-generationally. Between 6 and 8 percent of sons work in the public sector at ages eighteen and older. In Denmark, the nature of municipal, region, and state identification would include far too many false matches given the extensive public sector paired with large administrative units. Finally, an employer should be understood to mean an enterprise rather than a particular plant in both countries.

Our analysis is based on two complementary definitions of same firm employment across the generations. The first is a broad definition meant to reflect the network of employers of which the father has direct knowledge by virtue of having worked with them. We define a binary indicator of same firm employment that takes a value of 1 when the son at any particular age from sixteen to thirty in Denmark, and up to thirty-three in Canada, was in that year, or in any previous year, employed with any employer that also employed his father in any previous year back to the year the son was fifteen years old. This is a time-varying indicator, and we use its value when the son is in his early thirties as the basis for our analysis. We refer to this value as *ever same firm*.

Figure 18.1 offers the pattern in this indicator for sons in both countries from the age of sixteen. On the basis of this indicator, the proportion of same firm employment can only increase with time. At the age of sixteen, 11 percent of the Danish and 8 percent of the Canadian sons in our sample are working with an employer who had employed their fathers in the previous year. These proportions rise sharply in both countries during the teen years, reaching respectively 22 percent and 29 percent at age twenty. The intergenerational transmission of employers is, in other

Figure 18.1   Sons Employed at Some Point with Employer Fathers Worked for, by Son's Age

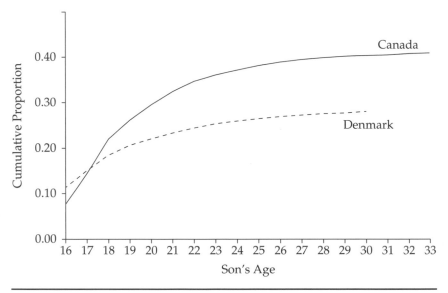

Source: Authors' calculations using Danish administrative data (documented in Statistics Denmark 2011 and described in Leth-Sørenson 1993) and Canadian administrative data (Corak and Piraino 2011, figure 1).

words, an important aspect of finding the first jobs teenagers hold. After about age twenty-three or twenty-four, the proportion of sons who have ever been employed with a previous employer of their fathers begins to level and does not increase very much after about age twenty-six. By their late twenties or early thirties, 28 percent of Danes and 40 percent of Canadians have at some point worked with an employer for which their fathers had also worked.[2]

The second indicator we derive is intended to reflect the permanent earnings of the son, and is based on the main employer, at age thirty or so. This is the employer accounting for the majority of the son's earnings over a three-year period. This in turn is related to the employer accounting for the majority of the father's earnings over the five-year period when the son was fifteen to nineteen years old. We refer to this as *same main employer*, and our intention is to relate this measure to the degree of intergenerational transmission of earnings. It is for this reason that we define the indicator over a period of successive years, reflecting the averaging in earnings we also undertake to reduce the role of transitory fluctuations and come closer to a measure of permanent income. In Denmark, we find that 4.0 percent of sons work for the same main employer as their fathers; in Canada, 5.6 percent do.

The slightly higher incidence of same firm employment in Denmark at the youngest ages could reflect the structure of apprenticeship programs, which facilitate the school to work transition more formally than in Canada. On the other hand, the higher overall proportions of same firm and same main firm employment in Canada may reflect the much larger geographic dispersion of employment combined with less mobility between regions. For example, if the labor market is segmented with high costs of mobility between potential employers, then it is more likely that simply by random chance sons will be employed with the same firms because of the limited job opportunities available in their region of residence. Corak and Piraino (2011) examine various aspects of this possibility and note through a series of counterfactual simulations that at the very most this accounts for 1 to 1.5 percentage points of the 5.6 percent incidence of same firm employment when job mobility is restricted to the same industry and finely defined region as the father. This leaves a significant fraction of the overall incidence open to family influences, but combined with a lower average firm size in Denmark may be large enough to explain some of the cross-country difference in the overall incidence.

Intergenerational Transmission of Employers and Paternal Earnings

The major objective of our analytical work is to document the gradient between parental earnings and the degree to which sons inherit their father's employer. Figures 18.2 and 18.3 present the incidence of same firm employment, for each of our two indicators, according to the percentile of the father's earnings distribution. The patterns are clearly similar across the two countries.

Figure 18.2 shows that the incidence of sons ever having worked for an employer that also employed the father follows a U-shaped pattern. Generally, the incidence is lowest in the middle part of the father's earnings distribution, and higher in the bottom and top 20 percent. The other notable pattern is the sharp spike in the incidence at the very top of the earnings distribution in both countries. In Denmark, the incidence of same firm employment rises distinctly above the 90th percentile, where it is always above 30 percent. But above the 95th percentile, it is well above this proportion increasing to 35 percent and just surpassing 50 percent at the top percentile. In Canada, the pattern is similar, about 45 percent of sons having had the same employer as their father when the father is in the 90th to 95th percentile of his earnings distribution, and rising to above 50 percent for higher-earning fathers before almost reaching 70 percent in the case of top percentile fathers.

Figure 18.2   Sons Employed at Some Point with Employer Fathers Worked for, by Fathers' Earnings

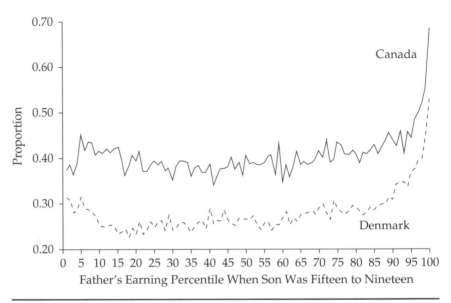

Source: Authors' calculations using Danish administrative data (documented in Statistics Denmark 2011 and described in Leth-Sørenson 1993) and Canadian administrative data (Corak and Piraino 2011, figure 2).

Figure 18.3 offers similar information for the incidence of the transmission of same main employers. In Denmark, the pattern is roughly constant throughout the paternal earnings distribution, increasing perhaps from generally below 4 percent to about that level. In Canada, there is a clear linear increase, rising steadily from about 4 to 5 percent in the lower fifth of the father's earnings distribution, to 6 to 8 percent in the upper third or so. But again, in both countries, the increase in the chances at the very top is noticeable, fully 10 to 15 percent of the sons of top percentile fathers employed as young adults at the same main employer that employed their fathers some ten to fifteen years earlier.

These bivariate relationships between paternal earnings and the chances that sons will have the same employer as the fathers are robust to a host of controls. We estimate a series of linear probability models of the incidence of same firm employment for both definitions that include a number of control variables common to the two countries. These include: the father's age; indicators for each of the father's sources of income; indicators for the number of employers the father had over a ten-year period; indicators for firm size; controls for the diversity of employment opportunities in the

Figure 18.3   Sons Employed as Young Adults with Same Main Employer as Fathers, by Fathers' Earnings

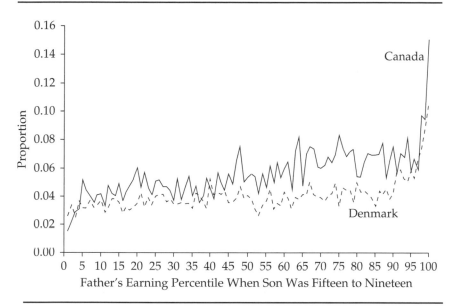

Source: Authors' calculations using Danish administrative data (documented ir Statistics Denmark 2011 and described in Leth-Sørenson 1993) and Canadiar administrative data (Corak and Piraino 2010, figure 1).

local labor market; an indicator of whether the father's firm was still in existence during the son's adulthood; the industry growth rates; two-digit SIC industry indicators; and detailed indicators of location, including a control for whether the son resided in an urban area.

Our main interest is in the results for two variables: the natural logarithm of the father's earnings (and its square), and an indicator for the presence of self-employment income. The former documents the gradient between income and the transmission of employers net of some basic controls associated mostly with industrial structure that may determine the chances sons will be employed with their father's firm. For example, as suggested, if the local labor market is not very diverse and if there is little interregional mobility, it is likely that sons will be employed with the same employer as their fathers by virtue of the fact that job opportunities are not available with many other firms. Similarly, sons are more or less likely to be employed in the same firm as their fathers if that firm is experiencing significant increases or decreases in employment by virtue of being in a growing or declining industry, or if firms tend to be large in size relative to the labor force. It is also sometimes noted that unionized firms may have implicit or explicit hiring rules that favor the children of employees (Shea 2000).

This said, we also highlight the role of self-employment income because its presence may indicate that the father could have direct control over the hiring process by virtue of firm ownership. The variable used is an indicator of the presence of self-employment income among the father's total income, and need not strictly have its origin in the same firm from which he obtained his earnings. We can only identify the employer that was the source of the earnings, and it is this employer that is used in deriving the incidence of the generational transmission of employers. To the extent that self-employed fathers also pay themselves earnings, the employer will be the same.

Table 18.1 presents a summary of the complete least squares regression results focused on these selected variables. In both countries, there is a clear quadratic relationship between paternal earnings and same firm employment for both definitions. The values of the coefficients suggest that the relationship is parabolic, always increasing and increasing at a greater rate with higher and higher levels of father's earnings. As such, the general patterns displayed in figures 18.1 and 18.2 seem, for the most part, to hold up in a multivariate context. Further, the relationship between the chances of being employed at the same employer as one's father are positively and strongly related to whether the father reported any self-employment income. In Denmark, the presence of self-employment income implies that the probability of same-firm employment is higher by 33.2 and 3.7 percentage points for respectively ever same employer and same main employer. We ascribe these rather large estimates to the incentives associated with tax filing where the self-employed can exploit the tax-free allowance for their sons by having them on the payroll. In Canada, the similar figures are 5 percentage points for ever same employer, off of an overall average of about 40 percent, and 0.5 percentage points for same main employer, compared to an average of just under 6 percent. As such, net of the influence of total paternal earnings, the presence of self-employment seems more strongly associated with the chances of ever getting a job with an employer the father had than with the chances of getting a career job with the same career employer as the father.

Intergenerational Transmission of Employers and Adult Earnings

The finding that there is a clear positive relationship between paternal earnings and the chances of firm employment raises the issue of how relevant the transmission of employers is to the intergenerational transmission of earnings. To document this relationship, we focus on the transmission of main employers, because these are most closely

Table 18.1   Linear Probability Models of Correlates of Sons Having Same Employer as Fathers

	Canada	Denmark
1. Sons ever having same employer as father		
Natural logarithm of father's permanent earnings	−0.486	−0.718
Natural logarithm of father's permanent earnings squared	0.0431	0.070
Indicator father having self-employment income	0.0476	0.338
2. Sons having same main employer as father		
Natural logarithm of father's permanent earnings	−0.242	−0.359
Natural logarithm of father's permanent earnings squared	0.0175	0.0220
Indicator father having self-employment income	0.0054	0.0370

Source: Authors' calculations using Danish administrative data (documented in Statistics Denmark 2011 and described in Leth-Sørensen 1993) and Canadian administrative data (Corak and Piraino 2011, tables 4 and 5).

Notes: Panel 1 reports results from a linear probability model with the dependent variable being a 0–1 indicator of whether the son at any point between the ages of fifteen and thirty worked for an employer for which his father had previously worked. The overall incidence of this occurring is presented as the last data point in figure 18.1, approximately 0.40 in Canada and 0.28 in Denmark.

Panel 2 reports results from a similar model, but with the dependent variable being a 0–1 indicator of whether the son's main employer in adulthood, the employer accounting for the majority of earnings, was the same main employer of the father when the son was a teenager. The overall incidence of this occurring is 0.056 in Canada and 0.041 in Denmark.

Other controls in both models include: indicators for presence of farming, fishing, and professional income; indicators for firm death and firm size; industry employment growth rate; average years of schooling in two-digit industry; urban indicator, province-region indicators; two-digit industry indicators; interactions between earnings, schooling, and self-employment income.

All results are statistically significant at the 95 percent level of confidence.

related to the adult earnings that form the basis for intergenerational earnings studies. Using Canadian data, Corak and Piraino (2011) report that the presence of same main employers across the generations does not appreciably change the overall average elasticity between father and son earnings in large measure because only about 6 percent of sons have the same main employers as their fathers. But their findings, and the results we document, suggest that this influence could well vary across the parental earnings distribution; the possibility of nonlinearities in the intergenerational elasticity being assumed away in the linear specification common in this literature. Accordingly, in the descriptive analysis that follows, we pay particular attention to differences across the paternal and child distributions and begin by focusing on certain parts of the transition matrices. But we also note that transition matrices and estimates of the average intergenerational earnings elasticity do not directly inform a discussion about equality of opportunity for the reasons highlighted by Roemer (2004), and we therefore then frame the analysis to address this issue.

Panel A of figure 18.4 presents slices of the full quartile transition matrix between father and son earnings for both countries.[3] The earnings quartiles of sons raised by bottom-quartile fathers are presented in the left panel of the figure, and that for sons raised by top-quartile fathers are offered in the right panel. These rows of the transition matrix are very similar between the two countries. In Canada, about 35 percent of sons born to bottom-quartile fathers become bottom-quartile adults; in Denmark, about 30 percent do so. The extent of upward mobility for these young men is even more similar: 37 percent of Canadians rise to the top half of the distribution, as do 39 percent of Danes, 16 percent in both countries managing the largest move to the top quartile. The similarities are also present at the upper end of the paternal earnings distribution. In both countries, there is more stickiness at the top of the distribution than at the bottom: almost 40 percent of sons raised by top quartile fathers also reaching the top quartile of the earnings distribution in the next generation. In both countries, 37 to 38 percent of these sons fall to the bottom half of the earnings distribution, 17 percent of Canadians and 21 percent of Danes falling fall to the bottom.

Panel B shows how these patterns are related to the intergenerational transmission of main employers, the left panel again indicating the situation of sons born to bottom-quartile fathers and the right indicating that of those originating in the top quartile. In both countries, the incidence of same main employer is about 3 to 4 percent for the children of the relatively poor fathers regardless of whether they remain poor or move to the very top of their earnings distribution (though at 2.3 percent a bit lower for Danes who manage to reach the top quartile). This is in sharp contrast to the experience of sons born to rich fathers. There is a clear gradient in the proportion having the same main employer as the father according to the relative earnings outcome of the son. Sons of top quartile fathers who fall to the bottom quartile are not very likely to have the same main employer as the father: only 2 to 3 percent do so, a proportion even less than bottom-quartile sons. In sharp contrast, this incidence is much higher if these sons remain in the top half of the earnings distribution, and particularly if they remain in the same quartile as their fathers. In Canada, almost 12 percent (or twice the overall average) of sons who are in the top quartile obtain

**Figure 18.4   Earnings Mobility and Transmission of Employers for Sons
Raised in Bottom- and Top-Earnings Quartiles**

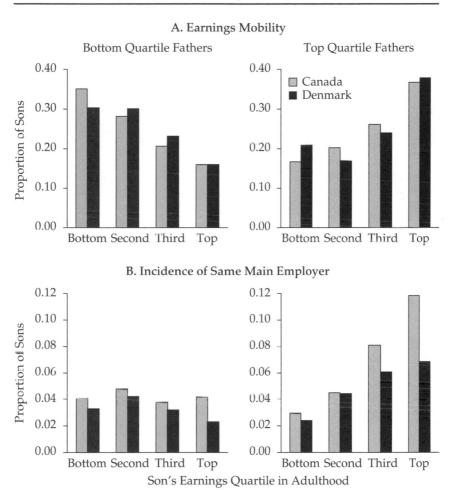

A. Earnings Mobility

Bottom Quartile Fathers

Top Quartile Fathers

B. Incidence of Same Main Employer

Son's Earnings Quartile in Adulthood

Source: Authors' calculations using Danish administrative data (documented in Statistics Denmark 2011 and described in Leth-Sørenson 1993) and Canadian administrative data (described in Corak and Piraino 2010).

their relatively high earnings from the same main employer that employed their father. Though there is also a clear gradient in the Danish context, the pattern is not as sharp as in Canada.

Table 18.2 offers evidence that is more directly related to equality of opportunity by presenting the results from quantile regressions of the standard linear model, but in a way that permits the intergenerational

Table 18.2   Intergenerational Earnings Elasticity and Impact of Same Main Firm Employment

	No Interactions		Fully Interacted Model			
	lnY	Constant	lnY	$lnY \times$ SameFirm	SameFirm	Constant
1. Canada						
10th percentile	0.328	5.86	0.309	*0.128*	−0.938	5.99
25th percentile	0.308	6.71	0.291	0.158	−1.43	6.83
50th percentile	0.253	7.48	0.238	0.177	−1.74	7.61
75th percentile	0.205	8.45	0.190	0.196	−2.01	8.59
90th percentile	0.170	9.05	0.158	0.190	−1.98	9.15
2. Denmark						
10th percentile	0.051	8.93	0.036	0.180	−1.84	9.29
25th percentile	0.132	9.65	0.123	0.135	−1.58	9.77
50th percentile	0.178	9.47	0.169	0.133	−1.62	9.56
75th percentile	0.195	9.49	0.188	0.138	−1.72	9.56
90th percentile	0.197	9.70	0.191	0.132	−1.67	9.77

Source: Authors' calculations using Danish administrative data (documented in Statistics Denmark 2011 and described in Leth-Sørensen 1993) and Canadian administrative data (described in Corak and Piraino 2010).
Notes: For the fully interacted model the reported coefficients are quantile regression estimates of the following model:

$$ln \ Y_{i,t} = \alpha + \beta \ lnY_{i,t-1} + \beta_1 \ lnY_{i,t-1} \times SameFirm_i + \gamma_1 SameFirm_i$$

where t indexes the son's permanent earnings and $t-1$ the fathers. *SameFirm* is a binary indicator of whether the son was employed by the same employer as the father. The model also includes controls for the father's age and age-squared. The no interactions model only has $lnY_{i,t-1}$ as a regressor.
All coefficients have margin significance levels of 0.000, except those italicized, which have a marginal significance level greater than 0.05.
For Canada, the sample size is 71,215; for Denmark it is 191,471.

earnings elasticity to change according to whether the son held a job with the same main firm as his father. The following fully interacted model is estimated at the 10th, 25th, 50th, 75th, and 90th percentiles:

$$ln \ Y_{i,t} = \alpha + \beta \ lnY_{i,t-1} + \beta_1 \ lnY_{i,t-1} \times SameFirm_i + \gamma_1 SameFirm_i + \varepsilon_i$$

where lnY_i is a measure of the natural logarithm of permanent earnings for an individual in family i, t indexes generations, and *SameFirm* is a binary indicator taking the value of 1 when the main firm is the same across generations. Our interest is with the coefficient, β_1, the interaction between paternal earnings and SameFirm, and how its value changes across the percentiles of the sons' earning distribution. If statistically significant, the implication would be that the intergenerational earnings elasticity is $(\beta + \beta_1)$ for those with the same main firm as their fathers.

The first two columns of the table also offer results from a model with no interaction effects.

Our interpretation of these results borrows from Nathan Grawe (2004), who suggests that the use of quantile regressions offers an appropriate way to empirically implement the concerns raised by Roemer (2004). Roemer states that "equality of opportunity . . . views inequalities of outcome as indefensible, ethically speaking, when and only when they are due to differential circumstances. Inequalities due to differential effort are acceptable" (2004, 50). Grawe echoes the view that a focus on average outcomes, as for example in the standard linear regression to the mean model, is not an appropriate indicator of equality of opportunity because abilities and preferences that have value in the market place will be correlated with the parents' economic circumstances. His interpretation of Roemer is to suggest "comparing children with similarly successful outcomes relative to other children born to similar families. That is, . . . [compare] the highest-, median-, or lowest-earning child born to low-earning parents to the highest , median-, or lowest-earning child born to high-earning parents" (Grawe 2004, 59). Quantile regression is one way of doing this. Equality of opportunity would be signaled by a low value for β among all sons who are successful in the labor market, those who for example have earnings at the 90th percentile. If a significant gradient between parent and child earnings exists for these high-achieving sons, then the suggestion is that in spite of having the abilities and preferences for labor market success the sons of low-income parents remain hampered by the economic circumstances of their family background, a situation that cannot be characterized as equality of opportunity.

The results for Canada show that the intergenerational earnings elasticity between fathers and sons falls at successively higher quantiles from about 0.3 at the 10th percentile to as low as 0.16 at the 90th. But this is only so in the absence of same firm employment. The results for the interaction term show that the intergenerational transmission of employers is a force working in the opposite direction. There is a greater stickiness in father-son earning outcomes for those who inherit their father's employer, with the increase in the slope being on the margins of statistical significance at the 10th percentile (the marginal significance level of a t-test is 0.065), but then rising in magnitude so as to double the elasticity at the 75th percentile and to more than double it at the 90th. At the 90th percentile, the intergenerational earnings elasticity is 0.158, but significantly higher, at 0.35, when the son is employed by the same main firm as the father. In this sense the results confirm the visual impression from figure 18.4. The suggestion is that high-achieving sons of low-earning fathers must have a greater endowment of characteristics valued in the marketplace than their counterparts with high-earning fathers: this endowment compensating them for not having access to the same parental resources associated with the intergenerational transmission of employers, and implying that their labor market outcomes would have been even better otherwise.

In Denmark, the overall pattern across the quantiles is the opposite, rising from lowest to highest. Paternal earnings are unrelated to the outcomes of the lowest-achieving sons, but much more so for the highest-achieving offspring: that is, higher-earning fathers are not any more able to influence the outcomes of their sons with the least potential than low-earning fathers, but they are more able to do so for sons with the greatest potential. This said, the magnitude of the elasticity at the higher quantiles is in the range of the Canadian findings. Further, the interaction term for same main employer is positive and statistically significant throughout the son's earnings distribution. Though the magnitude falls above the 10th percentile, at the 90th percentile, the overall intergenerational elasticity for those inheriting their father's main employer is about the same in the two countries: just under 0.35 in Canada, and just over 0.32 in Denmark.

Conclusion

Our results should be understood as descriptive, documenting the nature of the gradient in parent-child outcomes at the later stages of the child's life course and relating this to the structure of labor markets and how young adults make the transition from schooling to work. We find three very similar outcomes in Canada and Denmark, two countries that are characterized by relatively high levels of intergenerational earnings mobility.

First, the intergenerational transmission of employers is a common feature of the employment outcomes of the young cohorts of men we study, with 30 to 40 percent of young adults having at some point been employed with a firm that also employed their father. In large measure this is associated with the first jobs these individuals obtain during their teen years, but for four to about six percent it also refers to their main job in adulthood. We do not control for any family-specific characteristics or investments made during earlier years, and therefore the root causes of these patterns are not clear.

This said, these rather high levels in the incidence of sons ever having worked with the same employer as their fathers may not be out of line with some of the basic facts of how young people find jobs. Families and friends are often cited as the most important source of information for new jobs. Mark Granovetter (1995) was among the first to document this in a small-scale survey for a particular labor market, and Harry Holzer (1988) offers the theoretical underpinning by modeling the choice of search methods and suggesting that family and friends are a relatively productive and low-cost way of obtaining job offers. More recently, Linda Datcher Loury (2006) shows that close to the majority of jobs in the United States are found through family, friends, or acquaintances, and Lee Grenon (1999) reports that for Canada about one-quarter of successful job searches involves family or friends. These patterns may differ in a more structured European labor market, but the findings of Francis Kramarz and Oskar Skans (2007), whose methods are most closely related to our approach, suggest that they may be broadly applicable. These authors find that there is a high tendency for young adults in Sweden to find their first job in the very same plant that employs their parent.

The incidence of sons ever having worked with the same firm as their fathers in large measure reflects the job search process during the teen years. In both countries, this incidence does increase sharply up to about the age of twenty, and at least implies that the intergenerational inheritance of employers during these years may refer to temporary employment during the school to work transition. Even if this is the case, it can be understood as a type of parental investment that may have longer-term consequences as the sons inheriting a job may be more likely to gain work experience, job tenure, and associated general and firm-specific human capital. They may also avoid unemployment, and thereby can be imagined to gain a head start in establishing themselves in the labor market over the long term.

Our second major finding is that the intergenerational transmission of employers is positively associated with paternal earnings, rising distinctly and sharply at the very top of the earnings distribution. This is robust to a host of controls for the structure of the labor market and characteristics of the firms with which fathers are employed. This finding is new and builds on Corak and Piraino (2010, 2011) by showing that the pattern is robust across labor markets.

It may be that the network and other information that fathers offer their sons lowers search costs in particular sectors, and that job offers are more likely to be obtained in some firms if the father is or has been employed with those firms. Marco Caliendo, Arne Uhlendorff, and Ricarda Schmidl (2009) adapt Holzer's model in this way to account for the influence of network effects. Although particular firms may have explicit policies concerning the preferential hiring of the children of employees, this falls short of nepotism, in which parents are exerting direct control over the hiring process. Although we do find a strong positive relationship between parental self-employment and the intergenerational transmission of employers, the incidence of the former is not so great as to suggest that direct control over the hiring process is the main reason why 30 to 40 percent of sons at some point worked for the same firm as their fathers. Parental networks and information are a more likely story, and should be seen as another type of investment that parents make in the human capital of their children. But the consequences of this influence cannot be understood in isolation of the structure of labor markets.

This said, there is a sense that nepotism may be part of the explanation for some segments of the population, particularly at the very top, where we document distinct discontinuities in the relationship between paternal earnings and the chances of being employed with the father's employer. This finds some corroboration in the literature on firm succession. In particular, Morten Bennedsen and his colleagues (2007) examine the succession decisions of limited liability firms, both public and private, in Denmark between 1994 and 2002. They focus specifically on the impact on firm performance of family successions, but they also document over this period that one-third of successions were family-based, in which the new CEO was related through blood or marriage to the departing CEO. Our data may be picking up some of this dynamic, or the more general idea that at the highest earning levels parents are more likely to have control over the hiring process and use this in a way that is of benefit for their children. David Blanchflower and Andrew Oswald (2009), Thomas Dunn and Douglas Holtz-Eakin (2000), and Robert Fairlie and Alicia Robb (2007) describe the very high tendency of self-employed sons to have self-employed fathers and family members, and that this involves, at least with the American data used by Fairlie and Robb, the intergenerational transmission of firms in almost 50 percent of cases.

Our third finding is that the intergenerational transmission of employers has implications for the intergenerational transmission of earnings. The degree and pattern of intergenerational earnings mobility is very similar in Canada and Denmark, with very similar tendencies for those born to low- and high-income fathers to remain in low- and high-income employment as adults. But mobility out of the bottom has little to do with inheriting an employer for the father, whereas the preservation of high-income status is distinctly related to this tendency.

Although the interpretation of our findings is open to discussion, we follow the suggestions in some of the existing literature to relate the findings to empirical measures of equality of opportunity to suggest that the inheritance of employers cuts against this commonly held value. These findings also raise the importance of recognizing that child outcomes are related to the structure of labor markets, and therefore that the resources parents bring—though information, networks, or direct control of the hiring process—will influence the final transition children make in becoming self-sufficient and successful adults.

Notes

1. These restrictions are imposed to minimize the role of measurement error in earnings, as stressed in the literature on intergenerational earnings mobility (Solon 1989, 1992). We also require that the earnings of both sons and fathers must be above the bottom percentile thereby avoiding some suspected measurement errors in the data.

2. It should be noted that part of the pattern of change in the early years of the part of the life-course we examine could be due to a mechanical effect

reflecting the fact that we only begin to examine the father's employers when the son was fifteen years old. As the son ages, the incidence of same firm employment will rise because more years of information becomes available on the father's employment history. This said, this effect would appear to have worked itself out by the end of the period we examine, which is our main analytical concern.

3. The complete quartile transition matrices are appended as online appendix table 18A.1, available at: http://www.russellsage.org/Ermisch_et_al_OnlineAppendix.pdf.

We acknowledge with appreciation comments on earlier drafts of this chapter from Paul Gregg, James Wilson, the editors, and other members of the Cross-National Inheritance of the Transmission of Advantage network during presentations at meetings organized by the Russell Sage Foundation in New York and London. The financial support of the Russell Sage Foundation and the exemplary research assistance of Mikkel Sølvsten, as well as the advice of Patrizio Piraino, are also acknowledged with thanks. Corak is grateful for the financial support of the Social Sciences and Humanities Research Council of Canada through a Standard Research Grant.

References

Bennedsen, Morten, Kasper Meisner Nielsen, Francisco Pérez-González, and Daniel Wolfenzon. 2007. "Inside the Family Firm: The Role of Families in Succession Decisions and Performance." *Quarterly Journal of Economics* 122(2): 647–91.

Blanchflower, David G., and Andrew J. Oswald. 2009. "What Makes a Young Entrepreneur?" In *International Handbook on Youth and Young Adulthood*, edited by Andy Furlong. London: Routledge.

Caliendo, Marco, Arne Uhlendorff, and Ricarda Schmidl. 2009. "The Effects of Social Networks on Job Search Behavior and Labor Market Success." Unpublished working paper.

Corak, Miles. 2006. "Do Poor Children Become Poor Adults? Lessons from a Cross Country Comparison of Generational Earnings Mobility." In *Research on Economic Inequality*, vol. 13, edited by John Creedy and Guyonne Kalb. Amsterdam: Elsevier.

Corak, Miles, and Patrizio Piraino. 2010. "Intergenerational Earnings Mobility and the Inheritance of Employers." *IZA* discussion paper 4876. Bonn: Institute for the Study of Labor.

———. 2011. "The Intergenerational Transmission of Employers." *Journal of Labor Economics* 21(1): 37–68.

Datcher Loury, Linda. 2006. "Some Contacts Are More Equal than Others: Informal Networks, Job Tenure, and Wages." *Journal of Labor Economics* 24(2): 299–318.

Dunn, Thomas, and Douglas Holtz-Eakin. 2000. "Financial Capital, Human Capital and the Transition to Self-Employment: Evidence from Intergenerational Links." *Journal of Labor Economics* 18(2): 282–305.

Fairlie, Robert W., and Alicia M. Robb. 2007. "Families, Human Capital, and Small Business: Evidence from the Characteristics of Business Owners Survey." *Industrial and Labor Relations Review* 60(2): 225–45.

Granovetter, Mark. 1995. *Getting a Job: A Study of Contacts and Careers.* 2d ed. Chicago: University of Chicago Press.

Grawe, Nathan D. 2004. "Intergenerational Mobility for Whom? The Experience of High- and Low-Earnings Sons in International Perspective." In *Generational Income Mobility in North America and Europe,* edited by Miles Corak. Cambridge: Cambridge University Press.

Grenon, Lee. 1999. "Obtaining a Job." In *Perspectives on Labor and Income.* Ottawa: Statistics Canada.

Harmon, Colm, Ian Walker, and Niels Westergård-Nielsen. 2001. "Introduction." In *Education and Earnings in Europe.* Cheltenham: Edward Elgar.

Holzer, Harry J. 1988. "Search Method Use by Unemployed Youth." *Journal of Labor Economics* 6(1): 1–20.

Kramarz, Francis, and Oskar Nordström Skans. 2007. "With a Little Help from My . . . Parents? Family Networks and Youth Labor Market Entry." CREST working paper. Paris: INSEE.

Leth-Sørensen, Søren. 1993. "IDA: An Integrated Database for Labour Market Research." Copenhagen: Statistics Denmark.

Roemer, John E. 2004. "Equal Opportunity and Intergenerational Mobility: Going Beyond Intergenerational Income Transition Matrices." In *Generational Income Mobility in North America and Europe,* edited by Miles Corak. Cambridge: Cambridge University Press.

Shea, John. 2000. "Does Parents' Money Matter?" *Journal of Public Economics* 177(3): 155–84.

Solon, Gary. 1989. "Biases in the Estimation of Intergenerational Earnings Correlations." *Review of Economics and Statistics* 71(1): 172–74.

———. 1992. "Intergenerational Income Mobility in the United States." *American Economic Review* 82(3): 393–408.

Statistics Denmark. 2011. "Documentation of Database Contents–Integrated Database for Labour Market Research." Available at: http://www.dst.dk/en/Guide/documentation/Varedeklarationer/emnegruppe/emne.aspx?sysrid=1013 (accessed January 10, 2012).

PART V

CONCLUSIONS AND REFLECTIONS

Chapter 19

What Have We Learned?

JOHN ERMISCH, MARKUS JÄNTTI,

TIMOTHY SMEEDING, AND JAMES A. WILSON

T HE MOST important motivation for the CRITA project and the preceding chapters is the concern that rising income inequality will
have the long-run effect of reducing intergenerational mobility.
The concern is motivated by the tendency, observed for generations
born before 1970, for more unequal countries to have lower mobility.
These same countries have higher inequality now than at any time in
the past, excepting France, and the rank order of countries by annual
income inequality is about the same now as it was for older generations
(Brandolini and Smeeding 2009). This suggests that chances for mobility
may have become worse for the current generation of children because of
the rise in inequality since the 1970s.

Our aim in this book has been to examine the association between parents' socioeconomic status (SES) and outcomes during childhood that are
salient for intergenerational income mobility. We are especially focused
on more recent generations, primarily those who have been affected by
the rise in inequality. In an attempt to understand how and why mobility
is sustained at higher rates in some countries than in others, the chapters
of this book cover countries with very different levels of inequality and a
number of mobility-relevant outcomes between children's birth and their
adulthood. The conceptual framework is based on a life-course approach
in comparative perspective, allowing us to see where divergences in these
outcomes between high- and low-SES children occur in the life cycle and
how they evolve across several countries. Differences between countries
in these patterns suggest differences in how private and public institutions affect opportunities for individuals born into families at different
points along the income distribution. Another advantage of the cross-
national perspective is that genetic transmission in the outcome studied
(for example, cognitive ability) is likely to be the same across countries.[1]

It follows that cross-country differences will reflect different pre- and postbirth environments, including those that are policy driven as well as those that occur due to other properties of the country's environment for different SES groups, including aspects of population heterogeneity (for example, ethnic diversity) and institutions (for example, wage-setting practices or schooling systems).

In this chapter, we summarize the answers to our four main research questions, describe how future research can build on the present body of work, and consider the implications of study findings for policy. Policy responses to inequality in child outcomes in relation to family background and mobility concerns need to confront what James Fishkin (1983) called the liberal trilemma. He formulated three principles that command wide support:

- *The principle of merit.* There should be widespread procedural fairness in the evaluation of qualifications for positions (22).

- *Equality of life chances.* The prospects of children for eventual positions in society should not vary in any systematic and significant manner with their arbitrary native characteristics (32).

- *Autonomy of the family.* Consensual relations within a given family governing the development of its children should not be coercively interfered with, except to ensure for the children the essential prerequisites for adult participation in society (36).

These three liberal principles combine to form a trilemma because realization of any two can be expected to preclude realization of the third. Because the three criteria do not add up to a normative and coherent ideal, policy and value trade-offs are likely to be necessary (for another perspective on these ethical issues, see chapter 20 this volume). We believe, and the chapters in this volume suggest, that a great deal might be done in practice to increase equality of life chances without sacrificing either the principle of merit or the principle of family autonomy. Our comparative framework also helps illuminate what might be done. If some countries are delivering more equal life chances, then it is worth knowing how they are doing so in order to draw policy lessons from these findings that might apply to other countries with different cultures and institutions.

Research Questions

Overall, the book addresses four big research questions:

- Do differences by parental SES emerge, and if so, when?
- Do differences change over the life course?

- How do childhood differences contribute to intergenerational mobility?
- How do answers to these questions vary among countries?

This section is organized around the study's answers to the first three questions, with answers to the fourth being addressed within each subsection.

Do Differences by Parental SES Emerge, and When?

Gaps in outcomes by parental SES emerge early in childhood in all countries, as early as when we can first measure child characteristics or abilities. They exist for both cognitive and sociobehavioral outcomes and are usually larger for the former. They result from a combination of the influences of parenting and heredity (environment, including in utero environments, and genes), and are apparent and well measured by ages three to five in all the countries where we have data for these ages. We have direct evidence for the United States, Australia, Canada, the United Kingdom (chapter 4), and Germany (sociobehavioral only, chapter 5), and indirect evidence at slightly older ages for France (cognitive only, chapter 7), Finland, and Sweden (chapter 9). In no country do we find that high- and low-SES children start out equally prepared for schooling terms of cognitive abilities and social behavior. Rather, we consistently find that higher-SES children are better prepared for formal education in both dimensions.

The comparison across the four English-speaking countries at age five (chapter 4) indicates that differences in the environment matter. For cognitive outcomes, the disparities by family background are largest in the United States, followed by the United Kingdom and Australia, the smallest average differences being found in Canada. This pattern is illustrated in figure 19.1, in which we compare average vocabulary scores at age five between children whose parents have a middle level of education and those having high and low education, respectively. The gap between the least and most advantaged (the full bar in figure 19.1) is significantly larger (in a statistical sense) in the United States than that of each of the other three countries, and significantly smaller in Canada than in the United Kingdom, suggesting that the gradients, or profiles, of the disparity relationships also differ across nations. Despite large gaps between the most disadvantaged and the middle in all countries (the light grey segment of the bar), differences among countries in the overall cognitive gap also reflect variation in the degree to which the top of the SES distribution outperforms the middle (the dark grey segment of the bar).

SES gaps in social and behavioral development are markedly smaller than in cognitive outcomes, Canada exhibiting the smallest gaps. The largest disparity in sociobehavioral outcomes by SES is in the United Kingdom, where it is the greater level of behavioral problems of low-SES that is responsible for this finding. In both Germany and the United Kingdom,

Figure 19.1   Differences in Vocabulary Scores, by Parents' Education

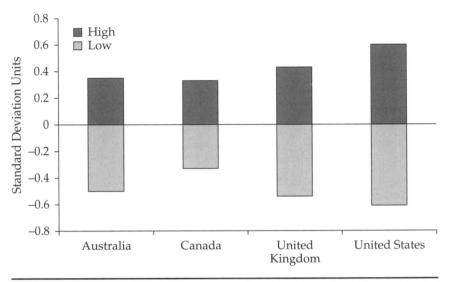

Source: Authors' calculations based on data from chapter 4, this volume.
Note: Differences presented in standard deviation units between average scores versus middle education.

some of the sociobehavioral gap arises because lower-SES mothers experience more partnership changes and family instability, and these are associated with more behavioral problems (chapter 5).

A relatively strong relationship between parental SES and either school achievement or cognitive test scores during adolescence exists for a large number of countries. It is evident in Sweden, the United Kingdom, Germany, Italy, Canada, and the United States (chapters 9 through 13 and chapter 17). Figure 19.2 illustrates the phenomenon by comparing the difference between the percentage of children in the top quartile of school or test score results and the percentage in the bottom quartile between children having parents with a middle level of education (the standard level expected in a country) and those with high (some tertiary education, a bachelor's degree or more) and low education, respectively.[2] It shows that the achievement gaps by parental education in adolescence are smaller in Canada and Australia than in the other countries (the full bar in figure 19.2). The dark grey bars indicate that the child's advantage from having highly educated parents is largest in the United States, England, and Sweden (in each of which the difference in the percentages in the top quartile and the bottom quartile is more than 40 percent). The largest disadvantage of having less-educated parents is in Germany, the United States, and England.

Figure 19.2   Differences in Top and Bottom Quartiles of Test Scores, by Parents' Education

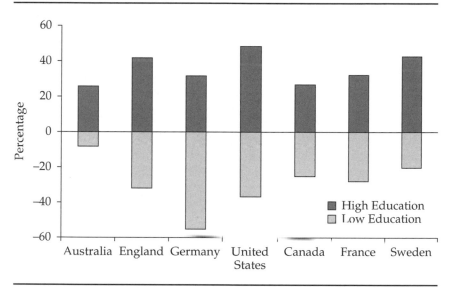

Source: Authors' calculations based on their own data.
Note: Australia and Canada observe the child at about age 15; England, about 14; Germany, about 17; United States, 13 to 16; France, about 11. Weighted data with exception of France. See chapter 12 for more detail.

Canada and Australia perform best in both of these dimensions. The meta-analysis of outcomes (chapter 2) also suggests significantly smaller gaps in Canada and Australia than the United States in the cognitive domain. In those chapters where direct comparisons can be made, similarities are more apparent than differences (chapters 9, 11, 14, and 17).

Do Differences Change Over the Life Course?

Several of the studies focusing on older children have attempted to observe changes in parent status–child attainment gradients as children age. Evidence concerning changes in the size of the SES gaps as the child ages is important to a better understanding of the proximal factors that drive the resulting child outcomes. Although gradients within countries clearly differ at early ages (figure 19.1), we find only limited evidence of fanning out—that is, the gaps becoming larger—as a child ages. Examination of changes between the ages of three to seven (United Kingdom) and four to nine (Australia) indicates relatively constant average gaps in both cognitive and sociobehavioral outcomes over these ages (chapter 6). In the United States, it appears that very large SES gaps narrow or hold constant up to age six and then widen, but the extent of the widening and the ages over which it occurs depends on whether achievement is measured in terms of absolute skill levels, such as number of questions answered correctly, or relative skill levels, such as standardized scores (chapter 10).[3] The absolute scores show gaps widening from age seven to fourteen, but not the standardized ones. The evolution of SES gaps in the United Kingdom from age seven to eleven is also not clear. For example, the gaps in standardized math scores widen over these ages, but standardized vocabulary scores change little (chapter 10).

There is robust evidence from three data sources that SES gaps in achievement for the United Kingdom become substantially bigger between the ages of eleven (the end of primary school) and fourteen (see chapters 10, 11, and 12). The widening gap after eleven is mainly related to the positive association between the quality of secondary school that children attend and their parents' SES, which is stronger than the association between primary school quality and parents' SES (chapter 12). The former correlation is driven by residential choices, which are constrained by incomes and house prices. In other countries, the SES gaps in outcomes are substantial but stay more or less the same through middle childhood and secondary school (chapters 9 and 11).

Generally, we do not find convergence in SES gaps at older ages and life stages. Thus, average differences in measurable child outcomes encountered early on in life persist throughout children's lives up to university age and likely beyond. Even in countries, such as France and Denmark (chapters 7 and 8), where universal early childhood education makes a difference in the disadvantage experienced by children with low-SES parents, this policy intervention lessens but does not erase the association of parental SES with child outcomes.

Changes in average gaps by parents' SES as children age occur because, for example, initially low-achieving children of high-SES parents may be more likely to improve as they get older than children of low-SES parents, or high achieving children of high-SES parents may be more likely to maintain their achievements than those with low-SES parents. Two chapters include a dynamic perspective and consider differences by parental SES in trajectories as the child ages. Examining ages three to seven in the United Kingdom and four to nine in Australia, chapter 6 finds that children of low-educated parents with poor early outcomes are more likely to persist at poor achievement levels, more so in the United Kingdom than Australia. Even among British children who started with similar outcomes, those with better-educated parents are doing better by age seven than their counterparts. English children of parents with higher education are more likely to improve their position in the distribution of secondary school tests between ages eleven and fourteen (chapter 12). It appears therefore that better chances of improvement in test results for adolescents with better-educated parents make an important contribution to the steeper parents' education profile at age fourteen compared with age eleven in England.

How Do Childhood Differences Contribute to Intergenerational Mobility?

The evidence suggests that childhood gaps contribute significantly to intergenerational correlations in education and income in all nations. We began the book by laying out a framework to help understand how advantage is transmitted over the life course from parents to their children. Chapters 3 and 9 put empirical flesh on this framework. In Sweden, the correlation between father's and son's midlife income is mediated by both cognitive ability and personality traits (measured when the son was eighteen). Although cognitive ability influences both sons' educational attainment and his earnings, attributes such as social maturity, emotional stability, and leadership capacity pay off directly in the labor market rather than through education. A rough estimate, based on Swedish data (chapter 3), is that children's measured cognitive ability accounts for about 20 percent of the correlation between father's and son's income. Children's personality traits and physical characteristics account for less than 20 percent, leaving more than 60 percent to more social and behavioral mechanisms underlying intergenerational income persistence. The mechanisms underlying this net association include unmeasured biological and environmental characteristics, the access of higher-income parents to superior social and economic contacts or networks, superior information possessed by higher-status parents, parental use of income and wealth to purchase child inputs that lead to future attainments, and perhaps nepotism.

The correlation between father's and son's final educational attainment is mainly mediated by cognitive ability, accounting for around two-fifths of the intergenerational education correlation in a number of countries (chapters 3 and 9). Again, the other side of the coin is that more than half of the intergenerational correlation in education remains unaccounted for by cognitive skills acquired in childhood, pointing to important influences of aspects of the child's environment correlated with parents' SES. Although it is unclear exactly what these other factors are that encourage intergenerational persistence, we can conclude from this finding that intergenerational persistence in SES is not mainly driven by differences in cognitive abilities by parental education or income group. Even those that exist overstate the impact of genetic transmission of cognitive ability, because cognitive abilities have been measured during childhood (in the Swedish study at age eighteen), meaning that there have been many years of environmental influences on the measure.

But differences between countries in intergenerational income mobility are not necessarily mainly driven by cross-country variation in the

Figure 19.3   Elasticity of Median Son's Earnings to Father's Earnings

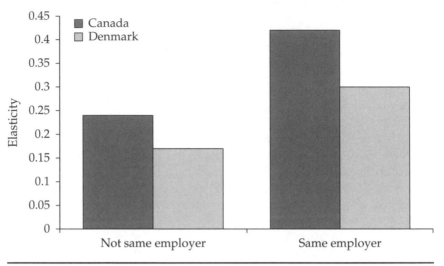

Source: Authors' calculations based on data from chapter 18, this volume, table 18.2.

relationship between parental SES and childhood achievements, such as grades during adolescence or final education attainment. For instance, chapter 17 strongly suggests that the weaker relationship between parental education and a child's earnings as an adult in Sweden than in the United Kingdom mainly arises because labor market returns to education in Sweden are lower than in the United Kingdom. Relationships between parents' education and child achievements earlier in life are similar in the two countries. Hence the structure of rewards for any given level of educational attainment or child achievement must also be taken into account when making cross-national comparisons of income mobility. This reward structure is heavily influenced by changes in earnings inequality, especially by the increasing premiums in pay for the highly educated that are found in almost all nations.[4]

Parental influence continues into adulthood in terms of getting good jobs: in both Canada and Denmark about 5 percent of sons have their main jobs with the same employer as their father, and the incidence of this phenomenon is much stronger at the top end of the father's earnings distribution (chapter 18). Figure 19.3 shows the association between father's earnings and son's median earnings, distinguishing between sons whose main job is in the same firm as their father and their counterparts who work in different firms. In both cases, mobility in earnings between generations is higher in Denmark than in Canada. When the son works in the same firm as his father, the association of his earnings with his father's is larger (mobility is smaller) than when he does not. Preservation of high-income status across generations in both countries is strongly related to the greater tendency of sons to have the same main employer among higher-income fathers, apparently reflecting both nepotism and the importance of networks in finding good jobs.

Policy Effects

Four chapters deal more directly with the influence of policies on intergenerational mobility. In France and Denmark there is causal evidence that universal preschool programs partially close the SES gap in school achievement and subsequent wages (chapters 7 and 8), more so in France than Denmark. Thus universal preschool education improves intergenerational mobility.

Chapter 13 focuses on a feature of some secondary school systems—early tracking into different types of secondary schools with specific educational curricula, typically characterized by either academic or vocational orientation. On the one hand, early educational choices may be more likely to reflect parental background than children's abilities, but, on the other hand, tracking by ability may weaken the influence of family background if tracking is truly ability-based. In both Italy and Germany, the association between parents' education and children' achievements before tracking takes place is strong—similar to that in other countries studied in this volume. There is also inequality by parental education in entry to tracks, and this does not weaken during school (for example, it exists for repeating grades and for changing tracks). Even after controlling for prior academic performance and school track, an association between university enrollment and parental SES exists for both countries, as it does for two countries without tracking—the United States and Canada (chapter 14). Overall, the influence of family background after initial tracking is stronger in the Italian system than the German one, and this appears to be related to more parental discretion (particularly absence of teachers' recommendations for tracking) and the absence of postsecondary vocational training in Italy.

Although we know little about college graduation from most chapters, chapter 15 indicates that an Italian reform led to a greater enrollment in tertiary education, thereby widening access, but also smaller rewards for those who chose the attractive shorter three-year program track over the longer five-year degree. Because children of higher-SES parents were more likely to complete the longer degree, the average returns from a university degree were larger among students from a higher-SES background than amongst those from a lower-SES background.

Summary

Although the United States stands out in having the largest SES gaps in mobility relevant skills and attributes, and Canada some of the smallest, despite their similarity of heritage, there are also many more similarities across these and other countries. We find that parents are important early in life, in school and related neighborhood choices, including secondary school systems with tracking. Evidence from France suggests that high-quality preschool experience—in terms of exposure to books, quality of preschool, formation of sociobehavioral (noncognitive) skills—has an effect of lessening the SES gradient. Education systems also matter, but the evidence indicates that their net effect is not to reduce the relationship between parental SES and child achievement, but to maintain or strengthen the patterns of differences in outcomes already evident at younger ages. Parental influence through networks continues into the labor market in early adulthood, but the size of earnings returns to ability and education may operate to reduce the midlife parent-child income correlation in some countries (for example, Sweden) and enhance it in others (for example, the United Kingdom and United States).

Our analysis of the unconditional bivariate relationships of different child outcomes with parental education that we report in chapter 2 suggests that the socioeconomic gradients in child outcomes are the highest in the United States. Although the country differences are not uniformly statistically significant, almost all point estimates consistently suggest the correlations are the highest in the United States across all outcome domains. Figure 19.4 summarizes the estimated country effects by showing the fitted correlation at adulthood in each of the domains. The only case in which the U.S. correlation is not the highest (furthest to the right) is socioemotional behavior. Here, the Swedish estimate, based on military enlistment data for noncognitive skills, has a greater latent correlation with parental education than is estimated for the United States.

To take us back to the beginning, what have we learned about trade-offs between inequality and mobility? Across nations, the winning country in mobility terms seems to be Canada (see chapter 2) with its low SES gradients all the way to the adulthood stage, even in a nation with above-average inequality. How much of this gradient is due to equal access to schooling, including early childhood education, is not answered, but new research suggests that Canadian policies that increase the generosity of child allowances at younger ages and those that subsidize tertiary degree attendance for the middle classes both produce better outcomes (Belley, Frenette, and Lochner 2011; Milligan and Stabile 2011). But even in high-mobility countries with relatively high inequality, such as Canada, or high-mobility–low–inequality Denmark, a gradient is still associated with working at parental places of employment, albeit mainly important for

Figure 19.4   Estimated Socioeconomic Gradients Across Countries, Fitted Correlations Against Country

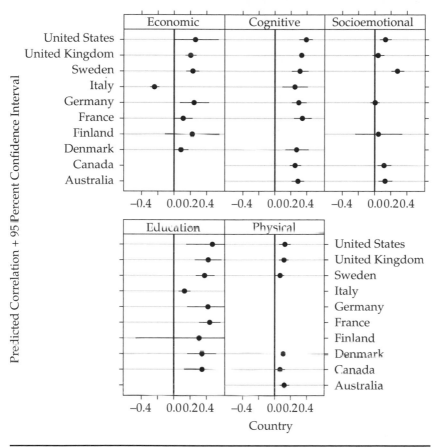

Source: Authors' calculations based on their own data.
Note: Countries with values to the right of the vertical line have lower mobility than those to the left of the line. The further to the right the dot is, the greater the parental SES effect on child outcomes.

the top of the distribution. At the other end of the mobility spectrum, the United Kingdom and the United States distinguish themselves from the rest, including Australia, Germany, and Italy—in terms of high inequality and low mobility. The steepest gradients of all are found in the United States for almost all outcomes (chapter 2).

We find that inequality in parental SES makes a difference in all nations and that these advantages are important before, during, and after schooling. Nations do, however, differ in how much parental advantage matters to children's outcomes. It may be that beyond some level of inequality, such as that found in the United States, the extent of cumulative advantage is such that policies designed to equalize opportunity, no matter how successful at early ages, are unable to overcome the starting position of children in high-SES families.

How Can We Advance the Next Generation of Research?

The research reported here is clearly incomplete. We were not able to compare the mobility of immigrants or the full effects of family structure and stability on mobility outcomes. We did not emphasize the important differences in educational outcomes between boys and girls, or the effects of family structure on outcomes.

Longer-term high-immigration countries, such as Canada and Australia, may have better outcomes because of institutions designed to foster inclusiveness, which also have strong positive effects on native low-SES children. Until we can define *immigrant* consistently across countries, and until we better understand the processes by which immigrants are selected into nations, we will not be able to factor out its effects. Family structure and stability may also be important for mobility, but comparable cross-national data on the stability of parental relationships across children's formative years in relation to parental SES is also difficult to find (see chapter 5 for the early years in Germany and the United Kingdom, where children are adversely affected by family instability).

Indeed, although we made every effort to find the most comparable data and highest-quality teams of scholars to carry out these cross-national comparisons, and though we found that reliance on parental SES as measured by educational attainment offered the greatest hope for comparability, many comparisons could not be made. We were limited in our comparisons of mobility across nations mainly by the lack of comparable high-quality data at our disposal. More and better use of administrative data in every country, such as that in Sweden (chapter 3), would clearly help every society understand better its own mechanisms of social mobility, even if researchers and policymakers are not interested in cross-national comparisons per se. If nations care about equality of life chances and the extent of the influence of parental advantage on mobility, they must collect the requisite survey or test data on child outcomes and the SES characteristics of the parents, with permission to link these data to various administrative registers where appropriate.

If nations believe that comparative research offers opportunities for understanding social processes (for example, the widely heralded success of PISA), additional effort will be needed to make sure that the data collected offer consistent cross-national measures of cognitive outcomes and achievements as well as sociobehavioral outcomes (behaviors, traits, and personality). For instance, in chapter 4, the Australian and U.K. surveys of early child outcomes are fully comparable for most such measures, but the United States and Canadian datasets had fewer good points of comparison. Also, studies designed for international comparability on outcomes, such as PISA, should aim to collect better measures of parental background that are also comparable across countries.

There is considerable scope for more small-scale comparative studies of two or more countries like those in this volume, particularly ones designed around particular institutions that differ between the countries (for example, preschool or secondary school systems). Natural experiments with wide external validity that shed light on the impact of particular policies and institutional features would also contribute to our understanding of intergenerational mobility.

What Are the Implications for Policy?

An important policy lesson from the research is that it is possible to provide more equal life chances than is the case in the United States and some other wealthy countries in ways that do not violate family autonomy or the principle of merit in assigning income positions (such as jobs) in society. But there are also limits to such policies as parental influences are evident at every stage of the life course. The experience of Canada reported in a number of chapters in this volume is an example of how policies and institutions might make a difference. Australia may be another case in point. Recall from chapter 1 (figure 1.1) that both of these countries have high intergenerational income mobility, similar to Sweden, Norway, and Finland, at the same time having higher income inequality compared with these Scandinavian countries.

Our study and earlier studies (Duncan et al. 2011) suggest that income inequality and income gradients per se make a difference in child outcomes. Andrea Brandolini and Timothy Smeeding (2009) find that patterns of increasing income inequality are mostly due to the top end of the distribution pulling away from the middle, whereas differences in incomes below the median vary across countries but are relatively stable. This suggests that the high-child-poverty countries (see chapter 2) might benefit from policies to improve economic well-being for low-income families. Higher child allowances and comprehensive polices to reduce poverty for low-income families with children are two such options. Jane Waldfogel (2010) finds that policies have increasingly reduced child poverty in the United Kingdom, producing better outcomes for low-income children, many of which are already evident. Such policy is also consistent with the findings in Kevin Milligan and Mark Stabile (2011), where higher-child-benefit programs in Canada had significant positive effects on child test scores, maternal health, and child mental health. Attacking

Figure 19.5   OECD SES Background Measure and PISA Reading Test Score, 2009

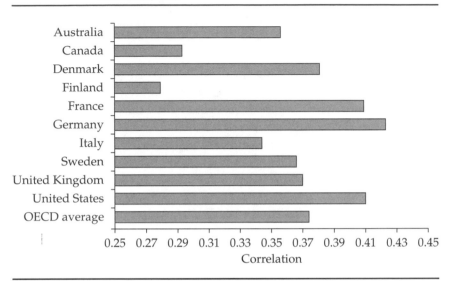

Source: Authors' calculations based on data from OECD (2010).

family economic well-being at the bottom of the distribution is another way to improve child outcomes and lessen high-low SES differences in achievements.

The educational system is likely to be the most widely used and acceptable policy tool we have for equalizing life chances. But the education system does not seem so far to achieve this goal. High-quality preschool experience—in terms of exposure to books, quality of preschool, formation of socioemotional (noncognitive) skills—has a positive influence everywhere. However, we also find that the net effect of education systems is not to reduce the relationship between parental SES and child achievement. At best, education systems may be offsetting existing processes of cumulative advantage in keeping the overall gradients stable as children age. We also find that parents play an important role at every stage of the life course—early in life, in school, and in related neighborhood choices, including secondary school systems with tracking.

We have seen that in Canada there are weaker relationships between parental SES and performance in cognitive tests before entering school (chapter 4) and during adolescence (chapters 12 and 14). These findings are echoed in the latest (2009) internationally comparative investigation of reading skills of fifteen-year-olds (OECD 2010). As figure 19.5 illustrates, Canada has one of the weakest associations between the OECD measure of student's socioeconomic background and PISA test results (also see

OECD 2010, figs. II.1.4, II.2.4, and II.3.6). Canadian policies and institutions appear to be operating to make children's life chances more equal. Again, the United States has one of the strongest correlations between PISA test results and parents' SES, along with France and Germany.[5] We have also seen that there are policies, such as universal preschool education, that reduce the influence of family background on children's life chances in a country with relatively low intergenerational mobility and above average inequality—France (chapter 7). Hence schooling can help reduce but not eliminate the disadvantages from having low-SES parents.

Although inequalities emerge early in life, reforming education systems may be able to reduce them. But there are limits to what policies might achieve without limiting family autonomy. We have direct evidence from England that higher-SES parents place their children in higher-quality secondary schools, mainly by moving to areas with better schools, and this sorting through residential selection produces the steeper gradient between pupil achievement and parents' education during secondary school compared with that at the end of primary school. One would be expected to face the same types of sorting if early childhood education became a part of the national public school system. More equal access to good secondary schools (such as through lottery allocation) could make a contribution, but, as long as variation in school quality is considerable, such a policy would be resisted by better-off parents because some would be forced to send their children to inferior schools (violating parental autonomy). A reduction in the variance of school quality through a leveling up would make a larger contribution. Finding the resources and ways to accomplish this, however, is a considerable challenge. Among other things, it requires that we know what makes a good quality school or preschool; for example, what role do pupils' peers or teacher qualifications play? What role do parents play in shaping a good school? These are research questions the answers to which are difficult to address, but are important for formulating education policy (see, for example, Duncan and Murnane 2011).

Reform of secondary school access is just one example of the constraint that family autonomy places on policies. We have seen that the SES gradient is observable at every childhood stage, explicitly or implicitly, even when getting a job. The parental role is embedded in each gradient, and it is unequal. In short, parents will do everything they can to give their children better outcomes—but not everyone is born to equally talented, equally educated, or equally well-off and behaviorally cogent parents. It is therefore in the personal interest of high-SES parents to maintain the status quo, and to even enhance their children's opportunities by making the gradient steeper at each stage of the life course. But though it might be efficient from an economic investment point of view and difficult to change politically and socially, it is important to find the policy levers that might reduce the inequalities that exist by the time children enter primary school. We have already mentioned preschool education, but some governments, such as those of the United Kingdom and the United States, are also discussing support for parents to improve their parenting skills in the general context of intervening early in a child's life, specifically, before age five (see Field 2010).[6] The limits of policy seem therefore to depend on increasing the evidence base about how much policy can accomplish for children who grow up in low-SES households.

Given the similarity of the association between parental background and achievements in many countries, we may be tempted to say that we cannot do much about these relationships, which has attendant implications for equalizing life chances. But policy changes should be monitored for their impact to extend the evidence base. For instance, England has legislated to raise university tuition fees by up to 200 percent from October 2012, thereby shifting support for university education from the taxpayer to the student. At the same time, loans to cover tuition fees are available and need not be paid back until the graduate earns £21,000 or more. Universities must also demonstrate that they have policies to widen access, including scholarship support for students with low-income parents, to charge the highest fees. The net effect on equality of access to university education is controversial. The new fees regime could reduce access of qualified lower-income students because they or their parents are less willing to assume the debt that needs to be incurred while studying than students with higher-income parents. On the other hand, that no loans need be repaid until the graduate is established in the labor market could improve access for students from less affluent backgrounds. Of course, we have also seen that who attains the academic qualifications for university entry is strongly related to parental background (chapters 12 and 17) even before we address university access and tempering its financial costs. But financial costs are important and seem to explain at least part of the differences in tertiary educational attainment between Canada and the United States (Belley, Frenette, and Lochner 2011).

It is also important that all aspects of reforms must be considered in evaluating their impact. For example, the university reform in Italy reduced inequality in university enrollment, but inequality in returns from a degree by parental SES increased when children of higher-SES parents chose a more lucrative longer-term degree (chapter 15).

We might also think of labor market policies that limit the scope for the operation of networks that give children of higher-income parents' advantages in getting better-paid jobs, evidence for which we encountered in Canada and Denmark (chapter 18). Such policies may move us closer to the principle of merit in assigning jobs as well as making life chances more equal, but they would clearly violate family autonomy. Here we see a clear conflict of our three principles in practice.

In chapter 20, John Roemer argues that family autonomy should be sacrificed in some cases. For instance, better preschools are likely a good way to lessen the gradient in learning for lower-SES children due to a leveling-up effect. In countries like the United States, where good preschools are already being heavily used by upper-SES parents, who can afford them, targeting subsidies to low-income children is probably preferred. A French style universal école maternelle is not likely to be fiscally or politically acceptable in the United States at this time, because higher-SES parents who can afford high-quality preschools that exclude low-SES children will see little benefit for their children in a universal system that levels the playing field. On the other hand, they might be willing to support high-quality preschooling subsidies for low-income children on equity grounds without violating parental autonomy.

Activist educational efforts in secondary and tertiary schooling and for school completion are needed to overcome parental advantages of money and place. Even in the United States, the Obama education bill will help meet the costs of tertiary education, and the Obama administration's race to the top provisions for secondary schools will, it is hoped, begin to level up the worst schools. But such changes, though adopted with some difficulty by President Barack Obama, must be maintained and perhaps even strengthened by future presidents and governors to at least keep the SES gradient from fanning out as children age.

In the end, we will never be able to eradicate SES differences in child outcomes, especially in highly unequal societies, and we will never be able to, or wish to, override parental autonomy. However, evidence does indicate that policy can help reduce barriers to intergenerational mobility, and increase equality of opportunity, even in the United States.

Notes

1. The genetic-environment distinction is, in fact, not so easy to make. Recent scientific papers have stressed the importance of genetic-environment interactions. Environment can trigger the expression of some genes, suppress gene expression in other cases, or enhance gene expression (Caspi and Moffitt 2006; Shanahan and Hofer 2005; Thomas 2010).

2. A note of caution is in order here because the comparability of test scores between countries is more questionable than that in figure 19.1. Some are cognitive ability tests in surveys and some are school achievement results. Further, the ages of measurement vary among the countries. Also, the Swedish data comes from a much older cohort than the others (for example, the 1973 cohort compared with the 1989–1990 cohort in England).

3. The raw scores allow for the variance in scores to change as the child ages, while the standardized scores impose a constant variance. Neither is inherently superior to the other.

4. Mary Daly and Robert Valletta (2008) find that earnings inequality and stability changed in the major OECD countries during the 1990s and 2000s, with greater gaps between the top and the middle of the earnings distribution and with more instability in earnings at the bottom of the distribution. See also Blanden, Haveman, and Wilson (2011), which finds that that the reward to greater educational attainment is higher in the United States than in the United Kingdom, suggesting that differences in rewards exist beyond those found for Sweden and the United Kingdom in chapter 17.

5. Interestingly, the correlation among countries between the correlation coefficient shown in figure 19.5 and average student performance on the PISA reading test is −0.74, and this is mainly driven by the conjunction of the high student performance of Canada and Finland and their low correlation of test results with SES background.

6. The report's two overarching recommendations are to 1.) establish a set of Life Chances Indicators that measure how successful we are as a country in making more equal life's outcomes for all children, and 2.) establish the Foundation Years, covering the period from the womb to five. The Foundation Years should become the first pillar of a new tripartite education system, with the Foundation Years leading to school years, leading to further, higher, and continuing education.

    Another review commissioned by the current U.K. government focused on early intervention (led by Graham Allen MP); see *Early Intervention: The Next Steps* and *Early Intervention: Smart Investment, Massive Savings* (http://www. cabinetoffice.gov.uk/news/graham-allen-launches-second-report-early-intervention; accessed October 21, 2011). The first report underlined that many of the costly and damaging social problems for individuals can be eliminated or reduced by giving children and parents the right type of evidence-based programs from infancy through age eighteen, and especially in their earliest years. The second report sets out how we can pay for those programs within existing resources and by attracting new nongovernment money.

    For the United States, see the provisions for Nurse Home Visiting for young children in at-risk families in the Obama health-care bill at http://www. house.leg.state.mn.us/comm/docs/PEWFederalHomeVisitingSummary.pdf (accessed October 21, 2011). See also Haskins, Paxson, and Brooks-Gunn 2009.

References

Belley, Phillipe, Marc Frenette, and Lance Lochner. 2011. "Post-Secondary Attendance by Parental Income in the U.S. and Canada: What Role for Financial Aid Policy?" *NBER* working paper 17218. Cambridge, Mass.: National Bureau of Economic Research. Available at: http://www.nber.org/papers/w17218 (accessed December 15, 2011).

Blanden, Jo, Robert Haveman, and Kathryn Wilson. 2011. "Understanding the Mechanisms Behind Intergenerational Persistence: A Comparison Between the

United States and UK." In *Persistence, Privilege, and Parenting: The Comparative Study of Intergenerational Mobility*, edited by Timothy M. Smeeding, Robert Erikson, and Markus Jäntti. New York: Russell Sage Foundation.

Brandolini, Andrea, and Timothy M. Smeeding. 2009. "Income Inequality in Richer and OECD Countries." In *The Oxford Handbook of Economic Inequality*, edited by Wiemer Salverda, Brian Nolan, and Timothy M. Smeeding. New York: Oxford University Press.

Caspi, Avshalom, and Terrie Moffitt. 2006. "Gene-Environment Interactions in Psychiatry: Joining Forces with Neuroscience." *Nature Reviews Neuroscience* 7: 583–90.

Daly, Mary, and Robert Valletta. 2008 "Cross-National Trends in Earnings Inequality and Instability." *Economics Letters* 99(2): 215–19.

Duncan, Greg J., and Richard Murnane, eds. 2011. *Whither Opportunity? Rising Inequality, Schools, and Children's Life Chances.* New York: Russell Sage Foundation.

Duncan, Greg J., Kjetil Telle, Kathleen M. Ziol-Guest, and Ariel Kalil. 2011. "Economic Deprivation in Early Childhood and Adult Attainment: Comparative Evidence from Norwegian Registry Data and the U.S. PSID." In *Persistence, Privilege, and Parenting: The Comparative Study of Intergenerational Mobility*, edited by Timothy M. Smeeding, Robert Erikson, and Markus Jäntti. New York: Russell Sage Foundation.

Field, Frank. 2010. *The Foundation Years: Preventing Poor Children Becoming Poor Adults.* The report of the Independent Review of Poverty and Life Chances. London: HM Government.

Fishkin, James S. 1983. *Justice, Equal Opportunity, and the Family.* New Haven, Conn.: Yale University Press.

Haskins, Ron, Christina Paxson, and Jeanne Brooks-Gunn. 2009. "Social Science Rising: A Tale of Evidence Shaping Public Policy." *Future of Children* policy brief. Princeton, N.J.: The Future of Children. Available at: http://www.future ofchildren.org/futureofchildren/publications (accessed November 18, 2011).

Milligan, Kevin, and Mark Stabile. 2011. "Do Child Tax Benefits Affect the Well-Being of Children? Evidence from Canadian Child Benefit Expansions" *American Economic Journal: Economic Policy* 3(August): 175–205. Available at: http://www. aeaweb.org/articles.php?doi=10.1257/pol.3.3.175 (accessed December 2, 2011).

Organisation for Economic Co-Operation and Development (OECD). 2010. *PISA 2009 Results: Overcoming Social Background—Equity in Learning Opportunities and Outcomes,* vol. 2. Paris: Organisation for Economic Co-Operation and Development.

Shanahan, Michael J., and Scott M. Hofer. 2005. Social Context in Gene-Environment Interactions: Retrospect and Prospect. Journals of Gerontology: Series B 60B (special issue): 65–76.

Thomas, Duncan. 2010. "Gene-Environment-Wide Association Studies: Emerging Approaches." *Nature Reviews: Genetics* 11(1): 259–72.

Waldfogel, Jane. 2010. *Britain's War on Poverty.* New York: Russell Sage Foundation.

Chapter 20

What Is the Justification of Studying Intergenerational Mobility of Socioeconomic Status?

JOHN ROEMER

THE STUDIES in this volume focus on the effect of socioeconomic circumstances—particularly those of the family that raises a child—on the child's performance, along a number of dimensions: in school at every level, in noncognitive behavior, and eventually in the labor market. The underlying presumption, though rarely stated explicitly, is that it is unfair if children from different social backgrounds systematically fare differently in life: it is a mark of inequality of opportunity. Fairness, therefore, would seem to require that the distribution of child outcomes be independent of the socioeconomic circumstances of the family that raises the child. The main institutions that may be used to rectify the disadvantages of being raised by poor or uneducated parents are schools. The statistical phrasing of this conception of fairness is that rows of the matrix of intergenerational transmission of socioeconomic status (SES) should be identical.

It is important to inquire more carefully into exactly what ethical view implies this conception of fairness or social justice. Parents transmit at least the following to their children: genes, wealth and material resources, knowledge, aspirations, and preferences. They also use their social connections to help their children. Most of the factors in this list are delivered or used with more or less intensity, depending on the parents' motivation and love for the child. To clarify, by aspirations, I mean parents' instilling in the child beliefs concerning whether he or she can succeed in various endeavors, and by preferences I mean values about how to live one's life (which can include occupational preferences). The distinction between preferences and aspirations may be difficult to measure, but I believe it is conceptually important.

If we partition the set of families into elements—call them types—defined by socioeconomic status or occupation or income of parents, it is extremely unlikely that the joint distribution of these resources will be identical across types. But the presumption behind the view that it is desirable to equalize the rows of the intergenerational transmission matrix is that all these differences in the distributions of resources across family types, which could be viewed as disadvantageous, should be compensated for, or counteracted, by the educational process. Is this, however, clearly desirable from an ethical point of view?

Perhaps the clearest case for compensation is to those children whose parents lack good social connections. In chapter 18 of this volume, Paul Bingley and his colleagues show that these connections may be very important in transmitting high levels of economic advantage from parents to children: in particular, that parents with high SES tend to transfer jobs to their children disproportionately. Most people would probably also say that the differential transmission of economic resources (wealth, and so on) to children should be compensated for by society. To the extent that schools can provide music lessons to children whose parents cannot afford them or books to children whose parents do not buy them, that is a good thing. My view is that it is an important role of schools to counter falsely pessimistic aspirations that some parents may relay to their children. And compensating children for the lack of knowledge transmission in their households is surely the most obvious role of schooling. This leaves genes, preferences, and parental love and motivation.

I focus on genes and preferences, which I believe raise complex issues. I discuss genes first—in particular, genes for cognitive and noncognitive abilities. It is difficult to separate genes from the social environment, because many studies have now shown that whether a particular gene is expressed depends on the environment outside the individual. For individuals exposed to similar environments, we may however attribute some difference in their performance to genes, and, with advances in biology, it may become feasible to identify specific genetic attributes which give rise to behaviors generating different outcomes across individuals. The argument for compensating children for an unlucky draw from the human gene pool is that the material conditions of a person's life should not be less abundant because of bad genetic luck. (Indeed, one might well argue that they who are genetically unlucky should enjoy material conditions better than those who are more genetically lucky, because the lucky ones derive pleasures from exercising their cognitive abilities in fulfilling and complex work, and from good social relationships, neither of which are so easily available to those who are unlucky in their endowments of these traits.) Two arguments stand against compensating those with an unlucky genetic draw, one emphasizing efficiency and the other self-ownership. The efficiency argument is that, from the social viewpoint, we should respect comparative advantage: that is, people should fill occupational slots in which they comparatively excel. The total output of goods and services will be larger in the economy if comparative advantage is respected; to attempt to train genetically untalented children so that they have equal chances of occupying high-paying jobs with more talented children would be expensive, rendering most people in society worse off than they would have been under the regime respecting comparative advantage. The self-ownership argument is that, from a moral viewpoint, a person has a right to benefit from his personal genetic constitution: it is an important part of what constitutes him as a person. This argument is presented in its most forceful form by Robert Nozick (1974).

I will not discuss the self-ownership argument further, for I believe it will not appeal to most of the readers of this volume. The comparative advantage argument, however, requires further discussion. One immediately sees that whether the comparative advantage argument appeals depends on one's overall view of social justice. Let us suppose, for the sake of argument, that if society does expend sufficient resources on relatively untalented children—call this situation A—it can improve the quality of their lives over what that quality would have been under the comparative-advantage regime—call that situation B. In A, fewer goods and services will be produced than in B, because society is spending resources on untalented children past the point where their marginal productivity equals that of more talented children, but the untalented ones will receive more of these goods than they would receive in B, whereas the talented ones (on average) will clearly have to receive fewer of them than they would receive in B.

Whether one prefers A to B depends on one's theory of distributive justice. If one is a utilitarian, someone who views justice as the maximization of average welfare, and if one believes that welfare is closely tracked by income, then one will prefer B. On the other hand, if one is a Rawlsian, who believes that justice comprises maximizing the welfare of the most disadvantaged class, then one will prefer A. (More generally, a prioritarian believes in giving priority to the worse off, if not the extreme priority that Rawls gives them. Prioritarianism is more egalitarian than utilitarianism and less egalitarian than Rawlsian maximin.) One's degree of overall inequality aversion will determine whether one favors A or B.

The concept of fairness that I enunciated in the first paragraph is not related in any simple way to inequality aversion. The rows of the intergenerational transmission matrix of SES might be equal, but the children who become adults of different social-economic stati could have very different income levels. That concept of fairness requires only that every child participates in the same lottery for adult socioeconomic status. This is entirely different from saying that the rewards to differential SES positions should be the same. Now, it is an important empirical observation that societies that have low overall economic inequality also are more fair, in the sense discussed here: the main examples are the Nordic countries. And presumably this is because low inequality between those of different SES in the parental generation implies that the joint distributions of the eight resources on which we are focusing are closer to being the same than they are in societies (like the United States) with more inequality across parental SES groups. Therefore, one of the important ways to achieve fairness in intergenerational transmission may be to lower overall inequality. This important point, however, does not nullify the claim that fairness in intergenerational transmission is conceptually distinct from overall equality.

So I conclude that it is not mandatory that one endorse the comparative-advantage argument: if one is sufficiently inequality-averse, then it is better to have fewer goods and services (a lower GDP per capita) and to have less inequality than to have a higher GDP per capita and more inequality. It is important to realize that the level of GDP per capita is not, as many economists claim, a measure of a society's efficiency. It is only a correct measure of social efficiency if one's view of the social good is the maximization of average income. Economists have sometimes allowed a particular and contestable social view (namely, utilitarianism) to infect their conception of efficiency, and this is unacceptable. For an egalitarian, the maximization of average output is not socially efficient. Here, the term *efficiency* must be modified by the adjective *social*. The concept of Pareto efficiency is quite different. Both the Rawlsian and the utilitarian will advocate Pareto efficient distributions of resources (namely, distributions of income in which it is impossible to make everybody better off). Both situations A and B may be Pareto efficient.

How do modern societies deal with these issues? It is clarifying to observe the debate over affirmative action in the United States—surely, other countries have had similar debates, but I am familiar with the American one. Affirmative action was initially implemented with respect to racial minorities. Opposition emerged with respect to affirmative action as practiced by universities in their admissions policies, and with respect to quotas of minorities in the hiring by firms. But the opposition in these two domains was very different. With respect to university admissions, the opponents did not oppose preferential admissions for disadvantaged groups, but said that race was not the right way of identifying disadvantage: rather, one should favor students from disadvantaged SES backgrounds. (California and Texas changed the affirmative action policies of their great public universities to reflect this view.) With respect to hiring, the opponents claimed that the best person should be hired for the job, independent of social background. In other words, in the case of college admissions, the opponents did not disagree with the principle of compensating SES disadvantage, but only with what they claimed was an incorrect diagnosis of disadvantage, and in the hiring case, they opposed the compensatory principle, and supported meritocracy—the most qualified person should get the job.

I see this debate as reflecting a view of social justice that says this: in the period of formation, children and young people should be compensated for the disadvantages associated with their backgrounds; but this stops at the labor market, where society should allocate its labor resources according to meritocracy (in the sense I have defined it). This is certainly a plausible view.

But notice that a meritocratic labor market does not imply a vastly unequal distribution of income: market incomes may still be reallocated through taxation. Whether a desirable degree of final economic equality in material resources can be achieved by redistribution through the provision of transfer payments and public goods depends in large part of the social ethos—the conception of justice that citizens hold. For it is this conception that will eventually be reflected in the tax structure of society.

I finally come to preferences, or values. Surely, we wish to protect children from the transmission of some kinds of preferences from parents: racist or sexist ones come to mind. But certain kinds of preference transmission seem entirely acceptable: parents who are teachers may instill in their children a desire to be teachers, and bankers may transmit to their children the desire to earn high incomes. The extent to which coal miners instill in their children the preference for coal mining because they think no other occupation is available to them should be compensated, because it is really a low and incorrect aspiration, but to the extent that it is because they love the coal-mining culture, it is a true preference. Is cognitive dissonance at work here? The question must be faced.

I believe parents have rights to transmit preferences of occupation and lifestyle to their children, if they are not the consequence of pessimistic aspirations: what is more important for a parent, than to attempt to pass on his values to his children? As long as we continue to believe in the family as an institution that has value for reasons other than the efficient formation of children, I think we should not attempt to compensate for the transmission of legitimate preferences. But the transmission of these preferences will surely have an effect on the incomes of children. This means that equality of the rows of the intergenerational transmission matrix is not necessarily ethically desirable.

I do not think that any of the studies in this volume investigate this question, that is, attempt to identify the extent to which intergenerational mobility is less than it would be under a random lottery because parents are transmitting legitimate preferences to their children that influence their occupational choices and incomes in a nonrandom way. I think it would be worthwhile to do so, though it would surely be a task to identify from the data the transmission of preferences, and to separate it, in particular, from the transmission of aspirations (it is aspirations based on false beliefs with which we are concerned). Lest one believe that this is a fine point that any empirical social scientist can ignore, I offer the case of the Roma. Surely, the transmission of preferences from Roma parents to children has massive effects on the children's lifetime incomes, and it is not clear to me that that transfer can be declared remediable because of cognitive dissonance or defeatist aspirations. This is a difficult question.

How much inequality in the rows of the intergenerational transmission matrix would remain if we effectively compensated children for all the circumstances that I have focused upon, but not for the transfer of legitimate values from parents? I do not know; the studies have not been done. In heterogeneous societies, a good deal of inequality of those rows might remain, for parents in heterogeneous societies perhaps have quite heterogeneous values. One must emphasize that this is an empirical question, and not use the idea as an excuse for relaxing the fight against inequality of opportunity. In homogeneous societies, I believe we will not produce less intergenerational mobility than we have today in those societies: the evidence is that the (relatively homogeneous) Nordic countries do not attempt to nullify the effect of parental transmission of preferences, and their intergenerational mobility is the highest in the advanced countries. Nevertheless, I think the conceptual point, that equalizing the rows of the intergenerational transmission matrix is not the summum bonum, is important. To the extent that we are pluralists and liberals, in the sense of John Rawls (1971), we must recognize the legitimacy of parents' transmitting to their children a variety of values, some of which will doubtless affect the children's material achievements. Because the distribution of these values is not independent of the socioeconomic status of the parents, we cannot hope to achieve complete equality of the rows of the intergenerational transmission matrix. If we do not assent to this view, we will have no good response to why we do not advocate dissolving families and raising children collectively.

References

Nozick, Robert. 1974. *Anarchy, State and Utopica.* New York: Basic Books.

Rawls, John. 1971. *A Theory of Justice.* Cambridge, Mass.: Harvard University Press.

Index

Boldface numbers refer to figures and tables.